Breakthrough Perspectives in Network and Data Communications Security, Design, and Applications

Indranil Bose
The University of Hong Kong, Hong Kong

INFORMATION SCIENCE REFERENCE

Hershey · New York

Director of Editorial Content: Kristin Klinger
Director of Production: Jennifer Neidig
Managing Editor: Jamie Snavely
Assistant Managing Editor: Carole Coulson
Typesetter: Michael Brehm
Cover Design: Lisa Tosheff
Printed at: Yurchak Printing Inc.

Published in the United States of America by
        Information Science Reference (an imprint of IGI Global)
        701 E. Chocolate Avenue, Suite 200
        Hershey PA 17033
        Tel: 717-533-8845
        Fax: 717-533-8661
        E-mail: cust@igi-global.com
        Web site: http://www.igi-global.com

and in the United Kingdom by
        Information Science Reference (an imprint of IGI Global)
        3 Henrietta Street
        Covent Garden
        London WC2E 8LU
        Tel: 44 20 7240 0856
        Fax: 44 20 7379 0609
        Web site: http://www.eurospanbookstore.com

Library of Congress Cataloging-in-Publication Data

Breakthrough perspectives in network and data communications security, design, and applications / Indranil Bose, editor.

    p. cm. -- (Advanced topics in buisness data communications and networks ; v. 1)

Includes bibliographical references and index.

Summary: "This book addresses key issues and offers expert viewpoints into the field of network and data communications, presenting research articles that address the most salient issues in network and data communications"--Provided by publisher.

ISBN 978-1-60566-148-3 (hardcover) -- ISBN 978-1-60566-149-0 (ebook)

1. Business enterprises--Computer networks. 2. Data transmission systems. 3. Computer networks. I. Bose, Indranil, 1968-

HD30.37.B736 2009

004.67--dc22

                        2008024194

British Cataloguing in Publication Data
A Cataloguing in Publication record for this book is available from the British Library.

Breakthrough Perspectives in Network and Data Communications Security, Design, and Applications is part of the IGI Global series named *Advances in Business Data Communications and Networking (ABDCN)* Series, ISBN: 1935-2638

If a library purchased a print copy of this publication, please go to http://www.igi-global.com/agreement for information on activating the library's complimentary electronic access to this publication.

Advances in Business Data Communication and Networking Series (ABDCN)

ISBN: 1935-2638

Editor-in-Chief: Indrail Bose, The University of Hong Kong, Hong Kong

Breakthrough Perspectives in Network and Data Communications Security, Design, and Applicatons

Indranil Bose, The University of Hong Kong, Hong Kong

Information Science Reference • copyright 2008 • 322pp • H/C (ISBN: 978-1-60566-148-3) • $195.00 (our price)

Modern organizations are critically dependent on data communications and network systems utilized in managing information and communications, vital to continuity and success of operations. Breakthrough Perspectives in Network and Data Communications Security, Design and Applications addresses key issues and offers expert viewpoints into the field of network and data communications, providing the academic, information technology, and managerial communities with the understanding necessary to implement robust, secure, and effective solutions. This much-needed addition to library and professional collections offers a matchless set of high quality research articles and premier technologies to address the most salient issues in network and data communications.

Business Data Communications and Networking: A Research Perspective

Jairo Gutierrez, University of Auckland, New Zealand

IGI Publishing • copyright 2007 • 388pp • H/C (ISBN: 1-59904-274-6) • $89.96 (our price)

The increasing business use of wireless and mobile technologies on a variety of devices has accelerated the need for a better understanding of the technologies involved. Business Data Communications and Networking: A Research Perspective addresses the key issues for businesses utilizing data communications and the increasing importance of networking technologies in business. Business Data Communications and Networking: A Research Perspective covers a series of technical advances in the field while highlighting their respective contributions to business or organizational goals, and centers on the issues of network-based applications, mobility, wireless networks, and network security.

The Advances in Business Data Communications and Networking (ABDCN) Book Series covers both guided and wireless communications of voice, data, images and video and their impact on the organizations in which they are used. Data Communications and Networks are no longer peripheral issues best left to the IT team, they are integral components of any modern information system and in many cases are essential to the success or failure of the organization. ABDCN aims to address the key issues for businesses utilizing data communications and the increasing importance of networking technologies in business. Through the ongoing release of breakthrough titles and research methodologies, this book series seeks to disseminate practical and theoretical information, which will enable readers to understand, manage, use and maintain business data communication networks more effectively.

Hershey • New York

Order online at www.igi-global.com or call 717-533-8845 x100 – Mon-Fri 8:30 am - 5:00 pm (est) or fax 24 hours a day 717-533-7115

Dedicated to my parents Santi Kumar Bose and Rama Basu

Editorial Advisory Board

Table of Contents

Detailed Table of Contents

Chapter I

Varadharajan Sridhar, Management Development Institute, India

This chapter deliberates the reasons for strategic outsourcing such as core competency, production economies, and transaction costs as presented in the literature and analyze these in the context of outsourcing model pioneered by an Indian mobile operator. The authors also explain vulnerabilities and risks associated with these outsourcing contracts and measures to be taken by the firm to mitigate their effects.

Chapter II

Sami J. Habib, Kuwait University, Kuwait

This chapter presents a computer aided integration tool, iCAD, that can predict a network evolution. The authors have used the term, network evolution, to mean predicting changes within the physical network topology as time evolves. iCAD is connected to four device libraries, each of which contains a distinct set of network technology devices, such as Ethernet hubs, ATM switches, IP routers, and gateways. As a network technology changes, each device library is updated. The cost and performance changes between the old and recent network technologies, enabling us to predict future changes to a first order; this chapter presents empirical results from 1999 until 2005 recording the network evolution progress, where the lower and upper bounds of network evolution came out to be 10% to 25% and 57% to 74% respectively in terms of network design cost reduction.

Chapter III

Hak Ju Kim, University of Houston–Clear Lake, USA

This chapter seeks to develop a richer understanding of the suitability of IP telephony in the Public Switched Telephony Network (PSTN) with an actual Local Exchange Carrier (LEC)'s case and network simulation. The authors also performed a simple real options analysis to evaluate a telecommunications network. The underlying network and associated data were derived from studies of an actual LEC. Through this experiment, we can get inference that IP has potential for a voice carriage.

Chapter IV

Abid Al Ajeeli, University of Bahrain, Bahrain
Yousif Al Bastaky, University of Bahrain, Bahrain

This chapter describes a detailed framework configuration infrastructure design for a high performance network. The configuration is described based on the new setup and migration requirements and it indicates how the design satisfies those requirements. The chapter explains the detailed configuration of the design process of the distribution layer switches and shows how these switches can be configured in the final implementation. The chapter also discusses the modifications that occurred during the implementation/migration phase.

Chapter V

Nurul I. Sarkar, AUT University, New Zealand
Catherine Byrne, Tonkin & Taylor Group Ltd., New Zealand
Nabeel A. Y. Al-Qirim, United Arab Emirates University, UAE

This chapter updates our previous research on GigE that has been documented as a case study of a large New Zealand organization. We focused on the level of GigE deployment, design, planning, implementation, network performance testing, problems encountered, and future plans. Our research findings show the feasibility and practicability of deploying GigE technology in high-speed networking applications, such as campus- and corporate-wide local area networks.

Chapter VI

M. Chandrasekaran, Directorate of Technical Education, India
R. S. D. Wahida Banu, Government College of Engineering, India

This chapter introduces and analyses a class of non-linear congestion control algorithms called polynomial congestion control algorithms. These generalize the Additive Increase and Multiplicative Decrease (AIMD) algorithms used for the TCP connections. The algorithms provide additive increase using a polynomial of the inverse of the current window size and provide multiplicative decrease using the polynomial of the current window size. There are infinite numbers of TCP-compatible polynomial algorithms by assuming polynomial of different order. This chapter analyses the interaction between the two models (named as MIMD-Poly and PIPD-Poly) of these generalized algorithms, for the wired (with unicast and multicast) and wireless TCP networks.

    Xabiel G. Pañeda, University of Oviedo, Spain
    David Melendi, University of Oviedo, Spain
    Roberto García, University of Oviedo, Spain
    Manuel Vilas, University of Oviedo, Spain
    Victor García, University of Oviedo, Spain

This chapter presents a method for performance analysis and configuration of audio/video-on-demand services. These kind of services makes use of an important number of resources, requires a constant quality of service and contents, and usually have important production costs. To maintain a good quality of service and at the same time, to make a profit for the content provider, services must have the optimum configuration. With this aim, the configuration process must be based on an accurate service behavioural analysis which evaluates the quality and the quantity of resources, contents and subscribers. This analysis can be performed using monitored information extracted from servers, proxies and network monitors, and predictions of a near future behaviour using laboratory experiments.

    Say Ying Lim, Monash University, Australia
    David Taniar, Monash University, Australia
    Bala Srinivasan, Monash University, Australia

As more and more servers appearing in the wireless environment provide accesses to mobile users, more and more demand and expectation is required by mobile users towards the available services. Mobile users are no longer satisfied with obtaining data only from one server, but require data from multiple servers either at the same or different locations. This eventually leads to the need for information gathering that span across several non-collaborative servers. This chapter describes some of the authors' researches in information gathering from multiple non-collaborative servers that may involve servers that not only accept direct queries from mobile users but also servers that broadcast data. They also look at how location dependent data plays an important role to mobile information gathering.

    Vilmos Simon, Budapest University of Technology and Economics, Hungary
    Sándor Imre, Budapest University of Technology and Economics, Hungary

In this chapter, the authors designed and implemented two algorithms: a location area forming algorithm (LAFA) and a cell regrouping algorithm (CEREAL), which can help guarantee QoS parameters in the next generation mobile networks. The authors used our realistic mobile environment simulator to generate input statistics on cell changes and incoming call for our algorithms and by comparing the values of the cost functions proposed, and recognized that a significant reduction was achieved in the amount of the signalling traffic, the location update cost was decreased by 40-60% in average.

This chapter proposes a very effective heuristic algorithm to address a variation of the cellular network expansion problem and discusses each algorithm step in detail. Although the input to the algorithm appears to be a binary integer programming problem, the proposed algorithm deals with several non-linear aspects. The solution specifies the connections of each component, cell sites, hubs, and mobile telephone switching office and satisfies the redundancy requirements for each cell site to ensure continued traffic flow in the event of a local overload or equipment failure. The algorithm reports the best feasible solution it finds, as well as lower and upper bounds on the cost of an exact solution. The authors hope that in presenting such an algorithm, designers of very large cellular network expansions will have a tool to obtain significantly good solutions in a reasonable time.

This chapter introduces a distributed system, called Wireless Proxy, to mitigate the effects of user mobility over streaming services on IEEE 802.11 wireless LANs (WLANs). It argues that a handoff procedure totally controlled by the client, depending on client mobility and configuration, can have negative effects over streaming services. In this way, mobile clients that remain associated with their current access point (AP) in poor channel conditions, severely affect the performance of streaming services. The presented distributed system monitors client mobility and induces mobile client handoffs when channel conditions worsen. Also, the system compensates streaming client and server underestimations of channel conditions. The obtained improvements using Wireless Proxy are experimentally tested using one of the most extended commercial streaming platforms and off-the-shelf Wi-Fi devices. The main contribution of the developed system is that it works with unmodified IEEE 802.11 wireless NICs and APs, such as the ones widely deployed nowadays.

In this chapter, the authors propose a new scheme for Multi User Detection (MUD) using Parallel Interference Cancellation (PIC) technique. This technique provides a good complexity, latency, and performance compromise. Among spread-spectrum techniques, the most popular one is the Direct-Sequence Code-Division Multiple-Access (DS-CDMA), where each active user's data is modulated (multiplied) by a unique code. This technique is suitable for Multi-Carrier (MC) Direct-Sequence Code-Division Multiple-Access (DS-CDMA) systems. We offer a new scheme of soft detectors whose performance is superior to that of the other famous suboptimal detectors. On each sub carrier, instead of making hard bit decisions of the other users in the current stage and regenerating and canceling the interference signal, a weighted sum of the soft outputs of the other users in the current stage is canceled from the soft output of the desired user.

    Ghassan Kbar, American University in Dubai (AUD), UAE
    Wathiq Mansoor, American University in Dubai (AUD), UAE

This chapter introduces a new radio resource management technique based on distributed dynamic channel assignment, and sharing load among Access Points (AP). Deploying wireless LANs (WLAN) at large scale is mainly affected by reliability, availability, fairness, scalability, and performance. These parameters will be a concern for most of managers who wanted to deploy WLANs. In order to address these concerns, a new radio resource management technique can be used in a new generation of wireless LAN equipment. This technique would include distributed dynamic channel assignment, and sharing load among Access Points (AP), which improves the network availability and reliability compared to centralized management techniques. In addition, it will help in increasing network capacities and improve its performance especially in large-scale WLANs. Analysis results using normal and binomial distribution have been included which indicate an improvement of performance resulted from network balancing when implementing distributed resources management at WLANs.

    Mieso K. Denko, University of Guelph, Canada

This chapter proposes a cooperative data caching and prefetching scheme for Mobile Ad Hoc Networks (MANETs). In this scheme, multiple hosts cooperate in both prefetching and caching commonly used data. To reduce communication and computational overhead, the authors use a clustering architecture for the network organization. A weak consistency based on time to live value was used to maintain data consistency. A hybrid cache replacement policy that uses frequency of access and the reference time was employed. The effects of cache size, mobility, and prefetching threshold on the network performance were investigated in a discrete event simulation environment. The contribution of intra-cluster and inter-cluster information to overall data accessibility ratio was also investigated. The simulation results indicate that the proposed scheme improves both data accessibility and query delay at relatively lower prefetch thresholds, larger cache sizes, and moderate mobility.

In this chapter, the authors survey fuzzy reasoning algorithm (FRA) as a highly adaptive algorithm used to achieve that goal. We present the various applications of that algorithm to ad-hoc routing protocols. In particular, the exposition includes a discussion of strength and weakness of these applications and how they can be improved.

In this chapter an enhanced algorithm, called Fuzzy-AQM, is suggested using fuzzy logic system to achieve the benefits of AQM. Uncertainty associated with queue congestion estimation and lack of mathematical model for estimating the time to start dropping incoming packets makes the Fuzzy-AQM algorithm the best choice. Extensive performance analysis via simulation showed the effectiveness of the proposed method for congestion detection and avoidance improving overall network performance.

Chapter XVII

The use of network traffic audit data for retrieving anomaly intrusion information and profiling user behavior has been previously studied, but the risk factors associated with attacks remain unclear. This study aimed to identify a set of robust risk factors via the bootstrap resampling and logistic regression modeling methods based on the KDD-cup 1999 data. Of the 46 examined variables, 16 were identified as robust risk factors, and the classification showed similar performances in sensitivity, specificity and correctly classified rate in comparison with the KDD-cup 1999 winning results that were based on a rule-based decision tree algorithm with all variables. The study emphasizes that the bootstrap simulation and logistic regression modeling techniques offer a novel approach to understanding and identifying risk factors for better information protection on network security.

Chapter XVIII

In Inter-Vehicle Communication (IVC) networks, the high mobility and lack of infrastructure pose major challenges in designing secure routing protocols. In this chapter, the authors present a new secure routing protocol called SERVEN (SEcure Routing in VEhicular Networks) that can achieve near-instantaneous secure communication in IVC networks. In particular, we concentrate on the design of the network setup phase of the protocol and we present simulation results using Network Simulator version 2.28 (ns-2.28). Secure setup means the appropriate formation of a network whose nodes are aware of each other and of the right topology. This is especially important for location-based routing protocols in IVC networks.

Chapter XIX

Antonios Alexiou, Research Academic Computer Technology Institute and University of Patras, Greece

Christos Bouras, Research Academic Computer Technology Institute and University of Patras, Greece

John Papagiannopoulos, University of Aegean, Greece

Dimitrios Primpas, Research Academic Computer Technology Institute and University of Patras, Greece

This chapter details the adoption of a broadband network in the region of Western Greece. The network consists of a fiber optic and Ethernet based infrastructure that is used in the metropolitan area of the city of Patras. It also includes a wireless broadband municipal network that is implemented in the city of Messatida. The main aim of the broadband network is to connect the public services related buildings in the region. At the same time, the designers want to create competition among access providers and content providers so that the end user can benefit from the advanced infrastructure and its associated services. Technical issues related to the creation and maintenance of the hierarchical broadband infrastructure such as choice of technology and interconnection are discussed in this chapter. Several contending business models are proposed and the open access model is selected due to the advantages that it can provide to the broadband project.

Preface

We are pleased to bring you this inaugural volume of Advanced Topics in Business Data Communications and Networking. The field of telecommunication is marked with rapid advances in wired and wireless technologies that enable sending and receiving of applications involving data and voice. Individuals involved in researching, improving, and using telecommunication and networking need a strong resource to provide ideas and information on the utilization and performance of the novel technologies that currently shape the field. Advanced Topics in Business Data Communications and Networking, Volume I presents a wide range of the most current research in the area of telecommunications and networking. This inaugural volume will assist researchers, educators, and professionals in understanding the necessary components for telecommunications and how to best adopt these elements into their own workplaces, and organizations throughout the world.

Chapter I, *"Strategic Outsourcing: Opportunities and Challenges for Telecom Operators"* by Varadharajan Sridhar of Management Development Institute, India addresses the issue of outsourcing in the context of telecommunications. Traditionally, firms outsource some or all of the non-core functions to vendors to reduce production cost. There are a large number of cases where information technology and associated processes are being outsourced and even off-shored to contractors in other countries so that firms acquire services at lower costs without sacrificing quality and efficiency. However, until recently telecom operators, have kept their core functions, such as network management, in-house. Rapid technological advances, high amounts of competition, dynamic markets, and the need for quick deployment of services have forced the operators to formulate innovative strategic outsourcing options. The author demonstrates through a case of a mobile operator in India, the issues and challenges of such strategic outsourcing options. He uses the case to describe how firms can mitigate the vulnerabilities of such outsourcing, including formulating clearly defined Service Level Agreements, and selecting suitable vendors.

Chapter II, *"Empirical Prediction of Computer-Network Evolution"* by Sami J. Habib of Kuwait University, Kuwait, discusses evolution of networks. As technology changes, networks evolve over time. It is impossible for a human network designer to evaluate all choices manually. The use of a computer aided design tool may be suitable for determining the tradeoffs in price, performance, and availability. This chapter discusses the use of the iCAD tool for determining network evolution. The tool is connected to four device libraries, each of which contains a set of devices such as Ethernet hubs, ATM switches, IP routers, gateways and their associated cost, capacity, number of ports, and type of wire. As technology changes, these device libraries are updated. The tool uses an evolutionary approach to determine the best network technologies in the presence of changing technology by maintaining the original devices and minimizing the upgrading cost. From the experiments it is found that Ethernet dominates ATM in the design of LAN and IP router dominates gateways for all site and backbone networks.

Chapter III, *"Suitability of IP Telephony in the Public Switched Telephone Network (PSTN): A Case Study"* by Hak Ju Kim, University of Houston–Clear Lake (USA) discusses IP telephony which is a prime example of converged service and holds a lot of promise in terms of low costs of operation as well as possibility of providing a number of value added services. Whether or not a company should convert its existing circuit switched-based telephony network to a packet switched IP telephony network is a debatable issue. The authors study a local telecommunications service provider that provides telecommunications services and equipment to residential and business customers. Using simulation tools, they discover that the IP telephony network would save about 73% of the link capacity of the circuit switched network. They also show that the same network could carry integrated service traffic at zero incremental cost. The value of the IP network is shown to be positive using the real options approach, and negative using the net present value approach. The researchers conclude that the profitability potential of IP networks is high and service providers will find such services to be quite lucrative.

Chapter IV, *"A Framework for High-Speed Networking"* by Abid A. Ajeeli and Yousif Al Bastaky, University of Bahrain, Bahrain, describes the construction of resilient networks. Resilient networks are important for organizations because they provide the maximum amount of availability without a lot of redundancy. The authors describe the building of such a high performance and resilient local area network for the University of Bahrain. This involved the upgrading of a legacy ATM network to a state-of-the-art gigabit network that connected the two campuses of the university at Sukhair and Issa-Town. The chapter includes an interesting discussion on how the switches are set up at the two campuses and also how virtual LANs are set up at the two campuses to minimize congestion in the network. By using a multi-layered approach that involved network hardware elements and network protocols, the design emphasizes resiliency. The network is built in such a way that it is able to support existing applications while providing a good opportunity for future growth as the needs of the two campuses change.

Chapter V, *"Updating on Gigabit Ethernet Implementation: The Case of a Large New Zealand Organization"* by Nurul I. Sarkar of AUT University, New Zealand, Catherine Byrne of Tonkin & Taylor Group Ltd., New Zealand, and Nabeel A. Y. Al-Qirim of United Arab Emirates University, UAE, reports a case study of a large New Zealand organization about the company's level and scope of Gigabit Ethernet (GigE) deployment, the problems the company encountered, network performance issues, and test results. The use of optical fiber for switch-to-switch connections have some obvious benefits, such as longer distance coverage, low attenuation, and less electromagnetic interference than the copper cables. However, the company under study used low-cost Cat 5e UTP cable as an alternative option to deliver 1 Gbps over 100 meters. The research findings show that the organization first achieved around 300 Mbps after the network upgraded to GigE. This limitation of the overall network throughput is mainly due to the low-end PC-based servers and the associated hardware. However, as expected with faster server hardware, the overall network throughput especially at server-to-server configuration is nearly up to 1 Gbps.

Chapter VI, *"Interaction Between MIMD-Poly & PIPD-Poly Algorithms and Other TCP Variants in Multiple Bottleneck TCP Networks"* by M. Chandrasekaran of Directorate of Technical Education, India, and R. S. D. Wahida Banu of Government College of Engineering, India, discusses two Polynomial Congestion Control Algorithms called MIMD-Poly and PIPD-Poly. The interaction between these two algorithms and other TCP variants in multiple bottleneck TCP Networks are presented. The chapter starts with the introduction and analysis of the non-linear congestion control algorithms that generalize the Additive Increase and Multiplicative Decrease algorithms. These algorithms provide additive increases using a polynomial of the inverse of the current size of window and multiplicative decreases using the polynomial of the current size of window. This chapter analyses the interaction between the two algorithms for the wired and wireless TCP networks. The compatibility of these algorithms is evaluated through simulations. The results of simulations are compared with other TCP variants and it is shown that both algorithms perform well.

Chapter VII, "*A Systematic Approach to the Analysis and Configuration of Audio/Video-on-Demand Services*" by Xabiel G. Pañeda, David Melendi, Roberto García, Manuel Vilas, and Victor García of University of Oviedo, Spain, presents research on audio/video streaming services that play an important role in the Internet. Users are interested in watching news and video clips or listening to their favourite songs. Due to this, companies are encouraged to deploy this type of services. However, maintaining them in good condition is not a simple task, at least for people with little experience in this field. This chapter presents a formal method for carrying out the main tasks in order to reach the best performance of the service, namely analysis and configuration. Analysis to evaluate the most interesting content, the resource consumption, and the QoS are defined. Using this information, the method proposes some processes to help the content producer and the system administrator configure the service. Following all the steps defined in the proposed method, both content providers and system administrators can manage a high performance audio/video service.

Chapter VIII, "*Mobile Information Processing Involving Multiple Non-Collaborative Sources*" by Say Ying Lim, David Taniar, and Bala Srinivasan of Monash University, Australia, describes how the information processing can be carried out when users are on the run. The information that mobile users need is not always available on a single server. So they need to query two or more different servers, obtain the information on their mobile device, and perform some operations on the gathered information in order to satisfy their information needs. Such downloading and combining of information from non-collaborative sources may be useful for various applications related to entertainment, tourism, and business sales. The authors study server strategy where a mobile user queries a server, on-air strategy where a server broadcasts to several mobile users, and a client strategy where a mobile device performs local operations on cached data. They propose various examples and cases where combinations of these strategies are used for retrieving information from non-collaborative sources and study them to show that location based data play an important role in mobile information processing.

Chapter IX, "*Network Planning Algorithms for Optimizing Signalling Load in Mobile Networks*" by Vilmos Simon and Sándor Imre of Budapest University of Technology and Economics, Hungary, describes design of mobile networks. In the next generation IP based mobile networks the cell handover will cause incremental signaling traffic, which can be critical from the point of view of delay variation. It will worsen the quality parameters of the real-time services, which are the backbone of next generation mobile commercial services. By designing and implementing location areas in a cellular mobile network, the number of handovers can be decreased significantly. The authors designed and implemented two Location Area Designing algorithms: a location area forming algorithm and a cell regrouping algorithm that can help to guarantee QoS parameters in next generation networks. They used a realistic mobile environment simulator to generate input statistics on cell changes and incoming call for the algorithms. By comparing the values of the cost functions proposed by them, they showed that significant reduction could be achieved in the amount of the signalling traffic, the location update, and the total cost.

Chapter X, "*A Heuristic Solution to the Large Scale Cellular Telecommunication Network Expansion Problem*" by Joon-Yeoul Oh of Texas A&M University-Kingsville, USA, and John P. Mullen of New Mexico State University, USA, provides a new algorithm for design of a cellular network. The increasing demand for cellular phone services often leads to a situation in which existing capacity is no longer adequate, resulting in such unpleasant experiences as unstable connections, blocked call attempts, and dropped calls. A common solution to this problem is network expansion, in which new physical components are placed to assure satisfactory network performance. An optimal solution would be one that does so at the lowest possible cost, but for even moderately large networks, solving such problems is extremely difficult or not practical. This research article presents a highly efficient heuristic algorithm that considers capacity and redundancy requirements, as well as cost. It finds a very good solution in minutes, instead of months or years, together with lower bounds on cost of an optimal solution. The article also demonstrates its relative efficiency and discusses each algorithm step in detail.

Chapter XI, *"Wireless Proxy: Distributed System to Mitigate the Effects of User Mobility Over Streaming Services on IEEE 802.11 Wireless LANs"* by Manuel Vilas, Xabiel G. Pañeda, David Melendi, Roberto García, and Victor García of University of Oviedo, Spain, describes wireless LANs that provide user mobility support. One problem associated with wireless LANs is the uncertainty associated with the process of handoff. Since users are responsible for choosing the time of handoff, it often results in periods of time when the mobile device remains connected to the old access point in spite of degradation of service. This severely affects the performance of streaming media. The authors propose a new method for automatic handoff of wireless LAN connection to a different access point that is available. This is done using a wireless proxy that monitors network conditions and initiates handoff when channel conditions detoriate. The authors test the method using commercial streaming platforms and off-the-shelf Wi-Fi devices and report that improvement in data rate after the handoff is almost instantaneous and the playback quality for audio/video services suffers little when using an automated distributed handoff system.

Chapter XII, *"Soft Decision Parallel Interference Cancellation for Multi-Carrier DS-CDMA"* by R. Radhakrishnan and K. R. Shankarkumar of Sri Ramakrishna Engineering College, and A. Ebenezer Jeyakumar of Government College of Engineering ,India, presents technical research on wireless communication. Mobile communication promotes greater personal security and communication from any remote place, time, or form in the world. Since a channel is very expensive, it is desirable to simultaneously allocate the available channel to multiple users. Multiple access schemes are used to allow many simultaneous users to share a common communication channel to communicate with each other. Multi-carrier DS-CDMA is found to be attractive in applications such as wireless networks, broadband local access and cellular telephony. However, the performance and capacity of a DS-CDMA system are limited by multiple access interference and near far problems. The authors propose a new technique for multi-user detection using Parallel Interference Cancellation. This technique provides a good compromise between complexity, latency, and performance.

Chapter XIII, *"Distributed Resources Management in Wireless LANs that Support Fault Tolerance"* by Ghassan Kbar and Wathiq Mansoor of American University in Dubai (AUD), UAE, discusses the management of resources in wireless networks. Wireless LAN technology provides flexibility and reliability for business computer users where wire-line installation proves impractical. Applying the proper Radio Resource management technique for wireless LANs will lead to better control of the wireless network performance in terms of reliability, availability, fairness, and scalability especially when deploying it on a large scale. Distributed Dynamic Resource Management deployed in mobile terminals and access points potentially improves the network availability and reliability compared to centralized management which is badly affected by single point of failure. In order to evaluate the performance of wireless LAN using Distributed Dynamic Resource Management, the system is analyzed using normal and binomial distributions under different conditions. The analytical results described in this chapter show a very good network performance when implementing distributed resources management technique for wireless LANs.

Chapter XIV, *"Cooperative Data Caching and Prefetching in Wireless Ad Hoc Networks"* by Mieso K. Denko of University of Guelph, Canada, states that caching and prefetching are predominantly used in wired networks in order to reduce network latency when answering queries through database lookup. The use of such techniques is also advisable for wireless ad-hoc networks for better network performance. The authors propose a clustering architecture that allows localized and adaptive caching in order to reduce the delay in access when the user remains mobile. Effectiveness of any caching approach is dependant on the cache replacement policy that is adopted and in this case the cache replacement policy uses frequency of access and time of access as the two important measures for deleting unpopular files. The adopted cooperative caching, prefetching, and cache replacement policy is tested in a network simulator that uses a particular type of ad hoc routing protocol. The results show that the proposed method performs quite well in terms of average data accessibility, average query delay, and network traffic overhead.

Chapter XV, "*A Survey on Fuzzy Reasoning Applications for Routing Protocols in Wireless Ad-Hoc Networks*" by Essam Natsheh of King Faisal University, Saudi Arabia, provides an analysis of mobile wireless ad-hoc networks that are networks without infrastructure. In these networks, every node must discover its local neighbors and through those neighbors it must communicate to nodes that are out of its transmission range. These networks suffer from all kinds of uncertainty, randomness, and fuzziness. This leads to the need for highly adaptive routing protocols that are adaptable to high variability and uncertainty for these types of networks. Recently, many researchers adaptively optimize the ad-hoc routing protocols functions and parameters using the fuzzy reasoning algorithm (FRA). The FRAs are proposed to overcome the shortcoming of ad-hoc networks. In this paper the author presents a survey of fuzzy reasoning based routing for mobile ad-hoc networks. He discusses the main problems that have been solved by this class of routing protocols and identifies some drawbacks of the proposed methods and possible solutions.

Chapter XVI, "*Fuzzy Linguistic Knowledge for Active Queue Management in Wireless Ad-Hoc Networks*" by Essam Natsheh of King Faisal University, Saudi Arabia, states that in a mobile ad-hoc network, every node can work as a router. Every node has protocols and services to request and provides services to other nodes with the capability to handle congestions. Traditionally, the congestion handling is done through Transmission Control Protocol. This protocol sends congestion signal when the node's queue is full. Some studies showed that early dropping of incoming packet before reaching the maximum queue length is an effective technique to avoid congestion and to minimize the packet latency. As an example, Active Queue Management drops incoming packets before the queue is full. Mobile ad-hoc networks suffer from high network congestion. This substantiates the need for queue management algorithms that are adaptable to high variability and uncertainty for these types of networks. The proposed fuzzy logic-based queue management algorithm overcomes the shortcomings of ad-hoc networks.

Chapter XVII, "*Risk Factors to Retrieve Anomaly Intrusion Information and Profile User Behavior*" by Yun Wang of Yale University, Yale-New Haven Health System & Qualidigm, USA and Lee Seidman of Qualidigm, USA, shows that analyzing network traffic audit data can lead to detection of the anomalous network connections and for profiling user behaviors. It is important to do so to uphold the security of corporate networks. The authors use a data mining approach using bootstrap resampling and logistic regression to study this issue. They use a benchmark data that consists of seven weeks of TCP dump network traffic data and two weeks of testing data with 34 types of attacks. The authors identify 16 important risk factors that can determine whether a connection is anomalous or not. An important contribution of the research is that the risk factors that reduced the full data by 65% is still able to predict anomalous connections quite well and show comparable performance to the full dimensional data in terms of metrics like sensitivity, specificity, and accuracy. The knowledge of the risk factors that are discovered in this research can be used to filter network traffic or to develop other advanced detection systems.

Chapter XVIII, "*Network Setup for Secure Routing in Inter-Vehicle Communication Networks*" by Rania Wehbi, Ayman Kayssi, Ali Chelab, and Zaher Dawy of American University of Beirut, Lebanon, describes communication in moving vehicles which is a challenging issue and falls under the realm of inter-vehicular communication. Inter-vehicular networks act as a wireless ad-hoc network where each vehicle acts as a node of the network. The issue of setup and maintenance of such networks is challenging because the vehicles are in motion and are passing through different location with differing connectivities. This research proposes a secure routing protocol called SERVEN that can achieve near instantaneous secure communication among vehicles. Different action steps of the protocol like hello, join, reply, challenge, not accept, accept, fired, and alert are fully described in this paper that explain step-by-step how this protocol works. Using a network simulator, the authors go on to show that for a network limited to 30 hops the time needed to accept a joining node is quite small and the bandwidth consumed in the worst case scenario is reasonable.

Chapter XIX, *"Metropolitan Broadband Networks: Design and Implementation Aspects, and Business Models"* by Antonios Alexiou, Research Academic Computer Technology Institute and University of Patras, Greece, Christos Bouras, Research Academic Computer Technology Institute and University of Patras, Greece, John Papagiannopoulos, University of Aegean, Greece, and Dimitrios Primpas, Research Academic Computer Technology Institute and University of Patras, Greece, details the adoption of a broadband network in the region of Western Greece. The network consists of a fiber optic and Ethernet based infrastructure that is used in the metropolitan area of the city of Patras. It also includes a wireless broadband municipal network that is implemented in the city of Messatida. The main aim of the broadband network is to connect the public services related buildings in the region. At the same time, the designers want to create competition among access providers and content providers so that the end user can benefit from the advanced infrastructure and its associated services. Technical issues related to the creation and maintenance of the hierarchical broadband infrastructure such as choice of technology and interconnection are discussed in this chapter. Several contending business models are proposed and the open access model is selected due to the advantages that it can provide to the broadband project.

The field of telecommunication and networking has become strategically important for most organizations within the past few years, and this continues to grow at a rapid pace. Professionals and educators alike will find that the Advanced Business Data Communication and Networking series is a constantly up-to-date tool necessary for understanding and implementing telecommunication and networking technologies into the daily lives of professors, researchers, scholars, professionals, and all individuals in general. An outstanding collection of the latest research associated with the effective use of wired and wireless networks, Advanced Business Data Communications and Networking, Volume I provides the latest research on telecommunication and their integral role in our ever-changing technological world.

Indranil Bose
Editor-in-Chief
Advances in Business Data Communication and Networking Series, Volume I

Chapter I
Strategic Outsourcing:
Opportunities and Challenges for Telecom Operators

Varadharajan Sridhar
Management Development Institute, India

ABSTRACT

Telecom operators have a wide variety of functions to perform including marketing of telecom products and services, managing their networks, providing after-sales customer service, and innovating new products and services in tune with fast changing technologies. Though until recently the telcos have kept their core network management functions in-house, there are recent announcements of large scale outsourcing of network management functions. As operators, especially those providing mobile services, have evolved from offering voice services to advanced data and video services, the Information Technology (IT) services required for appropriate management of these vale added service offerings have also become complex. Some carriers have also outsourced their IT functions to large IT services vendors. In this chapter we deliberate the reasons for strategic outsourcing such as core competency, production economies, and transaction costs as presented in the literature and analyze these in the context of outsourcing model pioneered by an Indian mobile operator. We also explain vulnerabilities and risks associated with these outsourcing contracts and measures to be taken by the firm to mitigate their effects.

INTRODUCTION

Outsourcing is defined as the process of commissioning part or all of an organization's assets, people, and/ or activities to one or more external service providers (Lee, 2006). Lee (2006) further points out that since outsourcing can make organization either agile and proactive, or sluggish and reactive, it is just not an operational decision but a strategic one with far-reaching consequences.

Quinn & Hilmer (1994) point out the following two strategic outsourcing approaches used by chief managers of organizations:

1. Concentrate the firm's own resources on a set of "core competencies" where it can achieve definable preeminence and provide unique value for customers.
2. Strategically outsource other activities—including many traditionally considered integral to any company—for which the firm has neither a critical strategic need nor special capabilities.

By doing the above, firstly, the firms maximize return on internal resources. Second, well developed core competencies provide formidable barriers against future and present competition. Third, the firms that outsource are able to fully utilize the external supplier's investments, innovations and specialized professional capabilities to their advantage. Fourth, this joint strategy decreases risk, shorten cycle times, lowers capital and operating expenditures for the firm.

Through out 1990s, large firms in the United States first began outsourcing non-core information technology (IT) services to large companies domestically, preferring to have these services provided securely and reliably from outside, rather that building up in house expertise. Outsourcing work mainly included software application development and maintenance.

Typically the IT services and their associated processes tend to be human intensive and are traditionally outsourced to countries where the labor costs are lower and from where the services could be delivered remotely without sacrificing quality and efficiency (Sridhar & Bharadwaj, 2006). Referred to as offshoring, the organization's products and services in this case are provisioned from locations in other countries (Davis, et al.,2006). Examples of such offshore outsourcing areas include customized software development, package software implementation, software product testing, customer care support services, IT infrastructure management and back office operations.

US companies expanded off-shoring through partnership, acquisitions and local subsidiaries. Thus they followed a less risky and more strategic approach of alliances by keeping the control with them. Their sourcing strategy more closely resembled the "in-sourcing" strategy of traditional offshore investments for global manufacturing. Sridhar & Bharadwaj (2006) discuss details on the model of growth of IT and IT Enabled Services outsourcing industry.

Strategic Outsourcing Models

Following are the three different outsourcing strategies pursued by firms (Lee, 2006):

Independent Outsourcing Strategy

In an independent strategy, relationships with external providers are tenuous, with interactions lasting for a very brief period of time. In this strategy, firms acquire resources externally but manage them internally. Firms develop indigenous competency thus minimizing dependence on external entities for critical organizational resources. This approach pursues a minimal outsourcing, buy-in contract and short-term duration strategy to gain outsourcing benefits by redirecting the business in to core competencies.

Arm's Length Outsourcing Strategy

An arm's length approach is based on non-idiosyncratic relationships with the presumption that sellers are interchangeable. These relationships commence with a detailed specification of each party's obligations. The control of unspecified obligations are vested on the provider. In order to minimize the exposure to provider opportunism, such relationships are loosely coupled, and long-term commitments are avoided. The outcome of such relationships is typically cost efficiency through the competitive pricing of services. In summary, this strategy focuses on improving the business' financial position by pursuing a selective outsourcing, fee-for-service contract, and medium-term approach.

Embedded Outsourcing Strategy

Embedded arrangements are superior in their ability to facilitate knowledge transfer and acquisition. The strength and stability of the relationships are derived in large part from both parties being committed to a long-term relationship. Opportunism is curtailed by the anticipated cost of foregoing a long-term relationship. Personal ties and emergent trust prevail and partners undertake joint problem solving. Hence the objective of this outsourcing strategy consists of comprehensive outsourcing, partnership, and long-term relationship to strengthen resource and flexibility in technology service that underpins the firm's business direction.

Though there are a number of studies on IT outsourcing as pointed out by Sridhar & Bharadwaj (2006), there is a dearth of studies of IT outsourcing practiced in different industry verticals such as manufacturing and telecom. In this chapter, we look specifically at the strategic outsourcing in the telecom industry. Telecom operators have a wide variety of functions to perform including marketing telecom products and services, managing their networks, providing after-sales customer service, innovating new products and services in tune with fast changing technologies. Though until recently the telcos have kept their core network management functions in-house, there are recent announcements of large scale outsourcing of network management functions. As operators, especially those providing mobile services have evolved from offering voice services to data and video services, the IT services required for appropriate management of these value added service offerings have also become complex. Some carriers have also outsourced their IT functions to large IT services vendors.

In this chapter, we discuss the motivations behind such outsourcing contracts, taking examples from a mobile service provider in India. In the next section, we discuss trends in outsourcing by telecom operators. Subsequently we discuss reasons for outsourcing by telecom operators citing examples from the Indian telecom industry on outsourcing contracts. We also discuss vulnerabilities of outsourcing and imitations effects. We conclude with future research directions.

TRENDS IN OUTSOURCING BY TELECOM OPERATORS

Following are the three different areas of outsourcing being pursued by the telecom operators:

1. **Network operations and management:** Network capacity planning and deployment, integrating network equipment, network maintenance, installation and fault repair, deployment of new network services.
2. **IT Management:** IT infrastructure management, desktop and server management, Operational Support Services (OSS), Billing Support Services (BSS), customer relationship management software development and implementation, deployment of new IT services.
3. **Customer Relationship Management:** Call centre services.

However, the nature and complexity of the above operations differ across different types of services (viz. mobile, fixed) offered by the telecom operators. The amount of outsourced work differs depending on the following models adopted by the telecom operators:

1. **Full Outsourcing:** The contracting partner takes full responsibility for the functions and services. Typically this involves transferring both staff and assets by the operator to

the contracting partner. Examples include Redstone which outsourced its entire UK operations to BT Wholesale, Hutchison "3" in Italy and the UK.

2. **Out-tasking:** In this model, the telco borrows skilled engineers and other resources from the contractors. However it retains full control and management of network operations and services. Examples include Movistar in Puerto Rico which out tasked the technical support functions to Lucent.

3. **Build Operate and Transfer:** The contractor takes responsibility for designing, building and deploying the network. After the services are commenced, the assets are transferred to the operator. This model is typically used for green field projects such as network build-out by new entrants or new network services such as 3G/4G by the incumbent operators. Examples include the technology upgrade of Eurotel of the Czech Republic.

4. **Managed Capacity:** The contractor takes responsibility to provide the operators with capacity to provide various service offerings. Examples include Bharti Airtel in India outsourcing capacity management to Nokia-Siemens and Ericsson.

Indian Mobile Market

Quick deployment, competition, advancement in technologies, and reduced cost of access has propelled the growth of mobile services in India much like in other emerging countries. Indian mobile subscriber base continues to grow and has reached about 225 million in December 2007 from about 142 million a year ago. Figure 1 illustrates the exponential growth of mobile services in India. India currently has the world's third largest mobile subscriber base in the world, and is slated to exceed that of the US by the end of this year to become the second largest in the world, next only to China. The compounded annual growth rate of

Figure 1. Growth of mobile services in India

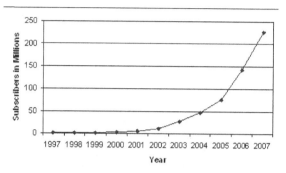

mobile subscriber base has been 84.2 percent over the last five years. Revenue from cellular mobile services touched $12.5 billion for the fiscal year ending March 2007 (Voice & Data, 2007).

However, Sridhar (2007) points out that intense competition, very low prices, very low Average Revenue Per User (ARPU), and high regulatory levies are characteristics of the Indian mobile industry. These have forced Indian telecom operators to adopt innovative methods to improve productivity and efficiency and reduce expenses.

Outsourcing by Bharti Airtel

In 2003, Bharti Airtel, the largest private telecom operator in India outsourced its network management and IT operations. In March 2003, Bharti outsourced its data centre operations, billing support systems, application development, and customer relationship management valued at $750 million in a 10-year contract with IBM (Singh & Dubey, 2004). Bharti's agreement with IBM was based on revenue sharing. Over a period of ten years, IBM would design, build up, and maintain Bharti's IT network in a full outsourcing model in exchange for a portion of Bharti's revenues (Martinez-Jerez, & Narayanan, 2006a). During the contract period, IBM would operate Bharti's data centre, its disaster recovery site at Chennai, India, and the billing that Bharti does in its licensed service areas around the country, its Customer Relationship Management programme, all applications development, as well as the IT help desk. IBM would also handle over 80% of Bharti Airtel's current programme and project management.

Bharti followed this with outsourcing network management to Ericcson (in 14 license service areas) and Nokia Siemens (in 7 license service areas) for a 3-year $724 million contract. During this period, Ericsson and Nokia Siemens would manage base stations (antennae, switches, routers, transmitters and receivers) within their areas of operation, deploy new base stations as required, roll out new networks and applications, and take on board roughly 800 of Bharti Airtel staff. They would also add new staff dedicated to Bharti Airtel as the network and business of Bharti expanded. As a result of these outsourcing contracts, Bharti Airtel would now just handle a few things: marketing, sales and distribution. Apart from that, it would just monitor its vendors, see that they stick to the parameters of the contracts, and make sure that they deploy and build only the best systems and networks for Bharti's operations (Singh & Dubey, 2004).

While the IBM outsourcing deal followed the full outsourcing model, the network management was on a managed capacity model. The success of this outsourcing model is explained in detail in Martinez-Jarez & Narayanan (2006b). We discuss the reasons for the outsourcing contract (for details on Bharti Airtel, the reader is referred to Appendix I).

REASONS FOR STRATEGIC OUTSOURCING

Core Areas of the Firm

Companies consistently make more money than their competitors only if they can perform some activities—which are important to customers—more effectively than anyone else. The argument of focusing on core competency is cited by many researchers (Lacity, et al, 1996; Mcfarlan & Nolan,

1995; Prahalad & Hamel, 1990; and Willcocks, et al 1995). In a qualitative research, Pinnington & Woolcock (1995) have found that the drivers for IT related outsourcing were cost control and reduction, focusing on core competencies, access to new expertise and technologies and improved flexibility.

Way back in 1989, when Kodak announced outsourcing data center operations to IBM, telecommunication services to the Digital Equipment Corporation, and PC support to Business Land, it created quite a stir in the IT Industry. Never before had such a well known organization, where IS was considered to be a strategic asset, turned it over to third party providers (Applegate & Montealegre, 1991). Kodak appears to have legitimized outsourcing, creating what is known as "The Kodak Effect." A number of high profile multi-billion dollar "mega-deals" were signed increasing the awareness of outsourcing.

What is Core for Bharti?

The Indian mobile industry is highly fragmented with as many as 6-9 operators in most of the service areas. Figure 2 illustrates the amount of competition and market power as indicated by the Herfindahl Hirschman Index (HHI). (viz. lower the HHI, more is the competition). With more than 85% of mobile subscribers being pre-paid, Bharti

Figure 2. Competition in mobile services in India

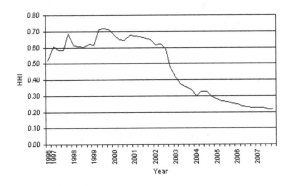

Figure 3. Growth of mobile subscribers of Bharti Airtel

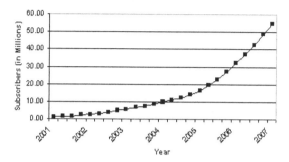

decided that acquiring and retaining customers is a very important core activity in which it should concentrate its energy and resources. Hence Bharti in its outsourcing strategy kept marketing, sales and distribution activities to itself so that they can dominate over their competitors in customer acquisition and retention.

Most of the telcos still consider their networks to be core to their business. This is especially true of government operators who consider networks to be their property and have been managing their erstwhile monopoly network operations by themselves. Though Bharti entered in to the telecom services market in 1995, the chief managers of the firm did not have the fixated idea of managing the network by them selves. Bharti created something akin to the "Kodak effect" in telecom outsourcing as it was watched by many operators world over for the success of it (Martinez-Jerez & Narayanan, 2006a). The shift in focus to concentrate resources on customer facing core activities seems to have paid of for Bharti. This is reflected in the growth in subscriber base of Bharti since 2003 as illustrated in Figure 3.

Maintaining Competitive Advantage

Quinn & Hilmer (1994) point out that the key strategic issue in insourcing versus outsourcing is whether a company can achieve a maintainable competitive edge by performing an activity, usually cheaper, better, in a more timely fashion or with unique capability on a continuous basis. They further pointed out that Ford Motor Company found that many of its internal suppliers' quality practices and costs were nowhere near that of external suppliers when it began its famous "best in class" worldwide benchmarking quality studies.

However outsourcing entails contractual risks such as vendor bankruptcy, vendor's inability to deliver, and contract breach by the vendor. To mitigate these, the firm engages in screening the vendor ex-ante and monitoring vendors ex-post. In screening, the firm's goal is to identify a potential vendor who is best suited for providing a certain service. Through proper screening, firms can reduce the risk of opportunism and adverse selection (Vitharana & Dharwadkar, 2007).

How Bharti Chose its Partners and Managed them?

Bharti chose Ericsson and Nokia Siemens, the top two mobile network equipment manufacturers for network management. Further, Bharti decided to partner with the best-in-class in managed IT services so that the technical aspects of developing and managing various IT services are also outsourced. IBM, the global leader in managed IT services, was selected to provide Bharti with complete and comprehensive end-to-end management of all of Bharti's hardware, software and applications requirements along with expert management of the IT infrastructure. Even while IT companies in India were going after large export IT off-shore contracts, IBM won the major domestic contract from Bharti due to expertise and world leadership (Sridhar, 2008).

Telecom technologies change rapidly and risk of technology obsolescence is very high in the industry. Outsourcing network management and capacity planning to equipment vendors like Ericsson and Nokia-Siemens, Bharti transferred the technology obsolescence risk to the vendors.

With constant growth in the market, Bharti was finding it difficult to recruit and train skilled manpower for its IT and network functions. However, large vendors such as IBM, Nokia-Siemens and Ericsson had huge skilled technical manpower and were in much better position to do the corresponding functions more efficiently than the telecom operators such as Bharti (Martinez-Jarez & Narayanan, 2006a).

The success of outsourcing is related to the service quality (Grover, et al, 1996). With highly trained manpower, the vendors of both IT and telecom were able to provide the much needed quality of services to Bharti.

Production Economies

Neoclassical economics regards any business organization as a production unit motivated by profit maximization. Williamson (1981) argues that a firm justifies sourcing options based on production economies. In the context of telecom and IT, a firm will choose to outsource or in source based on the comparative costs of internalizing the functions versus the price it has to pay vendors for the services (Saarinen & Vepasalainen, 1994). The propensity to outsource exists due to reduction in production cost as cited by Lacity, et al. (1996), Loh & Venkatraman (1992a), McFarlan & Nolan (1995). Although the reports in press and media tend to inflate the potential savings (Lacity & Hirschheim, 1993), the comparative cost advantages offered by vendors are a major factor in outsourcing services (Ang & Straub, 1998). Loh & Venkatraman (1992b) have empirically supported a positive relationship between IT cost structure and outsourcing. It is hypothesized by Ang & Straub (1998) that the higher the production cost advantage offered through IT outsourcing, the greater the degree of outsourcing. Thus the key compelling force driving the companies to outsource is savings due to reductions in direct wage costs and other operating expenses.

Murray & Kotabe (1999) have shown a negative relationship between asset specificity and internal sourcing of supplementary services. The result suggests that unlike product sourcing strategy where asset specificity and internal sourcing are positively related, supplementary services tend to be sourced externally to reduce fixed investment and increase operational flexibility.

How did Bharti achieve Production Economies?

In both network and IT outsourcing contracts, Bharti transferred its employees who were performing the functions outsourced to the payroll of the contracting partners. Soon after the outsourcing contract was signed up to 1000 engineers were transferred from Bharti to the vendors. According to one of the chief managers of Bharti these engineers were happier working for the technology companies than with the service providers. This apart from decrease in wage costs, improved efficiency of operations as well.

The managed capacity model with network vendors allowed Bharti the flexibility to pay the vendors on *Erlang* basis as and when the network capacity was up and running and was used. This avoided excess capital expenditure by Bharti on its network infrastructure deployed in anticipation of future demand. This also allowed Bharti a window of credit period and hence rationalized the capital expenditure in tune with the actual demand. The focus of the Indian mobile operators was switching from plain vanilla voice to value added services. Indian operators had to adopt 2.5G and 3G services to provide these services which required large capital expenditure (Martinez-Jarez & Narayanan, 2006a). The managed capacity model followed by Bharti protected it against such large expenditures.

Due to capacity based payment to network vendors, it was estimated that the capital expenditure of Bharti declined by as much as $730 million in 2007 (Singh & Dubey, 2004).

Transaction Costs

Quinn & Hilmer (1994) discuss that while outsourcing, analysts must include both internal transaction costs as well as those associated with external outsourcing. External transaction costs refer to the effort, time, and costs incurred in searching, creating, negotiating, monitoring and enforcing a service contract between buyers and suppliers (Mahoney 1992).

These transaction costs can erode comparative advantages in the production costs of vendors. However Ang and Straub (1998) have shown that both production cost and transaction costs are important in decision while outsourcing, however production costs are the overwhelming dominant factor, about six times as large as that of transaction costs. Considerable reduction in production cost with only marginal increase in transaction cost

increases propensity to outsource. If the products and services were to be internal, firms must back it up with continuing personnel development and infrastructure management.

How did Bharti Reduce Transaction Costs?

Due to high growth in mobile services, Chief Managers of Bharti were tendering, negotiating and working with the vendors every six months for network expansion. This resulted in (i) huge management bandwidth being spent on follow-up and other non-innovative, non-customer oriented activities and (ii) delays in deploying networks in a very competitive market place and (iii) unpredictable business models (Singh & Dubey, 2004). Quinn & Hilmer (1994) argue that one of the great gains in outsourcing is the decrease in

Table 1. Example SLAs Bharti had with Network Outsourcing Partners (Banerjee, 2008).

	Areas of Measurements	Target	Lower Control Limit	Upper Control Limit	No Reward Limit
1	Network Availability				
1.1	Network Availability of Switch	>99.95%	<99.93%	>99.97%	<99.5%
1.2	Network Availability of Radio Access	>99.2%	<99%	>99.4%	<98.5%
2	Available Network Capacity				
2.1	Switch Network Utilization	<70%	>55% &<65%	>80%	
2.2	Peak Processor Load during 24 hours	<70%	<60%	>80%	
2.3	Cells having utilization >=90%	<10%	<5%	>15%	
3	Network Accessibility				
3.1	Successful Call Rate	95%	<92%	>98%	<88%
3.2	Random Access Success Rate	95%	<92%	>98%	
3.3	Call Handover Success Rate	90%	<87%	>93%	
4	Voice Quality				
4.1	Percentage of cells having SQI samples between 16-30	95%	<93%	>97%	<88%
5	Customer Satisfaction Index				
5.1	No. of Network Related Complaints per 1000 Subscribers	<3	<2	>4	
5.2	Percentage of Network Related Complaints Resolved Within SLA	>90%	<85%	>95%	<80%

executive time for managing peripheral activities—freeing top management to focus more on the core of its business.

Bharti achieved this through well defined long term contracts with its vendors. However, managing and monitoring of the external partners required innovation in Service Level Agreements (SLAs). Detailed SLAs covering every aspect of outsourcing (for both IT and telecom) with associated penalties for non-conformance provided a framework for monitoring (Singh & Dubey, 2004). Examples of SLAs for the outsourced network management activities are included in Table 1. As is shown in the table, if any of the measurements fall below/ above certain threshold levels as indicated, there are penalties/ rewards as appropriate.

Along with SLAs, Bharti also defined Key Performance Indicators (KPIs) through which the performance of vendors were monitored and measured. By going for long term partnerships with select vendors of repute with detailed SLAs and KPIs, Bharti reduced the explicit transaction costs with the external vendors, thus making it a viable business model. It should be noted that the IT outsourcing with IBM was a full outsourcing model with corresponding set of SLAs. A list of over 100 SLAs were designed, implemented, measured and monitored by Bharti and IBM every month. The broad domains of SLAs included disaster recovery, infrastructure, projects, security and support (Details of some of the SLAs are provided in Martinez-Jerez & Narayanan, 2006b). Thus, by monitoring the SLAs and KPIs, Bharti ensured that the vendor fulfilled its obligations and guarded itself against potential vendor opportunism.

Vulnerabilities to Outsourcing

Quinn & Hilmer (1994) point out that there are vulnerabilities in outsourcing for the buyer as well. They point out, both the buyer (the firm) and the seller (the outsourcing contractor) entail some risks with respect to price, quality, time or other key terms of the contract. When there are many suppliers and mature market standards, a potential buyer is unlikely to be more efficient than the best available supplier. Another form of vulnerability is the lack of information available in the marketplace or from individual suppliers. For example, the seller might hide its inability to offer services due to lack of resources and/ or knowledge until it is too late for the customer to go elsewhere.

How did Bharti Manage Vulnerabilities?

Though the supplier market is matured for voice services, billing and operational support, advanced data offerings, and 3G services are still evolving and thus poses a risk for Bharti. However, Bharti minimized this vulnerability by outsourcing to the best-in-class such as IBM, Nokia Siemens and Ericsson who had enough resources to supply their respective products and services. After the outsourcing deal, Nokia Siemens moved its global Network Operations Centre to Chennai, India to deliver quality service. IBM today has one-fifth of its workforce in India accounting for the largest employee base next only to the US (Sridhar, 2008).

Another important vulnerability is the lack of buyers' competency to either assess or monitor sellers. The detailed SLAs along with Bharti's management expertise to monitor both the telecom and IT vendors' performance levels mitigated this vulnerability.

Degree of Sourcing Control

There is a constant trade-off between flexibility and control in outsourcing engagements. One of the main purposes of the network management outsourcing was to have suppliers assume certain classes of investments and risks, such as demand variability. However, at the same time, by outsourcing the core network management activities, Bharti faced "loss of control" over its services and the assets (both network and manpower). Quinn & Hilmer (1994) highlights that the outsourcing strategy can vary depending on the amount of control needed and degree of flexibility the buyer needed in responding to the market place to maintain competitive edge. As outsourcing grew in popularity, debate shifted from whether or not to outsource to how much to outsource (Lacity & Hirschheim, 1993).

Concerns during this stage of outsourcing evolution included whether outsourcing should be total or selective, service or asset, long or short term, involve single or multiple vendors. Bharti chose "long-term contracts" to have relatively high flexibility and lower control. Long term contracts also kept the suppliers interested in their services, thus minimizing the above mentioned vulnerabilities.

Adoption by Competitors

Firms see success of outsourcing contracts of competitors and imitate. Described as "jump on the bandwagon" (Lacity & Hirschheim, 1993) or "Kodak Effect" (Loh & Venkatraman, 1992a), such imitating behavior results in more companies going for outsourcing. Loh & Venkatraman (1992b) used diffusion modeling, in which there are two basic types of influences (internal and external) that drive the adoption of an innovation by members of a social system. They found evidence for internal sources of influence (outsourcing behavior of other firms) being better predictors for the observed distribution of outsourcing events than external sources (mass media reports and vendor sales figures) or mixed sources of influence (both external and internal). The internal influence model is structurally equivalent to the imitation model of Mahajan & Peterson (1985) which states that impetus for diffusion is an emulation of prior adopters by potential adopters.

Literature provides evidence to support that mimetic and normative institutional pressures lower governance and monitoring costs. When a firm realizes that most of its competitors outsource, it tends to adopt similar outsourcing practices in order to achieve legitimacy among its customers and business partners. In doing so, the firm is less likely to engage in comprehensive screening and monitoring, and instead use the same vendors and adopt standard, industry sanctioned monitoring practices (Vitharana & Dharwadkar, 2007).

As a support to the above arguments, major telecom operators in India have recently handed over large IT and network outsourcing contracts to the same set of vendors. Idea Cellular, India's fifth largest mobile operator, signed an IT outsourcing contract in 2007 with IBM for $500 million spread over seven years. Vodafone did the same with IBM for $1.5 billion. Aircel, which is owned by Maxis Telecom of Malaysia followed suit with outsourcing its IT services and Business Processes to Wipro, an Indian IT company (Sridhar, 2008). Similarly network management of Idea went to Ericsson while that of Vodafone was bagged by Nokia Siemens.

CONCLUSION

In this chapter we analyzed the strategic outsourcing by telecom operators and the reasons for the same. India's mobile telecommunications market is very dynamic and evolving. In a highly competitive market, Bharti had to continuously seek new opportunities from new products, services and market. It had to frequently add and change products and services in order that these would be the first in the market. This needed flexibility and innovation to be able to respond to the changing market environment. To function in this dynamic environment, Bharti looked for technological flexibility with an organic organizational structure. Hence it closely followed the "embedded outsourcing strategy" as explained in Lee (2006).

In this chapter, we only considered strategic outsourcing of network management and IT services related to the mobile services business. An important research question is to find out whether such outsourcing models can be successfully applied in other telecom businesses such as fixed line services as well.

This paper broadly validates reasons for outsourcing cited in the literature through a single case study. Though Martinez-Jerez & Narayanan (2006b) looked at Bharti's outsourcing deal and its subsequent impact over a one-year time period, longitudinal studies of the kind are rare to find. It will be interesting to look at cross section of such similar outsourcing contracts of the other firms over a time period so that the intended effects and actual effects can be ascertained. This is of even more interest when the network outsourcing market is expected to grow to $100 billion by 2010.

REFERENCES

Ang, S., & Straub, D. W. (1998). Production and Transaction economies and IS Outsourcing: A study of the US Banking Industry. *MIS Quarterly*, 535-552.

Applegate, L., & Montealegre, R. (1991). Eastman Kodak Organization: Managing Information System through Strategic Alliances. *Harvard Business School Case*, 9-192-030. Boston, Massachusetts.

Banerjee, J. (2008). *Outsourcing Operator Networks—Strategic Options*. Executive Management Programme Dissertation, Management Development Institute, India.

Davis, G., Ein-Dor, P., King, W., & Torkzadeh, R. (2006). IT Offshoring: History, Prospects and Challenges. *Journal of the Association for Information Systems*, 7(11), 770-795.

Grover, V., Cheon, M. J., & Teng , J.T.C.(1996). The effects of service quality and partnership on the outsourcing of information systems functions. *Journal of Management Information system*, 12(4), 89-116.

Khanna, T., Palepu, K., & Vargas, I. (2003). Bharti Tele-Ventures. Case No: 9-704-426. Boston, MA: Harvard Business School.

Lacity, M. C., & Hirschheim, R. (1993). *Information Systems Outsourcing: Myths, Metaphors and Reality*. New York, NY: John Wiley & Sons.

Lacity, M. C., Willcocks, L. P. & Feeny, D. F. (1996). The value of selective IT outsourcing. *Sloan Management Review.*, 37, 13-25.

Lee, J. (2006). Outsourcing Alignment with Business Strategy and Firm Performance. *Communications of the Association of Information Systems*, 17, 1124-1146.

Loh, L., & Venkatraman, N. (1992a). Diffusion of information technology outsourcing: influence sources and the Kodak effect. *Information Systems Research*, 3, 334-58.

Loh, L., & Venkatraman, N. (1992b). Determinants of IT outsourcing: A cross-sectional analysis. *Journal of Management Information Systems*, 9, 7-24.

Mahajan, V. & Peterson, R. (1985). *Models for Innovation Diffusion*, Sage Publications, Beverly Hills, CA.

McFarlan, F. W., & Nolan, R. L. (1995). How to manage an IT outsourcing alliance. *Sloan Management Review*, 36, 9-22.

Mahoney, J. T. (1992). Organizational economics within the conversation of strategic management. *Advances in Strategic Management*, 8, 103-156.

Martinez-Jerez, A., & Narayanan, V. G. (2006a). Strategic Outsourcing at Bharti Airtel Limited. One Year Later. Case No: 9-107-003. Boston, MA: Harvard Business School.

Martinez-Jerez, A., & Narayanan, V.G. (2006b). Strategic Outsourcing at Bharti Airtel Limited. Case No: 9-107-004. Boston, MA: Harvard Business School.

Murray, J. Y., & Kotabe, M. (1999). Sourcing strategies of US companies: a modified transaction—Cost analysis. *Strategic Management Journal, 20,* 791-809.

Pinnington, A., & Woolcock, P. (1995). How far is IS/IT outsourcing enabling new organizational structure and competences? *International Journal of Information Management, 15*(5), 353-365.

Prahalad, C. K., & Hamel, G. (1990). The Core Competence of the Corporation. *Harvard Business Review, 68*(3), 79-91.

Quinn , J. B., & Hilmer, F. G. (1994). Strategic Outsourcing. *Sloan Management Review, Summer* 43-55.

Saarinen, T., & Vepsalainen, A. P. J. (1994). Procurement Strategies for Information Systems. *Journal of Management Information Systems, 11*(2), 187-208

Sing, S., & Dubey, R. (2004). *The World's Top Off-shoring Locations.* Business Standard, Retrieved 4 October 2004 from World Wide Web http://www.businessworldindia.com.

Sridhar, V. (2007). Growth of mobile services across regions of India. *Journal of Scientific & Industrial Research, 66,* 281-289.

Sridhar, V. (2008). *Changing Landscape of the IT Industry.* Retrieved 16 February 2008 from World Wide Web http://www.economictimes.com

Sridhar, V., & Bharadwaj, S. (2006). Growth of Outsourced IT Enabled Services in India: A System Dynamics Approach. In Kehal, H. S., and Singh, V. P. (Eds.) *Outsourcing & Offshoring in the 21st Century: A socio economic perspective.* Hershey, PA, U.S.A.: Idea Publishing, 282-301.

Sridhar, V., Malik, A. (2007). Turning Copper in to Gold: Bharti Airtel's Fixed Line Service in India. *Asia Case Research Centre, University of Hong Kong,* Case Reference No: 07/329C.

Vitharana, P., & Dharwadkar, R. (2007). Information Systems Outsourcing: Linking Transaction Cost and Institutional Theories. *Communications of the Association for Information Systems, 20,* 346-370.

Willcocks, L. P., Fitzgerald, G., & Fenny, D. (1995). Outsourcing IT: The strategic implications. *Long Range Planning, 28*(5), 59-70.

Williamson, O. E. (1981). The Modern Corporation: Origin, Evolution, Attributes. *Journal of Economics Literature, 19,* 1537-1568.

APPENDIX I. BHARTI AIRTEL: ONE OF INDIA'S LARGEST TELECOM OPERATORS

Established in 1985, Bharti Airtel was a pioneering force in the telecom sector in India with many firsts and innovations to its credit. In 1995, Bharti was the first to launch mobile services in India's capital region of Delhi. Its brand "Airtel" became a household name across the country with "touching the lives of millions" as its byline. As of March 2006, Bharti's cellular subscribe base stood at about 21 million across all service areas accounting for 22 percent of the mobile subscriber base in India.

Having constructed 32,900 route kms of optic fiber network in the country, by 1998, Bharti Airtel had become the first private fixed line telephone service provider in the country. Bharti also was the first Indian company to provide comprehensive telecom services outside India in Seychelles and first private sector service provider to launch National Long Distance Services in India. The company further received license to provide International Long Distance service in April 2002, and became the first private telecom company in the country to own an undersea cable network of 3,200 kms from Chennai, India to Singapore. Bharti also was a founding member of the consortium of 15 global telecom operators that commissioned the South East Asia—Middle East—Western Europe—4 (SEA-ME-WE-4) fourth generation international network. At the time, Bharti Airtel had two main business units - Mobility and Infotel. While the Mobility section operated Bharti's cellular mobile services in the country, the Infotel section was divided into three types of services- fixed line services providing broadband and telephone service; National Long Distance and International Long Distance services; and enterprise services delivering end-to-end customized telecom solutions for corporate customers.

In 2004, with revenues touching US$1 billion, Bharti brought all the different services under its strong mobile services brand "Airtel". Under the new structure, while Airtel Mobile Services provided cellular mobile services, Airtel Broadband and Telephone services provided fixed line services and Airtel Enterprise and Carrier business unit provided enterprise services, national long distance and international long distance services.

Acknowledging the company's presence in the telecommunication sector, in 2005, world's largest mobile operator Vodafone forked out about US$ 1.5 billion for acquiring 10 percent stake in Bharti Airtel. By financial year ending March 2006, the company reported revenues of US$2.09 billion and notched in a net profit of US$424 million. Mobile services contributed to about 63% of the revenue while the Broadband & Telephone and Enterprise & Carrier business segments brought in the rest. In June 2006, Bharti Airtel was recognized as the "Best Indian Carrier" at the Telecom Asia Awards, 2006 (For further information on various operations of Bharti Airtel, the reader is referred to Sridhar & Malik, 2007 and Khanna, et al., 2003).

Chapter II
Empirical Prediction of Computer–Network Evolution

Sami J. Habib
Kuwait University, Kuwait

ABSTRACT

This article presents a computer-aided integration tool, iCAD, that can predict a network evolution. We have used the term a network evolution to mean predicting changes within the physical network topology as time evolves. iCAD is connected to four device libraries, each of which contains a distinct set of network-technology devices, such as Ethernet hubs, ATM switches, IP routers, and gateways. As a network technology changes, each device library is updated. Then, we have plotted the cost and performance changes between the old and recent network technologies, enabling us to predict future changes to a first order. This article presents empirical results from 1999 until 2005 recording the network evolution progress, where the lower and upper bounds of network evolution came out to be 10% to 25% and 57% to 74% respectively in terms of network-design cost reduction.

INTRODUCTION

The maintenance process of a network topology so that it can carry out all its communication tasks effectively and efficiently requires a steady tuning and upgrading. Therefore, how often and how to carry on such a process are questions yet to be answered. In other words, we want to identify a metric for predicting the network evolution and develop a design tool to carry on the prediction. Here we have defined a network-evolution metric

analogous to Moore's Law (Moore, 1965), which states that the number of transistors in an integrated circuit doubles every 18 months. We have stated that the cost of network-topology design when considering three types of network technologies is reduced at a lower rate of 10-25% and an upper rate of 57-74% in every 24 months.

The network-topology problem with technology considerations entails the allocation and integration of network devices (such as ATM switch, Ethernet hub, IP router, and gateway) that enable all clients to communicate and access file servers while minimizing the network-integration cost. Literally millions of possible network topologies can be considered for a given network. It is impossible for a human network designer to examine all possibilities for typical large installations. We have applied computer-aided design (CAD) techniques to design and redesign hierarchical computer networks to determine the network topology and network devices. The problem is known to be NP-complete (requiring an exponential number of steps to find an optimal solution) according to Gerla and Kleinrock (1977). The continual changes in the price, performance, and availability of network devices make the network-design process more difficult. The choices of network devices, which are made at a particular time, may not be appropriate a few months later.

The CAD tool, iCAD, is based on evolutionary approach. The tool creates an initial population of network topologies by selecting all network devices randomly. The software analyzes and evaluates each topology in the current population, selects the most fit topologies, modifies some, and discards the rest. New topologies are created by mutating existing topologies or by crossing over genetic material between two topologies. Then the optimization process continues. After several generations specified by the user, the tool terminates. The iCAD is connected to four device libraries, each of which contains a distinct set of network-technology devices, such as Ethernet hubs, ATM switches, IP routers, and gateways. Each device library contains information about device types and their attributes, such as cost, capacity, number of ports, and type of wire. As the network technology matures, the device library is updated. Thus, we have extended the usage of iCAD in Habib, Parker & Lee (2002) so that it can synthesize networks based on the current price and on the predicted future price. Because of this extension on iCAD, we are able to collect many empirical data regarding the network-design evolutions. In addition, we have insured that the

synthesized network, once designed, has been optimized for technologies available at the design time. We have examined the topological differences between the current network technologies and the future technologies. These differences would give guidance as to where the network should be upgraded in the future. Finally, we have upgraded existing design constraints by maintaining as much as possible of its original devices so that the upgrading costs are minimized. Maintaining as much as possible of the original devices is known as the legacy problem.

We have been observing and collecting the changes with the network technology, especially with respect to cost and capacity, for the past six years. Habib and Parker (2002) have recorded an initial study on the network evolution by comparing the outcomes from two sets of device libraries in years of 1999 and 2001. In this article, we have expanded our study by running iCAD with four different sets of libraries that go back to 1999, 2001, 2003, and 2005. We have plotted the cost and performance changes between networks designed with the old and recent network technologies. This enables us to predict future changes to a first order. The network-design cost has evolved at a decreasing rate from 10-25% to 57-74% for the past six years as our empirical data has shown. Over time, with more data points, the predictions will become more accurate.

The rest of the article is organized in four sections. The related work has been examined in following section. In "An Overview of the iCAD Tool," we describe the network design tool that is going to carry out all network evolution studies. The experimental results are presented in the section of the same name, and the section after that contains the conclusion.

RELATED WORK

The automatic-network evolution of physical-network topology has not been well researched and documented yet. However, the solution approaches to the network-topology-design problem are built on a wealth of research that can be classified into that of an abstract approach and that of a concrete approach. We have used the term *abstract* approach to mean determining only a set of links and their capacities to connect a set of nodes without specifying any type of network technology. On the other hand, we have used the term *concrete* approach to convey that at least one type of network technology is utilized to synthesize a network topology. Here we list many published papers that have addressed the design of network topology, either the abstract (Gerla & Kleinrock, 1977; Pierre & Legault, 1998; Saksena, 1989) or the concrete (Cosares, Deutsch, Saniee, & Wasem, 1995; Doshi, Dravida, & Harshavardhana, 1995; Elbaum & Sidi, 1996; Fahmy & Dougligeris, 1995; Gresht, 1989; Mitra, Morrison, & Ramakrishnan, 1998). These papers proposed many models and design methodologies for the network physical topology. We have studied and extended their models to be utilized for the network evolution even though none of these papers considered the network evolution. A few groups of researchers have attempted to examine the network evolution from different prospectives. The first group (Frogner & Cannara, 1999) has described a new way of achieving high accuracy in predicting network performance, where a network predictor is built for QoS networks, and it used a combination of network-component models and probabilistic analysis to predict the network performance. The predictor continuously monitors the quality of service, compares it with the expected or desired values and projects future values. Such a predictor uses the past data and performance measurements to predict the network behavior in the future, and it assumes that the network configuration and the policies are unchanged.

The second group (Vekiarides & Finkel, 1998) presented a NETCAP tool, which performed an analysis of Ethernet local area network (LAN) conditions and predicted the future performance of the LAN based on the prescribed changes. The third group (Beigi & Verma, 2001; Beigi, Calo, & Verma, 2004) of researchers from IBM Watson Researcher Center has presented network policies that enable the network administrator to determine whether adding, deleting, or changing a quality-of-service policy would affect the network performance. Network policies are a set of rules determined by the network administrator, to be used in configuring and sharing network resources between all users. A work by Verma (2002) has proposed to leverage the power of policies to simplify the provisioning and configuration of the different devices within the network. This simplification of the management functions is obtained via two elements of the policy-management tool and the policy architecture, namely centralization and business-level abstractions. *Centralization* refers to the process of defining all the device provisioning and configuration at a single point (the management tool) rather than provisioning and configuring each device itself. *Business-level abstractions* make the job of policy administrator simpler by defining the policies in terms of a language that is closer to the business needs of an organization rather than in terms of the specific technology needed to deploy it.

The last group of researchers from MIT and Cornell University (Nowell & Kleinberg, 2003) has defined and studied a basic computational problem underlying social-network evolution, the entitled link-prediction problem. Their problem states that, given a snapshot of a social network at time *t*, it seeks to accurately predict the edges that will be added to the network during the interval from time *t* to a given future time *t'*. In contrast to iCAD, the above articles analyze a network behavior for given policies, limit to one specific network technology, or predict the network performance. In other words, these papers identify the *need* for network evolution; however, they cannot *carry out* network evolution. With tool, we both identify and carry out the network evolution.

AN OVERVIEW OF THE ICAD TOOL

The prototype network tool consists of three main procedures as shown in Figure 1. An evolutionary approach is used to search the design space for a minimal three-level network cost that meets design and performance constraints. The first procedure generates an initial population of three-level network designs by selecting and integrating all network devices randomly. This procedure runs only one time and it insures that all topologies within the population are valid. The second procedure evaluates the cost and estimates the performance of each topology in the population. The third procedure mutates or interchanges portions of some selected topologies in the current population. The second and third procedures execute until the specified number of generations has been produced. The underlying model on which the iCAD tools are based is a large set of mixed-integer nonlinear constraints that must be satisfied to yield a correct design.

We have modeled a network as a three-level hierarchy (backbone, site, and group). The communication within a *group task* utilizes the lowest-level local area network (LAN) that connects a set of *clients* (workstations). The group tasks communicating within a *site task* use the intermediate-level network that connects a set of group LANs. The *backbone task* uses the highest-level network that connects all sites. An assumption is made that a network enterprise locates its clients in a manner where the most intense communications occur locally; moreover, the communications become less intense as the distances increase between the groups and sites. However, this might not be the case uniformly in all network enterprises. In order to perform all the collaborative group and site tasks, all clients need to communicate among themselves, and the network should provide the proper support to accomplish the global task within an acceptable time.

Figure 1. An overview of the iCAD tool

```
iCAD(CLT, CTM, TND, DL, EAP)
    /*CLT: is a table containing the client locations*/
    /*CTM: is a matrix containing the client traffic*/
    /*TND: represent a threshold network delay on the network performance*/
    /*DL: represents the four sets of network device libraries*/
    /*EAP: represents a set of parameters used by the evolutionary technique*/
Begin
    gen = 0;
    generate_initial_network_population();
    evaluate_network_population();
    while(gen < max_gen)
            begin
                    select_parents_for_next_offsprings();
                    perform_genetic_operations();
                    evaluate_network_population();
                    gen++;
            end
End
```

iCAD selects one network device for each network level (group, site, and backbone) and integrates all the selected network devices into a three-level network. We embedded a simple performance method (summing all the average delays of all network devices) within the tool to evaluate the synthesized networks (Bersekas & Gallager, 1992). In our formulation, the fitness function represents the total network cost, consisting of the summation costs of network devices, interconnections, and wires.

The output of iCAD is a population of optimized three-level network topologies. The inputs to the prototype network tool are application inputs and tool inputs. The application inputs include the client location table (CLT), client traffic matrix (CTM), and threshold network delay (TND). The CLT and CTM vary from application to application. The TND is a real value given by the designer to provide an upper bound for the average network delay (AND) of a synthesized three-level network topology. The tool inputs are the evolutionary approach's (EAP) parameters and device libraries (DL). The EAP's parameters refer to the population size (PS), number of generations (NG), crossover rate (CR), and mutation rate (MR). The PS indicates the number of candidate solutions that are used during the evolutionary-optimization process. The NG represents how often the evolutionary-optimization process will run. The crossover operator performs higher order transformations by combining parts from two networks (parents) to create a new pair of offspring. Thus, the crossover rate represents the probability of selecting the parents. The mutation operator performs unary transformations by changing a single feature in the network; therefore, the mutation rate represents the probability of selecting a topology for an alteration.

Description of Device Libraries

iCAD is connected to four libraries containing information about network-device types (ATM, Ethernet, IP router, and gateway) and their attributes such as cost, capacity, number of ports, and type of wire. In this article, we illustrate four sets of network libraries, which are collected and upgraded through the years, from 1999 to 2005. Table 1 summarizes iCAD's first network-library set (LIB99), which reflects the network device's status in the year 1999. The table shows four different network technologies with different ranges in communication bandwidth, number of ports, and costs.

Table 2 summarizes the updated iCAD's network device libraries (LIB01), which reflect the network components' status in the year 2001. This table contains network technologies similar to those shown in Table 1, but with different costs. Also, Tables 3-4 summarize the device libraries (LIB03) and (LIB05) that reflect the network components' status in the years 2003 and 2005 respectively.

From the four tables, we concluded that the prices of all network technologies dropped, but at different rates. Ethernet technology has dropped almost to 50% in cost from 1999 to 2001, while both ATM and IP router have dropped at the same rate of almost 25% in cost from 1999 to 2001. Ethernet technology has continued to drop 30% in cost from 2001 to 2003, but at slower rate than both ATM and IP router, which have dropped at the rate of 50% and 60% respectively. This is due to the maturity of ATM and IP-router technologies, which makes each the ultimate choice for high-speed networks. On the other hand, the Ethernet technology still offers a competitive choice due to legacy and high bandwidth such as GigaEthernet. However, the Ethernet technology is limited to three capacity selections (10Mbps, 100Mbps, and 1Gbps), and the price differences between them are huge. That could make ATM technology or IP router a more attractive choice during 2003, since both ATM and IP router offer more selections with different communication bandwidth. This makes ATM and IP router competitive with Ethernet. In 2005, the cost of

Table 1. LIB99, representing the status of network technology in 1999

Library Number	Network Technology	Number of Components Within Library	Range of Number of Ports	Range of Bandwidth, Mbps	Range of Cost ($)
1	Ethernet	36	2-32	10 – 1000	50 – 1,000,000
2	Gateway	25	2	1.5 - 1350	20 – 12,000
3	ATM	36	5-32	25 – 622	2000 – 250,000
4	IP Router	36	5-20	15 – 3000	1000 – 2,000,000

Table 2. LIB01, representing the status of network technology in 2001

Library Number	Network Technology	Number of Components Within Library	Range of Number of Ports	Range of Bandwidth, Mbps	Range of Cost ($)
1	Ethernet	36	2-32	10 – 1000	20 – 500,000
2	Gateway	25	2	1.5 - 1350	8 – 9,000
3	ATM	36	5-32	25 – 622	1500 – 200,000
4	IP Router	36	5-20	15 – 3000	700 – 1,400,000

Table 3. LIB03, representing the status of network technology in 2003

Library Number	Network Technology	Number of Components Within Library	Range of Number of Ports	Range of Bandwidth, Mbps	Range of Cost ($)
1	Ethernet	36	2-32	10 – 1000	14 – 350,000
2	Gateway	25	2	1.5 - 1350	4 – 4,500
3	ATM	36	5-32	25 – 622	750 – 100,000
4	IP Router	36	5-20	15 – 3000	280 – 560,000

Table 4. LIB05, representing the status of network technology in 2005

Library Number	Network Technology	Number of Components Within Library	Range of Number of Ports	Range of Bandwidth, Mbps	Range of Cost ($)
1	Ethernet	36	2-32	10 – 1000	10 – 100,000
2	Gateway	25	2	1.5 - 1350	4 – 2,000
3	ATM	36	5-32	25 – 622	600 – 75,000
4	IP Router	36	5-20	15 – 3000	50 – 75,000

all network technologies continued to drop up to 90% from 2003.

Network Cost Model

The network cost model (NCM) consists of the summation of device cost, interconnection cost and wire cost as shown in equation 1. The network-device cost (NDC) reflects all network devices (such as Ethernet hub, ATM switch, or IP router) needed to integrate the three-level network, and the device cost is listed within the device library. The network-interconnection cost (NIC) reflects the cost of protocol translators (gateways) that are needed to enable distinct group and site-network devices to communicate with each other, and distinct site and backbone-network devices to communicate with each other. The network-wire cost (NWC) reflects the cost of wires and cables that are needed to connect all network devices.

Minimize NCM = NDC + NIC + NWC   (1)

Network Performance Analysis

To determine the "goodness of fit" of each solution produced by iCAD, performance should be approximated rapidly during the evolutionary-optimization process. We utilized a network delay estimation that is based on a well-known formulation (Bersekas, 1992). This formulation views the network as a network of M/M/1 queues, where each group, site, and backbone is modeled as an M/M/1 queue. Summing all delays generated by all group tasks, site tasks, and the backbone task represents the average network delay (AND). Thus, a network's AND must satisfy the threshold network delay (TND), which is given by iCAD's user. This formulation has been used by many researchers for its simplicity and fast approximation for an average delay (Elbaum & Sidi, 1996; Gerla & Kleinrock, 1977).

To analyze an M/M/1 queue, we need the mean arrival rate (λ) and the mean service rate

(μ). In our case, λ represents the total traffic flow within a task (T_i) while μ represents the allocated network capacity for the network device (ND_i). λ is derived from the client traffic matrix (CTM), but μ is a decision parameter. Equation 2 estimates the total average network delay within the three-level network topology and Γ represents the total traffic within the three-level network infrastructure.

$$AND = \frac{1}{\Gamma} \sum_{i=1}^{N} \left(\frac{\lambda_i}{\mu_i - \lambda_i} \right) + PTO \qquad (2)$$

The term PTO stands for a *protocol translation (gateways) overhead*, which is the sum of all translation-process times between an Ethernet hub and ATM switch. This PTO occurs if an Ethernet hub and ATM switch are connected directly, for example.

EXPERIMENTAL RESULTS

The network tool iCAD was implemented in C++ on a SUN Blade 100. The software contains about 12,000 lines of code. The lowest network design cost found by the evolutionary approach that satisfied all design and performance constraints is the recommended solution to the problem. In all four experiments, a proportionate selection scheme was used in the evolutionary approach with the following parameters' values: population size (PS) = 250, number of generations (NG) = 3000, mutation rate (MR) = 0.05, and crossover rate (CR) = 0.80. A proportionate selection scheme (Michalewicz, 1994), which is a simple selection method, is used to compare each design's fitness function with the average fitness function of the entire population. The fitness function represents the network cost model (NCM), as stated in Equation 1. If a candidate network's fitness function is less than or equal to the average fitness function of the entire population, then this candidate network is kept for the next generation. Otherwise, the candidate network is selected for redesign. The convergence criterion used in our experiments is to terminate iCAD when the number of generations reaches the limit specified.

A hypothetical three-level network topology is considered in our study of the network evolution, as depicted in Figure 2. The three-level network represents the backbone, intermediate, and local area networks respectively. The network consists of eight local area networks (LAN), four intermediate networks, and one backbone network. The 65 clients' nodes are clustered around the 8 LANs as listed in Table 5. Such a type of network is an example of enterprise networks used by organizations, which have certain network requirements, such as high communication bandwidth, high-transfer rate and low delay bounds.

An enterprise network has rapidly become highly distributed collaborative activities involv-

Figure 2. A typical three-level network enterprise infrastructure

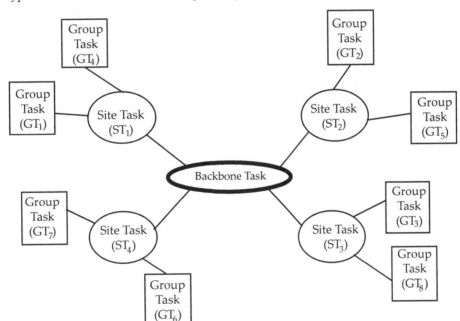

Table 5. Clients and groups clustering information

Site Tasks (ST)	Group Tasks (GT)	Client Tasks (CT)
1	1	1-10
	4	11-15
2	?	16-20
	5	21-30
3	3	31-40
	8	41-50
4	6	51-57
	7	58-65

ing teams of people in different locations. We used a typical midsize enterprise network—which contains 4 site tasks, 8 group tasks, and 65 client tasks as shown in Table 5—as our example.

Table 5 provides detailed information about the clustering of clients and groups. In the experiments, we focused on predicting network evolution for a three-level network topology with a local star backbone topology to connect its four sites.

A backbone network has three network choices: Ethernet hub, ATM switch and IP router.

The traffic flow is summarized by three parameters for each task: local traffic, outgoing traffic and incoming traffic, all of which are calculated from the client traffic matrix given by the user. The *local traffic* represents all the traffic flow within a task. The *outgoing traffic* represents all the traffic flow from a task to all other tasks. The *incoming*

Table 6. Traffic flow for site and group tasks

Task	Local Traffic (Mbps)	Outgoing Traffic (Mbps)	Incoming Traffic (Mbps)
site task 1	0.0	55.6	2.5
site task 2	0.0	15.0	21.3
site task 3	0.0	15.0	33.8
site task 4	4.2	7.5	35.6
group task 1	27.0	7.5	0.0
group task 2	2.0	2.5	2.5
group task 3	9.0	15.0	7.5
group task 4	8.0	48.1	2.5
group task 5	9.0	12.5	18.75
group task 6	4.2	7.7	16.6
group task 7	5.6	4.0	23.2
group task 8	9.0	0.0	26.3

Figure 3. Network-design cost versus performance over seven years

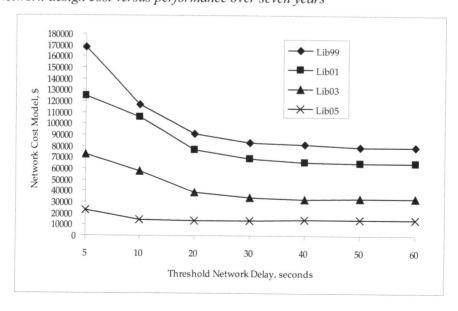

traffic represents all the traffic flow coming into a task from all other tasks. Table 6 shows the traffic flow given for the experiments and it is measured in megabits per second (Mbps). The traffic flow within the backbone task can be summarized by one parameter (backbone local traffic, BLT) or site traffic matrix (STM) depending on which topology is used. For the star topology, the backbone local traffic (BLT = 93.125 Mbps) represents all the traffic flow between all sites.

The relationship between the network-cost model (NCM) and the threshold network delay (TND) can be shown in Figure 3. The four curves represent the design cost when iCAD is connecting to LIB99, LIB01, LIB03, and LIB05 respectively. The seven points in each curve represent seven automatically produced network designs by iCAD with TND equal to 5.0, 10.0, 20.0, 30.0, 40.0, 50.0, and 60.0 seconds respectively. Each point in a curve represents an average of ten runs, where each run takes less than three minutes on a SUN Blade 100. The gaps between the four curves represent the shift in the network-design cost. The collected empirical data from 1999 to 2001 has shown a reduction rate in the range of 10.02% to 25.75% while from 2001 to 2003 the reduction rate has been shifted in the rage of 41.51% to 50.59%. The largest shift in the network-design cost occurs between 2003 and 2005, and the reduction rate is in the range 57.08% to 74.70%. We observed the domination of the Ethernet and IP router technologies over the ATM technology in the last few years, where the IP router technology leads in the interconnections among subnetworks, and the Ethernet technology takes over all local area networks (subnetworks).

Also, the plot in Figure 3 illustrates the classical inverse relationship between the network cost and delay. The tradeoff relationship between cost and delay was obvious from 1999 to 2003; however, it was obscure from 2003 to 3005. This is due to reduction in the manufacturing cost of all network technologies. The three-level network design cost is reduced by more than half, from $167,815.00 to

$78,960.13, when iCAD is connected to LIB99 and TND increases from 5.0 seconds to 60.0 seconds. When iCAD is connected to LIB01 and TND increases from 5.0 seconds to 60.0 seconds, the three-level network-design cost is reduced by almost half, from $124,609.00 to $64,400.10. When iCAD is connected to LIB03 and TND increases from 5.0 seconds to 60.0 seconds, the three-level network design cost is reduced by more than half, from $72,889.00 to $33,468.10. During 2005, the network-design cost went from $13,885.10 to $22,761.30 after tightening the threshold network delay from 60.0 seconds to 5.0 seconds.

The network *homogeneity factor* (HF) is an output parameter of iCAD ranging (0.0, 1.0]; HF = 1.0 indicates that all the allocated network devices are selected from the same technology. Otherwise, HF indicates the ratio of the maximum number of allocated network devices of the same technology to the total allocated network devices in the three-level network. In the case using LIB99 and TND = 60.0 seconds, the best network design has an estimated average network delay equal to 37.53 seconds and its HF is equal to 0.54, which indicates that 54% of the allocated network devices are an ATM technology. In the case using LIB01 and TND = 60.0 seconds, the best network design has an estimated average network delay equal to 35.46 seconds and its HF is equal to 0.54, which indicates that 54% of the allocated network devices are also an ATM technology. In the case using LIB03 and TND = 60.0 seconds, the best network design has an estimated average network delay equal to 35.46 seconds and its HF is equal to 0.46, which indicates that 46% of the allocated network devices are also an ATM technology. The ATM technology disappeared in all the designs while using LIB05, and the Ethernet technology dominates 62% of all allocated network devices.

In the case using LIB99 and TND = 5.0 seconds, the best network design has an estimated average network delay equal to 4.91 seconds and has its HF is equal to 0.45, which indicates

Table 7. Three network designs produced by iCAD while connecting to LIB99, LIB01, LIB03, and LIB05 respectively (threshold network delay = 60.0 seconds)

Tasks	Network Devices allocated from Using LIB99 by iCAD	Network Devices allocated from Using LIB01 by iCAD	Network Devices allocated from Using LIB03 by iCAD	Network Devices allocated from Using LIB05 by iCAD
Backbone	IP Router, 100Kpps, 5 ports, $7,000	IP Router, 100Kpps, 5 ports, $7,000	IP Router, 100Kpps, 5 ports, $2,800	IP Router, 100Kpps, 5 ports, $300
Site 1	IP Router, 50Kpps, 5 ports, $3,000	IP Router, 50Kpps, 5 ports, $7,000	IP Router, 50Kpps, 5 ports, $1,200	IP Router, 50Kpps, 5 ports, $150
Group 1	ATM, 45Mbps, 15 ports, $9000	ATM, 45Mbps, 15 ports, $7000	ATM, 45Mbps, 20 ports, $4500	Ethernet, 100Mbps, 14 ports, $1500
Group 4	ATM, 75Mbps, 10 ports, $8,000	Ethernet, 100Mbps, 6 ports, $4,200	Ethernet, 100Mbps, 6 ports, $2,940	Ethernet, 100Mbps, 6 ports, $500
Site 2	IP Router, 50Kpps, 5 ports, $3000	IP Router, 50Kpps, 5 ports, $3000	IP Router, 50Kpps, 5 ports, $1200	IP Router, 150Kpps, 5 ports, $500
Group 2	Ethernet, 10Mbps, 6 ports, $200	Ethernet, 10Mbps, 16 ports, $440	Ethernet, 10Mbps, 12 ports, $168	Ethernet, 10Mbps, 6 ports, $25
Group 5	ATM, 45Mbps, 15 ports, $9,000	ATM, 45Mbps, 15 ports, $7,000	ATM, 45Mbps, 15 ports, $3,500	Ethernet, 100Mbps, 14 ports, $1500
Site 3	IP Router, 50Kpps, 5 ports, $3,000	ATM, 75Mbps, 5 ports, $4,000	IP Router, 50Kpps, 5 ports, $1,200	IP Router, 150Kpps, 5 ports, $500
Group 3	ATM, 45Mbps, 15 ports, $9,000	ATM, 45Mbps, 15 ports, $7,000	ATM, 45Mbps, 15 ports, $3,500	Ethernet, 100Mbps, 14 ports, $1500
Group 8	ATM, 45Mbps, 15 ports, $9,000	ATM, 45Mbps, 15 ports, $7,000	ATM, 45Mbps, 15 ports, $3,500	Ethernet, 100Mbps, 14 ports, $1500
Site 4	IP Router, 50Kpps, 5 ports, $3,000	IP Router, 50Kpps, 5 ports, $3,000	IP Router, 50Kpps, 5 ports, $1,200	IP Router, 50Kpps, 5 ports, $150
Group 6	ATM, 45Mbps, 10 ports, $6,000	ATM, 45Mbps, 10 ports, $4,000	ATM, 45Mbps, 10 ports, $2,000	Ethernet, 100Mbps, 10 ports, $1000
Group 7	ATM, 45Mbps, 10 ports, $6,000	ATM, 45Mbps, 10 ports, $4,000	ATM, 45Mbps, 10 ports, $2,000	Ethernet, 100Mbps, 10 ports, $1000
Design Summary	Total Cost = $78,960.13 Average Network Delay = 37.53 seconds Homogeneity Factor = 0.54	Total Cost = $64,400.10 Average Network Delay = 35.46 seconds Homogeneity Factor = 0.54	Total Cost = $33,468.10 Average Network Delay = 35.46 seconds Homogeneity Factor = 0.46	Total Cost = $13,885.10 Average Network Delay = 14.10 seconds Homogeneity Factor = 0.62

that 45% of the allocated network devices are an Ethernet technology. In the case using LIB01 and TND = 5.0 seconds, the best network design has an estimated average network delay equal to 4.84 seconds and its HF is equal to 0.77, which indicates that 77% of the allocated network devices are also an Ethernet technology. In the case using LIB03 and TND = 5.0 seconds, the best network design has an estimated average network

delay equal to 4.94 seconds and its HF is equal to 0.38, which indicates that 38% of the allocated network devices are an IP router technology. The phenomena of the domination of Ethernet technology occurred during 2005 with HF equal to 62% of all allocated network devices. Tables 7 and 8 illustrate samples of the best eight network designs that are produced by iCAD using LIB99, LIB01, LIB03, and LIB05. Tables 7 and 8 illustrate

Table 8. Three network designs produced by iCAD while connecting to LIB99, LIB01, LIB03, and LIB05 respectively (threshold network delay = 5.0 seconds)

Tasks	Network Devices allocated from Using LIB99 by iCAD	Network Devices allocated from Using LIB01 by iCAD	Network Devices allocated from Using LIB03 by iCAD	Network Devices allocated from Using LIB05 by iCAD
Backbone	IP Router, 150Kpps, 5 ports, $11,000	IP Router, 150Kpps, 5 ports, $11,000	IP Router, 200Kpps, 5 ports, $6,800	IP Router, 150Kpps, 5 ports, $500
Site 1	IP Router, 150Kpps, 5 ports, $11,000	Ethernet, 1Gbps, 4 ports, $6,000	IP Router, 100Kpps, 5 ports, $2,800	IP Router, 150Kpps, 10 ports, $950
Group 1	ATM, 100Mbps, 15 ports, $15,900	Ethernet, 100Mbps, 15 ports, $12,000	ATM, 100Mbps, 15 ports, $6,750	Ethernet, 100Mbps, 14 ports, $1,500
Group 4	Ethernet, 1Gbps, 6 ports, $13,000	Ethernet, 1Gbps, 6 ports, $8,000	Ethernet, 1Gbps, 6 ports, $5,600	Ethernet, 1Gbps, 6 ports, $5,000
Site 2	IP Router, 100Kpps, 5 ports, $7000	Ethernet, 100Mbps, 4 ports, $3,000	IP Router, 100Kpps, 5 ports, $2,800	IP Router, 150Kpps, 5 ports, $500
Group 2	ATM, 75Mbps, 10 ports, $8,000	Ethernet, 100Mbps, 6 ports, $4,200	Ethernet, 100Mbps, 6 ports, $2,940	Ethernet, 100Mbps, 10 ports, $1,000
Group 5	Ethernet, 100Mbps, 12 ports, $13,000	Ethernet, 1Gbps, 12 ports, $14,000	ATM, 100Mbps, 15 ports, $6,750	Ethernet, 100Mbps, 14 ports, $1,500
Site 3	IP Router, 150Kpps, 5 ports, $11,000	IP Router, 150Kpps, 5 ports, $11,000	IP Router, 150Kpps, 5 ports, $4,400	IP Router, 200Kpps, 5 ports, $500
Group 3	Ethernet, 100Mbps, 12 ports, $13,000	Ethernet, 100Mbps, 12 ports, $9,000	ATM, 100Mbps, 15 ports, $6,750	Ethernet, 100Mbps, 14 ports, $1,500
Group 8	Ethernet, 100Mbps, 12 ports, $13,000	Ethernet, 100Mbps, 12 ports, $9,000	ATM, 150Mbps, 15 ports, $8,000	Ethernet, 100Mbps, 14 ports, $1,500
Site 4	IP Router, 100Kpps, 5 ports, $7,000	IP Router, 100Kpps, 5 ports, $7000	IP Router, 150Kpps, 5 ports, $4,400	IP Router, 150Kpps, 5 ports, $500
Group 6	Ethernet, 100Mbps, 8 ports, $9,200	Ethernet, 100Mbps, 8 ports, $5,600	Ethernet, 100Mbps, 8 ports, $3,920	Ethernet, 100Mbps, 10 ports, $1,000
Group 7	Ethernet, 1Gbps, 10 ports, $25,000	Ethernet, 100Mbps, 10 ports, $7,500	ATM, 100Mbps, 10 ports, $4,250	Ethernet, 100Mbps, 10 ports, $1,000
Design Summary	Total Cost = $167,815.00 Average Network Delay = 4.91 seconds Homogeneity Factor = 0.45	Total Cost = $124,609.00 Average Network Delay = 4.83 seconds Homogeneity Factor = 0.77	Total Cost = $72,889.00 Average Network Delay = 4.94 seconds Homogeneity Factor = 0.38	Total Cost = $22,761.30 Average Network Delay = 4.94 seconds Homogeneity Factor = 0.62

all the design decisions, which are automatically made by the evolutionary approach to minimize the network-design cost.

Table 7 illustrates all design decisions made by iCAD to produce the best network design with TND set to 60.0 seconds. There are *three* new design decisions that are made by iCAD when it uses LIB01. There are also *three* new design decisions that are made by iCAD when it uses LIB03. During the period of 2001 to 2003, and with regards to midlevel performance, ATM technology is more cost-effective than Ethernet technology. And for the same period, an IP router is the ultimate choice for the backbone and site networks due to its capability to connect heterogeneous network components without interconnection penalty. During the network-evolution process, the network cost goes down and the performance goes up. Also, in this case the network homogeneity factor has evolved from 54% to 46%. Glancing at the last column in Table 7, we observed only two network technologies that are used mainly: Ethernet and IP router.

The high-performance network designs are illustrated in Table 8, where all the design decisions were made by iCAD to produce the best network design, with TND set to 5.0 seconds. There are *six* new design decisions that are made by iCAD when it uses LIB01. There are *nine* new design decisionsthat are made by iCAD when it uses LIB03. In this case, the network homogeneity factor has evolved from 45% to 77% to 38% where an IP router and ATM switch are more cost-effective than Fast Ethernet and GigaEthernet Hubs. Also, an IP router is the ultimate choice for the backbone network due to its capability to connect heterogeneous network components without interconnection penalty.

However, our empirical data for 2005 shows a new trend for high-speed networks where an ATM technology was not allocated as illustrated by all design decisions made by iCAD in the last column in Table 8. The Ethernet technology dominates all local area networks and the IP router technology takes over all site and backbone networks. We consider the Ethernet to be the comeback technology, which expects to continue for many years the domination at the subnetwork domains. Also, the IP router will continue be the choice to interconnect subnetworks together; therefore, it eliminates the needs for gateways to interconnect heterogeneous network technologies.

CONCLUSION

We introduced a research test-bed tool for automatically synthesizing application-specific networks and observing the network evolution. In this article, we described a call for a network metric to examine the network evolution overtime. We have developed a number of network-device libraries over the past seven years for many different network technologies, such as Ethernet, ATM, and IP router. And we attached these libraries into an evolutionary design tool to select, integrate, and optimize a three-level enterprise network that can satisfy all design and performance constraints and at the same time minimizes the overall network-design cost.

As network technology changes, the design library is updated. By running the tool with the old and recent design libraries keeping the traffic flow constant, we plotted the cost and performance changes between the old and recent network technologies, which enabled us to predict the future change to a first order. The network evolution, which is represented by the gaps between the three cost-versus-performance curves, indicates that the network-design cost is decreasing at a doubling rate from 10.02-25.75% to 57-74% in every 24 months.

REFERENCES

Beigi, M., Calo, S., & Verma, D. (2004). Policy transformation techniques in policy-based systems management. In *Proceedings of the Fifth IEEE International Workshop on Policies for Distributed Systems and Networks*. Yorktown, NY.

Beigi, M., & Verma, V. (2001). Network prediction in a policy-based IP networks. In *Proceedings of the IEEE Globecom* (pp. 2522-2526). San Antonio, TX.

Bersekas, D., & Gallager, R. (1992). *Data networks* (2nd ed.). Englewood Cliffs, NJ: Prentice Hall Publishers.

Cosares, S., Deutsch, D., Saniee, I., & Wasem, O. (1995). Sonet toolkit: A decision support system for designing robust and cost-effective fiber-optic networks. *Interfaces, 25*, 20-40.

Doshi, B., Dravida, S., & Harshavardhana, P. (1995). Overview of INDT: A new tool for next generation network design. In *Proceedings of the IEEE Globecom*. Singapore.

Elbaum, R., & Sidi, M. (1996). Topological design of local area networks using genetic algorithms. *IEEE/ACM Transactions on Networking, 4*, 766-778.

Fahmy, H., & Douligeris, C. (1995). END: An expert network designer. *IEEE Network*, 18-27.

Frogner, B., & Cannara, A. (1999). Monitoring and Prediction of Network Performance. In *the Proceedings of the International Workshop on Advance Issues of E-Commerce and Web-Based Information Systems* (pp. 122-129). Santa Clara, CA.

Gerla, M., & Kleinrock, L. (1977). On the topological design of distributed computer networks. *IEEE Transactions on Communications, 25*, 48-60.

Gersht, A., & Weihmayer, R. (1990). Joint optimization of data network design and facility selection. *IEEE Journal on Selected Areas in Communications, 8*(9), 1667-1681.

Habib, S., & Parker, A. (2002). Computer-aided system integration tool for predicting enterprise network evolution. In *Proceedings of the Fifteen International Conference on Systems Engineering (ICSEng 2002)*, Las Vegas, NV.

Habib, S., Parker, A., & Lee, D. (2002). Automated design of hierarchical intranets. *Computer Communications, 25*(11-12), 1066-1075.

Michalewicz, Z. (1994) *Genetic algorithms + data structures = evolution programs*. Berlin, Germany: Springer-Verlag.

Mitra, D., Morrison, J., & Ramakrishnan, K. (1998). VPN Designer: A tool for design of multiservice virtual private networks. *Bell Labs Technical Journal, 3*(4), 15-31.

Moore, G. (1965). Cramming more components onto integrated circuits. *Electronics, 38*(8).

Nowell D. L., & Kleinberg, J. (2003). The link prediction problem for social networks. In *Proceedings of the Twelfth Annual ACM International Conference on Information and Knowledge Management (CIKM'03)* (pp. 556-559). New Orleans, LA.

Pierre S., & Legault, G. (1998). A genetic algorithm for design distributed computer network topologies, *IEEE Transactions on Systems, Man and Cybernetics, 28*, 249-258.

Saksena, V. (1989). Topological analysis of packet networks. *IEEE Journal on Selected Areas in Communications, 7*, 1243-1252.

Vekiarides, L., & Finkel, D. (1998). NETCAP: A tool for the capacity planning of ethernet LANs. In *Proceedings of the Sixth International Symposium on Modeling, Analysis and Simulation of Computer and Telecommunication Systems (MASCOTS 1998)* (pp. 198-203). Montreal, Canada.

Verma, D. (2002). Simplifying network administration using policy based management. *IEEE Network Magazine*.

This work was previously published in International Journal of Business Data Communications and Networking, Vol. 3, Issue 4, edited by J. Gutierrez, pp. 1-16, copyright 2007 by IGI Publishing, formerly known as Idea Group Publishing (an imprint of IGI Global).

Chapter III
Suitability of IP Telephony in the Public Switched Telephone Network (PSTN):
A Case Study

Hak Ju Kim
University of Houston–Clear Lake, USA

ABSTRACT

This article seeks to develop a richer understanding of the suitability of IP telephony in the Public Switched Telephony Network (PSTN) with an actual local exchange carrier (LEC)'s case and network simulation. We also performed a simple real options analysis to evaluate a telecommunications network. The underlying network and associated data were derived from our studies of an actual LEC. The preliminary result shows that an IP telephony network would save about 73% of the total link capacity of a circuit switched network and it could also carry some integrated services traffic at low incremental cost. The value of the IP telephony network was shown as positive under real options and as negative using net present value (NPV). We measured deferrable and irreversible value as well as the uncertainty value of an IP telephony network. Through this experiment, we can get inference that IP has potential for a voice carriage.

INTRODUCTION

Real options have been popular in academics (Amram & Kulatilaka, 1999; Brealey & Myers, 2002; Dixit & Pindyck, 1994; Graham & Harvey, 2002; Kauffman & Li, 2005), by recognizing its fundamental importance as a strategic decision-making tool. However, they do not feel the effect on how it leads to reframe the way they approach to solve a certain problem and to build in much more flexibility into their problems in practice.

The current telecommunications industry can be characterized as dynamic, aggressive, and uncertain (Antonelli, 1997; Bourreau & Dogan,

2001; Grover & Vaswani, 2000; Uri, 2000). This is particularly true for Internet-based businesses, due in large part to the ongoing development of IP-based technologies and declining costs (Leida, 1998; McKnight & Bailey, 1997; Odlyzko, 1998). Extrapolating from the growth of the Internet, some industry observers (Bos & Leroy 2001; Traupman, O'Connell, Minnis, Jadoul, & Huterer, 1999; Venken, Vleeschauwer, & Vriendt, 2001) expect that the primary network of the future will be IP-based. Included in this framework is voice traffic, which has been emerging as an Internet application in recent years.

The phenomenon of IP telephony (IPT) is interesting from many perspectives. Several previous studies (Marlatt, 1998; McKnight & Leida, 1998; Mier, 1998; Pospischil, 1998; Selsius Systems, 1998; Weiss & Hwang, 1998; Wong, 1999) have shown that the transmission and switching costs of this technology are lower than circuit switching, leading to speculation that IP technology will eventually replace circuit switching technology in the PSTN. The decision to undertake such a technological transition will surely be complex and multidimensional.

IPT is becoming an alternative to the telephone technology used by traditional telephone networks that have not changed substantially for decades. However where IPT can be a substitute for traditional telephony, it has a variety of challenges such as technical hurdles (Stone, 2003), pricing dilemma (Wieland, 2006), and policy environments (FCC, 2004). IPT also has many uncertainties, such as reduction in current growth rate, devaluating equipment and service by the short IP technology transition cycle, a fiercely competitive landscape of technology substitutes and innovations, and uncertain service demands by subscribers. Various policy issues are unresolved: the possibility of universal service obligation, access charge requirements, and treatment as a traditional telephone company. Enormous uncertainties create the opportunity to make decisions as states of nature are revealed.

The uncertainties associated with IPT suggest the real options approach would be useful. For example, when should an Internet company try to enter the IPT market? If it enters now, it may obtain a larger market share that it would not get by entering later, but it may lose money because of too small a total market. If it waits a few years, it will know if market growth will be high or low, but it has missed out on several years of sales and will probably obtain a reduced market share due to late entry. Under these types of uncertainties, IPT is ripe for a real options approach.

In this article, we will frame this problem based on the real options approach as a decision of capital investment under uncertainty. The goals of this article are two fold: (1) to demonstrate the application of the real options approach to telecommunications networks, and (2) to develop a richer understanding of the suitability of IP technology in the PSTN. In this article, we will apply a simple real options approach (i.e., Black-Scholes option model) to support this strategic investment decision, and a computer simulation (i.e., COMNET III) to determine the initial capital investment requirements. The underlying network and associated data are derived from our studies of an actual local exchange carrier (LEC).

Our model dimensioned the networks to carry the LEC's voice traffic. We then added integrated services traffic until the point where the delays of the network become acceptable (in the IP case). Traffic differentiation (prioritization) was applied for the voice traffic to support the toll-quality service. We expect that this article will be useful to network planners in network companies.

The preliminary result of our study shows that IP telephony network would save about 73% of the total link capacity of a circuit switched network and it could also carry some integrated services traffic at low incremental cost. The value of the IP telephony network was shown as positive under real options and as negative using NPV. We measured deferrable and irreversible value as well as uncertainty value of IPT network. Through this experiment, we can get inference that IP has potential for voice carriage.

The next section introduces the real options approach including concepts, factors, variables, indicators, application tools, and applying procedure. We then carry out network modeling and simulation. And then we assess IPT using the real options approach, especially Black-Scholes option pricing model.

REAL OPTIONS: AN OVERVIEW

Notion of Real Options

The typical traditional approaches (Brealey & Myers, 2006) to project evaluation and investments are net present value (NPV) method or decision-tree analysis (DTA). The NPV method is a standard method for financial evaluation of investment (projects). NPV calculates the difference between the present value of cash inflows from the investment and the present value of cash outflows initially invested. If the NPV of a project results in a positive amount, the project should be undertaken. However, if NPV is negative, the project should be rejected because net cash flows will also be negative. The NPV method explicitly assumes that the project will meet the expected cash flow without any intervention by management during the process. Rather, all the uncertainty can be handled by a single risk-adjusted discount rate. That is, there is no dynamics in a project. It is static; now or never.

Decision-tree analysis (Brealey & Myers, 2006) moves the analysis one step forward by allowing that decisions can be made after information has been received. But, as in the case of NPV, the appropriate risk-adjusted discount rate is virtually indeterminate. Using the firm's opportunity cost of capital is inappropriate if the project does not correlate with the company's cost of capital—another lesson for the telecommunications industry. Unbundled network elements

have different levels of risk. For example, the operator services element's risk/return is much different from the local loop element. To calculate the cost/price of these elements using the same discount rate would be incorrect.

The real options approaches (Amram & Kulatilaka, 1999; Carr, 1988; Dixit & Pindyck, 1994; McDonald & Siegal 1986; Pindyck, 1988; Trigeorgis, 1996) have emerged by the criticism of the traditional investment approaches (i.e., NPV and DTA) because of ignoring management's flexibility. Management's flexibility (Trigeorgis, 1996) is that managers can adapt decisions in response to unexpected market developments during the project period, such as waiting, staging, changing, abandoning, switching, and growing to investment.

Management's flexibility to make decisions as states of nature are revealed is assumed away by the traditional methodologies, like NPV and DTA. However, management discretion has value, which is not incorporated into the NPV. The real options methodology goes beyond this naive view of valuation and more closely matches the manner in which firms operate. It allows for the flexibility the firm has to abandon, contract, expand, or otherwise modify its actions after nature has revealed itself. This is the first lesson for the policymakers—if they wish to emulate the competitive process, they cannot rely on application of naive NPV method in investment decision of a project. The ability to value management's flexibility by the real options approaches has brought a revolution to modern corporate resource allocation (Amram & Kulatilaka, 1999).

Real options can be defined simply as opportunities to respond to changing circumstances of a project by management (Trigeorgis, 1996). These opportunities are rights but not obligations to take action in the future. Real options are differentiated from financial options because they involve real assets rather than financial assets. Most investments are like a call option on a common stock that gives the holder the right to make an investment and receive a project. It means that we will exercise the option of investment only if they are sufficiently deep in the money. Since their value fluctuates stochastically and most investments options (or opportunities) are not a "now or never" opportunity (Dixit & Pindyck, 1994), there is a value of waiting to invest.

The important factors that influence on the evaluation in the real options approach are uncertainty, irreversibility, and deferability (Trigeorgis, 1996). First, uncertainty is defined as the randomness of the external environment. It can be used to create value by managing opportunities to get more value and to avoid loss by identifying its source, trends, and evolution and then deciding the degree of their investments. Second, irreversibility is the possibility that the capital expenditures incurred in the project are partially or totally sunk costs when the investment decision is made. Third, deferability is the time value to delay the investment until favorable market conditions materialize.

To be consistent with the option pricing paradigm, it is assumed that there exists a certain date on which the project must be implemented, or exercise date. However, the investment costs on that exercise date can not be determined at present the same way as the strike prices on financial options are.

Previous Studies

There are several studies to value investments with a series of investment outlays. Most of the methods for valuing real options derived from financial option models, such as Black-Scholes option model (1973) and Cox-Ross-Rubinstein's binomial option model (1979) in financial market. Their approaches have greatly facilitated the actual valuation of options in practice. They showed that standard option pricing model with risk-neutral valuation can be alternatively derived under risk aversion, and that continuous trading opportunities enabling a riskless hedge or risk neutrality are not really necessary.

Margrabe (1978) developed an equation for the value of an option to exchange one risky asset for another within a stated period. The formula applies to American options, as well as European ones; to puts, as well as calls. One can apply the equation to options that investors create when they enter into certain common financial arrangements. Instead of Margrabe's one asset switching model, Stulz (1982) analyzed options on the maximum or minimum of two risky assets and Johnson (1987) extended Stulz's theory to several risky assets.

Further, Carr (1988) explored sequential exchange options, involving an option to acquire a subsequent option to exchange the underlying asset for another risky alternative. These papers opened up the potential to help analyze the generic option to switch among alternative uses, that is, switch among alternative inputs or outputs.

Pindyck (1988) analyzed options to choose capacity under product price uncertainty when investment is irreversible. Dixit (1989) considered a firm's entry and exit decisions under uncertainty, showing that in the presence of sunk or costly switching costs it combines Dixit's entry and exit decisions with Pindyck's capacity options for a multinational firm under volatile exchange rates. Kulatilaka and Marks (1988) examined the strategic bargaining value of flexibility in a firm's negotiations with suppliers.

Baldwin and Clark (2000) have been the first to observe that the value of modularity in computer system design can be modeled by the real options approach. Assuming that a product is designed in a modular fashion, they analyze the effect of modular design on product development performance by quantifying the value of modularity in terms of increased design flexibility. They apply the theory of real options to show that the mix-and-match feature of modular design can dramatically speed the rate of performance improvement.

Mathematical Option Models

How can the real options approach be used to supplement existing analysis process? Unfortunately, the level of quantitative analysis for real options is nowhere as advanced as the quantitative models for financial options. So, the real options approach will use the financial options models which are well developed in financial markets as a proxy model. We expect that the evaluation methodology for real options will be developed. We introduce two typical financial option models: black-scholes option model and binomial option model.

Black-Scholes Option Model: The Black-Scholes option model (B-S model) was produced as a solution for pricing European call options on stock in 1973. Although the B-S model was introduced 27 years ago, it is still widely used today despite its well-documented imperfections. The most obvious reason for this is its inherent simplicity. Indeed, the formula for pricing a basic option can be implemented on most modern calculators. The B-S model is used to measure both the value and risk of an option in relation to its underlying stock. There are the five parameters essential to the pricing of an option: the underlying stock price, the strike price, the time to expiration, the volatility of the stock, and the prevailing interest rate, during continuous time. The model is defined by:

$$C = SN(d_1) - X\, e^{(-rt)}N(d_2)$$

where C = Current Value of the Call Option

S = Current Stock Price
t = time until option expiration
X = option Striking Price
r = Risk-free Interest Rate
N = Cumulative Standard Normal Distribution
e = Exponential Function (2.71828)
$d_1 = [Ln(S/X) + (r+\sigma^2/2)t]/ \sigma\sqrt{t}$
$d_2 = d_1 * \sigma\sqrt{t}$

σ = Standard Deviation of Stock Returns
Ln = Natural logarithm

The first part of the model, $SN(d_1)$ is the present value of receiving the stock if it finishes above the strike price at expiration. This is found by multiplying stock price S by the change in the call premium with respect to a change in the underlying stock price $N(d_1)$. The second part of the model, $Xe^{-rt}N(d_2)$, is the present value of having to pay the strike price under the same condition. The fair market value of the call option is then calculated by taking the difference between these two parts. Indeed, if the stock finishes below the strike price at expiration of the call, then the call is worth less, but if it finishes above the strike price, then the call holder has to pay the strike price and will receive the stock in exchange.

Binomial Option Model: It is worthwhile exploring a simpler derivation of option price developed by Cox, Ross, and Rubinstein (1979) based upon a stochastic binomial process. The binomial approach is used to analyze finite-lived options in discrete time. It allows great flexibility in modeling various stochastic processes for the present value of future benefits and variation of conversion costs over time. The binomial option model is based on the approximation that the price of an underlying security (S) is only allowed to change to one of two values in each infinitesimally short time step. It is typical to express these two values as proportional increases or decreases in the price of S. A constant relative probability of an upward (or, equivalently downward) transition may be chosen, but it is found that the end result is independent of any such probabilities. We will therefore ignore probabilities entirely and for the moment restrict the discussion to the initial time step. The model can be expressed by:

$$C = S\Phi[a; n, p'] - Xr^{-n}\Phi[a; n, p],$$

where C = Current call value

S = Current stock price

X = the option's exercise price

Φ [, , ,] = Complementary binomial distribution

p (the hedging probability) $\equiv$ (r-d)/(u-d) and p' $\equiv$ (u/r)p,

$a \equiv$ the smallest non-negative integer greater than $\log(X/S\,d^{\,n})/\log(u/d)$

n = number of periods

If $a>n$, C = o.

The value of $\Phi[a;\, n,\, p]$ is the probability that the sum of n and p (Bernoulli random variables) will be greater than or equal to a. The variable a is an integer constant which is a function of X, S, d, u, and r; the p is functions of d, u, and r. The form of the expression for the price of the call is analogous to that found under the B-S model.

Suggested Procedure

There is no best way to apply the real options approach in every case because the underlying assets are not traded in the market and the uncertainty factors are different in each project. So, it is an important role of management to identify and analyze uncertainty factors. It does not mean that there is no value the applying procedure because well-framed process will help management to deliver realistic results. Then, how to apply the real options approach to our project? We suggest a general procedure, and then this procedure will be modified for each situation.

- *First step is to identify uncertainties.* For example, new services, market demand, price and cost, technology, competition, regulation, exchange rate, and so forth. However, we can not reflect these whole factors for evaluating our project. It is impractical to do that under limited time and resource in the real business world. We recommend them to be less than ten factors.

- *Second step is to analyze factors.* One way to analyze them is a SWOT analysis, which is a technique to analyze business risks using two by two matrixes. The endogenous business risks are classified by weakness and strength, while exogenous ones are classified by threat and opportunity.

- *Third step is to quantify the uncertainties.* This step is the most important, but the most difficult step because they are intangible. This is one of the main limitations in the real options approach. There is no guaranteed objectivity and transparency. For example, if several people evaluate the same factors, then are their results included a reasonable range. Maybe they will come out the different results respectively. Then who believe this real options approach? Is there no value to the real options approach? No. The reason is that the real options approach is the only methodology to explicitly consider the future opportunities (risks) and management's flexibility. Even though the numerical result may not coincide with true value, it reflects these intangible factors. So, a wrong numerical result is not worrisome because the real value of real options is to provide the intuitive meaning to management for strategic decision-making. However, it does not mean that we neglect the efforts to quantify these factors.

- *Fourth step is to choose and implement the methodology.* As yet, no real options evaluation methodology exists, so we borrow financial options pricing models which are used in the financial market. The typical techniques are Black-Scholes Option Model and Binomial Option Model.

- *Fifth step is to review the evaluation results.* Since the environment is changing rapidly, management should follow up and modify the result based on new information. This is why the real options approach is a dynamic technique.

Potentials of Real Options as a Strategic Decision-Making Tool

A strategic investment (Ganslandt, 2001; Horstmann & Markusen, 1987; Kulatilaka & Perotti, 1998; Smit & Trigeorgis, 1999; Spence, 1979) creates opportunities for a firm to invest or divest in subsequent time periods, depending on how opportunities unfold. Motivated by growing competition and uncertainty in the real world, managers are increasingly turning their attention to investments as productive assets rather than financial assets. Managers frequently must decide about resource allocations in general, for which there are many options. For example, managers can decide to: expand the production with a sunk cost of investment, maintain the current status, suspend production temporarily without direct costs, change materials and products, abandon an irreversible investment, and so forth. Thus a business is much more like a series of options (Trigeorgis, 1996) than it is like a series of static cash flows.

The real options approach is a strategic planning and valuation tool (Amram & Kulatilaka, 1999; Dixit & Pindyck, 1994; Luehrman, 1998; Trigeorgis, 1996) that helps managers make decisions. Since real options are used to both reduce risk and increase return, they play a role in hedging against uncertainties. The value of real options is not only in valuation, but also in the strategic management processes that allocates resources, for example, the development of an approach for implementing business strategies under the uncertainty. Telecommunications firms are required to make strategic decisions because of the necessary large investments in addition to business risks due the unexpected technology transitions.

With the rapid integration of computers and telephony (Asatani, 1998; Walters, 1999), telecommunication companies are faced with an uncertain future and unbridled competition. In these times, carriers must decide whether to enter a new market, how much to invest, and when to enter. These decision problems motivate the investment of telecommunications to be evaluated by the real options approach.

CASE STUDY OF A LEC

The company provides telecommunication services and equipment to residential and business customers in its service area as a local exchange carrier (LEC). The company served approximately 75,000 customers through its digital fiber-linked central offices. Historically the company has not experienced significant competition in its service area. However, as a result of the general telecommunications liberalization leading up to the Telecommunications Act of 1996, it has been experiencing increased competition of various sorts, including resellers of its local exchange services, large and users installing their own networks. Inter-exchange carriers (IXCs), satellite transmission services, cellular communications providers, cable television companies, competitive access providers (CAPs), and other systems.

The LEC's network (Figure 1) consists of two main switches (Nortel Network's DMS100/200/250), 26 remote switches (RSCs), and 26 remote line concentrating modules (RLCM). DMS main switching system can support 135,000 lines and several remote switches, but 17,069 lines and 20,547 lines are installed respectively, as of December 2004. RSC can extend a full complement of host switch features to subscribers up to 650 miles and carry out switching functions. The RLCM also can extend full DMS host office features and services up to 100 miles from a host switch. The daily average total calls are 1,445,698, with an average call holding time of 3.55 minutes (213 seconds).

Figure 2 shows a sequence of activities to operate and manage an actual LEC's network. Customer service activity includes receiving customer requests and assigning them to related

Figure 1. Network architecture of an actual local exchange carrier (LEC)

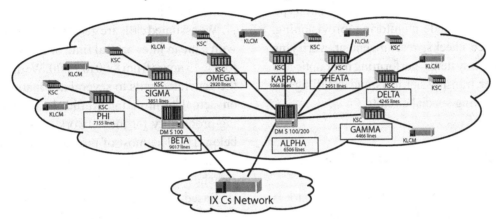

Figure 2. Activity map of network operation and management

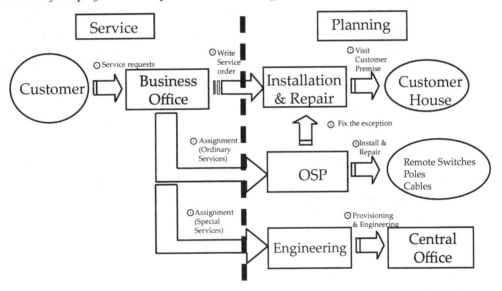

departments in the business office. Before assigning them, the department checks cable records and then writes a service order. CPE management activity includes visits to the customer premises for installation and a repair department. Service provisioning activity includes all the activities associated with a service order, from receiving the customer service requests to the actual service turn-up at the completion of the verification. In case of the LEC, the outside plant department (OSP) and network engineering department carry out these functions. Upon receiving facilities improvement requests from another business department, the OSP department begins to work according to the following steps: engineering, designing, installing, testing, inspection and turn-up, building in service area, and recording. At the same time, the network engineering department also receives a facilities improvement work order such as transmission equipment and special services (FX circuits, data circuits, etc.) from a business department, which then engineers and plans the implementation. This activity is carried out in the central office department. The typical activities include monitoring, provisioning, maintenance checks, rearrangement, verifying transmission systems, performing fiber optic and multiplexer, transmission tests, and installing and troubleshooting special circuits.

MODELING AND SIMULATION

In our study, COMNET III network simulator is used to model networks and then simulates the operation of the network and provides measures of network performance. COMNET III network simulation software (CACI, 1995) is one of the most popular network simulators in computer networking simulation studies. It uses a building-block approach, which is comprised of "blocks" or objects representing many of the objects used in real networks. For example, we can build network models by graphically selecting palette icons representing nodes (i.e., routers or switches), links (i.e., T1), protocols and traffic, and positioning them on the screen using a mouse.

In our study, we create three network models: advanced circuit switched network, IP telephony network, and integrated network.

Simulation Model I: Advanced Circuit Switched Network

For the advanced circuit switched network model, we dimensioned the network of an actual LEC. We aggregated various elements to simplify the simulation problem, but were careful not to

change significant factors, like network topology and traffic data.

We assumed calls are generated exponentially, with a mean inter-arrival time of 0.0412 seconds for the 15 hours from 8:00 to 23:00. We distributed the generated calls to several destinations based on actual terminating traffic data. The blocking probability for the network is engineered at below 1%. The most of the blocking occurs not in the switches but at the trunks between the switches.

Based on these assumptions, we built the network in the COMNET III simulator and compared the results with the real network. After a few iterations, we settled on a traffic matrix that resulted in the blocking results illustrated in Table 1; we felt that this validated the simulation model. The errors are due to the differences between our assumptions of traffic patterns and real traffic patterns, since we cannot accurately recreate the actual traffic patterns using statistical models. In blocking rate, the modeled network (1.9%) is much higher than actual network (0.24%). We believe that the network operation and management system (or software) for traffic flow control to reduce blocking rate exists in actual LEC's network, while not in our modeled network. However, this difference does not affect our simulation study because the blocking rate level of both networks is still low.

Simulation Model II: IP Telephony Network

For the IP telephony (IPT) network, we used the same network topology of the LEC. Even though

Table 1. Results of advanced circuit switched model

	Actual Network	Modeled Network
Originated Calls	926,039	924,120
Terminated Calls	519,659	520,890
Blocking Rate	0.24%	1.9%

this might yield a sub-optimal IPT network design, we can measure easily voice traffic migration effect from circuit switched network to IP network, and it allows us to ignore local loop issues between the two networks. The IPT network model assumed in our analysis is based on RTP/UDP/IP standardized in ITU H.323.

We focused the dimensioning of this network on basic voice switching and transport. Many technical issues must still be resolved before IP and circuit switched voice are close substitutes. We used the following assumptions:

- IP packets are compressed by 8Kbps based on G.729A Codec algorithm, which is a typical audio data compression standard for voice that compresses voice audio in chunks of 10msec.
- Vocoder generates 10 byte voice packets, two of which are aggregated for transmission in an IP packet.
- The RTP/UDP/IP protocol overhead is 40 bytes. RTP (Real-Time Transport Protocol) supports end-to-end delivery services of applications transmitting real-time data over IP networks (Casner, Frederick, Jacobsen, & Schulzrinne, 1996). RTP typically runs over UDP to utilize its multiplexing and checksum services.
- Voice packets are modeled by an *on-off* model, with a 350msec in "on" state and a 650msec in "silence" state, exponentially distributed respectively.
- The 99th percentile packet delay constraint is less than 50msec

Based on the above assumptions, we generate each 10 bytes voice packet with every 10msec through compression code and two voice packets (20 bytes payload) are enveloped in the 40 bytes RTP/UDP/IP header.

In the simulation, we found the average and 99th percentile delays for packets through the network. This delay was modeled using the delay

budgets in Table 2. We assumed that this would provide a connection quality that was approximately equivalent to circuit switched voice.

The source was initially modeled using an *"on-off"* speaker model. We found that, when aggregated, these could be modeled reasonably well by an exponential distribution, so that is what we used to reduce the running time of the simulation.

Now we attempt to reduce the number of links in the IPT network for calculating the reduced link costs from circuit switched network. As a result, we found that the link facilities of the circuit switched network could be decreased by about 73% before the delay on the IP network began to exceed the 50msec delay budget.

Simulation Model III: Integrated Service Network

Since a primary purpose of IP networks is to carry heterogeneous traffic, we incrementally added an integrated service traffic load without upgrading the switching hardware or transmission capacity any incremental hardware cost and measured the delay and delay jitter of IP telephony traffic. When the quality of the voice traffic became unacceptable, we found the network upgrade point.

We used traffic data measured on the Internet backbone's OC-3 trunks to determine the statistics of this traffic. We modeled a variety of Internet applications traffic, including HTTP, FTP, and DNS. The integrated traffic model parameters are summarized in Table 3. Since the traffic is aggregated from many sources, we assumed an exponential inter-arrival time of traffic flows of each application. We further assumed that all the

Table 2. Simulation outputs of IPT network

Performance Factors	Results
Average Link Utilization	4.15%
Average Variable Packet Delay	6.32msec
99% Variable Packet Delay	15.31msec

Table 3. Summary of integrated traffic parameters

Services	Parameters	Values
HTTP (Server > Client)	Percentage of Bytes Average Packet Length	70 791 bytes
HTTP (Client > Server)	Percentage of Bytes Average Packet Length	8 83 bytes
FTP and Other TCP	Percentage of Bytes Average Packet Length	17 600 bytes
DNS/UDP	Percentage of Bytes Average Packet Length	2 165 bytes
RTP/UDP	Percentage of Bytes Average Packet Length	3 401 bytes

traffic sources are uniformly distributed over the whole network.

Of these integrated services traffic, we configured IPT traffic with a higher priority. We then observed the effect on utilization and delay and delay jitter. The incremental non-voice traffic is modeled as a percentage of voice load (which is static). The unit of incremental integrated data traffic load is in percentage of the total bytes of aggregated integrated data traffic relative to the given IP telephony voice traffic load in bytes. As a result, up to 50% of non-voice load can be added onto the network without new investments.

NETWORK VALUATION

We used a simple real options approach to evaluate the LEC's network upgrade decision whether the current circuit switched network should be maintained, or should it be converted to an IPT network for the future. Since there are few standard approaches for real options analysis in telephony, we generate an appropriate method for this article. Since one of the goals of this article is to see the intuitive meaning of the real options approach instead of the exact correctness of it, we opt for a simple approach.

To that end, we chose the Black-Scholes option model (B-S model) because of its relative simplicity and proven methodology. To apply the

B-S model to the telecommunications network, we must find the value of five main variables: underlying network value, investment amount, volatility, risk-free rate, and the evaluation period.

Quantifying Uncertainties

Quantifying uncertainties is the most difficult step and the limitation of real options approach. It is very subjective and depends on the evaluator. For example, we know that competition will affect profits. Since competition in the local telephone market is a relatively new phenomenon—the company may find it difficult to estimate the impact of competition and to make appropriate competitive responses. Because of the quantification difficulties, we estimate these uncertainties using the *beta coefficient*, which is a measure of the volatility of a stock relative to the overall market, as a proxy. The beta coefficient for the LEC is 0.28. For the IPT network, we used the beta coefficients of ISPs because mostly IPT services are provided by ISPs and IPT services are a small portion in traditional telephone companies. The average beta coefficient of ISPs is 1.71.

Estimating Cash Flows

The network itself is not traded in the market and we can not directly value it because the network has an intangible value in addition to its physical value. So, we tried to measure it indirectly using the total discounted cash flows during the estimated life of the network.

The company is engaged in providing local network service, long distance and access service, telecommunications equipment selling and renting, directory advertising, billing, and other services. However, we used revenues of local and long distance services for later comparison to the IP telephony network. To forecast the revenue of advanced circuit switched network, we computed a compound annual growth rate (CAGR) from 1993 to 2005. Since the company has grown steadily and continuously during the past seven years, we assume that it will continue to grow during the evaluation period. The average growth rate was 6.87% for subscribers and 6.41% for revenue from 1993 to 2005.

For forecasting the revenue of the IPT network, we assumed that the IPT will grow exponentially until the evaluation period because the IPT is still in the development stage. Scott's formula and Schuster's network diffusion model (1998) were used to estimate IPT subscribers. The saturation point for IPT in this company's service area is the same as 80% of total households because the Internet penetration is expected to be 80% of total households in 2006 and the market share for the company is 20% of that. The saturation for IPT subscribers to estimate IPT subscribers is estimated as not exceeding the Internet hosts' saturation capacity. Since the company's total number of subscribers in 2006 is 78,565 subscribers, the number of IPT subscribers is 62,852 which is the 80% of total LEC subscribers.

Based on the results of our simulation, the current link capacity savings (73%) in IPT network is included in the revenue as an opportunity cost.

The operating costs for circuit switched network were estimated the same way (CAGR) of revenue for it since operating costs are related to the revenue. For the IPT network, we used the average operating costs of nine ISPs during the past three years, since we could not find a typical

ISP. The methodology used for average costs was moving average method.

The capital investment was only considered the difference of equipment (i.e., switching equipment) to perform the circuit-switching (i.e., DMS, RSC, and RLCM) and IPT functionality (i.e., router, gateway, and DSLAM) because facilities building and others were already invested as sunk costs and trunk costs are already reflected as a opportunity revenue in the IPT network. We assumed that the initial investment for circuit switched network was current book value of actual LEC's equipment. The equipment of the circuit switched network was valued at about $16 million, as of December 2005. The annual investment is assumed to be $2 million, since the company has put one million into the two main switches for additional capacity and features. These investments are necessary for the LEC to maintain the current facilities and to operate normally. The initial investment of IPT network was estimated about $36 million.

The life of telephone central office equipment can be derived in several ways. According to IRS documents, the product life of telephone switching equipment is 18 years. Given the pace of technological change, we are doubtful that such long depreciation schedules will be sustainable in the future. In this article, we will use 10 years. For the advanced circuit switched network, it is assumed that the first investment amount is the current book value of the LEC's equipment that actually performs the circuit-switching functionality (i.e., DMS, RSC, and RLCM).

For the cost of capital, the weighted average cost of capital (WACC) was used. The value for debt percentage was calculated by the company's average value during past five years from 1995 to 2005. The cost of debt is based on estimated long-term debt interest rate for future five years in the company's annual report. The capital asset pricing model (CAPM) was used to calculate the cost of equity. The risk-free rate and market interest rate was 5.43% and 9.98%, respectively.

We used a beta coefficient to measure volatility as a proxy. As the LEC has grown continuously without difficulty, it is shown a very low beta value (0.28). However, the beta value of ISPs providing IP telephony have high beta (1.71) because ISPs are new entrants in telecommunications with new technologies. They face more substantial risks. Finally, the evaluation period was six years from 2006 to 2012 because the average remaining life of a circuit switched network was six years. The

Table 4. Cost of capital

	Circuit Switched Network	IP Telephony Network
Debt of Total Assets	66.80 %	66.80 %
Cost of Debt	5.68 %	5.68 %
Risk-free Interest Rate	5.38 %	5.38 %
Beta Coefficient	0.28	1.71
Market Interest Rate	9.98 %	9.98 %
Cost of Equity	6.38 %	11.23 %
Cost of Capital	5.49 %	8.73 %

Figure 3. Cash flows of circuit switched network

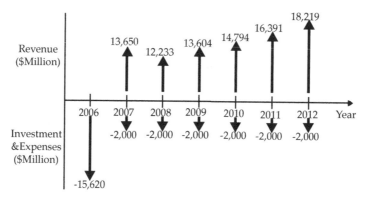

Figure 4. Cash flows of IP telephony network

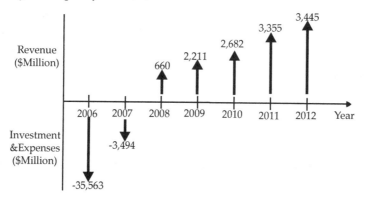

Table 5. The option value of network models

	Circuit Switched Network	IP Telephony Network
Network Value	$83M	$5M
Investment	$24M	$20M
Risk-free Interest Rate	5.38%	5.38%
Volatility	0.28	1.71
Periods	6 years	6 years
$N(d_1)$	0.99545	0.96813
$N(d_2)$	0.97271	0.00978
Net Present Value (NPV)	$55M	-$15M
Option Value	$11M (call) $55M (put)	$20 M(call) $29 M(put)

Table 6. Uncertainty effect

Year	2006	2007	2008	2009	2010
Volatility	1.37	1.54	1.71	1.88	2.05
Value	$4.5M	$4.8M	$5.0M	$5.1M	$5.2M

Table 7. Deferrable and irreversible effect

Year	2006	2007	2008	2009	2010
Deferability	$44.5M	$60.9M	$79.7M	$104.9M	$126.5M

Table 8.

Year	2006	2007	2008	2009	2010
Irreversibility	$24.5M	$24.6M	$24.7M	$24.7M	$24.7M

summarized cost of capital is shown in Table 4.

Figure 3 and Figure 4 show the estimated cash flows and investment schedule of the circuit switched network and IP telephony network. Using these assumptions, we applied the Black-Scholes option model to the two telecommunications networks: circuit switched network and IP telephony network. We used a Microsoft Excel spreadsheet to apply the Black-Scholes option model and enter the value of five main variables. We then measured three effects (i.e., uncertainty, deferrability, and irreversibility) in the IP telephony network. The *uncertainty effect* can be measured by the change of volatility, which represents the risks of the underlying network value. Since the high uncertainty means high volatility, we can see the decrease of potential loss by increasing the volatility. The *deferability effect* can be shown by delaying the investment in IP telephony. We will see the increase of real options value by delaying the investment. The *irreversibility effect* can be measured by selling the IP telephony network.

The measured loss is the irreversible loss of the IP telephony business.

Option Value of Network Models

The results are shown in Table5. The net cash flows for circuit switched network was very positive for $83 million and option value is $72 million. So, option premium (that is, option value-NPV) is only $11 million. The main reason is that $N(d_1)$ value (0.99545) is nearly the same with $N(d_2)$ value (0.97271), which means that the company has little flexibility to increase profits or to decrease losses, since the circuit switched network has no significant uncertainty.

By comparison, the IP telephony network showed a negative in NPV (-$15 million), but a positive ($5 million) in options value. So, option premium is $20 million. Option premium for IP telephony network ($20 million) is bigger than that of circuit switched network ($11 million). Based on this result, we can get inference that IP telephony network has high uncertainty and so management can increase a potential profit or decrease a potential loss through his/her management's flexibility.

In the circuit switched network, even though the call (buy) value for $66 million is much bigger than the put (sell) value for $0.1 million, option premium is opposite (call premium < put premium). This means that the circuit switched network gets is currently profitable, but that it may be attractive to sell it in the future because of a huge put (sell) premium. Meanwhile, the IP telephony network incurs a loss during its first several years, but it has a high call (buy) premium since it has a potential in the future. This result can explain why the price of Internet stocks is high despite their recurrent losses.

Uncertainty Effect

The uncertainty effect can be measured by changing the volatility because it is a proxy of uncertainty. We decreased and increased it by 10% and 20%, respectively, in the volatility of IP telephony network model. As the results are shown in Table 7, high volatility (uncertainty) increases the real options value. This means that it is worthwhile to invest in high potential businesses like IP telephony.

Deferrable Effect

Delaying investment in the IP telephony network also increases the real options value (Table 8). This means that as management gets new information related to IP telephony, they can update their decisions, which increases the potential profit or decreases the potential loss. However, we are doubtful about this effect because it does not consider the market power of other competitors. That is, if we enter the IP telephony market now, we get a larger market share than we would by entering later.

Irreversible Effect

The company may choose to abandon the business if the IP telephony market is unfavorable. In this case, the company may sell (put) its business. We assumed that we can sell the whole equipment in market because the IP market is very competitive. As seen in Table 9, this irreversible effect does not influence the value of the IP network as time passes. This means that IP telephony can decrease the loss of investment because of its potential.

CONCLUDING REMARKS

We simulated the integrated circuit switched network with IP telephony and implemented a simple real options approach to compare the investments. The conclusions of this analysis are:

- IP telephony could save about 73% of the total link capacity of a circuit switched network and it could also carry some integrated services traffic at zero incremental cost, while the circuit switched network would require a significant investment in order to offer competing services. This means that the profitability of carriers will be enhanced in IP telephony based carriers, as compared to circuit switched carriers. It may well be that this potential growth in profitability is what is ultimately compelling for telcos and their shareholders. This is a fairly strong result.

- The value of IP network was shown as positive using real options and as negative using NPV. This supports arguments favoring the potential of IP telephony. We evaluated the deferrable and irreversible value as well as uncertainty value of IP network.

There is clearly much more work that must be done to apply real options analysis to telecommunications networks, as well as to understanding the technical and economic issues around IP telephony. These preliminary results suggest that a compelling business case for IP telephony exists and that carriers should be studying whether and how to convert their networks to this new technology. It also suggests that the regulatory issues raised by IP telephony will not go away.

REFERENCES

Amram, M., & Kulatilaka, N. (1999). *Real options: Managing strategic investment in an uncertain world*. Boston: Harvard Business School Press.

Antonelli, C. (1997). A regulatory regime for innovation in the communications industries. *Telecommunications Policy, 21*(1), 35-45.

Asatani, K. (1998). Standardization on multimedia communications: Computer-telephony-integration-related issues. *IEEE Communications Magazine, 36*(7), 105-109.

Baldwin, C., & Clark, K. (2000). *Design rules: The power of modularity*. MIT Press.

Black, F., & Scholes, M. (1973). The pricing of options and corporate liabilities. *Journal of Political Economy, 81*, 637-659.

Bos, L., & Leroy, S. (2001). Towards an all-IP-based UMTS system architecture. *IEEE Network*, 36-45.

Bourreau, M., & Dogan, P. (2001). Regulation & innovation in the telecommunications industry. *Telecommunications Policy, 25*(3), 167-184.

Brealey, R. A., & Myers, S. C. (2002). *Capital investment and valuation*. McGraw-Hill.

Brealey, R. A., Myers, S. C., & Allen, F. (2006). *Principles of corporate finance*. McGraw Hill.

CACI. (1999). COMNET III user's manual. *CACI Products Company*.

Carr, P. (1988). The valuation of sequential exchange opportunities. *Journal of Finance, 23*(5), 1235-1256.

Casner, S., Frederick, R., Jacobsen, V., & Schulzrinne, H. (1996). *RTP: A transport protocol for real time applications*. ftp://ftp.isi.edu/in-notes/rfc1899.txt

Cox, J. C., Ross, S. A., & Rubinstein, M. (1979). Option pricing: A simplified approach. *Journal of Financial Economics*, 229-264.

Dixit, A. K. (1989). Entry and exit decisions under uncertainty. *Journal of Political Economy, 97*(3), 620-638.

Dixit, A. K., & Pindyck, R. S. (1994). *Investment under uncertainty*. Princeton, NJ: Princeton University Press.

Dixit, A. K. & Pindyck, R. S. (1995). The options approach to capital investment. *Harvard Business Review*.

Federal Communications Commission. (2004). *Notice of proposed rulemaking in the matter of IP-enabled services.* WC Docket Number 04-36.

Ganslandt, M. (2001). *Strategic investment and market integration* (IUI Working Paper Series 560). The Research Institute of Industrial Economics.

Graham, J. R., & Harvey, C. R. (2002). How do CFOs make capital budgeting and capital structure decisions. *Journal of Applied Corporate Finance, 15*(1), 823.

Grover, V., & Vaswani, P. (2000). Partnerships in the U.S. telecommunications industry. *Communications of the ACM, 43*(2), 80-89.

Horstmann, I. J., & Markusen, J. R. (1987). Strategic investments and the development of multinationals. *International Economic Review, Department of Economics, University of Pennsylvania and Osaka University Institute of Social and Economic Research Association, 28*(1), 109-121.

Johnson, H. (1987). Options on the maximum or the minimum of several assets. *Journal of Financial and Quantitative Analysis, 22*(3), 277-283.

Kauffman, R. J., & Li, X. (2005). Technology competition and optimal investment timing: A real options model. (forthcoming). *IEEE Transactions on Engineering Management, 52*(1), 15-29.

Kulatilaka, N., & Marks, S. (1988). The strategic value of flexibility: Reducing the ability to compromise. *American Economic Review, 78*(3), 574-580.

Kulatilaka, N., & Perotti, E. (1998). Strategic growth options. *Management Science, 44*(8), 1021-1031.

Leida, B. (1998). *A cost model of internet service providers: Implications for internet telephony and yield management.* MIT Master Thesis.

Luehrman, T. A. (1998). Strategy as a portfolio of real options. *Harvard Business Review,* 89-99.

Margrabe, W. (1978). The value of an option to exchange one asset for another. *Journal of Finance, 33,* 177-186.

Marlatt. (1998). IP telephony sees price wars. *Internet World.* http://www.interworld.com/print/19998/04/06/ ispworld/19980406-wars.html

McDonald, R., & Siegel, D. (1986). The value of waiting to invest. *Quarterly Journal of Economics, 101,* 707-727.

McKnight, L. W., & Bailey, J. P. (Eds.). (1997). *Internet economics.* Cambridge, MA: MIT Press.

McKnight, L. W., & Leida, B. (1998). Internet telephony: Costs, pricing, and policy. *Telecommunications Policy, 22*(7), 555-569.

Mier, E. (1998). Voice-over-IP: Getting started. *Business Communications Review, 28*(5).

Odlyzko, A. (1998). The economics of the Internet: Utility, utilisation, pricing, and quality of service. *AT&T Labs – Research.*

Pospischil, R. (1998). Fast internet: An analysis about capacities, price structures and government intervention. *Telecommunications Policy, 22*(9), 745-755.

Pindyck, R. S. (1989). Irreversible investment, capacity choice, and the value of the firm. *American Economic Review, 2,* 969-985.

Selsius Systems. (1998). A fundamental shift in telephony networks. Selsius Systems. http://www.selsius.com/literature/sales_literature/ip_pbx.pdf

Shuster, M. S. (1998). Diffusion of network innovation: Implications for adoption of internet services. *MIT Internet Telephony Consortium Semiannual Meeting, Helsinki, Finland,* 20-22.

Smit, H. T. J., & Trigeorgis, L. (1999). Growth options, competition and strategy: An answer to the market valuation puzzle. In L. Trigeorgis (Ed.), *Real options and business strategy: Applications to decision making.* Risk Books.

Spence, A. M. (1979). Investment strategy and growth in a new market. *Bell Journal of Economics, 10*(1), 119.

Stone, A. (2003). Has VoIP arrived? *IEEE Internet Computing,* 1011.

Stulz, R. (1982). Options on the minimum or the maximum of two risky assets. *Journal of Financial Economics, 10,* 161-185.

Traupman, E., O'Connell, P., Minnis, J., Jadoul, M., & Huterer, M. (1999). The evolution of the existing carrier infrastructure. *IEEE Communications Magazine, 37*(6), 134-139.

Trigeorgis, L. (1996). *Real options: Managerial flexibility and strategy in resource allocation.* Cambridge, MA: MIT Press.

Uri, N. D. (2000). Measuring productivity change in telecommunications. *Telecommunications Policy, 24*(5), 439-452.

Venken, V., Vleeschauwer, D., & Vriendt, J. (2001). Designing a DiffServ-capable IP-backbone for the UTRAN. In *Proceeding of the 2nd International Conference on 3G Wireless Beyond,* San Francisco.

Walters, R. (1999). *Computer telephony integration.* Artech House, Inc.

Weiss, M. B. H., & Hwang, J. (1998). Internet telephony or circuit switched telephony: Which is cheaper? *The 26th Telecommunications Policy Research Conference,* Alexandria, VA.

Wieland, K. (2006). The VoBB dilemma: What can incumbents do about voice over broadband? *Telecommunications Magazine.*

Wong, W. (1999). Telcos to push IP telephony in 1999. *CNET News.* http://www.news.com/News/Item/0,4,30542,00.html

This work was previously published in International Journal of Business Data Communications and Networking, Vol. 3, Issue 3, edited by J. Gutierrez, pp. 39-56, copyright 2007 by IGI Publishing, formerly known as Idea Group Publishing (an imprint of IGI Global).

Chapter IV
A Framework for High–Speed Networking

Abid Al Ajeeli
University of Bahrain, Bahrain

Yousif Al Bastaky
University of Bahrain, Bahrain

ABSTRACT

This chapter describes a detailed framework configuration infrastructure design for a high performance network. The configuration is described based on the new setup and migration requirements and it indicates how the design satisfies those requirements. The chapter explains the detailed configuration of the design process of the distribution layer switches and shows how these switches can be configured in the final implementation. The chapter also discusses the modifications that occurred during the implementation/migration phase. The design of the framework incorporates resiliency into the network core in order to manage problems effectively. This will enable user access points to remain connected to the network even in the event of a failure. This incorporation aims to provide services and benefits to users without impediments.

INTRODUCTION

A computer network is simply a system of interconnected computers. This chapter emphasizes on the design and implementation of one type of computer networks, which is the local area network (LAN). It is a group of computers and associated devices that share a common communication line or wireless link and typically share the resources of a single processor or server within a limited geographic area. Usually, the server has applications and data storage that are shared by multiple computer users to optimize network traffic.

Network traffic has increased dramatically during the last few years due to the confluence of several factors (Regnier et.al, 2004). These factors are:

- Businesses are using networks to access resources, such as enterprise storage, that were previously directly connected.
- Web services and the World Wide Web have moved increasing amounts of business activity to a networked paradigm.
- Messaging is becoming a prevalent means of sharing data and services.
- Clusters-rather than large server systems-are becoming the default means of creating large computing resources.
- The sheer volume of data has risen dramatically due to the increased use of audio and video resources, and real-time data acquisition, including, especially, radio frequency identification (RFID) tag tracking.

Major local area network technologies include Ethernet, Token Ring, and Fiber Distributed Data Interface (FDDI). Ethernet is by far the most commonly used LAN technology. A number of corporations use the Token Ring technology. FDDI is sometimes used as a backbone LAN interconnecting Ethernet or Token Ring LANs. Another LAN technology, ARCNET, was the most commonly installed LAN technology, and is still used in the automation industry.

The Framework composed of a suite of application programs, which is kept on the LAN server. Users who need an application frequently can download it once and then run it on their local hard disk. Users, in each department, can order printing and other services as needed through applications run on the LAN server. A user can share files with others at the LAN server and a LAN administrator maintains read and write access. A LAN server may also be used as a Web server.

The proposed network design has a wireless LAN that is sometimes preferable to a wired LAN because it is cheaper to install and maintain. The implementation supports a Resilient Packet Ring (RPR), which is a network topology, developed as a new standard for fibre optic rings. The Institute of Electrical and Electronic Engineers (IEEE) began the RPR standards (IEEE 802.17) development project in December 2000 with the intention of creating a new Media Access Control layer for fibre optic rings (Ward, 2002).

In order to provide readers with more information on network models, we sketch the interfaces, which identify seven layers of communication types as in Figure 1.

Each layer depends on the services provided by the layer below it down to the physical layers, which define network hardware such as the network interface cards and the wires that connect the cards together.

The network model shown in Figure 1 can be used as a background for the layered of hardware and software that handles packet processing. When a network interface card (NIC) receives a data packet, it initiates a series of interactions with the system processor to handle the data payload and deliver it to the appropriate application as in Figure 2.

The motivation is to design and build a network infrastructure to deal with scalability issues for a network to scale for future upgrade leveraging high speed Gigabit Infrastructure with ability to grow to 10 Gigabit per second. The result is that the framework will have a network ready for future technologies such as IPv6 and MPLS. Other motivation is the manageability power added to the network with enterprise management system, which will result in better productivity

Figure 1. The OSI network mode

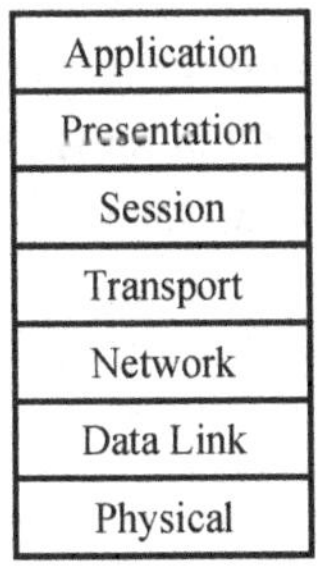

Application
Presentation
Session
Transport
Network
Data Link
Physical

Figure 2. Layered stack of applications

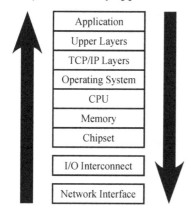

of the staff, faster fault isolation and response as well as proactive management planning for future applications.

The Gigabyte System Network is the highest bandwidth and lowest latency interconnect standard, providing full duplex dual 6400 megabit (800 megabyte) per second of error-free, flow-controlled data. The technology is ideal wherever organizations require timely movement of large amounts of information including scientific and technical computing, high-definition television (HDTV), data mining, transaction processing, video and film archiving, and storage management (HNF, 1998).

The rest of the chapter is organized as follows. Section 2 provides related works and background details on network organization, high performance, and resiliency. Section 3 discusses the ways of building network connectivity and topology; Section 4 provides discussion details of WAN connectivity. The IP addressing and VLANs - layer 3 design is outlined in section 5. Section 6 discusses network management issues; Section 7 provides a brief conclusion with some discussions of future research directions in this area.

RELATED WORK

Networks have proliferated in many walks of life and have become an integral part of the corporate world. Ubiquitous computing and internet-capable cellular phones have provided people with the ability to remain connected with individuals, even if they are away from a wired office environment. Numerous researchers continue to develop and outline new design technologies including software, hardware, routers, and countless other products (Netcraft, 2004; Tanenbaum, 1996) With wide use of computers in the corporate world, the speed and convenience of using them to communicate and to transfer data have forever altered the landscape of how people conduct businesses.

Xerox Corporation originally created Ethernet in 1973. Originally, it ran at 3 Mbps and was called X-Wire. In 1979, Xerox and Digital Equipment Corporation joined forces, along with Intel Corporation, to standardize and promote the use of a 10-Mbps version called DIX. In 1983, the Institute of Electrical and Electronics Engineers (IEEE) approved the first 802.3 standard, which was, for the most part, the same technology as the DIX standard.

The deployment of networked service applications such as collaborative tools and LAN-based video conferencing has created the need for a cost-effective and high-performance network infrastructure (Netcraft, 2004). This led to the advancement of network technologies from ATM to Gigabit Ethernet (GbE) (Chowdhry, 1997), which is the latest in a line of successful Ethernet technologies. It is very similar to its predecessors, but faster. Data travels across GbE at 1000 Ebps, which is a 100 times faster than the original Ethernet.

Intel (Intel, 2006) discussed the emergence of multi-Gigabit Ethernet and showed how it enables data centers to accept more transactions and provide faster response. To take full advantage of this network capacity, Intel advised data center managers to consider the impact of high-traffic volume on server resources. A compelling way to efficiently translate high bandwidth into increased throughput and enhanced quality of service is to rely on Intel I/O Acceleration Technology (Intel, 2006).

Network availability plays a crucial role in the design of network systems today, especially given the popularity of distributed applications facilitated by the Internet. The all-IP network essentially acts as the "system bus" to these applications. In a chapter published by ZNYX Networks, Inc ("ZNYX Networks," 2001) claims that a preferable design would include an automated system that circumvents faults to reduce challenges facing system designers.

As applications became more network intensive and user connection speeds grew, network administrators recognized the need to connect switches to each other at higher speeds. This was to prevent congestion on the inter-switch links. Initially, this was done with technologies such as Fibre Distributed Data Interface (FDDI) and later with ATM.

In 1992, work began on a higher-speed version of Ethernet, keeping the same basic characteristics of the original, but working at 100 Mbps. This was originally designed not to replace the backbone technologies of FDDI and ATM, but to give servers a higher-speed connection to the network. It became very popular as a backbone technology, however, because it did not require any kind of translation or conversion of format. It was Ethernet all the way from the desktop to the server and made network administration much easier (Plessel, 1999; Krunz, 1998).

Nortelnetworks (Nortel networks, 2004b) has engineered a network infrastructure to provide sufficient bandwidth resources to the end users. The network was designed for the mission-critical function of information transfer system. The resiliency network was aimed to ensure that those resources are consistently available. Resiliency and redundancy, however, are not the same thing. Redundant networks often have two of every

network element. Resilient networks are comprised of network devices that provide reliable fail over mechanisms—either within the device or by working in concert with other network elements so that all network devices can be utilized simultaneously.

A redundant network, as defined by Nortelnetworks, is not always the most resilient. Redundant network elements can increase network complexity and can be expensive to implement. A truly resilient network provides the maximum amount of network uptime without requiring an entire duplicate network. As a result, Nortelnetworks designed a healthcare network infrastructure with a network resiliency to maximize network uptime. Healthcare organizations, furthermore, seek proper implementation and operation to ensure sustainable operational performance of the network. In this case a framework for planning, implementing, operating, and maintaining such a network must be incorporated (Nortel networks, 2004b).

The chapter produced by Cisco Systems, Inc., and Network Appliance, Inc., (NetApp) highlights key market drivers for IP-connected network-attached storage, and elaborates on some common deployment scenarios in customer environments (Ahmed, Godbole, & Vishwanathan, 2004). Faster online response for users is one of the key drivers for customer retention and loyalty in an e-business environment. For example, the "eight-second-rule" states that if a Web page does not completely load within eight seconds, customers might not return to the Web site, leading to lost revenue. While performance is typically addressed at several levels in the infrastructure design, networked storage, in the mean time, plays an important role in meeting overall performance goals(Ahmed, Godbole, & Vishwanathan, 2004; *Houdt, & Blondia, 2005*).

IDC confirmed (IDC, 2004) that networked storage grew from US$6 billion in 1999 to approximately US$32 billion in 2004 (CAGR = 51.3%) while direct-attached storage shrunk from US$14 billion in 1999 to approximately US$9 billion in 2004 (CAGR = -10%).

Liu claims that (Liu & Yang, 2004) the widespread use of the Internet and the maturing of digital video technology have led to the increase in various streaming media applications. In order to support multimedia communication, it is necessary to develop routing algorithms that make decisions based on multiple Quality of Service (QoS) parameters achievable. However, the problem of QoS routing is difficult because finding a feasible route with two independent path constraints is NP-complete problem (Koyama et al., 2004).

Liu (Liu & Yang, 2004) confirmed that QoS routing algorithms for broadband networks must be adaptive, flexible, and intelligent for efficient network management. Some researchers (Koyama et al., 2004) proposed a multi-purpose optimisation method for QoS routing based on Genetic Algorithm (GA). The simulation results in (Koyama et al., 2004) show that the proposed method has a good performance and therefore is a promising method for QoS routing.

Ilija Hadzic and Edward Szurkowski (Hadzic & Szurkowski, 2005) discussed Ethernet as deployed in metropolitan area networks (MANs) as a lower-cost alternative to SONET-based infrastructures. MANs are usually required to support common communication services, such as voice and frame relay, based on legacy synchronous TDM technology in addition to asynchronous packet data transport. The chapter of (Hadzic & Szurkowski, 2005) addressed the clock synchronization problem that arises when transporting synchronous services over an asynchronous packet infrastructure, such as Ethernet.

A novel algorithm for clock synchronization is presented combining time-stamp methods used in the network time protocol (NTP) with signal processing techniques applied to measured packet inter-arrival times. The algorithm achieves the frequency accuracy, stability, low drift, holdover performance, and rapid convergence required for viable emulation of TDM circuit services over Ethernet (Liu & Yang, 2004; Koyama et al., 2004; Hadzic & Szurkowski, 2005).

Resilient links protect network against an individual link or device failure by providing a secondary backup link that is inactive until it is needed. A resilient link comprises a resilient link pair that contains a main link and a standby link. If the main link fails, the standby link immediately takes over the task of the mail link. Herbert (Herbert, 2003) in his chapter "issues in Resilient Network Design" outlined the misleading possibilities of packet flooding. The packet flooding effect can contrive to mislead network administrators and engineers as to the true utilisation levels on the switches, and cause unnecessary hardware upgrades to take place.

NETWORK CONNECTIVITY AND TOPOLOGIES

Physical network topology refers to the characterization of the physical connectivity relationships that exist among entities in a communication network. Discovering the physical layout and interconnections of network elements is a prerequisite to many critical network analysis tasks, including reactive and proactive resource management, server siting, event correlation, and root-cause analysis. For example, consider a fault monitoring and analysis application running on a central IP network management platform. Typically, a single fault in the network will cause a flood of alarm signals emanating from different interrelated network elements. Knowledge of element interconnections is essential to filter out secondary alarm signals and correlate primary alarms to pinpoint the original source of failure in the network (Bejerano et al., 2003; Katzela & Schwarz, 1995, Yemini et al., 1996). Furthermore, a full physical map of the network enables a proactive analysis of the impact of link and device failures.

Network Topology Diagrams

A network topology is the method in which nodes of a network are connected by links. A given node has one or more links to others, and the links can appear in a variety of different shapes. The simplest connection is a one-way link between two devices. A second return link can be added for two-way communication. Modern communication cables usually include more than one wire in order to facilitate this, although very simple bus-based networks have two-way communication on a single wire.

A *logical topology* describes the possible connections between pairs of networked endpoints that can communicate. This is useful in describing which endpoints can communicate with which other endpoints, and whether those pairs capable of communicating have a direct physical connection to each other

Network topology is determined only by the configuration of connections between nodes; it is therefore a part of a graph theory. Distances between nodes, physical interconnections, transmition rates, and/or signal types are not a matter of network topology, although they may be affected by it in an actual physical network. Figure 3 shows a number of topologies ("Guide Network," 2008).

Real life topology applications consist of hybrid network topology. Hybrid networks use a combination of two or more topologies in such a way that the resulting network does not have one of the standard forms. For example, a tree network connected to a tree network is still a tree network, but two star networks connected together exhibit hybrid network topologies. A hybrid topology is always produced when two different basic network topologies are connected.

The design of advanced network technology is usually based on hybrid topologies. The hybrid topologies are required because we deal with different network technologies, different network architecture, and different distribution switch layers with different speeds and load sizes.

Implementation

This section describes a project that aims to design and implement a Local Area Network infrastructure for the UOB upgrading from the legacy ATM network to a state of the art gigabit

Figure 3. Network topology examples

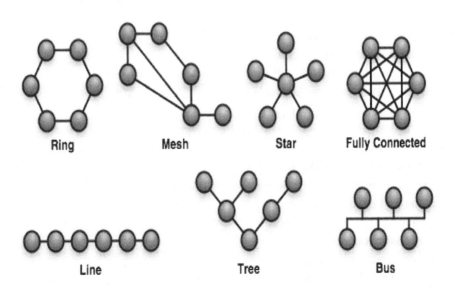

and a 10/100 desktop network in the two University sites, Sukhair and Issa-town. The university's two campuses, located near the capital of Manama, offer a full range of study in subjects ranging from electrical engineering to business and education. UoB is also undergoing rapid growth, having added several institutes and expanded from four to nine colleges in the past four years. During this time, enrolment has doubled from 10,000 to 20,000 students, with continued growth projected well into the future.

To facilitate this expansion, UoB originally invested more than $1.3 million to network its campuses with Asynchronous Transfer Mode (ATM) technology from Nortel Networks. Recently, however, increased traffic seriously decreased network throughput, hampering administrative and e-learning applications. Students had difficulty registering on-line; grades could not be submitted and processed in a timely fashion; access to e-libraries was sporadic. Moreover, the Nortel ATM infrastructure was incapable of creating additional virtual LANs (VLANs) and otherwise scaling to satisfy UoB's rapidly escalating needs, rendering the network obsolete in just four years.

For the above reasons, we started our system by planning, designing and implementing a network topology that provides the highest application performance and network availability. Availability is the proportion of time that a system can be used for productive work. However, network reliability is required to achieve availability. Reliability is defined as the provisional probability that an element will operate without fault in a given period ("Network Level," 2001).

Furthermore, the system is based wholly on (3Com) core and edge switches technology. The aim is to support local switching on modules, reducing congestion and enabling intensive applications to run faster. Multiple VLANs segregate network traffic and ensure maximum efficiency. Hardware routing reduces packet loss and latency time, allowing flawless transfer of mission-critical

data as well as enterprise resource management applications and videoconferencing.

There are a total of n1 + n2 + ...nk Intermediate Distribution Interface wiring closets (IDFs) in Sukhair and 18 IDFs in Issa-town, each terminates the end user connections. There is one new switch (3Com) in each IDF, which works as an aggregator to the existing L2 switches that provide user connectivity. The switch also provides connectivity to some users at 10/100/1000 Mbps (in some sites, it's 10/100 Mbps using 4400 switches).

The above diagram in Figure 4 can be used as a base for the UOB network, which is connected to one of the Batelco networks, which have a backbone that is connected to other networks. The University of Bahrain is located at two different sites: Sukhair and Issa town. Sukhair site consists of many buildings spread over 10 km wide. Issa town, furthermore, has more than 40 detached buildings. This concept is outlined in figure 4.

Two core switches (3Com 7700R) are to be used at the core of the network, one as a core of Sukhair site and the other as an Issa-town core switch. Both will provide connectivity between the wiring concentrator and server farm switches. Whenever available, the wiring closets with 4924 switches are connected to the core with two gigabit links as link aggregates to the related core.

All of the equipment is managed by a management system, the 3Com Network Director (3ND).

Figure 4. View of Internet–connected networks

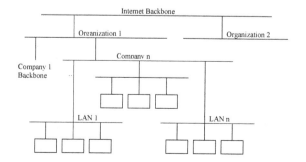

Network Interconnectivity

Physical connectivity is determined between elements such as switches and routers in a multiple subnet communication network. Each element has one or more interfaces each of which is physically linked with an interface of another network element. Address sets are generated for each interface of the network elements, wherein members of a given address set correspond to network elements that can be reached from the corresponding interface for which the given address set was generated.

Connectivity mechanisms between various UoB sites are outlined in figure 5 and figure 6. The figures show, for example, the interconnectivity between the IDF wiring closets and the Switch 7700R cores in both sites; Sukhair and Issa-town as well as the server farm closet.

The server farm aggregation is designed and implemented using two Giga ports per 4924 switch to provide redundant connectivity for servers. The server aggregators are linked to the Switches 7700R core with 2Gbps.

In Sukhair, we designed the network to be of 99 VLANs. Each VLAN has 253 nodes. The VLANs distribute traffic load using either 1 Gigabit links or aggregated links. In Issa Town, the network design follows similar principles adopted in Sukhair site in which connectivity uses single links or aggregated links as in buildings 15, 28, and the library.

Wherever two links are connected, the traffic between edge stacks and core is utilizing two aggregate links to the core. Core switches in Sukhair and Issa-town are connected to each other via ATM links on Nortel switches.

Sukhair Campus Switches Set-Up

A network switch is a small hardware device that joins multiple computers together within one local area network (LAN). Technically, network switches operate at layer two (Data Link Layer) of the OSI model.

Network switches appear nearly identical to network hubs, but a switch generally contains more "intelligence" (and a slightly higher price tag) than a hub. Unlike hubs, network switches are capable of inspecting data packets as they are received, determining the source and destination device of that packet, and forwarding it appropriately. By delivering each message only to the connected device it was intended for, a network switch conserves network bandwidth and offers generally better performance than a hub.

As with hubs, Ethernet implementations of network switches are the most common. Mainstream Ethernet network switches support 10 Mbps, 100 Mbps, or 10/100 Mbps Ethernet standards.

Different models of network switches support differing numbers of connected devices. Most consumer-grade network switches provide either four or eight connections for Ethernet devices. Switches can be connected to each other. Such "daisy chaining" allows progressively larger number of devices to join the same LAN (Mitchell, 2008).

Each building, in Sukhair site, has one or more 4924 distribution layer switches acting as an aggregator for current building edge switches. As in Figure 5, Sukhair Core terminates connections of different buildings in Sukhair campus. Today, most of these buildings are connected with one Gigabit link. Some buildings with high-density users act as distribution links for two or more buildings. High-density buildings are connected by dual links as an aggregated link.

Sukhair 4924 distribution switches are set to have all front ports untagged in user VLAN. They are also used to terminate users and user edge switches "Nortel, 3Com and Cisco edge switches". The Gigabit uplink from the back is tagged on the Interconnect VLAN. VLAN and IP design will be described in detail in section 5.

Figure 5. UoB—3Com Network—Sukhair Site

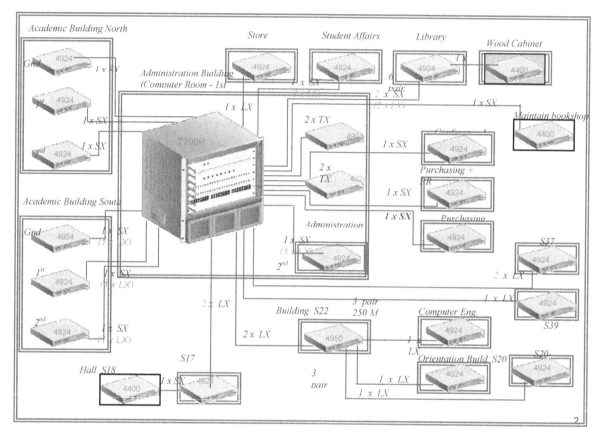

Issa Town Campus Switches Setup

Each of Issa Town buildings has a 4924 distribution switch acting as an aggregator for current building edge switches as well as terminating some power users. As per Figure 6, Issa Town Core terminates connections of different buildings in Issa Town campus. Most of these buildings are connected by one Gigabit link. Some of the high- density users' buildings are connected by dual links as an aggregated link or acting as distribution switches for more than one building

Similar to Sukhair, Issa Town core switch has been equipped with dual switch fabric for redundancy as well as 2 × 20 port 1000 BaseX and 1 × 20 port 10/100/1000 for servers and routers connectivity.

Issa Town 4924 distribution switches are set to have all front ports untagged in user VLAN and shall terminate users and user edge switches "Nortel, 3Com and Cisco edge switches". The Gigabit uplink from the back is tagged on the Interconnect VLAN. VLAN and IP design will be described in detail in section 5.

WAN INTERCONNECTIVITY SETUP

Wan Interconnectivity includes Inter Campuses link between Issa Town and Sukhair as well as Internet connectivity. The Inter campus link is using ATM to connect the two campus locations via Batelco at OC3—155Mbps speed. As the connection is established through Nortel C5000

Figure 6. UOB Network based on 3Com Giga Ethernet Solution- Issa Town

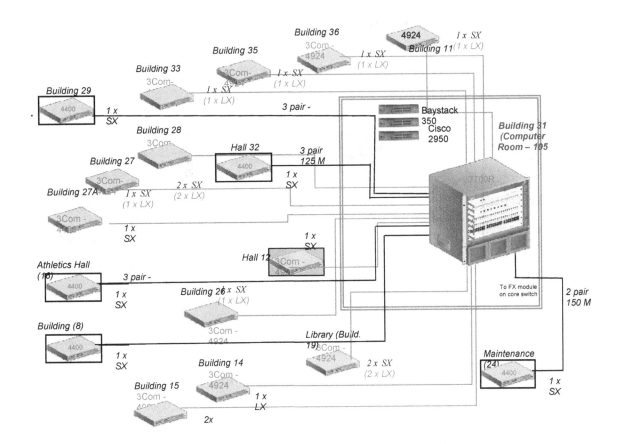

and C1400 switches, 3Com network design keep the connectivity via WAN VLAN connects directly to Nortel in both sides. WAN VLAN is an isolated network on VLAN 1 on each 4007R that connects at 100Mbps speed to the C5000 in both sides. A Gigabit speed can also be used instead. However, the limitation will be in Batelco connection to 155Mbps. Figure 7 illustrates WAN Connectivity Based on ATM

The WAN link is divided into 2 VCIs (Virtual Circuits), one carries Normal Inter Campuses data and the other carries data with regards to the registration and Oracle access VLAN. Filtering is implemented on the C5000 on both sides to classify and manage routing through the two VCIs.

IP ADDRESSING AND VLANS: LAYER 3 DESIGN

In order to understand the modification carried out on the IP schema, a brief description is introduced below. TCP/IP (Transport Control Protocol / Internet Protocol) is the language of the Internet. Agents can perform assigned tasks on the Internet when they learn to "speak TCP/IP". A host, for example, that has TCP/IP functionality (such as Unix, OS/2, MacOs, or Windows NT) can easily support applications that use the network.

IP is a "network layer" protocol that allows the host to actually "talk" to each other. Such things as carrying datagram, mapping the Internet address

Figure 7. UoB network WAN connectivity based on ATM

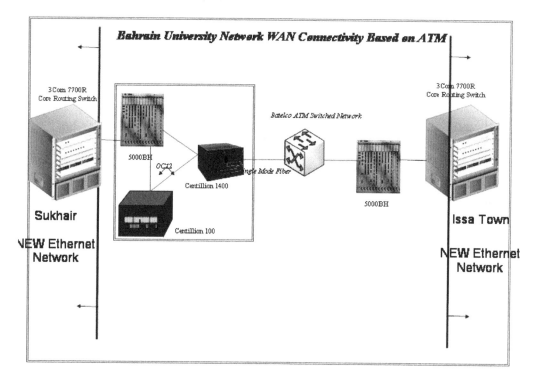

(such as 10.2.3.4 to a physical network address such as 08:00: 69:0a:ca: 88), and routing, which takes care of making sure that all of the devices that have Internet connectivity can find the way to each other (Curtin, 1997).

In our design, some changes have been applied to the IP scheme in both, Sukhair and Issa-town sites. The key characteristic is to have the IP Scheme reflect the building number as convenient as possible. All user VLANs / subnets are in range of 192.168.x.0, where x is the building number. Some buildings have names and not numbers or have extended numbers such as A20, S18 and in this case the IP scheme of these buildings will not reflect the geo-location.

As the design employs Layer 3, additional VLANs are used as Interconnect VLANs. Interconnect VLANs are used to carry the RIP routing information. The Interconnect VLANs are in IP

range of 172.16.x.0 and they only exist between 7700 Core and 4924 Layer 3 Distribution. The Distribution switches update the cores through the communications with routing information protocol. However, alternative default route has been implemented in each of the 4924 distribution switch to the core.

The IP Addressing of the Interconnect VLAN carries the same third octet number in the native user VLAN. However, LAN ID is the third octet number plus 1000, i.e. Building 39 has a user VLAN (39) 192.168.39.0 and its interconnect VLAN (1039) to the core is 172.16.39.0

In Issa Town campus the VLANs start with 100 to avoid repetitive VLANs across the 2 campuses, i.e. Building 11 has a VLAN 111. Also for Inter-connect, VLANs start with 1100, therefore the associated Interconnect VLAN to the same building 11 will be 1111.

The Interconnect VLANs have only two IP addresses each

VLAN Interface in 7700R	VLAN Interface in 49xx Distribution
172.16.x.1	172.16.x.254

The Routing Information Protocol (RIP) is only enabled on these two interfaces.

For Users of VLANs, the 4924 distribution switches act as a Gateway L3 border. The 4924 addressing for VLAN users (VLAN Interface L3 Address) would be 192.168.x.1

Figure 8 shows RIP routing in Sukhair site. Issa Town RIP routing will also follow a similar concept.

Servers reside in VLAN 100 and VLAN 19 "Public VLANs". They utilize 4924s as distributed servers VLANs and route through the 7700. In addition to the server VLANs, the 7700 core will have two server VLANs including:

- VLAN 3 "Oracle VLAN", and
- VLAN 4 "DHCP VLAN".

Both servers utilize the UTP 10/100/1000 modules.

There is only one exception for building 22, which is a distribution for 3 Buildings S20, S21 and S20A. Therefore, the RIP domain has been extended to carry Layer 3 information across the 4950 to the 4924s.

Issa Town IP scheme is following the same concept with a small change of adding a 100 to the building number. Some buildings with high density have more than one VLAN. These building are not numbered in sequence and have been set after consultation with Issa Town network administrator.

The network is primed to support planned improvements with a minimum additional cost when network upgrading is needed. However, in addition to converging voice and data, the design

Figure 8. VLANS layer 3 design

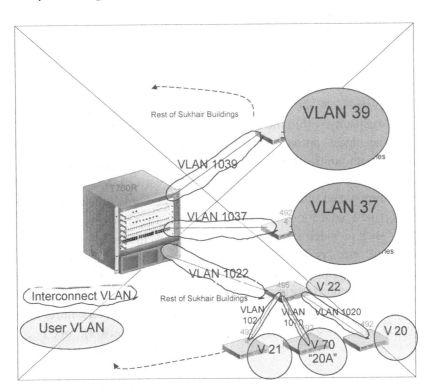

process took into consideration future expansions so we planned 3com wireless systems to connect students in dormitories, cafeterias, and meeting rooms.

The administration and management of network processes within an organization can dramatically reduce cost and increase efficiency of the network. Management can properly support applications ranging from registration to instructional material delivery planning. This can help show a significant saving in teacher and administrative time and benefits the university as staff can spend less time on routine tasks and more on helping the university to reach its key objectives (Barrett, & King, 2005). A security plan must be put into place, and users need to be educated and trained. Access control lists confine users to areas of the network for which they are authorized and layer 3 protocol authentication prevents unauthorized users from entering the network, ensuring that sensitive students' data and payroll are safe from prying eyes.

As UOB is growing fast, the new design will sufficiently be able to extend for new requirements in the near future. The design addresses capacity/performance and protocols In terms of capacity, the new network supports upgrade capacity in certain ways: ability to move forward to 10 Gigabit in the Network Core and ability to scale for 100% upgrade capacity within the current equipment Building block approach open the limit for scalability with multi-tier network architecture In terms of Applications, UOB is planning to gradually renew and update its infrastructure to support new educational based real time applications such as video streaming, IP telephony, e-learning, etc. As Networking Technology change to cope with new application demand, the new network supports current and near future technologies such as IPv6 and MPLS for open Internet world "Internet 2".

NETWORK MANAGEMENT

All of the network devices should be managed from a single console. This console should display graphical topology information, and should provide details of switch configuration, status and link utilization. The used network management tools provide proactive management for the whole network with comprehensive real-time as well as historical reporting mechanisms.

3Com 3ND is used to manage the network. The Network Management workstation is supplied by ABK as per the specification below. The Recommended specification is advisable. The PCs are standalone and are used for the sole purpose of the network management.

	Minimum	Recommended
IBM PC or compatible	500MHz Pentium III	2.4GHz Pentium IV
RAM	512MB	1GB or more
Free hard disk space	2GB	4GB
Graphics capabilities	1024x768/256 colours	1024x768 /64K colours
CD-ROM drive	Yes	Yes
Network adapter card	Yes	Yes

Network management include also grouping and grouping policies, methods for keeping the network running smoothly and efficiently, knowing what to look for and how to fix it is a necessity skill ("Network Management", 2006).

The design of the network at UOB campuses provided a manageable solution to network growing problems by integrating network resilience into core networking devices. This resiliency integration into the network core enables user access points to remain connected to the network even in the event of a failure. To ensure the availability of the network, one needs to measure it using the following equation:

$$Availability = MTBF / (MTBF + MTTR)$$

This equation shows that availability can be improved by either increasing MTBF or by reducing MTTR. Where MTBF is the Mean Time Before Failure, which is the average time from an initial fault free state, *and* MTTR is the Mean Time To Repair, which is the average time taken to diagnose a failure and repair it.

Availability is quantified using the percentage of uptime (or expected down time) provided by a system. For example, a system with 99.9% availability would expect to have about nine hours of downtime a year. A system with 99.999% availability, often referred to as 5 nines availability, limits downtime to about 5 minutes a year.

It is impossible to create systems that never fail, so minimizing MTTR values will increase availability. Carrier class systems have traditionally provided MTTR targets of less than 50 milliseconds, which is the specification for SONET ring recovery time.

Core converged applications can provide the services and benefits they were designed to without impediments (Nortel Network, 2004a).

Having the new network equipment will facilitate extending high speed Internet to everywhere, added global outreach for students to access Internet for education. The network is now ready for e-learning application including video and audio multicast with real-time application aware network devices.

CONCLUSIONS AND RECOMMENDATIONS

The chapter described a framework for designing and implementing LAN infrastructure in general. It also described our experienced in designing and implementing the infrastructure at the University of Bahrain. The chapter showed how the switching mechanisms were set up at both campuses. The server farm aggregation was implemented using two Giga ports per 4924 switches. This approach was aimed to provide redundant connectivity for servers.

The chapter emphasized the importance of network resiliency, which is a multi-layered process that allows campus services to support existing applications while providing a solid foundation for the future network growth. Working towards five 9s resiliency starts in the network core with network hardware elements, design, and protocols working together to ensure reliability. By ensuring the maximum amount of resiliency in the most heavily used area of the network, network managers can feel confident that applications like IP Telephony, multicasting, and collaboration tools can provide the network resources when and where they are needed.

There are two issues that need to be tackled in the future upgrading.

1. **RIP routing update issue:** In Post implementation testing, an issue of RIP updates from 7700 are inconsistent and sometimes information may be lost. This drawback has been experienced with VLANs 10xx where xx is from 24 to 99. This draw back has been dealt with in the current design by implementing a static default router in the 4924 switch to forward the traffic to the 7700, which is an alternative to RIP routing. We recommend fixing this issue in the upcoming release of the 7700 distribution layer switch.

2. **Intercampus routing:** As the Inter-Campus routing over Batelco ATM utilizes the legacy old equipment of Nortel C5000 and C1400 switches. Upgrading these switches to ATM routers (3Com 6000) is necessary in order to provide a framework for end-To-end 3Com environment, fully manageable environment, and the ability to set end-to-end QoS and filtering.

REFERENCES

A Guide to Network Topology. (2008). Retrieved January 26, 2008, from *http://learn-networking.*

com/network-design/a-guide-to-network-topology.

Ahmed, I., Godbole, R., & Vishwanathan, S. (2004). An Open Standards Approach to Network-Centric Storage, Retrieved 12, July, 2005 from *www.netapp.com.*

Barrett, D., & King, T. (2005). *Computer networking illuminated.* Jones and Bartlett Publishers, Inc.

Bejerano, Y., Breitbart, Y., Garofalakis, M., & Rastogi, R. (2003). Physical Topology Discovery for Large Multi-Subnet Networks. *Bell Labs, Lucent Technologies, IEEE INFOCOM 2003.*

Chowdhry, P. (1997, September). Can Gigabit Ethernet and RSVP Beat ATM. *PCWeek Magazine.*

Curtin, M. (1997). Introduction to Network Security, Retrieved March 6, 2008 from *http://www.interhack.net/pubs/network-security/network-security.html.*

Hadzic, I., & Szurkowski, E. S. (2005). High-Performance Synchronization for Circuit Emulation in an Ethernet MAN. *Journal Of Communication and Networks, 7*(1), pp.1-12.

Herbert, J. (2003). *Issues in Resilient Network Design,* March 2003, International Network Services Inc.

HNF, (1998). *High Performance Networking Forum,* Retrieved November, 17, 2007 from *www.hnf.org.*

Houdt,B. V., & Blondia, C. (2000). Performance Evaluation of the Identifier Splitting Algorithm with Polling in Wireless ATM Networks. *International Journal of Wireless Information Networks, 7*(2).

IDC. (2004). 2000 *Disk Storage System Forecast & Analysis (1999-2004),* Report (IDC #B23768).

Intel. (2006). Accelerating High-Speed Networking with Intel® I/O Acceleration Technology, Retrieved January 10, 2008 from *http://www.idgconnect.com/networking/networkmanagement/accelerating_high_speed_networking_with_intel_i_o_acceleration_technology.*

Katzela, I., & Schwarz, M. (1995). Schemes for Fault Identification in Communication Networks. *IEEE/ACM Transactions on Networking, 3*(6), 753–764.

Koyama, A., Barolli, L., Capi, G., Apduhan, B. O., Arai, J. & Durresi, A. (2004). An efficient multi-purpose optimization method for qos routing using genetic algorithm. *Journal of Interconnection Networks, 5*(4), 409-428..

Krunz, M. (1998). Lecture Notes for ECE 564—fall 1998. *Broadband Networks and Multimedia Communications.* University of Arizona.

Liu, F., & Yang, C. (2004a). Proxy Design for Improving the Efficiency of Stored MPEG-4 FGS Video Delivery over Wireless Networks. *Journal of Communication and Networks, 6,* 280-286.

Mitchell, B. (2008). Your Guide to Wireless/Networking, Retrieved January 28, 2008 from compnetworking.about.com/od/hardwarenetworkgear/g/bldef_switch.htm.

Netcraft Ltd. (2004). June 2004 Web Server Survey, Retrieved September 21, 2005 from *news.netcraft.com/archives/Web Server Survey.html.*

Network Management Basics. (2006). Retrieved March 16, 2008 http://www.cisco.com/univercd/cc/td/doc/cisintwk/ito_doc/nmbasics.htm .

Network Level Resiliency for High Availability (HA) in Ethernet Networks, (2001). Retrieved January 11, 2008 from *www.znyx.com.*

Nortel Network. (2004a). Designing a Resilient Network, Retrieved January, 10, 2008. From *http://www.nortel.com/products/01/passport/8600_rss/collateral /nn107680-031804.pdf.*

Nortel networks. (2004b). High-Availability Network for the Healthcare Industry, Retrieved February 19, 2008 from *www.nortelnetworks. com.*

Plessel, M. (1999). IEEE and Gigabit Ethernet Alliance Announce Formal Ratification of Gigabit Ethernet Over Copper Standard. *Gigabit Ethernet Alliance Press Release*, Published by the Institute of Electrical and Electronics Engineers, Inc.

Tanenbaum, A. S. (1996). *Computer Networks*, 3rd ed. Prentice Hall, Inc.

Regnier, G. et al. (2004, September). TCP Onloading for Data Server. *IEEE Computer*, 46.

Ward, M. (2002). Resilient Packet Ring, Retrieved March 1, 2008, from *http://searchnetworking. techtarget.com/sDefinition/0,,sid7_gci754865,00. html.*

Yemini, S., Kliger, S., Mozes, E., Yemini, Y., & Ohsie, D. (1996, May). High Speed and Robust Event Correlation. *IEEE Communications.*

ZNYX Networks, Inc. (2001). *Network Level Resiliency for High Availability (HA) in Ethernet Networks.* Retrieved January 30, 2008 from *www. znyx.com.*

Chapter V
Updating on Gigabit Ethernet Implementation:
The Case of a Large New Zealand Organization

Nurul I. Sarkar
AUT University, New Zealand

Catherine Byrne
Tonkin & Taylor Ltd., Auckland, New Zealand

Nabeel A. Y. Al-Qirim
United Arab Emirates University, UAE

ABSTRACT

Ethernet network technology is still one of the most popular LAN technologies in use today by many organizations and educational institutions worldwide. The throughput offered by the 10 and 100 Mbps Ethernet is inadequate for supporting high bandwidth applications such as real-time multimedia and Web applications. Gigabit Ethernet (GigE) technology provides 1000 megabits per second (i.e., one gigabit per second) at a more reasonable cost than the other technologies of comparable speed, therefore it is a natural upgrade strategy for many legacy Ethernet networks. This chapter updates our previous research on GigE that has been documented as a case study of a large New Zealand organization. We focused on the level of GigE deployment, design, planning, implementation, network performance testing, problems encountered, and future plans. Our research findings show the feasibility and practicability of deploying GigE technology in high-speed networking applications, such as campus- and corporate-wide local area networks.

INTRODUCTION

To meet the growing demand for high-bandwidth networking applications, such as multimedia and web services, has challenged network researchers to design network architectures capable of delivering a quality of service to end users. The demand for high bandwidth to the desktop has also grown for many end users requiring for an even high-speed network technology at the backbone. The deployment of GigE at organizations will enable the development of many bandwidth-intensive interdisciplinary applications, standards-based quality of service features, fast routing, and ease of management makes GigE an ideal solution for the next generation network technology.

GigE is an evolution of the original Ethernet design which has been around for more than 30 years. The first ratification of the Ethernet standard is known as IEEE 802.3 Carrier Sense Multiple Access with Collision Detection (CSMA/CD) access method and Physical Layer Specifications (TechFest, 2001). This specification is for 10 Mbps (i.e., 10BASE 2) over thin coaxial cable of maximum length 185 meters. Since then the standard has improved to include new media systems for 10 Mbps (e.g. 10BASE-T), then 100 Mbps (i.e., Fast Ethernet), and now 1000 Mbps, known as GigE. The 10 GigE has also been standardised by the IEEE in June 2002 (802.3ae, 2002; Meirosu et al., 2005).

A detailed discussion of GigE technology including 1 and 10 GigE and their performance measurements can be found in many networking literature (Cheng, Yu, & Sincoskie, 2005; Hughes-Jones, Clarke, & Dallison, 2005; Intel Corporation, 2003a; McNamara, 2001; Stallings, 2007; Zeadally & Zhang, 2004). Bakes et al. (2003) described a case study of GigE technology and its applications at the NASA Glenn Research Center.

In this chapter we update our research on GigE that has been documented as case study of a large New Zealand organization considering upgrade to GigE focusing on the level and scope of GigE deployment, network design and implementation, network performance improvement, problems encountered, and future plans (Sarkar, Byrne, & Al-Qirim, 2006). This case study approach may be useful to other organizations interested in upgrading their current networks to GigE. Professionals interested in the GigE technology could benefit from the experience of the organization in this study in adopting and diffusing the GigE technology.

The remainder of this chapter is organized as follows. An overview of GigE is presented first. We then discuss the deployment considerations of GigE. A case study of a large New Zealand organization focusing on the level and scope of GigE deployment are described. The network performance and test results are presented followed by brief discussion and conclusion.

OVERVIEW OF GIGABIT ETHERNET

GigE supports four different physical layer implementations, three to which are defined in the IEEE 802.3z standard (802.3, 1998). The fourth is defined in the IEEE 802.3ab standard (802.3ab, 1999). IEEE 802.3z provides the specifications for the 1000BASE-LX, 1000BASE-SX, and 1000BASE-CX physical layers which, together, are generally referred to as 1000BASE-X. 1000BASE-LX networks support three types of optical fibre and 1000BASE-SX networks support two types. 1000BASE-LX can operate over a pair of 10 μm (core diameter) single mode fibres, or 50 or 62.5 μm multimode fibres, and uses long-wavelength (1300 nm nominal) lasers.

An overview of various GigE standards is presented in Figure 1. The frame format of a typical GigE is shown in Figure 2.

Figure 1. Gigabit ethernet standards

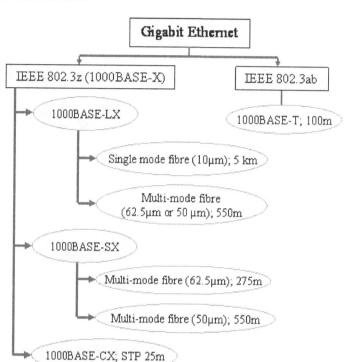

Figure 2. Gigabit Ethernet frame format

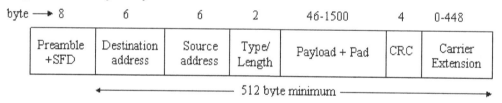

GIGABIT ETHERNET DEPLOYMENT CONSIDERATIONS

The three important factors (Intel Corporation, 2003b; Janowski, 2003; Serenbetz, 1998) that are necessary for the proper deployment of GigE are: (1) transmission media selection; (2) testing existing cabling; and (3) identifying potential bottlenecks.

For implementing a GigE, either UTP Cat 5 or better or fibre optic cables can be used. The choice of cables depends on factors such as distance coverage, physical location and environmental effects. The GigE has been approved for 550m and 5 km lengths for fibre optic and 100m for UTP Cat 5, Cat 5e and Cat 6 copper cables. So, if the distance between two devices is longer than 100m, then fibre optic cable will be more appropriate than the copper cables. However, the fibre optic cable may still be the better choice for applications requiring a short distance communication (less than 100m) because the fibre optic cable is not affected by electromagnetic interference, and is less vulnerable to security breaches. But, fibre optic cables are more expensive, difficult to install and since most organizations already have existing UTP Cat 5 or 5e, making copper cables often the most cost-effective choice for many companies upgrading to GigE (Janowski, 2003; Tan, 2000).

According to Tan (2000), GigE technology such as 1000BASE-T (i.e., 1Gbps over twisted-pair) will be the likely choice for many organizations. The question may arise as to whether copper cables (e.g., Cat 5e) or optical fibre cables are to be installed for upgrading to GigE. While many argue (Higgins, 2003; Hochmuth, 2003; Tolly, 2003) that using Cat 6 does not warrant the extra expense, others argue see e.g., (Corporation, 2003) that Cat 6 allows for 10 Gigabit use and should therefore be used for new installations to provide some future proofing. Although 10 GigE is not a standard for copper wiring, the industry community sees it as an important issue and an IEEE 802.3 Working Group has been established. However, Cat 6 cable has several advantages over Cat 5e, including tighter tolerance on impedance variations, higher bandwidth (250 MHz), and better performance.

Table 1 compares the performance of Cat 5, Cat 5e and Cat 6 cables (Anixter & Intel Corporation, 2003). The typical frame error rates in column 2 of Table 1 represent the transfer of 1 million 1518-byte packets over a 100BASE-T link using a marginal Ethernet adapter and switch port.

If existing copper cable is to be used for GigE, then it is important that all cables must be tested to meet the performance criteria for GigE. As Janowski (2003) points out cable testing should include connectors, patch and fly leads. Testing for crosstalk and return loss is also required when using existing cabling, as these issues do not affect both 10BASE-T and 100BASE-T as the pairs used do not have bi-directional traffic (Sweeney, 2000; Vanderlaan, 1999). The test parameters are included in the TIA/EIA 568-B.1 standard, including the far-end crosstalk and return loss that were not included in the original Cat 5 standard.

According to Janowski (2003) and Chapin (2001), another issue is the standard 32-bit PCI architecture, as this only handles up to 133 megabytes per second, whereas 64-bit PCI-X buses

Table 1. Performance comparison of Cat 5, Cat 5e and Cat 6 twisted-pair cables

Cabling	Typical frame errors	Errors (%)	Improvement over Cat 5 (%)
Cat 5	200,000	5	
Cat 5e	100,000	3.5	50
Cat 6	17,000	0.4	92

can handle up to 1 gigabyte per second. There are several PCI-X buses available in the market (e.g. AMD 750, Intel Xeon and Itainuim2), but is not a common configuration for PC-based workstation. This is one of the bottlenecks that need to be considered when deploying GigE. Another potential bottleneck is that the devices connected to network such as printers are not to have Gigabit capabilities. The availability of PCI Express from Intel Corporation and the more widespread adoption of PCI-X may resolve some network bottlenecks.

Deployment Steps

The industry best practice for deploying GigE as outlined in (Gigabit Ethernet Alliance, 1998; Intel Corporation, 2003a; McNamara, 2001) seems to be that the deployment is carried out in the following order:

- **Switch-to-switch and switch-to-router connections:** This requires a decision on whether layer 2 or layer 3 switches are to be used. Layer 3 switches allow for the linking of subnets without the use of a router.
- **Switch-to-server connections:** All servers on the GigE switch should have Gigabit capable network interface cards (NICs).
- **Switch-to-high performance workgroups:** Whether this step is carried out depends on the company requirements. If a company requires Gigabit performance to desktop then,

according to GigE Alliance (Gigabit Ethernet Alliance, 1998) and McNamara (McNamara, 2001), the first area that needs to be upgraded is the groups/departments that requires connection between high performance workstations and switches.

- **Switch-to-other users:** If this were going to be done, it would be the last step in the implementation.

Figure 3 shows an example of a best practice implementation of a GigE network for a large organization.

CASE STUDY

This research is exploratory in the sense that there was no prior research in New Zealand to guide this research endeavour. Therefore, this research

adopted the case study methodology proposed by Yin (1994). Yin's (1994) views are that case studies are the preferred research strategy to answer how and why type questions and using interviews would also be acceptable by the interpretivist school (Walsham, 1995). The strength of case studies is the ability to capture a greater number of variables than is possible with any of the other strategies. The case study approach is important to this study in exploring the application of this novel GigE technology in organizations.

In summary, this research adopts Yin's (1994) case study design in studying one single case (holistic) represented here by a large environmental and engineering consultancy firm (unit of analysis) that has been in business for more than 45 years. As requested by the management of this company, the real name of the company and the interviewee was suppressed. Closed-ended and open-ended questions were used during the in-depth interview with the IT manager of the company.

Figure 3. A typical corporate gigabit ethernet infrastructure

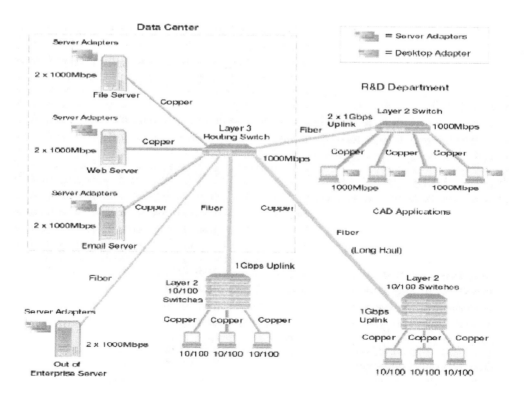

Case Background

The company in this study has 10 regional offices in New Zealand with a headquarters in Auckland. The company has also affiliated companies in Malaysia and Philippines. This company specialises in environmental, geotechnical, water resources and civil infrastructure work such as tunnelling, storm water, waste management and roading.

Currently there are 325 employees in New Zealand consisting of 287 consultants and 38 support staff. All staff members are highly computer literate and most of them are very sophisticated users. The nature of the business requires a robust and responsive IT infrastructure with flexibility to meet the fluctuating demands of project work.

To get some insights about the level of deployment of GigE, we conducted an interview with an IT manager of the organization under study. The interview questionnaire used in this study consists of three sections with a total of 32 questions (see Appendix for interview questionnaire).

The first section (questions 1 to 16) of the interview questionnaire was designed to get an insight into the existing network infrastructure of the company under study. This was supported by asking about the number of PCs and laptops and the operating systems they used in questions 2 to 5; number of servers on the LAN and server OS, in questions 8, and 9; network topology and cabling in questions 14 and 15. The second section (questions 17 to 26) of the interview questionnaire was designed to gather some information about the upgrade to GigE. This was supported by asking about what is being upgraded to GigE, in question 17; whether the existing wiring system is going to be used for GigE, in questions 18 to 20; and the networking devices including routers and switches that need to be upgraded, in questions 21 to 22. The third section (questions 27 to 32) of the interview questionnaire was designed to get information about GigE design, planning and implementation. This was supported by asking about reasons for upgrade, in question 27; what

services will use GigE and planned implementation, in questions 28 and 29; and the overall cost for upgrade and data rate after upgrade to GigE, in questions 31 and 32.

Existing Network Infrastructure

The existing network infrastructure (before upgrade to GigE) is an extended star physical topology with a star Intermediate Distribution Frame (IDF) on each floor of the building, joined to a central star Main Distribution Frame (MDF). Each star IDF uses a mixture of 3Com Ethernet 3 switches (24-port 10/100 Mbps) and 10 Mbps Hubs. A D-Link DES-5024 24-port 10/100 Mbps switch serves the central star. The cabling for all parts of the topology consists of either Cat 5 or Cat 5e. There is no record of where each type is used and none of the cabling has been certified. The protocols used on the network are TCP/IP and IPX/SPX.

Each of the organization's offices runs a LAN which is connected to head office via a VPN running over Fibre, Wireless and DSL. These links are also used for the Internet access for the company. However in the head office a separate 4Mbps fibre line is also being used for the Internet connectivity (*Telecom NZ Links*, 2004). Mako Systems are used as routers, firewalls and VPN access end points. Microsoft's ISA Server is used for VPN services for mobile users and for publishing Internet facing servers.

At the head office, there are twenty servers in total of which 19 are Windows 2003 servers, and one Windows 2008 server. Table 2 lists the 20 servers: (1) fifteen servers as shown in column 1 are linked to company LANs; (2) two servers are connected to both the company's LANs and externally is shown in column 2; and (3) the remaining three servers are external to the company LANs and are used for communication and accessing PMCRS (Project Management and Communication Reporting System)(see column 3).

Table 2. Sixteen servers currently operating at the head office

Server connected to LAN	Server connected to LAN and externally	External server
SQL server (2)	VPN server	Web server
File server (2)	ISA server	Mail server
Print server (1)		SQL server
Domain Controllers (2)		
Application Servers (5)		
Intranet server (1)		
Archival storage server (1)		
Legacy financial server (1)		

At the head office there are 220 PC-based workstations and 54 laptops. All computers are operating under MS Windows XP, The configuration for each workstation ranges from Intel P4 3.0 MHz to Core 2 Duo, with 1GB to 2GB of RAM. Hard disk drives are 120GB with a speed of 7,200 rpm. All computers have DVDs, sound cards and 1GB Marvel network cards.

All computers in the organization are configured with MS Windows XP via a scripted install and a standard set of software via Microsoft Installer (MSI) and group policies. Then through the use of further group policies computers are installed with the specialist software required by the users. Basically the bulk of installations are covered by four further group policies as follows:

- ArcGIS
- Geotechnical software (about 12 applications by different vendors)
- Administrative assistants (software required by the administrative support staff in each Group).
- Accounts software (applications required only be the accounts staff)

With the use of Active Directory Services and distributed file systems, the distribution of new and upgraded applications is controlled by MSIs and group policies across all offices via the VPN. While not a 24/7 operation, users do have requirements and expectations of having the system available 7 days a week and for most of the evening. Administrative activities are run from midnight to 4am in the morning, so there is little time available for planned down time.

Reasons for Upgrade

According to the IT Manager of the organization under study, there are three main reasons for upgrading to GigE.

- **Relocation of offices:** The IT Group had moved to a new location about three years ago but the central switches stayed at the old location. To cope with company's current growth, servers are splitted over both locations. The re-wiring would allow all servers and the switches on the star MDF to move to one location.

- **High bandwidth applications:** Due to increased use of images with design packages such as ArcGIS, Land Development, AutoCAD, 12D and MOSS, as well as photographs in reports, has led to the requirement for more bandwidth.

- **Replacement of hubs and switches:** Wanted to install more Ethernet Switches to replace all the Hubs and 10 Mbps switches.

Goals and Requirements

The overall goals for upgrading to GigE are: (1) streamline the wiring from the star MDF to the star IDFS; and (2) provide, in the first instance, more bandwidth on the backbone and gradually to users. To achieve successful rollover to GigE, the organization undertook the following three phases:

- Deciding on a design
- Implementation
- Testing

The factors influencing the process revolved around past experience, budget constraints and newness of the technology. The reason the organization has not replaced all hubs with switches is because of the problems that they have had getting good support in New Zealand for their current switches. So this is an important factor in the choosing of new switches. The switch supplier has to have a strong presence in New Zealand—not just for selling but for ad-hoc support as well. However budget constraints means that cost has to be taken into account in this decision. The decision to use a consultant to design the upgrade has been made despite the organization usually doing design work themselves. The reason for this is based on two issues: (1) time is a factor since all IT staff members are heavily committed to other projects for several months; and (2) newness is another factor—use of GigE technology is still new, so the company wanted another view.

As the IT Manager stated "even if they only endorse the design we have in place already, it would be worth the piece of mind". As the star MDF's location is being shifted, re-wiring will be necessary. Given this and the fact that no further plans for relocation are likely to occur in the foreseeable future, the decision was made to plan for future bandwidth growth requirements. As discussed earlier, both Cat 5 and Cat 5e would be capable of running Gigabit. Fibre optic cable was considered but the benefits versus the cost were not warranted according to both the consultants and the IT Manager.

The specification requirements for the servers had been investigated and although the current servers only have 32-bit bus PCI capability, the IT Manager had already decided that even though this would cause a bottleneck, access speeds would still be faster than fast Ethernet and upgrades to a higher speed PCI bus can be done as the technology becomes available. So the design mandate given to the consultants was to design a system that in the first instance provided switch-to-switch Gigabit connections, allowing however the ability to extend to the desktop when and if required in the future. The other requirement was for the heavy demand servers (total six servers) to have Gigabit connection to the switches on the star MDF.

Design and Planning

The consultants were asked to assess the entire current topology as well as replacing the main star. The design they submitted did not change the topology in any significant way. The only difference was the addition of extra cables between the star MDF and star IDFS, where currently there are two; the new design had four cables. The use of the four cables allows for redundancy as well as for growth. The consultant's recommendation for switches met the organization's requirements of a strong New Zealand presence and budget constraints.

All floors would have their 10/100 switches and/or hubs replaced with one 10/100 switches which also have two Gigabit ports, with an option for two more. One of these ports would be used for the connection to the backbone. In the future a Gigabit switch can be added at each of the star IDFS for any group of users that require GigE to the desktop. These switches will use one of the remaining three cables at each star.

Figure 4. Connection configuration for the main switches

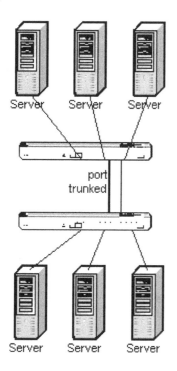

Figure 5. Workstation-to-server configuration before upgrade to GigE

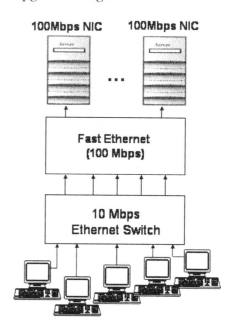

The use of two switches at the main star allows for redundancy and for increased bandwidth for server access. The connection configurations for these switches are shown in Figure 4. These switches are layer-3 switches, which allows for any expansion of the network in the future. The high usage servers will connect directly to these switches.

The rest of the switches are layer-2 switches as the cost of layer-3 switches is not warranted. The total cost of the switches and installation was in the 40 to 60 thousand-dollar range.

Implementation

The implementation requires new wiring to be run between all floors to the star MDF in the computer room. This can all be done without disruption to the existing network. However the wiring ducts between the floors has been concreted in, ap-

parently for fire safety reasons, so this will have to be drilled through out of work hours because of the noise disruption. The switch at each star IDF can be placed in the existing frame and connected to the new backbone cable before cutover. However this will require some reorganization of the current frame configuration so that the new switches can be patched tidily from the patch panel. This work will be done on a Sunday, after a week's notification, to minimise impact on the users. The new frame for the star MDF will be installed and all switches and panels transferred at the same time.

Prior to cutover to the new wiring and switches, the network cards in the servers will have to be replaced with 100/1000 NICs. This is scheduled to be done as part of the routine maintenance over the month prior to cutover. The cutover was scheduled for one Saturday. Testing the new star topology had been completed but the unknown

Figure 6. Workstation-to-server configuration after upgrade to GigE

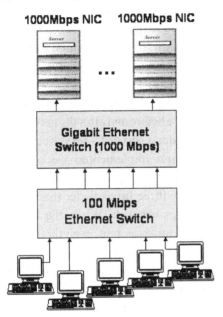

Figure 7. Comparison of network throughput performance before and after upgrade to GigE under workstation-server configuration.

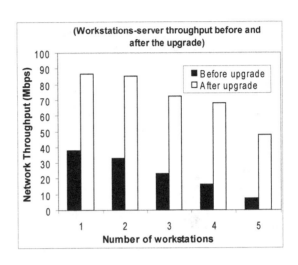

was the new main star interacting with the existing cabling of the other stars. So although one evening should have been enough time, doing the cutover on a Saturday gave all weekend before lack of system caused by any problems would impact on the business.

The cutover consisted of changing the patch leads from the existing switches and hubs at each IDF to the new switches and of connecting the high usage servers to the switches at the MDF. This was all carried out successfully and workstations in each star were used to run various applications with speeds compared to similar tests done before cutover. An increase in speed was not necessarily expected in this low load situation but was a check that there was not a decreased performance indicating some problem. However the following morning the network went down and testing showed that a particular star was the problem. Resetting the switch restarted the network but the consultants decided that a

"loopback" problem existed, that is one of the stars somewhere had two routes to the servers that were on the problem star. The cabling was again checked and completely re-patched but the problem re-occurred within 24 hours. Resetting fixed the problem again but the consultants were adamant that it could not be the switch as all the switches had undergone testing in their lab for a week before installation. However after more testing by the organizations IT staff and several more outages (impact reduced by taking all servers off the problem star), the IT Manager insisted on replacing the switch. No further problems occurred once the switch was replaced. The network performance is described next.

Performance Test Results

The organization under study was particularly interested in the network throughput performance improvement operating under high traffic condi-

Figure 8. Comparison of network throughput performance before and after upgrade to GigE under server-server configuration

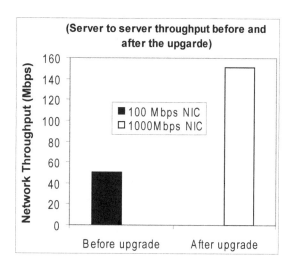

tions, as this was one of the main reasons for upgrading to GigE.

The workstation-to-server configurations before and after upgrading to GigE are shown in Figure 5 and 6, respectively.

The network performance was tested by transferring a 596 MB file under the following network configurations: (1) workstation-to-server; and (2) server-to-server. In the first configuration, two or more servers (with identical configuration including 1000 Mbps NIC) were connected to a GigE switch and all workstations were communicating with the servers via 100 Mbps Ethernet switch (Figure 6). In the second configuration, two servers (with identical configuration including 1000 Mbps NIC) were linked to a GigE switch. In each case, the file transmission time was recorded and the network throughput was computed by dividing the file size by the transmission time.

Figure 7 compares network throughput performance before and after upgrade to GigE under workstation-to-server configuration. We observed that the network throughput performance has increased significantly after the network upgrade to GigE. The network throughput performance

improvement is even more significant as the number of workstation communicating with servers increased. For example, when five workstations are communicating with the servers on the GigE, the network throughput is around six times larger than the existing 10/100 Mbps network (i.e., before upgrade to GigE).

In Figure 8, we compare network throughput performance before and after the network upgrade to GigE under a server-to-server configuration.

When first implemented we observed that the network throughput under the GigE was approximately three times faster than the existing 10/100 Mbps network. While the improvement in data transmission rate, even though it was not ten times faster than the fast Ethernet, was still acceptable to the company's operation because it provided an increased productivity. However, it was considered that much of this limitation to the overall network throughput was due to the low-end PC-based servers and associated hardware including bus architecture, RAM, and GigE cards. It was found that with faster server hardware (the biggest improvement to speed was when network cards became integrated on the motherboard's chipset). The overall network throughput especially at server-to-server configuration increased to nearly 1 Gbps.

Included in the performance testing was a P4 3GHz machine with hyperthreading enabled and an onboard GigE NIC. This computer was the fastest in all the tests, even though it was running over Cat 5e. The onboard network card must have been the difference and further studies showed this to be true. The third party consultant tested the cables using a Fluke Networks DSP-4100 cable tester, and all the cables passed the requirements.

DISCUSSION AND CONCLUSION

Gigabit Ethernet technology is a viable option for campus- and corporate-wide backbone networks, as well as for desktops, workgroups and server connections where legacy Ethernet LAN technologies are no longer able to provide adequate bandwidth and services.

This chapter described a case study of a large New Zealand organization about the company's level and scope of Gigabit Ethernet (GigE) deployment, the problems the company encountered, network performance and test results. While the use of fibre optic cable for switch-to-switch connections may have some obvious benefits such as longer distance coverage, less electromagnetic interference, and high noise immunity than the copper cables. The most common low-cost Cat 5e UTP cable can be used as an alternative option to deliver 1 Gbps (i.e. 1000BASE-T) over 100 meters.

Our findings show that the organization under study first achieved around 300 Mbps after the network upgraded to GigE. This limitation of the overall network throughput was mainly due to the low-end PC-based servers and the associated hardware. However, as expected with faster server hardware the overall network throughput especially at server-to-server configuration was nearly up to 1 Gbps. Originally, while the improvement in data transmission rate was not ten times faster than the fast Ethernet, it was still acceptable to the company's operation since it provided an increased productivity. However with the better server configurations and faster server hardware that has been introduced full advantage of GigE capacity has been achieved.

Our analysis and findings reported in this chapter serve two main purposes. Firstly, we believe that our findings, as reported in this chapter, can be a useful resource, aiding managers to make an informed decision about the deployment of GigE technology to upgrade their campus and/or corporate LAN infrastructure. Secondly, this case study can be used in the classroom as a real-world example, when teaching high-speed networking courses. We believe that this chapter also contributes to filling a research gap in how

a large New Zealand organization and similar organizations elsewhere upgrade their networks to GigE to meet the current and future needs of high-speed networking requirements. A survey with a larger number of organizations is planned as an extension of the present study.

REFERENCES

802.3, I. (1998). *Information Technology - Telecommunications and information exchange between systems-Local and Metropolitan Area Networks - Specific requirements - Part 3: Carrier Sense Multiple Access with Collision Detection (CSMA/CD) Access Method and Physical Layer Specifications.*Unpublished manuscript, New York.

802.3ab, I. (1999). *Supplement to IEEE Std 802.3, Physical Layer Parameters and Specifications for 1000 Mb/s Operation over 4-pair of Category 5 Balanced Copper Cabling, Type 1000BASE-T.*Unpublished manuscript, New York.

802.3ae. (2002). *IEEE Std. 802.3ae-2002 Amendment: Media Access Control (MAC) Parameters, Physical Layers and Management for 10 Gb/s Operation.*Unpublished manuscript.

Anixter & Intel Corporation. (2003). *Gigabit Ethernet over Copper Cabling.* Retrieved June 17, from http://www.personal.psu.edu/staff/r/y/ryb2/gige/Gigabit%20Ethernet%20over%20cabling.pdf

Bakes, C. M., Kim, C. M., & Ramos, C. T. (2003). An assessment of Gigabit Ethernet technology and its applications at the NASA Glenn Researcg Center: A case study.*Journal of Engineering and Technology Management, 20,* 245-272.

Chapin, S. J. (2001). *To InfiniBand ... And Beyond.* Retrieved May 27, 2003, from http://www.networkcomputing.com/1205/1205ws2.html

Cheng, J. Z., Yu, H.-C., & Sincoskie, W. D. (2005). Meeting the broadband access infrastructure demands: The promise of Gigabit Ethernet. *Technological Forecasting and Social Change, 72*(1), 1-10.

Corporation, I. (2003). *Evolution of Gigabit Ethernet: From the Server to the Desktop*. Retrieved June 6, from http://www.intel.com/network/connectivity/resources/doc_library/white_papers/Gigabitevolution.pdf

Gigabit Ethernet Alliance. (1998). *Gigabit Ethernet: Accelerating the standard for speed*. Retrieved June 6, 2003, from http://www.10gea.org/GEA-Accel1999_rev_wp.pdf

Higgins, T. (2003). *Need-To-Know: Gigabit Ethernet - Part 1*. Retrieved June 6, from http://www6.tomshardware.com/network/20030304/Gigabit-04.html

Hochmuth, P. (2003). *Category 6 cabling not ready*. Retrieved May 27, from http://www.nwfusion.com/news/2002/128588_01-07-2002.html

Hughes-Jones, R., Clarke, P., & Dallison, S. (2005). Performance of 1 and 10 Gigabit Ethernet cards with server quality motherboards. *Future Generation Computer Systems, 21*(4), 469-488.

Intel Corporation. (2003a). *Evolution of Gigabit Ethernet: From the Server to the Desktop*. Retrieved June 6, from http://www.intel.com/network/connectivity/resources/doc_library/white_papers/Gigabitevolution.pdf

Intel Corporation. (2003b). *Gigabit Ethernet: Technology and Solutions*. Retrieved May 27, from http://www.intel.com/network/connectivity/resources/doc_library/white_papers/Gigabit_Ethernet/Gigabit_Ethernet.pdf

Janowski, D. D. (2003). Gigabit Ethernet: Making the Switch. *PC Magazine, 22,* 113-121.

McNamara, K. (2001). *Gigabit Ethernet*. Retrieved June 17, 2003, from http://beradio.com/micro-sites/magazinearticle.asp?mode=print&magaszinearticleid=13

Meirosu, C., Golonka, P., Hirstius, A., Stancu, S., Dobinson, B., Radius, E., et al. (2005). Native 10 Gigabit Ethernet experiments over long distances. *Future Generation Computer Systems, 21*(4), 457-468.

Sarkar, N. I., Byrne, C., & Al-Qirim, N. (2006). Gigabit Ethernet implementation: the case of a large New Zealand organization. *International Journal of Business Data Communications and Networking, 2*(4), 59-77.

Serenbetz, J. (1998). Assessing network infrastructure. *NetWorker, 2,* 40-46.

Stallings, W. (2007). *Data and computer communications* (8th ed.). New Jersey: Prentice Hall.

Sweeney, T. (2000). *Gigabit Ethernet Over Copper: Time To Test That Cat-5 Cabling*. Retrieved June 17, 2003, from http://www.internetweek.com/indepth/indepth050800-1.htm

Tan, T. C. (2000). Gigabit Ethernet and structured cabling. *Electronics & Communication Engineering Journal, 12*(4), 156-166.

TechFest. (2001). *TechFest Ethernet Technical Summary*. Retrieved May 27, 2003, from http://www.techfest.com/networking/lan/Ethernet1.htm

Telecom NZ Links. (2004). Retrieved June 3, 2004, from http://www.telecom.co.nz/content/

Tolly, B. (2003). *Gig E to the desktop: Bargain or boondoggle?* Retrieved June 6, from http://www.nwfusion.com/columnists/2003/0217tolly.html

Vanderlaan, P. (1999). *Installation Effects Upon Alien Crosstalk and Equal Level Far End Crosstalk*. Retrieved May 27, 2003, from http://bwce-com.belden.com/college/techpprs/ieacectp.htm

Walsham, G. (1995). Interpretive case studies in IS research: Nature and method. *European journal of Information Systems, 4,* 74-81.

Yin, R. (1994). *Case Study Research Design and Methods*: California: Sage Publications.

Zeadally, S., & Zhang, L. (2004). Enabling gigabit network access to end users. *Proceedings of the IEEE, 92*(2), 340-353.

APPENDIX: INTERVIEW QUESTIONNAIRE

Section 1: Existing System

1. Each of your offices operates a LAN. Are they joined by a WAN?   Y/N
   If Yes, briefly describe how this is configured and what equipment/software is used.

2. How many workstations are on the LAN being investigated for upgrading to Gigabit Ethernet?

3. How many laptops (not already included in the above figures)?

4. What OS is used in workstations? Please give number for each OS (Tick all that apply).
   | Win98 | WinNT | Win 2000 |
   | WinXp | Unix/Linux | Other (please specify) |

5. What OS is used in laptops (if not included in Q4 above)? Please give number for each OS.
   | Win98 | WinNT | Win 2000 |
   | WinXp | Unix/Linux | Other (please specify) |

6. Are the Win98 computers going to have their OS changed? Y/N

7. In general what are the specifications of workstations that will use Gigabit Ethernet?
   | PCI Bus (MHz) | RAM (type e.g. DDR & size) |
   | HDD transfer rate | CPU speed | CPU type |

8. How many servers are on the company LAN?

9. What OS is used for file servers? Please give number for each OS
   | WinNT | Win 2000 |
   | UNIX | LINUX | NetWare |

10. What are the specifications of servers that will use Gigabit Ethernet?
    | PCI Bus (MHz) | RAM (type e.g. DDR & size) |
    | HDD transfer rate | CPU speed & type |

11. What protocols are used on the LAN?

           TCP/IP   IPX/SPX

           NetBui   Other (please specify)

12. Which of the following are used on the current network? Please specify brand/model and how many.

           Routers   Ethernet switches   Hubs

           Repeaters   Bridges

13. Are VLANs used? Y/N

14. What wiring topology is used?

             Star   Bus   Ring

             Tree   Other _____

15. What kind of cabling is currently used? Have they been certified?

           Cat 3   Certified Y/N   Cat 5   Certified Y/N

           Cat 5e   Certified Y/N   Cat 6   Certified Y/N

        Fibre optic   Certified Y/N   Coax   Certified Y/N

16. Define the LAN backbone—please describe or provide a diagram.

Section 2: What is Being Upgraded?

17. What is being upgraded to Gigabit Ethernet?
  - Entire LAN   Y/N
  - Segment(s)   Y/N

    If segment(s), please specify (i.e. backbone plus one department)

18. Is the existing wiring going to be used?   Y/N

19. If No to Q18 please specify why.

20. If Yes to Q18 has it been tested to check that it will meet Gigabit Ethernet requirements? Y/N

21. Is any of the equipment listed in Q12 being replaced? Y/N

22. If Yes to Q21 please list the new equipment—brand/models and numbers

        Routers   Ethernet switches   Hubs

        Repeaters   Bridges

23. Is there any other equipment being installed not mentioned in Q22 above?   Y/N
    If yes, please specify

24. What changes will be required for the servers?

25. Will any redundancy be built into the network topology?   Y/N
    If so where and how?

26. What will the structure of the network be once the installation has been completed?
    Please describe or provide a diagram.

Section 3: Planning and Implementation

27. What are the reasons for upgrading to Gigabit Ethernet?

28. What services/applications will use Gigabit Ethernet and why?

29. What are the planned implementation steps?

30. How is the cutover being planned?

31. What was the cost of the upgrade?

        < $20,000 $20,001–$40,000 $40,001–$60,000

        $60,001–$80,000 $80,001–$100,000   > $100,001

32. What were the bandwidth/data rate, before and after the upgrade to Gigabit Ethernet:

        Server level: Before: _____   After: _____

        User level: Before: _____   After: _____

        Backbone: Before: _____   After: _____

Chapter VI
Interaction Between MIMD–Poly & PIPD–Poly Algorithms and other TCP Variants in Multiple Bottleneck TCP Networks

M. Chandrasekaran
Directorate of Technical Education, India

R. S. D. Wahida Banu
Government College of Engineering, India

ABSTRACT

This chapter introduces and analyses a class of non-linear congestion control algorithms called polynomial congestion control algorithms. These generalize the Additive Increase and Multiplicative Decrease (AIMD) algorithms used for the TCP connections. These algorithms provide additive increase using a polynomial of the inverse of the current window size and provide multiplicative decrease using the polynomial of the current window size. There are infinite numbers of TCP-compatible polynomial algorithms by assuming polynomial of different order. This chapter analyses the interaction between the two models (named as MIMD-Poly and PIPD-Poly) of these generalized algorithms, for the wired (with unicast and multicast) and wireless TCP networks. TCP compatibility of these algorithms is evaluated using the simulations of the implementations of the proposed two models. Simulations are done using ns2, a discrete event simulator. The model MIMD-Poly is proved to be TCP-compatible. The results of simulation are compared with that of the TCP variants such as TCP/Tahoe, TCP/Reno, TCP/New Reno, and TCP/Vegas. The Comparison shows that both algorithms perform better in terms of throughput.

INTRODUCTION

During the last decade, computer networks have been growing very tremendously. Large number of computers gets connected to both private and public networks. In most of these networks the protocol stack used is TCP/IP. In spite of the rapid growth and explosive increase in traffic demand computer networks in general, Internet in particular is still working without collapse.

Also the growth of the Internet has sparked the demand of several applications, which require the stability of the Internet. For achieving such a success and to have the stability of Internet, mechanisms are developed to reduce transmission errors, to provide better bandwidth sharing of sources that use common bottleneck links, to reduce the Round Trip Time (RTT) and mainly to provide the congestion control by the transport layer protocol i.e. TCP (Transmission Control Protocol). TCP's end-to-end congestion control mechanism reacts to packet loss by adjusting the number of outstanding unacknowledged data segments allowed in the network (Jacobson, 1988; Widmer et al., 2001). Such algorithms are implemented in its protocol, TCP. (Comer, 1991; Stevens, 1994; Allman & Paxson, 1999). In the existing algorithms, increasing the congestion window linearly with time increases the bandwidth of the TCP connection and when the congestion is detected, the window size is multiplicatively reduced by a factor of two (Yang & Lam, 2000).

TCP is not well suited for several emerging applications including streaming and real time audio and video because it increases end-to-end delay and delay variations (Jin et al., 2001).

This paper analyzes a new class of nonlinear congestion control algorithms for Internet Transport Protocols and applications. It seeks to develop a family of algorithms for applications such as Internet audio and video that does not react well to rate reductions, because the rate reduction technique used for these applications will result into the degradation in user-perceived quality (Allman & Paxson, 1999; Floyd & Fall, 1999). This analysis results into get good understanding of TCP-compatible congestion control algorithms by generalizing the Additive Increase and Multiplicative Decrease (AIMD) algorithms. The authors analyze the proposed algorithms in a simulated wired TCP network.

One of the current challenges of the Internet is to allow universal access to multimedia transmissions, even for receivers located within networks of different bandwidth and other characteristics. Multicast allows one single transmission to be delivered to a large number of receivers over a network (Seada et al., 2002). Congestion control is a major requirement for multicast to be deployed in the current Internet. This paper analyses the performance of the proposed congestion control algorithms in a wired network that employ multicast routing strategies.

With the proliferation of mobile computing devices, the demand for continuous network connectivity regardless of physical location has created greater interest in the use of mobile ad hoc networks (Sundaresan et al., 2003; Holland & Vaidya, 1999). This paper also analyze the performance of the proposed algorithms in Mobile Ad hoc Networks that uses TCP and compares the performance of the two proposed models with the standard AIMD algorithms implemented for TCP networks.

In all the simulations, the proposed two models are named as MIMD-Poly and PIPD-Poly. They are compared with the TCP variants such as TCP/Tahoe (called as TCP), TCP/Reno, TCP/NewReno, TCP/Vegas and the comparisons are simulated in ns2, the discrete event driven simulator that is used by most of the network researchers.

This paper is structured as follows. The basic AIMD congestion control rules and the existing TCP congestion control algorithms are discussed first. Then the next section discusses about the proposed generalized congestion control algorithms called Polynomial algorithms and the two models – MIMD-Poly and PIPD-poly.

This is followed by the analysis of the proposed algorithms and the model MIMD-Poly is proved to be TCP-friendly by deriving its throughput variations in terms of packet loss rate. Simulation of a wired TCP network with Dumbbell topology and with different sources employing the various congestion control mechanisms is performed and is presented. A multicast wired TCP network is simulated. The various multicast routing protocols such as centralized multicast and dense mode are simulated and the performance of the proposed algorithms in such environment is discussed in the following section. Implementation details, simulation and analysis of the proposed models for Mobile Ad hoc Networks are given next. This paper is finally concluded.

WINDOW BASED CONGESTION CONTROL FOR TCP NETWORKS

The state of art of the network congestion shows that it is a very difficult problem because there is no way to determine the network condition. The congestion occurs when there is a lot of traffic in the networks. Rapidly increasing bandwidths and great variety of software applications have created a recognized need for increased attention to TCP congestion control mechanisms (Kirov, 2005).

TCP is a connection-oriented protocol that offers reliable data transfer as well as flow and congestion control. (Allman & Paxson, 1999). TCP maintains a congestion window that controls the number of outstanding unacknowledged data packets in the network. Sending data consumes slots in the window of the sender and the sender can send packets only as long as free slots are available (Fall & Floyd, 1996).

On start-up, TCP performs slowstart, during which the rate roughly doubles each round-trip time to quickly gain its fair share of bandwidth (Wang & Crowcroft, 1991). In steady state, TCP uses the AIMD mechanism to detect additional bandwidth and to react to congestion. When there

is no indication of loss, TCP increases the congestion window by one slot per round-trip time. In case of packet loss, indicated by a timeout, the congestion window is reduced to one slot and TCP reenters the slowstart phase. Packet loss indicated by three duplicate ACKs results in a window reduction to half of its previous size.

The AIMD algorithm may be expressed as given in (Jin et.al., 2001; Bansal & Balakrishnan, 2001; Yang & Lam, 2000).

$$
\begin{aligned}
I: \quad & W_{t+R} \leftarrow W_t + \alpha; \alpha > 0 \\
D: \quad & W_{t+\delta t} \leftarrow (1 - \beta) W_t; 0 < \beta < 1
\end{aligned}
\tag{1}
$$

Where:

- $I \rightarrow$ Increase in window as a result of the receipt of one window of acknowledgement in a round-trip-time (RTT) and
- $D \rightarrow$ Decrease in window size on detection of congestion by the sender
- $W_t \rightarrow$ Window size at time t
- $R \rightarrow$ RTT of the flow and
- α and $\beta \rightarrow$ Increase and Decrease Rule constants.

There are many variations to these algorithms so as to gain more bandwidth by adjusting the window size (Kirov, 2005; Moraru et al, 2007). The ns2 simulator has implementations of many such variants (Simulator, 2000). The algorithm represented by equation (1) is implemented as TCP/Tahoe, simply called as TCP (Yang & Lam, 2000). The other variants implemented are TCP/Reno, TCP/NewReno, TCP/Vegas, and TCP/SACK etc. These algorithms vary in slowstart and congestion avoidance phases.

POLYNOMIAL CONGESTION CONTROL ALGORITHMS

This section discusses the properties of the proposed polynomial congestion control algorithms.

The authors noted that the window adjustment policy is only one component of the congestion control protocol derived from polynomial algorithms. Other mechanisms such as congestion detection (loss, ECN etc.), retransmissions (if required), estimation of Round-trip-time etc., remain the same as TCP (Floyd, 1995). The proposed algorithms mainly aim in increasing the window size faster and to gain the bandwidth quicker.

The authors generalized the AIMD rules in the following manner, in order to study and understand the notions of TCP—compatibility and the trade off between the increase and decrease rules.

The polynomial rules are given below:

$$I: \quad W_{t+R} \leftarrow W_t + (\alpha / W_t)^k + (\alpha / W_t)^{2k} + (\alpha / W_t)^{3k} + ...; \quad \alpha > 0$$
$$D: \quad W_{t+\delta t} \leftarrow W_t - (\beta W_t)^l - (\beta W_t)^{2l} - (\beta W_t)^{3l} - ...; \quad 0 < \beta < 1$$
$$(2)$$

These rules generalize the class of all congestion control algorithms based on window size adjustment. Now for the analysis of the algorithms the above rules are restricted into a Model as given below.

$$I: \quad W_{t+R} \leftarrow W_t + (\alpha / W_t)^k$$
$$D: \quad W_{t+\delta t} \leftarrow W_t - (\beta W_t)^l$$
$$(3)$$

The above rules are named as MIMD-Poly. For various values of k and l the above rules show the forms of various increase and decrease rules:

1. For k = 0, l = 1 the rules show AIMD.

$$I: \quad W_{t+R} \leftarrow W_t + 1$$
$$D: \quad W_{t+\delta t} \leftarrow W_t - \beta W_t$$
$$(4)$$

2. For k = -1, l = 1 the rules show Multiplicative Increase and Multiplicative Decrease (MIMD)

$$I: \quad W_{t+R} \leftarrow W_t + W_t / \alpha$$
$$D: \quad W_{t+\delta t} \leftarrow W_t - \beta W_t$$
$$(5)$$

3. For k = -1, l = 0 the rules show Multiplicative Increase and Additive Decrease (MIAD)

$$I: \quad W_{t+R} \leftarrow W_t + W_t / \alpha$$
$$D: \quad W_{t+\delta t} \leftarrow W_t - 1$$
$$(6)$$

4. For k = 0, l = 0 the rule show Additive Increase and Additive Decrease (AIAD)

$$I: \quad W_{t+R} \leftarrow W_t + 1$$
$$D: \quad W_{t+\delta t} \leftarrow W_t - 1$$
$$(7)$$

By including the higher order terms polynomial algorithms of different orders are obtained. The following rules are obtained by considering the first two terms in the general equation (2). The rules shown in equation (8).

$$I: \quad W_{t+R} \leftarrow W_t + (\alpha / W_t)^k + (\alpha / W_t)^{2k}; \quad \alpha > 0$$
$$D: \quad W_{t+\delta t} \leftarrow W_t - (\beta W_t)^l - (\beta W_t)^{2l}; \quad 0 < \beta < 1$$
$$(8)$$

The above rules are named as PIPD-Poly. Using the above second order polynomial rules and assuming various values of k and l the following general polynomial algorithms are obtained.

1. For k = 0, l = 0 we get:

$$I: \quad W_{t+R} \leftarrow W_t + 2$$
$$D: \quad W_{t+\delta t} \leftarrow W_t - 2$$
$$(9)$$

These rules show AIAD.

2. For k = 1, l = 1 we get:

$$I: \quad W_{t+R} \leftarrow W_t + (\alpha / W_t) + (\alpha / W_t)^2$$
$$D: \quad W_{t+\delta t} \leftarrow W_t - (\beta W_t) - (\beta W_t)^2 \quad (10)$$

These rules show PIPD.

3. For k = 0, l = 1 the rules show Additive Increase and Polynomial Decrease (AIPD) and

4. For k = 1, l = 0 the rules show Polynomial Increase and Additive Decrease (PIAD).

By choosing different values of α and β in equations (3) and (8), they became the members of the polynomial family. By including the higher order terms, polynomial increase and decrease algorithms of different orders are obtained that may be used for the window size adjustment for the congestion avoidance phase.

ANALYSIS OF THE ALGORITHMS: MIMD-POLY AND PIPD-POLY

The polynomial algorithms are implemented and represented by equations (3) and (8). They are represented as MIMD-Poly and PIPD-Poly in section 3. Both of these algorithms are implemented to study the variation of window size and the resulting throughput with respect to time. The algorithm begins in the slowstart state (Wang & Crowcroft, 1991). In this state, the congestion window size is doubled for every window of packets acknowledged. Upon the first congestion indication, the congestion window size is cut in half and the session enters into the polynomial congestion control state (Yang & Lam, 2000; Fall & Floyd, 1996; Kirov, 2005).

In this state the congestion window size is increased by $[(\alpha / W_t)^k + (\alpha / W_t)^{2k} + (\alpha / W_t)^{3k} + ...]$ for each new acknowledgement received, where W_t is the current congestion window size. The algorithm reduces the window size when congestion is detected. Congestion is detected by two events: (i) triple-duplicate ACK and (ii) time-out. If by triple-duplicate ACK, the algorithm reduces the window size by $[(\beta W_t)^l - (\beta W_t)^{2l} - (\beta W_t)^{3l} - ...]$. If the congestion indication is by time-out, the window size is set to 1.

Figure 1. Functional form of window vs. time curve

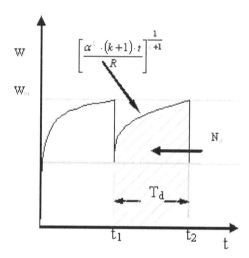

The window size and throughput of these algorithms are compared with the standard congestion control algorithms for TCP. (Jin et.al., 2001; Fall & Floyd, 1996; Moraru et.al., 2007). The authors have used the TCP variants available in ns2 such as TCP/Tahoe, TCP/Reno, TCP/NewReno and TCP/Vegas for comparison (Simulator, 2000).

TCP Friendliness of MIMD-Poly: A Proof

This section analyzes the throughput of the polynomial algorithm as a function of the loss-rate it experiences for which the MIMD poly algorithm is assumed. The analysis is similar to the analysis explained in (Jin et.al., 2001; Bansal & Balakrishnan, 2000). Using the Increase rule of MIMD-Poly algorithm and by linear interpolation of window size between Wt and W_{t+R} is given by,

$$\frac{dW}{dt} = \frac{\alpha^k}{W^k \cdot R} \tag{11}$$

$$\frac{W^{k+1}}{k+1} = \frac{\alpha^k \cdot t}{R} + C \tag{12}$$

where C is the constant of integration. The functional form of this curve is shown in Figure 1.

The two parameters which are of interest are T_d and N_d marked in the figure 1; where T_d is the time between two successive packet drops, and N_d is the number of packets received between two successive drops.

Let W_m be the maximum value of the window W_t at time t_2, at which congestion occurs. Then the expressions for T_d and N_d are evaluated as given below:

$$T_d = t_2 - t_1$$

$$T_d = \frac{R}{\alpha^k (k+1)} \left[W^{k+1} - \left(W_m - \beta^l W_m^l \right)^{k+1} \right]$$

$$T_d = \frac{R \cdot W_m^{k+1}}{\alpha^k \cdot (k+1)} \left[1 - \left(1 - \beta^l W^{l-1} \right)^{k+1} \right]$$

$$T_d = \frac{R \cdot W_m^{k+1}}{\alpha^k \cdot (k+1)} \left(\beta^l \cdot W_m^{l-1} \right)^{k+1}$$

$$T_d \approx \frac{\beta^l \cdot R}{\alpha^k \cdot (k+1)} W_m^{k+l} \qquad (13)$$

N_d is the shaded area under the curve in Figure 1.

$$N_d = \frac{(k+1)^{\frac{1}{k+1}}}{R} \int \left(\frac{\alpha^k \cdot t}{R} \right)^{\frac{1}{k+1}} dt \qquad (14)$$

Calculating the integral, we get

$$N_d = \frac{\beta^l}{\alpha^k} W_m^{k+l+1} \qquad (15)$$

The average throughput, λ of a flow is the number of packets sent between successive drops (N_d) divided by the duration between drops (T_d). The packet loss probability $p = 1/ N_d$. Writing λ and p in terms of W_m and by substituting the expressions for N_d and T_d yield:

$$\lambda \propto 1/p^{1/k+l+1} \qquad (16)$$

This implies that for polynomial Model MIMD poly to be TCP-compatible as per (Bansal et al., 2000), λ must vary as $1/ p^{0.5}$, and hence k+l

= 1. This analysis can be extended to find the throughput of the PIPD polynomial algorithm also. The authors restrict with the MIMD-Poly and in future they will be attempting to prove the TCP-compatibility of the throughput relation for the PIPD and other polynomial models.

Simulation of Packet Drops

The variations of window size with time for the MIMD-Poly and PIPD-Poly algorithms are studied by using the ns2 simulations. The network topology, consisting of a source node (n0) connected to a receiver node (n3) through two routers (n1 and n2) as shown in figure 2, is used for analyzing the performance of the algorithms during packet drops.

In figure 2 a TCP agent is attached to the source node and a TCP/Sink is attached to the receiver node. The links are assumed to be bidirectional with a bandwidth of 1Mbps. The link connecting the two routers is assumed with a buffer capacity of 20 and with Drop Tail buffer management algorithm. The data packets generated by an FTP Source are connected to the source node.

The TCP agents are implemented with the MIMD-Poly and PIPD-Poly increase and decrease rules. These rules are implemented into the TCP agent program *tcp.cc*. The two algorithms are selected by choosing the values for the TCP/Agent variable *windowOption_*. If *windowOption_* is 9, then MIMD-Poly is chosen and if it is 10, then PIPD-Poly is chosen. The selective packet drops is simulated and the effects of these drops on window size variations are recorded. The figures 3 and 4 show the window size vs. time plot for the simulated packet drops for MIMD-Poly and PIPD-Poly. The packets with sequence numbers 50,150 and 700 are dropped. In MIMD-Poly algorithm the packets are dropped at the time instances $T_1 = 0.78s$, $T_2 = 1.205s$ and $T_3 = 4.428s$. In PIPD-Poly algorithm the packets are dropped at the time instances $T_1 = 0.78s$, $T_2 = 1.205s$ and $T_3 = 3.577s$. The plots given in figures 3 and 4

Figure 2. Topology to simulate the packet drops

Figure 3. Window size variation of MIMD-Poly Algorithm for the simulated packet drops

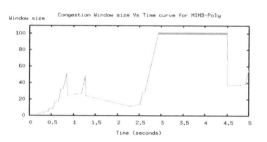

Figure 4. Window size variation of PIPD-Poly Algorithm for the simulated packet drops

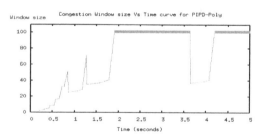

show that the two algorithms use the increase and decrease rules given by equations (3) and (8). The window size of the PIPD-Poly algorithm increases faster than the MIMD-Poly algorithm during the congestion avoidance phase.

PERFORMANCE EVALUATION OF POLY ALGORITHMS IN WIRED TCP NETWORKS

This section presents the results of the ns2 simulation of various polynomial algorithms in wired

TCP networks (Simulator, 2000). The authors start by investigating the connections running the TCP-compatible polynomial algorithms MIMD-Poly and PIPD-poly. The simulations use the topology shown in Figure 5.

It consists of 12 TCP connections sharing multiple bottleneck links, where all connections have an almost identical round-trip propagation delay equal to 20ms. Each polynomial flow uses a modified TCP with AIMD algorithm replaced by the polynomial family; other mechanisms like slow-start and time-out remain unchanged as already mentioned in section 4 of this paper. Each source always has data to send, modeled using the network simulators "FTP" application. On simulation the values of window size and throughput are observed and the figures and graphs display this information.

The results are obtained using the Drop Tail buffer management algorithm at the bottleneck gateway (Floyd & Jacobson, 1993; Kokje & Kakadia, 2007). Figure 6 shows the variation of window size over a simulation period of 500 sec for TCP, TCP/Reno, TCP/NewReno, TCP/Vegas, and MIMD-Poly and PIPD-Poly models. The results show that both congestion control algorithms are TCP-compatible and MIMD-Poly consumes more bandwidth than PIPD-Poly.

Figure 7 shows the throughput of the TCP, TCP/Reno, TCP/NewReno, TCP/Vegas, MIMD-Poly and PIPD-Poly. The throughput (λ) is modeled by,

$$\lambda = \frac{c \cdot s}{R \cdot \sqrt{p}} \qquad (17)$$

where s is the segment size, R *is* the round trip time, p is the packet loss rate and c is a constant value commonly approximated as $1.5\sqrt{2}/3$. The graphs show that the throughput of MIMD-Poly and PIPD-Poly are high compared with that of all the variants of TCP.

Figure 5. Dumbbell topology with multiple bottleneck links

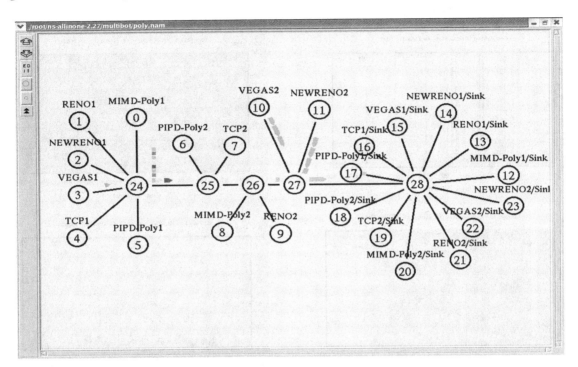

PERFORMANCE EVALUATION OF POLY ALGORITHMS IN WIRED TCP NETWORKS WITH MULTICAST ROUTING PROTOCOLS

Multicasting is very much essential to share the same information among a group of interconnected users. Distribution of real time audio and video to a group of hosts who have joined a distributed conference is an example of the application of multicasting (Seada et.al., 2002). This multicast traffic will be sharing the network bandwidth with other data traffic. Hence the protocols designed for data transfer should take care of such situations.

To examine the performance of the proposed algorithms MIMD-Poly and PIPD-Poly in interacting with the multicasting, a network with dumbbell topology as shown in Figure 8 is simulated. Two multicasting groups are formed: one with node n0 as the source and nodes n8, n9 and n10 as receiving members forming group0,

the other with node n1 as the source and n11 and n12 as receiving members forming group1. The receiving members can join or leave the group at any time. The simulation scenario for the members to join and leave is randomly chosen.

For the multicast groups the CBR traffic is attached to the source nodes. To study the interaction of the TCP traffic, agents of the TCP variants such as Tahoe, Reno, New Reno and Vegas along with the proposed Poly algorithms are attached to these sources and FTP data traffic is sent through these source nodes. These data traffic contend to share the bandwidth of the bottleneck link with the multicast traffic. The simulation results of the TCP sources such as window size and throughput are recorded.

Two multicast routing strategies are assumed for the simulations. One is the Centralized multicast mode (Ctrm) and the other is the Dense Mode (DM). In Dense mode, two variations such as PIM-DM and DVMRP are used. The main difference between these two variations is that DVMRP

Figure 6.Window size vs. Time of TCP, TCP/Reno, TCP/NewReno, TCP/Vegas, MIMD-Poly and (d) PIPD-Poly. (α =1.75 and β=0.1)

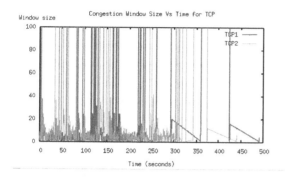
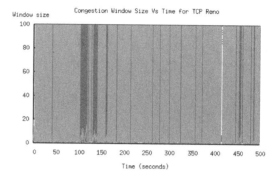

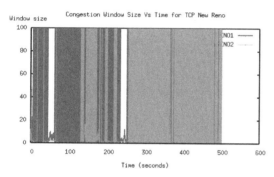
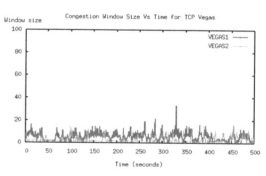

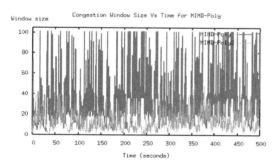
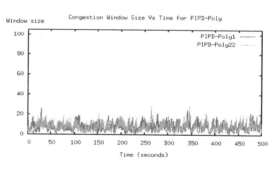

maintains parent-child relationships among nodes to reduce the number of links over which data packets are broadcast (Simulator, 2000).

The results of the simulations i.e. the window size vs. time graphs for all the TCP sources are plotted. The Figures 9 and 10 show the window size variations of TCP variants such as Tahoe, Reno, New Reno, Vegas, MIMD-Poly and PIPD-Poly with the two multicast routing strategies Ctrm and DM. The results show that the two proposed algorithms behave similar to other TCP variants with an improvement in total throughput.

PERFORMANCE EVALUATION OF POLY ALGORITHMS IN MOBILE AD HOC NETWORKS

A Mobile Ad hoc Network is a network in which a group of mobile computing devices communicate among themselves using wireless radios, without the aid of a fixed networking infrastructure (Allman & Paxson, 1999). They can be used anywhere that a fixed infrastructure does not exist, or is not desirable. Mobile ad hoc networks provide

Figure 7.Throughput vs. Time of TCP, TCP/Reno, TCP/NewReno, TCP/Vegas, MIMD-Poly and (d) PIPD-Poly. (α =1.75 and β=0.1)

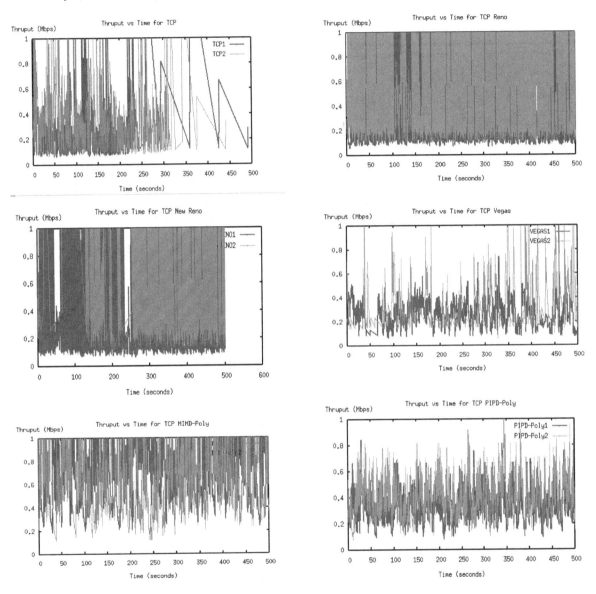

Figure 8. Dumbbell topology used for Multicast network

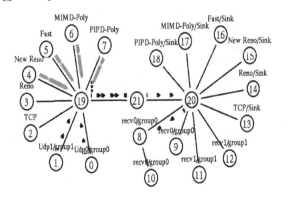

Figure 9.Window size vs. Time of TCP, TCP/Reno, TCP/NewReno, TCP/Vegas, MIMD-Poly and PIPD-Poly. (Multicast Centralized mode)

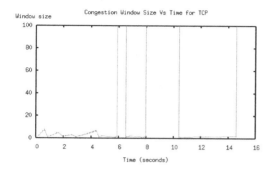
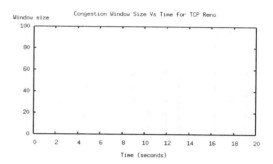
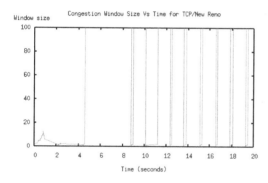
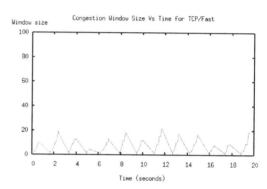
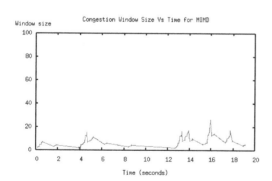
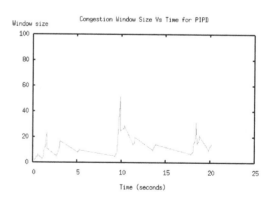

an extension to the Internet. Since TCP/IP is the standard network protocol on the Internet, its use over mobile ad hoc network is a certainty (Sundaresan et.al., 2003; Holland & Vaidya, 1999). The performance of the proposed window based Polynomial congestion control algorithms over the mobile ad hoc networks are analyzed and compare with the standard algorithms implemented for TCP, TCP/Reno, TCP/NewReno and TCP/Vegas (Fall & Floyd,1996; Moraru et al., 2007).

A topology containing 12 nodes, mobility scenario, which creates a random movement to the nodes, is simulated. Figure 14 shows two snapshots of the topology used at different simulation instants. It shows the mobility simulated with different sources delivering the TCP packets.

The simulations assumed the following routing algorithms used for Mobile ad hoc networks: Dynamic Source Routing (DSR), Dynamic Destination Sequenced Distance Vector (DSDV)

Figure 10. Window size vs. Time of TCP, TCP/Reno, TCP/NewReno, TCP/Vegas, MIMD-Poly and PIPD-Poly. (Multicast Dense mode)

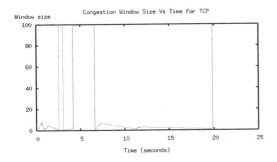

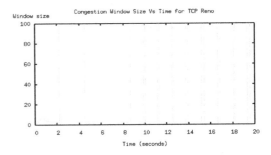

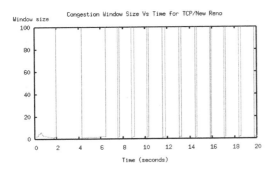

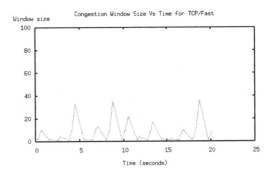

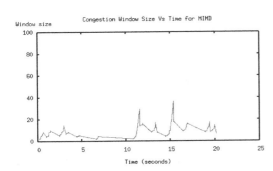

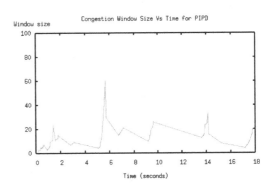

Routing, Ad-hoc On-demand Distance Vector (AODV) Routing (Sundaresan et al., 2003; Chen et al., 2003). The same topology and mobility scenario is assumed for each routing algorithms. The window based polynomial congestion control algorithms are simulated in each case. The performance of the two models MIMD-Poly and PIPD-Poly are recorded.

Along with the sources implemented with standard TCP, TCP/Reno, TCP/NewReno and TCP/Vegas. Figures 11, 12 and 13 display the window size adjustment using these algorithms. The throughput is evaluated based on the equation (17). The results show that the PIPD-Poly and MIMD-Poly algorithms improved the total throughput regardless of the routing method used. Figure 14 shows the total throughput of TCP, TCP/Reno, TCP/New Reno, MIMD and PIPD congestion control algorithms in wired networks with unicast and multicast traffic in mobile ad-hoc networks.

Figure 11.Window size vs. Time of TCP, TCP/Reno, TCP/NewReno, TCP/Vegas, MIMD-Poly and PIPD-Poly (Mobile Ad Hoc AODV)

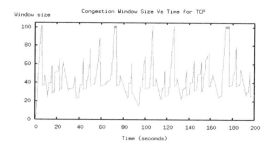
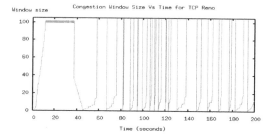

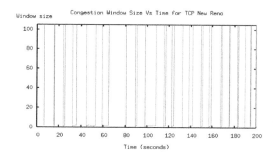
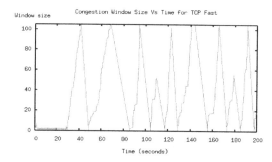

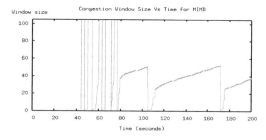
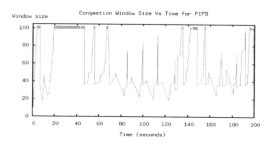

The results show better long-term throughput for the proposed algorithm in all the cases.

CONCLUSION

This paper presents and evaluates a family of nonlinear congestion control algorithms, called polynomial algorithms such as MIMD-Poly and PIPD-Poly. These polynomial algorithms generalize the familiar class of linear algorithms. The authors showed that for one of the restricted model of the polynomial family, MIMD-Poly, the throughput $\lambda \infty 1/p^{1/k+l+1}$, where p is the packet loss rate it encounters. This shows that the model is TCP compatible.

The simulation results showed good performance and interactions between polynomial algorithms (MIMD-Poly and PIPD-Poly) and TCP using standard algorithms in wired and mobile ad hoc networks. The algorithms MIMD-Poly and PIPD-Poly obtain higher long-term throughput than the standard algorithms for TCP, TCP/Reno, TCP/NewReno and TCP/Vegas. The figures 6, 9,

Figure 12. Window size vs. Time of TCP, TCP/Reno, TCP/NewReno, TCP/Vegas, MIMD-Poly and PIPD-Poly (Mobile Ad Hoc DSDV)

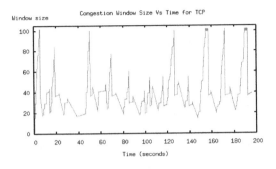
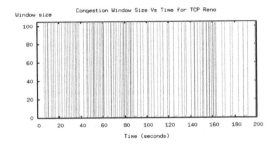

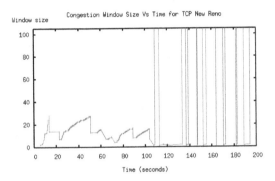
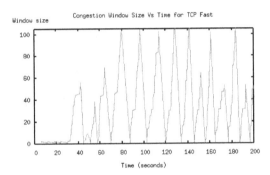

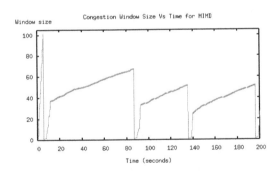
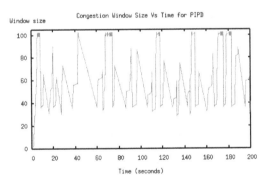

10,11, 12 and 13 show the variation of congestion window with respect to time for the TCP, TCP/Reno, TCP/NewReno, TCP/Vegas, TCP/MIMD and TCP/PIPD algorithms in the case of wired network (with unicast and multicast) topology shown in figure 5 and 7 and in the case of Mobile Ad hoc networks. Figure 15 displays the total throughput for the various TCP variants in wired and mobile ad hoc networks. The topology of the mobile ad hoc network is shown in Figure 14.

The authors believe that the results presented in this paper lead to an understanding of the issues involved in the increase and decrease phases of a congestion control algorithms.

Figure 13.Window size vs. Time of TCP, TCP/Reno, TCP/NewReno, TCP/Vegas, MIMD-Poly and PIPD-Poly (Mobile Ad Hoc DSR)

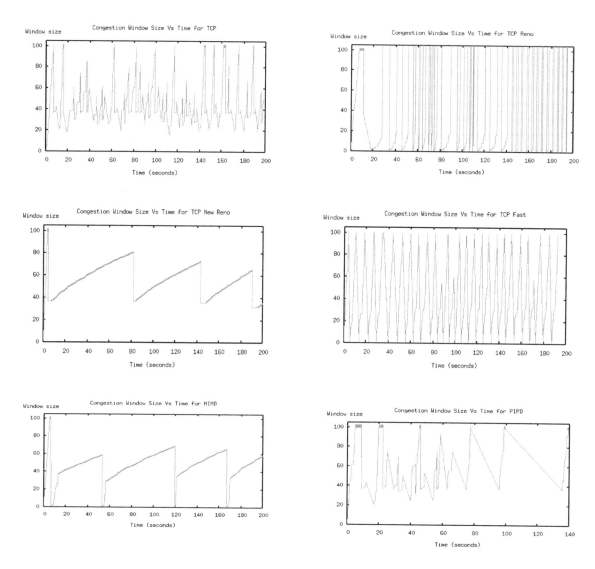

Figure 14. Snapshots of topology at two different instants of time

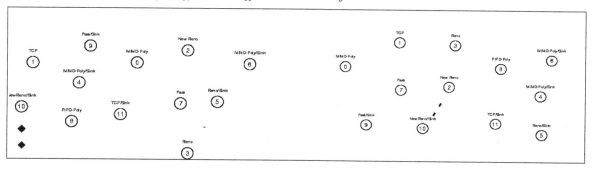

Figure 15. Total throughput of TCP Variants

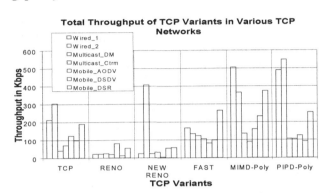

REFERENCES

Allman, M., & Paxson, V. (1999, April). TCP congestion control. *Internet Engineering Task Force, RFC 2581.*

Bansal, D., & Balakrishnan, H. (2000, May). TCP-friendly congestion control for real-time streaming applications. *Technical Report MIT-LCS-TR-806, MIT Laboratory for Computer Science.*

Bansal, D., & Balakrishnan, H. (2001, April). Binomial congestion control algorithms. *Proceedings of IEEE INFOCOM.*

Chen, K., Xue, Y., & Nahstedt, K. (2003, May). On setting TCP's congestion window limit in mobile ad hoc networks. *Proceedings of the IEEE International Conference on Communication, Anchorage, Alaska.*

Comer, D. E. (1991). *Internetworking with TCP/IP* (Volume I). Englewood Cliffs, New Jersey: Prentice Hall

Fall, K., & Floyd, S. (1996, July). Simulation-based comparisons of Tahoe, Reno, and SACK TCP. *Computer Communications Review.*

Floyd, S. (1995, October). TCP and explicit congestion notification. *ACM Computer Communication Review, 24,* 8-23.

Floyd S., & Fall, K. (1999, August). Promoting the use of end-to-end congestion control in the Internet. *IEEE/ACM Transactions on Networking, 7*(4), 458–472.

Floyd, S., & Jacobson, V. (1993, August). Random early detection gateways for congestion avoidance. *IEEE/ACM Transactions on Networking, 1*(4).

Holland, G., & Vaidya, N. H. (1999, August). Analysis of TCP performance over mobile ad hoc networks. *Proceedings of the ACM MOBICOM, Seattle, WA, USA.*

Jacobson, V. (1988, August). Congestion avoidance and control. *ACM Computer Communication Review, 18,* 314-329.

Jin, S., Guo, L., Matta, I., & Bestavros, A. (2001, July). A spectrum of TCP-friendly window-based congestion control algorithms. *Technical Report BU-CS-2001-015, Computer Science Department, Boston University.* Available at: http://www.cs.bu.edu/techreports/2001-015-spectrum-tcp-friendly.ps.Z.

Kirov, G. (2005). A simulation analysis of the TCP control algorithms. *Proceedings of the International Conference on Computer Systems and Technologies.*

Kokje, T., & Kakadia, V. (2007). Analysis of congestion control strategies for TCP variants using droptail and RED queuing disciplines. *Unpublished Technical Report, Department of Computer Science University of Southern California, Los Angeles.*

Moraru, B., Copaciu, F., Gabriel Lazar, G., & Dobrota V. (2007). Practical analysis of TCP implementations: Tahoe, Reno, NewReno. *Unpublished report, Technical University of Cluj-Napoca.*

Seada, K., Gupta, S., & Helmy, A. (2002, July). Systematic evaluation of multicast congestion control mechanisms. *Proceedings of the SPECTS.*

Seada, K., & Helmy, A. (2002, March). Fairness evaluation experiments for multicast congestion control protocols. *Technical Report 02-757, University of Southern California, CS Department.*

Simulator. (2000). ns-2 Network Simulator. Available at: http://www.isi.edu/nsnam/ns/.

Stevens, W. R. (1994, November). TCP/IP illustrated (Volume 1). Reading, MA: Addison-Wesley.

Sundaresan, K., Anantharaman, V., Hsieh, H-Y., & Sivakumar, R. (2003, January). ATP: A reliable transport protocol for ad hoc networks. *Proceedings of the ACM Mobihoc.*

Wang, Z., & Crowcroft, J. (1991, January). A new congestion control scheme: Slow start and search (Tri-S). *ACM Computer Communication Review, 21,* 32-43.

Widmer, J., Denda, R., & Mauve, M. (2001, May). A survey on TCP-friendly congestion control. *IEEE Network.*

Yang, R. Y., & Lam, S. S. (2000, November). General AIMD congestion control. *Proceedings of the ICNP.*

Chapter VII
A Systematic Approach to the Analysis and Configuration of Audio/Video-on-Demand Services

Xabiel G. Pañeda
University of Oviedo, Spain

David Melendi
University of Oviedo, Spain

Roberto García
University of Oviedo, Spain

Manuel Vilas
University of Oviedo, Spain

Victor García
University of Oviedo, Spain

ABSTRACT

This chapter presents a method for performance analysis and configuration of audio/video-on-demand services. These kind of services makes use of an important number of resources, requires a constant quality of service and contents, and usually have important production costs. To maintain a good quality of service and at the same time, to make a profit for the content provider, services must have the optimum configuration. With this aim, the configuration process must be based on an accurate service behavioural analysis which evaluates the quality and the quantity of resources, contents and subscribers. This analysis can be performed using monitored information extracted from servers, proxies and network monitors, and predictions of a near future behaviour using laboratory experiments. To systematize both analysis and configuration, a method must be developed in order to help service managers attain a good performance and at the same time, make a profit for their companies. All this systematic method goals are based on the principle that "a satisfied client provides more profit". Other elements such as data sources, input data, and initial configuration should also be included. Moreover, the methodology is prepared to be extensible, and adaptable to new configuration possibilities, data, analyses, or goals.

INTRODUCTION

The boom of the World Wide Web combined with the bandwidth increase in subscribers' accesses has given rise to the appearance of a new complementary service: the Internet video. There are two types of video services on the Internet: live-video and video-on-demand. Live video services deliver information just in time for the user who is connected. Information could have been previously recorded and stored, or can be captured and broadcasted live; in either case, the information can only be seen once. Only one type of interaction is possible, the pause, and its behaviour is similar to a TV broadcast. On the other hand, the principles of video-on-demand are totally different. Users request the information at any time and the server delivers it exclusively. This system allows users to interact with information: Pauses, backward and forward jumps are allowed. Its behaviour is similar to that of a videotape.

Most video services on the Internet are based on streaming technology and, in spite of the important number of advantages, this technology presents some problems linked to the usage of resources and production costs. Video delivering consumes an important bandwidth in the network and requires a constant quality of service. To maintain this quality under control and select the most interesting contents, the use of a good analysis methodology is fundamental. The analysis systems must provide the necessary information to ensure the correct configuration of the streaming services. Two different aspects appear when a service must be configured. The first is related to the service provider, who must improve the service by working on contents. The second is linked to the network operator, who has to manage service architecture, routing, bandwidth, etc.

In this paper, a systematic approach to the analysis and configuration of audio and video-on-demand services is presented. The aim is to

provide a useful tool to help both the network operator and the content provider in their configuration tasks. The designed method specifies the process for the different application phases and additional elements such as data sources, inputs, goals and extensibility process definitions. Moreover, aspects such as the use of models and emulators to predict near future performances are considered.

The rest of the paper is organized as follows: In section 2 other related work will be analysed. The developed method will be described from sections 3 to 15. The case study will be presented in section 16 and, finally, conclusions will be presented in section 17.

RELATED WORK

In spite of the complexity and relative immaturity of streaming technology, a wide range of deployments of audio and video services has been developed in recent years.

A lot of organizations, from digital newspapers to public companies, are interested in these types of services in order to obtain a new way of attracting the attention of a wider audience. Nevertheless, the special characteristics of streaming services, such as the delivery of continuous information, the high consumption of resources and the need for stable conditions during the delivery of contents make them very sensitive to channel errors and delays. For these reasons several works have addressed the detailed analysis of streaming traffic over different technologies (Louginov & Radha, 2002), (Cranley & Davis, 2005), (Guo, Tan, Chen, Xia, Spatscheck, Zhang, 2006) and (Chung & Claypool, 2006), presenting interesting results from the point of view of network operators and the management of streaming flows.

It is well known that the success of a video on-demand service, and therefore the consumption of resources in each service device, depends on user behaviour; the higher the number of accesses the greater the profit, but also the probability of having performance problems. Unfortunately, human behaviour depends on several parameters that affect the perception of the session quality; some of them subjective (Pereira, 2005) and some others objective (Vicari & Kohler, 2006). For this reason, one of the most important tasks in the analysis of a streaming service is the characterization of user accesses. User behaviour is deeply influenced by the type of offered contents (Costa, Cunha, Borges, Ramos, Rocha, Almeida & Ribeiro-Neto, 2005). This influence can be easily observed by comparing the results shown in (Almeida, Krueger, Pager and Vernon, 2001), that analyzes the workload of an educational server, and (Chesire, Wolman, Voelker and Lavy, 2001), that analyzes traffic targeted on different servers on the Internet. Also, user behaviour patterns can be influenced by the availability of the contents. (Veloso, Almeida, Meira, Bestavros and Jin, 2002) perform an analysis of user behaviour on a live streaming service, studying the main causes of the difference between stored media and live media user accesses. At the same time, the popularity of the contents is not only influenced by the subject but also by the life cycle of the content (Cherskasova & Gupta, 2004). Therefore, the behaviour of the users has implications on the design of the architecture of a streaming service (Yu, Zheng, Zhao & Zheng, 2006). To evaluate the performance of the service in future situations or when new architectures are being designed, workload generators (Jin & Bestavros, 2001) have been developed.

Streaming services are difficult to manage and configure. Hundreds of different parameters can influence the evolution of the service; from the saturation of the network to the subject of the contents. One important aspect where some studies have appeared is the metric design for video services (Arias, Suárez, García, Pañeda, & García, 2002), (Dalal & Perry, 2003), (Ivanovici

& Beuran, 2006), (Casale, Cremonesi, Serazzi & Zanero, 2006), (Brotherton, Huynh-Thu, Hands & Brunnström, 2006) and (Keynote, 2006). They have transformed the analyses, which used the number of visits and the loss of packets as the only metrics. However, these metrics are difficult to use in real services because they are based on data which is not provided by server logs. Some of the presented metrics require feedback from the clients and in other cases require the synthetic generation of requests targeted on the multimedia servers.

Some companies have developed tools to analyze and manage streaming services (Keynote, 2006), (AudioWeb, 2006). Although some interesting metrics are presented, their way of analyzing streaming services does not consider the important relationships between content providers, service providers and network operators. To achieve an optimal service configuration several organizations and different sources of information (Van der Raadt & Gardin, 2005) and (Menascé & Almeida, 2000) must be coordinated. One of the most important relationships established between these entities is the *SLA* (Service Level Agreement). For this reason, this aspect has also been studied previously (Chieng, Marshall, Ho & Parr, 2001) and (Cherskasova, Tang & Singhal, 2004).

In spite of the interesting results shown in these papers, there has not been a deep research oriented to design techniques which helps managers improve their services. Most of the services are configured based on service administrators' experience, however not all of them have enough experience. This paper intends to compensate the lack of systematic methods for the analysis and configuration of real audio/video-on-demand services. The complete process is covered and several specific metrics have been designed to maintain the quality of service and select the most appropriate contents to be offered.

GENERAL DESCRIPTION

To carry out this task the method specifies: participant entities, input data, goals, analysis processes based on monitoring information and predictions, analysis metrics and configuration tasks, including the initial configuration. This method is oriented to audio/video on demand services with different types of information which is updated periodically. The main targets are audio/video services of information media, such as TV, newspapers, magazines, etc, and network operators, such as cable network operators or traditional communication operators

PARTICIPANT ENTITIES

The method defines a set of participant entities which provide input data and receive the results generated by the application process. These entities are the following: main network operator, external network operator, service administrator, user, user of the main operator, external user, content provider, network monitor and service device.

INPUT DATA AND SERVICE CLASSIFICATION

The source data needed to feed an accurate analysis must be obtained from several entities. For example, the content provider generates information about contents such as title, theme, etc; on the other hand, service devices provide access information, such as delivered bytes, access times, lost packets, etc. However, in most cases all the data is not available. The method classifies services into six groups, based on the entities that provide source data. Table 1 shows the proposed service classification. Data provided by source entities can be quite abundant. However, the minimum necessary information is presented in Table 2.

Table 1. Service classification

Accesses	Contents	Users	Networks		Networks
	Accesses	Contents	Devices		Devices
		Accesses			Users
			Accesses	Users	Contents
				Accesses	Accesses
Basic	Content Oriented	Service Oriented	Resource Oriented	User Oriented	Complete

Table 2. Minimum information

Accesses	Timestamp, time delivered, bytes delivered, destination, origin, packet loss, buffer reloads, users' device (PC, PDA, etc).
Content	Publication date, theme.
Users	Connection type.
Service devices	Utilization of different elements (CPU, memory, hard disk, licenses, etc).
Network	Exploitation and features in its different sections.

METHOD LIFE CYCLE

The life cycle, which is shown in Figure 1, passes through several stages when the method is applied to a service. Initially, it begins with the service deployment. In this stage, the service which is going to be analyzed and configured, starts to run, servers are installed, contents stored and the initial configuration is defined. Once the service is running, it must be classified based on the data available to perform the analysis. Once the service is classified, the initial performance stage begins. In this step the monitoring and services analysis provide the first information about service performance. However, the number of users and contents is not sufficient to obtain accurate results. When the service evolution allows enough analysis information to be gathered, the life cycle can jump to the stable performance stage. The last step in the life cycle is the Service Death where the service ends. During the initial performance and stable performance stages the service can be reclassified if new information can be obtained for the analysis process.

Figure 1. Method life cycle

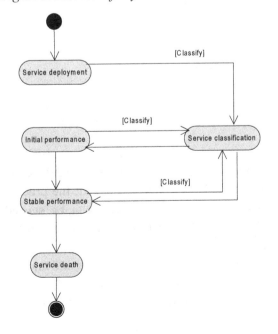

APPLICATION PROCESSES

The method has two types of application processes, one called iterative synchronous process, which is oriented to be used by human users, and another called reactive asynchronous process, which is oriented to automatic application by using some type of expert system. Differences between them are focused on the coordination between the phases of the process. While the former is synchronized, the latter is unsynchronized, thanks to the use of several intermediate stores.

Iterative Synchronous Process

This application process, which is shown in Figure 2, is divided into three main synchronized tasks. The first is the goals and SLA (*Service Level Agreement*) definition task where the targets must be established. The second is the analysis task where the system performance is evaluated in order to extract the best configuration parameters. The third is the configuration task where behavioural parameters can be modified to improve the quality of service.

The iterative application process begins with the goals definition task. At first, both network operator and content provider must define the values of performance which need to be reached. These goals can be revised in the following process iteration if necessary. However, once the process has started, the modification of goals will be independent for content provider and network operator, due to the variability of their expectations. The evolution of the process may require modifications both on the part of the network operator and/or the content provider.

The next task is that of analysis, which is divided into five phases. The first requires an important amount of basic analysis. This phase is subdivided into four different parts: user analysis, quality analysis, content analysis, and resource analysis. Each analysis will be composed of several tests which extract information about

Figure 2. Iterative synchronous process

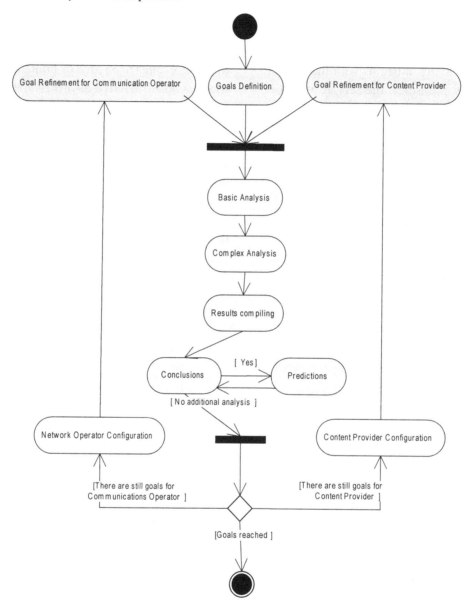

different behavioural characteristics. The results will be combined in the next phase to perform complex analyses, which are composed of multi-dimensional analyses and data mining processes. Their results will be compiled to obtain summarized information and to reach conclusions about service behaviour. To complete the conclusions, further analyses based on predictions will be developed, using models and laboratory experi- ments to analyze alternative situations different to the real ones. When the conclusions indicate that the goals have been achieved, the process concludes and a new process can be started with new goals. If there are still goals pending, the next task is configuration. Two independent parts, one for the network operator and another for the content provider, form the configuration task. The reason for this division is because the former must configure resources while the latter needs to configure contents. The network operator part includes three phases: network resources configuration, computer resources configuration and architecture service definition. On the other hand, the content provider part includes content creation, content modification and environment configuration. Once the configuration tasks are finished the original goals can be modified, if they are considered too optimistic, to adapt them to more realistic values. This process is devised to be applied over long periods (weeks or months) due to the complexity of the tasks which must be performed in it. This process is called synchronized since all the phases start when the previous ones have finished.

Reactive Asynchronous Process

The other application process, shown in Figure 3, is the reactive asynchronous process. This is oriented to an automatic application using an expert system. The process uses several intermediate stores to grant independence to all the phases. The final effect is a set of unsynchronized phases which are activated by different types of events.

Some of the tasks to be carried out when an event occurs are very complex; in these cases, a trigger is used to activate them in specific periods. That is the case of complex analysis, result compiling and conclusion obtaining phases. All of them are activated by a control process which coordinates their execution.

Figure 3. Reactive asynchronous process

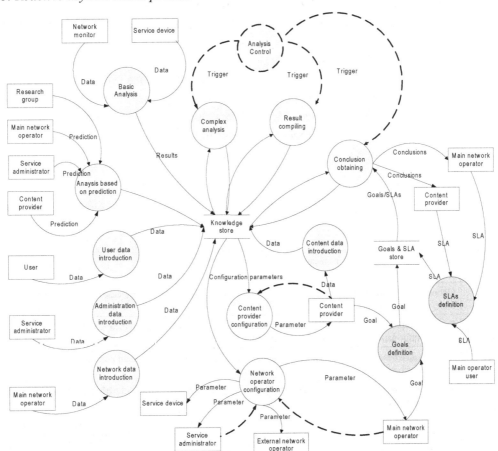

GOALS AND SLA DEFINITIONS

Goals Definition

One of the most important tasks in the configuration process is goals definition. The content provider often tries to make a profit through the service. On the other hand, the communication operator wants to obtain income from the content provider, and the lowest resource consumption possible. In all cases, the success of the service will depend on the parameters presented in Table 3.

Some of these goals are not different from those of the web services. However, the difference in the type of information, discrete in Web, and continuous in video, makes other goals necessary to evaluate the service correctly. This is the case of reproduction length and quality. A service, whose users watch all the video, cannot be considered equal to another where users hardly visualize just a few seconds, even though the latter has more visits. In the first case, users show a greater interest, and their probability of returning to the service is high. Moreover, the complexity of the service architecture is higher in streaming services due to the important consumption of resources.

At the beginning of the method process, values for some of these parameters need to be

established. When the values are reached, a new process will be started with new goals.

SLAs Definition

A Service Level Agreement includes an important number of different elements which establish the relation between service provider (and network operator) and subscribers. Some of these elements are related to the quality of service evaluation. These elements can be analyzed using the metrics and evaluated using the tests included in this work. In this phase the target values for these metrics are established and their fulfilment will be checked in the conclusion obtaining task.

ANALYSIS METRICS

Historically this type of services has been analyzed using metrics derived from web services. However, web services provide discrete information (a page, a file, etc) while audio/video services provide continuous information. Although these metrics can be useful, sometimes they can cause misunderstanding in the analysis conclusions. For example, a typical metric in web services is the number of visits (reproductions for audio/video

Table 3. Goals

Number of reproductions	Obtaining many reproductions means a greater interest on the part of the users.
Number of different users	Obtaining a large number of users expands the popularity of the service, and increases the probability of receiving more visits in the future.
Duration of reproductions	Providing reproductions with 100% or more (backward jumps) of video length means that users are satisfied with both the information provided and the quality of the reproductions.
User's loyalty and value	Building up a base of loyal users is very important because they ensure a constant number of reproductions. Moreover, the success of the newly generated information is higher.
Quality of reproductions	Achieving reproductions without interruptions, with only the initial buffer reload, with a clear sound, etc, allows users to appreciate the contents for their quality.
Resources consumption	The cost of resources (network, computers, software) used in this kind of services is very high. Therefore, minimizing the resources consumption is one of the main goals for the network operator. The quality must be maintained at an acceptable cost.

services). In audio/video services this metric must be used consciously, because a reproduction with 0 seconds transmitted can be considered as valid as a reproduction where 100% of the audio/video has been delivered. Obviously, they are very different. In the first case the reproduction is a failure, while in the second it is an important success. This metric can show the initial interest of the users but can never be used to evaluate service success.

This method defines a great variety of metrics specifically designed or adapted for audio/video services. The metrics have been classified into four groups: content, quality of service, user and resource metrics. In this section some of the most important will be presented.

Content Analysis Metrics

Interest: In order to evaluate the interest of users, which is generated by the contents provided, the number of different users' requests is counted. When users demand videos, they show their interest for the information offered. However, once the reproduction has started, the user can lose interest due to many reasons.

Success: To analyze the success of the service, the delivered time of contents is measured. This metric will reflect how much time users have been reproducing the audio/videos of the service.

Performance: The quantity of audio/video produced in a period can greatly affect the success of a service. For that reason a specific metric has been designed which evaluates service performance depending on the time of audio/video produced. Its formula is the following:

$$performance = \frac{success}{time\ produced}$$

Impact: This metric tries to analyze how the users have received the delivered information. Despite the fact that this metric evaluates

success as well as the previous ones, it is more accurate because video length is compared with the delivered time (% reproduced). Its formula is the following:

impact = %reproduced users

The metric of impact tries to establish the success of the audio/video, by using the percentage of visualized video and the number of different users who have reproduced it. This metric provides an index to evaluate the evolution of the service, which is far more reliable than the number of accesses. It is also important to know if users are satisfied or not with the reproduced audio/video

Quality of Service Analysis Metrics

Packet Loss Rate: This metric compares the number of lost packets with the total number of sent packets. Its formula is the following:

$$packet - lost\ rate = \frac{lost\ packets}{sent\ packet}$$

Reload Rate: One of the most important elements when an audio/video is served is the quality perceived by the user. Many of the problems produced during audio/video distribution can be corrected thanks to the client reproduction buffer (e.g. unordered or delayed packets). However, when the packets loaded in the buffer cannot compensate these mistakes, the reproduction must be stopped to reload the buffer. That is the moment when the user detects the problem. To evaluate the quality of service perceived by the users, a metric has been designed to compare the time needed to reload the buffer with the time of reproduced audio/video. The formula is the following:

$$reload\ rate = \frac{reload\ time}{reproduced\ time}$$

Not all buffer reloads have to be counted to calculate the metric. All the reloads that occur just after a play interaction must be considered as acceptable (initial loads) and must not be included in the reload time. Figure 4 shows these two types of buffer reloads.

Reloads per reproduction: Sometimes, a more simplified metric can be used to evaluate the cuts in the reproduction. A very simple metric can be to count the number of buffer reloads (without acceptable reloads).

Startup time: Latency is a classic metric for performance analysis of Internet services. Based on this metric, the startup time concept has been defined as the period between the first interaction and the beginning of the reproduction. Figure 5 shows the messages interchanged by server and client during that period.

User Analysis Metrics

User Value 1: Calculating user value is a relatively difficult task. Experts in data mining do not agree on the method of calculation. Our method proposes two possibilities, depending on whether the time of reproduced audio/video is considered more important than the number of reproduced audio/videos or vice versa. In the former case, the user value is evaluated through the time of delivered video.

User Value2: In the latter case, the number of reproductions is considered more important than the time of reproduced contents. Then the user value is calculated by multiplying the number of reproductions by the reproduced percentage.

Figure 5. Startup time

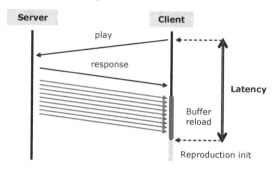

Resource Analysis Metrics

Throughput: Throughput is a classic metric in computer performance analysis. To adapt it to this type of services, it will be considered as the number of bytes per time unit.

Bandwidth Consumed: The bandwidth consumption is a classic metric in Internet service analysis. In this type of services, this element is of great importance due to the bandwidth required to transmit this type of information.

Simultaneous Streams: This metric evaluates the number of active reproductions in a given period. A reproduction can be in two states, active or paused. When it is active, a data stream between client and server (or proxy) is established. When a reproduction is paused, no bandwidth is being consumed. It is quite important to determine the consumption of resources in the network in order to analyze the number of requests active in a given moment.

Figure 4. Buffer reload types

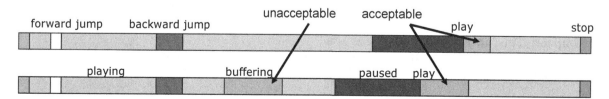

ANALYSIS BASED ON MONITORING INFORMATION

From the point of view of the source information, there are two types of analyses. One based on monitoring information extracted from the real service, and another with information extracted from lab experiments. The first is composed of several tests classified depending on the number of input variables and their complexity. According to this, the methodology defines three groups of tests: basic, multidimensional and data mining.

Basic Analysis

The basic analysis is divided into four different groups. Each task is carried out to analyze one element of the whole system. So there are four tasks: content, quality, users and resource analysis. Each of them is composed of several tests which extract information about different behavioural features. Some of them are listed below:

- **Content Analysis:**
  - **Interest test:** This test analyzes the interest of users before the beginning of their video reproductions. To carry out this analysis, the interest metric previously presented is used.
  - **Success test:** Using the success metric presented in the previous section this test evaluates the success of an audio/video or a set of audio/videos.
  - **Impact test:** One of the most important elements when a service is analyzed is the impact which is produced on the public. To check this parameter, the metric presented in the previous section is used.
  - **Reproduced percentage test:** This test analyzes the percentage of audio/video reproduced. In spite of its simplicity, this test can provide interesting knowledge about the profitability of

the effort undertaken in the production of contents.

  - **Performance test:** By using the metric presented in the previous section this test evaluates the performance of an audio/video or a set of audio/videos.
  - **Length suitability test:** This test aims to detect if the selected length for the audio/videos is suitable or not. It is difficult to check if an audio/video is too short. However, this test enables us to know if an audio/video is too long. Thanks to the use of a reproduction length histogram, it is possible to know if users watch the audio/video until the end or not. Figure 6 shows the reproduction length histogram of a real service. The histogram is a combination of two distributions, one for users who are not very interested and another for those who are very interested. If the reproductions with problems are not considered in the histogram, the length can be checked using the weight of both distributions. If the first distribution is heavier then the audio/video is too long. Otherwise the length is correct.
  - **Fast leaving test:** This test calculates the percentage of reproductions with less than 10 seconds of visualized video. Below this limit, the user has no interest in the contents, due to a lack of quality or disappointing information.
  - **Leaving before the end test:** This test analyzes the evolution of reproductions which have finished before the end of the audio/video. The aim is to know whether users leave videos due to disappointment or for other reasons.
  - **Inter-arrival time test:** This test evaluates the cacheability of audio/videos. When an audio/video receives an important number of requests in a short

Figure 6. Length suitability

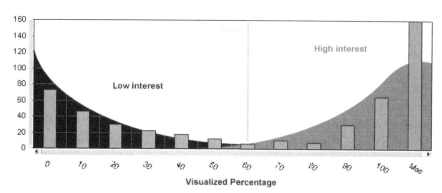

period of time, it can be interesting to load it in a cache. These caches can belong to the server or a proxy in an intermediate point of the network.

○ **Popularity test:** This test compares access distribution with the generalized Zipf-like distribution for different values of θ. The expression of a Zipf-like distribution is the following (where 0≤θ≤1 and n is the number of audio/videos):

$$P(i) = \frac{C}{i^\theta}, \quad C = \frac{1}{\sum_{i=1}^{n} \frac{1}{i^\theta}},$$

- **Quality Analysis:**
  ○ **Mistaken reproduction test:** This test calculates the number and percentage of reproductions with 0 seconds of reproduced audio/video. It is used to know how many reproductions have been erroneous because the user does not have a suitable program to listen to or watch the audio/video.
  ○ **Real quality reproduction tests:** These tests calculate the number and the percentage of reproductions with lost and delayed packets. The results can be presented as a histogram or evolution time series. Reproductions with these problems reflect transmission

difficulties. Despite the fact that these incidences may not be appreciated by the users, they must be considered to avoid future problems.

○ **Perceived reproduction quality tests:** This test analyzes the quality of reproductions from the user's point of view. It uses the two metrics which have been defined in the previous section for this purpose.

○ **Latency test:** This test analyzes the evolution of the latency metric. In spite of this being an important quality parameter in interactive services, the perceived reproduction quality test is much more important. Anyway its values should be low enough to prevent users from leaving the service due to excessive waiting.

- **User Analysis:**
  ○ **Number of users evolution test:** This test counts the number of different users who have requested a video in a given period.
  ○ **User access profile test:** One important element to predict future demand and book the necessary resources to support it is determined when users access the service. This test analyzes when users prefer to access the service.

o **Users value test:** By using one of the metrics presented in the previous section, this test evaluates the value of users. It helps managers decide the importance of a user or a group of users.

o **User loyalty test:** This test checks the number of users and the number of reproductions they have made. To analyze loyalty, users are classified according to their number of reproductions. The obtained graph generates a skew which shows loyalty. If the skew is concave the majority of users are not loyal. If convex, the service has loyal users.

o **User origin test:** This test aims to detect the origin (Internet connection provider) of users. This parameter helps to know the quality of their access line, when this information cannot be obtained directly from clients. Furthermore, user origin is important to decide the location of proxies (caches and load balancers).

o **User connection quality test:** This test classifies users by their access lines. It is essential to know user's bandwidth during the production of the videos. These must be coded with lower bandwidth consumption than that available to the users of the service.

o **Device test:** This test classifies users according to their access devices (This information can be obtained from the operating system version). The use of multimedia services from mobile devices has increased considerably and it is quite important to know how many users access from a mobile device, such as a PDA or mobile telephone (low capacity, few resources), or from a PC (high capacity).

• **Resource Analysis:**

o **Bandwidth usage:** One of the most important parameters to maintain the quality of service is the bandwidth. This test analyzes the bandwidth consumed in different points of the network which connects users with servers. Moreover, the bandwidth usage in the servers output and in the proxies input/output is also analyzed. It is standard practice that network operators fix a limit in the bandwidth that a server (or proxy) can consume in its network connection. This limit aims to prevent a peak in the consumption that may affect other services which are plugged into the same connection. This test analyzes the consumed bandwidth so that more can be requested if necessary.

Figure 7. Bandwidth usage in a network head-end

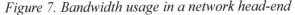

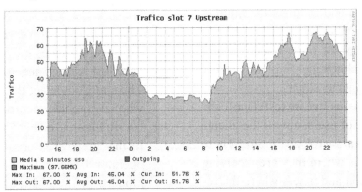

- ○ **Total bandwidth usage:** This test analyzes the evolution of the bandwidth usage in different points of the communication networks where the traffic generated by the service passes. The information provided is useful to detect networking bottle-necks which generate low quality in the service. Figure 7 shows a chart extracted from the head-end in a real HFC network.

- ○ **Memory, CPU and disk usage test:** Memory and CPU tests are important in service device performance analysis. To avoid situations where servers and proxies, which support the services, have performance problems, the memory and CPU utilization must be under control. Moreover, the secondary memory must be evaluated. Due to the size of video files, the storage capacity is an important parameter in this type of services.

- ○ **Throughput test:** This test analyzes the throughput of every device used in the service architecture. The main goal is to help determine the best architecture for the service, evaluating if a device is necessary or it can be eliminated.

- ○ **Simultaneous clients test:** This test evaluates the load which each device of the service architecture supports. The test has two main goals, to evaluate the devices capacity (combined with other tests) and to know the number of licences which are being used in a given period of time. Usually, commercial technologies limit the number of simultaneous clients.

- ○ **Simultaneous stream test:** Due to the behaviour of users, not all the clients connected are active all the time. There are periods where they are receiving information and others where the re-

Figure 8. Lost packet evolution by network operator

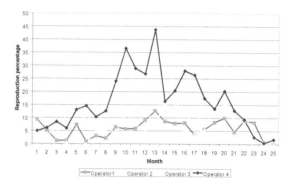

production is paused. This test is useful to know the number of streams which a device can serve simultaneously. Combined with other tests we will be able to evaluate the capacity of the devices.

Multidimensional Analysis

Sometimes, it is necessary to cross examine the results of different analyses to achieve more precision. Their main goal is to determine the best service configuration parameters. These analyses are called multidimensional analyses and are performed by merging basic analyses results and/or raw source data. The methodology defines an amount of multidimensional analyses related with quality, the access network, themes, users, etc. Some of the most important are the following:

- **Network Operators versus lost packets:** This test evaluates the reproductions which have lost packets according to the operator. The aim is to detect the origin of the clients who have problems reproducing the audio/videos. In Figure 8 an evolution graph is shown. In this graph it is possible to observe how operator 1 shows very high percentages in months 10, 11 and 12. Later, with the results of this test, the content provider realized that the quality of the videos was too high for this operator. The quality in new contents was reduced and the percentage decreased gradually.

- **Network Operators versus user value:** This test detects the network operators with the most valuable users. This information is important, for example, when the content provider plans to make changes in the quality parameters.

- **Network Operators versus popularity:** Popularity is a parameter linked with cache management. Usually, caches are distributed in different networks, and it is important to know the popularity of the contents for each network. As well as the basic test, real data is compared with the Zipf distribution.

- **Transferences between themes:** This test analyses whether users reproduce audio/videos with different subjects. For instance, it tries to determine if users who usually reproduce news, also reproduce films or video-clips. This knowledge is important to keep the clients satisfied. If the majority of users reproduce a theme, for example political news, the content producer will try to focus its production on this subject. However, it is not always possible to do this, since there are periods without this type of news. In these cases, it is useful to know what other themes interest the public in order to drive the production process.

Data Mining

The analysis process includes a data mining phase. To generate knowledge extracting information from the source data, the methodology uses the process presented in (Berry, & Linoff, 2000). This phase permits the generation of predictive information for the future and thus obtain accurate information about previous behaviour.

Figure 9. Process to develop lab experiments

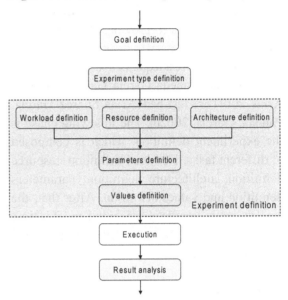

ANALYSIS BASED ON PREDICTION

This part of the analysis is oriented to evaluate different situations which may appear in the real service in a near future. With the results of the tests the administrator will have useful information to try to avoid problems in the future service performance.

To develop the test, the method specifies two types of experiments: emulations (Busari & Williamson, 2002) and simulations (Jin, & Bestavros, 2001). The former uses test-beds to analyse future scenarios, while the latter uses simulation models. Defining situations which can appear in a near future, the experiments can detect undesired situations and can provide important results to predict future performances, all of which allows managers to reach a more robust and reliable configuration for their services.

The method defines a process to develop this type of experiments. This process, shown in Figure 9, is divided into different steps. The first step is in charge of specifying the service. Its type and characteristics have to be determined.

The second is the goals definition. At this time it is necessary to decide what kind of information the experiment has to provide. Once the goals are clear, it is necessary to decide which type of experiment is more adequate: to use a simulation model (García, Pañeda, García, García, García & Arias, 2001) or a test-bed (Arias, Suárez, García, Pañeda, García, 2002b). The following phase is the experiment definition, which is composed of different tasks: workload definition, resource definition, architecture definition, parameters definition and values definition. After that, the experiment is completely specified and it is time to execute it. Finally, an analysis of the results must be performed.

Goal Definition

The first step is to answer the following questions: what is the aim of the experiment? What information are we interested in?

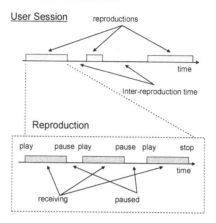

Figure 10. User behaviour

To answer these questions, the outputs of the experiment must be defined. These outputs will be expressed by means of the metrics defined in the previous sections. Elements such as bandwidth consumed in a point of the network, throughput, CPU usage, etc will be considered.

Table 4. Parameters to be determined

Media delivered time: audio/video time delivered throughout the reproduction.
Pause number: number of pauses in a reproduction.
Pause time: length of a pause.
Pause start-time: time in the audio/video when the pause appears.
Inter-reproduction time: time between two reproductions of the same user.
Reproductions per session: number of reproductions carried out by a user in a given period of time.
Inter-session time: time between two user sessions.
Length, position and number of forward jumps.
Length, position and number of backward jumps.
Quality of audio and video streams: This parameter can either be defined using: Frames per second and frame size, or bandwidth consumed per second.
Number of audio/videos: number of audio/video files offered in the service.
Popularity of the audio/videos: criteria used to decide which audio/video the user selects.
Length of the audio/videos.
Packet size (only for simulations models): size of the audio and video packets. Sometimes, there are different sizes due to the codec used to generate the audio or the video stream.
Inter-packet time (only for simulations models): time between two packets of the same type.
Background traffic: traffic which is going to be fed into the analyzed network, not generated by the service under study. Only necessary in some types of experiments, where the main goal is to test the service behaviour in a network where other types of traffic compete with the service's own traffic.

Table 5. Elements to be determined

Number of servers, location in the network, and load balancing policies.
Number of proxies, location in the network, and cache policies.
Transport protocol between each service device (TCP, UDP, etc).
Number of clients and location in the network.
Number of producers and location in the network (Only in live services with online generated information).

Type of Experiment Definition

The second step in the method application process is the definition of the type of experiment.

Two types of experiments can be performed: a simulation model or a testbed can be used. Depending on the type of experiment, it is necessary to define different parameters

Experiment Definition

The experiment definition is composed of five tasks. Three of them, workload, architecture and resource definition, are oriented to define the base for the experiment. The others, parameters and values definition, are used to characterize the analysis which is going to be performed.

Workload Definition. To perform a useful experiment, an accurate workload must be defined (García, Pañeda, García, Melendi. & Vilas, 2007) (Pañeda, García, Melendi, Vilas, & García, 2007). Most of the necessary data is extracted from real services. The rest must be established as parameters which will be defined later using different values to characterize the experiment. The workload definition is divided into two different parts: user behaviour and content characteristics.

Figure 10 shows the behaviour of a user in a service based on streaming technology. To clearly define an experiment, the parameters of Table 4 must be specified.

Architecture Definition

This phase includes two different parts that must be taken into consideration. The first is the network architecture, and the second is the service architecture. Table 5 presents different questions which must be determined when dealing with service and network architectures.

Resource Definition

In this step the quantity of resources, both in service devices (servers, proxies, etc) and in the communication network must be established.

Parameters Definition: In this phase one or more elements must be determined as parameters. The values for these parameters are not extracted from the real service; instead, they will be defined arbitrarily depending on the goal of the experiment.

Values Definition: In this phase a set of values for each parameter of the experiment must be defined. The process is the following: **Determine the maximum and the minimum value** and **establish the criteria for the intermediate values**. For instance, determining the gap between them using a particular distribution: Linear; Exponential; Free. When there is more than one parameter, there are two possibilities to combine them: **blind combination** (generating all the possibilities with all the parameters) and **intelligent combination** (eliminating those combinations which are not interesting).

Results Analysis: The last phase is the results analysis. The results from lab experiments are not different from the analyses of the information gathered from the real service. So the results can be evaluated in the same way as the analyses based on monitoring information.

Table 6. Qualities table

Quality	% of the best Q	Operator/access line	User %	Usage %	PRQ (%)
180 kbps	100	Telefonica (512)	5	35,15	1
		Telefonica(256)	25	70,31	7
90 kbps	50	Telefonica(512)	5	17,58	1
		Telefonica(256)	25	35,15	7
		Telecable(128)	60	70,31	9

Figure 11. Traffic distribution graph

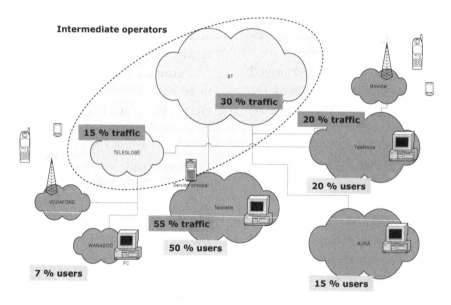

RESULTS COMPILATION AND CONCLUSION OBTAINING

Results Compilation

Results compilation is the task which is responsible for coordinating all the results obtained in the previous stages. By combining analysis test results, several lists, graphs and tables are created to help reach conclusions:

Themes and length table: This table presents a row with the different themes produced in the service, presenting the following data: theme, interest, success, impact, average length, and average reproduction length.

Qualities table: This table presents the users that can reproduce the qualities offered in the service and their quality problems. A quality is presented in a row with the following data: quality, percentage of the best quality, operator and type of line. Each type of line has associated to it: user percentage, percentage of the line capacity used and perceived reproduction quality in percentage. An example is shown in Table 6.

Traffic distribution graph: The scheme presents the operators that own the networks used to deliver the information (intermediate operators and final operators). Traffic and user percentages are written as shown in Figure 11.

Table 7. Lists and graphs

List of recommended qualities	The list will be defined in the following way: **One quality for each type of users**. The difference between the line capacity and the quality proposed must be greater than 20%. If the results of the analysis show quality problems the difference must be increased. **Intermediate qualities**. If the distance between qualities is greater than 25%, new qualities will be introduced with intermediate characteristics.
List of most interesting themes	This list presents the themes ordered by the interest metric. For each theme the recommended length is calculated with the formula: 120% of the average reproduction length, considering only the valid reproductions without unacceptable buffer reloads.
Bottle-neck graph	This graph is defined by adding to the traffic distribution graph the values of perceived reproduction quality in percentage for each operator and informing the operators where quality problems are high.
Overload resources table	A row with each overloaded resource is defined with the following information: average utilization percentage, maximum utilization percentage and the overload period.

Table 8. Content modifications

Length decrease	The video can be cut without cost, to adapt it to the new specifications.
Quality modification	If the original video is available, generating a new video in streaming format is relatively easy and cheap.
Cacheability allowing	If the number of reproductions is low, it is a good decision to deny the cacheability of the video, as saving the videos in cache consumes important resources, and it does not improve the quality if the video is rarely requested.
Removing a video	When there is no free space in the server disk or this video is harmful to the service (bad quality), removing the information can be a good option.

Conclusions Achievement

This task is divided into three different phases. One oriented to evaluate if the goals have been satisfied, another oriented to evaluate the current configuration, and the last oriented to introduce external information.

Goals and SLA evaluation: This phase evaluates if the goals have been reached. A table is used for this purpose. The table has a row for each goal with the following values: goal, target value, reached value and fulfilment percentage. If all the goals have been satisfied the analysis and configuration process stops. Moreover, the fulfilment of the SLAs is individually checked for each subscriber. If the targets are not achieved, a report must be sent to the subscriber.

Evaluation of the current configuration: Some questions must be answered in this phase: *Are the qualities used in the audio/videos appropriate? What themes must be produced preferen-* *tially? Are there bottle-necks in the distribution network? Are the service devices overloaded?* To help answer these questions, the lists and graphs in Table 7 can be defined.

External Information Introduction: Although this method has a clear technical aim, it can not be forgotten that the final goal of content providers and network operators is to make a profit from the services. This phase of conclusion achievement is used to add external data, such as economic information which can modify the conclusions obtained through the analysis process. To this aim, it can be useful to define a table with action/cost.

CONTENT PROVIDER CONFIGURATION

This section describes the configuration process specified in the method. A video service can be

Table 9. *Network problems*

Point	Solution
User access line	Decreasing video bandwidth requirements
Intermediate point	Cache installation or workload balance
Server access line	Workload balance
External operator	Cache installation or decreasing video bandwidth requirements

Table 10. *Architecture elements*

Function	Problem
Cache	Important number of reproductions from network or a subnet
Workload balancing	High traffic in an intermediate point, in the server connection line; overload in the existing servers
Redundant servers	Connectivity problems in the server access line. Server unavailable

configured in two different situations: firstly, when goals have not been reached and the service must be reconfigured; and secondly, during the initial configuration. For the first situation the process must be based on results which were achieved in the analysis task. However, for the latter, the configuration of the service cannot be based on these results and market research must be carried out.

Content Creation: In this task new contents will be developed following the criteria determined in the analyses. These criteria are the following: theme of the video, length and quality. Quality will be defined by using the list of recommended qualities. The selection of the theme will not only deal with the list and tables established in the conclusion achievement task, but also with external factors. For example, it is impossible to produce news if there is nothing to report. So, using the order established in the tables the most interesting theme will be chosen. The length will depend on the selected theme.

Content Modification: The content modification is one of the most difficult problems due to two main reasons: impossibility to obtain the original material to repeat the production; and the cost of making a new production, mainly when contents are not hits yet. However, there are some modifications without a high cost, which are presented in Table 8.

NETWORK OPERATOR CONFIGURATION

This task is composed of three phases: one to configure the service architecture, another to alter network resources, and lastly where an increase in computational resources is applied to the service. Since all these phases are not independent they will be applied in a circular process until no more changes are necessary.

Network Resources: This configuration task involves bandwidth modifications. Usually, bandwidth has to be increased; however, when reserved resources are underused, a decrease is logical. To solve the lack of bandwidth in the output of video servers, an increase may be requested to the network operator or the workload may be balanced using a redundant server. This problem is more difficult to solve when the lack of bandwidth is located in the user connection. In this case, commercial problems prevent the increase, so the best solution is to change the requirements of the video. When the problems are in an intermediate point of the network, introducing a proxy can be a good solution to cache the most reproduced videos. Table 9 shows possible solutions for the lack of bandwidth.

Computational Resources: There are two types of computational resources, hardware resources and software resources. The hardware configuration task allows network operators to

Figure 12. Extensibility process

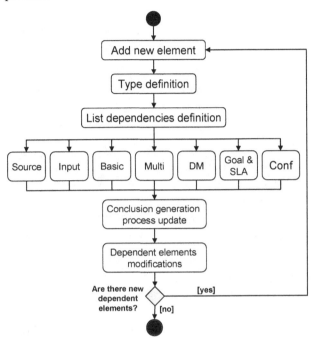

modify the power of their computers, such as increasing the number of CPUs, expanding the memory, and even sometimes changing the whole computer or adding a redundant computer. The software configuration task is carried out in order to change program versions (server, proxy) and mainly to increase or decrease the number of licenses. Commercial technologies usually limit the number of simultaneous clients who may be connected to the server. It is common to increase the number of licenses as the number of clients increases. Both computational and network resources are closely related to service architecture. A modification in the architecture can render unnecessary or insufficient the resources previously reserved for the service.

Service Architecture: Sometimes, increasing the number of resources in the network or in service devices is not the best solution. In these cases, a modification in the service architecture can improve service performance. Two entities can be introduced: caches, and additional servers. These elements are recommended in the cases

presented in Table 10. A bottle-neck graph can be used to determine the best location for every new device.

EXTENSIBILITY

The evolution of technology can render any analysis and configuration process obsolete. New goals, elements to be configured, analysis tests, sources and input data can appear and the processes must be updated. The presented method specifies an extensibility process to incorporate these new elements. This process, presented in detail in (Pañeda, 2004), organizes the tasks, and causes others which may be necessary when a new element is added. Figure 12 shows the process. When a new element is added, a list of dependencies must be defined in order to avoid inconsistencies. If new elements are introduced or some of the existing are modified, the method considers these activities in this process.

CASE STUDY

Description

The presented study has been performed on the video-on-demand service of **La Nueva España Digital** (www.lne.es) which is one of the most successful news services in Spain. This digital service has an important number of accesses and has reached the 8th position in the ranking of digital news sites in Spain. In 2001, www.lne.es presented its video-on-demand service (http://tv.lne.es) developed by the **Computer Science Department of the University of Oviedo**.

The multimedia section of www.lne.es has an architecture formed by two servers (Suárez, Pañeda & García, 2002). One is the streaming server and the other supports the web pages used to access the videos, the analysis system and is the redundant streaming server.

Helix of **RealNetworks** (RealNetworks. 2002) is the technology used to stream the videos delivered on demand when a subscriber performs a request. The analysis server stores all the modules of the analysis tool (García, Pañeda, García, Melendi, Vilas, 2007), including the database, the web server, loaders and analyzers.

The multimedia service contents have been classified in 9 subsections according to their subject and they are the following: *News, Music, Tourism, Science, Cinema, Comedy, Leisure, Sports* and *Others*. The lengths range from 30 seconds, the shortest, to more than an hour the longest. Currently, the service has approximately 1,500 videos which are available with a quality of 250 kbps (using Surestream technology).

Results

After applying the presented method over a period of four years, the LNE TV streaming service has evolved very positively and achieved a very high performance (success, number of users, quality of service, etc). These results are of special importance since the number of videos produced daily has been the same throughout this period, which has allowed LNE to increase their income without additional investment. The method has been applied using the Iterative Synchronous Process with periods of approximately one month. Using the information provided by the analysis tool the team has gathered enough information to act over the system. The most important modifications in the system configurations have been:

Figure 13. Evolution of the number of requests per section

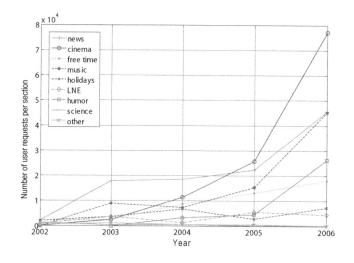

Table 11. Evolution of success, interest and impact metrics during the last 5 years

Year	2002	2003	2004	2005	2006
Success	1.300.896	4.833.532	5.825.509	6.982.283	16.341.246
Interest	9.340	40.848	61.123	97.011	229.605
Impact	817,68	4.824,94	4.894,41	8.777,77	37.708,70

Figure.14. Requests per session

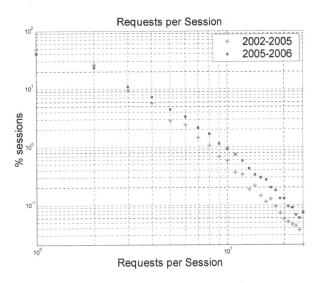

The quality used to code the videos. It has been increased from 90 kbps to 250 Kbps passing by 120, 150, 180 and 220.

- The servers out-bandwidth. It has been increased form 1Mbps to 18Mbps.
- The content production has been focused on the subjects which had previously generated more interest and their length has been adjusted based on the reproduction percentage study. Since it is not always possible to produce the subject the journalists want, the lists with the most interesting topics can help to choose the best option each time. The content production has been focused on these subjects with the results shown in figure 13. The most valuable sections are currently more valuable than they used to be and others with little success have been closed.

- The presentation has been modified several times and SMILs have been introduced to make sequences of videos (E.g. trailers of the week).

These actions have produced different results in service performance. Part of them (produced until July of 2004) were presented in detail as a case study in (Pañeda, 2004). Some of the most interesting results are the following:

- The success of the service has increased exponentially. Due to the content subjects selection we have more users and more valuable users. In Table 11 the evolution of the success, interest and impact metrics during the last five years are shown.
- The user value is another parameter which has been improved. One of the generators of

this effect has been the inclusion of SMIL files which have increased the number of videos reproduced in the same session. Figure 14 shows the increase in 2005 when this new presentation element was introduced.

- Quality problems have been reduced to marginal values thanks to the study of the most suitable qualities.
- The consumption of resources has not reached the limits of any service device. Increases in the servers bandwidth have always been ordered in advance thanks to the resource tests which show consumption tendencies.

CONCLUSION

The configuration of video on demand services is a complex process, due to the high resource consumption, the cost of the production of contents and the difficulties of managing continuous information. Nowadays, this task is principally based on manager's experience. However, a formalization of the steps which must be followed can help to decrease this component, and, above all, can facilitate the job of inexpert administrators. The developed method has been used to configure the video-on-demand services of La Nueva España Digital (www.lne.es) for 5 years. After this period of guided analysis and configuration, an important improvement in the quality of service and a great number of satisfied users has been reached. This systematic approach to the analysis and configuration has detected the most interesting themes, the most useful quality for videos and the resources consumption in a clear and organized way. The results provided have allowed their administrators to decide the best configuration for the service, in spite of their lack of experience in this type of services.

FUTURE WORK

The next step in this work is to extend the method to deal with live audio/video services. This type of service has specific characteristics and new analysis, roles and classifications have to be introduced. One member of our research group has designed a methodology in his PhD Thesis (Melendi, 2007) to deploy these services, and our current target is to integrate both to generate a complete methodological process. Also, this combination can resolve one of the weakest tasks in the current design, which is the specification of the service deployment.

Apart from that, since the method is being used in real systems, where their characteristics and the underlying technology are improving continuously, modifications and improvements will be necessary. Currently, the research group is working on the definition of more accurate analysis in different areas, such as users and predictions.

ACKNOWLEDGMENT

This research has been financed by the network operator **Telecable** and **La Nueva España** (Grupo Editorial Prensa Ibérica) within the projects of NuevaMedia, Telemedia, ModelMedia and MediaXXI and the **Spanish National Research Program** within the project FUTURMEDIA (TSI2007-60474).

REFERENCES

Almeida, J. M., Krueger, J., Pager, D. L., & Vernon, M. K. (2001). *Analysis of Educational Media Server Workloads*. Paper presented at ACM NOSSDAV. New York, USA.

Arias, J. R., Suárez, F. J, García, D. F., Pañeda, X. G., & García, V. G. (2002). *A Set of Metrics for Evaluation of Interactive News-on-Demand Systems.* Paper presented at ACM Multimedia Conference. Juan Les Pins, France

Arias, J. R., Suárez, F. J, García, D. F., Pañeda, X. G., & García, V. G. (2002b). *Evaluation of Video Server Capacity with Regard to Quality of the Service in Interactive News-On-Demand Systems.* Paper presented at PROMS-IDMS2002. LNCS 2515. Coimbra, Portugal.

AudioVideoweb (2006). AudioVideoweb.com LLC, Retrieved 12th of November from http://www.audiovideoweb.com/

Berry, M., & Linoff, G. (2000). Mastering Data Mining. Wiley & Sons.

Brotherton, M. D, Huynh-Thu, Q., Hands, D. S., & Brunnström, K. (2006). Subjective Multimedia Quality Assessment. *IEICE Transactions on Fundamentals of Electronics, Communications and Computer Sciences*, Vol. E98-A, Number 11.

Busari, M., & Williamson, C. (2002). A Synthetic Workload Generation Tool for Simulation Evaluation of Web Proxy Caches. Computer Networks: *The International Journal of Computer and Telecommunications Networking*, 38(6), 779-794.

Casale, G., Cremonesi, P., Serazzi, G., & Zanero, S. (2005). *Performance Issues in Video Streaming Environments.* Paper presented at IEEE QEST'05.

Cherkasova, L., & Gupta, M. (2004). Analysis of Enterprise Media Server Workload: Access Patterns, Locality, Content Evolution and Rates of Change. *IEEE/ACM Transactions on Networking*, 2004.

Cherkasova, L., Tang, W., & Singhal, S (2004). *An SLA-Oriented Capacity Planning Tool for Streaming Media Services.* Paper presented at DSN2004.

Chesire, M., Wolman, A., Voelker, G., & Lavy, H. (2001). *Measurement and Analysis of a*

Streaming-Media Workload. Paper presented at USENIX Symposium on Internet Technologies and Systems.

Chieng, D., Marshall, A., Ho, I., & Parr, G., (2001). Agent-Enhanced Dynamic Service Level Agreement in Future Network Environment. *Lecture Notes in Computer Science, 21*(16).

Chung, J., & Claypool, M., (2006). Empirical Evaluation of the Congestion Responsiveness of Real Player Video Streams. *Kluwer Multimedia Tools and Applications, 31*(2).

Costa, C., Cunha, I., Borges, A., Ramos, C., Rocha, M., Almeida, J., Ribeiro-Neto, B., (2005). Analyzing Client Interactivity in Streaming Media. *Paper presented at IEEE MMSP'05.*

Cranley, N., & Davis, M. (2006). *Performance Evaluation of Video Streaming with Background Traffic over IEEE 802.11 WLAN Networks.* Paper presented at ACM WMuNEP'06, Montreal, Quebec, Canada.

Dalal, A. C., &Perry, E., (2003). A New Architecture for Measuring and Assessing Streaming Media Quality. Paper presented at PAM 2003.

García, M/, Pañeda, X. G/, García, D. F/, García, D. F., García, V. G., & Arias, J. R, (2001). *A Tool for Performance Prediction of an HFC Operator Based on a Queuing Network Model Simulation.* Paper presented at SPECTS-2001. Orlando, USA.

Guo, L., Tan, E., Chen, S., Xia, Z., Spatscheck, O., & Zhang, X. (2006). *Delving into Internet Streaming Media Delivery: A Quality and Resource Utilization Perspective.* Paper presented at IMC 2006.

Ivanovici, M., & Beuran, R. (2006). *User Perceived Quality Assessment for Multimedia Applications.* Paper presented at OPTIM'06.

Jin, S., & Bestavros, A., (2001). *GISMO, A Generator of Internet Streaming Objects and Workloads.* Paper presented at ACM SIGMETRICTS.

Keynote (2006). Streaming Perspective StreamQ, Retrieved 12th of November from http://www.keynote.com/

Loguinov, D., & Radha, H. (2002). Retransmission Schemes for Streaming Internet Multimedia: Evaluation Model and Performance Analysis. *ACM SIGCOMM Computer Communication Review (CCR), 32*(2).

Loguinov, D., & Radha, H. (2001). *Measurement Study of Low-bitrate Internet Video Streaming.* Paper presented at ACM SIGCOMM Internet Measurement Workshop. San Francisco, USA.

Melendi, D. (2007). Configuración, despliegue y evaluación de servicios de audio y video en directo sobre redes heterogéneas *(Configuration, Deployment and Evaluation of Live Audio and Video Services over Heterogeneous Networks).* PhD Thesis. University of Oviedo.

Mena, A., & Heidemann, J., (2000). *An Empirical Study of Real Audio Traffic.* Paper presented at IEEE Infocom, pp. 101-110. Tel-Aviv, Israel.

Menascé, D. A., & Almeida, V. A. F, (2000). *Scaling for E-Business: Technologies, Models, Performance and Capacity Planning.* Prentice Hall.

Pañeda, X., (2004). Análisis, modelado y configuración de servicios de video bajo demanda sobre redes de cable *(Analysis, modeling and configuration of video-on-demand services over cable networks).* PhD Thesis. University of Oviedo.

Pañeda, X. G., Melendi, D., Vilas, M., García, R., García., V, & Rodríguez, I. (2007, September). FESORIA: An integrated system for analysis, management and smart presentation of audio/video streaming services. *Multimedia Tool and Applications.* DOI:

Pañeda, X. G., García, R., Melendi, D., Vilas, M., García, V. (2007). Popularity analysis of a video-on-demand service with a great variety of subjects. Influence of the subject, video characteristics and new content publication policy. *International Journal of Advanced Media and Communication.* InderScience Inc.

Pereira, F., (2005). *A Triple User Characterization Model for Video Adaptation and Quality of Service Experience.* Paper presented at IEEE MMSP'05.

RealNetworks (2002). Helix Universal Server Administration Guide.

Suárez, F. Pañeda, X. G., & García, V. G. (2002). *Low Cost, Highly Available, High Performance Talks-on-Demand Sytems.* Paper presented at ACM International Multimedia Conference. Juan les Pins, France. 2002.

Van der Raadt, B., Gardin, T., & Yu, E. (2005). Exploring Web Services from a Business Value Perspective. Paper presented at IEEE RE'05.

Veloso, E., Almeida, V., Meira, W., Bestavros, A. & Jin, S. (2002, November). *A Hierarchical Characterization of a Live Streaming Media Workload.* Paper presented at ACM Internet Measurement Workshop (IMV)..

Vicari, N., & Kohler, S., (2006). *Measuring Internet User Traffic Behaviour Dependent on Access Speed.* Paper presented at IP Traffic Measurement, Modelling and Management.

García, R., Pañeda, X. G., García V., Melendi, D., & Vilas, M. (2007). Statistical characterization of a rela video on demand service: User behaviour and streaming-media workload analysis. *Simulation Modelling Practice and Theory.* Elsevier.

Yu, H., Zheng. D., Zhao, B. Y., Zheng, W., (2006). *Understanding User Behaviour in Large-Scale Video-on-demand Systems.* Paper presented at EuroSys2006.

Chapter VIII
Mobile Information Processing Involving Multiple Non-Collaborative Sources

Say Ying Lim
Monash University, Australia

David Taniar
Monash University, Australia

Bala Srinivasan
Monash University, Australia

ABSTRACT

As more and more servers appearing in the wireless environment provide accesses to mobile users, more and more demand and expectation is required by mobile users toward the available services. Mobile users are no longer satisfied with obtaining data only from one server, but require data from multiple servers either at the same or different locations. This eventually leads to the need for information gathering that spans across several non-collaborative servers. This article describes some of our researches in information gathering from multiple non-collaborative servers that may involve servers that not only accept direct queries from mobile users but also servers that broadcast data. We also look at how location dependent data plays an important role to mobile information gathering.

INTRODUCTION

The direction of the mobile technology industry is beginning to emerge and advance at a rapid pace as more mobile users have evolved (Myers & Beigl, 2003). Interests in mobile technology have grown exponentially over the last few years and are greatly influenced especially by the dramatic reduction in the cost of hardware and protocol standardization (Hurson & Jiao, 2005; Kapp, 2002). The increase in progression and advancement of mobile technology has created a new paradigm of computing called mobile computing in which people are allowed to be connected wirelessly to access data anytime, anywhere without having to worry about the distance barrier (Lee, Zhu, & Hu, 2005; Lee et al., 2002; Madria, Bhargava, Pitoura, & Kumar, 2000). Users have also become more productive with the achievement of mobility since they are able to access a full range of resources regardless of where they are located and where they are able to get hold of real time information.

The emerging growth of the use of intelligent mobile devices (e.g., mobile phones and PDAs) opens up a whole new world of possibilities, which includes delivering information to mobile devices that are customized and tailored according to their current location (Gutting et al., 2000; Tsalgatidou, Veijalainen, Markkula, Katasonov, & Hadjiefthymiades, 2003; Xu et al., 2003). Mobile queries are requests for certain information that are initiated by mobile users to the appropriate servers from their mobile devices. Query processing in a mobile environment may involve join processing from either single or several different servers with the mobile devices (Liberatore, 2002; Lo, Mamoulis, Cheung, Ho, & Kalnis, 2003). In addition, mobile queries can be performed regardless of where the users are located and the results obtained are influenced by the location of the user. Data that are downloaded from different locations would be different and there is a need to bring together these data according to a user who may want to synchronize the data that are downloaded from different location to be consolidated into a single output. Thus, the intention is to take into account location dependent factors, which allow mobile users to query data without facing location problems (Song, Kang, & Park, 2005; Tse, Lam, Ng, & Chan, 2005; Xu, Tang, & Lee, 2003). This concept is associated with location dependent query.

One of the main objectives of this article is to demonstrate the importance of allowing mobile users who believe that obtaining data from a single server is not enough and may need further processing with data that are obtained from other servers. Furthermore, the user may get data from several servers that are from the same or different providers. In other words, there are times when the user has the desire to gather data from several non-collaborative servers into their mobile devices (Lo, et al, 2003; Malladi & Davis, 2002). Mobile devices have made it capable for mobile users to process and retrieve data from multiple remote databases by sending queries to the servers and then process the multiple data gathered from these sources locally on the mobile devices (Mamoulis, Kalnis, Bakiras, & Li, 2003; Ozakar, Morvan, & Hameurlain, 2005). By processing the data locally, mobile users would have more control over what they actually want as the final result of the query. They can therefore choose to query data from different servers and process them locally according to their requirements. Also, by being able to obtain specific data over several different sites, it would help bring optimum results to mobile user queries. Furthermore, by driving away the computation on the client device, the bandwidth computation may also be reduced.

Example 1: A mobile user may want to know where the available vegetarian restaurants are in the city he or she is currently visiting. There are two major servers (e.g., tourist office and the vegetarian community) that may give information about the available vegetarian restaurants. First, using his or her wireless PDA, he or she would download information broadcast from the tourist office. Then, he or she would download the information provided by the vegetarian community. After obtaining the lists from the two information providers, he or she may perform an operation on his or her mobile device that joins the contents from the two relations obtained earlier from the two non-collaborative organizations. This illustrates the importance of assembling information obtained from multiple non-collaborative sources in a mobile device in order to obtain more comprehensive information.

This article investigates the need for information gathering spanning several non-collaborative servers that may bring to mobile users. Furthermore, due to the various nature of how a server may disseminate their data (e.g., through ad-hoc queries or data broadcasting), this article also evaluates the query processing methods involving the previously mentioned strategies.

In this article, we first present an insight of the background of mobile environment, non-collaborative servers, and prospective applications for information gathering from multiple sources. By formulating the taxonomy, it helps to give understanding of the possible database operations that can be performed on the mobile devices. We will also describe the process of information gathering that results from multiple servers that involves location dependent data, which are then followed by a system prototype. Finally, the last section concludes the article. Note that in this article we use the term mobile client, mobile user, and users interchangeably.

BACKGROUND AND PRELIMINARIES

Before discussing more details, the process of information gathering, and its rationale, this section would first introduce some background and preliminaries related to mobile query processing in a typical mobile environment, which involves multiple non-collaborative servers. Firstly, this section provides some introductory knowledge on the wireless environment covering what constitutes the architecture of a typical mobile computing environment, followed by the usefulness of obtaining information from multiple sources and lastly the prospective application of this study.

Mobile Computing Environment: A Background

Mobile computing has provided mobile users the ability to access information anytime, anywhere.

It enables mobile users to query databases from their mobile devices over the wireless communication channels (Imielinski & Badrinath, 1994). In general, mobile users with their mobile devices and servers that store data are involved in a typical mobile environment (Lee et al., 2005; Madria et al., 2000; Wolfson, 2002). Each of these mobile users communicates with a single server or multiple servers that may or may not be collaborative with one another. This server is also known as mobile base station (MBS), which the mobile users communicate to in order to carry out any activities such as transaction and information retrieval. The servers supply its services to a wide range of users who are within the active region through a wireless interface. Thus, mobile users have to be within a specific region to be able to receive a signal in order to connect to the servers.

Figure 1 depicts a mobile environment architecture where two servers are involved, *S1* and *S2,* in location *A* and location *B* respectively. Mobile users move freely within the different region to obtain different data by accessing the different servers via sending a query and receiving the results back to the mobile device upon completion of processing.

Example 2: A property investor, while driving his or her car, downloads a list of nearby apartments for sale from a real-estate agent. As he or she moves, he or she downloads the requested information again from the same real-estate agent. Because his or her position has changed since he or she first inquires, the two lists of apartments for sale would be different due to the relative location when this investor was inquiring the information. Based on these two lists, the investor would probably like to perform an operation on his or her mobile device to show only those apartments that exist in the latest list, and not in the first list.

Hence, in a typical mobile environment, it is unacceptable to meet with situations where

Figure 1. Mobile environment architecture

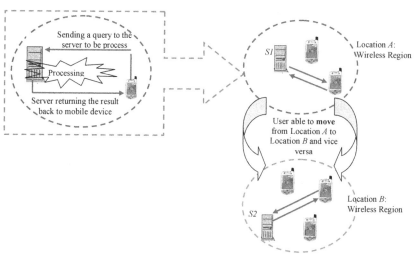

a mobile user is currently obtaining data from a current active region and is still not feeling satisfied with the result. This leads to the need of further processing with other data that can only be obtained from other servers that may or may not be collaborative to each other.

Overview of Non-Collaborative Servers

The term collaborative usually relates to the traditional distributed databases whereby the desire to integrate the data of a particular enterprise and to provide centralized and controlled access to that data (Bell & Grimson, 1992; Ceri & Pelagatti, 1984; Özsu & Valduriez, 1999). The technology of distributed database may not be appropriate for use in the mobile environment, which involves not only the nomadic clients, which move around, but also non-collaborative servers, which are basically servers that are maintained by different organizations (Lo et al., 2003).

Therefore, non-collaborative servers would refer to servers that do not know each other and do not have any relation between one another. There are basically just individual server providers, which disseminate data to the users and they do not communicate with one another. Since each

server can just be an independent service provider, often these independent servers are specialized within the domain of the information they are providing.

An example of such a server that disseminates information on restaurants normally just focuses on the restaurants information and limited supporting information, which can sometimes be included (e.g., how to get there--the transportation is just supporting information since it does not exactly show the route on how to get there from a particular location the user is currently at). Therefore, there is still a need to obtain full information from multiple servers, which in this case are the restaurant and transportation servers separately.

In addition, not all service providers are supported by the usage of a mediator (Lo et al., 2003). Therefore, information obtained from other independent non-related service providers needs to be processed individually. It is not a fair assumption that all service providers are linked through a mediator. Hence, in our research, we focus on independent service providers, which refers to non-collaborative servers. Thus, it is vital to consider gathering information from non-collaborative servers because it is often not enough to just get data from a single server.

Prospective Applications

Information gathering in the context of mobile environment is a source where collecting various data together regardless of whether it is related or not related as long as it is useful for the mobile users. There exists several significant influences of information gathering from multiple sources that lies on personal applications. Next, we show summarized lists of some promising applications that bring great impacts to mobile users.

- **Entertainment applications:** Shopping appears to be a popular trend and hobby. Often shoppers would prefer to go to shops that give the lowest price for the item they are interested in buying. Many shops in the same shopping complex may sell the same item, but they are different companies and they are not related with one another. Thus, with the ability of getting the information, especially the pricing for the desired item, separately from the various shops could aid users in deciding which shops to go to that offers a better price.

Example 3: A mobile user who is currently in a shopping complex is interested in a buying a tennis racquet. There are two different sports shops in the complex, sports shop *A* and sports shop *B,* that sell the tennis racquet that the user wants to buy. So first, by sending a query to shop *A,* he or she obtains a list of the prices for the tennis racquet. Then he or she sends a query to shop *B,* which again he or she will get a list of prices for the tennis racquet. So with these two lists, the mobile user can do a local processing, which compares the matching racquets and displays the shop that gives a lower price for the respective racquets that are being matched.

- **Tourism applications:** Tourism brings value added in terms of economical growth to not only the country, but also the physical relationship between the visitor and the producer of a good or service. Tourism is an important element to boost the country's reputation and economy. Thus, it is important to give both local and international travelers the best and most convenient. Giving the ability of information gathering from multiple sources tends to emerge as valuable services to the mobile travelers regardless of where their current geographical coordinates.

Example 4: An international tourist, while traveling to a foreign country, does not know the where abouts of the tourist attraction spots. He or she looks for famous tourist spots recommended by both the transport office and tourism office. First, using his or her wireless PDA, he or she would download information broadcast from the tourism office to get a list of the famous tourist spots. Then, he or she would download the information provided by the transport office to get information on the available transportation. Once he or she obtains the lists from the two information providers, he or she may perform an operation on his or her mobile device that joins the contents to match the tourist spots together with transport information on how to get there.

- **Emergency responses applications:** There are times especially when someone on the highway is having trouble with their car and needs to find the nearest possible petrol station that offers car services as soon as possible. In this circumstance, the person on the highway can use his or her mobile device to make a query as he or she travels along the highway to look for a petrol station that offer car services. This comes into the category of emergency cases, as it is rare and is not needed all the time.

Example 5: A traveler currently in location *A* wants to know where the nearest gas station is (petrol kiosk) and using the mobile device, they downloaded a list of available petrol kiosk nearby to his or her current surrounding location. As they travel further until they arrive in location *B*, he or she makes another query to get another list of petrol kiosk, but this time the list is somewhat different since he or she has been driving and the location has moved from *A* to *B*. Therefore, based on these two lists, the traveler wants to display only those petrol kiosks that provide car service regardless of whether it is in *A* or *B*.

- **Double checking applications:** Data that are stored in the servers that are to be disseminate to the public can sometimes be outdated due to the company that manages the data being closed down or other undesired catastrophes. If the users are still able to query for the data, part of the data may not be accurate anymore since it has not been maintained and updated well. This will make the data worthless if the users download it. Therefore, a certain degree that allows the users to see the data that is downloaded are obtained from a reliable source or not may be useful if the ability of processing data that are obtained from one server together with another list of data obtained from another server as a double checking precaution.

Example 6: This example requires an assumption of one property that can be handled by several estate agents. A user obtains a list of properties in the city that are ready for sale from real-estate agent *A*. Without knowing, real-estate agent *A* has just been declared bankrupt and the lists that are currently in the server have not been updated since. Thus, some of the properties that the user has downloaded have actually been sold. Without knowing all this, since the user is able to obtain another list of properties in the city from another agent, which is agent *B*, this list would have been able to be used as a reference list to the previous list that was obtained from agent *A*. Since one property can be handled by several agents, the

properties for sale in the city between list *A* and list *B* should be the same. The only difference may be the price on whether the agent is selling it cheaper or more expensive than the other. Thus, by seeing the difference in the availability of the properties between the two lists, this information can appear to the mobile user that one or the other is not correct since we have to assume one property is to be handled by several agents.

In summary, we can see from the previous sample application domain that obtaining from a single place is not sufficient enough to provide the desired results to the mobile users. The mobile users often require several data that are non-related with one another to be gathered and processed together so that a higher level and meaningful information can be obtained. By giving more flexibility to the mobile users to "mix-and-match" non-related data from several servers proves to return a more comprehensive result that is able to satisfy the needs of the users. Therefore, information gathering from multiple non-collaborative servers brings benefits and gives a good prospect for users to achieve a higher quality and productive information.

MOBILE USER QUERIES

The context of mobile user queries in this article is that the mobile queries contain operations that are being carried out when multiple lists of data are obtained from multiple servers (Lim, Taniar, & Srinivasan, 2006). In this section, we will present a taxonomy of the mobile user queries in two elements namely (i) *non-location-based on-mobile queries* and (ii) *location-based on-mobile queries*.

- In non-location-based on-mobile queries, the need to obtain constructive information often requires mobile users to download lists from multiple sources to be integrated and processed together. In a mobile environment, joins are used to bring together information from two or more different information sources. It joins multiple data from different servers into a single output to be displayed on the mobile device. The idea of this is basically to ensure mobile users have the ability to reduce the query results with maximum return of satisfaction because with the additional post-processing, the output results can be greatly reduced based on the user's requirements and needs before the final display on the device.

Consider Example 1 presented earlier where it shows how a join operation is needed to be performed on a mobile device as the mobile user downloads information from two different sources, which are the tourist office and the vegetarian community. In this case, two pieces of information might be joined on the restaurant IDs from the two different lists. This therefore, illustrates a simple on-mobile join case, where it is basically a process of combining data from one relation to another.

- Location-based on-mobile queries have become a growing trend due to the constant behaviour of mobile users who move around. Location-dependent processing is of interest in a number of applications, especially those that involve geographical information systems (Cai & Hua, 2002; Cheverst, Davies, & Mitchell, 2000; Jung, You, Lee, & Kim, 2002; Tsalgatidou et al., 2003). An example query might be "to find the nearest petrol kiosk" or "find the three nearest vegetarian restaurants." As the mobile users move around, the query results may change and would therefore depend on the location of the issuer. This means that if a user sends a query and then changes his or her location, the answer of that query has to be based on the location of the user issuing

the query (Seydim, Dunham, & Kumar, 2001; Waluyo, Srinivasan, & Taniar, 2005). Location dependent processing involves the circumstances when mobile users are in the situation where they download a list when in a certain location and then they move around and download another list in their new current location. Or another circumstance might be a mobile user might already have a list in his or mobile device but moves and needs to download the same list again but from a different location. In any case, there is a need to synchronize these lists that have been downloaded from a different location.

Consider Example 2 presented earlier. It shows an example of how location dependent queries processes are being carried out. With the two different lists on hand that the investor currently had based on the properties in the two different locations, the investor would probably like to perform some kind of database operation on his or her mobile device. The difference in the list is due to the moving location from one point to another point by the investor.

MODELS OF INFORMATION PROCESSING

There are times when a user may need to query several non-collaborative servers in order to obtain a more comprehensive list of data. The user may need to perform some database operations locally on the mobile device based on the list of data that has been downloaded from the remote databases.

Figure 2 models the various strategies that the server can adopt. *Server strategy* involves mobile users sending queries to the server for processing (Seydim et al., 2001). It relates to processing to be taken by the server to process and return the results based on the mobile user queries. *On-air strategy* is similar to traditional broadcasting

Figure 2. Query processing strategies

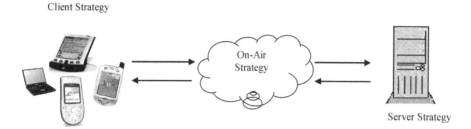

techniques whereby the sets of database items are broadcasted through the air to a large number of mobile users over a single channel or multiple channel (Tran, Hua, & Jiang, 2001; Triantafillou, Harpantidou, & Paterakis, 2001). With the set of data on the air, mobile users can tune into one or more channel to get the data. *Client strategy* relates to maintaining cached data in the local storage and being able to have the ability to do local processing if queries results are being sent back to the mobile device and stored in the cache memory. Thus, efficient cache management is critical in mobile query processing (Cao, 2003; Elmargamid, Jing, Helal, & Lee, 2003; Xu, Hu, Lee, & Lee, 2004; Zheng, Xu, & Lee, 2002).

Lists of information can be obtained from servers that distribute their respective data using various strategies such as server strategy, on-air strategy, and client strategy. Each of the available servers has their associated query processing strategies and they can be processed together regardless of whether part of the servers use a different strategy.

Example 7: Suppose a mobile user wants to know the timetable for the transportation services to a particular event. Each of the transportation timetables, as well as the event, is stored in different servers and maintained by two different organizations. Transport servers would deal with transportation data while an event server would deal with current events that are happening. Therefore, in order to know the transportation timetable for a particular event, the user has to

gather data from the two different servers, which is first sending a query to obtain the event list into the mobile device, and then sending another query to the transport server to obtain the list of transportations. Now these two lists are in the mobile device and are ready to be processed locally to match the transportation timetable onto the respective events. This exemplifies the importance of assembling information from multiple servers into a single information, which is the desired result as the outcome on the PDA.

Assuming that both transport and event servers are individual servers that accept direct query from the users, Figure 3 models an illustration of how two different lists are obtained from two different sources to be processed locally. This achieves the object of processing information obtained from multiple non-collaborative servers.

In the following sub section, we will uncover several case studies and explain how multiple non-collaborative servers that use the different strategies integrate its results into useful information for the mobile users. Just for illustration and simplicity purposes, we only illustrate situations where there are only two servers that are in use.

Case Study 1: Both Servers use Server Strategy

Without acknowledging the current standing location of the user, we would like to allow the user to be able to carry out simple database

Figure 3. Example of assembling information from two different servers

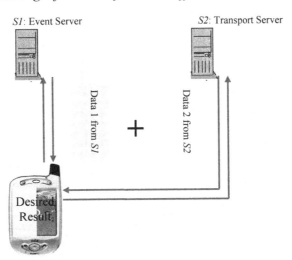

operations locally on the mobile device such as simple join between the different lists of data that are downloaded into the mobile device from the remote databases. We would first examine cases where the two different servers that the users need to obtain its information from to be integrated together are both using server strategies as being modeled in Figure 4.

Server strategy has limited functionalities since it provides dedicated point-to-point connections in accepting the mobile users request directly. This is due to the limited bandwidth that is available. Therefore, if suddenly there are many users wishing to send a request to the same server, the server may be congested. Thus, server strategy may cause an increase in exceeding usage of bandwidth especially when too many data requests are being sent out by the mobile users. The overwhelming mobile users requests may affect the query performance. This can easily cause a scalability bottleneck with a large mobile user population.

As far as the cost remains a major concern to a wide majority of mobile users, obtaining data via server strategy may be expensive or cost effective. This is because mobile users are establishing a direct communication to the server, which is how server strategy provides exclusive point-to-point communications between the user and server, which in this case the server processes the query that is being sent by the mobile users and returns the results back to the mobile users (Sun, Shi, & Shi, 2003).

In addition to the previous issues that users may face when obtaining data from servers that accept direct requests, there are several other additional complexities such as deciding which servers to download first in order to reduce memory consumptions and minimize transfer costs as well worthless or unnecessary data transfers. The techniques obtained from servers indicate there is a need to download in advance at least a list of data from one side of the server to the mobile device. Due the limitation of memory, it would be wise to use a technique that is able to utilize the minimum memory. Both response and access time are also a major concern because they may slow down the results from the query especially when the number of requesting queries is increasing.

Figure 4. Example of on mobile query processing

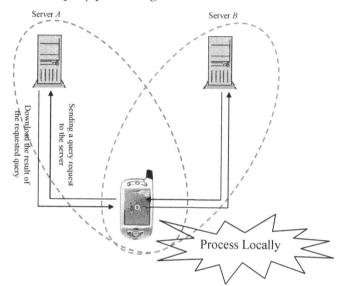

Case Study 2: Server Strategy and On-Air Strategy

There are situations when certain data are broadcast on a public wireless channel, which requires the user to tune into the broadcast channel to filter out the relevant data. Users have no control in issuing queries directly to the servers. Therefore, we are concerned with how users can efficiently obtain their specific request without being able to send a query to the servers that use the broadcasting system. In this system, by broadcasting it actually lets an arbitrary number of users access the data simultaneously. Therefore, this may be acquainted with issued of over population in accessing a particular data that may slow down the access. In other words, when encountering a multiple non-collaborative servers setting, some servers may not able to accept queries that are directly issued by the mobile users but rather provide data broadcasting.

Figure 5 illustrates an example of a server that supports data broadcast in conjunction with another server that supports direct query. Example, in order to gather data from the two non-collaborative servers, whereby one server supports data broadcast and another server supports direct query, the mobile users would need to tune into the wireless channel to obtain the desired data from the server that supports data broadcast and issue a query to the other server, which accept direct query.

When determining the on-air strategy to be used over server strategy or client strategy, one important issue is to determine an optimal broadcast sequence for the data items that are to be distributed to the mobile users. This refers to data broadcast scheduling, which one must look at in order to have minimal access time and minimal tuning time in receiving the required data items. By prioritizing the data items and using a good selection mechanism can reduce the broadcast cycle length, which eventually is able to reduce the query response time (Chung et al., 2001; Lee, Lo, & Chen, 2002). The data items can be characterized as both "hot" and "cold" and this can be the determinant of which data item should be given a higher priority over the others (Zhang & Gruenwalk, 2002).

Another alternative to the selection mechanism, in taking into account of reducing response time, is to have more than one broadcast channel

Figure 5. Example of on mobile querying broadcasted data

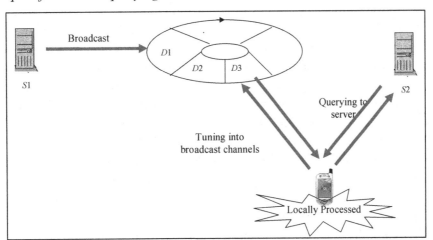

whereby the broadcast data can be distributed to more than one broadcast channel. In most cases, data items are broadcast over a single channel as it avoids additional issue of the organization of data and allocation while having more than one channel (Imielinski, Viswanathan, & Badrinath, 1997). Furthermore, the use of a single channel appears to be more problematic especially when there are a large number of data items to be broadcast, thus, with the adoption of multiple channels to broadcast data, the chance of reducing long delays before obtaining the desired data items can be achieved.

The next factor that could help reduce response time would be concerning the organization of the data items especially when retrieving multiple data items is required. An illustration of such a situation can be a mobile client wants to send a query to retrieve multiple stock prices concurrently. This is an example of multiple data items retrieval and in order to retrieve such query in a more efficient way, the need to consider the semantic relationship between the data items is required (Chung et al., 2001; Ren & Dunham, 2000). However, in order to predict which data item that the mobile client would be interested in next is difficult because

there is not much knowledge of any future query that is available. Existing related work has investigated the use of access graphs to represent the dependency of the data items (Lee et al., 2002). Other existing algorithms that have been investigated to identify the most effective organization of the data items includes heuristics algorithm (Hurson et al., 2005) and randomized algorithm (Bar-Noy, Naor, & Schieber, 2000).

The last possible deciding factor for query response time can be determined by incorporating broadcast indexing scheme. Indexing scheme can reduce tuning time for the mobile client to access their required data item (Lee, Leong, & Si, 2002). By applying this scheme, mobile clients can conserve their battery life and thus, results in energy saving because the clients can switch to "doze" mode and back to "active" mode only when he or she knows the desired data item is about to arrive.

Although the on-air strategy appears to be more scalable in comparison to the server strategy, there are still limitations that it brings to the users because most users would find it easier to send a direct request to a specific server. In addition, since the data that are being broadcast are usually open to the public, there are privacy issues that may arise. Thus, if the mobile user wants to obtain private data, they would have to rely on the server strategy rather than the on-air strategy. Therefore, by being able to incorporate strategies that are able to accommodate the request of the users to bring it more flexibility like how server strategy does for the users maybe beneficial.

Case Study 3: Server Strategy and Client Strategy

Caching frequently accessed data in a client's local storage becomes prominent in improving the performance and data availability of data access queries (Chan, Si, & Leong, 1998). This is made available by caching the frequently accessed data items in the local mobile device storage as well as when frequent disconnection occurs, the query can still be partially processed from caches and at least some of the results from the previous queries can be returned to the users (Lee et al., 2002). This is because the mobile device is able to keep the existing data and if the user needs the same exact data, the downloading can be minimized if the mobile device recognizes that the data has been previously loaded into the device. Caching at the mobile client helps in relieving the low bandwidth constraints imposed in the mobile environment (Kara & Edwards, 2003). Issues that characterize the caching mechanism would include cache granularity, cache coherence, and cache replacement.

Figure 6 shows whenever a user issues a query, it first searches its cache and if a valid copy is found in the cache, it will return the results immediately. Otherwise it can also search the client's other local cache for the required results or it can be obtained either through the server or broadcast (on-air) strategy. Thus, it is often important to have cache management because often a user may download similar data repeatedly from the same source.

In general, the main limitation that limits the ability of having to cache everything on the mobile device mainly lies on the limited memory capacity. Therefore, one of the challenges that concerns the local cache memory is to exploit algorithms that can maximize the cache capacity to reduce the repeated transfer cost as much as possible and increase the respond time to the user's queries request. As we are concerned, the existing works on caching for mobile devices are still not sufficient for the new nomadic types of queries. A vast range of existing has been greatly being done on the issue of cache replacement and

Figure 6. Example of on mobile querying with cache data

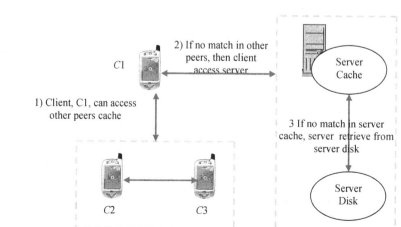

cache granularity and employing them into several possible cases in the real mobile environment situations. Index caching has been popular to save memory caching to improve query response time as well as managing space more efficiently, which is significant for location dependent queries. A few related works to this have also been done (Xu et al., 2003; Xu et al., 2004; Zheng et al., 2002). We also need to identify which mobile device has the request cache data that the other mobile users can access, as well as to make sure the cache data is still up to date before allowing the other interested users to access it (Elmargamid et al., 2003).

LOCATION DEPENDENT QUERY PROCESSING

Whenever a user moves from one location to another, the objects being queried can turn out to be different according to their geographical coordinates. Hence, location dependent plays an important role (Saltenis & Jensen, 2002; Sistla, Wolfson, Chamberlain, & Dao, 1997; Waluyo et al., 2005). It is important to show the mobile user, who is moving from one location to another location frequently, that the queries he or she

sends, depends on the location that he or she is querying from.

Figure 7 shows that when a user is in location *A,* the query results are P1, P2, P3, P4, and P5, but as he or she moves toward location *B* and send the query again, the results now are P5, P6, P7, and P8. This shows that the change of user's query results are reflected by the change of the user's location. Basically with this, two query results that are obtained from Query 1 and Query 2 respectively, the user would like to process them together on the mobile device to obtain the just the desired data.

The main problem in this location dependent are the consistency problems that may arise, especially when the database is updated in the midst of processing a query. Furthermore, in order to ensure the shortest path, whereby we will first go for the server that stored the desired results, which can be obtained faster and easier or that can be obtained nearest to our current geographical coordinate compared to obtaining from another server. So, it is crucial to ensure the mobile users are able to obtain the shortest path to the desired destination. Some other issues would involve information processing when the results of the queries are obtained from different locations. We also need to learn how we are able to select

Figure 7. Example of on mobile location dependent query processing

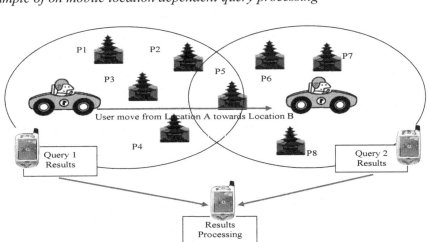

the server to perform the query that is available from different locations so that we can answer the query more efficiently and correctly.

One important issue can be illustrated as follows. For instance, there are two locations, *A* and *B*. The user has a query in mind and based on the optimization in regards to the shorter path theory, the user will need to download information from location *B* and then send to location *A* for processing. But at the moment, the user is in location *A* and is going to location *B* soon. So, if following the optimization theory, this will require the user to first go to location *B* to download the desired data, and then move back to location *A* even though the current location of the user is now in *A*. In this method, there may arise a risk; maybe by the time the user goes to location *B*, the desired item is no longer available or there may have been network congestion and so on. If this occurs, the user would waste their time going to location *B* to get the desired data. Thus, we may need a different processing method where the user can start downloading from location *A* or just the partial key until the cache is full, and then when going to location *B*, send the request to *B* to download the remaining items based on the key that is already in the cache.

For example, in Case Study 1, which involves querying to different servers that are utilizing the server strategy, it is obvious that in order to minimize the cost, we need to first download the list that has fewer records and then send it to the other server for matching. But if the location aspect is there, it might not be possible to choose which server to access first because it is dictated by the relative location. So this arises one important issue that needs to be looked at to what are the other aspect besides selecting servers that contain fewer records to be downloaded first.

Another example, based on Case Study 2, where we involve two servers in different locations, where the server in location *A* does not accept queries but the server in location *B* accepts queries. The issue may occur if the user is required to get the data from location *B* first, which accepts queries and then send to the server in location *A* that does not accept queries. This may create a problem because once we obtain the desired results from location *B* through sending a query to request the desired data, the results will then be sent to our mobile device. However, with this data, we are required to send to the server in location *A*, maybe to perform some comparison but that server does not accept queries, but only broadcasts data out to the mobile user. So our problem would be how can we then select another better technique that can reverse the situation so that we can get tune into the broadcast channel to get the data first and then only send the obtained data to the server to be process for the final results.

The last example based on Case Study 3 where caching is involved, a mobile user is currently in location *A* and wants to obtain data from location *A* before moving to location *B*. It might be a good idea while in location *A*, that the user requests the desired data from peer mobile users whether they have data from location *B* (maybe just partial), so that the user can "borrow" this data before having to personally go to location *B* to get those data. Or if they can only obtain location *B* data partially from the peer mobile user during their visit in location *A*, they can still benefit from less downloads transfer when they go to location *B* to obtain the desired data since they already have partial key, they can just request the exact information that is needed based on the partial key.

Existing related work has been done on computing the shortest path search by using compact exit hierarchy (CEH) and applying semantic location model (Lee et al., 2005), thus the issue is whether the method can be integrated into the situation when the need of combining the results with the other list of information are needed. Other previous work relates to investigating techniques in decreasing the access time and to also have the organizing time shorter especially when there are a number of updates at once and quick enough to respond to the users. Also being done in past research work about improving the consistency of data and response time for the mobile users in retrieving the required data. Since location dependent query deals with geographical coordinates of the mobile users, it is important to also look at minimizing movements of users. This refers to helping reduce the mobile user having to go back to the previous location to obtain additional data if he or she forgets when he or she was there before.

IMPLEMENTATION AND SYSTEM PROTOTYPE

We have implemented our proposed methods on a mobile environment whereby the server and mobile device architecture consists of two desktop computers, which act as servers of two different locations, and a PDA as a mobile device, which wirelessly connects to both servers. Initially the PDA is connected to one server and requests the data from that server. When the PDA is moved, it requests data from the second server. In this environment, we have simulated location-based query processing. The database in the servers uses MS SQL server, and both servers provides

the mobile device with an access to the database. We use C# programming language within the .NET framework to program our proposed methods. Initially, the development is purely done at a desktop, and without involving the PDA. The testing was done using the Pocket PC emulator, which comes with the Visual Studio .Net. Once the testing is complete, the deployment is done by transferring down the executable from PC Emulator to the real PDA through the MS Active Sync, in which it copies not only the executable program, but also the visual .Net run time

In this section, we describe a query-processing prototype that involves multiple non-collaborative servers. This prototype is built on the idea from Example 1. Basically the prototype shows a sample interface design on how the final product would appear on the mobile user's PDA. Recalling Example 1, the mobile user is interested to know all vegetarian restaurants that are available in the country he or she is currently located. The mobile user is interested in obtaining recommendations from both servers, the tourist office and the vegetarian community servers. In this prototype design, we do not incorporate any location dependent processing and we assume that the current country (location) is Australia.

Figure 8. Final output of prototype design

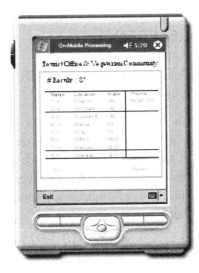

Figure 8a models the final display on the PDA for the mobile user and Figure 8b models a sample screen shot of informing user the next page is being processing.

From this prototype, we can see that it only shows the basic features, which are the results in tabular format that is simple and straightforward. This can be a limitation especially when in today's world, multimedia has emerged as an important component in human interaction. A lot of people are demanding multimedia features now due to the vast benefits on what multimedia information can bring to the mobile users. Not only does the incorporation of multimedia elements enhance the appearance and make the information more interesting, but it also gives a better interaction between the user and the device. For instance, a person who is blind may not read what is displayed on the PDA screen, but with the ability to incorporate multimedia feature, the results can be translated into "voice" talk instead of just displaying the results. This shows one importance on what multimedia information can bring around to the mobile users.

CONCLUSION AND FUTURE DIRECTION

In this article, we have presented possible applications that will be beneficial for information gathering from multiple non-collaborative sources. A brief taxonomy of the possible database operations involving multiple sources is also presented. We have also demonstrated not every server that is available in the wireless environment accepts direct queries from the users. There are some situations when the servers do not have the ability to accept direct queries and we need to process that data together with data that are obtained based on direct queries. As the wireless and mobile communication of mobile users has increased, location has become a very important constraint. A list of data obtained from different locations

brings in different contents, and hence, there is a need to efficiently make these different lists of data into a single valuable piece of information for mobile users. All the issues and limitations have been outlined accordingly to where the lists of data are obtained via server, on-air, or client strategies. A sample prototype is being designed to demonstrate where the project may be applied in real life application.

Our future work is to further investigate the gathering processing techniques to further optimize the response and the data processing that is obtained from the non-collaborative servers. Since there are several issues that arise regardless of whether the lists are obtained from the server, on-air, or client strategy, they are difficult and very challenging to overcome. Thus, further investigation on choosing the right technique for each strategy according to situations should be done individually before processing several lists that are obtained from various strategies together. In addition, individually evaluating the best technique to obtain certain lists of data from each strategy should also be done to obtain the suitable technique. It is also beneficial to explore on the issues of scalability in terms of the servers that are needed to process together maintain the same efficiency or improve efficiency even though *n* servers are involved.

REFERENCES

Bell, D., & Grimson, J. (1992). *Distributed database systems*. Addison-Wesley.

Cai, Y., & Hua, K. A. (2002). An adaptive query management technique for real-time monitoring of spatial regions in mobile database systems. In *Proceedings of 21ˢᵗ IEEE International Conference on Performance, Computing, and Communications* (pp. 259-266).

Ceri, S., & Pelagatti, G. (1984). *Distributed databases: Principles and systems*. New York: McGraw-Hill.

Chan, B. Y., Si, A., & Leong, H. V. (1998). Cache management for mobile databases: Design and evaluation. In *Proceedings of the International Conference on Data Engineering (ICDE)* (pp. 54-53).

Cheverst, K., Davies, N., Mitchell, K., & A., F. (2000). Experiences of developing and deploying a context-aware tourist guide. In *Proceedings of the 6th Annual International Conference on Mobile Computing and Networking* (pp. 20-31).

Elmargamid, A., Jing, J., Helal, A., & Lee, C. (2003). Scalable cache invalidation algorithms for mobile data access. *IEEE Transactions on Knowledge and Data Engineering, 15*(6), 1498-1511.

Gutting, R. H., Bohlen, M. H., Erwig, M., Jensen, C. S., Lorentzos, N. A., Schneider, M., & Vazierginiannis, M. (2000). A foundation for representing and querying moving objects. *ACM Transactions on Database Systems Journal, 25*(1), 1-42.

Hurson, A. R., & Jiao, Y. (2005). Data broadcasting in mobile environment. In D. Katsaros, A. Nanopoulos, & Y. Manolopaulos (Eds.), *Wireless information highways.* London: IRM Press Publisher.

Jung, II, D., You, Y. H., Lee, J. J., & Kim, K. (2002). Broadcasting and caching policies for location-dependent queries in urban areas. In *Proceedings of the of the 2nd International Workshop on Mobile Commerce* (pp. 54-59).

Kapp, S. (2002). 802.11: Leaving the wire behind. *IEEE Internet Computing, 6.*

Lee, D. K., Xu, J., Zheng, B., & Lee, W. C. (2002). Data management in location-dependent information services. *IEEE Pervasive Computing, 2*(3), 65-72, July-Sept.

Lee, D. K., Zhu, M., & Hu, H. (2005). When location-based services meet databases. *Mobile Information Systems, 1*(2), 2005.

Lee, K. C. K., Leong, H. V., & Si, A. (2002). Semantic data access in an asymmetric mobile environment. In *Proceedings of the 3rd Mobile Data Management* (pp. 94-101).

Liberatore, V. (2002). Multicast scheduling for list requests". In *Proceedings of IEEE INFOCOM Conference* (pp. 1129-1137).

Lim, S. Y., Taniar, D., & Srinivasan, B. (2006). A taxonomy of database operations on mobile devices. *Handbook of Research on Mobile Multimedia*, accepted for publication, 2006.

Lo, E., Mamoulis, N., Cheung, D. W., Ho, W. S., & Kalnis, P. (2003). In *Processing ad-hoc joins on mobile devices*. Technical report, The University of Hong Kong (2003). Retrieved from http://www.csis.hku.hk/~dbgroup/techreport

Madria, S. K., Bhargava, B., Pitoura, E., & Kumar, V. (2000). Data organisation for location-dependent queries in mobile computing. In *Proceedings of ADBIS-DASFAA* (pp. 142-156).

Malladi, R., & Davis, K. C. (2002). Applying multiple query optimization in mobile databases. In *Proceedings of the 36th Hawaii International Conference on System Sciences* (pp. 294-303).

Mamoulis, N., Kalnis, P., Bakiras, S., & Li, X. (2003). Optimization of spatial joins on mobile devices. In *Proceedings of the SSTD.*

Myers, B. A., & Beigl M. (2003). Handheld computing. *IEEE Computer Magazine, 36*(9), 27-29.

Özsu, M. T., & Valduriez, P. (1999). Principles of distributed database systems (2nd ed.). Prentice Hall.

Ozakar, B., Morvan, F., & Hameurlain, A. (2005). Mobile join operators for restricted sources. *Mobile Information Systems, 1*(3).

Ren, Q., & Dunham, M. H. (2000). Using semantic caching to manage location-dependent data in mobile computing. In *Proceedings of the 6th*

International Conference on Mobile Computing and Networking (pp. 210-221).

Seydim, A.Y., Dunham, M. H., & Kumar, V. (2001). Location-dependent query processing. In *Proceedings of the 2nd International Workshop on Data Engineering on Mobile and Wireless Access (MobiDE'01)* (pp. 47-53).

Si, A., & Leong, H. V. (1999). Query optimization for broadcast database. *Data and Knowledge Engineering, 29*(3), 351-380.

Sistla, A. P., Wolfson, O., Chamberlain, S., & Dao, S. (1997). Modeling and querying moving objects. In *Proceedings of the 13th International Conference on Data Engineering* (pp. 422-432).

Saltenis, S., & Jensen, C. S. (2002). Indexing of moving objects for location-based services. *Proceedings of ICDE* (pp. 463-472).

Song, M., Kang, S. W., & Park, K. (2005). On the design of energy-efficient location tracking mechanism in location-aware computing. *Mobile Information Systems, 1*(2), 109-127.

Tran, D. A., Hua, K. A., & Jiang, N. (2001). A generalized design for broadcasting on multiple physical-channel air-cache. In *Proceedings of the ACM SIGAPP Symposium on Applied Computing (SAC'01)* (pp. 387-392).

Triantafillou, P., Harpantidou, R., & Paterakis, M. (2001). High performance data broadcasting: A comprehensive systems "perspective." In *Proceedings of the 2nd International Conference on Mobile Data Management (MDM 2001)* (pp. 79-90).

Tsalgatidou, A., Veijalainen, J., Markkula, J., Katasonov, A., & Hadjiefthymiades, S. (2003). Mobile e-commerce and location-based services: Technology and requirements. In *Proceedings*

of the 9th Scandinavian Research Conference on Geographical Information Services (pp. 1-14).

Tse ,P. K. C., Lam, W. K., Ng, K. W., & Chan, C. (2005). An implementation of location-aware multimedia information download to mobile system. *Journal of Mobile Multimedia, 1*(1), 33-46.

Waluyo, A. B., Srinivasan, B., & Taniar, D. (2005). Research on location-dependent queries in mobile databases. *International Journal of Computer Systems Science & Engineering, 20*(3), 77-93, March.

Wolfson, O. (2002). Moving objects information management: The database challenge. In *Proceedings of the 5th Workshop on Next Generation Information Technology and Systems (NGITS)* (pp. 75-89).

Xu, J., Hu, Q., Lee, W. C., & Lee, D. L. (2004). Performance evaluation of an optimal cache replacement policy for wireless data dissemination. *IEEE Transaction on Knowledge and Data Engineering (TKDE), 16*(1), 125-139.

Xu, J., Tang, X., & Lee, D. L. (2003). Performance analysis of location-dependent cache invalidation schemes for mobile environments. *IEEE Transactions on Knowledge and Data Engineering (TKDE), 15*(2), 474-488.

Xu, J., Zheng, B., Lee, W. C., & Lee, D. L. (2003). Energy efficient index for querying location-dependent data in mobile broadcast environments. *Proceedings of the 19th IEEE International Conference on Data Engineering (ICDE '03)* (pp. 239-250).

Zheng, B., Xu, J., Lee, D. L. (2002). Cache invalidation and replacement strategies for location-dependent data in mobile environments. *IEEE Transactions on Computers, 51*(10), 1141-1153.

This work was previously published in International Journal of Business Data Communications and Networking, Vol. 3, Issue 2, edited by J. Gutierrez, pp. 72-93 , copyright 2007 by IGI Publishing, formerly known as Idea Group Publishing (an imprint of IGI Global).

Chapter IX
Network Planning Algorithms for Optimizing Signalling Load in Mobile Networks

Vilmos Simon
Budapest University of Technology and Economics, Hungary

Sándor Imre
Budapest University of Technology and Economics, Hungary

ABSTRACT

In the next generation IP-based mobile networks, one of the most important QoS parameters are the delay and the delay variation. The cell handover causes incremental signaling traffic, which can be critical from the point of view of delay variation. It worsens the quality parameters of the real-time services, which are the backbone of next generation mobile commercial services. We have designed and implemented two algorithms: a location area forming algorithm (LAFA) and a cell regrouping algorithm (CEREAL), which can help us to guarantee QoS parameters in the next generation mobile networks. We used our realistic mobile environment simulator to generate input statistics on cell changes and incoming call for our algorithms and by comparing the values of the cost functions proposed by us, we recognized that significant reduction was achieved in the amount of the signaling traffic, the location update cost was decreased by 40-60% in average. To confirm the results obtained by the realistic mobile environment simulator, a vehicular mobility simulator was used for generating the input to the algorithms for realistic vehicle mobility behavior. The same was recognized, that by employing our LA forming schemes, a significant reduction was attained in the signalling traffic that causes delay and delay variation, helping us improving QoS parameters in general.

INTRODUCTION

Signalling delay and the delay variation are very important service quality parameters of the next generation, IP based mobile networks. The cell handovers in mobile networks causes an incremental signalling message overhead (Akyildiz, Mcnair, Ho, Uzunalioglu, and Wang, 1998), which affects the delay variation and it is critical in the case of timing-sensitive real-time media applications. The signalling overhead is caused because the location information of a mobile is maintained by registration (Wong & Leung, 2000), where the mobile terminals update their location area information to their home agents (Location Management). The determination of the location of the user is also important, because the demand of mobile Location Dependent Information Services (LDIS) has fueled in recent years. (Jayaputera & Taniar, 2005) proposed a new approach to generate a query result for Location-Dependent Information Services. Another scope is when the users location moves from one base station to another and the queries cross multi-cells, (Jayaputera & Taniar, 2005) gave an approach of mobile query processing in these situations.

The determination of the optimal number of cells in each location area (LA) is a very important task, but the optimal partition of cells into LAs is an NP-hard problem. There was an important contribution in the determination of the optimal number of cells in an LA (Saraydar, Kelly, and Rose, 2000), but they were not focusing on the selection of the optimal set of cells for each LA. Therefore we propose a solution to obtain the optimal partition of cells for every LA.

The location area structure means that we can join several cells into one administrative unit, so-called location area, and in this way the cell border crossings inside this domain will be hidden for the upper hierarchical levels. Signalling overhead will be produced only when we cross a domain border, but that is rarer than a cell handover, thus the traffic of signalling messages will be reduced (Cayirci & Akyildiz, 2003).

The question arises: What size the LA should be? Both, increasing and decreasing the size have their own benefit. On the one hand if we join more and more cells into one LA, then the number of LA handovers will be smaller, so the number of location update messages sent to the upper levels will decrease. However in the case of numerous cells belonging to a single LA, an incoming call will cause lots of paging messages (Zhang, Castellanos, and Campbell, 2002), since we must send one to every cell to find where is the mobile user inside that LA. That will increase the load of base stations.

On the other hand if we decrease the number of cells, then we do not need to send so many paging messages (hereby we will load less links and the processing time will decrease, too), but then the number of LA changes will increase.

Accordingly we must search for the optimal compromise between these two conflicting aspects (Kameda & Li, 2000).

The LA management is classified according to its use of time, distance, movement profile information in its paging and location update procedures. The location update can be performed due to the time elapsed since the last registration process (Jun & Ho) or the number of cell boundary crossings measured since the previous update (Tsai & Hsiao, 2001). (Wong & Leung, 2001) recommend a distance-based scheme, where the location update will be performed, when a mobile user moves a threshold number of cells away from the cell where the last registration process was carried out. The hybrid of distance-based and zone-based is studied by (Casares-Giner & Mataix-Oltra, 2002). (Bar-Noy, Kessler, and Sidi, 1995) have compared time-, distance-, and movement based schemes in terms of location management cost, and they have shown that the distance-based one performs best. However, its implementation is hard since the distance of the mobile terminal has to be computed dynamically as it moves from cell to cell.

In this paper we propose a zone-based LA solution, since they are used in all the deployed cellular mobile systems.

Our aim was to decrease the amount of administrative messages, so we designed an LA forming algorithm (LAFA) based on the statistical probabilities of the moving directions (Simon, Huszák, Szabó, and Imre, 2003) chosen by the mobile users. We have implemented this graph algorithm, using the cell border crossing probabilities as input. We propose a mobility simulator developed by us, for the generation of a realistic border crossing and incoming call pattern as an input for our algorithm. Furthermore we propose a cell regrouping algorithm (CEREAL), too, for a refinement optimization, using an error function defined for the LA partitions, which was produced by the LA forming algorithm. The implemented program calculates the cost functions (see Section 5) of the random and of our LA forming algorithm, in the function of the paging and location update importance weights.

This paper is organized as follows: the mathematical description of our paging and location update cost function is introduced in Section 2. The LAFA is presented in Section 3. In Section 4 we give the CEREAL for the optimal refinement, while in Section 5 our results are shown and discussed. In Section 6 we draw conclusions.

COST STRUCTURE

Most of the references (Madhow, Honig, and Steiglitz 1995), (Xie, Tabbane, and Goodman 1993) related to the location area design are focused on how to determine the optimal number of cells for an LA. In this paper we presented an algorithm which can give us the optimal partition of cells into LAs.

Although there had been earlier attempts to optimize location update cost or paging cost or a combination of them in (Akyildiz, Ho, and Lin 1996), (Abutaleb & Li, 1997), (Merchant & Sen-

gupta, 1995) however the aspect of minimizing the location update cost with a heuristic algorithm (LA forming algorithm) first, and after using that basic partition as an input to a regrouping algorithm, which will minimize the aggregated cost function, was not considered there. So, we have split this complex problem into two sub problems to optimize the location update cost and the aggregated cost, one after another. We defined the location and paging cost functions differently than in the above mentioned related works, because of the handling of the two sub problems.

The Paging Cost Function

On the arrival of an incoming call, the mobile switching center sends a paging message to every base station under its control, in order to find out the called mobile terminal (MT) (Bhattacharje, Saha, and Mukherjee, 2004). So each cell in the given LA will carry all the paging traffic associated with the called MTs within that LA. In order to characterize a network configuration we define a paging cost function for the lth LA by which we can describe the bandwidth seized by the paging operations in a given interval:

$$C_{p_l} = \sum_{i=1}^{K} N \cdot \lambda_i \cdot B_p \, , \qquad (1)$$

where

- N is the number of cells in the given l^{th} LA
- λ_i is the incoming call rate to the given i^{th} MT
- B_p is the paging cost
- K is the number of MTs in the lth LA

With equation (1) we can determine cost of the traffic induced by paging messages for a given LA, generated by the incoming calls in the given interval. The total paging cost for the LAs in our system:

$$C_p = \sum_{l=1}^{M} C_{p_{ll}} = \sum_{l=1}^{M} \sum_{i=1}^{K} N \cdot \lambda_i \cdot B_p = \sum_{l=1}^{M} N \cdot B_p \cdot \sum_{i=1}^{K} \lambda_i$$

$$(2)$$

where M is the number of LAs in our system.

Location Update Cost Function

We define a location update cost function for our network, which will help us to determine the LA handovers caused by the mobile users crossing the LA boundary (Chiussi, Khotimsky, and Krishnan, 2002), which generates additional location update traffic, namely they need to inform their home agents about their new location (Akyildiz, Mcnair, Ho, Uzunalioglu, and Wang, 1999).

The location update cost for the kth LA:

$$C_{lu_k} = B_{lu} \cdot \sum_{j=1}^{B} q_j ,$$

$$(3)$$

where:

- B_{lu} is the cost required for transmitting a location update message
- q_j is the intensity of cell boundary crossings on the jth boundary
- B is the number of the exterior cell border-lines

The total location update cost for the LAs in our system:

$$C_{lu} = \sum_{l=1}^{M} C_{lu_k} = \sum_{l=1}^{M} B_{lu} \cdot \sum_{j=1}^{B} q_j ,$$

$$(4)$$

where M is the number of LAs in our system.

Our final goal is to maximize the intra-domain traffic, because in this way we can decrease the number of the LA handovers, and therefore the total amount of administrative messages. We can reduce the number of handovers by joining the cells, along the dominant moving directions. This LA forming principle will be introduced in the Section 3.

To evaluate the algorithms we need the minimized expectation value of the aggregated cost function, with variable weight factors, which takes into consideration both aspects of forming LAs:

$$\min E \left\{ w_1 \cdot C_p + w_2 \cdot C_{lu} \right\}$$

$$(5)$$

On the basis of the importance of paging or rather location update cost, we can use different weights, and in that way we can dynamically vary the sizing based on the actual point of view and the required QoS parameters.

Because of the expectation value is a homogeneous linear operator, the Equation (5) expression becomes:

$$\min \left(w_1 \cdot E \left\{ C_p \right\} + w_2 \cdot E \left\{ C_{lu} \right\} \right)$$

$$(6)$$

THE LOCATION AREA FORMING ALGORITHM (LAFA)

We model our network with the $G(V, E)$ graph, where the cells are the graph nodes $v \in V$, and the cell border crossing directions are represented by the edges $e \in E$ of the graph (see Figure 1).

Definitions

- If $\{v_1, v_2\} \in E$ then the cells represented by v_1 and v_2 are adjacent.
- If $\{v_1, v_2\}$ and $\{m_1, m_2\}$ are the end points of $e, f \in E$, and $\{v_1, v_2\} \cap \{m_1, m_2\} \neq 0$, then the cell border crossing directions e, f are adjacent.
- If the set of nodes of graph F is consistent with the set of nodes of graph G and the edges of graph F are an acyclic subset of edges of graph G, the graph F is the spanning tree of the graph G.
- If the weight function $c : E \rightarrow \Re$ is defined on the edges and the sum of its edge weights is maximal among the spanning trees of

Figure 1. The representation of the mobile system by a graph

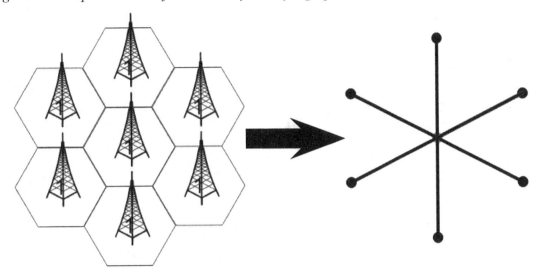

graph G, the graph F is the maximum weight spanning tree of the graph G.

The Algorithm

A moving direction matrix can be defined to every cell, which contains the statistical probabilities of the moving directions chosen by the mobile users, when they step across the cell borders. This mobility pattern database can be obtained by measurements, which is attainable for the mobile operators. In our case we have developed a mobility simulator (Section 5), which serves us a realistic cell boundary crossing and incoming call pattern as an input to our algorithms.

We define weights to the edges of the graph G, not negative real numbers in the range [0,1], based on the probability matrix, namely the weight of the edges is consistent with the cell border crossing probabilities.

We must divide graph $G(V, E)$ into subgraphs $G(V, E)$, so that the subgraphs contain the maximum weight spanning tree. The set of edges of those maximum weight spanning trees will give us the cell groups which compose the LAs.

Starting from the $s = 1$ initial point, we choose from edges joint to the node s, the one, which has

the biggest weight (c_{max}), if there is more than one biggest weight, then we choose one of them randomly and include it into the set of edges L_1 ($L_1 = \{e_1\}$) (Figure 2). The two nodes connected by this edge are included into set $U_1 = \{s_1, v_1\}$. In the next step, we search for the second largest weight (if there is more than one, we choose it in the same way as in the first step), and we examine those two nodes belong to the U_1 set. If both are in the set V/U_1, then the edge, which connects them, is included into the L_2 set of edges ($L_{21} = \{e_2\}$) and the two belonging nodes into the set U_2. If one of them is in the set U_1, then we must make an evaluation step.

We must check if inequality

$$\frac{c_m}{\frac{1}{n} \cdot \sum_{i=1}^{n} c_i} > K \qquad (7)$$

is satisfied, where c_m is the weight of the examined edge, and c_i are the weights of edges in the U_1 set. K is the lower bound, given by us. If the inequality is satisfied, the edge can be included into this set ($L_1 = \{e_1, e_2\}$). If the inequality is not satisfied, this edge can not be included into this set, namely the cell which is represented with this node, can

Figure 2. Joining the two nodes (cells) into one set (LA)

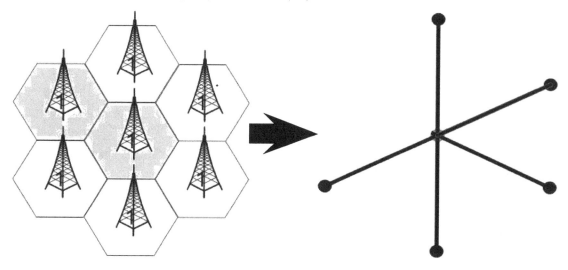

not be joint into this LA. Another upper bound can be used, we can give the maximum number of cells in one LA.

In this way we can join the cells which are in the same dominant moving directions, so the number of domain handovers can be decreased (highways, footpaths, etc.).

We run this algorithm until we get the U_i partition of nodes V, so this partition will give us the groupings of cells into clusters, namely the D_i location areas.

THE CELL REGROUPING ALGORITHM (CEREAL)

The partition of cells is an NP-hard problem, therefore we propose a heuristic algorithm. Therefore we have developed a regrouping algorithm, which would help us to refine the cell grouping in cases when it is necessary.

Definitions

- For cell i, $Y_i = (Y_1, Y_2)$ is a two dimensional probability variable, where $Y_{i1} = q_{iF}$, q_{iF} is the border crossing intensity of the cell i

and $Y_{i2} = \sum_{j=1}^{N} \lambda_j$, where λ_j is the expectation value of the incoming call distribution, and

N is the number of the mobile terminals in the cell i.

- The LAFA gives us a partition of cells $\{D_1, D_2, ..., D_M\}$ in location areas, where M is the number of areas in our mobile system. Then $Y = \bigcup_{i=1}^{M} D_i$ and $D_i \cap D_j = 0$, if $i \neq j$.

The Algorithm

If $|D_i|$ is the number of cells in the given D_i location area, then we can define the center of the area by

$$\overline{D_i} = \frac{1}{|D_i|} \sum_{Y_l \in D_i} Y_l . \tag{8}$$

We can define the distance of the Y_j cell from the D_i location area as

$$d\left(Y_j, D_i\right) = d\left(Y_j, \overline{D_i}\right) = \left(\sum_{l=1}^{2} \left(Y_j - \overline{D_l}\right)^2 \right)^{1/2} . \tag{9}$$

A very important parameter in our regrouping algorithm will be the error function of our location area system

$$W(D_1,...D_M) = \sum_{i=1}^{M} \sum_{Y_j \in D_i} d^2(Y_j, D_i). \qquad (10)$$

Our goal is to minimize the error function by transposing the cells into adjacent location areas, and by this we can reduce the distances among them, what will result in a significant reduction of location update and paging costs.

Steps:

1. The calculation of the initial area centers and the initial error function ($\overline{D}_i$, $W(D)$)

2. For the first cell (Y_1) and the adjacent location areas (D_i), given by our location area forming algorithm, we calculate:

$$\Delta(D_i, Y_1) = \frac{|D_i| \cdot d^2(Y_1, D_i)}{|D_i| + 1} - \frac{|D(Y_1)| \cdot d^2(Y_1, D(Y_1))}{|D(Y_1)| - 1} \qquad (11)$$

where $D(Y_i)$ is the location area, which contains the Y_i cell.

We can prove that if we re-group the Y_1 cell from the $D(Y_i)$ location area to the D_i area, the error function of our location area system will change by exactly $\Delta(D_i, Y_1)$.

So if

$$\min_{\substack{1<i<M' \\ D_i \neq D(Y_1)}} \Delta(D_i, Y_1) = \Delta(D_k, Y_1) < 0, \qquad (12)$$

where M' is the number of the location areas which are adjacent with cell Y_1, then we transpose the cell Y_1 from location area $D(Y_1)$ to D_k.

Calculate the new location area centers and add the $\Delta(D_k, Y_1)$ to the former error function value.

3. Iterate the 2nd step for every Y_1.

4. If there are no more cells to transpose, we can stop, otherwise repeat step 2.

This regrouping algorithm will give us the final LA partition, which will minimize the inter LA movement, and by this the signalling load, too.

QUANTITATIVE ANALYSIS

Optimal partition of cells into LA-s is an NP-hard problem, so we could give only a quantitative analysis of the problem and evaluate our algorithm with a mobility simulator in two different mobility environments.

In this section we will present our cost evaluation results, using the mobility simulator, as an input generator for our algorithms. The simulator produces cell changing and incoming call statistics, which are used to run our algorithms and to calculate the cost functions.

The Mobility Simulator

We developed a simulator (see screenshot in Figure 3), which will give us a realistic cell boundary crossing and incoming call database in a given mobile system, as an input to our algorithms. In the simulator we can give an arbitrary road grid, covered by cells of different size (for example WLAN, UMTS, GSM cell). We can choose between mobile terminals of different velocities, and we can give the incoming call arrival parameter to every mobile.

This way we can design different types of mobility environments (rural environment with highways or a densely populated urban environment with roads and carriageways), and grids of cells adapted to these environments. The mobile terminals will move on that road grid, choosing randomly a point on the road, just like in a real life. Because in everyday action the mobile users typically move to manage their duty tasks or entertainment (for example workplace, school, cinema, bank), and they want to arrive there in the shortest time, so we implemented the Dijkstra's algorithm, to find the shortest path of mobile terminals to their

Figure 3. A designed urban environment in our mobility simulator, with a road grid covered by cells

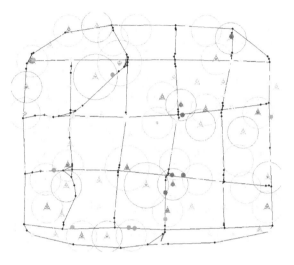

wanted destination. For every mobile terminal an incoming call arrival parameter is defined. When a call arrives to the mobile, the program assigns it to the cell where the mobile is in that moment. It is the same case when a mobile terminal changes a cell, the simulator register the cell's identifier in the base station transition matrix. On the end of the simulation; we get a cell boundary crossing and an incoming call distribution for every cell in our system.

With this database, which is a good representation of the mobility patterns in real life, we can run our LA forming algorithm, and evaluate it by the defined location update cost function (4).

Simulation Results

We compared the performance of a random LA partition and the LA forming algorithm, by using two typical mobility environments.

We designed a rural and an urban mobility environment in our mobility simulator, the first one is rarely populated, but on the belonging highways a big number of mobile terminals are moving with high speeds, while the second environment is densely populated, with mobile terminals moving

with smaller velocities. In the rural environment the average cell size is larger then in the urban, accordingly there is a smaller number of cells. We run the simulation on a moderate sized example network, the rural mobile system consisted of 99 base stations, while in the urban system was about 123 base stations. Then we stored the output of the simulation, namely a cell boundary crossing matrix (base station transition matrix) and the incoming call distribution for every cell. This database was the input of our LA forming program, which designed a LA partition for both mobility environments.

1. **Employing only the LAFA:** Based on these LA partitions, we computed the location update cost (in total number of handovers between the LAs in the simulation period), and we computed the same cost for a randomly designed LA partition, where we can give the number of cells in one LA, and then the program designs an LA partition. It is important to point out, that the randomly designed LA do not mean that the cells are joined by a random way, the cells joined to the same LA are on the dominant moving directions, so the random LA-s can be considered as a planed partition, but not the optimal one. So the results are compared to these planed structures, not to haphazard partitions.

For the rural environment the results of the simulation are given in Figure 4, where the Upper Bound of LA axis represent the number of cells given in the random design or rather the additional upper bound of cells which was given in the LAFA, when Equation (7) is satisfied. In Figure 4 the location update cost decreases as the upper bound becomes higher, but then the paging cost will increase, too. So in the random partition we can decrease the location update cost if we increase the size of the LAs, but then the paging cost will be a serious problem. A significant advantage of the LAFA is that it reduces the location update cost very significantly, by not increasing the number of cells in one LA, so the paging cost can be kept on a lower level. In the

Figure 4. The location update cost in rural environment, in random and algorithmically partition

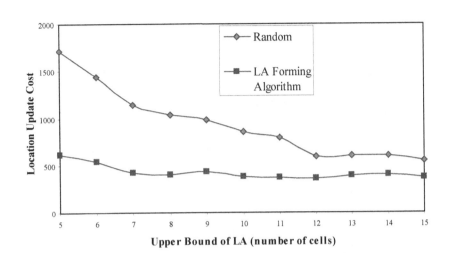

domain of 5-10 cells in an LA, our new scheme reduces the inter LA traffic by 40-60 percents on the average.

In Figure 5 the results for the urban environment can be seen. It is very similar to the rural, however the location update cost is remarkably reduced, without increasing the paging signalling load. The decrease is very significant in the interval of five to eleven cells. In the interval between 12 and 15, does mean that by increasing the number of cells the location update cost does not decrease, but the Equation(7) is not satisfied so the algorithmic LAs are already finished, so the cost does not change.

Another simulation was done to investigate the effect of the value of parameter K (7), which can be dynamically modified, depending on the model we want to deploy. It changes in the (0,1) interval, as it converges to 1, the size of the LA-s are decreasing, so we expected that the location update cost will increase significantly as the parameter K increases. The Figure 6 shows the results obtained in the rural environment, as the value of parameter K is increasing, the location update cost of the random partition is increasing too, the cost of the LAFA is not increasing till $K = 0.5$ value, but after it follows the cost of the

random partition. So the algorithm outperforms the random partition in every value of parameter K, especially for the lower values that are characteristic for our algorithm. The minimum of the location update cost is reached for the value 0.4 of parameter K.

In the urban environment the results are more effective, the cost of the LAFA is lower by 30-40% (see Figure 7), depending on the value of parameter K. The minimum is reached in at value of 0.5 of parameter K.

2. **Employing both algorithms:** We examined what will happen if we employ our regrouping algorithm on the initial partitioning obtained by the LAFA. We measured the total cost, the sum of the location update and paging cost versus the value of parameter K which was employed in the LAFA.

Figure 8 shows the total cost in the rural environment. It can be seen that in the case of the total cost the effect of increasing the value of parameter K is just the opposite of that in case of the location update cost. The reason is that by increasing the value of parameter K, the size of the LA-s is getting smaller, so the paging cost is decreasing significantly. So the LAFA is not so effective anymore, but the CEREAL is still out-

Figure 5. The location update cost in urban environment, in random and algorithmically partition

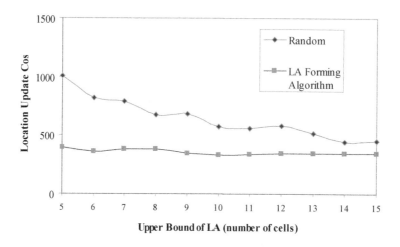

Figure 6. The location update cost versus the value of parameter K (rural)

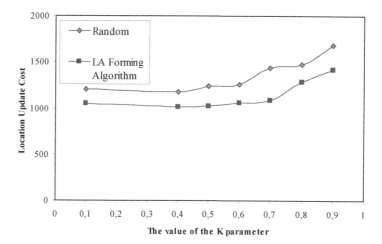

Figure 7. The location update cost versus the value of parameter K (urban)

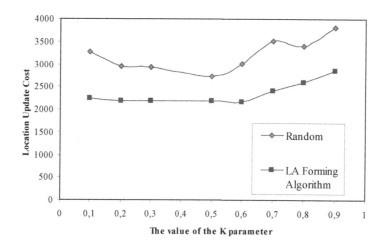

performing the other two partitioning methods significantly, in some cases over 50%.

The Figure 9 shows the total cost versus K parameter in the urban environment. It is the same case, the CEREAL decreases the amount of the total cost by 30-40%, and it does not depend on the value of parameter K.

Depending on our objective we can deploy either the LA forming algorithm or the regrouping algorithm. If we want to decrease the location update cost, the LA forming algorithm is the solution, however if we want to decrease the total cost, we need to employ the regrouping algorithm.

QUANTITATIVE ANALYSIS RESULTS USING THE VEHICULAR MOBILITY SIMULATOR

To confirm the results obtained by the mobility simulator, we used a vehicular mobility simulator for generating the input metrics for the LA forming and regrouping algorithm. This is an extendable JAVA mobility simulator that can simulate the behaviour of mobile users on a given street plan in a realistic way, using an extended version of the Nagel-Schreckenberg model (Nagel & Shreckenberg, 1992). The environment physically limits the

Figure 8. The total cost versus the value of parameter K (rural)

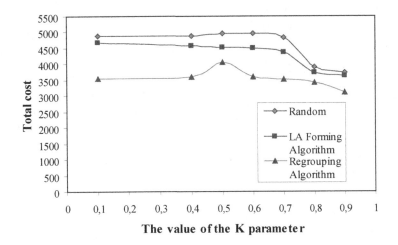

Figure 9. The total cost versus the value of parameter K (urban)

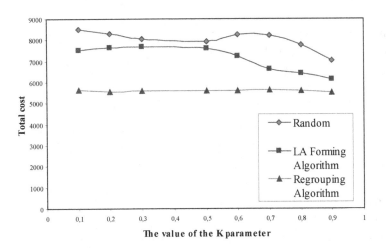

freedom of users (e.g. cars, trains), they can only move inside certain areas and react to the changing environment and the behaviour of other vehicles. For example, if a car approaches a traffic jam at a junction, it has to slow down and eventually stop. Every other car on the same road is affected by this: they have to slow down or stop as well. In this way, the simulator can, to a certain extent, mimic real vehicular movements in a (semi-) urban environment. The mobility simulator applies the Dijkstra algorithm for every vehicle to determine the path to their destination. The cost of each road is determined by its length, its speed limit and the number of vehicles on it. In this way, the main roads with higher speed limit will be preferred. Additionally, in case of a traffic jam, the vehicles will try to avoid this congested road and choose an alternative road to get to their destination. At the beginning of the simulation, the vehicles are placed on the map and will be assigned a given call arrival intensity, a destination and a maximum speed. After the simulation, cell change and call arrival intensity matrices will be produced and fed to the LA forming algorithm.

We compared the performance of the reference LA partition (already introduced) and the LA forming algorithm, by using two typical mobility environments for urban areas (two urban environments, see Figure 10).

In the Manhattan city model, two roads (bold) have a higher speed limit, which makes them more attractive for drivers. Each junction has traffic lights in order to avoid dead locks. In the European city model, the inner ring (bold) is more likely to be chosen as destination. This represents the morning rush hour situation where people converge to work in the city centre.

Furthermore, four classes of traffic conditions were defined ranging from low to high average vehicle density and from low to high call arrival rate per vehicle (Poisson distribution, calls per hour) (Table 1). Note that during the simulation, the local vehicle density will be much higher, especially in the area around junctions. A number

Figure 10. The Manhattan city model and the European city model with main roads in bold

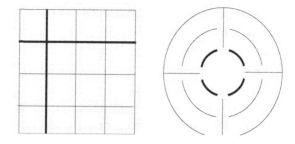

of cells with diameter of 0.78 km were deployed on the city map, such that coverage was total.

A) Employing only the LAFA: Once the LA partitions have been determined, the location update cost was computed (in total number of handovers between the LAs in the simulation period), and the same cost was computed for the reference LA partition, where the number of cells in one LA were predefined. The value for the lower bound K was set to 0.5.

For the European city model the results of the simulation are given in Figure 11, where the call arrival and MT density axis represent the four classes, combining the two means of call arrival rate and two different vehicle densities. Obviously, the more vehicles in the environment, the higher the total LA update cost for the network. Figure 11 shows that the LA forming algorithm can significantly reduce the location update cost, even in high call arrival rate.

In Figure 12 the results for the Manhattan city model are depicted. Again, the location update cost is remarkably reduced, but not so significantly as

Table 1. Mobility simulation parameters

	Vehicle density		Call arrival rate (λ)	
	Manh.	*Euro.*	*Manh.*	*Euro.*
Class I	0.5%	0.4%	1	1
Class II	0.5%	0.4%	8	8
Class III	3.3%	2.8%	1	1
Class IV	3.3%	2.8%	8	8

Figure 11. The location update cost for the European city model

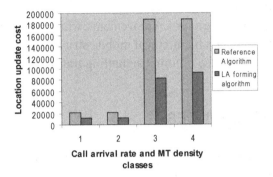

Figure 12. The location update cost for the Manhattan city model

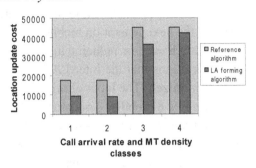

Figure 13. The total cost for the European city model

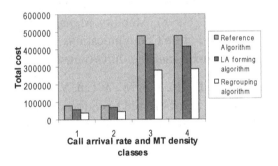

Figure 14. The total cost for the Manhattan city model

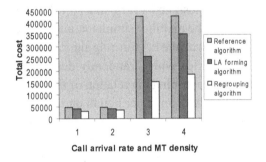

in the previous model. Due to the Manhattan grid pattern, the vehicles have much more alternative routes to choose from. This increases the total number of LA changes and the LA update cost.

B) Employing both algorithms: We have examined what will happen if the regrouping algorithm is employed on the initial partitioning obtained by the LA forming algorithm. We measured the total cost, the sum of the location update and paging cost, for the four classes.

Figure 13 shows the total cost for European city model. The LA forming algorithm is not so effective any more (because it is developed for reducing the location update cost, not the total cost), but the regrouping algorithm is still outperforming the other two partitioning methods significantly, in some cases more than 40%.

In the Figure 14 the Manhattan city model total cost is displayed. Again, the regrouping algorithm proves to be very effective in reducing the signalling cost.

One the end the conclusion is the same like in the case, when we used the mobility simulator, if the objective is to decrease the location update cost, the LA forming algorithm is the solution, however if we want to decrease the total signalling cost, we need to employ the regrouping algorithm.

CONCLUSIONS

An important benefit of optimized LA planning is preventing needless radio resource usage (Demirkol, Ersoy, Caglayan, and Delic 2004), but the most important is that we can support global QoS parameters, like signalling delay and delay variation, which can be critical in time sensitive services of the next generation mobile systems.

It can be achieved by reducing the signalling cost, which means that the inter LA movement must be minimized. The input of this algorithm was obtained by a mobility simulator developed by us that produces network information (base station transition matrix, incoming call distribution to every cell) in a realistic manner. We also proposed a cell regrouping algorithm, which uses the LA partitions obtained by our algorithm, like an initial step.

To evaluate the performance of our new scheme, we designed a rural and an urban environment in the mobility simulator, and with this database we run the LA forming algorithm. Then we compared it with a randomly designed LA structure, examining the relation of the location update cost with an upper bound on the number of cells.

The simulation results show that the LA forming technique reduces the location update cost by 40-60 percents. The regrouping algorithm performs well if we want to decrease the total cost of our system, it can reduce the total cost by 30-40%, sometimes over 50%. We recognized, by comparing the random algorithm and our LA forming one that a significant reduction was attained in the signalling traffic that causes delay and delay variation, helping us improving QoS parameters in general. To confirm the results obtained by the mobility simulator, we used a vehicular mobility simulator for generating the input to the algorithms (base station transition matrix, incoming call distribution to every cell) for realistic vehicle mobility behavior. On the end we get the same results like in the previous case.

Due to the difficulty of the problem our future research plan is to use simulated annealing to obtain the optimal LA partitions, in reasonable running times. In this case we will examine the minimization of the location update cost, subject

to the paging cost, as an inequality constraint (using constrained optimization). Another research direction is to develop an optimization algorithm based on the inter-LA movements, which will help us to plan a hierarchical mobile structure which results in the minimal signalling traffic.

REFERENCES

Abutaleb, A., & Li, V. O. K. (1997). Paging Strategy Optimization in Personal Communication Systems. *Wireless Networks, 3,* 195-204. Amsterdam, The Netherlands: Baltzer.

Akyildiz, F., Mcnair, J., Ho J., Uzunalioglu, H., & Wang, W. (1998). Mobility Management in Current and Future Communications Networks. *IEEE Network Magazine,* July/August.

Akyildiz, I. F., Ho, J. S. M., & Lin, Y. B. (1996, August). Movement Based Location Update and Selective Paging for PCS Network. *IEEE/ACM Trans. Networking, 4*(4), 629-638.

Akyildiz, I. F., Mcnair, J., Ho, J. S. M., Uzunalioglu, H., & Wang, W. (1999). Mobility Management in Next Generation Wireless Systems. *Proc. IEEE, 87*(8), 1347-1385.

Bar-Noy, A., Kessler, I., & Sidi, M. (1995, July). Mobile users: To update or not to update?. *Wireless Networks, 1*(2), 175-185.

Bhattacharje, P. S., Saha, D., & Mukherjee, A. (2004, July). An Approach for Location Area Planning in a Personal Communication Services Network (PCSN). *IEEE Transactions on Wireless Communications, 3*(4), 1176-1187.

Casares-Giner, V., & Mataix-Oltra, J. (2002, May). Global Versus Distance-Based Local Mobility Tracking Strategies: A Unified Approach. *IEEE Trans.Veh.Technol., 51,* 472-485.

Cayirci, E., & Akyildiz, I. F. (2003). Optimal Location Area Design to Minimize Registration

Signalling Traffic in Wireless Systems. *IEEE Transactions on Mobile Computing*, 2(1), January-March.

Chiussi, F. M., Khotimsky, D. A., & Krishnan, S. (2002, September). Mobility Management in Third-Generation All-IP Networks. *IEEE Communications Magazine*, *40*(9), 124-135.

Demirkol, I., Ersoy, C., & Caglayan ,M. U., Delic, H. (2004, May). Location Area Planning and Cell-to-Switch Assignment in Cellular Networks. *IEEE Transactions on Wireless Communications*, *3*(3), 880-890.

Jayaputera, J., & Taniar, D. (2005). Query Processing Strategies for Location-Dependent Information Services. *International Journal of Business Data Communications and Networking*, vol. 1, no. 2, pp. 17-40

Jayaputera, J., & Taniar, D. (2005). Data Retrieval for Location-Dependent Query in a Multi-cell Wireless Environment. *Mobile Information Systems: An International Journal*, IOS Press, *1*(2), 91-108.

Jun, L. D., & Ho, C. D. On Optimum Timer Value of Area and Timer–Based Location Registration Scheme. *IEEE Commun. Letters*, 5, 1106-1110.

Li, J., Kameda, H., & Li, K. (2000, June). Optimal Dynamic Mobility Management for PCS Networks. *IEEE/ACM Trans.Networking, 8*(3), 319-327.

Madhow, U., Honig, M. L., & Steiglitz, K. (1995). Optimization of Wireless Resources for Personal Communications Mobility Tracking. *IEEE/ACM Trans. Networking*, 3(6), 698-707.

Merchant, A., & Sengupta, B. (1995, October). Assignment of Cells to Switches in PCS Networks. *IEEE/ACM Trans. Networking*, 3(5), 521-526.

Nagel, K., & Shreckenberg, M. (1992). A cellular automaton model for freeway traffic. *J. Phisique I, 2*(12), 2221-2229.

Saraydar, C. U., Kelly, O. E., & Rose, C. (2000, September). One-Dimensional Location Area Design. *IEEE/ACM Trans. Networking, 49*(5), 1626-1632.

Simon, V., Huszák, Á., Szabó, S., & Imre, S. (2003). Hierarchical Mobil IPv6 and Regional Registration Optimization, International Conference on Parallel and Distributed Computing. Euro-Par 2003, 26th-29th August, Klagenfurt, Austria, Published at Springer, Lectures Notes in Computer Sciences; 2790, ISBN 3-540-40788-X, pp. 1137-1140.

Tsai, J. T., & Hsiao, H. H. (2001). Performance of Movement-Based Location Update and One-Step Paging in Wireless Networks with Sparsely Underlaid Microcells. *Proceedings of IEEE GLOBECOM*, San Antonio, TX, Nov. pp. 642-647

Wong, V., & Leung, V. (2001, October). An Adaptive Distance-Based Location Update Algorithm for Next Generation PCS Networks. *IEEE J. Select. Areas Commun., 19*, 1942-1952.

Wong, V. W. S., & Leung, V. C. M. (2000, September). Location Management for Next-Generation Personal Communications Networks. *IEEE Network Magazine*, 18-24.

Xie, H., Tabbane, S., & Goodman, D. (1993, May). Dynamic Location Area Management and Performance Analysis. *Proceedings of the 43rd IEEE Vehicular Technology Conference*, 533-539

Zhang, X., Castellanos, J., & Campbell, A. (2002, March). Design and Performance of Mobile IP Paging, ACM Mobile Networks and Applications. *Special Issue on Modeling Analysis and Simulation of Wireless and Mobile Systems*, 7(2).

Chapter X
A Heuristic Solution to the Large Scale Cellular Telecommunication Network Expansion Problem

Joon-Yeoul Oh
Texas A&M University-Kingsville, USA

John P. Mullen
New Mexico State University, USA

ABSTRACT

This chapter proposes a very effective heuristic algorithm to address a variation of the cellular network expansion problem and discusses each algorithm step in detail. Although the input to the algorithm appears to be a binary integer programming problem, the proposed algorithm deals with several non-linear aspects. The solution specifies the connections of each component, cell sites, hubs, and mobile telephone switching office and satisfies the redundancy requirements for each cell site to ensure continued traffic flow in the event of a local overload or equipment failure. The algorithm reports the best feasible solution it finds, as well as lower and upper bounds on the cost of an exact solution. Preliminary testing indicates that it generates very good results, in spite of its very short execution time. The authors hope that in presenting such an algorithm, designers of very large cellular network expansions will have a tool to obtain significantly good solutions in a reasonable time. In addition, because the expansion problem presented here is a knapsack problem, the authors anticipate that this heuristic might have other applications in solving similar large-scale problems.

INTRODUCTION

Over the years, significant technology improvements have been achieved in the field of cellular telecommunications. However, existing cellular network systems often cannot satisfy the sharply increasing demand due to the growing number of subscribers. For instance, some calls may not be connected during a peak time or frequent drop-calls may occur due to the limited coverage areas. Even if a system would normally be adequate, heavy phone call activity due to the evacuation from a natural disaster can cause a connection difficulty.

The cellular network expansion problem (CNEP) deals with the way to increase the capacity of existing cellular telecommunication network systems. There are two general ways to solve this problem. One is cell site splitting and the other is cell site addition.

The main idea behind cell site splitting is to split a large cell into a number of smaller cells to maximize the theoretical and practical capacity of the cell sites (Goodman, 1997). Depending on the density and distribution of traffic throughout the network, such systems can employ various sizes of cell sites. Generally, large cell sites are used to provide services to areas with low subscriber density. For high subscriber density locations, multiple smaller cell sites are used to provide services. In lightly populated areas, the diameter of a cell site can be up to 30km, whereas in the most densely populated areas, smaller diameters, 2km and 1km, are in use (Gardiner, 1995; Rappaport, 1996; William, 2001). This expansion method is the most commonly used.

In the case of cell site addition, new cell sites are created in areas that were originally not covered. The main concerns are the determination of the optimal number of cell sites and the location of the new cell sites. In 1992, AT&T Network Systems had a contract with the Pilipino Telephone Corporation (Piltel) to expand Piltel's cellular network. For the $82 million contract, AT&T

provided 1000 equipments including switching offices and cell sites (Bona, 1992). Cellular South in Mississippi also installed more than 100 cell sites to provide better coverage and clarity with $38 million investments for two years (Rankin, 2004). DIGITAL Telecommunications Philippines Inc. is planning to increase its cell sites to 4,000 in 2008 and they anticipate an increase of customers from the present five million to ten million with the cellular network expansion plan (Sanchez-Lacson, 2008).

Whether employing cell splitting or cell site addition, a designer faces three main challenges; determining a set of optimal connections to Mobile Telephone Switching Office (MTSO), estimating the required capacity of each MTSO, and deciding on the redundancy requirements. In other to ensure that a connection path will exist in the event of a component failure or local overload, the redundancy requirement specifies the minimum number of connections between a cell site and MTSO. For instance, if the value of redundancy requirement for a cell site is 2, then the cell site must be connected to two MTSOs each of which can satisfy its half of the capacity requirement for that cell site, in addition to the requirements of all the other sites connected to it. If there is a disconnection or an overload in one route, the users in the cell site still can still communicate, using the other MTSO connection. Figure 1 shows an example of possible new connections due to the system expansion. The hexagons show the coverage area of each cell site. The smaller hexagons are the new coverage areas due to the cell splitting. The cell sites are interconnected to a MTSO in a star or a daisy-chain manner, and the MTSOs are usually interconnected each other in a ring shape. With a daisy chain configuration, the capacity of the wire/fiber link is a big concern since a link connecting two sites might have to carry traffic that is of no concern to either site. The cellular telecommunication network also is connected to the Public Switching Telephone Network (PSTN), which allows connections to

Figure 1. New connections due to the system expansion

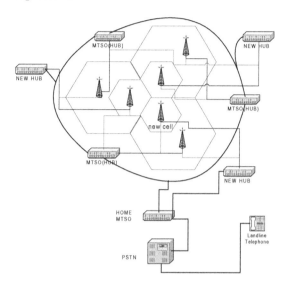

a landline phone. Computationally, it is difficult to determine the optimal MTSO connections for each cell site (split and/or new) while satisfying demand, MTSO capacity and redundancy requirements. Cost is another key factor that needs to be considered for the optimization effort. Hence, a most desirable or optimal solution would be a set of connections that would satisfy the number of cell site installations, MTSO connections, and redundancy requirements at a lowest cost.

MATHEMATICAL MODEL FOR THE CELLULAR TELECOMMUNICATION NETWORK EXPANSION PROBLEM

Dutta and Kubat proposed an optimal network connection model satisfying network capacity, but did not consider each individual hub capacities (1999). The formulation below considers each hub's capacities. Let H be the number of existing hubs, G be the number of new cell sites, and N be the number of new hubs. Let c_{ij} be the connection cost between hub i and cell site j, and let r_j be the redundancy requirement at cell site j. Let S_i be the remaining capacity at hub I, and x_{ij} be a binary

variable which is equal to one if hub i and cell site j are connected, and otherwise zero. The variable I_i is the one time cost to be spent if a new hub is installed and y_i is a binary variable which is equal to one if hub i is installed and zero, otherwise. The problem of selecting optimal connections and hubs can be stated as shown in Box 1.

To allow greater solution efficiency, the problem can be restated as follows. First, the decision variable, x_{0j}, indicates whether or not there is a connection between the new cell site j and hub 0. Thus, Eq (1.2) can be written:

$$x_{0j} = r_j - \sum_{i=1}^{H+N} x_j, \quad \text{where } j = 1,2,...,G.$$

Substituting this into the objective function, we get: (see Box 2).

The above minimization problem is equivalent to the maximization of (see Box 3).

Because $\sum_{i=1}^{G} \left(c_{0j} \, r_j \right)$ is the sum of given constants, the initial formulation may be simplified to: (see Box 4)

Let $K = N + H$, and $y_k = 1$ for all existing hubs. Then, the first and second terms in the objective function can be combined with Constraints (2.2) and (2.3) and the problem stated as shown in Box 5.

This formulation of the cellular network expansion problem is a knapsack problem (Corman, 2001; Dutta, 1999). Generally, the computational time to solve knapsack problems grows exponentially with problem size. In this case, the number of possible solutions with K hubs and G cell sites with the redundancy requirements r_j, where $j = 1,2,...,G$, is $\binom{K}{r_1} \times \binom{K}{r_2} \times \binom{K}{r_3} \times \cdots \times \binom{K}{r_G}$. Therefore, when K and G are large, this would lead to a very long computational time. Thus, heuristic methods are commonly used to solve telecommunication network system design problems, as well as other large scale combinatorial optimization problems (Bazaraa, 1993; Corman, 2001; Murty, 1995).

Box 1.

$$\text{Min} \quad \sum_{i=0}^{H}\sum_{j=1}^{G} c_j \ x_j + \sum_{i=H+1}^{H+N}\sum_{j=1}^{G} c_j \ x_j + \sum_{i=H+1}^{H+N} I_i y_i \qquad (1.1)$$

$$\text{Subject to} \quad \sum_{i=0}^{H+N} x_i = r_j, \quad \text{where } j=1,2,...,G, \qquad (1.2)$$

$$\sum_{j=1}^{G}\left(\frac{d_j}{r_j}\right) x_j \le S_i, \quad \text{where } i=0,1,...,H, \qquad (1.3)$$

$$\sum_{j=1}^{G}\left(\frac{d_j}{r_j}\right) x_j \le S_i y_i, \quad \text{where } i=H+1, H+2,...,H+N, \qquad (1.4)$$

where x_{ij} and y_i are binary variables. Constraint (1.2) reflects the redundancy requirement at each cell site. Technically, any solution in which the sum of the x_{ij} in (1.2) is at least r_j would be feasible. However, because adding unnecessary connections would never lead to a lower-cost solution, there is an equality relation in that constraint. As noted below, stating (1.2) as a set of equalities permits a more concise statement of the problem. Constraints (1.3) and (1.4) ensure the solution does not exceed the capacity of existing hub and new hub, respectively. Also, the total capacities of cell sites connected to hub i must not exceed its capacity. Because the demand will be distributed over all hubs connected to a site, the demand for each cell site is divided by the redundancy requirement of that cell site. Thus, the ratio value, (d_j/r_j), is assigned to hub(s) according to the redundancy requirement. Note that if the requirements in (1.2) and both of the capacity constraints are satisfied, the demand of each cell site is also satisfied.

Box 2.

$$\text{Min} \quad \sum_{j=1}^{G} c_{0j}\left[r_j - \sum_{i=1}^{H+N} x_i \right] + \sum_{i=0}^{H}\sum_{j=1}^{G} c_j \ x_j + \sum_{i=H+1}^{H+N}\sum_{j=1}^{G} c_j \ x_j + \sum_{i=H+1}^{H+N} I_i y_i$$

$$= \quad \text{Min} \quad \sum_{j=1}^{G}\left(c_{0j} r_j \right) + \sum_{i=0}^{H}\sum_{j=1}^{G}\left(c_j - c_{0j} \right) x_j + \sum_{i=H+1}^{H+N}\sum_{j=1}^{G}\left(c_j - c_{0j} \right) x_j + \sum_{i=H+1}^{H+N} I_i y_i$$

Box 3.

$$= \quad \sum_{j=1}^{G}\left(c_{0j} r_j \right) + \text{Max}\left\{ -\sum_{i=0}^{H}\sum_{j=1}^{G}\left(c_j - c_{0j} \right) x_j - \sum_{i=H+1}^{H+N}\sum_{j=1}^{G}\left(c_j - c_{0j} \right) x_j - \sum_{i=H+1}^{H+N} I_i y_i \right\}$$

Box 4.

$$\text{Max} \quad -\sum_{i=0}^{H}\sum_{j=1}^{G}\left(c_j - c_{0j} \right) x_j - \sum_{i=H+1}^{H+N}\sum_{j=1}^{G}\left(c_j - c_{0j} \right) x_j - \sum_{i=H+1}^{H+N} I_i y_i \qquad (2.1)$$

$$\text{Subject to} \quad \sum_{j=1}^{G}\left(\frac{d_j}{r_j}\right) x_j \le S_i, \quad \text{where } i=0,1,...,H, \qquad (2.2)$$

$$\sum_{j=1}^{G}\left(\frac{d_j}{r_j}\right) x_j \le S_i y_i, \quad \text{where } i=H+1, H+2,...,H+N, \qquad (2.3)$$

Box 5.

$$\text{Max} \qquad \sum_{k=1}^{K}\sum_{j=1}^{G}\left(c_{0j}-c_j\right)x_k - \sum_{k=1}^{K}I_k y_k \qquad\qquad (3.1)$$

$$\text{Subject to} \quad \sum_{j=1}^{G}\left(\frac{d_j}{r_j}\right)x_k \le S_k y_k, \quad \text{where } k=0,1,...,K. \qquad (3.2)$$

HEURISTIC SEARCH ALGORITHM FOR THE CELLULAR NETWORK EXPANSION PROBLEMS

Dutta and Kubat (1999) insisted that if the cellular network is enlarged, the installation of new hubs is more cost effective than that of a new home MTSO. They used a heuristic for the cellular network connection problem considering the ring capacity, which they tested using two sets of sample problems. For the first problem set, there were 5 hubs and 10 cell sites and in the second, there were 20 and 10 hubs and 50 cell sites. They compared the heuristic solutions to the corresponding solutions using the LINGO software package and Lagrangian lower bound. The average deviation rates between the Lagrangian lower bound and heuristic solution for problem set 1 and 2 were 2.1% and 0.7%, respectively.

Lagrangian relaxation is the most common procedure used to solve the network design, expansion, and allocation problems (Bazaraa, 1993). Tragantalerngsak, et al. (2000) proposed a Lagrangian relaxation based on branch and bound algorithm for their solution. Sherali, et al. (2000) developed a network model and applied reformulation-linearization technique with a Lagrangian dual/relaxation procedure, and Chang, et al. (2001) used Lagrangian relaxation and subgradient optimization techniques for the channel allocation in cellular mobile systems.

Heuristic approaches, such as genetic algorithms, tabu search, and simulated annealing, are other popular methods for the optimization of network design and expansion (Gen, 2000;

Rayward-Smith, 1996). Deeter and Smith (1998) used a genetic algorithm to optimize a reliable communication network design. Adickes, et al. (2002) proposed a method for the optimization of radio frequency data communication technology using a genetic algorithm. However, none of these papers consider the limits imposed by the hub capacities.

This article proposes a new algorithm, the Heuristic Search Algorithm (HSA) to efficiently address all aspects of the expansion problem stated above. At one level, the HSA is similar to the transportation simplex algorithm (TSA). However, the TSA cannot be applied directly to the cellular network expansion problem because redundancy requirements each cite to be connected to multiple hubs, rather than a single destination. In addition, the TSA cannot deal with potential hubs, which may or may not be selected. The HSA addresses all of these difficulties.

Tables 1 concisely shows the problem in a tableau form similar to that of the TSA. There is a row for each hub and a column for each cell site. All limits and costs are listed. The pairs (c_{ij}, x_{ij}) represent the connection costs, c, and the current value of x for that particular cell site and hub. This article will make frequent reference to this table in the discussion below.

The proposed HSA consists of five processes; 1) finding the lower limit and identifying scarce resources, 2) finding an initial solution by using penalty search, 3) improving the initial solution by using the profit search, 4) reallocating the connections in an attempt to find a better solution, and 5) reallocating the scarce hubs in an attempt

Table 1. Tableau form of the site expansion problem

	cell site 1	cell site 2	...	cell site G	initial cost	capacity
hub 0	(c_{11}, x_{11})	(c_{12}, x_{12})	...	(c_{1G}, x_{1G})	I_1	S_1
hub 1	(c_{21}, x_{21})	(c_{22}, x_{22})	...	(c_{2G}, x_{2G})	I_2	S_2
...	...	...	...	...	...	...
hub H	(c_{H1}, x_{H1})	(c_{H2}, x_{H2})	...	(c_{HG}, x_{HG})	I_H	S_H
redundancy	r_1	r_2	...	r_G		
demand	d_1	d_2	...	d_G		

to find an even better solution. The interactions among these procedures are depicted in Figure 2. The procedures and their interactions are described in detail below.

Procedure 1: Global Optimal Search, Ignoring Demand and Capacity Constraints

The first procedure of the HSA is to find a global optimal solution without considering the hub capacity constraints. This simplified problem may be stated as shown in Box 6.

Because there is no limitation on hub capacity, this procedure simply finds a solution each cell site by selecting the cheapest hubs, r_j, available to that site and setting the corresponding $x_{ij} = 1$. This process occurs in the other of cost, so for each cell, the last connection selected is donated (i^*, j^*). This connection has a cost which is greater than or equal to every other selected connection for that cell and less than or equal to every other connection that was not selected. Below, these are referred to as $c_{i^*j^*}$ and $x_{i^*j^*}$.

After finding a solution to the simplied problem, the procedure identifies scarce hubs. Let `colsum[j]` be the sum of the x_{ij} in each column. If $S_i^{(k)}$, the remaining capacity of hub i, is negative at the end of procedure 1, that hub is identified as a scarce hub and the binary variable `scarce[i]` is set to 1. Otherwise, `scarce[i]` will remain zero.

Figure 2. Heuristic search algorithm flow chart

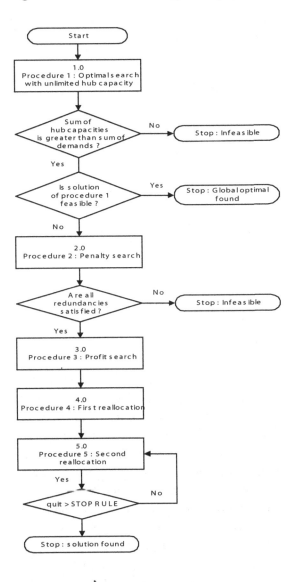

Box 6.

$$\text{Max} \qquad \sum_{i=0}^{K}\sum_{j=1}^{G} c_j\, x_{jk} + \sum_{i=0}^{K} I_i y_i \qquad\qquad (4.1)$$

$$\text{Subject to} \quad \sum_{i=0}^{G} x_{jk} = r_j, \quad \text{where } j = 0,1,...,G. \qquad\qquad (4.2)$$

Procedure 1: find an optimal solution, ignoring hub capacity constraints;

initialization: k, $x_{ij} = 0$, `scarce[i]`$= 0$, $S_i^{(0)} = S_i$ for all i, j;

begin 1

   for $j = 1$ to G **do**

   begin 2

      while $\sum_{i=0}^{K} x_{ij} < r_j$ **do**

      begin 3

        $c_{i*j*} = \min \{c_{ij} \mid x_{ij} = 0\}$;

          set $x_{i*j*} = 1$;

        $k = k + 1$;

        $S_i^{(k)} = S_i^{(k-1)} - (d_j/r_j)$;

   end 3;

   end 2;

   for $i = 0$ to K **do**

   begin 4

      if $S_i^{(k)} < 0$;

         set `scarce[i]`$= 1$;

   end 4;

end 1;

After finishing procedure 1, the HSA performs two tests. The first is to check the feasibility of the problem. The second test is to check the feasibility of the initial solution of the problem. This algorithm performs this procedure even if a problem is infeasible, so the analyst can check why the problem becomes infeasible. Also, from the result of procedure 1, one can predict the future location(s) of new hub(s). If the solution at the end of procedure 1 passes the first and the second test, it is a global optimal solution. If a problem passes the first feasibility test, but the solution

from procedure 1 does not pass the second feasibility test, procedure 2 starts. Finally, the solution obtained in procedure 1 establishes a lower limit on the objective function since no other solution, satisfying the redundancy requirements, can have a lower cost than this solution.

Procedure 2: Penalty Search

The second procedure attempts to find an initial solution that satisfies the demand, capacity, and redundancy requirement constraints. The Penalty Search is similar to Vogel's approximation method (Hiller, 2005) which finds an initial feasible solution for the transportation simplex algorithm by examining penalties associated with different choices. However, the approach in the HSA differs in order to deal with the redundancy requirements. This modified method is called the "penalty search" below. The "penalty" is defined as a difference between a "smallest cost" and a "next smallest cost" at each column and row. Let the penalty for row i be p_i, and the penalty for column j be p_j. Then, as seen on the pseudo code of procedure 2, the process to calculate p_i and p_j is almost the same as Vogel's approximation method except for updating the value of x_{ij}, $r_j^{(k)}$, $S_i^{(k)}$. The symbol ** is used in procedure 2 to distinguish its solution from that of procedure 1.

Procedure 2: penalty search;

initialization: k, p_i, p_j, $x_{ij} = 0$, $r_j^{(k)} = r_j$, $S_i^{(k)} = S_i$ for all i, j;

if $\sum_{i=0}^{G} x_{kj} = r_j$, then $p_i = -1$

if $S_i < \min(d_j / r_j)$, then $p_j = -1$

begin 1

    while any p_i or $p_j \neq -1$ **do**

    begin 2

        for $j = 0$ to G **do**

        initialization: `space[j]` = 0;

        begin 3

            if $x_{ij} = 0$ with $S_i^{(k)} \geq (d_j / r_j)$

            `space[j]` = `space[j]` + 1;

    end 3;

    if `space[j]` = $r_j^{(k)}$

        for $j = 0$ to G **do**

            $x_{ij} = 1$ if $x_{ij} = 0$ with $S_i^{(k)} \geq (d_j / r_j)$;

    calculate p_i for all rows with $p_i \neq -1$;

    $p_{i*} = \max \{p_i\}$;

    if $p_{i*} > p_{j*}$

        $i** = i*$;

        select $j**$ such that $c_{i**j**} = \min \{c_{i*j} | p_j \neq -1\}$;

    else

        $j** = j*$;

        select $i**$ such that $c_{i**j**} = \min \{c_{ij*} | p_i \neq -1\}$;

    $x_{i**j**} = 1$;

    $k = k + 1$;

    $r_{j**}^{(k)} = r_{j**}^{(k-1)} - 1$;

    $S_{i**}^{(k)} = S_{i**}^{(k-1)} - (d_{j**} / r_{j**})$;

    if $r_j^{(k)} = 0$, then $p_{j**} = -1$;

    if $S_{i**}^{(k)} < \min(d_j / r_j)$, then $p_{i**} = -1$;

    end 2;

end 1;

At the end of procedure 2, the HSA performs a third feasibility test to check whether the initial solution from procedure 2 is feasible or not. If the solution satisfies the redundancy requirement for each cell site and the capacity for each hub, the solution is an initial feasible solution (IFS), and procedure 3 starts. Otherwise, the problem is infeasible, and the program quits. If the program quits at this point, only the value of the lower limit and its associated solution are provided.

Procedure 3: Profit Search

The third procedure starts with the IFS obtained from the penalty search and tries to find a better solution. This part of the HSA attempts to replace higher cost connections with lower cost ones, subject to capacity constraints. Therefore, it is called "profit search." The "profit" is defined as a positive difference value between the cost associated with some $x_{ij} = 1$, say x_{ij*}, and the cost of some other $x_{ij} = 0$, say x_{i*j*}, within column j^*, where $c_{ij*} > c_{i*j*}$ and $S_{i*}^{(k)} \geq (d_{j*} / r_{j*})$. Note that procedure 3 may revise the value of i^* if an improved solution is found. Let the profit for column j^* at step k be $P_{j*}^{(k)}$, the biggest profit in column j^* be MP_{j*} and the biggest profit among all columns be MP_{j**}. Then, the profit search performs as shown in Box 7.

The HSA repeats procedure 3 until there are no more profits in any column. Since the flows are reallocated within the same column, the redundancy requirement and demand constraints for each cell site are not violated. Also, since the flows are reallocated only to hubs with available capacities, the capacity constraints for each hub are not violated. Therefore, each iteration of this procedure generates a feasible solution. Only the last solution is saved and used in the next procedure. The total cost of the solution from procedure 3 is always less than or equal to the IFS.

Procedure 4: First Reallocation

The fourth procedure attempts to find better connections based on the reallocation of flows from the scarce hubs, which are identified in procedure 1, to others. The "loss" is defined as a positive difference between c_{ij} with $x_{ij} = 1$ in scarce hub i, say c_{ij*}, and one of c_{ij} with $x_{ij} = 0$ in non-scarce hubs, say c_{i*j*}, within each column, where $c_{ij*} > c_{i*j*}$ and $S_{i*}^{(k)} \geq (d_{j*} / r_{j*})$. Then, let $N_{j*}^{(k)}$ be the loss in column j^*, MN_{j*} be the smallest loss in column j^*, and NP_{j**} be the smallest loss among all columns. (see Box 8)

Box 7.

Procedure 3: profit search;
while $P_j^{(k)} > 0$ for all j **do**
begin 1
    initialization: $P_j^{(k)}$, M_j, $MP_j = 0$ for all j, k = 0;
    for $i = 0$ to K **do**
    begin 2
        for $j = 1$ to G **do**
        begin 3
            if $x_{ij} = 1$
                $j^* = j$;
                for $t = 0$ to K **do**
                begin 4
                    $k = k + 1$;
                    select i^* such that $P_{i^*}^{(k)} = \max \{c_{tj^*} - c_{i^*j^*}\}$,
                    where $t \neq i^*$, $x_{i^*j^*} = 0$, $c_{tj^*} > c_{i^*j^*}$, $S_{i^*}^{(k)} \geq (d_{j^*} / r_{j^*})$;
                end 4;
            if $P_{j^*}^{(k)} > 0$, and $P_{j^*}^{(k)} > P_{j^*}^{(k-1)}$
                $MP_{j^*} = P_{j^*}^{(k)}$;
            select row such that min $\{c_{i^*j^*} \mid MP_{j^*}\}$;
                $i^{**} = i^*$;
            select column such that min $\{c_{tj^*} \mid MP_{j^*}\}$;
                $t^* = t$;
        end 3;
        end 2;
    $M_{j^{**}} = \max \{MP_{j^*} \mid MP_{j^*} > 0$ for all $j^*\}$;
    select row such that min $\{c_{i^{**}j^*} \mid MP_{j^{**}}\}$;
        $i^{***} = i^{**}$;
    select column such that min $\{c_{t^*j^{**}} \mid MP_{j^{**}}\}$;
        $t^{**} = t^*$;
    $x_{t^{**}j^{**}} = 0$;
    $S_{t^{**}}^{(k)} = S_{t^{**}}^{(k-1)} + (d_{j^{**}} / r_{j^{**}})$;
    $x_{i^{***}j^{**}} = 1$;
    $S_{j^{***}}^{(k)} = S_{j^{***}}^{(k-1)} - (d_{j^{**}} / r_{j^{**}})$;
end 1;

This may initially lead to a higher cost, but it has the potential to find a lower cost because a procedure that is similar to that of procedure 3 is repeated after the reallocation. So, the total cost of procedure 4 is always less than or equal to that of procedure 3. The results of procedure 4, a total cost and solution, are saved. The solution of procedure 4 is also feasible because no constraints are violated.

Box 8.

Procedure 4: first reallocation of the demands from scarce hubs;
while `scarce[i]` = 1 for all *j* **do**
begin 1
    initialization: $N_j^{(k)}$, *k*, NP_j, $MN_j = 0$;
    for *i* = 0 to *K* **do**
    begin 2
        if `scarce[i]` = 1
        for *i* = 1 to *G* **do**
        begin 3
            if x_{ij} = 1
            $j^* = j$;
            for *t* = 0 to *K* **do**
            begin 4
                $k = k + 1$;
                select *i** in non-scarce hubs such that $N_{j^*}^{(k)} = \max\{c_{i^*j^*} - c_{tj^*}\}$,
                where *t* = `scarce[i]`, $x_{i^*j^*} = 0$, $c_{tj^*} > c_{i^*j^*}$, $S_{i^*}^{(k)} \geq (d_{j^*}/r_{j^*})$;
            end 4;
            if $N_{j^*}^{(k)} < N_{j^*}^{(k-1)}$
                $MN_{j^{**}} = N_{j^*}^{(k)}$;
            select row such that $\min\{c_{i^*j^*} \mid N_{j^*}\}$;
                $i^{**} = i^*$;
            select column such that $\min\{c_{tj^*} \mid N_{j^*}\}$;
                $t^* = t$;
        end 3;
    end 2;
    $NP_{j^{**}} = \max\{MN_{j^*} \mid MN_{j^*} > 0 \text{ for all } j^*\}$;
    select row such that $\min\{c_{i^{**}j^{**}} \mid NP_{j^{**}}\}$;
        $i^{***} = i^{**}$;
    select column such that $\min\{c_{t^*j^{**}} \mid NP_{j^{**}}\}$;
        $t^{**} = t^*$;
    $x_{t^{**}j^{**}} = 0$;
    $S_{t^{**}}^{(k)} = S_{t^{**}}^{(k-1)} + (d_{j^{**}}/r_{j^{**}})$;
    $x_{i^{***}j^{**}} = 1$;
    $S_{i^{***}}^{(k)} = S_{j^{***}}^{(k-1)} - (d_{j^{**}}/r_{j^{**}})$;
    do procedure 3;
    save total cost and solution;
end 1;

Procedure 5: Second Reallocation and Finalization

This procedure performs three tasks. The first task is to identify the second scarce hubs. The second task is to reallocate the connections away from scarce hubs. The third one is to find the lower total cost by using the profit search. Let STOP RULE be the predefined variable with the value of 3, scarce2[i] indicate which hubs are second scarce hubs; that is the hubs with scarce capacities at this point have scarce2[i] = 1. This program will stop when quit > STOP RULE. Then, the fifth procedure performs as shown in Box 9.

Initially, the solution from procedure 4 is considered the best previous solution. At the end of procedure 5, the total cost of the current solution is compared to that of the previous best. If the total cost of the current solution is greater than or equal to the previous total cost, the variable, quit, is increased by one, and the HSA keeps the previous solution and total cost as an upper limit. Otherwise, the HSA keeps the current solution at the best so far and does not increase the value of quit. Also, if the current solution is better, the HSA updates the upper limit on cost. Unlike procedure 4, procedure 5 is repeated as long as the value of the variable, quit, is less than the value of the predefined variable, STOP RULE. The value of STOP RULE can be any positive

Box 9.

```
Procedure 5: second reallocation of the connections from scarce hubs;
initialization: quit = 0, STOP RULE = 3;
while quit < STOP RULE do
begin 1
    initialization: scarce2[i] = 0;
    for i = 0 to K do
    begin 2
        if S_i^(k) at the end of previous procedure less than any (d_j / r_j) in row i
            scarce2[i] = 1;
    end 2;
    while all the second scarce hubs are checked do
    begin 3
    do begin 1 in procedure 4 with scarce2[i] instead of scarce[i];
    end 3;
    do procedure 3;
    save total cost and solution;
    if current total cost ≥ previous total cost
        quit = quit + 1;
        upper limit = previous total cost;
        solution of upper limit = previous solution;
    else
        upper limit = current total cost;
        solution of upper limit = current solution;
end 1;
```

integer value. However, a higher value of STOP RULE makes the elapsed time longer, and a lower value of STOP RULE may result in a higher total cost. After completing procedure 5, the HSA generates an output report that contains the lower limit and its solution found in procedure 1, the upper limit and its solution found in procedure 5, and elapsed time.

TEST RESULTS AND ANALYSIS

The Heuristic Search Algorithm was written in the C programming language and implemented on a PC with a 233 Mhz Pentium processor and 160 Mb RAM memory. To test the efficiency of the HSA, five problem sets were implemented. The first two problem sets are small size problems, which have 48 to 150 variables, and the next two problem sets are medium size problems, which have 3200 variables. The last problem set is a large size problem that has 10000 variables. The total number of problems for all problem sets was over 200.

Both the solutions and the execution time of the HSA were compared to the branch and bound algorithm used by LINGO 7, commercial version. For small and medium size problems, the results of the HSA were compared to the solution of LINGO software. However, because the version of LINGO 7 that we used could only solve problems that have up to 3200 binary variables, the solutions of the large size problems were analyzed based on the lower and upper limits found from the HSA.

The data, such as connection cost, demands for cell sites, redundancy requirements, initial cost, and capacity for MTSOs, are generated by using Microsoft © Excel's landbetween(lower limit, upper limit) command. Table 3 shows the data range for the problem sets.

For problem set 1, the HSA and LINGO found the same optimal solution that LINGO found in most of test problems. The total deviation rate was almost zero. The average number of iterations was about 25 iterations for the HSA, and zero iteration for LINGO. The average elapsed time of the HSA was 0.59 minute while that of LINGO was 1.47 minutes.

The problems in set 2 have 10 hubs and 15 cell sites. The test data ranges for the set 2 are the same as set 1 except the capacity ranges for the existing hubs. The HSA found an optimal solution in 85% of test cases. The average deviation ratio for this problem set was 10^{-6}. This is likely to be very small, relative to uncertainties in estimated costs. The HSA solved the problems within about 1.5 seconds and LINGO took 2.8, which is not a significant time difference.

The problems in set 3 have 3200 variables with 50 hubs and 64 cell sites. The HSA had a little bit larger deviation ratios than the small size problems in this problem set. However, the aver-

Table 2. Data range for problem sets

	Range	
	LL	**UL**
Connection Cost	10	50
Capacity of hub 0 (MTSO)	100,000	
Capacity of existing hubs	300	800
Capacity for new hubs	1000	1500
Redundancy for cell sites	1	3
Demand for cell sites	300	400
Initial cost for new hubs	200	300

LL = Lower Limit,   UL = Upper Limit

Table 3. Test results for Problem Sets 1, 2, and 3 (number shows the average values)

	HSA		**LINGO**		**d.r.**
	Iterations	**Time (sec)**	**Iteration**	**Time (sec)**	
Problem set 1	24.13	0.59	0	1.47	0
Problem set 2	78.25	1.40	77.53	2.8	10^{-6}
Problem set 3	370.2	4.60	262.3	5.6	4×10^{-6}

d.r. = deviation ratio = (Upper limit solution – Optimal solution) / Optimal solution

Table 4. Test results for Problem Set 4

	HSA				LINGO			d.r.
	Lower	Upper	Iteration	Time	Opt	Iteration	Time	
4.1	3576	3789	889	35.7 sec	3750	55,498,421	42 hrs	7×10^{-5}
4.2	3492	3805	977	17.0 sec	–	102,664,390	147 hrs	–
4.3	3774	4123	1038	15.8 sec	4085	65,321,382	45 hrs	9×10^{-5}

Lower = Lower limit solution, Upper = Upper limit solution, Opt = optimal solution

age deviation ratio was only 4×10^{-6}. Both the HSA and LINGO solved the problems in about five seconds.

The problems of set 4 have 32 hubs and 100 cell sites. This problem set has the same number of variables as problem set 3. However, problem set 4 has fewer hubs and more cell sites than the problem set 3. The same data range was used as in problem set 3. For test problem 4.2, LINGO failed to find an optimal value because of a memory shortage. The best value (not optimal value) reported by LINGO after running 147 hours and 35 minutes was 3971, which is 4.36% larger than the HSA's upper limit, and the number of iterations was 102,664,390. For test problems 4.1 and 4.3, LINGO found optimal solutions, but the elapsed time was 42 hours and 45 hours respectively, while in all three cases, the HSA found a solution in less than a minute. This set demonstrates the point at which the HSA performs much faster than the LINGO program.

Problem set 5 has ten test problems. Each problem has 100 hubs and 100 cell sites, so the total number of variables is 10,000. Since our version of LINGO 7 could not solve a problem size of 100×100, the upper limit of the HSA was compared to the lower limit of the HSA. To distinguish the deviation rate used in the problem set 5 from that of other problem sets, Δ is used for the symbol of the deviation ratio instead of d.r. The Δ is defined as the difference between the upper and lower limit divided by upper limit.

Table 5. Test results Problem set 5

HSA		Δ
Iteration	Time (sec)	
458.7	45.7	10^{-6}

$\Delta = $ (Upper – Lower) / Lower

Also, given that in practice a designer would not run both algorithms, this is a practical measure of an answer's quality.

Since a solution associated with the lower limit would not be feasible, (upper – lower) / upper was used for the value of Δ instead of (upper – lower) / lower. The average value of Δ was 10^{-6}. The HSA took around 46 seconds to solve the problem size of 100×100, which is less than 2% of the time it took LINGO to solve the smaller problems in Set 4.

CONCLUSION

As the number of cellular phone users increases, the system becomes crowded. To continue providing high quality services to its users, the system capacity needs to be increased. Methods such as the installation of new cell sites and the splitting of existing cell sites are used. In order for these methods to work, newly installed or split cell sites must be connected to at least one hub. To ensure the traffic flow, even during peak time, and to prevent any disconnections between cell sites and hubs, each cell has a redundancy requirement. Satisfying the new connections and the redundancy requirements can make hub capacities scarce, which can lead to expensive connection costs. This paper presents a model of the cellular telecommunication network connection cost which considers redundancies, presents a knapsack formulation of that problem and proposes the "Heuristic Search Algorithm (HSA)" as a practical way to solve large network expansion problems.

The solutions of the HSA were compared to the solutions generated by the LINGO software. The computational results indicated that the HSA found an optimal solution in most cases, and provided an extremely high quality solution in others. The HSA provides a lower and upper limit on the cost of an optimal solution, as well as the remaining capacity of each hub. Because it is very difficult to find an optimal solution for large problems, the information provided by the HSA is very useful to decision makers in deciding whether to install new hubs and determining the locations of the new hubs.

Compared to an exact approach, as represented by the LINGO software, the HSA is much less limited on the number of variables; hence it can be applied to a large size problem. Also, for the medium size problem, the test results indicated that the HSA found a very good solution in a much shorter elapsed time, compared to that required by the LINGO. As the size of the problem increases, the LINGO's computational time increases dramatically. Although there is a version of LINGO which is virtually unlimited in problem size, it handles very large problems by storing variables on the computer's hard drive, which can even further increase run time. Thus, the HSA can provide a solution to very large problems that LINGO could not provide within a reasonable amount of time.

While the HSA may not find an optimal solution, it will find a feasible solution, if one exists, and establish an upper bound on the cost of an exact solution. It will also find a lower bound on the optimal solution cost, which may or may not have a corresponding feasible solution. Nevertheless, if the bounds are close, a decision maker can select the HSA's approximate solution, knowing that it is a very good feasible solution to the network expansion problem. Also, because the HSA runs so very quickly, a designer has time to explore multiple alternative plans. In addition, the HSA establishes a benchmark, against which other feasible solutions might be measured. In conclusion, the heuristic search algorithm is time efficient and cost effective and has great potential for solving this version of the cellular network expansion problem, as well similar large-scale knapsack problems.

REFERENCES

Adickes, D. M., Billo, E. R., Norman, A. B., Banerjee, S., Nnaji, O. B., & Rajgopal, J. (2002). Optimization of indoor wireless communication network layouts. *IIE Transactions, 34(9)*, 823-836.

Bazaraa, M. S., Sherali, H. D., & Shetty, C. M. (1993). *Nonlinear Programming: Theory and Algorithms* (2nd Ed.). New York: John Wiley & Sons.

Bona, K. A. (1992). *AT&T to provide equipment to expand Philippine cellular system - AT and T Network Systems*. Retrieved Feb 20, 2008 from http://findarticles.com/p/articles/mi_m3457/is_n14_v10/ai_12445255.

Calhoun, G. (1992). *Wireless Access and the Local Telephone Network*, Boston: Artech House.

Chang, K., & Kim, D. (2001). Optimal prioritized channel allocation in cellular mobile systems. *European Journal of Operational Research, 28,* 345-356.

Corman, H. T., Leiserson, E. C., Rivest, L. R., & Stein, C. (2001). *Introduction to Algorithms* (2nd Ed.). Boston: McGraw Hill.

Deeter, L. D., & Smith, E. A. (1998). Economic design of reliable networks. *IIE Transactions, 30(12)*,1161-1174.

Dutta, A., & Kubat, P. (1999). Design of partially survivable network for cellular telecommunication systems. *European Journal of Operational Research, 118(1)*, 52-64.

Gardiner, J., & West, B. (1995). *Personal Communication System and Technologies*, Boston: Artech House.

Gen, M., & Cheng, R. (2000). *Genetic Algorithm and Engineering Optimization*, New York: John Wiley & Sons.

Goodman, D. J. (1997). *Wireless Personal Communication Systems*, Boston: Addison Wesley.

Hiller, F., & Lieberman, G. (2005). *Introduction to Operations Research* (8th Ed.). New York: McGraw Hill.

Murty, K. (1995). *Operations Research: Deterministic Optimization Models*. Upper Saddle River: Prentice Hall.

Rankin, T. (2004). *Cellular South Expands CDMA 1XRTT Network; Data Rollout Planned for Quarter Three*. Retrieved Feb 20, 2008 from

http://findarticles.com/p/articles/mi_m0EIN/is_2004_June_1/ai_n6050795.

Rappaport, T. S. (1996). *Wireless Communications: Principles and Practice*. Upper Saddle River: Prentice Hall.

Rayward-Smith, V. J., Osman, I. H., Reeves, C. R., & Simth, G. D. (1996). *Modern Heuristic Search Methods*. New York: John Wiley & Sons.

Sanchez-Lacson, E. (2008). *Digitel earmarks $350M for expansion*. Retrieved Feb 20, 2008 from http://business.inquirer.net/money/breakingnews/view_article.php?article_id=113888

Sherali, H. D., Lee, Y., & Park, T. (2000). New modeling approaches for the design of local access transport area networks. *European Journal of Operational Research, 127(1)*, 94-108.

Tragantalerngsak, S., Holt, J., & Ronnqvist (2000). An exact method for the two-echelon, single-source, capacitated facility location problem. *European Journal of Operational Research, 123(3)*, 473-489.

William, L. C. (1993). *Mobile Communications Design Fundamentals*, (2nd Ed.). New York: John Wiley & Sons.

William, L. C. (2001). *Lee's Essentials of Wireless Communications*. New York: McGraw Hill.

Chapter XI
Wireless Proxy:
Distributed System to Mitigate the Effects of User Mobility Over Streaming Services on IEEE 802.11 Wireless LANs

Manuel Vilas
University of Oviedo, Spain

Xabiel G. Pañeda
University of Oviedo, Spain

David Melendi
University of Oviedo, Spain

Roberto García
University of Oviedo, Spain

Victor García
University of Oviedo, Spain

ABSTRACT

This article introduces a distributed system, called wireless proxy, to mitigate the effects of user mobility over streaming services on IEEE 802.11 wireless LANs (WLANs). It argues that a handoff procedure totally controlled by the client, depending on client mobility and configuration, can have negative effects over streaming services. In this way, mobile clients that remain associated with their current access point (AP) in poor channel conditions, severely affect the performance of streaming services. The presented distributed system monitors client mobility and induces mobile client handoffs when channel conditions worsen. Also, the system compensates streaming client and server underestimations of channel conditions. The obtained improvements using wireless proxy are experimentally tested using one of the most extended commercial streaming platforms and off-the-shelf WiFi devices. The main contribution of the developed system is that it works with unmodified IEEE 802.11 wireless NICs and APs, such as the ones widely deployed nowadays.

INTRODUCTION

One of the user access technologies that has achieved a greater commercial impact is that of wireless LAN (WLAN) based on IEEE 802.11 standards. In spite of the broad set of applications of this technology and the current support for user mobility, it still has some special characteristics which need to be considered. Wireless stations, prior to the transmission or reception of data, have to carry out several tasks: search for the best AP, perform an authentication and, then, associate with this AP. In a general situation, the same process has to be repeated every time a client roams from the coverage area of one AP to a new one. Unlike UMTS networks, in IEEE 802.11 networks the client manages the handoff procedure and takes decisions about the best moment to perform a handoff and the best AP to associate to. Since the elements of the network have no control over handoff, during handoffs clients cannot receive data and may lose packets.

This simple handoff management of IEEE 802.11 wireless LANs has side effects on streaming services. It is well known that streaming services need stable and reliable network conditions (throughput and delay). Several adaptation techniques have been designed in order to deal with punctual transmission problems and adjust consumptions to meet network conditions. In most of these techniques streaming clients and servers use network probes to analyze network conditions, and to calculate the most appropriate delivery rate. Depending on manufacturers' implementations of the IEEE 802.11 standard, different models of wireless NICs present different behaviours. Some mobile wireless stations try to maintain the connection with their current AP in the presence of extremely poor channel conditions even if a better AP is obtainable. This causes unnecessary periods of high loss rates during which streaming clients' network probes result in underestimations of actual network conditions. When the perceived channel quality goes below

a predefined threshold, the station changes its access point and, during handoff latency, stops receiving data. Even after this handoff, video playback presents long periods of poor quality and sometimes user sessions stop.

The first step to mitigate user mobility effects is to force handoffs of conservative clients that remain associated even in bad channel conditions. Introducing this type of control in the network infrastructure, the handoff process is performed independently of the wireless station manufacturer or configuration. The second step is to compensate the effect of handoff latencies over the estimations of network conditions made by mobile streaming clients, by modifying or adapting the results of their network probes.

In this article, a distributed system to improve the experience of the users of streaming services in wireless networks, called wireless proxy, is proposed. This distributed system is based on the compensation of client underestimations of channel conditions and the mitigation of the effects of mobile clients over static clients. These two goals are achieved by filtering or forwarding delivery rate messages and by inducing mobile station handoffs based on estimations of user mobility. In this way, handoff is performed independently of wireless client configurations, by only analyzing channel conditions. The main contribution of our system is that it works with unmodified IEEE 802.11 wireless NICs and APs, adding extra elements in the network to analyze and control user mobility.

The rest of the article is organized as follows. First previous works in the same field are analyzed. A description of the problems detected during the streaming of high quality contents over WLANs is performed. Next a solution to mitigate the problems previously exposed is proposed. The results of the experimental tests carried out are then shown. Finally, conclusions and future work are presented.

RELATED WORK

One of the most challenging issues of current 802.11 networks is the support of user mobility, mainly due to handoff latencies and performance anomalies. The reduction of the effects of user mobility over different types of services has been intensively researched previously. We can classify previous works in this field into three main groups: a first group that presents solutions based on configuration optimizations or technological modifications in IEEE 802.11 networks, a second group that analyzes streaming services performance over wireless LANs and a last group based on the development of systems or protocols capable of mitigating handoff latency effects maintaining current wireless technologies.

IEEE 802.11 Technology Modifications to Reduce Handoff Latency

Wireless stations select the moment to start searching for a better AP based on a threshold in the signal perceived. Changing this threshold, Velayos and Karlsson (2003) try to improve handoff latencies. Mhatre and Papagiannaki (2006) propose changing currently used methods to estimate the moment to trigger a handoff, for a smart and continuous monitoring of channels.

The majority of the time spent during a handoff is dedicated to the search phase. Mishra, Shin, and Arbaugh (2003) propose techniques to reduce the duration of this search phase based on caching the channels where other APs are detected. Shin, Forte, Singh, and Schulzrinne (2004) added to this AP caching in wireless stations an advanced algorithm for AP search. Synchronization between APs operating in the same channel using SSID (service set identifier) beacon broadcasts is proposed in Ramani and Savage (2005) as the way to improve the search phase. This is performed by listening on a particular channel exactly when SSID broadcasts are going to happen. If wireless stations search for activity in other channels, while normally remaining associated to one AP, they can discover the location of other APs of the same network (Liao & Gao, 2006).

Other works concentrate their efforts on improving the authentication phase. In Pack and Choi (2004) and in Kassab, Belghith, Bonin, and Sassi (2005) the authors propose mobility prediction algorithms based on the pre-authentication of wireless stations on multiple APs.

The use of a shared channel for all the users of the same cell in IEEE 802.11 WLANs means that users connected with poor channel conditions reduce the performance of other users connected with better channel conditions. This effect, called *performance anomaly*, is analyzed in Yang, Lee, Jan, Chang, and Sunghyun (2006). The authors develop new methods based on the modification of CSMA/CA (carrier sense multiple access/collision avoidance) parameters depending on the selected modulation for the transmission/reception of frames.

In spite of the contributions of the solutions presented in these works, all the proposed improvements require changes in currently deployed wireless LAN technologies. Also, the analyses are mainly focused on Layer 2 handoff latencies. In this article the mitigation of handoff latencies and user mobility effects is focused on from a different perspective, working with off-the-shelf wireless clients and APs.

Streaming Services Performance Over IEEE 802.11 Networks

The success of a video on-demand service depends on the user's perceived quality. User experience in a mobile environment is influenced, at least, by the initial buffering size and the client estimations of network conditions. While the buffer is used to isolate clients from temporary deteriorations of network conditions, client estimations are used to adapt multimedia flow consumptions to the real status of the network. In spite of the interest of characterizing handoff latencies in WiFi networks, the effects of client mobility on streaming sessions require deeper analysis.

Koucheryavy, Moltachanov, and Harju (2003) analyze the performance of live video streaming services in IEEE 802.11b networks. This analysis points out that RSSI low values may lead to severe problems in session establishment. Cranley and Davis (2005) evaluate the performance of streaming services in the presence of different types of background traffic, obtaining some interesting conclusions about IEEE 802.11 network maximum throughput. The influence on the playback quality of users with poor channel conditions on users with good channel conditions is the target of Bai and Williamsom (2004). The influence of handoff over RealNetworks live streaming services is analysed by Vilas, Pañeda, Melendi, García, and García (2006). In this work the authors point out that live streaming services offering high quality contents (512Kbps or higher) are severely affected by user mobility; after a handoff the playback of contents presents poor quality during long periods of time.

Systems and Protocols to Mitigate User Mobility Effects Over Streaming Services

Taking into account the fact that streaming services performance is severely affected by the changing conditions of the mobile environment, a third group of works is focused on mitigating these effects by developing new systems and protocols, maintaining unaltered IEEE 802.11 technology.

Yang, Chen, Sun, Gerla, and Sanadidi (2006) propose a new protocol for the delivery of real-time video over wireless links. This protocol is specially designed to deal with high packet loss rates and the effects of multiple users sharing a common channel. On the other hand, our solution works with protocols currently used in commercial streaming services, and does not imply changes

either in the streaming clients or the servers.

Another group of works proposes advanced architectures to reduce roaming effects on streaming services. Zenel (1999) proposes media and protocol adaptations to meet channel conditions. Bruneo, Villani, Zaia, and Puliafito (2003) develop a distributed system to improve streaming service performance on user mobility cases. This system predicts user handoffs and controls the state of the streaming session to reduce packet loss and negative effects. In Bellavista and Corradi (2004) and Bellavista, Corradi, and Giannelli (2005), the authors propose an advanced system based on the prediction of user mobility using information obtained from the client. In this way, a personalized agent can move to the new cell with the client and also the client can increase the size of the buffer based on its handoff prediction. All these solutions need the introduction of new software in wireless stations or APs, requiring the user to install new software or the APs to be able to run additional software. Nevertheless, it is very difficult to convince users to reconfigure their devices or to install new specific software just to improve the performance of streaming services on large infrastructure WLANs composed of multiple APs, as this is a very specific case. Moreover, reprogramming APs to run specific software is not possible in most of the commercial devices.

The solution presented in this article, the wireless proxy, does not introduce extra pieces of software on wireless clients or APs and does not impose changes on currently deployed IEEE 802.11 wireless LANs. Also, streaming clients and servers do not need to be modified or adapted to meet WLANs special characteristics.

USER MOBILITY EFFECTS OVER STREAMING SERVICES

The IEEE 802.11 standard describes the physical and MAC Layers, establishing basic mechanism but maintaining some parameters without a standard specification. These parameters are set by manufacturers. Examples of this type of manufacturer dependent parameters are the threshold to predict handoff, the process of changing channel speeds and the number of retransmissions that the ARQ has to perform. These parameters have a significant impact on the performance obtained in 802.11 networks. From our measurements, some wireless cards are configured with an extremely low threshold to proceed with a handoff (RSSI lower than -85dBm). Such a conservative threshold causes mobile clients to remain associated to an AP in very poor channel conditions even when a better association with a different AP is possible. In this situation, the packet loss rate for the mobile station increases due to channel conditions. At the same time, these clients cause a deterioration of the performance obtained by other users of the same cell (Heusse, Rousseau, Berger-Sabbatel, & Duda, 2003). Stations with low RSSI values transmit at very low speed, probably performing several retransmissions, saturating the channel and affecting the other users of the same cell.

Experimental Testbed

To complete the analysis performed in Vilas, et al. (2006) of RealNetworks live streaming services we have deployed a simple WiFi infrastructure composed of two APs. These APs are tuned in non-overlapping channels with their coverage areas overlapped. If the better AP is selected, wireless users always access the network using high-speed modulations (RSSI>-65dBm). Both APs are connected by an Ethernet core composed of two 100Mbps LAN switches linked by one 1Gbps trunking port. In the wired side of the network, two streaming services were deployed using the two most extended commercial platforms (RealNetworks and Windows Media). Contents are available on-demand and live with an encoding quality of 1Mbps. Tests were performed with 1.5Mbps of background traffic in each cell

simulating the activity of other users. During the tests, activity of other wireless networks in the surrounding area, tuned in non-overlapping channels, was detected.

Results

The main conclusion of the performed experiments is that, independent of the streaming platform and the type of service, clients with low handoff thresholds suffer a strong deterioration in playback quality after handoff. Video playback after handoff is composed of a set of static pictures during a period of several minutes and sometimes the streaming session hangs. As can be seen in Figure 1, this behaviour is reflected in the delivery rate measured before, during, and after handoff of a mobile client. One of the simplest alternatives that the streaming servers have to adjust the delivery rate, specified by the client, is to drop video frames maintaining audio quality unaltered as described in Wu, Hou, Zhu, Zhang, and Peha (2001). This adjustment after roaming is caused by the streaming client, who sends an RTSP (real time streaming protocol) message to the server indicating a new value for the delivery bandwidth; this parameter is set to a value several times lower than the encoding quality. This behaviour is due to streaming client underestimation of network conditions caused by temporary effects of the handoff procedure. Li, Li, Claypool, and Kinicki (2005) points out that network probes do not react well in the presence of very variable conditions like those present in wireless links. In our tests, if the streaming session does not hang, the negative effects caused by handoffs last for an average period of 2 minutes and can reach values up to 10 minutes. Various messages with underestimations of channel conditions are sent from the client to the server several minutes after handoff, indicating lower values than encoding quality.

Furthermore, streaming sessions of static users are negatively affected by the mobility of other users. They also suffer a drop in session quality as severe as that of mobile users which may even lead to their streaming session finishing. This is due to performance anomaly of CSMA/CA wireless networks (Heusse et al., 2003).

In Table 1 a summary of the obtained results is shown. Results are classified by tested platform and by delivery type (on-demand or live). Providing that both streaming platforms present playback problems in the presence of user mobility and that the network probes used by both platforms are different, the detected negative effects seem to be intrinsic to current commercial streaming technology and thus, the behaviour is not platform dependent.

WIRELESS PROXY

To decrease the roaming effects in streaming services, multiple solutions can be designed.

One possible solution to avoid client buffer starvation is to increase the client buffer size. This increase presents two main problems: it requires the intervention of the users and produces higher latency times. Also, new streaming clients and multimedia servers specifically designed for the characteristics of IEEE 802.11 LANs can be developed to mitigate these problems. However, it is not a realistic solution to consider having different clients and servers to support access from different networks.

The development of an intermediate device aware of the type of access network being used and its characteristics can be a better solution. Proxy solutions help to maintain lighter clients and servers only specialized in streaming itself. This element, based on obtained knowledge about user connection conditions, can adapt the result of network probes used by streaming clients and servers to the real conditions of the network. Also, this proxy can take decisions about the best moment to perform a handoff. This behaviour differs from the typical proxy (*RTSP Proxy Kit*, n.d.) which temporarily stores some contents to reduce the consumption of resources.

Since channel estimations are platform dependent, we have developed a solution for RealNetworks platforms. In a RealNetworks platform, the session is controlled by using RTSP and the delivery of contents is performed by using RDT (real data transport). The estimated values for the delivery rate travel from the client to the server in an RTSP Setup message and can be easily intercepted by the wireless proxy. A similar solution can be developed for Windows Media. For instance, when RTSP and RTP are used, it is possible to generate RTCP (real-time transport control protocol) packet trains in the proxy instead of in the client, isolating the server from client mobility and its effects (Nichols, Claypool, Kinicki, & Li, 2004).

The wireless proxy can obtain knowledge about connection conditions of wireless stations in different ways. For example, its decision can be based on the information provided by a set of passive wireless *sniffers* monitoring wireless channel activity for each of the clients (Yeo, Youssef, Henderson, & Agrawala, 2005). These sniffers can report about client channel conditions to the wireless proxy by using a wired interface. Another possibility to obtain the right set of information about the wireless side of the network is to poll, using SNMP (simple network management protocol), the APs of the infrastructure (*Cisco DOT11 MIB*, n.d.). Using this information the wireless proxy is aware of the real state of each client connection.

WLAN administrators are capable of de-associating stations manually by using AP management interfaces. In all the APs that we have tested, this function is fulfilled by sending a de-authentication frame to the target wireless station. If this frame is received in a mobile station when a better AP is reachable, this wireless station changes its association to the new AP. To our knowledge, it is not possible to define, in off-the-shelf commercial APs, an automatic generation of de-authentication frames when client channel conditions go below a predefined threshold. For this reason, IEEE 802.11 APs are not used to force mobile stations handoff in our system.

Wireless Proxy Architecture

The architecture of the system is described in Figure 2 and the conceptual model is shown in Figure 3. The *WP* (wireless proxy) is composed of three different elements: *MC* (mobility control), *DFs* (data forwarders) and *HI* (handoff inductors).

Each time the WP detects a new request, an independent DF is launched to exclusively control one streaming session. DF is in charge of analyzing the interchange of messages between client and servers and maintaining all the necessary connections. Each DF has an *FF* (forwarding flag) associated, managed by MC to control user signaling. If FF is set, DF only acts as a transparent element between client and server. If FF is unset, DF filters those signaling messages related with delivery rate adjustments originated in the client, constructs a correct answer and sends it to the client. For a detailed description see "Data Forwarder" and "Mobility Control" subsections.

MC monitors APs and their associated clients to predict user mobility. MC, using SNMP, periodically polls APs to know their associated clients and their RSSI. This periodicity can be tuned depending on the typical speed of user mobility. With these values, MC estimates client mobility, sets/unsets FF and generates a message to the HIs, indicating that it is necessary to force the handoff of a certain client. During handoffs, clients underestimate channel conditions and try to adjust the quality of contents. The MC, based on its knowledge of client mobility, improves user experience by filtering the adaptation messages of the clients. These messages are only filtered during a period of time equal to a timer called *MT* (mobility timer) activated by the proxy when a mobile user is detected.

HI is the element that forces client roaming between APs using de-authentication WLAN management frames. This roaming induction is only performed when MC detects a mobile user that is suffering poor channel conditions. MC sends a message to the HIs indicating both the AP and station MACs, and, after that, HIs send a de-authentication management frame to the client. This role can be played by any wireless device capable of generating wireless LAN management frames impersonating APs (for a detailed description of HI see "Handoff Inductor" subsection).

In the following subsections, detailed descriptions of the wireless proxy, data forwarder, mobility control and handoff inductor modules are provided. After that, the mobility prediction algorithm used in the proxy is detailed. Finally, the experimental results of the streaming performance using wireless proxy are presented.

Wireless Proxy (WP)

WP performs the following tasks:

1. Launch a thread, MC, with a list of target APs.
2. Listens for new connections in RTSP/TCP port 554.
3. For each new connection it creates an independent thread DF in charge of analyzing, filtering or forwarding the messages of these streaming sessions. Additionally, it maintains a relationship between clients' MAC and an FF.
4. Return to step 2.

Data Forwarder (DF)

DFs perform the following tasks:

1. Analyze RTSP/TCP client session establishment messages and open an

RTSP/TCP connection with the server. Go to Step 2.

2. Receive packets from the client and from the server:

    a. If the packet is an RTSP/TCP message received from the client, go to Step 3.

    b. If the packet is an RTSP/TCP message received from the server, it is directly forwarded to the client except for the RTSP Setup message with the selection of data transport protocol and ports. This message is analyzed and modified with the goal of opening the correct ports to receive data from the server and redirecting it to the client. After that, go to Step 2.

    c. If the packet is an RDT packet received from the server, it is forwarded to the client. After that, go to Step 2.

    d. If the packet is an RDT packet received from the client, it is forwarded to the server. After that, go to Step 2.

3. Analyze RTSP/TCP messages received from the client:

    a. If the message is an RTSP Setup containing data transport protocol and port specifications, analyze this message and open one port to receive/send data from/to the server and a second one to receive/send data from/to the client. After that, forward the message with the modified port information to the server and go to Step 2.

    b. If the message is an RTSP Setup with the *Delivery Bandwidth* parameter, DF polls its FF. The correct FF value is set by MC. If this FF is set, the message is redirected to the server since it comes from network overload. If the FF is not set, the message is filtered and a correct answer to the client is sent, since it is generated by a client underestimation of channel conditions. After that go to Step 2.

    c. If the message is not included in types (a) or (b), it is directly forwarded to the server. After that go to Step 2.

Mobility Control (MC)

MC performs the following task:

1. Poll APs to discover their associated clients and RSSI. The periodicity of this polling can be tuned depending on user mobility speed.

2. Based on these values, the proxy can estimate bandwidth availability in each cell and obtain conclusions about user mobility cases (see "User Mobility Prediction" subsection).

    a. If one client is detected as mobile, go to Step 3.

    b. If no client is detected as mobile in one cell and the MT is not active, FF is cleared for all the clients in that cell. Then return to Step 1.

3. The proxy has to activate FF for all the DF of the same cell to compensate the underestimations of mobile clients and the effects on static clients. After that, it has to activate the MT after which the conditions of the channel would have been recovered. Also, a message is sent to the correct HI to force the client handoff to a better AP. After that, go to Step 1. This MT is the second tuneable parameter of WP.

Handoff Inductor (HI)

WiFi networks use management frames to control client authentication and association to an AP. The structure of these management frames is detailed in the IEEE 802.11 standards and one of their functions is to de-associate or de-authenticate clients. When a wireless client is de-associated, this client searches for a new AP with a better RSSI and tries to reassociate. If no better AP is available, the client tries to reassociate with the same AP. In our test environment, APs use de-authentication management frames to de-associate clients only after the administrator manually types the right command on the AP interface.

To our knowledge, on commercial APs it is not possible to define a triggered generation of de-authentication frames based, for example, on clients' RSSI. These de-authentication messages can be automatically generated by an extra element (HI) that runs operating systems such as Linux or MAC OS and some special wireless drivers that permit raw injection of frames in the network (*Airjack*, n.d.). This extra element has two network interfaces (see Figure 2): one Ethernet card attached to the wired network and one IEEE 802.11 interface. Using the wired card the HI is capable of receiving messages from the MC. After analyzing these messages, the HI generates the right management frames for wireless stations using the wireless interface.

In a WLAN planned to support user mobility in all the desired area, the coverage areas of APs must overlap. Analyzing the network deployment, it is possible to obtain the perceived client RSSI in each point and from each AP. From this analysis, we can obtain a minimum RSSI value for the best AP selection in each point, and use this value as a threshold to predict handoffs. If the obtained threshold is less than -70dBm, new network planning and AP placement is needed in order to avoid performance anomalies and unwanted effects of mobile users over static users. From a pragmatic perspective, the value to force handoffs has to be slightly lower than the value obtained from the analyses, in order to avoid de-associated clients reassociating with the same AP. If the value to force handoffs is equal to the lowest value obtained in the analyses, handoff induction presents a 1020% effectiveness. With 5dB lower value, this effectiveness reaches 85%.

Planning the network as described, clients can receive signals using high-speed modulations and, when the selection of an AP is not the best possible, the HI can force a client handoff to a better AP. This information about client mobility is obtained from the MC. When the MC detects user mobility and RSSI going under a tuneable threshold, it sends a message to all the HI of the system, indicating the MAC address of the client to de-associate and the MAC address of the AP to which that client is currently associated.

User Mobility Prediction

User mobility prediction is a research field which has concentrated a lot of work in recent years (Duong, Dadej & Gordon, 2005; Ghosh, Beal, Ngo, & Qiao, 2006; Kassab et al., 2005; Pack & Choi, 2004). With the goal in mind of providing access in all the desired area using high-speed modulations, a simple but useful mobility detection algorithm has been implemented in the proxy. This mobility algorithm was derived from the analysis of the RSSIs of different wireless users (mobile and static). Some of these measurements are shown in Figure 4. As can be seen, when the client is moving away from the origin AP without handoff induction, the RSSI goes down. Due to the conservative behaviour of wireless hardware the client remains associated with the origin AP under extremely poor channel conditions. When the RSSI goes under -80dBm, the client considers other options. Since the coverage areas of APs overlap and the access in all the desired area is provided with high-speed modulations, when the client reassociates with a new AP the RSSI reaches a very high value. For static users, the RSSI presents smaller variations (between 1 and 8dB) even in the presence of mobile obstacles such as people moving in the surrounding area.

From the analysis of this behaviour, the mobility prediction algorithm considers three different user mobility cases:

1. **Mobile user roaming between different APs:** This situation can be identified because the RSSI of a mobile wireless client reaches values under a tuneable threshold as can be

seen in Figure 5. If one client is detected as mobile, and it is predicted that it is going to change its association, its FF has to be reset. Furthermore, the MC has to reset the FF of all the users due to the negative effects introduced by the mobile user. Also, in this situation, the MC interacts with HI, showing that a client is moving and that an induction of handoff would be helpful. The value of consecutive measurements has to be low in order to produce a high percentage of correct predictions since the prediction of mobility is needed for a useful handoff induction.

2. **Static client:** This situation can be identified because the RSSI is nearly stable and higher than the threshold value. In this situation two possible cases can be detected: low channel loads and high channel loads. With low channel loads, the client does not need to readjust the delivery bandwidth except for the case of a user performing mobility in the same cell that is described previously. With high channel loads, clients send messages to the server for the readjustment of the delivery bandwidth; if no client is moving from one AP to another, delivery rate setup messages are forwarded to the server as they are generated due to channel overload. If after a handoff, a previously mobile client is detected as static, the wireless proxy has to maintain FF cleared during MT. This time has to be long enough to allow the client to receive sufficient data to compensate previous underestimations.

3. **Mobile user going out of the coverage zone:** This situation is also characterized by a decrease in the RSSI. It is extremely complicated to distinguish this situation from the previous, due to the fact that the system wants to anticipate the roaming effects. The default proxy policy is the same as in "Mobile user roaming between different APs".

EXPERIMENTAL EVALUATION OF WIRELESS PROXY

Experimental Setup

We have developed various tests with off-the-shelf WiFi equipment to analyze streaming service performance in the presence of client mobility using the wireless proxy. We have also tested network overloads caused by SNMP AP polling.

The testbed was composed of three IEEE 802.11g APs, placed in the most appropriate areas to provide access at high-speed modulations, support user mobility and minimize interferences. The coverage areas are overlapped with a non-overlapping channel tuning. The three APs are connected by an Ethernet core composed of two 100Mbps LAN switches linked by one 1Gbps trunking. In the wired side of the network, one Helix Server (*Helix Server Project*, n.d.) was installed. Contents are available on-demand and live with qualities of 512Kbps, 768Kbps, and 1Mbps. With this deployment, the lowest value of RSSI to communicate in optimal conditions is -65dBm.

The maximum number of wireless stations considered in the test was 6 (2 mobile, 2 static. and 2 for background traffic generation). The wireless clients considered are laptop computers with two different types of interfaces: integrated 802.11b/g Intel wireless NIC, Cisco Aironet 802.11b/g PCMCIA. This type of mobile client is selected to avoid the strong restrictions related with processor capabilities and battery energy consumption of contemporary small portable devices.

The role of HI is played by two PCs equipped with a wireless Z-Com 802.11 PCMCIA interface but can be played by other devices that support Linux and Airjack drivers. The selected operating system for HI was an Ubuntu Linux distribution. To generate de-authentication frames impersonating APs, Airjack drivers were installed and associated with the Z-Com PCMCIA. Since

Airjack permits the injection of frames in different channels, only one HI is needed in our testbed to generate de-authentication frames in the channels used by APs.

Background traffic is generated on a PC attached to the wired side of the network and directed to two of the laptop computers using *iperf* (Tirumula, Qin, Dugan, Ferguson, & Gibb, n.d.). Generated background traffic varies from 1Mbps to 11Mbps directed to each of the laptops. The aim of this background traffic is to emulate the activity of other users of the same cell.

Wireless Proxy Configuration

Since the worst value of RSSI when the best AP is selected was -65dBm, the value to force handoffs was set to -70dBm. The time between consecutive measurements was set to 1.5 seconds since the average speed of a user walking is around 56Km/h. In our tests, MT was set to 15 seconds since with this value the client receives enough data to compensate previous underestimations. To avoid problems in raw frame injection reliability, each frame was retransmitted 10 times.

Results

In all the tests, the subjective quality of audio/video playback is improved both in mobile and in static clients. Session hangs are reduced to approximately 1%.

The improvements obtained in the tests are shown in Figures 5 and 6, respectively. Table 2 shows the characteristics of the contents delivered during our tests. They have been obtained for a mobile client performing one handoff while other static users are maintaining streaming sessions both in origin and destiny cells. Both audio and video streams present an average delivery rate before handoff equal to the encoding quality. When the client is moving away from the origin AP, channel conditions deteriorate and some data packets are lost. Nevertheless these losses are not appreciable in the delivery rate since channel capacity, in the worst conditions achieved in the experiments, is several times higher than the encoding quality.

During the few seconds of effective handoff, the client fails to receive data and that is reflected in received data rate. After the effective handoff time, thanks to the use of the WP, the data rate is recovered almost instantaneously. That is achieved by isolating the server from client underestimations of channel conditions by filtering delivery rate adjustments. Fast bandwidth recovery is another symptom of good playback quality perceived by mobile clients. Handoff times are not affected by handoff induction using de-authentication management frames since handoff latencies are the same with and without HI (values around 2 seconds). The utility of handoff induction is described in the analysis of static client sessions.

In Figure 7, the results obtained for a mobile client performing two handoffs with traffic loads of 10.38Mbps in origin and destiny cells are shown. The moment of time when the mobile station is forced to perform a handoff is marked with a vertical dashed line. As can be seen, in the second handoff the effective roaming time presents an increase due to extra traffic load. The same effect is described in Velayos and Karlsson, (2004). Filtering of signaling messages improves user experience even in the presence of such negative conditions.

In Figure 8, the delivery rate for a static user requesting 1Mbps content under the coverage area of AP-1, with extra traffic load of 10.38Mbps, and a mobile user performing three consecutive handoffs (AP1 to AP2, AP2 to AP3 and AP3 to AP2) is shown. Forcing mobile client handoff with the HI, the effects of mobile users are reduced since handoff is induced when RSSI falls below -65dBm. This represents a significant improvement compared to the RSSI values where clients perform roaming without HI (-80dBm). As can be seen, the negative effects over static users have been significantly reduced and when handoff induction is successful in the first trial they are almost totally avoided.

Network Overhead Analysis

Analyzing SNMP messages and their size, values of 95 bytes (SNMP GET) and 115 bytes (SNMP RESPONSE) are obtained at MAC level. Analyzing packet sizes and inter-arrival times, average data rate is around 10Kbps per monitored AP. This data rate consumption is negligible compared with the typical transmission speed of current LANs.

CONCLUSION

Client mobility has a great influence on network probes used by commercial streaming clients to estimate channel conditions. The management of handoff in WiFi networks and the conservative behaviour of WiFi hardware produce long periods of poor playback quality when some wireless clients move through the coverage area of different APs. These problems can be avoided by adapting the messages interchanged between current streaming clients and servers to meet real channel conditions.

In this article, the usefulness of the adaptation of the messages interchanged between client and server is analyzed. An intermediate element, a wireless proxy, developed for one of the most extended commercial platforms is presented. With this intermediate element, client playback experience is improved, reducing the effects of client mobility.

Additionally, handoff induction can be a helpful technique in order to avoid user mobility effects and performance anomalies in wireless LANs, even in the presence of other types of traffic different to those of streaming services. In this way, handoff is not totally dependent on client configurations and the network decides the best moment to handoff from one cell to another.

FUTURE WORK

In spite of the interest of the results obtained, deeper analyses of wireless proxy have to be carried out. To perform an experiment to evaluate the system considering 20 or 30 clients is not an easy task and leads to two different strategies: to deploy the service on a real hot-spot with a high number of mobile users, or to develop system models to obtain results based on simulation. Also, the inclusion of more advanced mobility prediction algorithms and new techniques for content buffering in the intermediate element, have to be considered. The reliability and scalability of the solution has to be studied, analyzing aspects such as the percentage of success of the mobility prediction algorithm or the reliability of SNMP messages with competing traffic.

Due to the unreliability of raw frames injection, the percentage of success of this technique has to be carefully evaluated, obtaining the optimal value for the number of retransmissions to assure the correct reception of the frame in the mobile station. Other options to generate management frames, such as LinuxAP (Malinen, n.d.), also need to be evaluated. Also, different options for monitoring conditions of client connections have to be considered. For example, the introduction of a wireless sniffer capable of analyzing channel activity may be a better solution than SNMP polling. Thus, mobility prediction does not depend on manufacturer extensions of SNMP daemons.

ACKNOWLEDGMENT

This research has been financed by the network operator Telecable and La Nueva España within the projects of NuevaMedia, Telemedia, ModelMedia and MediaXXI and the Spanish National Research Program within the project INTEGRAMEDIA (TSI2004-00979). Special thanks to Intel Corporation for providing the hardware necessary for this analysis.

REFERENCES

Airjack. (n.d.). Retrieved March 29, 2006, from http://sourceforge.net/projects/airjack

Bai, G., & Williamsom, C. (2004). *The effects of mobility on wireless media streaming performance*. Paper presented at Wireless Networks and Emerging Technologies (WNET), Banff, AB, Canada.

Bellavista, P., & Corradi, A. (2004). *A QoS management middleware based on mobility prediction for multimedia service continuity in the wireless internet*. Paper presented at IEEE Int. Symp. on Computers and Communications (ISCC) 2004, Alexandria, Egypt.

Bellavista, P., Corradi, A., & Giannelli, C. (2005). *Mobile proxies for proactive buffering in wireless internet multimedia streaming*. Paper presented at IEEE International Conference Distributed Computing Systems Workshops, Washington, DC.

Bruneo, D., Villari, M., Zaia, A., & Puliafito, A. (2003). *VoD services for mobile wireless devices*. Paper presented at IEEE ISCC 2003, Kemer, Antalya, Turkey.

Cisco DOT11 MIB. (n.d.). Cisco DOT11 Association MIB. Retrieved March 29, 2006, from http://www.cisco.com

Cranley, N., & Davis, M. (2005). *Performance evaluation of video streaming with background traffic over IEEE 802.11 WLAN networks*. First ACM Workshop on Wireless Multimedia Networking and Performance Modelling, Montreal, Quebec, Canada.

Duong, H., Dadej, A., & Gordon, S. (2005). Proactive context transfer and forced handover in IEEE 802.11 wireless LAN based access networks. *ACM SIGMOBILE Mobile Computing and Communications Review, 9*, 32–44.

Ghosh, J., Beal, M. J., Ngo, H. Q., & Qiao, C. (2006). *On profiling and predicting locations of campus-wide wireless network users*. Paper presented at ACM/SIGMOBILE MobiHoc 2006, Florence, Italy.

Helix Server Project. (n.d.). Retrieved March 29, 2006, from https://helix-server.helixcommunity. org/

Heusse, M., Rousseau, F., Berger-Sabbatel, G., & Duda, A. (2003). *Performance anomaly of 802.11b*. Paper presented at IEEE Infocom 2003, San Francisco.

Kassab, M., Belghith, A., Bonnin, J., & Sassi, S. (2005). *Fast preauthentication based on proactive key distribution for 802.11 infrastructure networks*. Paper presented at ACM WMuNeP 2005, Montreal, Quebec, Canada.

Koucheryavy, Y., Moltachanov, D., & Harju, J. (2003). Performance evaluation of live video streaming in 802.11b WLAN environment under different load conditions. *Lecture Notes in Computer Science, 2889*, 30–41.

Li, M., Li, F., Claypool, M., & Kinicki, R. (2005). *Weather forecasting—predicting performance for streaming video over wireless LANs*. Paper presented at ACM NOSSDAV 2005, Stevenson, WA.

Liao, Y., & Gao, L. (2006). *Practical schemes for smooth MAC layer handoff in 802.11 wireless networks*. Paper presented at IEEE WoWMoM 2006, Niagara Falls, Buffalo, NY.

Malinen, J. (n.d.). *HostAP driver*. Retrieved August 7, 2006, from http://hostap.epitest.fi/

Mhatre, V., & Papagiannaki, K. (2006). *Using smart triggers for improved user performance in 802.11 wireless networks*. Paper presented at ACM Mobysis 2006, Uppsala. Sweden.

Mishra, A., Shin, M., & Arbaugh, W. (2003). An empirical analysis of the IEEE 802.11 MAC layer handoff process. *ACM SIGCOMM Computer Communication Review, 33,* 93–102.

Nichols, J., Claypool, M., Kinicki, R., & Li, M. (2004). *Measurements of congestion responsiveness of Windows Media streaming media.* Paper presented at ACM NOSSDAV'04, Kinsale, County Cork, Ireland.

Pack, S., & Choi, Y. (2004). Fast handoff scheme based on mobility prediction in public wireless LAN systems. *IEEE Proceeding–Communications, 151,* 489–495.

Ramani, I., & Savage, S. (2005). *SyncScan: Practical fast handoff for 802.11 infrastructure networks.* Paper presented at *IEEE Infocom* 2005, Miami, FL.

RTSP Proxy Kit. (n.d.). Retrieved March 29, 2006, from http://sourceforge.net/projects/rtsp

Shin, S., Forte, A. G., Singh, A., & Schulzrinne, H. (2004). *Reducing MAC layer handoff latency in IEEE 802.11 wireless LANs.* Paper presented at ACM MobiWAC 2004, Philadelphia.

Tirumula, A., Qin, F., Dugan, J., Ferguson, J., & Gibbs, K. (n.d.). *Iperf: Testing the limits of your network.* Retrieved March 29, 2006, from http://dast.nlanr.net/Projects/Iperf

Velayos, H., & Karlsson, G. (2004). *Techniques to reduce IEEE 802.11b handoff time.* Paper presented at IEEE ICC 2004, Paris.

Vilas, M., Pañeda, X. G., Melendi, D., García, R., & García, V. (2006, May). *Influence of effective handoff latency on live streaming services.* Paper presented at CITA2006, Monterrey, Mexico.

Wu, D., Hou, Y. T., Zhu, W., Zhang, Y., & Peha, J. (2001). Streaming video over the internet: Approaches and directions. *IEEE Transaction on Circuits and Systems for Video Technology, 11,* 282301.

Yang, D., Lee, T., Jan, K., Chang, J., & Sunghyun, C. (2006). Performance enhancement of multirate IEEE 802.11 WLANs with geographically-scattered stations. *IEEE Transactions on Mobile Computing, 5,* 907919.

Yang, G., Chen, L., Sun, T., Gerla, M., & Sanadidi, M. (2006). Smooth and efficient real-time video transport in presence of wireless networks. *ACM Transactions on Multimedia Computing, Communications, and Applications (TOMCCAP), 2,* 109–126.

Yeo, J., Youssef, M., Henderson, T., & Agrawala, A. (2005). *An accurate technique for measuring the wireless side of wireless networks.* Paper presented at WiTMeMo 2005, Seattle, WA.

Zenel, B. A. (1999). A general purpose proxy filtering mechanism for the mobile environment. *ACM Wireless Networks, 5,* 391409.

This work was previously published in International Journal of Business Data Communications and Networking, Vol. 3, Issue 3, edited by J. Gutierrez, pp. 1-18, copyright 2007 by IGI Publishing, formerly known as Idea Group Publishing (an imprint of IGI Global).

Chapter XII
Soft Decision Parallel Interference Cancellation for Multi-Carrier DS-CDMA

R. Radhakrishnan
Sri Ramakrishna Engineering College, India

K. R. Shankarkumar
Sri Ramakrishna Engineering College, India

A. Ebenezer Jeyakumar
Government College of Engineering, India

ABSTRACT

In this chapter, we propose a new scheme for Multi User Detection (MUD) using Parallel Interference Cancellation (PIC) technique. This technique provides a good complexity, latency, and performance compromise. Among spread-spectrum techniques, the most popular one is the Direct-Sequence Code-Division Multiple-Access (DS-CDMA), where each active user's data is modulated (multiplied) by a unique code. This technique is suitable for Multi-Carrier (MC) Direct-Sequence Code-Division Multiple-Access (DS-CDMA) systems. We offer a new scheme of soft detectors whose performance is superior to that of the other famous suboptimal detectors. On each sub carrier, instead of making hard bit decisions of the other users in the current stage and regenerating and canceling the interference signal, a weighted sum of the soft outputs of the other users in the current stage is canceled from the soft output of the desired user. This is the input to the next stage, then at the last stage, the interference canceled outputs from all the sub carriers are combined (Maximal Ratio Combining) to form the decision statistics. We derived expressions for the Bit Error Rate (BER) on Rayleigh fading channels. Analytical results are found for different stages in the proposed PIC scheme. The simulation results show that the proposed scheme offers good interference cancellation than the other filter receiver. The complexity of this scheme grows linearly with the number of users. Moreover, this scheme is much faster than other receivers such as Successive Interference Cancellation (SIC).

INTRODUCTION

An important aspect of the air interface of a cellular telephone system is the multiple access method. Each user of the cellular system is given a separate channel, and how they are different is determined by the multiple access method. In a cellular system employing Direct Sequence Code Division Multiple Access (DS-CDMA), all users use the same frequency at the same time (Viterbi, 1995). Before transmission, the signal from each user is multiplied by a distinct signature waveform. The signature waveform is a signal which has a much larger bandwidth than the information bearing signal from the user. The CDMA system is thus a spread spectrum technique (Scholtz, 1982). All users use different signature waveforms to expand their signal bandwidth. At the base station, the sum of all the broadband signals is received. To demodulate a signal from a specific user, the received signal is correlated with the signature waveform of that user. To solve the problems with the conventional receiver a different type of multi-user detector has been designed (Short & Rushforth, 1990; Verdu, 1998; Xie, Short, & Rushforth, 1990).

Multi-carrier modulation is currently used in many wireless systems for transmission of data for telephone network and cellular radio (Bingham, 1990). MC-DSCDMA technique offers many advantages like robustness in fading interference, spectral efficiency, down link Bit Error Rate (BER) and non-contiguous bandwidth operations (Shinusuke Hara & Prasad, 1997). The modulated signal can be generated with the aid of the Fast Fourier Transform (FFT) at the cost of low receiver complexity.

Studies have been made to analyze the performance of multi-carrier DS-CDMA systems. It is known that Multiple Access Interference (MAI) limits DS-CDMA system capacity (Cooper & Nelleton, 1978), and that any technique, which can suppress/cancel MAI, can increase the capacity of system. Multi-user detectors exploit the inherent structure in the MAI to estimate and cancel the MAI to improve detection performance. Much of the research is aimed at finding an appropriate trade off between complexity and performance. Important linear sub optimum multi-user detectors including decorrelating detector and MMSE detectors were tried to remove the MAI (Shimon Moshavi & Bellcore, 1996; Sergio Verdu, 1998). The major disadvantages of the linear sub optimal detection were (i)The number of large computations needed to invert the matrix especially for asynchronous case (ii) Need to estimate the recovered amplitude or phase

Owing to the large complexity involved in the optimum detection, several sub optimal approaches had been studied (Zhenuhua Xie et al, 1990; Proakis, 1995; Alexandra Duel Hallen et al, 1995; Verdu, 1998). Non-linear sub optimum multi-user detectors, including Successive Interference Canceller (SIC) and Parallel Interference Canceller (PIC), make tentative decisions on the bits of the users using any detector.

SIC cancels the interference estimate one after another whereas PIC cancels the interference simultaneously (Tero Ojanpera, 1997; Sergio Verdu, 1998). The performance of SIC will be better if unequal received power of the user is available at the receiver and PIC was better if the user with equal power (Jefery G. Andrews & Meng, 2004). The SIC detector imposes only modest additional complexity and has the potential of providing a significant performance over single-user detector. In contrast to the SIC based multi-user detector, the Parallel Interference Cancellation (PIC) (Viterbi, 1971) aided detector estimates and subtracts the MAI imposed by all interfering users from the signal of the desired user in parallel (Ginnakis, Hua, Stoica, & Tong, 2000; Kondo & Milstein, 1996).

In recent years, there has been an increased interest in the subtractive type interference cancellers, SIC and PIC was the two important detectors in the group.

Successive Interference Cancellation (SIC)

In SIC, all the users were ranked according to their received signal power and processed by the matched filter or RAKE receiver to obtain the data estimates. The transmitted signal was reconstructed using Hard Decision (HD) bits/symbols, estimates of the user and the spreading sequence. Then the estimated reconstructed signal of the user was subtracted from the composite multiuser received signal (Pulin Patel & Jack Holtzman, 1994). Two different methods were suggested to implement the practical SIC scheme. However, SIC first cancelled strongest interferences and then weakest, due to this a bit delay was imposed in each cancellation stage (Seskar et al, 1998; Lai and Shynk, 2000). Analytic bit error probabilities for SIC in Rayleigh fading channels indicates that the performance of SIC decreased with increased tracking error (Lin Fang & Laurence B. Milstein, 2000)

The error propagation due to wrong decision and followed by error probability for next users could be minimized by increasing magnitude of Log Likelihood Ratio (LLR) scheme (Sang Wu Kim & Young-Jun Hong, 2003). The scheme considered both signal strength and instantaneous multi-user interference for cancellation. The effect of channel estimation error on the average BER for various LLR base was also examined (Xiaodang Ren et al, 2003). It is observed that the scheme very well supports overload systems. Two different models with high capacity, low complexity and robust SIC systems were considered one was an uncoded system with an Interference Cancellation block and an optimum power control. The second model was realized by using low rate super orthogonal codes and Maximum Likelihood Sequence Estimation (MLSE) with Viterbi decoder. Numerical results showed that the described scheme was very effective in mitigating a multipath channel (Jeffreey Andrews & Meng, 2004).

Simplicity, compatible with current commercial systems, adaptable with error correcting codes and spectral efficiency are some of the advantages of SIC. Few disadvantages are (i) Signal must be estimated and subtracted out from the composite signal before decoding the next user, under this circumstance if the signal estimation is inaccurate and further decoding is not reliable (ii) Successive process consumes time (iii) Ordering of user powers is a must (iv) The capacity of the system drops off owing to more multipath components

Parallel Interference Cancellation (PIC)

The main advantage of PIC over SIC is that it does not require the power estimates of all users to be updated after each cancellation stage and the processing delay is the same for all the users. In contrast to the SIC based multi-user detector, the PIC aided detector estimates and subtracts the MAI imposed by all interfering users from the signal of the desired user in parallel (Viterbi, 1971; Varanasi & Aazhang, 1990).

Multi-carrier DS-CDMA system that applied repetition coding and maximal ratio combining to achieve the performance of systems in the absence of narrow band interference. In which the symbols transmitted over the 'M' multi-carrier tones were modulated by a rate 1/M convolutional encoder instead of repetition codes (Kondo & Milstein, 1994; Rowitch & Milstein, 1995). This system effectively suppresses the interference and very robust also. Interference cancellation can further be improved iteratively, such a technique is called multistage receivers (Fawer & Aazhang, 1995; Divsalar & Simon, 1996; Kondo & Milstein, 1996; Latva Aho, 1996).

It is noted that regeneration of the interference PIC requires the estimation of various parameters including time, amplitude and phase of all users (Michael Bucherer et al, 1996). In real-time applications, the system would experience phase jitter and time errors, which affects interference cancellation and BER. However, analysis did not considered other practical degradation factor which affects mobile receiver performance (Divsalar et al, 1998).

If the tentative data decisions are used for the interference estimations, then this scheme is called multistage Hard Decision-Parallel Interference Cancellation (HD-PIC). If tentative data decisions are not used, then the scheme is called Soft Decision-Parallel Interference Cancellation (SD-PIC) (Ginnakis et al, 2000; Achem Nahler et al, 2000; Vivek Bharadvaj & Michael Buehrer, 2001; Thomos Hesse & Schulz, 2002; Ghotbi & Soleymani, 2002). These studies consider hard decision IC receivers, where hard bit decisions were made on the output of the Matched Filters (MFs) which was then used to regenerate and cancel the MAI in parallel. Error in these bit decisions and inaccuracies in the parameters such as amplitude, timing and phase could significantly degrade the performance of HD-PIC.

A new multistage PIC, consisting of combination of soft and hard partial PIC with parameter estimation was demonstrated (Mohsen Ghotbi & Soleymani, 2002). Normally in the first stage, the accurate knowledge of power and phase was not used but in the subsequent stages, accurate power and phase estimation could improve the performance. From the review of literature on various solution methodologies for solving the problem of interest, it is clear that they need suitable improvements for them to effectively explore the complex space. A new partial parallel interference cancellation by integrating frequency diversity combining is demonstrated recently (which is termed as FDC- PPIC). It acquires superior performance improvement over Matched Filter (MF) receiver of multi-carrier DS-CDMA. FDC- PPIC is more potential for future application (Guoxioing Xu & Liangcai Gan, 2005). In order to decrease the influence on reception performance resulted from incorrect decision of the interference

users' information bits in parallel interference cancellation process, a neural network based design to correct the interference cancellation factor is also proposed (Yanping Li et al, 2006). Due to the dominance of fading in determining system performance, it has been observed that different PIC techniques (PPIC, FDC-PPIC, and Neural Network based) have similar optimum performance, all very close to conventional PIC (David W. Matolak & Beibei Wang, 2007).

In this article, a new scheme of soft detectors whose performance is superior to that of the other famous suboptimal detectors is offered. On each sub carrier, instead of making hard bit decisions of the other users in the current stage and regenerating and canceling the interference signal, a weighted sum of the soft outputs of the other users in the current stage is canceled from the soft output of the desired user. This is the input to the next stage then at the last stage. The interference canceled outputs from all the sub carriers are combined (Maximal Ratio Combining-MRC) to form the decision statistics. We derived expressions for the Bit Error Rate (BER) on Rayleigh Fading channels.

Demand for wireless data services and applications is taking off around the world and this is where Multicarrier CDMA fits in. MC-CDMA consistently provides better capacity for video and data communications than the other commercial technologies. In GPS Pseudolites transmissions are envisaged to provide better than one meter location accuracy for various applications. A main drawback with the ground-based pseudolite transmission is the effect of interference in multipath environment. We note that use of MC-CDMA for GPS Pseudolite transmission can be beneficial in combating the effect of interferences.

The rest of the article is organized as follows. In Section II, system model and PIC scheme are presented. Section II presents BER analysis of the PIC scheme. Analytical and simulation results are presented in Section III. Finally, conclusion is presented in Section IV.

Multi-Carrier Transmitter

In the multi-carrier transmitter, the spreading is serial to parallel converted and each modulates 'M' carriers rather than a single carrier, that is the number of sub carrier in the system is equal to the number of chips per bit. In these systems spreading sequences are applied in the frequency domain by mapping different chips of the spreading sequence to different sub carrier frequencies, rather than the time domain and such systems are called multi-carrier DS-CDMA systems.

The Multi-carrier DS-CDMA transmitter for 'K' users is shown in Figure 1 and the transmitted signal for *k*-th user is given by:

$$S_k(t) = \sqrt{2E_{Ck}} \sum_{i=-\infty}^{\infty} b_k^i a_k(t-iT) \sum_{m=1}^{M} Cos(\omega_m t + \theta_{k,m})$$

(1)

where E_{Ck} is the transmitted energy/chip for *k*-th user

b_k^i is *i*-th transmitted bit of *k*-th user
T is one bit duration
M is number of sub carrier
ω_m is *m*-th sub carrier frequency

$\theta_{k,m}$ is the phase of the *m*-th sub carrier of *k*-th user, which is uniformly distributed over $[0, 2\pi)$

$a_k(t)$ is the signature waveform of user *k* is given by

$$a_k(t) = \sum_{n=0}^{M-1} C_k^{(n)} h(t-nMT_c)$$

(2)

where $C_k^{(n)}$ is the spreading sequence of *k*-th user

N is the processing gain
$h(t)$ is the impulse response of the chip wave shaping filter assumed to satisfy the Nyquist condition

and $\int_{-\infty}^{\infty} |H(f)|^2 df = 1$ and $T = NMT_c$

T_c is one chip duration in a single carrier system ($M = 1$).

Multi-Carrier Receiver

The receiver for this system provides a correlator for each sub carrier, and the outputs are combined using a maximal ratio combiner, as shown in Figure 2. The channel is assumed to be a slowly varying frequency selective Rayleigh channel with delay spread of T_m. The bit error performance of this multi-carrier DS-CDMA system has been analyzed assuming perfect knowledge of the phases of all the sub carriers at the receiver. The channel in each sub band is assumed to be slow-varying, flat Rayleigh channel with transfer

Figure 1. Multi-carrier DS-CDMA Transmitter of K Users

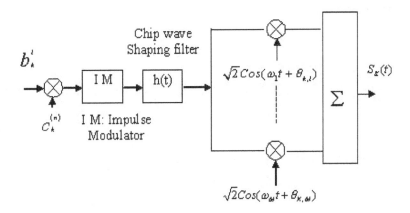

function $\zeta_{k,m} = \alpha_{k,m} \exp(j\beta_{k,m})$ where $\{\alpha_{k,m}\}$ are i.i.d Rayleigh random variables with unit second moment, and $\{\beta_{k,m}\}$ are i.i.d uniform random variables over $[0, 2\pi)$, for both user 'k' and sub carrier 'm'.

The received signal is given by Box 1.

Practically phase estimates are mostly imperfect because of channel fading and interference condition. Either unspread waveforms or spread waveforms can be sent on the multiple sub carriers in an MC system.

Interference Cancellation in Multi-Carrier DS-CDMA

The capacity of the DS-CDMA system is limited by MAI, and any technique which can suppress or cancel MAI can increase DS-CDMA system capacity. To combat MAI, the following approaches may be used (i) Designing of good radio link (ii) Employing techniques such as, sectorization, antenna tilts etcetera, to decrease the interference experienced by each user (iii)

Owing to the non-zero cross correlation of the users code receiver

MUDs exploit the inherent structure of MAI to estimate and cancel the MAI. Recently, there has been an increased interest in suboptimal multi-user detectors owing to the high complexity of optimum MUDs. Nonlinear suboptimal MUDs including SIC and PIC are the two important detectors in the group. These detectors have a number of attractive features.

Successive Interference Cancellation

In SIC all the users have been ranked according to their received signal power, with the highest power user being labelled as user 1 and the lowest power user being labelled as user 'K'. User data are demodulated sequentially so that the strongest user data are demodulated first and the weakest user last. The matched filter or RAKE receiver is used to process the received composite signals which provide an estimate of the data of one user.

Box 1.

$$r(t) = \sum_{k=1}^{K} \sqrt{2E_{ck}} \sum_{i=-\infty}^{\infty} b_k^i a_k(t-iT) \sum_{m=1}^{M} a_{k,m} Cos(\omega_m t + \theta'_{k,m}) + n_\omega(t) \qquad (3)$$

where $\theta'_{k,m} = \theta_{k,m} + \beta_{k,m}$
$n_\omega(t)$ is White Gaussian Noise with power spectral density of $\eta_0/2$.

Figure 2. Multi-carrier DS-CDMA Receiver for K Users

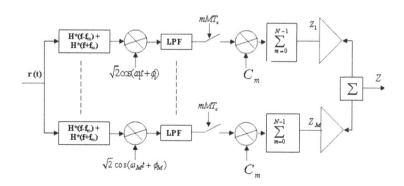

Figure 3. Structure of successive interference cancellation

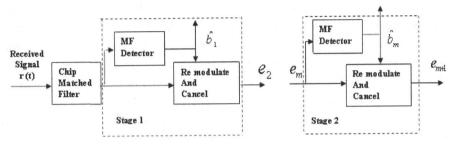

The transmitted signal of this user is then reconstructed using both the hard decision bits/symbols, and also the estimates of the Channel Impulse Response (CIR) and the spreading sequence. Then the received signal is subtracted from the composite multi-user received signal, and this difference signal becomes the input to the next stage as shown in Figure 3. This procedure is repeated until the lowest power (weaker) user namely k-th user's signal is demodulated.

Though the SIC has the potential of providing a significant performance improvement over the conventional single user detector, it has the drawback of more delay for the demodulation of the last user. The interference cancellation benefit is not uniform for all the users, that is, the last user gets the maximum cancellation benefit and the first user gets no cancellation benefit. The successive structure not only requires less hardware but also more robust in doing cancellation.

Parallel Interference Cancellation

Figure 4 shows the structure of PIC. In each cancellation stage, the signal of each user is reconstructed by invoking the data estimated from the previous cancellation stage. Then, for each user the reconstructed signals of all the other users are subtracted from the received composite signal and the resultant signal is processed by the RAKE receiver or matched filters, in order to obtain the new set of data for each 'K' user which is to be used in the next interference cancellation stage. The reconstruction, cancellation and re-estimation operations are repeated as many times as the system complexity becomes low.

The advantages of PIC is, its complexity grows linearly with the number of users, small delay compared to SIC and not required power estimates of all users, which is to be updated after each cancellation stage. However, it is observed

Figure 4. Structure of parallel interference cancellation

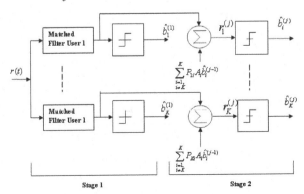

that regeneration of the interference in SIC and PIC requires the estimation of various parameters like delay, amplitude and phases of all users.

A significant amount of research has been done in the analysis and simulation of HD-PIC for Multi-carrier DS-CDMA. However, performance of HD-PIC is significantly degraded by inaccuracies in the estimation of parameters. Hence, a new PIC scheme which directly uses the soft output of the matched filters for cancellation is introduced and the proposed scheme does not require the estimation of parameters.

SYSTEM MODEL

Since 1990 the multi-carrier modulation has been used in many wired and wireless applications.

The basic principle is to divide the transmitted bit stream into many different sub streams and send these over to many sub channels, whereas the sub channel is orthogonal under ideal propagation conditions. The data rate and bandwidth of each sub channel is much less than the total data rate and bandwidth.

The Figure 5 shows the multi-user multistage PIC demodulator on the m-th sub carrier (there are M such demodulators, one on each sub carrier) and Figure 6 shows the maximal ratio combined outputs from all sub carrier of k-th user and bit decision for k-th user. In the first stage of m-th sub carrier demodulator, conventional matched filters for all the users are provided as shown in Figure 5.

The first stage is followed by $L - 1$-th stage of cancellation wherein stage, on each sub carrier,

Figure 5. Multistage PIC demodulator on m-th sub carrier

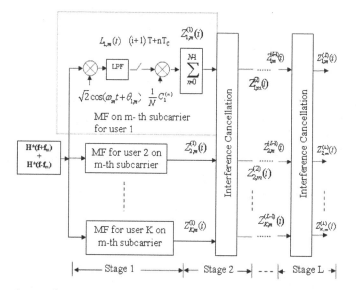

Figure 6. Maximal ratio combiner

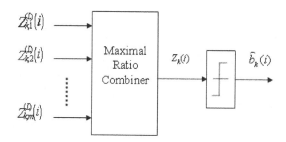

a weighted sum of the soft outputs of the other users in the current stage is subtracted from the soft output of the desired user. The bit decision statistics is performed at the stage '*L*' after maximal ratio combining of all IC stage outputs, as shown in Figure 6. However, there is no interference cancellation at the first stage.

Derivations of PIC

The analytical expressions for the bit error rate at the output of second and third stages of the PIC receiver are derived as follows. The LPF output of *m*-th sub carrier for *k*-th user,

$$L_{k,m}(t) = LPF\{r'_m(t)\sqrt{2}\, Cos(\omega_m t + \theta'_{k,m})\}$$

is given in Box 2.

The power spectral density of $n^0_{k,m}(t)$ is $\eta_0/2$. Without any loss of generality, the system decision for *i*-th bit of k-th user is analyzed. Let $Z^{(1)}_{k,m}(i)$ denote the soft output of *i*-th bit of k-th user ($k = 1, -$, 3, ..., *K*) on m-th sub carrier ($m = 1, 2, 3, ..., M$) of j-th stage ($j = 1, 2, 3, ..., L$) of the PIC receiver.

The soft output of *i*-th bit of *k*-th user on m-th sub carrier of the first stage, $Z^{(1)}_{k,m}(i)$ is given by

$$Z^{(1)}_{k,m}(i) = \frac{1}{N} \sum_{n=0}^{N-1} C_k^{(n)} L_{k,m}\left(iT + nMT_c\right) \quad (7)$$

The output $Z^{(1)}_{k,m}(i)$ consists of three components namely, information signal, MAI and Noise. Therefore equation (7) is written as

$$Z^{(j)}_{k,m}(i) = S_{k,m}(i) + I_{k,m}(i) \quad (8)$$

where $S_{k,m}(i) = \sqrt{E_{ck}}\, b_k^i\, \alpha_{k,m}$ \quad (9)

$$I_{k,m}(i) = \frac{1}{N} \sum_{k'\neq k} V_{k',k,m}(i)\, \rho_{k',k} + n_{k,m}(i) \quad (10)$$

$$V_{k',k,m}(i) = S_{k',m}(i)\, Cos(\theta'_{k',m} - \theta'_{k,m}) \quad (11)$$

$$\rho_{k'k} = \sum_{n=0}^{N-1} C_k^{(n)} \sum_{n=0}^{N-1} C_k^{(n')} x((n-n')MT_c) \quad (12)$$

$$n_{k,m}(i) = \frac{1}{N} \sum_{n=0}^{N-1} C_k^{(n)} n^0_{k,m}(iT + nMT_c) \quad (13)$$

and the variance of $n_{k,m}(i)$ is $\eta_0/2N$.

Box 2.

$$L_{k,m}(t) = \sum_{k'=1}^{K} \sqrt{E_{ck'}} \sum_{i=-\infty}^{\infty} b_{k'}^i a_{k',m} Cos(\theta'_{k',m} - \theta'_{k,m}) g_{k'}(t - iT) + n^0_{k,m}(t) \quad (4)$$

where $g_{k'}(t) = \sum_{n=0}^{N-1} c_{k'}^{(n)} x(t - nMT_c)$ \quad (5)

$n^0_{k,m}(t) = LPF\{n'_{\omega m}(t)\sqrt{2}\, Cos(\omega_m t + \theta'_{k,m})\}$ \quad (6)

$x(t) = F^{-1}|H(f)|^2$

$r'_m(t)$ and $n'_{\omega m}(t)$ are the output of m-th band pass filter after passing $r(t)$ and $n_\omega(t)$ through it respectively.

Output Statistics of Second Stage Cancellation

The main objective of the interference cancellation is to estimate the MAI of k-th user in parallel and cancel the estimate from k-th user's total signal. The first stage soft outputs $Z_{k,m}^{(1)}(i)$ are fed as input to the second stage where cancellation is performed. Referring to equation (10), the knowledge of $V_{k'k,m}(i)$ and $\rho_{k'k}$ are used to compute MAI. An estimate of $V_{k'k,m}(i)$ is obtained by multiplying by $Z_{k,m}^{(1)}(i)$ with a factor $G_{k,m}^{(1)}$ and $\rho_{k'k}$ is determined by the knowledge of the spreading sequences of all the users.

That is,

$$\hat{V}_{k'k,m}(i) = Z_{km}^{(1)}(i)\, G_{k'm}^{(1)} \tag{14}$$

where $G_{k,m}^{(1)}$ is given by

$$G_{k',m}^{(1)} = \frac{1}{N} Cos(\theta'_{k',m} - \theta'_{k,m})\, \rho_{k'k} \tag{15}$$

Using the approximate estimate of $V_{k'k,m}(i)$ in (11), the interference cancelled output of the second stage, can be obtained as

$$Z_{k,m}^{(2)}(i) = Z_{km}^{(1)}(i) - \sum_{\substack{k'=1,\\k'\neq K}}^{k} \hat{V}_{k'k,m}(i) \tag{16}$$

In addition, the approximate cancellation can be explained by considering the soft outputs of the first and second user and it is given by

$$Z_1^{(1)}(i) = S_1 + \frac{1}{N}S_2\, Cos(\theta'_2 - \theta'_1)\rho_{21} + n_1 \tag{17}$$

$$Z_2^{(1)}(i) = S_2 + \frac{1}{N}S_1\, COS(\theta'_1 - \theta'_2)\rho_{21} + n_2 \tag{18}$$

In order to cancel the component of second user in the first user output an estimate of $V_{21} = \frac{1}{N}S_2\, Cos(\theta'_2 - \theta'_1)$ is needed. The estimate of V_{21} can be obtained by the equation shown in Box 3.

The interference cancelled output of the second stage for the first user is given by

$$Z_1^{(2)} = Z_1^{(1)} - \hat{V}_{21} \tag{20}$$

Referring to equations (17), (19) and (20), it is observed that the cancellation in equation (4.22) perfectly removes the 2nd user component from the first stage output of the 1st user. However, in the cancellation process, the $\frac{1}{N^2}S_1S_2\, Cos(\theta'_2 - \theta'_1)Cos(\theta'_1 - \theta'_2)\, \rho_{12}\rho_{21}$ term in equation (19) is introduced at second stage output in equation (20), hence the cancellation is

Box 3.

$$
\begin{aligned}
\hat{V}_{21} &= Z_2^{(1)} \frac{1}{N} Cos(\theta'_2 - \theta'_1)\rho_{21} \\
&= \frac{1}{N}S_2\, Cos(\theta'_2 - \theta'_1)\rho_{21} \\
&\quad + \frac{1}{N^2}S_1S_2 Cos(\theta'_2 - \theta'_1)Cos(\theta'_1 - \theta'_2)\rho_{12}\rho_{21} \\
&\quad + \frac{1}{N}n_2\, Cos(\theta'_2 - \theta'_1)\rho_{21}
\end{aligned}
\tag{19}
$$

imperfect. However, since this newly introduced term is proportionate to $1/N^2$, and the value of processing gain (N) is typically large, the effect of this term is quite small. However, interference cancellation performance can further be improved by using additional PIC stages.

In the cancellation process, k-th user signal component remains unaltered whereas the interference component is altered. The interference statistics and the noise terms at the second stage output is given important. Equation (16) can be written as

$$Z_{k,m}^{(2)}(i) = Z_{km}^{(1)}(i) - \sum_{\substack{k'=1, \\ k'=K}}^{K} \widehat{V}_{k',k,m}(i) = \sqrt{E_{ck}} \, b_k^i \, \alpha_{k,m} + W_k^{(2)}(i)$$

(21)

where

$$W_{k,m}^{(2)}(i) = n_{k,m}(i) - \frac{1}{N} \sum_{\substack{k'=1, \\ k' \neq K}}^{K} Cos(\theta'_{k',m} - \theta'_{k,m}) \, \rho_{k'k} \, I_{k,m}$$

(22)

For large values of K, $I_{k,m}(i)$ can be approximated as a Gaussian random noise with zero mean and variance

$$Var\{I_{k,m}(i)\} = \sum_{k' \neq K} \frac{E_{ck}}{2N^2} \, \rho_{k'k}^2 + \frac{\eta_0}{2N}$$ (23)

The variance and noise for the k-th user $\eta_{k,m}^{(2)}$ at the second stage output can be obtained as

$$\eta_{k,m}^{(2)} = \frac{\eta_0}{2N} + \sum_{\substack{k'=1, \\ k' \neq K}}^{K} \frac{1}{2N^2} \, \rho_{k'k}^2 \, Var\{I_{k,m}(i)\}$$

(24)

Output Statistics of Third Stage Cancellation

The performance of PIC can be further improved by using additional stages. However, second or third stages of cancellation are adequate to achieve performance close to the best possible

performance. Increasing the number of stages beyond three stages improves the performance only marginally, while increasing the complexity and delay. Accordingly, the performance up to stages three is analyzed which takes the second stage soft outputs $Z_{k,m}^{(2)}(i)$ in refer to equation (16) as its input.

Further, the interference caused by the imperfect cancellation in the second stage is cancelled in the third stage like second stage. Here also, an imperfect estimate of the interference term is obtained like second stage and which is used in the cancellation. Further, the estimate of the third stage IC is added to the second stage output in order to cancel the negative imperfect cancellation term introduced in the second stage cancellation. Hence, the k-th user output at the third stage interference cancelled output $Z_{k,m}^{(3)}(i)$ can be written as shown in Box 4.

Using the Gaussian approximation as before, $\eta_{k,m}^{(3)}$ is obtained as

$$\eta_{k,m}^{(3)} = \frac{\eta_0}{2N} + \frac{\eta_0}{2N^2} \sum_{\substack{k'=1, \\ k' \neq K}}^{K} \rho_{k',k}^2 + \frac{1}{2N^4} \sum_{\substack{k'=1, \\ k' \neq K}}^{K} \rho_{k',k}^4 \, \eta_{k,m}^{(2)}$$

$$+ \frac{1}{4N^4} \sum_{\substack{k'=1, \\ k' \neq K}}^{K} \sum_{\substack{k''=k', \\ k'' \neq 1}} \rho_{k'',k}^2 \, \eta_{k'',m}^{(2)} \rho_{k,k''}^2$$ (29)

Maximal Ratio Combining and BER

The bit decision is made on the maximal ratio combined output at the final stage. A perfect knowledge of the channel fading gain of k-th user is assumed, hence, the output of the PIC followed by the MRC is given by

$$Z_k = \sum_{m=1}^{M} g_{k,m} \, Z_{k,m}^{(L)}$$

(30)

where $g_{k,m}$ Channel fading gain

In order to maximize the signal-to-noise ratio, $g_{k,m}$ is set to be

Box 4.

$$Z_{k,m}^{(3)}(i) = Z_{k,m}^{(2)}(i) + \sum_{k'=1}^{K} Z_{k',m}^{(2)}(i)\, G_{k',m}^{(2)}(i) \qquad (25)$$

$$= \sqrt{E_{ck}}\, b_k^i\, \alpha_{k,m} + n_{k,m}(i) - \frac{1}{N} Cos(\theta_{k',m}' - \theta_{k,m}')\rho_{k',k}\, I_{k,m}(i)$$

$$+ \sum_{k'=1}^{K} Z_{k',m}^{(2)}(i)\, G_{k',m}^{(2)}(i)$$

$$= \sqrt{E_{ck}}\, b_k^i\, \alpha_{k,m} + n_{k,m}(i) - \sum_{\substack{k'=1,\\ k'\neq K}}^{K} n_{k',m}(i)\, G_{k',m}^{(1)}(i) + \sum_{k'=1}^{K} W_{k',m}^{(2)}(i)\, G_{k',m}^{(2)}(i)$$

$$= \sqrt{E_{ck}}\, b_k^i\, \alpha_{k,m} + W_{k,m}^{(3)}(i)$$

where $W_{k,m}^{(3)}(i) = n_{k,m}(i) - \sum_{\substack{k'=1,\\ k'\neq K}}^{K} n_{k',m}(i)\, G_{k',m}^{(1)}(i) + \sum_{k'=1}^{K} G_{k',m}^{(2)}(i)\, W_{k',m}^{(2)}(i) \qquad (26)$

$$G_{1,m}^{(2)}(i) = \frac{1}{N^2} \sum_{k'=2}^{K} Cos(\theta_{1,m}' - \theta_{k',m}')\, \rho_{k',1}^2 \qquad (27)$$

$$G_{k,m}^{(2)}(i) = \frac{1}{N^2} \sum_{\substack{k'=1,\\ k'\neq K}}^{K} Cos(\theta_{k',m}' - \theta_{1,m}')\, Cos(\theta_{k',m}' - \theta_{k',m}')\, \rho_{k'1}\, \rho_{k,k'} \qquad (28)$$

where $k = 2, ..., K$

Then the 3rd stage output for k-th user $\eta_{k,m}^{(3)}$ variance of the interference and noise is given by
$\eta_{k,m}^{(3)} = Var\{W_{k,m}^{(3)}(i)\} = E\{W_{k,m}^{(3)}(i)\}^2$

$$g_{k,m} = \frac{E\{Z_{k,m}^{(L)}|\alpha_{k,m}\}}{Var\{Z_{k,m}^{(L)}|\alpha_{k,m}\}} \qquad (31)$$

It is assumed that $\{\alpha_{k,m}\}$ vary sufficiently slowly so that the conditional mean and variance of $Z_{k,m}^{(L)}$ $Z_{k,m}^{(L)}$ can be accurately estimated to compute $g_{k,m}$ in the above. The signal-to-noise ratio at the MRC output γ_k, conditioned on $\overline{\alpha}_k = [\alpha_{k,1}, ..., \alpha_{k,m}]^t$ can be written as:

$$\gamma_k = \frac{E^2\{Z_k|\overline{\alpha}_k\}}{Var\{Z_k|\overline{\alpha}_k\}} \qquad (32)$$

where $\gamma_{k,m} = E_{ck}\alpha_{k,m}^2/\eta_{k,m}^{(L)}$ is the instantaneous SNR on m-th sub carrier. Since $\{\alpha_{k,m}\}$ are i.i.d. Rayleigh random variables the power density function of γ_k is given by

$$f_{\gamma k}(x) = \frac{x^{M-1}\ell^{-x/\overline{\gamma}}}{(M-1)!\overline{\gamma}^M} \qquad (33)$$

where $\bar{\gamma} = E_{ck} E\{\alpha^2_{k,m}\}/\eta^{(L)}_{k,m}$ is the average SNR per sub carrier. The average bit error probability is then given by

$$P_{e=} \int_0^\infty Q(\sqrt{2x}) \, f_{\gamma k}(x) \, dx \qquad (34)$$

a closed form solution of which can be obtained as

$$P_e = \left[\frac{1}{2}(1-\mu)\right]^M \sum_{m=0}^{M-1} \binom{M-1+k}{k} \left[\frac{1}{2}(1+\mu)\right]^m \qquad (35)$$

where $\mu = \sqrt{\dfrac{\bar{\gamma}}{1+\bar{\gamma}}}$

Convolution Coded PIC Scheme

The proposed PIC scheme is extended to a convolutionally coded multi-carrier DS-CDMA system and its performance is analyzed. A convolutionally coded multi-carrier DS-CDMA transmitter is shown in Figure 7.

The user data bits are converted into 'R' coded symbols by an encoder. The output code symbols are interleaved and serial-to-parallel converted, so that coded symbols were transmitted simultaneously. Then each of the 'R' code symbols multiplied by the user specific spreading sequence modulates 'M' sub carriers, which results in 'RM' sub carriers.

The coded symbols are mapped on to 'RM' sub carriers using several ways. Suppose $R = 4$ and $M = 2$ each data bit is encoded into $R = 4$ code symbols which are mapped on to $RM = 8$ sub carriers. One simple way of mapping is to transmit the first code symbol on the first and second sub carriers, the second code symbol on the third and fourth sub carriers, third code symbol on the fifth and sixth sub carriers and the fourth code symbol on the seventh and eighth sub carriers.

Another way of mapping is to transmit the first code symbol on the first and fifth sub carriers, the second code symbol on the second and sixth sub carrier, the third code symbol on the third and seventh sub carrier, and the fourth code symbol on the fourth and eight sub carriers. This method maximizes the minimum sub carrier distance for the code symbols. The transmitted signal for k-th user is given by

$$S_k(t) = \sqrt{2E_{ck}} \sum_{i=-\infty}^{\infty} \alpha_k(t-iT) \sum_{m=1}^{RM} b^i_{k,[m]R} \, Cos(\omega_m t + \theta_{k,m}) \qquad (36)$$

where $T = NRMT_c$ is the symbol period $[m]_R = 1 + (m-1, \mod R)$, $\{b^i_{k,1}, b^i_{k,2}, ..., b^i_{k,R}\}$ are k-th users binary convolutional code symbols transmitted during the time interval $[iT,(i+1)T]$.

For K synchronous users in the system, the received signal is given in Box 5.

The convolution coded multi-carrier DS-CDMA receiver consists of bank of 'RM' PIC

Figure 7. Coded multi-carrier DS-CDMA transmitter

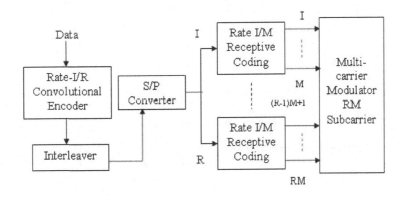

Box 5.

$$r(t) = \sum_{k=1}^{K} \sqrt{2E_{ck}} \sum_{i=-\infty}^{\infty} \alpha_k(t - iT) \sum_{m=1}^{RM} b_{k,[m]R}^i \, \alpha_{k,m} \, Cos(\omega_m t + \theta'_{k,m}) + n_\omega t \qquad (37)$$

Figure 8. PIC Receiver for Coded Multi-carrier DS-CDMA

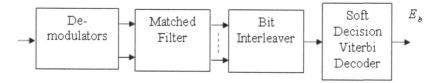

demodulators, followed by a symbol demapper as shown in Figure 8. The symbol demapper remapps the 'RM' sub carriers into 'R' sub carrier groups, and each group consists of 'M' sub carriers which carries the same code symbol.

The demodulator outputs are deinterleaved by the bit deinterleaver, then the output is fed into the soft decision Viterbi decoder. Convolutional codes are widely used in many practical applications of communication system design. Viterbi decoding is predominantly used for short constraint lengths ($K \leq 10$). It is well known that minimum free distance can be increased either by decreasing the code rate or constraint length.

The cancellation process in the 'M'-stage PIC demodulator is the same as that for the uncoded systems shown in Figure 5 except that code symbols are considered here instead of uncoded data bits. Also, the MRC and hard bit decision as shown in Figure 6 are not performed here. Instead, the demodulator receives the input from last stage which is 'RM' soft outputs corresponding to the 'RM' sub carrier, where the outputs from sub carriers which carry the same code symbols are combined as follows

$$Z_k^n(i) = \sum_{m \in \{A_n\}} \alpha_{k,m} \, Z_{k,m}^{(L)}(i) \qquad (38)$$

where $Z_k^n(i)$, $n = 1, 2, ..., R$ is the demapper output corresponding to the n-th convolutionally coded symbol.

$\{A_n\} = \{n, n + R, ..., n + (M - 1)R\}$ represents the set of sub carrier which carry the n-th coded symbol.

The conditional mean and variance of $Z_k^n(i)$ are given by

$$E[Z_k^n(i) | b_{k,n}^i, \overline{\alpha}] = \sqrt{E_{ck}} \, b_{k,n}^i \sum_{m \in \{A_n\}} \alpha_{k,m}^2 \qquad (39)$$

$$Var[Z_k^n(i) | \overline{\alpha}_u] = \sum_{m \in \{A_n\}} \alpha_{k,m}^2 \, \eta_{k,m}^{(l)} \qquad (40)$$

where $\alpha_k = [\alpha_{k,1}, ..., \alpha_{k,RM}]$

The soft outputs from the mapper/deinterleaver $Z_k^n(i)$, $n = 1, ..., R$, $i = 1, 2, ...P$ are fed as input to the soft decision Viterbi decoder. If the decoder chooses that path which has the maximum path metric (the branch metrics, $\mu_i^{(r)}$ and path metrics of r-th path, $U^{(r)}$ respectively) it is given as

$$\mu_i^{(r)} = \sum_{N=1}^{R} Z_k^n(i) \, d_{n,i}^{(r)}, \quad and \quad U^{(r)} = \sum_{i=1}^{P} \mu_i^{(r)} \qquad (41)$$

where $d_{n,i}^{(r)}$ n-th coded symbol of r-th trellis path at time index i.

At the receiver, after demodulation with proper interleaving of the coded symbols, an upper bound on the coded BER performance can be obtained using the transfer function of the convolutional code used.

$$d_{n,i}^{(r)} P_e < \frac{dT(D_1,...D_M,B)}{dB}\Big|_{B=1,D_n=\prod_{m\in\{A_n\}}\frac{1}{(1+\bar{\gamma}_c)}}$$

$$(42)$$

where, $\bar{\gamma}_c \triangleq E_{ck}/2\eta_k^{(L)}$ and $T(D_1, D_2, ..., D_M, B)$ is the transfer function of the convolutional code used.

Figure 9. Rate-1/2, rate-1/4 and rate-1/8 convolutional encoders of constraint length 3

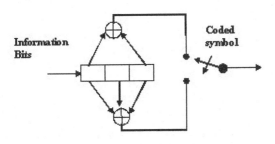

Rate-1/2 Convolutional Encoder

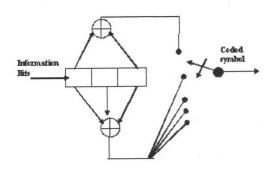

Rate- 1/4 Convolutional Encoder

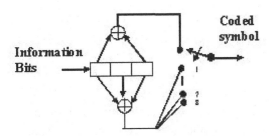

Rate- 1/8 Convolutional Encoder

The convolutional encoder with rate-1/2, 1/4 and 1/8 is shown in Figure 9, with constraint length 3. The list of parameters of rate 1/n convolutional codes is given in Tables 1, 2 and 3.

PERFORMANCE RESULTS

The BER performance of the proposed soft decision PIC with uncoded and coded schemes is presented in this section. The BER performances at various stages are compared by assuming perfect channel estimation at the receiver. No cancellation is performed in the first stage ($L = 1$) and only filtering of each sub carrier is performed. Cancellation is performed in the second ($L = 2$) and third ($L = 3$) stages of the PIC, which is followed by MRC of all the sub carrier outputs. Figure 10 shows the plot of BER Vs number of user (K), at various interference cancellation stages ($L = 1, 2, 3$) for the uncoded systems with $M = 2$, $N = 32$ and $E_b/\eta_0 = 15dB$

The Figure 10 shows the plots corresponding to both the analytical results evaluated through equation (35), as well as the results obtained through bit error simulations using random binary sequences for spreading. From Figure 10, it is observed that the proposed PIC receiver with two stages ($L = 2$) gives significant BER performance improvement than the conventional matched filter receiver and further enhancement is obtained by one more additional stage of cancellation ($L = 3$). It is further observed that the approximate analytical results agree well with the simulations.

Figure 11 compares the BER performance of the PIC receiver for uncoded system for different values of the number of sub carriers (M) and processing gains (N), at the second and third stages of the PIC. Three cases ($M = 1$, $N = 64$), ($M = 2$, $N = 32$), ($M = 4, N = 16$) are considered to keep the total system bandwidth same. The ($M = 1, N = 64$) scheme corresponds to the single-carrier scheme. Owing to the time diversity benefit of the multi-carrier system, the performance of the proposed

Table 1. Rate 1/2 maximum distance code

Constraint length k	Generators in Octal		d_{free}	Upper bound on d_{free}
3	5	7	5	5
4	15	17	6	6
5	23	35	7	8
6	53	75	8	8
7	133	171	10	10
8	247	371	10	11
9	561	753	12	12
10	1,167	1,545	12	13
11	2,335	3,661	14	14
12	4,335	5,723	15	15
13	10,533	17,661	16	16
14	21,675	27,123	16	17

Table 2. Rate 1/4 maximum free distance code

constraint length k	Generators in Octal				d_{free}	Upper bound on d_{free}
3	5	7	7	7	10	10
4	13	15	15	17	13	15
5	25	27	35	37	16	16
6	53	67	71	75	18	18
7	135	135	147	163	20	20
8	235	275	313	357	22	22
9	463	535	733	745	24	24
10	1,117	1,365	1,633	1,653	27	27
11	2,387	2,353	2,671	3,175	29	29
12	4,767	5,723	6,265	7,455	32	32
13	11,145	12,477	15,537	16,727	33	33
14	21,175	23,175	35,527	35,537	36	36

PIC improves as the number of sub carriers is increases. The performance with ($L = 3$) is better than that with ($L = 2$) because of the additional interference cancellation stage.

The BER performance of convolutionally coded PIC is shown in Figure 12 and 13. In Figure 12 upper bounds on the coded BER evaluated refer to equation (42) are plotted for rate 1/2, 1/4, and 1/8 convolutional codes and different number of sub carriers ($M = 2, 4, 8$) at $N = 32$ and $E_b/\eta_0 = 15dB$. Different combinations of R and M, ($R = 2, M = 4$), ($R = 4, M = 2$) and ($R = 8, M = 1$) with 8 sub carriers for three different systems are considered.

For all these three systems, the BER performance at various stages of the PIC ($L = 1, 2, 3$) is also shown in Figure 12. It is observed that for all the three coded systems, the proposed technique

Table 3. Rate 1/8 maximum free distance code

constraint length k	Generators in Octal				d_{free}	Upper bound on d_{free}
3	7	7	5	5	21	21
	5	7	7	7		
4	17	17	13	13	26	26
	13	15	15	17		
5	37	33	25	25	32	32
	35	33	27	65		
6	57	73	51	37	36	36
	75	47	67	137		
7	153	111	165	173	40	40
	135	135	147	137		
8	275	275	253	371	45	45
	331	235	313	357		

Figure 10. BER performance of the PIC receiver for uncoded system analysis and simulation plots for different stages

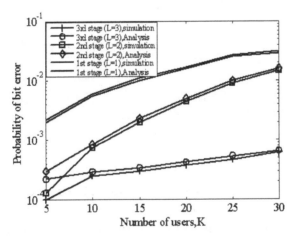

provides significantly improved BER performance compared to the conventional matched filter receiver. Also, for a given number of interference cancellation stages, the performance of the ($R = 2$, $M = 4$), ($R = 4$, $M = 2$) systems is similar to the lowest rate code, but the performance of ($R = 8$, $M = 1$) system is slightly better. In order to keep the system bandwidth constant, a larger 'M' and smaller 'R' are preferred to maintain more frequency diversity benefit and less time diversity benefit. Otherwise, to keep the desired performance for a given system bandwidth a low rate codes with larger 'R' gives more time diversity benefit and less frequency gain due to smaller 'M'.

Figure 11. BER performance of the PIC receiver for uncoded system analysis plots for different sub carriers

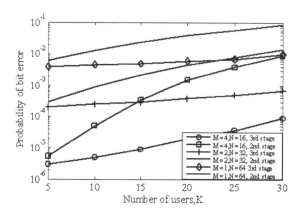

Figure 12. Upper bound of the PIC receiver for coded system with different code rates

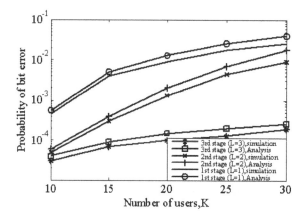

Figure 12 points out a possible complexity trade-off between the systems having different values of 'R' and 'M'. In Figure 13 shows the comparison of theoretical upper bounds and simulation BER results for various stages of cancellation for R=2, M=1, N=32, and $E_b/\eta_0 = 15dB$.

From the above results, it is concluded that analytical values are found to agree well with the simulation results thus, the proposed PIC receiver effectively cancels the MAI and improves the BER performance both for uncoded and coded systems.

CONCLUSION

The performance of a parallel interface cancellation (PIC) scheme for multi-carrier DS-CDMA systems has been presented and analyzed. At each cancellation stage in the proposed PIC scheme, on each sub carrier, a weighted sum of the soft outputs of the other users in the current stage is canceled from the soft output of the desired user to form the input to the next stage. At the last stage, the interference canceled outputs from all the sub carriers are maximal ratio combined to form the decision statistic.

Figure 13. Comparison of the analytical bounds on coded systems for different stages of PIC

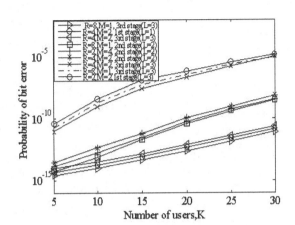

The scheme has the advantage of not requiring the amplitude estimates of the other users. The performance of the proposed technique is analyzed in terms of throughput and signal-to-interference noise ratio. The analytical expressions for the BER at different stages in the proposed PIC scheme on Rayleigh fading channels have been derived, for uncoded as well as convolutionally coded systems. Analytical results have been shown to agree well with the simulation results. The proposed PIC receiver has proved its capacity to effectively cancel the MAI significantly improve the BER performance compared to conventional MF-MRC receiver, for uncoded as well as coded systems.

Simulation validates the successful implementation and feasibility of the proposed solution methodology as a better alternative for existing parallel interference cancellation techniques.

REFERENCES

Achem, N., Irmer, R., & Fettweis, G.P. (2000). Parallel interference cancellation with reduced complexity for multi-carrier spread spectrum FCDMA. *Proceedings of IEEE 6th International Symposium on Spread Spectrum Techniques and Applications*,353-357.

Alexandra, D-H., Holtzman, J., & Zvonar, Z. (1995). Multi-user detection for CDMA systems. *IEEE Personal Communications, 2*(2), 46-58.

Bingham, J. (1990). Multi-carrier modulation for data transmission: An idea whose time has come. *IEEE Communication Magazine*, 5-14.

Bucherer, M., Kaul, A., & Woerner, B. D. (1996). Analysis of DS-CDMA parallel interference cancellation with phase and timing errors. *IEEE Journal on Selected Areas in Communications, 4*(8), 1522-1535.

Cooper, G. R., & Nelleton, R. W, (1978). A spread spectrum technique for high capacity mobile communication. *IEEE Transaction on Vehicular Technology, 27*, 264-275.

David, W. M., & Beibei, W. (2007). Efficient Statistical Parallel Interference Cancellation for DS-CDMA in Rayleigh Fading Channels. *IEEE Transaction on Wireless Communications, 6*(2), 566-574.

Divsalar, D., & Simon, M. (1996). A new approach to parallel interference cancellation for CDMA.

IEEE Proceedings of GLOBECOM, London, U.K, 1452-1457.

Divsalar, D., Simon, M., & Raphaeli, D. (1998). Improved parallel interference cancellation for CDMA. *IEEE Transactions on Communication,* 46 (2),258-268.

Fawer, U., & Aazhang, B. (1995). Multi-user receiver for code division multiple access communication over multipath channels. *IEEE Transactions on Communication,* 43(234), 1556-1565.

Ginnakis, G. B., Hua, Y., Stocia, P., & Tong, L. (2000). *Signal Processing Advances in Wireless and Mobile Communications VOL: 2 Trends in single- and Multi-user systems, Prentice Hall, New Jersey.*

Guoxioing, X., & Liangcai, G. (2005). Parallel interference cancellation with frequency diversity combining for multi-carrier DS-CDMA. IEEE International Symposium on Microwave, Antenna, Propagation and EMC technologies for Wireless Communications. (MAPE 2005), 1(8-12), 297-300.

Jefery, G., Andrews, T., Meng, T. H. Y. (2004). Performance of multi-carrier CDMA with successive interference cancellation in a multipath fading channel. *IEEE Transactions on Communication Technology,* 52(5), 811-822.

Kondo, S., & Milstein, L. B. (1996). Performance of Multicarrier DS-CDMA systems. *IEEE Transaction on Communication,* 44(2), 238-246.

Kondo, S., & Milstein, B. (1994). Multi-carrier DS-CDMA systems in the presence of partial band interference. *IEEE Military Communication Conference, MILCOM-94,* 2, 588-592.

Lai, K. C., & Shynk, J. J. (2000). Error-rate analysis of the adaptive successive interference canceller for DS-CDMA signals. *Proceedings of IEEE International Conference on Acoustics, Spread and Signal Processing (ICASSP)'2000.*

Latva-Aho, M., Juntti, M., & Heikkila, M. (1996). Parallel interference cancellation receiver for DS-CDMA systems in fading channels. *IEEE 8th International Symposium on Personal, Indoor and Mobile radio Communications,* 2, 559-564.

Lin, F., & Milstein, L. B. (2000). Successive interference cancellation in multicarrier DS/CDMA. *IEEE Transactions on Communications,* 48(9),1530-1540.

Mohsen, G., & Soleymani, M. R. (2002). Multi stage PIC with power and phase estimation. *Proceedings of IEEE Vehicular Technology Conference' 2002,* 3,1716-1726.

Proakis, J. G. (1995). *Digital communications.* McGraw-Hill.

Pulin, P., & Holtzman, J. (1994). Analysis of a simple successive interference cancellation scheme in a DS/CDMA system. *IEEE Journal on selected areas in Communications,* 12(5),796-807.

Rowitch, D. N., & Milstein, L. B. (1999). Convolutionally coded Multicarrier DS-CDMA systems in a multipath fading channel--Part II: Narrowband interference suppression. *IEEE Transaction on Communication,* 47(11), 1729-1736.

Rowitch. D. N., & Milstein, L. B. (1995). Convolutional coding for direct sequence multi-carrier CDMA. *IEEE Proceedings of Military Communication, San Diego, CA (pp. 55-59).*

Sang, W. K., & Young-Jun, H. (2003). Log-Likelihood ratio based successive interference cancellation in CDMA systems. *IEEE vehicular Technology Conference'03,* 4, 2390-2392.

Scholtz, R. A. (1982). The origins of spread spectrum communication. *IEEE Transaction on Communication,* 30(5), 822-854.

Seskar. I, Pedersen, K. J., Kolding. T. E., & Holtzman, J. (1998). Implementation aspects of successive interference cancellation. *ACM Wireless Networks.*

Shimon, M., & Bellcore. (1996). Multi-user detection for DS-CDMA communications. *IEEE Communications Magazine*, 124-136.

Shinusuke, H., & Prasad, R. (1997). 'Overview of Multi-carrier CDMA. *IEEE Communications Magazine*, 126-133.

Tero, O. (1997). Overview of multi-user detection /Interference cancellation for DS-CDMA. *IEEE International Conference on Personal Wireless Communications'97*, 115-119.

Thomos, H., & Schulz, W. (2002). Parallel interference cancellation applied to an asynchronous MC-CDMA systems. *Proceedings of IEEE Vehicular Technology Conference' 2002*, 2, 689-693.

Varanasi, M. K., & Aazhang, B. (1990). Multistage detection in asynchronous Code Division Multiple Access communications. *IEEE Transactions on Communications*, 38(4), 509-519.

Verdu, S. (1998). *Multi-user detection*. Cambridge Univ. Press.

Viterbi, A. J. (1971). Convolutional codes and their performance in communication systems. *IEEE Transaction on Communication, COM-19*, 751-772.

Viterbi, A. (1995). *CDMA: Principles of spread spectrum communication*. Addison-Wesley.

Vivek, B., & Buehrer, M. R. (2001). Acquisition in CDMA systems using parallel interference cancellation. *IEEE 58th Vehicular Technology Conference' 2004*, 2,1078-1081.

Xiaodang, R., Shidong, Z., Yan, Y., & Zucheng, Z. (2003). A new successive interference cancellation for asynchronous CDMA. *IEEE GLOBE-COM'03*,1, 252-256.

Xie, Z., Short, R. T., & Rushforth, C. K. (1990). A family of suboptimum detectors for coherent Multi-user communications. *IEEE Journal on Selected Areas in Communication, 8*, 683-690.

Yanping L., Yongbo Z., & Huakui, W. (2006). Partial parallel interference cancellation multi-user detection using recurrent neural network based on Hebb Learning Rule. *The Sixth world congress on Intelligent Control and Automation (2006) WCICA-2006*, 1, 2989-2992.

Zhenhua, X., Short, R. T., & Rushforth, C. K. (1990). A family of sub-optimal detectors for coherent multi-user communications. *IEEE Journal on Selected Areas in Communications*, SAC-8 (4), 683-690.

Chapter XIII
Distributed Resources Management in Wireless LANs that Support Fault Tolerance

Ghassan Kbar
American University in Dubai (AUD), UAE

Wathiq Mansoor
American University in Dubai (AUD), UAE

ABSTRACT

This chapter introduces a new radio resource management technique based on distributed dynamic channel assignment, and sharing load among Access Points (AP). Deploying wireless LANs (WLAN) at large scale is mainly affected by reliability, availability, fairness, scalability, and performance. These parameters will be a concern for most of managers who wanted to deploy WLANs. In order to address these concerns, a new radio resource management technique can be used in a new generation of wireless LAN equipment. This technique would include distributed dynamic channel assignment, and sharing load among Access Points (AP), which improves the network availability and reliability compared to centralized management techniques. In addition, it will help in increasing network capacities and improve its performance especially in large-scale WLANs. Analysis results using normal and binomial distribution have been included which indicate an improvement of performance resulted from network balancing when implementing distributed resources management at WLANs.

INTRODUCTION

WLAN technology is rapidly becoming a crucial component of computer networks that widely used in the past few years. It provides mobility as well as essential network services where wire-line installation proved impractical. Wireless LAN technology evolved gradually during the 1990s, and the IEEE 802.11 standard was adopted in 1997 (Crow, 1997; IEEE 802.11, 1997). The inclusion of the newer IEEE 802.11g versions of the standard offers a firm basis for high performance wireless LANs. Companies and organizations are investing in wireless networks at a higher rate to take advantage of mobile, real-time access to information. While first generation IEEE 802.11 technology is adequate for residential and small office/home office (SOHO) customers, the same is not always true for enterprise customers. In fact, some chief information officers (CIOs) and information technology managers are reluctant to deploy wireless LANs. Among their concerns are security, reliability, availability, scalability, fairness, performance under heavy load, deployment, mobility, and network management. While security is often mentioned as manager's greatest worry about wireless, some of their other concerns such as, reliability, availability, performance, and deployment, can be addressed through radio resource management techniques. The use of such techniques would encourage the rapid deployment of wireless infrastructure with much greater flexibility than has previously been available. The current wireless network products do not scale as well as they might in large-scale enterprise networks. IEEE 802.11 wireless networks have become increasingly popular and more widely deployed. This put pressure to expand the functionality of wireless LAN equipment to become suitable for large scale. A Scalable Network Resource Allocation Mechanism with Bounded Efficiency Loss has been proposed by (Ramesh, 2006) to guaranty a fully efficient allocation when users are price taking. In this

paper, users choose the rate at which they want to send data, and links set prices according to the marginal cost of the total rate allocated. While such a scheme is efficient when all users are price taking, there is a loss of efficiency when users are able to anticipate the effects of their choices on the link prices. Although IEEE 802.11 task groups and study groups are working to improve the standard, there is a need for lots of improvement to suit the future functionality that will be added to Wireless equipments.

Enterprise managers want to deploy wireless networks with several important qualities. These include; high security, fairness, highly reliable and available WLANs with very little downtime, and high performance (i.e., be capable of high throughput and low latency). The ideal wireless network is to have reliability, availability, and performance criteria to be similar of wired enterprise networks. In addition, it should be possible to deploy wireless networks very quickly and without the need for extensive and time-consuming site surveys. Furthermore, the networks should have the flexibility needed to support load balance and changes in the radio environment. Radio resource management (RRM) forms the basis of quality of service (QoS) provisioning for wireless networks (Kayiazakos, 2004). It is an intense research area due to the wireless medium's inherent limitations and the increasing demand for better and cheaper services. There are many benefits of RRM: timely guarantees of resources for key applications, enhanced network planning and management, and efficient bandwidth utilization. A joint scheduling, routing and congestion control mechanism for wireless networks, that asymptotically guarantees stability of the buffers and fair allocation of the network resources, has been addressed by (Atilla, 2006). Resource allocation for orthogonal frequency-division multiple-access relay network with multiple source nodes, multiple relay nodes, and a single destination node has been addressed by (Guoqing Li, 2006). However, in a practical relay system, a large number of nodes may be present and the centralized allocation scheme requires non-negligible signaling overhead. Load imbalance and consequent unfair bandwidth allocation can be greatly reduced by intelligent association control. An efficient solution to determine the user-AP associations for max-min fair bandwidth allocation has been suggested by (Yigal Bejerano, 2007) to provide fairness and load balancing in WLAN. This paper proposes load balancing techniques for obtaining optimal max-min fair bandwidth allocation, where the overall network throughput can be increased. It uses algorithm to compute a fractional association solution, in which users can be associated with multiple APs simultaneously. Improving the mobility management has been addressed in (Ush-Shamszaman, 2005) based on dividing the location management into two levels, intra and inter mobility. This will reduce the amount of signaling traffic, but still didn't address the problem of reliability and availability. Supporting security, reliability and QoS in dynamic environment has been discussed in (DaSilva, 2004) using modified routing protocol OSPF-MCDS over WLANs. It manages the bandwidth allocation using a decentralized policy-based network management scheme. In this approach load balancing would be improved but at the expense of generating more traffic between the APs required to exchange signaling needed for the protocol OSPF-MCDS. In addition, there would increase of latency for terminal association moving across the boundary of multiple APs.

WLAN performance is dependent on the radio propagation environment in which the wireless LAN operates. The radio propagation environment may change from time to time, affecting connection speeds and error rates. In a manufacturing environment, for example, where the multipath environment changes as equipment is moved about, it is quite possible for a link to fail completely even if the mobile is stationary. Network management personnel in information technology departments are often unable to man-

age the network all the way to the user's mobile computer, and may be dependent on users to notify them of some types of problems. On the other hand many CIOs' see network management solutions as to extend all the way to users' laptops and other handheld devices. In WLANs, when AP is called on to serve a high number of users, it is likely to become overloaded, and the resulting congestion may significantly degrade the service received by users dependent on that AP. These issues in network management that are affected by unpredictable network load lead to problems of reliability and availability. The ideal is for WLANs is to provide similar reliability and availability, and, to the extent possible, wireless LAN designers strive to provide the kind of service to which wired network users have become accustomed. Wireless users are likely to experience slower service, which is the result of the often lower transmission speeds and higher error rates on wireless links. Raw data rates on wireless LANs are typically lower than those on Ethernet networks. For example, at one time most Ethernet networks provided 10 Mb/s service to users. At that time, wireless LAN technology provided no more than 1 or 2 Mb/s raw data rate to the user. Today the numbers have increased considerably, but there is still a gap. Ethernet networks can provide 100 Mb/s or even 1000 Mb/s service to users. While IEEE 802.11n promises higher speeds, wireless LANs currently in use operate at speeds up to 11 Mb/s in the case of IEEE 802.11b, and up to 54 Mb/s in the case of IEEE 802.11a/g. But these numbers make wireless LANs sound much faster than they really are. So, for example, an IEEE 802.11b link may step down from the data rate of 11 Mb/s to 5.5, 2, or even 1 Mb/s according to network congestion. Overhead bits dramatically reduce the effective data rate available as described in (IEEE 802.11, 1997; IEEE 802.11a, 1999; O'Hara, 1999; Van Nee, 1999). Congestion further reduces the throughput experienced by a user because AP and the mobile computers it serves share a single radio channel. As with Ethernet, when the traffic level or number of active computers is high, congestion occurs, and poor performance is the result. With switched Ethernet, however, each station can have a segment of its own. On the other hand, all stations using an IEEE 802.11 AP share the same bandwidth resource, and congestion is likely to be particularly severe in areas of high user density (Hills, 2004; O'Hara, 1999). It is highly desirable for wireless LAN equipment to include provisions to mitigate this problem and try to eliminate or reduce the effect of congestion.

Deploying WLANs seems easy, but in fact, the deployment of a well designed, large-scale wireless LAN requires a careful site survey and design, which can be difficult and time consuming. This is due of selection of AP locations and assignment of radio channels to the APs. The design of WLAN is usually based on signal strength measurements and on consideration of radio propagation issues. This is challenging because the building is a three-dimensional space, and an AP located on one floor of the building may provide signal coverage to adjacent floors of the same building and perhaps to other buildings. Firstly, selection of AP location should be done to provide complete coverage of the target space without undue coverage overlap. Consideration of the characteristics of the radio propagation environment in which the wireless LAN is being deployed can be difficult but is important in a WLAN design (Hills, 2001). In a coverage-oriented design one would like to space the APs as far apart as possible while still providing complete coverage of the target space. This will minimize equipment and installation costs, and it will also allow the minimization of coverage overlap between APs operating on the same radio channel. Such "co-channel overlap" degrades performance (Hills, 2001). Secondly, channel assignment is normally done in a way that minimizes co-channel overlap. This is because, with carrier sense multiple access with collision avoidance (CSMA/CA), the IEEE 802.11 multiple access scheme, co-channel overlap causes interaction between stations in different cells, degrading

performance (Hills, 2001). A good site survey and design for a large-scale enterprise WLAN requires radio expertise. Since most data communications personnel lack this kind of expertise, enterprise organizations often provide personnel with the necessary training or hire an outside company to handle deployment. Careful site survey and design are time consuming but are important to the successful deployment of first-generation wireless LAN networks. Although many customers attempt to shorten the process, they may experience performance problems resulting from a less than adequate design. Mathematical models to tackle the WLAN planning problem has been done by (Sandro Bosio, 2007) with the aim of maximizing network efficiency by taking into account the inter-AP domain interference and the access mechanism. Both the single-channel and the multiple-channel WLAN planning problems are considered. The general side result coming from their analysis is that the efficiency of a multi-AP WLAN can be highly impaired by the effect of the interference among APs' domains, thus a wise planning strategy should aim at minimizing such effect.

Centralized management architecture has addressed the above issues to improve reliability, availability, performance, and deployment effectiveness in enterprise and other large-scale wireless LANs (Hills, 2004). These improvements arise from the radio resource management algorithms contained in the software running on the intelligent switches that control APs. In this approach, the software controlling the APs attempts to optimize performance without having any direct control over client behavior, and this limits the effectiveness of the approach. The above article discussed how radio resource management is beginning to be used to mitigate some of the problems in enterprise wireless LANs. However, centralized management still suffer form availability problem if the centralized node failed. A solution to this problem has been addressed in this paper using distributed network management that have the same benefit described in (Hills, 2004), (reliability, availability, performance and deployment effectiveness in enterprise and other large-scale WLANs), but at higher network availability and fault tolerance as would be described in the following sections.

DISTRIBUTED WLAN NETOWRK MANAGEMENT ARCHITECTURE

In a first-generation IEEE 802.11 wireless LAN, the network's intelligence is distributed among the APs. However, managing the association between mobile terminal and AP is controlled by the mobile terminal according to signal strength. This management strategy wouldn't involve the AP in making the decision for the association which might result in overloading some AP while other AP might be under-loaded, and consequently causing congestion at some APs. In addition,

channel frequency allocation for AP is done at the design and deployment stage. Radio resource management techniques that apply centralized management (Hills, 2004), require access to information that must be gathered across a number of APs, and the techniques involve control decisions that apply to a number of APs, not just one. The centralized management would reduce the congestion but it suffers from low network availability if the central point failed.

In order to reduce the congestion at the AP and at the same time maintain high network availability, distributed dynamic network management across multiple APs has been suggested in this paper as described in Figure 1. As shown in Figure 1, the dotted circle indicating the coverage of a particular AP. This coverage might overlap with adjacent AP, where interference is caused if both APs are running at the same channel radio frequency. At the same time mobile terminal falling within the overlapped region would have the choice to have association with either AP. To solve the

Figure 1. Distributed APs management techniques

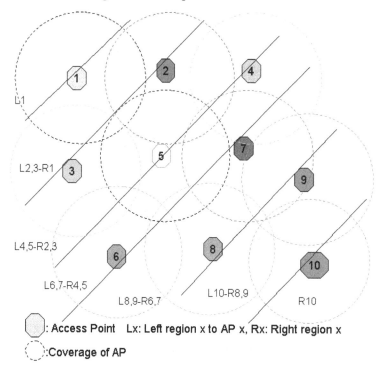

problem of interference, adjacent APs should be assigned different channel radio frequency. This can be done statistically through the design and deployment phases, or through dynamic channel assignment. The distributed dynamic channel assignment described in the next subsection has the advantage of dynamically allocating different channel frequency to different AP. This would reduce the interference and provide high network availability at the same time.

The coverage region of every AP is divided in 2 regions, left hemisphere and right hemisphere. This region division would be used to distributed load among adjacent APs that have coverage overlap, where mobile terminal would choose to associate with one AP according to its location in the left or right hemisphere of the AP as described in the subsection (Load Balancing and Channel Association). This will reduce congestion and provide load balancing between different APs.

Distributed Dynamic Channel Assignment

The performance of a network depends, in part, on the assignment of radio channels to APs. This assignment is often done using a manual process in which the designer attempts to assign the channels in a way that minimizes co-channel overlap. The coverage areas, and therefore the channel assignments, are dependent on among other things such as the radio propagation environment. Since the radio propagation environment changes, so one cannot be sure that the channel assignments valid at the time the network was designed will continue to be valid. However, distributing channel assignment between APs according to its channel frequency that minimize the overlap between these frequencies would reduce the interference between these channels as described in Table 1. In this table, the assignment of channel frequency to adjacent APs, are spread from minimum frequency to maximum which cause

less interference between these APs. Example Adjacent APs 2, 2, 3 are assigned channel number 1, 6, 11 consecutively, and APs 4, 5, 6 are assigned channel number 2, 7, 10 consecutively. Distributed Dynamic Channel Assignment would add extra flexibility to assign a proper channel number to different AP dynamically according to AP index number where its channel frequency is assigned according to its index as mapped in Table 1. This dynamic assignment would help in replacing failed AP with another one using the same index number. Each AP requires having an index number that can be set at the initialization stage.

Distributed dynamic channel assignment would be done according to AP index belonging to the same network, where all APs are assigned unique index starting from 1 at left hand side and increment by one for the next adjacent AP. Then the AP would be assigned a channel frequency according to Table 1 assignment. Since there are 11 to 14 channel frequencies (Crow, 1997; IEEE 802.11, 1997; Van Nee, 1999) available for use according to different standard (North America, Most Europe, France, Japan), different frequency would be assigned for the first 11 APs, then these frequencies can be re-assigned for the remaining APs that exceed 11, where interference is unlikely since these APs assigned the same frequency are not adjacent and therefore would not cause signal interference. In addition, that interference between the first 11 channel frequencies would be minimum since adjacent AP assigned frequency are distributed to have non adjacent frequencies as described in Table 1.

Load Balancing and Terminal Association

Since an AP and its associated clients share a limited bandwidth resource, APs can become overloaded, leading to congestion and poor network performance. On the other hand, a client may be able to communicate quite successfully

Table 1. AP Frequency allocation and indexing

Channel Number	Channel Frequency (GHz)	AP Index associated with Channel number for minimum interference
1	2.412	1
2	2.417	4
3	2.422	7
4	2.427	9
5	2.432	11
6	2.437	2
7	2.442	5
8	2.447	8
9	2.452	10
10	2.457	6
11	2.462	3

with two or more APs but at expense of possibly causing congestion at some AP. Thus, one would like to have a wireless LAN that is capable of distributing client associations among APs more or less uniformly so that no one AP is overloaded. WLAN equipment with this capability can enhance network performance considerably. Association between a client and an AP begins with an association request that is initiated by the client. This association request is normally preceded by the client's transmitting one or more probe requests on channels it selects. In each of these probe requests, the client asks for a response from all APs operating on that channel and able to receive the client request. This tells the client which APs are within radio range, and the signal strengths received from the APs give an indication of which APs will be able to provide higher-quality service. Before sending an association request, a client should also have previously sent an authentication request that has been granted. The method by which a client decides with which AP to request association is not specified in the IEEE 802.11 standard. In addition, client cards produced by different manufacturers, use different algorithms for requesting an association.

However, the association between mobile terminals in distributed dynamic management can be controlled not only according to signal strength which cause network congestion at some AP, but also according to its location in the right or left hemisphere of the AP. To determine the location of mobile terminal within the network map, the same procedure described in (Kbar, 2005) can be used for wireless terminal and compared to the coordinate of the AP that detected its strong signal. This management technique works according to distributing the load between adjacent APs where mobile terminal fall within the overlapped region would be associated only with one AP located to its right hemisphere. If mobile terminal located within the overlapped region, the signal strength would not be used to determine to which AP it will associate with. In fact, the mobile terminal location would be used to distributed load to different AP, where it will associate with AP that is located at the right hemisphere of itself. As shown in Figure 1, if mobile terminal located anywhere within the region of AP-1 without overlapping with other AP, it always associate with this AP-1. However, if it locates within the overlapped region of AP-1, and AP-2, it will associate with AP-2 where the terminal is located at the left hemisphere of AP-2. The golden role here is to associate all mobile terminals, that are falling within 2 APs (overlap region), with AP that locates at the right of the terminal, or the left hemisphere of the AP. In other word the AP in the right of the terminal (left hemisphere of AP region) would be the winner to associate mobile terminals located in the overlap region with other AP. These actions expected to significantly improve the performance of the WLAN. They also will make the site survey and design process easier because these techniques can, to some degree, compensate for errors in designing the network.

ANALYSIS RESULTS USING NORMAL DISTRIBUTION

For proving that our method is decreasing the load on heavily congested area where there are a lot of APs in the regions, we focus on AP-5 in figure 2 since it is in the center where there are a lot of terminals which will heavily decrease the bandwidth available to them. Let us assume that there are 10 terminals as shown in the Figure 2. They are usually associated with AP-5 in the normal association method since they all are closer to AP5.

While using our method only the 5 on the left hemisphere of AP5 will be associated with AP-5 plus another one on the right hemisphere is associated with AP-5 since it is within the coverage of AP-5 only. The other four will be associated to AP4, AP6, AP7 and AP8 with one each since they are located on the right hemisphere of AP-5 and on the left hemisphere of other APs. This example shows that 60% of the terminals associate with AP-5, and 40% of the terminals associated with other APs. Considering the same assumptions of 40 % of the terminals might associate with other APs according to uniform distribution when there are 20 terminals, 30 terminals, 40 terminals and 50 terminals, we can draw the distribution of terminal association as shown in Figure 3. The graph in figure 3 shows the relationship between number of terminals and the number of the associated terminals to AP-5 for both the distributed method and the strength based method.

It is clearly shown in Figure 3 that around 60% of the terminals are associated with AP-5 in case of using distributed method, while around 75% to 100% of the terminals are associated with AP5 when using strength based method. We assume a uniform distribution of the terminals within the region since the random distribution is not a reliable condition for evaluation. The result also proves that by using distributed method there

Figure 2. Load balancing

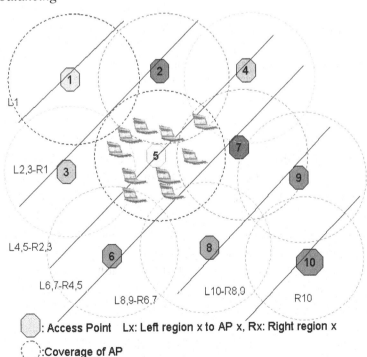

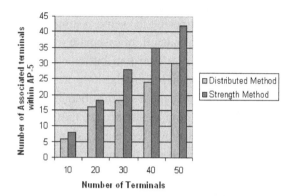

Figure 3. Association distributions

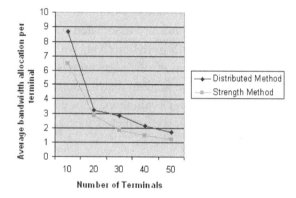

Figure 4. Average bandwidth allocation

will be better utilization of the bandwidth over the strength method as shown in Figure 4. Under the assumption that the maximum bandwidth of AP is 54 Mb/sec according to IEEE-11g standard, as shown in Figure 4 the average bandwidth allocation per terminal is 9 Mb/sec when using the distribution method for total number of 10 terminals, while the average bandwidth drops to 6.5 Mb/sec using the strength method under the same condition of total 10 terminals. The difference in bandwidth allocation gets close to each other, using the 2 methods when the number of terminals increases to 50. As shown in Figure 4, the average bandwidth allocation per terminal is 1.5 Mb/sec when using the distribution method for total number of 50 terminals, while the average bandwidth drops to 1.2 Mb/sec using the strength method under the same condition of total 50 terminals.

The last AP-10 would accept all associations since terminals falling within its right hemisphere don't have other choice to get association with other APs. This will increase the load for the last AP to the same level as the strength method.

WLAN with Fault Tolerance

WLAN with multiple AP suffers from network availability when one or more AP failed. This will cause some mobile terminals falling within the area of the failed AP to lose connection and become unable to use the network. In order to reduce the congestion at the AP and at the same time maintain a high network availability, distributed dynamic network management with fault tolerance across multiple APs has been suggested in this section as described in Figure 5. As shown in Figure 5, the dotted circle indicating the coverage of a particular AP. This coverage might overlap with adjacent AP, where interference is caused if both APs are running at the same channel radio frequency. At the same time mobile terminal falling within the overlapped region would have the choice to have association with either AP. Each AP has 2 coverage areas; low coverage as shown in the dotted circle for AP-2, Ap-4, and AP-5, and high coverage as shown in the blue solid circle of AP-1, and in the grey solid circle of AP-7. The AP-1 and AP-7 have also low coverage area as shown in the dark grey solid circle, and pink solid circle for AP-1 and AP-7 consecutively. The solid circle for AP-3, with dashed pattern indicates a failed AP, where its coverage has been substituted by the high coverage area of AP-1 and AP-7. This technique improve the WLAN performance by providing high network availability and fault tolerance through broadcasting 2 coverage levels by every AP to substitute for the failed AP coverage.

In order for the architecture shown in figure 5 to work, each AP should operate in 2 level of coverage power. Each AP would also detect the failed neighbor AP through continuous broadcast management signal that occurs at specific interval of time, where each AP will broadcast its available network table for all adjacent APs that have sensitive antenna to detect it. The available network table would be updated by each AP when it receives broadcast from neighboring APs, where after few broadcast events the table would contain a list of all operating APs that belong to the same network as explained in the following sequence diagram in Figure 6. Assume in this diagram that AP-1 has joined the WLAN and broadcasted its own availability network table (that contains list of known AP {1}) to neighboring APs (AP-2, and AP-3). It also receives broadcast from AP-2 and AP-3. The management signal received from AP-2 would contain a list of all APs (2, 4*, and 5*) that are neighbor to AP-2, where 4* is the list of APs for AP-4 that had been received previously at AP-2 from AP-4. The list 4* indicating another list of AP-4 that contains the list of APs

that are neighbor of AP-4 which are AP-5 and list of AP-7 (7*). The list from AP-5 (5*) would also contain the list of AP-5 that are neighbor of AP-5 which are (3, 4, 6, 7, 8). At the same time the list received from AP-7 would contain the list of APs that are neighbor to AP-7 which are (4, 5, 8, 9). Eventually, the availability table at AP-1 would contain a list of all APs that are belonging to the same network. The other APs would also update their availability table which also would include the list of all APs of the same network.

If one of the AP failed (example Ap-3 as shown in Figure 5), all of its neighbor APs (AP-1, and AP-7) would not receive a regular broadcast from it. If AP-1 and AP-7 didn't receive broadcast management signal from its neighbor AP-3, they will assume a failure on AP-3 and adjust their coverage power to operate at high level. This will allow AP-1, and AP-7 to cover the area of the failed AP-3 as shown in Figure 5 (blue solid circle, and grey solid circle).

Figure 5. Distributed APs management techniques with fault tolerance

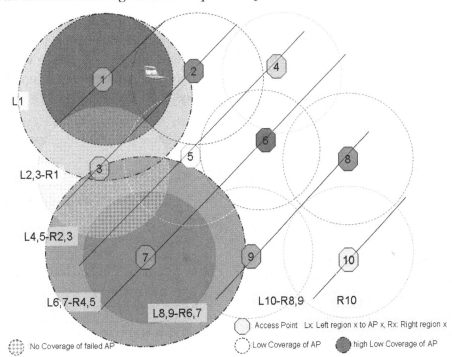

Figure 6. Sequence of broadcast management signal at AP

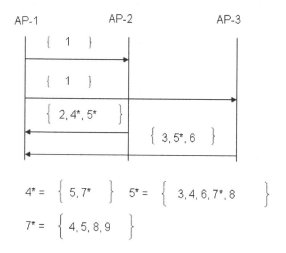

ANALYSIS USING BINOMIAL DISTRIBUTION

The binomial distribution gives the discrete probability distribution $P_p(n/N)$ of obtaining exactly n successes (terminal falling only within a particular AP range eg. AP-5) out of N Bernoulli trials or terminals falling within the coverage of a particular AP and its neighbors APs (where the result of each Bernoulli trial is true with probability p and false with probability $q = 1 - p$). The binomial distribution is therefore given by:

$$P_p(n/N) = \binom{N}{n} p^n q^{N-n} \qquad (1)$$

$$= \frac{N!}{n!(N-n)!} p^n (1-p)^{N-n}, \qquad (2)$$

where $\binom{N}{n}$ is a binomial coefficient.

Assume that the desired probability of terminals falling within one Access Point (eg. AP-5) only is $p = 0.8$. Therefore the probability of failure is $q = 1 - p = 0.2$. The total number of terminals (trials) is $N = 50$. According to binomial distribu-

tion of formula 2, the probability of at least up to i terminals is falling within only one AP (eg. AP-5) is:

$$p(x \leq i) = \sum_{k=0}^{i} \frac{n!}{(n-k!)k!} p^k (1-p)^{n-k} \quad (3)$$

The probability that more than i terminals are falling within the same AP is given by:

$$p(x > i) = 1 - p(x \leq i) = 1 - \sum_{k=0}^{i} \frac{n!}{(n-k!)k!} p^k (1-p)^{n-k}$$

$$(4)$$

Applying formula 4 in (http://www.stat. sc.edu/~west/applets/bionmialdemo.html), we can obtain the probability for more than i terminals are falling within AP-5 according to different value of i {i=20 to 48} as shown in Figure 7. As shown in this figure, the probability would reach one when desired probability is 0.8 if the number of terminals is 32. The number of terminals would increase to 42 if the desired probability increases to 0.95.

According to distributed management and using binomial distribution, the total number of terminals that are only falling within AP-5 can be obtained by the following formula as shown in Figure 8:

Figure 7. Probability distribution

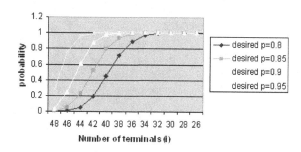

Figure 8. Total number of terminals at different desired probability

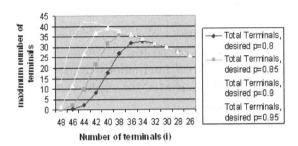

As shown in Figure 8, the maximum total number of terminals depends on the desired probability. When the desired probability is 0.95, the maximum number is 43 terminals. This number drops to 32 when the desired probability is reduced to 0,8.

Figure 9. Number of terminals associated with same AP

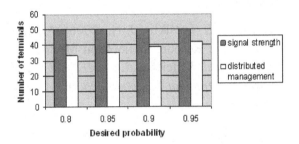

$$T = i \times p(x > i) \qquad (5)$$

As shown in Figure 8, the maximum total number of terminals depends on the desired probability. When the desired probability is 0.95, the maximum number is 43 terminals. This number drops to 32 when the desired probability is reduced to 0,8.

Using signal strength terminal management the total number of terminals that are falling within AP-5 is N. Hence the advantage of using distributed management is reducing the number of terminals associated with a particular AP (eg. AP-5) by:

$$N - T = N - i \times p(x > i) \qquad (6)$$

As shown in Figure 9, the total number of terminals falling within the same access points using signal strength is N (50 terminals) independent of the desired probability. The total number of terminals using distributed management depends on the desired probability, where the total number would be 32 at desired probability of 0.8, and it increases to 43 when the desired probability increases to 0.95. Hence, the total number of terminals falling within the same AP using distributed management drops by 1-32/50 (35%). This would allow terminals to have better bandwidth allocation using the distributed management scheme.

CONCLUSION

The architecture that has been described has the potential to improve performance, and deployment effectiveness in enterprise and other large-scale wireless LANs, and at the same time maintain a high network availability and reliability through network fault tolerance that is based on dynamic power coverage assignment. These improvements arise from the distributed dynamic resource management deployed in mobile terminals and APs.

The suggested technique assists the APs to optimize its performance by dynamically allocating different frequency to adjacent AP in order to reduce the signal interference. In addition, the association between mobile terminals and AP are distributed to different APs according to their location in the left or right hemisphere of the AP. This will reduce the congestion in APs and consequently improve the WLAN large-scale network performance. Furthermore, fault tolerance has been provided through the dynamic power coverage assignment, where AP updates its network availability table through network signal management. This network signal management would be used by the AP to update its availability table that has list of all APs connected to the same network. When one of the AP failed, it will be detected by its neighbor APs and automatically adjust their power coverage to high level after 2 consecutive periods to cover the area of the failed AP. This will allow mobile terminals falling within the area of failed AP to remain connected to this WLAN.

REFERENCES

Atilla, Eryilmaz, & Srikant R. (2006). Joint Congestion Control, Routing, and MAC for Stability and Fairness in Wireless Networks. *IEEE Journal on Selected Areas in Communications. 24*(8), 1514- 1524.

Crow, B. P., Widjaja, I., Kim, L. G., & Sakai, P. T. (1997). *IEEE 802.11 Wireless Local Area Networks. IEEE Communication Magazine, 35*(9), 116–26.

DaSilva, L. A., Midkiff, S. F., Park, J. S., Hadjichristofi, G. C., & Davis, N. J. (2004). Network Mobility and Protocol Interoperability in Ad Hoc Networks. *IEEE Communications Magazine.*

Guoqing, L., & Hui, L. (2006). Resource Allocation for OFDMA Relay Networks With Fairness Constraints. *IEEE Journal on Selected Areas in Communications, 24*(11), 2061-2069.

Hills, A. (2001). Large-Scale Wireless LAN Design. *IEEE Communication Magazine, 39*(11), 98–104.

Hills, A. (2004). Radio Resource Management in Wireless LANs. *IEEE Radio Communications.* http://www.stat.sc.edu/~west/applets/binomialdemo.html

IEEE 802.11 (1997). IEEE Standard. *Wireless LAN Medium Access Control (MAC) and Physical Layer (PHY) Specifications.*

IEEE 802.11a (1999). *IEEE standard. Wireless LAN Medium Access Control (MAC) and Physical Layer (PHY) Specifications: High Speed Layer in the 5 GHz Band.*

Kbar, G., & Mansoor, W. (2005). *Mobile Station Location based on Hybrid of Signal Strength and Time of Arrival.* International Conference on Mobile Business ICMB2205, Sydney. Australia July 11-13.

Kyriazakos, S., & Karetsos G.(2004). Practical resource management in wireless systems. *Book reviews IEEE Communications Magazine.*

O'Hara, B., & Petrick, A. (1999). *The IEEE 802.11 Handbook: A Designer's Companion.* IEEE Press.

Ramesh, J., & Tsitsiklis, J. N. (2006). A Scalable Network Resource Allocation Mechanism With Bounded Efficiency Loss. *IEEE Journal on Selected Areas in Commmunications, 24*(5), 992-999.

Sandro, B., Antonio, C., & Matteo, C. (2007). Radio Planning of Wireless Local Area Network. *Transactions on Networking, 15*(6), 1414-1427.

Ush-Shamszaman, Z., & Abdur, R. M. (2005). A mobility management scheme in all-ip integrated network. *Proceedings of the 23rd IASTED International Multi-Conference Parallel and Distributed Computing And Networks.* 15-17.

Van, N. R., Awater, G., Morikura, M., Takanashi, H., MA Webster, M., & Halford, K. (1999). New High-Rate Wireless LAN Standards. *IEEE Communication Magazine, 37*(12), 82–88.

Yigal, B., Seung-Jae, H., & Li (Erran) Li (2007). Fairness and Load Balancing in Wireless LANs Using Association Control, IEEE. *IEEE/ACM Transactions on Networking, 15*(3), 560-573.

Chapter XIV
Cooperative Data Caching and Prefetching in Wireless Ad Hoc Networks

Mieso K. Denko
University of Guelph, Canada

ABSTRACT

This article proposes a cooperative data caching and prefetching scheme for Mobile Ad Hoc Networks (MANETs). In this scheme, multiple hosts cooperate in both prefetching and caching commonly used data. To reduce communication and computational overhead, we use a clustering architecture for the network organization. A weak consistency based on time to live value was used to maintain data consistency. A hybrid cache replacement policy that uses frequency of access and the reference time was employed. The effects of cache size, mobility, and prefetching threshold on the network performance were investigated in a discrete event simulation environment. The contribution of intra-cluster and inter-cluster information to overall data accessibility ratio was also investigated. The simulation results indicate that the proposed scheme improves both data accessibility and query delay at relatively lower prefetch thresholds, larger cache sizes, and moderate mobility.

INTRODUCTION

In the past few years, most of the research devoted to MANETs has focused on the development of routing protocols to increase connectivity among mobile hosts in a constantly varying topology (Johnson & Maltz, 1996; Perkins & Bhagwat, 1994). Although development of routing pro-

tocols is one of the main challenges that must be addressed, improved data accessibility is the ultimate goal of such networks. In order to enable quick deployment of MANETs, development of reliable and efficient data management schemes suitable for this network environment is crucial. Data caching and prefetching techniques used in traditional wireless networks can be extended to be used in MANETs. In this article, we investigate the use of caching and prefetching techniques for improving data accessibility and reducing latency in MANET environments.

Caching has been utilized extensively in wired networks, such as the Internet, to increase the performance of Web services (Fan et al., 1998; Rousskov & Wessels, 1999; Wang, 1999; Wessels & Claffy, 2005). However, existing cooperative caching schemes cannot be implemented directly in MANETs due to host mobility and resource constraints that characterize these networks. Consequently, new approaches have been proposed to tackle these challenges (Cao, Yin, & Das, 2004; Hara, 2002; Lim, Lee, Cao, & Das, 2003; Papadopoui & Schulzrinnr, 2001; Wang, 2005; Yin & Cao, 2006). These approaches have been introduced to increase data accessibility and reduce query delay in MANETs. A cooperative cache-based data access scheme is subsequently proposed for ad hoc networks (Cao et al., 2004; Yin & Cao, 2006). Three caching techniques, namely CacheData, CachePath, and HybridCache, are utilized as caching approaches. In CacheData, the intermediate hosts, which are located along the path between the source host and the destination host, cache frequently accessed data items. In CachePath, the intermediate hosts record the routing path information of passing data. CachePath only records the data path when it is closer to the caching host than the data source. The HybridCache technique represents a combination of CacheData and CachePath. This technique performs better than either the CachePath or CacheData approach. The cache replacement algorithm in HybridCache is based upon the access frequency of a data item and the distance to the same cached copy or to the data source. However, due to the inherent mobility of the host, such distances can change frequently. Moreover, the authors did not consider prefetching and multiple data sources in their study. In Lim et al. (2003), a similar approach is proposed for data caching in a network that integrates ad hoc networks with the Internet.

In Hara (2002), a replica allocation scheme with periodic data item updates is proposed. This scheme focused on improving data accessibility with the main goal of decreasing the data access failure in response to network division. The schemes presented in Sailhan and Issarny (2003) and Wang, (2005) are based on a specific routing protocol. The scheme in Sailhan and Issarny (2003) used popularity, access cost, and coherency as criteria to replace cached data items when a mobile host's cache space is full. In Wang (2005), a transparent cache-based mechanism based on a new on-demand routing protocol called dynamic backup routes routing protocol (DBR2P) is proposed. The routing protocol and the cache mechanism allow the caching of data. In order to guarantee data access, this scheme allowed the cached data to be moved to a backup host in response to a link failure. Another study proposed the implementation of an architecture similar to cooperative caching, which defines two protocols to share and disseminate data among mobile hosts (Rousskov & Wessels, 1999). However, the scheme focused on data dissemination in a single-hop rather than cooperative caching in a multi-hop environment. Another study utilized a novel architecture for database caching based on the separation of queries and responses (Artail, Safa, & Pierre, 2005). The experimental results indicated that the scheme improved data accessibility by reducing response time in the presence of host mobility.

Cooperative caching is an effective mechanism for increasing data accessibility in both wired and wireless networks. However, caching alone is not sufficient to guarantee high data accessibility and low communication latency in dynamic systems with limited network resources. In this article, we propose an integrated cooperative caching and prefetching mechanism for MANETs.

This article provides the following contributions to increasing the efficiency of data management in MANETs. First, we use a clustering architecture that allows localized and adaptive data caching and prefetching mechanisms to increase data accessibility and reduce latency in the presence of host mobility. Second, we use a cache replacement policy that combines both frequency of access and latency of access to the cached data. Thus, eviction of data in the cache depends on a metric that combines the optimal combination of access frequency and time of reference with a configurable parameter. Third, the proposed cooperative caching and prefetching architecture is flexible and does not rely on any specific routing protocol. Fourth, the article provides an analysis of the contribution of intra-cluster and inter-cluster information to the data accessibility ratio.

The remainder of this article is organized as follows. Section 2 presents the proposed system architecture. Section 3 presents the cooperative caching and prefetching strategies. Section 4 presents the cache replacement policy and data consistency management. Section 5 presents the results of performance evaluation based on simulation experiments. Finally, Section 6 presents conclusions and future research work.

THE PROPOSED SYSTEMS ARCHITECTURE

Network Model and Assumptions

The network consists of mobile hosts that form clusters. The network connectivity is maintained using a periodic Hello message that is exchanged among one-hop neighbors. Other information such as the data stored at a host, host's role (cluster head, data source, or caching agent) are exchanged among neighbors. The clustering algorithm is used for cluster management. These tasks include cluster head election, monitoring cluster membership changes, and facilitating inter-cluster communications. We assume that each host has a cache of a fixed capacity and cached data can be accessed by any other host. Data caching and prefetching

operations are carried out cooperatively to avoid extra communication overhead.

The Architecture

Cooperative caching is particularly attractive in environments where the network is constrained in terms of bandwidth, power, and storage. Cooperative caching offers several benefits since it can enable efficient utilization of available resources by storing different data items and sharing them among themselves. Cooperative caching additionally improves performance by increasing data accessibility and reducing communication latency.

In this study, we consider data management in a large ad hoc network. The network organization is based on a clustering architecture with a cluster head. Hosts that allow communication between two clusters are called gateways. Figure 1 gives an example of the proposed architecture with two clusters. We used cooperative clusters with cluster heads (CH). Each cluster has a CH, data source (DS), caching agents (CAs), and mobile hosts (MHs). The DS generates data items needed by other MHs in the network. Multiple data sources store different data items. The hosts that act as DSs are known to the CHs and local CAs. For clustering, we used the lowest ID clustering algorithm proposed in Gerla and Tsai, 1995. However, any existing distributed clustering algorithm can be

Figure 1. The cluster architecture

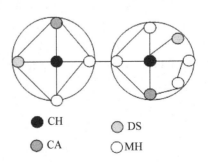

used. We used a secondary cluster head to cope with cluster head changes and data loses (Lu, 2005).

Cache Placement and Host Organization

Each host has its own caching manger (CM) and prefetching manager (PM). The PM uses information from the CH and other hosts to make prefetching decisions. The PM maintains a list of data items to be fetched based on the implementation of the data prefetching algorithm and sends request to neighbors or to the CH. The CM monitors cache size, cached data lifetime, and cache replacement operation. It uses a cache replacement algorithm to maintain a list of data items to be replaced when other data items are fetched.

When a host does not have the required data, it forwards the request to its neighbors, then to the CA, DS, or CH. Each cluster maintains information on a local data source (DS). When a MH receives the requested data item, it will decide whether the data item should be cached.

A data item is placed at a specific host in the cluster. A fixed threshold distance metric of k-hop will be used for deciding a CA. The number of hops is adjusted based on host mobility and link characteristics. Larger hop lengths are used for less mobile and more stable networks. For example, maintaining three-hop neighborhood information in a dynamic network will cause more update overhead than maintaining one-hop neighborhood information since more transmission is involved. Moreover, the link may be changed before it is used the next time. In general, cache placement at the CA is carried out based on distance metric, cache replacement algorithms, and capacity constraints.

COOPERATIVE CACHING AND PREFETCHING STRATEGIES

Cooperative caching involves cache placement, cache replacement, data request-reply operations, and cache consistency. The data request-reply operation also known as data search can be performed proactively or based on demand. Most existing solutions in data management for MANETs consider cooperative caching without prefetching. In this article, we consider cooperative caching with prefetching.

Types of Cooperative Caching

We consider two types of host cooperation. The first type of cooperation involves cooperative data access and storage. Neighbor hosts store different data items and serve any request made for such data items by any host interested in the data. The second form of host cooperation involves cooperative prefetching and cache placement. When the data item is prefetched from a DS or CA, the data can be cached at any other CA if it is fresh relative to the existing data item. In other words, the existing data item can be updated by a CA in the cluster, even if the request for data was not initiated by it. However, such updates are only performed locally within a cluster.

Data query and reply is forwarded on a hop-by-hop basis. The data request begins at a local cluster. If the request fails, the search will continue through other clusters until the DS or any CA containing fresh data responses to the query. The query reply is forwarded on a reverse route in the same manner. The request will be unsuccessful only when the network is partitioned. The solution for this problem involves data replication. This specific problem was already discussed both in the literature and in our own earlier work (Feldmann, 1999; Hara, 2002; Lu, 2005). Although disconnected operation is a norm (not an exception) in MANETs, permanent failure due to battery power depletion or network partition could result in a complete loss of data if no replicated copy is available.

Prefetching Strategies

Caching becomes more effective if the requested data item is available in the cache when needed. Strategies for proactively prefetching the most frequently accessed data within the cache or prefetching frequently needed data upon the expiry of Time-To-Live (TTL) can significantly improve network performance by reducing latency. To reduce communication overhead, we use the prefetch-on-mis scheme when the value of TTL expires for a particular data item.

We propose implementation of a prefetching strategy that works at two levels. The first level of prefetching is performed between hosts and caching agents, whereas the second level of prefetching is performed between CAs and the CH.

1. **Prefetching between MHs and CAs:** A host that frequently needs a particular data item will prefetch the data from the CA or DS if the data has not already been cached in its neighbor. Under such a circumstance, a host will become a CA. It will notify its CH, its neighbors, and the CAs in its cluster, of its status change and the ID of the data it is storing.

2. **Prefetching between CAs and CHs:** If a CA has an expired data item, it will prefetch the item from other CAs or DSs in its cluster. If the CA cannot find a fresh data item from within its cluster, it will send its request to the CH, which will in turn request the data from other clusters. The pseudocode for Request-Reply is shown in Figure 2.

In the Request-Reply process, any host that receives a data item request will first check its own cache space and its validity and then decide whether to send data to the requester or forward the query to the other host or CH.

Figure 2. Data request-reply

```
Begin
    When a mobile host, N, requests a data item,
D:
    Call cache_avail;
    If a copy of D exists in its cache and valid
then
        Return D;
    Else
        Requests D from Neighbors/CA/DS
        If D exists and still valid then
            Return D;
        Else // no data in the cluster
        Requests D through CH;
End
```

The Prefetching Algorithm

The performance of prefeching depends on the quality of the prediction mechanism used. The algorithm should be adaptive and it should use distributed information gathering mechanisms. We used a popularity-based prediction algorithm. The PM maintains the required statistics and implements the prefetching algorithm.

By prefetching frequently accessed data in the local cache within a cluster, latency can be reduced significantly. The frequency of access to data is determined based on the past access history for a particular data item. Based on these statistics, the data items that are most likely to be needed in the near future will be prefetched and cached. To achieve this, hosts maintain frequency of access request statistics for each data item.

Each host maintains a Node Prefetching Index (NPI) for each data item (D_i) as follows:

$$NPI(D_i) = \frac{n_i}{N_k}, i \geq 1 \qquad (1)$$

where N_k is the total number of distinct access requests at the host k, n_i is the total number of distinct requests for the data item (D_i). The value NPI shows the ratio of access to the data. Hence, a higher value of the NPI provides evidence of the popularity of that data at the host.

Each caching agent fetches the data item if the data is popular, which is determined by the cumulative prefetching index (CPI) using a predefined threshold. For each data item (D_i), the value of CPI is computed as follows:

$$CPI(D_i) = \sum_{i=1}^{k} \left(NPI(D_i)\right) \qquad (2)$$

where k is the number of hosts. The fetch index is adjusted based on past access history and an update will be sent to all CAs in the cluster. These indexes are updated whenever the data item is accessed.

CACHE REPLACEMENT AND DATA CONSISTENCY

Cache Replacement Algorithm

The primary purpose for cooperative cache placement is to avoid duplicated storage of the same data item at neighbor hosts. This reduces data access costs in terms of the number of hops required for data transmission to obtain the data. A clustering architecture is suitable for partitioning the network into smaller and more manageable groups.

Cache placement determines whether a received data item should be cached. However, when a MH's cache space is full and a new data item should be cached, cache replacement will determine which cached data item should be removed from the cache space.

Cache replacement algorithms play a major role in determining the performance of a caching scheme. There are two scenarios in which cache entries could change. The first scenario occurs when the data stored in the cache becomes invalid. In this case, the invalid data item is replaced. If the data is popular, it will be prefetched and placed in the cluster for future use. The second scenario occurs when a MH's cache space is full and a data item has to be cached. In this case, the existing data should be evicted and replaced by

new data. The MH has to decide which data item in its cache space should be removed to make room for the new data item. Thus, our proposal involves prefetching the required data item and distributing it to hosts for caching in designated CAs. The data item would be cached in the CAs by replacing expired TTLs or by evicting existing data using cache replacement algorithms.

If all data items are valid, a cache replacement algorithm is used to evict cache content and store new data items. Most existing cache replacement schemes use policies such as least recently used (LRU) and least frequently used (LFU). In the LRU policy, the least recently accessed cached data is replaced, while in the LFU policy, the least frequently accessed data is replaced. The LRU may replace data that has not been accessed for a long time, even if this data may be needed by multiple hosts later. This is plausible, since hosts can join or leave the network randomly and they do so frequently. Furthermore, LFU alone may not be useful since the frequency of access may not be stable in a dynamic network. Consequently, we used the combined metric that allows replacing the least frequently used data with the least recent references.

The LRFU Cache Replacement Policy

To avoid removing data that may be needed soon, we used a cache replacement algorithm that makes use of both frequency and latency of access information. This hybrid cache replacement policy combines LRU and LFU and is known as the least recently-least frequently used (LRFU) algorithm. LRFU removes data items that have the smallest combined values for both frequency and latency of access. If multiple data items have the same frequency of access, then one of them will be evicted based on their TTL value.

According to the LRFU policy, each host assigns a value called combined recency and frequency (CRF) that estimates the probability that the data will be accessed in the future. Past references to the data contribute to this value based on a weighing function, F(x), where x is the time span between past references and the current time.

The CRF value of a data item, D, at time t_c is computed as follows (Lee et al., 1997):

$$CRF_{tc}(D) = \sum_{i=1}^{k} F(t_c - t_{bi}) \qquad (3)$$

where F(x) is a weighing function and $\{t_{bi}\}$, i, 1... k, are the reference times of data items D and $t_{b1} < t_{b2} < t_{b3} < ... \leq t_c$.

The LRFU policy differs from LRU in that it takes other references into account. Furthermore, LRFU differs from LFU in that the contribution of each reference depends on its latency. As the weighting function, we used the function:

$$F(x) = \left(\frac{1}{5}\right)^{\delta x} \qquad (4)$$

where x is the difference between the current time and reference time and δ is a control parameter.

It is evident from the above weighing function that F(x) approaches the LFU as δ approaches zero, and it approaches LRU as δ goes to one. By varying the control parameter δ, the performance of the LRFU policy can be improved.

Cache Consistency Management

Data items stored in the DS are classified as either dynamic data or static data. The value of a dynamic data item changes frequently, while the value of a static data item does not. The cache consistency check ensures that the cached data is consistent with the original data at the DS. Because static data items seldom change, the network traffic caused by an update broadcast is minimal. By dividing data items into static data and dynamic data, the overhead caused by maintaining cache consistency will be greatly reduced.

For dynamic data, a simple weak consistency (Alex, 1992; Wessels & Claffy, 1998; Yin & Cao, 2005) model based on the TTL mechanism is used. The DS assigns a TTL value to all dispatched data items. The TTL value of a data item is computed at the DS as follows:

$$TTL = \min \{\lambda(current - created), \rho\} \qquad (5)$$

where λ and ρ are predefined constants. The parameters, *Current and created* refer to the current time and the creation time of the data item respectively. The parameter ρ represents a predefined threshold. To determine whether the TTL value of a data item is valid, a host computes the Current TTL (CTTL) as follows:

$$CTTL = (TTL - (current - initial)) \qquad (6)$$

where *current* is the time when this data item was found in cache space, and *initial* is the time when this data item was dispatched from the DS. If the value of CTTL is less than or equal to zero, this data item expires. Otherwise, it is considered valid. When the TTL expires, the data is removed from the cache and the entry is marked with a flag to indicate the invalid status. This information will be sent to neighbors to avoid any request to this data later.

PERFORMANCE EVALUATION

The implementation was run in the Network Simulator (2005) environment in order to evaluate the proposed architecture. Using the hybrid cache replacement policy, we evaluated the performance of integrated cooperative caching and prefetching with cooperative caching. We used the AODV protocol (Perkins, Belding-Royer, & Chakeres, 2005) as the ad hoc routing protocol. Host mobility was modeled using the Random Waypoint model (Broch, Maltz, Johnson, Hu, & Jetcheva, 1998).

Performance Metrics

The performance metrics used in our simulation study were average data accessibility ratio (DAR), average query delay (AQD), and average network traffic overhead (NTO). We investigated the effects of cache size, pause time, number of clusters, and prefetching overhead on these performance metrics. The simulation parameters with their default values are summarized in Table 1. In the simulation, co-operative caching with prefetching, cooperative caching with no prefetching (CCNP), and simple caching schemes (NCC) were investigated at various parameter settings.

1. **Data accessibility ratio (DAR):** The data accessibility ratio is defined as the ratio between the total number of data item requests and the total number of successfully received data items.
2. **Average query delay (AQD):** The average query delay is the average time interval between the generation of a query and the receipt of the query reply.
3. **The percentage network traffic overhead (NTO):** The percentage network traffic overhead is defined as the ratio of the increase in the total number of data transmitted with integrated caching and prefetching and the total number of data transmitted without prefetching. This metric can be used to measure the efficiency of prefetching.

Table 1. Simulation parameters

Parameter	Default value/range
Network Area(m)	1500 × 1500
Network Size	200
Transmission Range(m)	250
Number of DS/cluster	3
Number of CA/cluster	3-5
Host Speed (m/s)	0-20
Pause Time (s)	200-2000
Cache Size(KB) in MHs	100 – 1800
Simulation Time(s)	2000

There is a trade-off between hit ratio and traffic increase. Since each cached data item has an expiry time, the overhead is lower than a mechanism that stores all data for the entire duration until it is replaced. When fetched data can be used by multiple hosts, the increase in data prefetching decreases since data will not be prefetched multiple times. Hence, the hit ratio increases without an increase in network traffic. A good prefetching scheme should result in a high hit ratio without causing much additional traffic.

Discussion of Simulation Results

Figures 3-9 show the results of a performance evaluation from the experiments. The results are summarized in four categories.

1. **Simulation experiments on data accessibility:** The effects of cache size, pause time (PT) and the control parameter (δ) on data accessibility were investigated.

Figure 3 shows that the data accessibility ratio increases with an increase in cache size for all caching schemes. Cooperative caching with prefetching (CCPF) performs better at larger cache sizes due to the increased number of spaces available for caching after data fetching. The DAR includes within cluster data hits (local cache hit, neighbor cache hit, and remote cache hit). The results indicate improvements made by prefetching over cooperative caching (CCNP) and simple caching schemes (NCC).

Figure 4 shows that DAR increases proportionally to pause time. This occurs because the higher pause times indicate lower mobility. Thus, the CA will be relatively static, resulting in better data accessibility. On the other hand, the results show that cooperative caching with prefetching (CCPF) generally outperforms (by an approximate 20% increase in DAR) the scheme with only cooperative caching (CCNP). At higher pause times, data miss is only caused by a lack of the required data in the CA and not by mobility.

Figure 3. Data accessibility ratio cache size

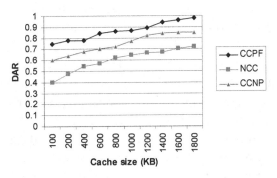

Figure 4. Data accessibility ratio as a function of pause time

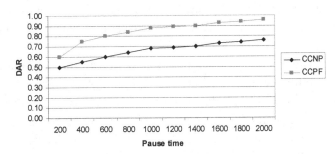

Figure 5. Data accessibility ratio as a function of cache size for different values of δ

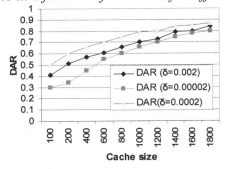

Figure 6. Average query delay as a function of cache size

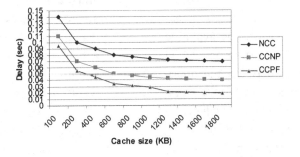

Figure 5 shows the effect of the combined frequency and latency control parameter (δ) for the LRFU cache replacement algorithm. The purpose of this experiment was to find a more suitable value for δ that would increase the performance of the cache replacement policy. The smaller value of δ (0.00002) was closer to LFU policy, whereas the larger value of δ (0.002) was closer to the LRU policy. The results in Figure 5 show that when the value of δ is 0.0002, the LRFU policy performs better than the other two cases at all cache sizes. The results also show that at a higher cache size, the rate of increase is low since there is sufficient space for caching and the cache replacement policy has less effect. This occurs because of a decreased cache miss due to the lack of prefetched data. As the value of δ increases, the data accessibility increases until it reaches a maximum level, beyond which the level of increase is negligible. The maximum value of data accessibility depends on both the cache size and the value of δ. Hence, the determination of a more appropriate value for δ depends on the cache size and weighing function.

2. **Simulation experiments on average query delay:** The effects of cache size and pause time on the average query delay were investigated.

Figure 6 shows that the CCPF consistently outperforms other schemes at all cache sizes. However, the difference in the delay is small at both ends of the cache size spectrum (lowest and highest). At lower cache sizes, both policies result in an equally sharp reduction of delay, while at higher cache sizes, the cache replacement policy has little effect since the available space can accommodate the existing or fetched data items. The difference between the query delays is relatively higher at larger cache sizes. This is because more data can be prefetched and cached when the cache size is large than when it is small. The results indicate improvements made by

prefetching over cooperative caching and simple caching schemes.

Figure 7 shows that there is a decrease in average query delay associated with increased pause time for both schemes. However, cooperative caching with prefetching performed better than cooperative caching without prefetching. The schemes differ little at higher pause times (lower mobility) and indicate that the delay remains constant. In MANETs, the number of hops is closely related to the communication latency. Therefore, if more requests are fielded by a mobile host's own cache or by its immediate neighbors, then the query delay will be much shorter than if the request is fielded by a remote DS.

3. **Simulation experiments on network traffic:** Although prefetching increases data accessibility, it also introduces network traffic. The effects of prefetch thresholds on network traffic and data accessibility were investigated. The prefetch threshold shows the length of time required to perform prefetching. A threshold value of zero indicates no prefetching, while a threshold value of 1.0 indicates perfect prefetching. Prefetching was performed on the expiry of the TTL value, mobility of immediate neighbor holding the data, and on cache miss. The decision of which data item to fetch also depends on the prefetch index maintained at each host. Figures 8 and 9 show the NTO and DAR for various numbers of clusters (NC), respectively. In all experiments, the NTO was higher for larger numbers of clusters and lower for smaller numbers of clusters at all prefetch threshold levels. This is because data prefetching may involve transmission across multiple clusters, which are located a number of hops away. On the other hand, results in Figure 9 show that DAR decreased with an increase in the prefetch threshold. However, the rate of decrease was similar at all clusters after the threshold of about

Figure 7. Average query delay as a function of pause time

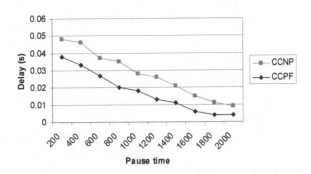

Figure 8. Average network traffic overhead as a function of prefetch threshold

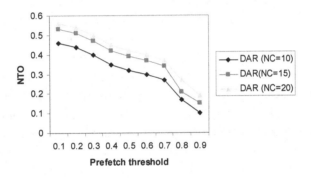

Figure 9. Average data accessibility ratio as a function of prefetch threshold

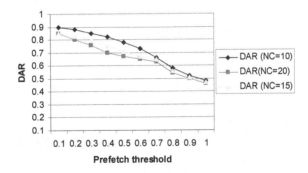

0.6-0.7. Threshold values above 0.7 do not exhibit any significant differences. The fact that higher DAR was observed at relatively lower numbers of clusters indicates that communication delay in inter-cluster communication was reduced, and that more caching agents can be located within the same cluster. These results imply that short prefetch threshold values result in higher data accessibility, but this occurs at the expense of higher network traffic. However, by choosing a suitable threshold value, a balance between both can be achieved. Our experiments indicate that a threshold value below 0.7 and above 0.1 was able to achieve an optimal balance between the data accessibility and the network traffic increase for various numbers of clusters.

4. **Simulation experiments on hit ratio by source:** To see the percentage of queries satisfied from local cluster and external clusters, we compiled separate statistics for intra-cluster and inter-cluster query responses.

We considered both cooperative caching with prefetching and without prefetching. The results are shown in Table 2. In this table, Local Hit Ratio (LHR) refers to the ratio of successful requests replied from local cache. Global Hit Ratio (GHR) refers to the number of requests satisfied from other clusters. This experiment was carried out using PT = 1400KB, PT = 1800KB and MH speed = 18 m/s. The last column of the table gives the average (AVG) data accessibility from both local and global sources.

The results show that with cooperative caching and prefetching (CCPF) schemes, less data items are fetched from external clusters to satisfy queries. The results also show that cooperative caching with prefetching ensures a greater data

accessibility ratio than the scheme that uses only cooperative caching. In these simulation experiments, an approximate 25% gain (with PT=1400) and 23% gain (with PT = 1800) was achieved from intra-cluster information (local hit). Also about a 7% gain was observed when the PT value increases from 1400 to 1800. However, due to host mobility and wireless link characteristics, it is difficult to achieve 100% data accessibility in MANETs.

CONCLUSION

In this article, we proposed and evaluated a cooperative caching and prefetching scheme for MANETs. The architecture for enabling cooperative data caching and a prefetching algorithm were both presented. Additionally, a cache replacement policy based on combined metrics for data access frequency and reference time was also presented. A simulation based experimental study was carried out to evaluate the performance of the proposed scheme using average data accessibility, average query delay, and network traffic overhead. The results confirm that caching coupled with prefetching increases the data accessibility ratio and reduces query delay. In future work, we intend to enhance the proposed scheme by adapting it to the integrated ad hoc network and the Internet environment and evaluate performance in an implementation testbed.

ACKNOWLEDGMENT

This research was supported in part by the Natural Sciences and Engineering Research Council of Canada (NSERC) Discovery Grant No. 046940.

The authors are grateful to the anonymous referees for their valuable suggestions, which improved the quality of the article.

Table 2. DAR by source (internal and external clusters) of successful query and AVG for each caching scheme

Scheme	PT=1400		PT=1800		DAR
	LHR	GHR	LHR	GHR	AVG
CCNP	56%	14%	65%	12%	73.5%
CCPF	81%	9%	88%	7%	92.5%

REFERENCES

Alex, V. (1992). A good file system. In *Proceedings of USENIX File System Workshop* (pp. 1-12).

Artail, H., Safa, H., & Pierre, S. (2005). Database caching in MANETs based on separation of queries and responses. In *Proceedings of the IEEE International Conference on Wireless and Mobile Computing, Networking, and Communications* (pp. 237-244).

Broch, J., Maltz, D. A., Johnson, D. B., Hu, Y. C., & Jetcheva, J. (1998). A performance comparison of multi-hop wireless ad hoc network routing protocols. In *Proceedings of* ACM MobiCom (pp. 85-97).

Cao, G., Yin, L., & Das, C. R. (2004). Cooperative cache-based data access in ad hoc networks. *IEEE Computer Society, 37*(2), 32-39.

Das, S., Perkins, C., & Royer, E. (2000). Performance comparison of two on-demand routing protocols for ad hoc networks. In *Proceedings of IEEE INFOCOM* (pp. 3-12).

Fan, L., Cao, P., & Almeida, J. (1998). Summary cache: A scalable wide area web cache sharing protocol. In *Proceedings of ACM SIGCOMM,* ACM Press (pp. 254-265).

Feldmann, A., Caceres, R., Douglis, F., Glass, G., & Rabinovich, M. (1999). Performance of Web proxy caching in heterogeneous bandwidth environments. In *Proceedings of the 18th Conference of the IEEE Computer and Communications Society* (pp. 107-116).

Gerla, M., & Tsai, J. T. C. (1995). Multicluster, mobile, multimedia radio network. *Wireless Networks, 1*(3), 255-265.

Hara, T. (2002). Replica allocation in ad hoc networks with periodic data update. In *Proceedings of the 3rd International Conference on Mobile Data Management* (pp. 79-86).

Johnson, D., & Malta, D. (1996). Dynamic source routing in ad hoc wireless network. In *Mobile Computing*, edited by T. Imielinski & H. Korth, Kluwer Academic Publishers, Chapter 5, (pp. 153-181).

Lee, D., Choi, J., Choe, H., Noh, S. H., Min, S. L., & Cho, Y. (1997). Implementation and performance evaluation of the LRFU replacement policy. In *Proceedings of the 23rd Euromicro Conference* (pp. 106-111).

Lim, S., Lee, W. C., Cao, G., & Das, C. R. (2003). A novel caching scheme for internet based mobile ad hoc networks. In *Proceedings of the IEEE International Conference on Computer Communications and Networks (ICCCN)*, (pp. 38-43).

Lu, H., & Denko, M. K. (2004). Reliable data storage and dissemination in mobile ad hoc network. In *Proceedings of the International Workshop on Theoretical and Algorithmic Aspects of Wireless Ad Hoc, Sensor and Peer-to-Peer Networks* (pp. 81-86).

Lu, H., & Denko, M. K. (2005). Replica update strategies in mobile ad hoc networks. In *Proceedings of the 2nd IEEE/IFIP International Conference on Wireless and Optical Communications Networks* (WOCN 2005).

Network Simulator. (2005). Retrieved from http://www.isi.edu/nsnam/ns/

Papadopoui, M., & Schulzrinne, H. (2001). Effects of power conservation, wireless coverage and cooperation on data dissemination among mobile devices. In *Proceedings of ACM MobiHoc* (pp. 117-127).

Perkins, C., & Bhagwat, P. (1994). Highly Dynamic Destination-Sequenced Distance-Vector routing (DSDV) for mobile computers. In *Proceedings of ACM SIGCOMM* (pp. 234-244).

Perkins, C. E., Belding-Royer, E. M., & Chakeres, I. (2003). Ad Hoc On Demand Distance Vector

(AODV) routing. IETF Internet draft, draft-per-kins-manet-aodvbis-00.txt, (Work in Progress).

Rousskov, A., & Wessels, D. (1999). Cache digests. *Computer Networks and ISDN Systems, 30*(22-23), 2155-2168.

Sailhan, F., & Issarny, V. (2003). Cooperative caching in ad hoc networks. In *Proceedings of the 4th International Conference on Mobile Data Management* (pp. 13-28).

Wang, J. (1999). A survey of Web caching schemes for the Internet. *ACM SIGCOMM, Computer Communication Review, 25*(9), 36-46.

Wang, Y. et al. (2005). A transparent cache based mechanism for mobile ad hoc networks. In *Proceedings of the 3rd International Conference on Inform Tech and Applications (ICITA'05)* (Vol. 2, pp. 305-310).

Wessels, D., & Claffy, K. (1998). ICP and the squid Web cache. *IEEE JSAC, 16*(1998), 345-357.

Yin, L., & Cao, G. (2006). Supporting cooperative caching in ad hoc networks. *IEEE Transactions on Mobile Computing, 5*(1), 77- 89.

This work was previously published in International Journal of Business Data Communications and Networking, Vol. 3, Issue 1, edited by J. Gutierrez, pp. 1-15 , copyright 2007 by IGI Publishing, formerly known as Idea Group Publishing (an imprint of IGI Global).

Chapter XV
A Survey on Fuzzy Reasoning Applications for Routing Protocols in Wireless Ad–Hoc Networks

Essam Natsheh
King Faisal University, Saudi Arabia

ABSTRACT

The challenge in creating a routing protocol for ad-hoc networks is to design a single protocol that can adapt to the wide variety of conditions that can be present in any ad-hoc network environment. The routing protocol must perform efficiently in environments in which it suffers from high nodes mobility and many wireless transmission constraints. Because it is often impossible to know in advance what environment the protocol will find itself in, and because the environment can change unpredictably, the routing protocol must be able to adapt automatically. In this chapter, we survey fuzzy reasoning algorithm (FRA) as a highly adaptive algorithm used to achieve that goal. We present the various applications of that algorithm to ad-hoc routing protocols. In particular, the exposition includes a discussion of strength and weakness of these applications and how they can be improved.

INTRODUCTION

Mobile wireless ad-hoc networks are networks without infrastructure, where every node works as a router. In these networks, every node must discover its local neighbors and through those neighbors it will communicate to nodes that are out of its transmission range (multi-hop routing).

These networks suffer from all kinds of uncertainty, randomness and fuzziness. This uncertainty is due to high bit error rate (BER) in the wireless channel, increased collisions due to the presence of hidden terminals, signals interference and attenuation, location dependent connection, uni-directional links, and frequent link breaks due to nodes mobility. This emerges the need for high adaptive routing protocols with adapting capabilities to high variability and uncertainty for these types of networks.

Recently, many researchers adaptively optimize the ad-hoc routing protocols functions and parameters using the fuzzy reasoning algorithm (FRA). The FRAs are proposed to overcome the above shortcoming in ad-hoc networks. The routing protocol parameters can be determined more accurately and dynamically by fuzzy reasoning, instead of static values. The application of fuzzy reasoning to ad-hoc networks problems allows us to specify these parameters using "if...then..." type of linguistic rules.

In this paper we present a survey of fuzzy reasoning based routing for mobile ad-hoc networks. We outline the main problems that have been solved by this class of routing protocols and discuss some drawbacks of the proposed methods and possible solutions. Our survey is only on fuzzy reasoning applications for ad-hoc routing protocols and we will not report its applications to other layers of wireless ad-hoc networks. Surveys on fuzzy reasoning applications for wired telecommunication networks exist in (Ghosh et al., 1998) and for ATM networks in (Sekercioglu et al., 2001).

The remainder of this paper is structured as follows: we present a review of current research efforts classified according to the routing optimization targets. A later sections discusses the validity of the performance metrics that may be used in fuzzy reasoning, implementation complexity of the fuzzy reasoning algorithms, compatibility between conventional and fuzzy-based routing protocols, the paper's conclusion, and then further researches possibilities.

REVIEW OF CURRENT RESEARCH EFFORTS

The major challenges that the FRAs tried to optimize in ad-hoc routing field are: routes costs estimation, QoS-based routing, energy-aware routing, position-based routing, zone-based routing, clustering, parameters configuration and routes local repair. A detailed discussion on each of these optimization targets are given below. This classification of FRAs according to the routing optimization targets is not mutually exclusive and some methods fall in more than one class.

Routes Costs Estimation Techniques

In this technique the route cost is calculated for every available route. Some performance measures are used to estimate the stability of the routes. The fuzzy reasoning is used to map the relation of route stability and its cost. The route with a high cost will be considered as a best route and it will be used for data forwarding.

Rea and Pesch (2004a) used fuzzy reasoning for caching decision in Dynamic Source Routing (DSR) protocol. They combined four routes stability metrics (link strength, link capacity, node energy and number of hops) into a single decision: *To cache* or *Not To Cache* the routes. They proved the effectiveness of this method (Rea and Pesch, 2004b). To distinguish between routes when multiple routes are available, they used fuzzy weighting of cache entries in (Rea and Pesch, 2004c). More improvements are done in (Rea and Pesch, 2005) using fuzzy adaptive cache expiration policy to dynamically adapt a static cache timeout values. The cache timeout is calculated by increasing/decreasing the static timeout with respect to the routes' fuzzy weight. However, the values of cache timeout can be more accurately calculated by fuzzy mapping the correlation between cache timeout and routes stability parameters.

Ma *et al.* (2004) used fuzzy Petri net and its reasoning mechanism for routes selection. Firstly they define certainty factor between each neighboring node that is obtained by computing the relative velocity and the relative motion distance, then they utilize the reasoning mechanism of fuzzy Petri net to find a route with the highest reliability. However, using relative velocity as mobility metric is not recommended as discussed in (Boleng *et al.*, 2002). This metric requires velocity information from other network nodes beside it is not feasible to compute. In (Chiang and Huang, 2004), the authors used fuzzy Petri net and Global Position System (GPS) information to get a snapshot of the complete network topology. Also, this technique is not recommended since it requires global network knowledge that places an added demand on the network.

In (Rong *et al.*, 2005) and (Zhigang *et al.*, 2005), the authors proposed a fuzzy applicability method for routes selection. Fuzzy applicability shows the approximate degree of two fuzzy sets. In ad-hoc networks, it denotes the approximate degree of two neighboring nodes, and it is the standard to judge whether a link is proper for communicating between the two hosts. It can be calculated using GPS location information. Similar work is done in (Zhao and Wang, 2004b) using fuzzy linear regression method. Fuzzy linear regression makes it possible to extract linear relationships from small data sets, with fewer hypotheses than statistical linear regression. However, these researches used mathematical models to map GPS information to the routes selection decision and missed the strength of the fuzzy systems that is fuzzy reasoning.

Marwaha *et al.* (2004) used fuzzy reasoning to achieve multiple routing objectives while selecting a route. The objectives they considered are to (i) minimize end-to-end delay; (ii) maximize packet delivery; and (iii) maximize the lifetime of the batteries. They achieved that using signal strength, battery power and buffer occupancy as a metrics to calculate the routes coast. Although the objective of this type of protocols is to have one rule-base that satisfies multiple routing criterions, it is difficult to find real relationship between some of these criterions. For example, trying to create a relationship between the packets end-to-end delay and the lifetime of the batteries

is unreliable and extend the reality. In fact, this type of indirect relationship needs to be proven before formatting the rules of FRA.

QoS-Based Routing Protocols

Quality of service (QoS) is the performance level of a service offered by the network to the user. The goal of QoS providing is to achieve better network traffic delivery and at the same time optimal network resources utilization. The users require different kinds of services from the network. These services can be categorized using the service requirement as: maximum bandwidth, minimum delay, minimum delay jitter, and minimum packet lose rate.

Recently, there have been considerable efforts in the area of supporting QoS by fuzzy reasoning in ad-hoc networks. The works that exist tend to be based on queues scheduling algorithms, route selection depending on QoS parameters, and route selection depending on traffic parameters (load-aware algorithms). These are discussed in the following subsections.

A. Queues Scheduling Algorithms

Scheduling algorithms tried to guarantee QoS by minimizing the packets' wait time in the queues. The choice of scheduling algorithm to determine which queued packet to process next have a significant effect on overall end-to-end performance of ad-hoc routing protocols.

In (Gomathy and Shanmugavel, 2004a; Gomathy and Shanmugavel, 2004b; Gomathy and Shanmugavel, 2005a; Gomathy and Shanmugavel, 2005b), the authors proposed a method to give every queued packet a priority index calculated using the FRA with three traffic characteristics: queue length, data rate and packet's deadline. Although this method showed higher QoS guarantee than conventional scheduling algorithms, it doesn't distinguish between real-time and multimedia traffic and data and routing control traffic.

To overcome the previous drawback, Thankakan *et al.* (2001) proposed a model handle multiple queues where each queue is for specific classes of traffic and they used fuzzy reasoning to manage these queues. Khoukhi and Cherkaoui (2005) proposed an advanced model that includes a set of mechanisms: admission control for real-time traffic, a FRA for best-effort traffic regulation, and three schemes for real-time traffic regulation. However, in that model some bandwidth loss was experienced in overall network capacity due the increased complexity. Other work that used fuzzy controller to allocate wireless resources to higher priority real-time traffic and optimally allocates remaining resources to non-real-time traffic found in (Bandara *et al.*, 2000; Bandara *et al.*, 2002). This work needs to be justified with wireless ad-hoc networks.

Most of the real-time traffic support in wired networks relies on the availability of precise link utilization information. In ad-hoc networks, however, all traffic within a mobile node's transmission range contends for medium access. Hence the shared nature of wireless communication channels makes resource estimation more difficult. Multi-hop interference introduces further challenges to the problem, making it complex to accurately determine the available resources. However, without sufficiently accurate resource prediction, it is difficult to provide multimedia services with satisfactory quality.

Node mobility also brings new obstacles to real-time traffic support in ad-hoc networks. The movement of a node on an active path often leads to a link break, and subsequently loss of packets. The packet loss after the link break, accompanied by increased packet transmission delay during a consequent route repair, significantly impacts the QoS of multimedia services.

B. Route Selection Depending on QoS Parameters

In (Wong and Wong, 2002), the authors proposed a fuzzy-decision-based protocol with support for prioritized service differentiation packet routing. The idea of this protocol is that it classifies the traffic to five prioritized classes depending on the QoS parameters. After that, it uses the fuzzy reasoning to calculate how 'fit' each path to these classes of traffic. However, this protocol increased the routing load about 30% and need more investigation and improvement.

Zhang *et al.* (2004) proposed a complicated algorithm contains three sub-fuzzy controllers: (i) fuzzy request controller investigates the QoS required by the traffic, (ii) fuzzy route state controller investigates the QoS provided by routes, and (iii) fuzzy matching controller matches between the two previous controllers. Thus, the complication in this algorithm makes it not scalable and is not suitable for more than 10 nodes network.

Raju *et al.* (2000) proposed the idea of fuzzy connection admission (FCA) algorithm that uses the fuzzy reasoning to map the relationship between QoS parameters and the maximum number of generated probes (routing control messages). They extend this idea in (Raju *et al.*, 2002) and presented a fuzzy route probing inference system to give a rank to all paths using QoS parameters. After that, the protocol split probes to these routes according to the values of the routes rank. In (Raju *et al.*, 2004), the authors modified FCA algorithm to generate certificates (permissions to search for feasible routes) and then distributed them to the probes. Actually, in ad-hoc routing protocols the use of probes to check the nodes connectivity depend on the time of their consecutive sending not on their numbers. Therefore, this work needs to be investigated within real ad-hoc routing protocols to prove its effectiveness.

C. Route Selection Depending on Traffic Parameters (Load-Aware Algorithms)

Load-aware routing protocols consider the load (traffic rate) as the main route selection metric and monitor the congestion status of active routes to reconstruct the path when nodes of the route have their interface queue overloaded.

Kwan *et al.* (2003) used fuzzy reasoning to decide the congestion status (traffic rate) of the network. They used the linguistic variable for the number of nodes, queue length sizes and traffic priority to estimate fuzzy relation for the traffic congestion of a path. After that, they used a tree search on path states to provide an optimal solution for the balance between the need to preserve network resources and real-time requirements.

Other researchers used fuzzy reasoning to balance the network traffic between multiple paths. In (Alandjani and Johnson, 2003) this is achieved by using traffic load metrics (traffic importance and network congestion) while in (Liu *et al.*, 2005) it is achieved by using paths stability metrics (energy consumption, buffer occupation, signal strength, and number of intermediate nodes). In these algorithms the traffic will be split over the paths for load balancing, the traffic will be sent simultaneously over a plurality of the paths, or even it will be rejected due to cost/benefit considerations.

Energy-Aware Routing Protocols

The idea of these protocols is to use the energy parameters to direct the network traffic to non-critical nodes (nodes having high residual energy or less data). This will save the network nodes' battery lifetime of the low battery nodes and hence it will increase the overall network lifetime.

Balakrishnan and Johnson (Balakrishnan and Johnson, 2005) used fuzzy reasoning to allow every node to decide weather or not to forward the traffic to the next node in the route depending on its remaining energy and the traffic intensity. In this method, the source nodes will not know the status of the non-forwarder nodes making the possibility of data losing in the network to be high. To overcome that, in (Liang and Ren, 2005; Liang, 2005) used fuzzy reasoning to make it possible for the source node to add adjacent nodes to the route depending on: the distance between the adjacent node and the destination, the adjacent node remaining energy and its degree of mobility. In (Xia and Liang, 2005), the authors enhanced the previous method to balance traffic delay and nodes energy by electing the nodes with the highest three possibilities as the relay nodes and then elect the node with the highest possibility as the target node.

In (Yusuf and Haider, 2005), the authors used more advanced technique by making the forwarding decision to be the costs of the links. Links with the highest cost will be chosen at forwarding time. To calculate links costs, the authors used fuzzy reasoning with five energy and traffic metrics. However, using five inputs to the FRA needs to be carefully investigated to demonstrate the inter-relationship between them. Validating this relationship is extremely difficult.

Position-Based Routing Protocols

Position-based routing algorithms use the *physical* location information of the nodes for routing. The routing decision at each node is then based on the destination's position and the position of the forwarding node's neighbors.

Due to the frequent nodes movements in ad-hoc networks, Nikaein and Bonnet (2002) used *location server* to maintain a database of current nodes location information. They used fuzzy reasoning to trigger location update and search procedures. The trigger rate is determined as a function of node's speed and distance from the origin. This function describes node behaviors and it is computed after each movement. However, using the location server makes the ad-hoc network miss its main characteristic that is a network without infrastructure.

Zone Routing Protocol

The zone routing protocol (ZRP) proactively maintains routes within a local region of the network (routing zone). The ZRP can be configured for a particular network through adjustment of a single parameter, the routing zone radius.

Pearlman and Haas (1999) presented a study demonstrating the effects of node velocity, nodes density and route query rate on the performance of the ZRP. Huang *et al.* (2005) used these three metrics to create a rule-base used via a fuzzy inference system (Huang *et al.*, 2005) and evolving fuzzy neural networks (Huang *et al.*, 2004) to dynamically adjusted routing zone radius values. The proposed methods built in Bluetooth-based mobile ad-hoc networks effectively reduced the space cost when compared with conventional methods.

In (Wang and Olariu, 2004), the authors proposed the two-zone routing protocol (TZRP) as an extension to ZRP. In TZRP, each node maintains two zones: a *crisp zone* for proactive routing and efficient bordercasting, and a *fuzzy zone* for heuristic routing using imprecise locality information. The authors used a heuristic method to calculate the fuzzy zone and its radius. However, using the fuzzy reasoning to calculate that is more effective due to its nature to map the imprecise locality information.

Clustering Protocols

Clustering is a technique to divide nodes into several groups that randomly move in the network. This technique can reduce the communication overhead and can easily manage the network resources of an ad-hoc network.

Habetha and Walke (2002) proposed a clustering algorithm based on fuzzy reasoning can trigger several predefined topology changes by the output

variables of the fuzzy rules. These output variables are: creation, deletion, or drift of a cluster, and installation, deletion, or handover of forwarder. Each output variable indicates in the form of a linguistic variable whether the respective topology change should be carried out or not.

In (Zhao and Wang, 2004a; Hwang *et al.*, 2002), the authors proposed clustering algorithms and used fuzzy reasoning to calculate the link lifetime between the neighboring nodes. They calculate it using distance and speed in (Zhao and Wang, 2004a) and signal strength and direction of the relative motion in (Hwang *et al.*, 2002).

Liang (Liang, 2003a; Liang, 2003b; Liang, 2003c) used fuzzy reasoning for master/controller election for each cluster in the network. Rules antecedent is the node distance to the cluster centroid and its remaining battery capacity, and consequent is the possibility that this node will be elected as a master/controller.

Fuzzy Configuration of Routing Protocols Parameters

In this technique the fuzzy reasoning is used to dynamically configure the protocols parameters instead of using static values. The dynamical configuration can adapt to the changing of the network topology and improve the protocol performance. In other hand using static parameters for the protocols in ad-hoc environment that suffer from frequent change of network topology and different traffic intensity may degrade the routing protocols performance.

Wang *et al.* (2005) used a fuzzy reasoning to dynamically configure five routing parameters of AODV (Ad hoc On-demand Distance Vector) routing protocol. They used mathematical models to represent nodes moving mode and their traffic mode. These models were used to categorize the network environments to 9 categorize. The fuzzy reasoning was used to estimate the nodes membership degree in these environments. Depending on the node membership degree, the values of the protocol parameters are increased or decreased.

Actually, the fuzzy reasoning can be used more effectively to accurately calculate the real values of protocol parameters that map the status of the node and its links. We did this to dynamically adapt routes lifetimes (Natsheh *et al.*, 2005; Natsheh *et al.*, 2006a), 'Hello' messages interval time (Natsheh *et al.*, 2006b) and active queue management for congestion control (Natsheh *et al.*, 2007).

Local Repair Techniques

In conventional ad-hoc routing protocols, once a link between two nodes in a route is broken, the whole route is broken and the source node starts to search for alternative routes. If routing protocols support local repair; once a link breaks between two nodes on a route, the upstream node of the link break tries to recover the route by searching for alternative node that can reach through it to the destination. Another possible method is to monitor the links and avoid any breaks by finding alternatives and stronger links. This could be done by monitoring the links in the route and predicting the links break before it happens and find alternative nodes for the *weak* links.

Venkatesh *et al.* (2005) used fuzzy reasoning to dynamically optimize the routes length that may change significantly due the mobility of the nodes in ad-hoc networks. They used nodes speed and pause-time as a metrics for the need of routes shortage and the shortage decision is done according to the number of entries of neighbor table and time-stamp of these entries. However, the performance of this technique can be improved, if more accurate metrics reflecting links stability status are considered and more accurate output decision reflecting the needs for routes update.

Even if this local repair field is one of the most suitable ad-hoc routing techniques, for fuzzy reasoning, there is no further research done to improve this technique. Actually, to avoid links breaks or to choose alternative links, the protocol needs a fuzzy decision according to nodes mobility and links parameters. This fuzzy decision can be achieved optimally by fuzzy reasoning.

VALIDITY OF THE PERFORMANCE METRICS

The validity of a measurement metric is the extent to which the metric measures what it is supposed to measure. Normally, after researchers decide to use fuzzy reasoning to optimize some of ad-hoc networks parameters, they search for metrics that can optimally used to map the parameter under study. The strength of the fuzzy reasoning comes from the strength of the correlation between the parameter under study and the metrics used to measure it. Besides real representation of the parameters, these metrics must be reliable, valid and can be measured in the real environment. Boleng *et al.* (2002) presented five standard characteristics that must be satisfied in any performance metrics. These characteristics are:

1. Computable in a distributed environment without global network knowledge.
2. A good indicator of the parameter under study.
3. Feasible to compute.
4. Independent of any specific protocol.
5. Computable in real network implementations.

It's noticed that some metrics used in the literature don't meet the five standard characteristics. Table 1 shows some of these metrics and the characteristics they failed to achieve.

Simulator parameters as a pause-time (Venkatesh *et al.*, 2005) (Wang *et al.*, 2005) and a network map size (Wang *et al.*, 2005) may not be present in an implementation of the routing protocols in a real network. As a result, it is apparent that using these parameters to be an input to the fuzzy algorithm fail requirement 5.

Table 1. Performance metrics used in literature and the characteristics they failed to achieve

Performance Metric	Failed Characteristic
Pause-time (Venkatesh et al., 2005) (Wang et al., 2005)	5
Numbers of nodes in the network (Wang et al., 2005) (Kwan et al., 2003)	1
Network map size (Wang et al., 2005)	5
Relative velocity (Ma et al., 2004)	1, 3

In (Ma *et al.*, 2004), the authors presented mobility metric based on the relative velocity between nodes. This metric violates requirement 1 by requiring velocity information from other network nodes. Similarly, using the numbers of nodes in the network as an input metric (Wang *et al.*, 2005) (Kwan *et al.*, 2003) requires global network knowledge and violates requirement 1. In addition, the relative velocity metric also violates requirement 3 because is not necessarily feasible to compute. Communicating velocity and direction among all nodes and calculating the resulting relative velocity will be the most difficult in these network conditions (Boleng *et al.*, 2002).

IMPLEMENTATION COMPLEXITY OF THE FUZZY REASONING ALGORITHMS

Using FRAs with ad-hoc routing protocols we may achieve comparable or better run-time computation than purely conventional methods. This can be achieved using one of the following methods:

1. **Lockup table:** The input-output relationship of the fuzzy reasoning engine for FRA of Fuzzy-AQM is illustrated in Figure 1 (Natsheh *et al.*, 2007). This relationship can be stored as a lookup table which will result in a very fast execution.

2. **Fuzzy logic interpreter:** Instead of implementing the FRA using a high level language with its local interpreter and compiler, an

Figure 1. The input-output relationship of the Fuzzy-AQM

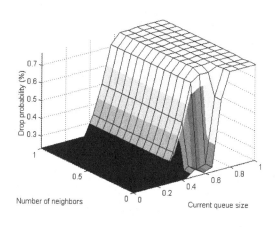

interactive computing environment based on a fuzzy logic interpreter can be used to minimize the calculation overhead (Bonissone, 1992).

3. **Dedicated fuzzy hardware:** FRAs based on dedicated hardware can deliver much higher performance than those based on general-purpose computing machines (Hung, 1995).

COMPATIBILITY BETWEEN CONVENTIONAL AND FUZZY-BASED ROUTING PROTOCOLS

The FRAs are compatible with conventional ad-hoc routing protocols in the sense that a node that uses FRA (an "intelligent" node) may communicate with a node that uses conventional routing protocols (standard node), as there are no changes in the protocols messages format.

CONCLUSION

This paper has reviewed the current research efforts in FRAs to ad-hoc routing protocols including: routes costs estimation, QoS-based routing, energy-aware routing, position-based routing, zone-based routing, clustering, parameters configuration and routes local repair.

The analysis of the proposed methods shows the current promise of fuzzy reasoning in most functions of ad-hoc routing protocols. The analysis has also revealed the limitation of the proposed methods and suggests future enhancement and work to effectively get the strength of the fuzzy reasoning. It focuses on the validity of the performance metrics and outlines its characteristics.

FURTHER RESEARCH

Numerous areas for future research are described throughout literature review section, with the improvement of current applications of fuzzy reasoning in ad-hoc routing protocols and the development of general framework among the most exciting opportunities.

Increased fuzziness of the routing protocols for ad-hoc networks will always be possible. With the applications presented in this study, hopefully this fuzziness can be directed towards the areas that will improve the performance of the protocols in rough environments of high mobility or numerous wirelesses constrains.

Future FRAs may use neural or other learning schemes to help them to optimize the membership functions. This method may enhance the performance of routing protocols due to its more accurate parameters generated by FRAs. However, it must be examined carefully due to the expected complexity that may slow down the routing protocols.

Although the routing metrics used in this study effectually measured the topology changes, there is a need to examine the possibility of using various media access techniques as a routing metrics. The wireless media techniques will determine the various radio frequency (RF) channel distortions that include path loss, multi-path effects, noise, and dropped messages due to message collisions. Thus, future work may include understanding the RF channel and extending the routing metric used by the FRA to accurately map the wireless environment of ad-hoc networks.

Overall, the work presented here has given us an insight into how ad-hoc routing protocols parameters might be more accurately and dynamically determined by FRA, instead of using inaccurate static values. Therefore, more research studies could focus on using FRA to optimize other parameters of ad-hoc routing protocols.

REFERENCES

Alandjani, G., & Johnson, E. E. (2003). Fuzzy Routing in Ad Hoc Networks. *Proc. of IEEE Int'l Conf. on Performance, Computing, and Communications*, 525–530, Phoenix, AZ, April 9-11.

Balakrishnan, M., & Johnson, E. E. (2005). Fuzzy Diffusion for Distributed Sensor Networks. *Proc. of the IEEE Military Communications Conference*, 1–6, Oct. 17-20.

Bandara, J., Shen, X., & Nurmohamed, Z. (2000). A Fuzzy Resource Controller for Non-Real-Time Traffic in Wireless Networks. *Proc. of the IEEE Int'l Conf. on Communications*, *1*, 75–79, June 18-22.

Bandara, J., Shen, X., & Nurmohamed, Z. (2002). Resource Allocator for Non Real-Time Traffic in Wireless Networks Using Fuzzy Logic. *Wireless Personal Communications*, Kluwer Academic Publishers, Netherlands, *21*, 329–344.

Boleng, J., Navidi, W., & Camp, T. (2002). Metrics to Enable Adaptive Protocols for Mobile Ad Hoc Networks. *Proc. of the Int'l Conf. on Wireless Networks (ICWN '02)*, 293-298.

Bonissone, P. P. (1992). A compiler for fuzzy logic controllers. In *Fuzzy Eng. Toward Human Friendly Sys. IFES'91*, IOS Press.

Chiang, T., & Huang, Y. (2004). Multicast Routing Representation in Ad Hoc Networks Using Fuzzy Petri Nets. *Proc. of the 18th Int'l Conf. on Advanced Information Networking and Applications, 2*, 420–423, March 29-31.

Ghosh, S., Razouqi, Q., Schmacher, H. J., & Celmins, A. (1998). A Survey of Recent Advances in Fuzzy Logic in Telecomunications Networks and New Challenges. *IEEE Trans. on Fuzzy Systems, 6*(3), 443–447.

Gomathy, C., & Shanmugavel, S. (2004a). An Efficient Fuzzy Based Priority Scheduler for Mobile Ad hoc Networks and Performance Analysis for Various Mobility Models. *Proc. of the IEEE Wireless Communications and Networking Conference, 2*, 1087–1092, March 21-25.

Gomathy, C., & Shanmugavel, S. (2004b). Effect of Packet Scheduling and Evaluation of Fuzzy Based Priority Scheduler on Ad hoc Network Unicast Communication. *Proc. of the IEEE Int'l Conf. on Signal Processing and Communications*, 506–510, Atlanta, USA, Dec. 11-14.

Gomathy, C., & Shanmugavel, S. (2005a). Supporting QoS in MANET by a Fuzzy Priority Scheduler and Performance Analysis with Mixed Traffic. *Proc. of the 14th IEEE Int'l Conf. on Fuzzy Systems*, 31–37, Nevada, USA, May 22-25.

Gomathy, C., & Shanmugavel, S. (2005b). Supporting QoS in MANET by a Fuzzy Priority Scheduler and Performance Analysis with Multicast Routing Protocols. *EURASIP Journal on Wireless Communications and Networking, 3*, 426–436.

Habetha, J., & Walke, B. (2002). Fuzzy Rule-Based Mobility and Load Management for Self-Organizing Wireless Networks. *International Journal of Wireless Information Networks, 9*(2), 119-140.

Huang, C., Lai, W. K., Hsiao, S., & Liu, H. (2005). A Self-Adaptive Zone Routing Protocol for Bluetooth Scatternets. *Computer Communications, Elsevier, 28*(1), 37-50.

Huang, C., Lai, W. K., Hsiao, S., Liuand, H., & Luo, R. (2004). A Bluetooth Routing Protocol Using Evolving Fuzzy Neural Networks. *International Journal of Wireless Information Networks, Springer, Netherlands, 11*(3), 131-146.

Hung, D. L. (1995). Dedicated Digital Fuzzy Hardware. *IEEE Micro, 15*(4), 31–39.

Hwang, I., Liu, C., & Wang, C. (2002). Link Stability-Based Clustering and Routing in Ad-Hoc Wireless Networks Using Fuzzy Set Theory. *International Journal of Wireless Information Networks, 9*(3), 201–212.

Khoukhi, L., & Cherkaoui, S. (2005). Fuzzy-MARS: A Fuzzy Logic Approach with Service Differentiation for Wireless Ad hoc Networks. *Proc. of the IEEE Int'l Conf. on Wireless Networks, Communications, and Mobile Computing, 2*, 839–844, June 13-16.

Kwan, M., Dogancay, K., & Jain, L. (2003). Fair Multi-path Selection for Real-Time Video Transmission in Ad-Hoc Networks Using Artificial Intelligence. *Proc. of the Design and Application of Hybrid Intelligent System, 104*, 830-841, Melbourne, Australia, Dec. 14-17.

Liang, Q. (2003a). A Design Methodology for Wireless Persona Area Networks with Power Efficiency. *Proc. of the IEEE Wireless Communications and Networking, 3*, 1475–1480, March 16-20.

Liang, Q. (2003b). Designing Power Aware Self-Reconfiguring Topology for Mobile Wireless Personal Area Networks Using Fuzzy Logic. *IEEE Transactions on Systems, Man, and Cybernetics—Part C: Applications and Reviews, 33*(3), 390–394.

Liang, Q. (2003c). Clusterhead Election for Mobile Ad Hoc Wireless Network. *Proc. of the 14th IEEE Proceedings on Personal, Indoor and Mobile Radio Communications*, 2, 1623–1628, Sept. 7-10.

Liang, Q. (2005). Fault-Tolerant and Energy Efficient Wireless Sensor Networks: A Cross-Layer Approach. *Proc. of the IEEE Military Communications Conference*, 1–7, Oct. 17-20.

Liang, Q. & Ren Q. (2005). Energy and Mobility Aware Geographical Multipath Routing for Wireless Sensor Networks. *Proc. of the IEEE Wireless Communications and Networking*, 3, 1867–1871, March 13-17.

Liu, H., Li, J., Zhang, Y., & Pan, Y. (2005). An Adaptive Genetic Fuzzy Multi-path Routing Protocol for Wireless Ad-Hoc Networks. *Proc. of the 1st ACIS Int'l Workshop on Self-Assembling Wireless Networks (SAWN 2005)*, 468–475, Maryland, USA, May 23-25.

Ma, H., Hu, Z., & Wang, G. (2004). A Reliable Routing Algorithm in Mobile Ad Hoc Networks Using Fuzzy Petri Net. *Proc. of the IEEE Global Telecommunications Conference Workshops*, 80–84, 29 Nov.-3 Dec..

Marwaha, S., Srinivasan, D., Tham, C. K., & Vasilakos, A. (2004). Evolutionary Fuzzy Multi-Objective Routing for Wireless Mobile Ad Hoc Networks. *IEEE Congress on Evolutionary Computation (CEC2004)*, 2, 1964 –1971, USA, June 19-23.

Natsheh, E., Jantan, A. B., Khatun, S., & Subramaniam S. (2006b). Fuzzy Reasoning Approach for Local Connectivity Management in Mobile Ad-hoc Networks. *International Journal of Business Data Communications and Networking (IJBDCN)*, 2 (3), 1–18.

Natsheh, E., Jantan, A. B., Khatun, S., & Subramaniam S. (2007). Intelligent Reasoning Approach for Active Queue Management in Wireless Ad-hoc Networks. *International Journal of Business Data Communications and Networking (IJBDCN)*, 3 (1), 16–33.

Natsheh, E., Jantan, A., Khatun, S., & Subramaniam S. (2005). A Fuzzy-Based Routes Lifetime Estimation for Ad-hoc Networks. *Proceeding of the 6th International Arab Conference on Information Technology (ACIT'2005)*, 413–419, Amman, Jordan, Dec. 6–8.

Natsheh E., Khatun S., & Jantan A. (2006a). Adaptive Fuzzy Route Lifetime for Wireless Ad-hoc Networks. *The International Arab Journal of Information Technology (IAJIT)*, 3 (4), 285–292.

Nikaein, N., & Bonnet, C. (2002). ALM- Adaptive Location Management Incorporating Fuzzy Logic for Mobile Ad Hoc Networks. *Proc. of 1st Annual Mediterranean Ad Hoc Networking Workshop*, Sardegna, Italy, Sept. 4-6.

Pearlman, M. R., & Haas, Z. J. (1999). Determining the Optimal Configuration for the Zone Routing Protocol. *IEEE Journal of the Selected Areas in Communications*, 17(8), 1395–1414.

Raju, G. (2004). Intelligent Distributed Routing Under Constraints and Imprecise State Information. *Proc. of the IEEE Int'l Conf. on Systems, Man and Cybernetics*, 4, 3630-3634, Oct. 10-13.

Raju, G. & Hernandez, G. (2002). Routing in Ad Hoc Networks. *Proc. of the IEEE Int'l Conf. on Systems, Man and Cybernetics*, 2, 291-295, Oct. 6-9.

Raju, G., Hernandez, G., & Zou Q. (2000). Quality of Service Routing in Ad Hoc Networks. *Proc. of the IEEE Wireless Communications and Networking Conference*, 1, 263-265, Sept. 23-28.

Rea, S., & Pesch, D. (2004a). Multi-metric Routing Decision for Ad Hoc Networks using Fuzzy Logic. *M-Zones White Paper June 04*, white paper 06/04, Ireland.

Rea, S., & Pesch, D. (2004b). Multi-Metric Routing Decisions for Ad Hoc Networks using Fuzzy Logic. *Proc. of the 1st IEEE Int'l Symposium on Wireless Communication Systems*, 403–407, Mauritius, Sept. 20-22.

Rea, S., & Pesch, D. (2004c). Fuzzy Logic based Multi-Metric Route Management for Ad-hoc Networks using Realistic Mobility Model. *Second International Workshop on Management of Ubiquitous Communications and Services (MUCS 2004)*, Dublin, Ireland, Dec. 13-14.

Rea, S., & Pesch, D. (2005). Fuzzy Logic Routing with Load-Balancing using a Realistic Mobility Model. *Proc. of the IEEE 61st Vehicular Technology Conference*, 3, 2105–2109, 30 May-1 June.

Rong, H., Zhigang H., & Hao, M. (2005). A Reliable Routing Algorithm Based on Fuzzy Applicability of F sets in MANET. *Proc. of the 11th Pacific Rim International Symposium on Dependable Computing (PRDC'05)*, 245-249, Dec. 12-14.

Sekercioglu, A., Pitsillides, A., & Vasilakos, A. (2001). Computational Intelligence in Management of ATM Networks: A Survey of Current State of Research. *Soft Computing Journal*, 5, 257-263.

Thankakan, K., Thumthawatwom, T., & Santiprabhob, P. (2001). Intelligent Scheduling Management for QoS-Enabled Wireless Ad Hoc Network With Fuzzy Rule-Based System. *Proc. of the Joint 9th IFSA World Congress and 20th NAFIPS Int'l Conf.*, 5, 2983-2988, Vancouver, Canada, July 25-28.

Venkatesh, C., Yadaiah, N., & Natarajan, A. M. (2005). Dynamic Source Routing Protocol Using Fuzzy Logic Concepts for Ad Hoc Networks. *Academic Open Internet Journal*, Bulgaria, 15, 1–14.

Wang, C., Chen, S., Yang, X., & Gao, Y. (2005). Fuzzy Logic-Based Dynamic Routing Management Policies for Mobile Ad Hoc Networks. *Proc. of the IEEE Workshop on High Performance Switching and Routing*, 341–345, May 12-14.

Wang, L. & Olariu, S. (2004). A Two-Zone Hybrid Routing Protocol for Mobile Ad Hoc Networks. *IEEE Transactions on Parallel and Distributed Systems*, 15(2), 1105–1116.

Wong, Y. F., & Wong, W. C. (2002). A Fuzzy-Decision-Based Routing Protocol for Mobile Ad Hoc Networks. *Proc. of the 10th IEEE Int'l Conf. on Networks (Icon 2002)*, 317-322, Singapore, Aug. 27-30.

Xia, X., & Liang, Q. (2005). Latency and Energy Efficiency Evaluation in Wireless Sensor Networks. *Proc. of the IEEE 62nd Vehicular Technology Conference*, 3, 1594–1598, Sept. 25-28.

Yusuf, M., & Haider, T. (2005). Energy-Aware Fuzzy Routing for Wireless Sensor Networks. *Proc. of the IEEE Int'l Conf. on Emerging Technologies*, 63–69, Islamabad, Pakistan, Sept. 17-18.

Zhang, X., Cheng, S., Feng, M., & Ding, W. (2004). Fuzzy Logic QoS Dynamic Source Routing for Mobile Ad Hoc Networks. *Proc. of the 4th IEEE Int'l Conf. on Computer and Information Technology (CIT'04)*, 652-657, Sept. 14-16.

Zhao, C., & Wang, G. (2004a). Fuzzy-Control-Based Clustering Strategy in MANET. *Proc. of the Fifth World Congress on Intelligent Control and Automation*, 2, 1456–1460, June 15-19.

Zhao, C., & Wang, G. (2004b). Routing Protocol Based on Fuzzy Regression for MANET. *Proc. of the 3rd Int'l Conf. on Machine Leaning and Cybernetics*, 1811–1815, Shanghai, China, Aug. 26-29.

Zhigang, H., Rong, H., & Hao, M. (2005). A Route Reliability Algorithm for Mobile Ad Hoc Networks. *Proc. of the Int'l Conf. on Wireless Communications, Networking and Mobile Computing*, 2, 787–790, Sept. 23-26.

Chapter XVI
Fuzzy Linguistic Knowledge for Active Queue Management in Wireless Ad–Hoc Networks

Essam Natsheh
King Faisal University, Saudi Arabia

ABSTRACT

Mobile ad-hoc network is a network without infrastructure, where every node has its own protocols and services for powerful cooperation in the network. Every node also has the ability to handle the congestion in its queues during traffic overflow. Traditionally, this was done through Drop-Tail policy, where the node drops the incoming packets to its queues during overflow condition. Many studies showed that early dropping of incoming packet is an effective technique to avoid congestion and to minimize the packet latency. Such an approach is known as Active Queue Management (AQM). In this chapter an enhanced algorithm, called Fuzzy-AQM, is suggested using fuzzy logic system to achieve the benefits of AQM. Uncertainty associated with queue congestion estimation and lack of mathematical model for estimating the time to start dropping incoming packets makes the Fuzzy-AQM algorithm the best choice. Extensive performance analysis via simulation showed the effectiveness of the proposed method for congestion detection and avoidance improving overall network performance.

INTRODUCTION

Mobile ad-hoc network is a network without infrastructure where every node can work as a router. Every node has protocols and services to request and provide services to other nodes with the congestion handling capability. Traditionally,

the congestion handling is done through Transmission Control Protocol (TCP). This protocol sends congestion signal (drop incoming packets) when the node's queue is full (queue length is maximum). Some studies (Braden, 1998; Floyd, 1993) showed that early dropping of incoming packet before reaching the maximum queue length is an effective technique to avoid congestion and to minimize the packet latency, *e. g.* Active Queue Management (AQM) drops incoming packets before the queue is full in contrast to traditional queue management which starts dropping only when the queue in overflowed.

Mobile ad-hoc networks suffer high network congestion due to high bit error rate (BER) in the wireless channel, increased collisions due to the presence of hidden terminals, interference, location dependent connection, uni-directional links, frequent path breaks due to mobility of nodes and the inherent fading properties of the wireless channel (Murthy, 2004). This substantiates the need for high adaptive AQM algorithms with adapting capabilities to high variability and uncertainty for these types of networks. The proposed fuzzy logic based AQM (called Fuzzy-AQM) is such types of algorithms to overcome the above shortcoming in ad-hoc networks. The application of fuzzy logic to the problem of congestion control allows us to specify the relationship between queue parameters and packets dropping probability using "if... then..." type of linguistic rules. The fuzzy logic algorithm would be able to translate or interpolate these rules into a nonlinear mapping.

In this study, the focus is to investigate the impact of the traditional and Fuzzy-AQM algorithms on the ad-hoc network. The considered strategy is as follows: when the congestion is detected, the node uses one of the AQM policies to drop the incoming data packets. Meanwhile, it allows the control packets to pass to the queue using Drop-Tail policy. Therefore, the data packets are dropped first when the packets drop probability exceeds a certain threshold while the control packets are still acceptable until the queue is full.

Control messages are preferred to pass to the queue during congestion time for the following reasons:

1. Control messages are used to update the changes of the network topology. Therefore, they prevent data packet to be transmitted through broken paths.

2. Data packets are "connection oriented", that is, guaranteed delivery to their destinations by TCP. In contrast, control messages are "connectionless"; that is, the dropped message will not be retransmitted again.

3. Control message size is very small compared to data packet. Normally in ad-hoc routing protocols, control message size is 64 bytes while data packet is 512 bytes, *i. e.* the control message takes small space in the queue and fast processing time in the node.

The rest of this paper is organized as follows. Section II summarizes related work on the common AQM polices issues and focuses on previous implementations of fuzzy AQM policies. Followed by congestion in ad-hoc networks, the fuzzy dropping algorithm as a new AQM policy (Fuzzy-AQM), performance analyzes of the proposed algorithm, and finally the conclusions.

RELATED WORK

The most famous AQM algorithm is Random Early Detection (RED) (Floyd, 1993). The RED algorithm manages the queue in an active manner by randomly dropping packets with increasing probability as the average queue size increases. It maintains two thresholds that determine the rate of packet drops: a lower threshold (denoted by min_{th}) and an upper threshold (denoted by max_{th}). For each packet k arrives to the queue, the drop probability for that packet $p_d(k)$ is given by:

$$p_d(k) = \begin{cases} 0 & \text{if } q_c < \min_{th} \\ \dfrac{avg - \min_{th}}{\max_{th} - \min_{th}} \max_p & \text{if } \min_{th} \leq avg < \max_{th} \\ 1 & \text{if } avg \geq \max_{th} \end{cases}$$

where q_c is current queue size, *avg* is current average queue size and max_p is maximum drop probability.

Some previous studies showed the difficulties of choosing the RED parameters (May, 1999; Iannaccone, 2001; Misra, 2000). Other studies showed that there is no significant benefit to RED over Drop-Tail for the web traffic (Iannaccone, 2001; Brandauer, 2001; Christiansen, 2001). Those drawbacks are the main reasons to default disable of the RED function (or some vendor-specific variant of RED, e.g. Cisco's Weighted RED (WRED) (Cisco, 2002)) in most of the available routers today. To overcome these drawbacks, extensions of the RED algorithm had been proposed to make it more robust and/or adaptive, for example, Stabilized RED (SRED) (Ott, 1999), Flow RED (FRED) (Aweya, 2001), Dynamic RED (DRED) (Lin, 1997) *etc.* The most famous dynamic configured RED is the Adaptive RED (ARED) algorithm proposed by Floyed *et al.* (Floyd, 2001). In ARED, the max_p is configured dynamically to keep the average queue size *avg* within a target range.

Many studies used the fuzzy logic system to dynamically calculate the drop probability behavior of AQM policy. Wang *et al.* (Wang, 2003) proposed Adaptive Fuzzy-based RED (AFRED) algorithm to calculate p_d using the current queue size as the only input for the fuzzy system. Some other studies calculate p_d based on Fuzzy Explicit Rate Marking (FERM) algorithm using two queue state inputs: the current queue size 'q_c' and its rate of change 'Δq_c'. The FERM was implemented in (Pitsillides, 1997) for ATM networks, while in (Rossides, 2003; Chrysostomou, 2003) it was implemented for differentiated services (DiffServ) networks.

In (Ren, 2002; Chrysostomou, 2003; Yanfei, 2003; Fatta, 2003; Aoul, 2004; Lin, 2005; Al-Frihat, 2005), the authors calculate p_d using Fuzzy Proportional Derivative Controller (FPDC) with two inputs: the error 'e' (which is the difference between the current queue size and the desired queue length) and the change of the error 'Δe' (which is the difference between the current er-

ror and the previous error). A conventional fuzzy controller use (e, Δe) as inputs to observe the controlled system response and its parameters. These parameters are overshoot, rise-time and settle-time. This set of parameters is not only used to evaluate the stability, but the performance of a system as well, and often is given in specification. Using the same inputs (e, Δe) to calculate p_d of AQM is meaningless and the fuzzy "if...then..." rules will not accurately represent the queue system behavior.

Li *et al.* (Li, 2003) have used the current average queue size '*avg*' and its variance 'Δavg' as the input for the Fuzzy Logic Adaptive RED (FLARED) algorithm to adaptively modifying the changes of step-size of the parameter max_p. This scheme tune only one parameter of ARED algorithm and its drawback is the lack to tune other ARED parameters.

In this study, we have used fuzzy logic system to calculate p_d in ad-hoc networks using: the current queue size and the number of neighboring nodes. This scheme can be generalized to be used in any network where the number of neighbors' nodes represents the number of communication links, or precisely number of TCP sessions. Table 1 compares various schemes to design fuzzy AQM algorithms.

Table 1. The fuzzy AQM schemes

Fuzzy AQM Scheme	Congestion Metric	Optimized Variable
AFRED	Current queue size 'q_c'	Drop Probability
FERM	q_c and its change 'Δq_c'	Drop Probability
FPDC	Error 'e' and its change 'Δe'	Drop Probability
FLARED	Average queue size '*avg*' and its change 'Δavg'	Δmax_p
Our scheme: Fuzzy-AQM	q_c and node neighbors density 'n_d'	Drop Probability

CONGESTION IN AD-HOC NETWORKS

In ad-hoc networks, congestion control is handled through transport layer protocols. The connection-oriented transport layer protocol used in ad-hoc networks is Transmission Control Protocol (TCP). The objectives of this protocol include the setting up of an end-to-end connection, end-to-end delivery of data packets, flow control and congestion control. TCP uses window-based flow control mechanism. The sender maintains a variable size window whose size limits the number of packets the sender can send. The destination sends acknowledgment (ACK) for packets that are received. When the window size is exhausted, the sender must wait for an ACK before sending a new packet based on a sliding window principle. This waiting time is known as retransmission timeout (RTO) period. If the ACK does not arrive within the RTO period, then the sender will assume the packet is lost. The loss of packet is due to the congestion in the network which will yield TCP to start the congestion control mechanism.

Mobile ad-hoc networks experience dynamic changes in the network topology due to unrestricted mobility of nodes. The topology changes lead to frequent changes in the connectivity of wireless links and hence routes reestablishment may be repeated very often. This route reestablishment process takes a significant amount of time. The route reestablishment time is a function of transmission range of the nodes, distance between the source and destination, number of intermedi-

ate nodes between the source and destination and node's velocity. If the route reestablishment time is greater than RTO period of the source node, then it will not receive the ACK and assumes congestion in the network, followed by retransmission of the lost packets and initiation of the congestion control mechanism (Murthy, 2004). A schematic illustration of congested ad-hoc network is shown in Figure 1. The source sends its data packets through node A, which passes those packets to node B then to the destination. As soon as the link between the source and node A is broken, it starts route reestablishment process and creates a direct link with node B. If this processing time is less than RTO, the source will receive the ACK and send other data packets, or it will resend the previous lost packets.

FUZZY-AQM ALGORITHM

In this section, concepts and rules of the proposed Fuzzy-AQM algorithm for ad-hoc networks are introduced. In the following two subsections, we studied the effect of some node parameters on packets drop probability. These parameters are used in subsection C to create the rules of the fuzzy system. Method to design their membership functions is presented in the later subsection. Overall system design and its implementation complexity are presented in subsection E and F. Compatibility of the proposed algorithm with other conventional algorithms discussed in the last subsection.

A. Effect of Current Queue Size on Drop Probability

Current queue size q_c is the most used indicator in AQM policy for estimating the probability of dropping the incoming packets. The drop probability p_d can be calculated as (Plasser, 2002):

Figure 1. Congestion in ad-hoc networks

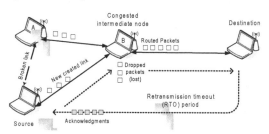

Figure 2. Drop probability for the coming load

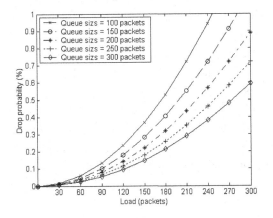

$$p_d = \frac{2N^2}{(CT_p + q_c)^2} \qquad (2)$$

where N is a load factor, C is a transmission capacity (in packets/seconds) and T_p is a propagation delay (in seconds). Assuming a 10 Mbps (2500 packets/sec) transmission capacity with a 100 msec propagation delay, Figure 2 shows the relation between p_d and the load for various queue sizes. It is evident that the probability of a packet dropping increases as the load increases. More packets in the queue wait for processing as load increases. Thus, it can be stated that when the used space of the queue is high, p_d of incoming packets is also high and vice versa. Consequently the following rules are proposed:

R1: If q_c is low then p_d ought to be low
R2: If q_c is medium then p_d ought to be high
R3: If q_c is high then p_d ought to be high

B. Effect of Node Neighborhood Density on Drop Probability

In ad-hoc networks, the traffic is categorized as: data packets and control messages. The control messages are used to continuously update the nodes about the topology changes (new created

or lost links). For example, if a node has two neighbors that means it will receive two Hello messages every second from them. Besides, receiving a route request messages, a route breaks messages, or data packets. If that node has ten neighbors, this means it will receive, in every second, ten Hello messages beside bulk amount of control messages and data packets. Hence, it is clear that the traffic pass through the nodes with few neighborhoods is less than the others with many neighbors.

In Equation 2, the load N can be written as:

$$N = \sum_{i=0}^{n} \lambda_i \qquad (3)$$

where λ_i denote flow's rate from the neighbor node i and n is the number of neighbors. The congestion will happen at:

$$p_d = 1 \quad if \sum_{i=0}^{n} \lambda_i > C \text{ and } q_c = q_m \qquad (4)$$

where q_m is the maximum queue size. Hence, if the neighbors' density (n_d) of a node's is high, the node's queue will be full quickly and increases the probability of congestion and vice versa. Consequently the following rules are proposed:

R4: If n_d is low then p_d ought to be low
R5: If n_d is medium then p_d ought to be high
R6: If n_d is high then p_d ought to be high

C. The Rule-Base for Fuzzy Drop Probability

To fulfill the fuzzy sets theory, the previous six rules (R1 to R6) can be combined within a 2-dimensional rule-base to control p_d adaptively as presented in Table 2. For example, according to Table 2 the first rule is:

IF q_c is *Low* AND n_d is *Low* THEN p_d is *Low*

D. Membership Functions for the Fuzzy Variables

After defining the fuzzy linguistic 'if-then' rules, the membership function (MF) corresponding to each element in the linguistic set should be defined. For example, if the queue size is 5 k bytes and q_c equal to 2 k bytes, using conventional concept, it implies q_c is either 'low' or 'medium' but not both. In fuzzy logic, however, the concept of MFs allows us to say the q_c is 'low' with 80% membership degree and 'medium' with 20% membership degree.

The MFs we propose to use for the fuzzy inputs (q_c, n_d) and the fuzzy output (p_d) are illustrated in Figure 3. These MFs are used due to their economic value of the parametric and functional descriptions. In these MFs, the designer needs only to define one parameter; *midpoint*. These MFs mainly contain the *triangular* shaped MF. This function is specified by three parameters (a, b, c) as follows:

$$triangle(x; a, b, c) = \begin{cases} (x-a)/(b-a) & for\ a \leq x \leq b \\ (c-x)/(c-b) & for\ b \leq x \leq c \\ 0 & elsewhere \end{cases} \quad (5)$$

where $a = midpoint/2$, $b = midpoint$, $c = 3 \times midpoint/2$ and x is the input to the fuzzy system. The

remaining MFs are as follows: Z-shaped membership to represent the whole set of low values and S-shaped membership to represent the whole set of high values.

Maxpoint is the maximum queue size in q_c–MF (Table 2), and it is the number of the network's nodes in n_d–MF.

Midpoint of q_c–MF is a threshold that indicates whether the queue is going to be full soon. The threshold is simply set to 60% of the queue size. The optimal value for this variable depends in part on the maximum average delay that can be allowed by the nodes.

Tseng *et al.* (Tseng, 2003) argue about the cost-effectiveness to have large ad-hoc networks. They proved by simulation that practical sizes of ad-hoc networks would range within about five nodes. Therefore, for n_d–MF, *midpoint* should be equivalent to five nodes.

E. Fuzzification, Inference and Defuzzification

The fundamental diagram of the fuzzy system is presented in Figure 4. Fuzzification is a process where crisp input values are transformed into membership values of the fuzzy sets (as described in the previous section). After the process of fuzzification, the inference engine calculates the

Figure 3. Membership functions used for the fuzzy variables

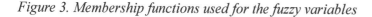

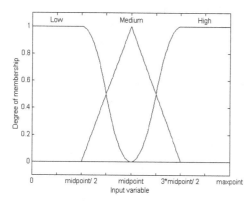

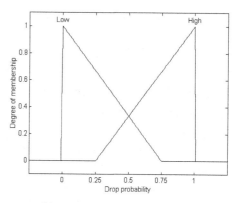

(a) MFs used for the input variables   *(b) MFs used for the output variable*

Figure 4. Block-diagram for the basic elements of the Fuzzy-AQM

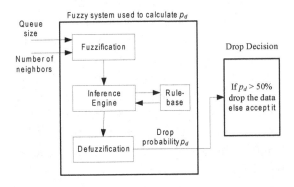

fuzzy output using the fuzzy rules described in Table 2. Defuzzification is a mathematical process used to convert the fuzzy output to a crisp value; that is, p_d value in this case.

The fuzzy logic system has been simulated using C++ programming language. There are various choices in the fuzzy inference engine and the defuzzification method. Based on these choices, several fuzzy systems can be constructed. In this study, the most commonly used fuzzy system, *Mamdani* method, is selected; for further details on this system see (Yager, 1994).

Formally, the rule-base (Table 2) of the Fuzzy-AQM algorithm can be rewritten in the following format:

$$IF \ q_c \ is \ A_{i1} \ AND \ n_d \ is \ A_{i2} \ THEN \ p_d \ is \ B_i \quad (6)$$

where A_{i1}, A_{i2}, and B_i are the linguistic labels *Low*, *Medium*, and *High* of the ith rule.

Mamdani method is used as the fuzzy inference engine, where Min ($\wedge$) operator is chosen as AND connective between the antecedents of the rules as follows:

$$\tau_i = A_{i1}(x_1) \wedge A_{i2}(x_2) \quad (7)$$

where τ_i is called the *degree of firing* of the ith rule for the input values: $x_1 = q_c$ and $x_2 = n_d$. The next step is the determination of the individual rule output F_i (fuzzy set) which is obtained by:

$$F_i(y) = \tau_i \wedge B_i(y) \quad (8)$$

The third step is the aggregation of rules outputs to obtain the overall system output F (fuzzy set), where Max ($\vee$) operator is chosen as OR connective between the individual rules:

$$F(y) = \vee_i F_i(y) = \vee_i (\tau_i \wedge B_i(y)) \quad (9)$$

To use this algorithm in the ad-hoc network environments, a fourth step needs to be added to get a crisp single value for p_d. This process is called *defuzzification*. Center of area (COA) (Yager, 1994) is chosen as the defuzzification method as follows:

$$p_d = \frac{\sum_{j=1}^{m} F(y_j) \times y_j}{\sum_{j=1}^{m} F(y_j)} \quad (10)$$

here y_j is a sampling point in the discrete universe output F, and $F(y_j)$ is its membership degree in the MF.

F. Implementation Complexity of the Fuzzy Algorithm

Using fuzzy logic system with AQM we may achieve comparable or better run-time computation than purely conventional methods. This can be achieved using one of the following methods:

1. **Lockup table:** The input-output relationship of the fuzzy reasoning engine for Fuzzy-AQM is illustrated in Figure 5. This relationship can be stored as a lookup table which will result in a very fast execution.

2. **Fuzzy logic interpreter:** Instead of implementing the fuzzy system using a high level language with its local interpreter and compiler, an interactive computing environment based on a fuzzy logic interpreter can be used to minimize the calculation overhead (Bonissone, 1992).

Figure 5. The input-output relationship of the Fuzzy-AQM

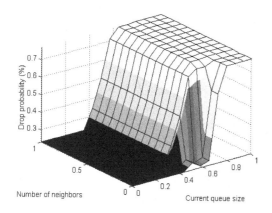

3. **Dedicated fuzzy hardware:** Fuzzy systems based on dedicated hardware can deliver much higher performance than those based on general-purpose computing machines (Hung, 1995).

A. Compatibility Between Conventional and Fuzzy AQM

The proposed Fuzzy-AQM algorithm is compatible with conventional AQM algorithms in the sense that a node that uses Fuzzy-AQM (an "intelligent" node) may communicate with a node that uses conventional AQM (standard node), as there are no changes in the protocols messages format.

PERFORMANCE ANALYSIS OF FUZZY-AQM

C. Simulation Environment

Simulation of the proposed AQM design was done using *OMNeT++* version 2.3 with *Ad-Hoc simulator* 1.0 (available at: http://www.omnetpp. org/). The *OMNeT++* is a powerful object-oriented modular with discrete event simulator tool.

Each mobile host is a compound module which encapsulates the following simple modules: an application layer, a routing layer, a MAC layer, a physical layer, and a mobility layer.

Application layer: This module produces the data traffic that triggers all the routing operations. In all scenarios, 15 nodes are enabled to transmit. The traffic is modeled by generating a packet burst of 64 packets sent to a randomly chosen destination that stays the same for all the burst length. The rate of each burst sending packets is 3 packets/sec. The time elapsed between two application bursts is normally distributed in [0.1, 3] sec. The packet size is 512 bytes.

Routing layer: The routing model is the heart of the simulator. This model depicts the Ad-hoc On-demand Distance Vector (AODV) routing protocol, all of its functions, parameters and their implementation (Perkins, 2003).

MAC layer: The simple implementation for this layer has been used. The outgoing messages (from routing layer) are let pass through to the physical layer. The incoming one (from physical layer) instead is delivered to the routing layer with an *MM1 queue* policy with queue size 5k bytes. When an incoming message arrives, the module checks a flag that indicate if the routing layer is busy or not. If so the message will be saved in the queue using Drop-Tail, Adaptive RED, or Fuzzy-AQM algorithm. Note that Drop-Tail is a special case of AQM with the following condition:

$$p_d = \begin{cases} 1 & \text{if } q_c = q_m \\ 0 & \text{otherwise} \end{cases} \qquad (10)$$

The parameters of Adaptive RED (see notation in (Floyd, 2001)) are set at $min_{th} = 1.5k$ bytes, $max_{th} = 3k$ bytes, $max_p = 0.01$, $w_q = 0.002$, $\alpha = max_p/4$, and $\beta = 0.9$. When the routing layer is not busy, the MAC module picks the first message from the queue and sends it upward.

Physical layer: It deals with the on-fly creation of links that allow the exchange of messages among the nodes. Every time a node moves from its position, an interdistance check on each node is performed. If a node gets close enough (depending on the transmission power of the moving nodes) to a new neighbor, a link is created between the two nodes with the following properties: channel bandwidth is 11 Mb/s (IEEE 802.11a) and delay is 10 μ s. Each node has a defined transmission range chosen from a uniformly distributed number between [90, 120] m.

Mobility layer: The *random waypoint* model was adopted for the mobility layer. It is one of the most used mobility pattern in the ad-hoc network simulations. This is because of its simplicity and its quite realistic mobility pattern. In this mobility model, a node randomly selects a destination. On reaching the destination, another random destination is targeted after 3 seconds *pause time*. The speed of movement of individual nodes range between [2, 12] m/sec. The direction and magnitude of movement was chosen from a uniformly distributed random number.

Three different network sizes are modeled: 700m×700m map size with 25 and 35 nodes and 800m×800m map size with 45 nodes. Each simulation run takes 300 simulated seconds. Multiple runs were conducted for each scenario and collected data was averaged over those runs.

Performance Metrics

The following metrics were used for measuring performance:

- **Drop Ratio:** The percentages of packets that are dropped from the queue due to overflow (congestion) to the total arrival in the queue.
- **Invalid Route Ratio:** calculated as follows:

$$Invalid\ Route\ Ratio = \frac{\sum_{i=1}^{n} Number\ of\ invalid\ routes}{\sum_{i=1}^{n} Number\ of\ valid\ routes} \quad (12)$$

Each time a route is used to forward a data packet, it is considered as a valid route. If that route is unknown or expired, it's considered as invalid route.

- **Average End-to-End Delay:** Average packet delivery time from a source to a destination. First, for each source-destination pair, average delay for packet delivery is calculated. Then the whole average delay is calculated from average delay of each pair. End-to-end delay includes the delay in the send buffer, the delay in the interface queue, the bandwidth contention delay at the MAC layer, and the propagation delay.
- **Routing Overhead:** calculated as follows:

$$Overhead = \frac{\sum_{i=1}^{n} Number\ of\ SentCtrlpkt\ by\ source}{\sum_{i=1}^{n} Number\ of\ received\ data\ by\ destination} \quad (13)$$

where n is number of nodes in the network and *SentCtrlPkt* is control packets used by AODV and described in Table 3. This metric can be employed to estimate how many transmitted control packets are used for one successful data packet delivery. We use it to study the effect of AQM algorithms on the efficiency and scalability of the routing protocol.

Table 3. Control packets used by AODV

Message	Description
RREQ	a Route Request message
RREP	a Route Reply message
RERR	a Route Error containing a list of the invalid destinations
RREP_ACK	a *RREP* acknowledgment message

SIMULATION RESULTS AND EVALUATIONS

A. Drop Ratio Details

The average control messages drop ratio for the proposed Fuzzy-AQM algorithm is less than other conventional algorithms as shown in Figure 6 (a). The percentage of Fuzzy-AQM improvement compared to Drop-Tail and Adaptive RED algorithms is: 93.9% and 74.5% for 25 nodes, 65.8% and 33.5% for 35 nodes, and 75.1% and 49.7% for 45 nodes respectively.

This improvement of the fuzzy algorithm is a result of choosing the neighbors' density parameter to estimate the size of incoming traffic and hence start the early dropping policy as needed. Despite the data packets drop ratio of Fuzzy-AQM is little bit higher than adaptive RED, as shown in Figure 6 (b), this is enough to produce a higher enhancement in the control messages drop ratio. This enhancement is a result of the wide difference between the size of data packets (512 bytes) and control messages (64 bytes). Consequently, at congestion time, dropping one data packet allows the queue to accept eight control messages.

Drop-Tail algorithm doesn't have any mechanism to distinguish between data and control packets like other AQM algorithms. Moreover, the number of control messages in ad-hoc network is much higher than data packet; to provide continuous update of topology changes. Those two reasons affect a high control messages drop ratio for the Drop-Tail algorithm as shown in Figure 6 (a).

B. Invalid Route Ratio Details

The Fuzzy-AQM algorithm has less average invalid route ratio compared to other conventional AQM shown in Figure 7. This decrement of the proposed algorithm is about: 20.3% and 23.1% for 25 nodes, 31.1% and 14.6% for 35 nodes, and 22.4% and 12.9% for 45 nodes respectively.

Information about route breaks is broadcasted as an RERR message. The Fuzzy-AQM algorithm allows more control messages to pass the queue to the upper routing layer as shown in Figure 6. This increased number of received control messages helps the nodes with Fuzzy-AQM to be more accurate to topology changes and have precise updated routing tables, hence, have less invalid routes.

Figure. 6. Drop ratio comparison

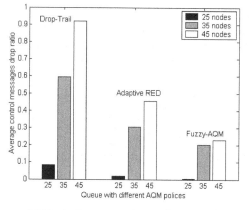

(a) Control messages drop ratio comparison

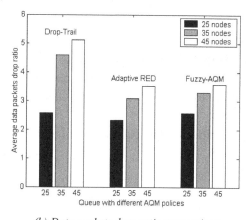

(b) Data packets drop ratio comparison

Figure 7. Invalid route ratio comparison

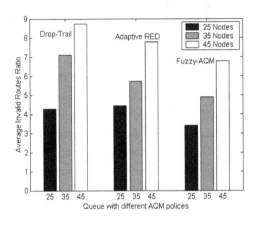

Figure 8. Average end-to-end delay comparison

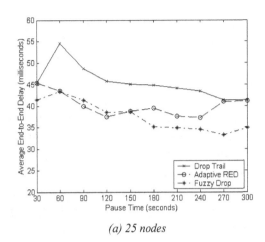

(a) 25 nodes

C. Average End-to-End Delay Details

Figure 8 indicates that the proposed Fuzzy-AQM algorithm has lower average end-to-end delay compared to other conventional algorithms. This decrement is approximately: 17.2% and 6.3% for 25 nodes, 24.1% and 11.6% for 35 nodes, and 33.6% and 21.6% for 45 nodes respectively.

The nodes that have conventional AQM algorithms have higher invalid route ratio (Figure 7), therefore they suffer longer routing delay to recover from broken paths and discover new ones. To recover a broken path, an RERR message must first be launched from the intermediate nodes to tell the source node about the broken link. The source node deletes the corresponding entry from its routing table. The RREQ must then be broadcasted from the source to the destination, and an RREP consequently has to be transmitted back to the source. Data packets are buffered at the source node during this process and the duration of their buffering adds more time delay to the end-to-end delay. The nodes with Fuzzy-AQM algorithm, on the other hand, have reliable routing tables that minimize the need to this recovery process.

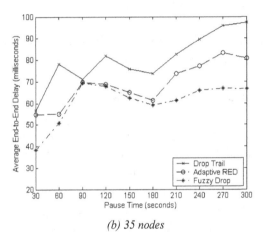

(b) 35 nodes

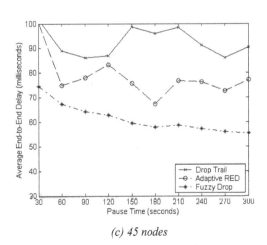

(c) 45 nodes

D. Routing Overhead Details

As expected, the AQM algorithms don't have major effect on the routing protocol efficiency or scalability as shown in Figure 9. These algorithms maximize the number of 'received' control messages meanwhile they have no effect on 'sent' control messages (see Equation 10). This is because the control messages used in AODV are broadcast messages; that is, they will not be resent if they are dropped or lost.

The Drop-tail algorithms has worst routing overhead ratio as the number of node increase as a result of increasing data packets drop ratio which is clear in figure 6 (b). Meanwhile, the data packets dropping ratio is nearly the same for adaptive AQM algorithms (ARED and Fuzzy-AQM) that results in no major difference in routing overhead ratio.

E. Drop Probability Values

In Drop-Tail algorithm, p_d always take a static value of 1 to start packet dropping at overflow. In Adaptive RED algorithm, p_d increases linearly between the two thresholds min_{th} and max_{th} in dependent on the average queue size 'avg'. Some studies, (Plasser, 2002), (Ohsaki, 2004), showed that using linear p_d function can result in forced

drops when q_c exceeds max_{th} or link under-utilization when q_c decreases to zero. This is an evident that the original linear drop function does not perform well within a wide range of loads.

The p_d values used by the proposed Fuzzy-AQM for randomly chosen node in the 25 nodes simulated network are shown in Figure 10. It is evident that the drop function is non-linear and a high load requires a disproportionately higher p_d than a low load to keep the queue size in the same range. Non-linearity of p_d function is also clear in the input-output relation (Figure 5).

Figure. 10. Drop probability values used by a node

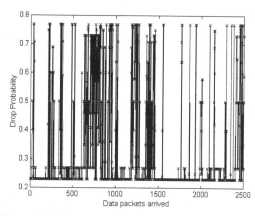

Figure 9. Routing overhead comparison

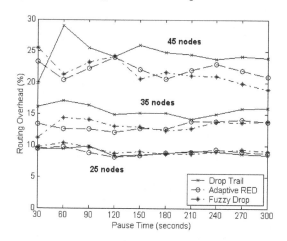

Figure 11. Average p_d values used by 25 and 35 nodes networks

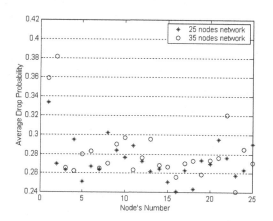

The comparison between the average p_d values used by every node in the 25 nodes and the 35 nodes networks is shown in Figure 11. Due to higher neighbors' density, 35 nodes network have higher p_d values than 25 nodes network. This is a result of increasing in number of control messages.

CONCLUSION AND FUTURE WORK

In this study, a novel AQM algorithm (Fuzzy-AQM) based on fuzzy logic system was suggested. This algorithm for early packets dropping is implemented in wireless ad-hoc networks in order to provide effective congestion control by achieving high queue utilization, low packet losses and delays. The proposed scheme is contrasted with a number of well-known AQM schemes through a wide range of scenarios. From the simulation results, the efficiency of the proposed fuzzy AQM policy in terms of routing overhead, average end-to-end delay and average packet losses are pronounced than other AQM polices, with capabilities of adapting to high variability and uncertainty in the mobile ad-hoc networks.

Inspired by this work, a possible future extension is to examine ways to methodically improve the adaptiveness of Fuzzy-AQM algorithm. Fuzzy-AQM maps the relationship between drop probabilities and the nodes' input traffic. There are many other potential parameters can be examined in ad-hoc environment for doing so. For example, the node can keep track of its mobility parameters such as speed, direction, or transmission range and change RED queue aggressiveness accordingly. The fuzzy system could infer the number of expected connections based on these parameters. When a large number of connections are present, queue lengths can fluctuate considerably in a short period of time. In such case, trigger congestion notification in time is necessary in order to minimize packet loss.

REFERENCES

Al-Frihat, J. (2005). Advanced queue management algorithms for computer networks. *Studies in Informatics and Control Journal, 14*(2) 111-116.

Aoul, Y. H., Nafaa, A., Negru, D., & Mehaoua, A. (2004). FAFC: Fast Adaptive Fuzzy AQM Controller for TCP/IP Networks. *Proceedings of IEEE Global Telecommunications Conference, 3,* 1319-1323.

Aweya, J., Ouellette M., & Montuno, D. Y. (2001). A control theoretic approach to active queue management. *Computer Networks, 36*(2-3), 203-35.

Bonissone, P. P. (1992). A compiler for fuzzy logic controllers. *Proceedings of the International Fuzzy Engineering Symposium (IFES'91),* 706-717, IOS Press.

Braden, B. et al. (1998). Recommendations on queue management and congestion avoidance in the Internet. *Request for Comments (RFC) 2309.*

Brandauer, C., Iannaccone, G., Diot, C., Ziegler, T., Fdida, S., & May, M. (2001). Comparison of tail drop and active queue management performance for bulk-data and Web-like Internet traffic. *Proceedings of the 6th IEEE Symposium Computers and Communications,* Hammamet.

Christiansen, M., Jeffay, K., Ott, D., & Smith, F. D. (2001). Tuning RED for Web traffic. *IEEE/ACM Transaction on Networking, 9*(3), 249-264.

Chrysostomou, C., Pitsillides, A., Hadjipollas, G., Sekercioglu, Y. A., & Polycarpou, M. (2003). Fuzzy logic congestion control in TCP/IP best effort networks. *Proceedings of the Australian Telecommunications, Networks, and Applications Conference (ATNAC'03),* Melbourne, Australia.

Chrysostomou, C., Pitsillides, A., Rossides, L., Sekercioglu, Y. A., & Polycarpou, M. (2003). Congestion control in differentiated services networks using Fuzzy-RED. *IFAC Journal Control Engineering Practice, 11*(10), 1153-1170.

Cisco Systems. (2002). *Weighted random early detection on the Cisco 12000 Series Router.*

Di Fatta, G., Hoffmann, F., Lo Re, G., Urso, A., (2003). A genetic algorithm for the design of a fuzzy controller for active queue management. *IEEE Transactions on Systems, Man, and Cybernetics--Part C, 33*(3), 313-324.

Floyd, S., & Jacobson, V. (1993). Random early detection gateways for congestion avoidance. *IEEE/ACM Transaction Networking, 1*(4), 397-413.

Floyd, S., Gummadi, R., & Shenker, S. (2001). *Adaptive RED: An algorithm for increasing the robustness of RED's active queue management.* Retrieved January 18, 2008, from http://www.icir.org/floyd/red.html

Hung, D. L. (1995). Dedicated digital fuzzy hardware. *IEEE Micro, 15*(4), 31-39.

Iannaccone, G., May, M., & Diot, C. (2001). Aggregate traffic performance with active queue management and drop from tail. *ACM SIGCOMM Computer Communication Review,* July.

Li, Z., Zhang, Z., Addie R., & Clerot, F. (2003). Improving the adaptability of AQM algorithms to traffic load using fuzzy logic. *Proceedings of the Australian Telecommunications, Networks, and Applications Conference (ATNAC'03),* Melbourne, Australia.

Lin, D., & Morris, R. (1997). Dynamics of random early detection. *Proceedings ACM SIGCOMM.*

Lin, W., Wong, A., & Dillon, T. (2005). A novel Fuzzy Logic Controller (FLC) for shortening the TCP channel roundtrip time by eliminating user buffer overflow adaptively. *Proceedings of the 28th Australasian Computer Science Conference (ACSC2005),* 38, 29-38, Newcastle, Australia.

May, M., Bolot, J., Diot, C., & Lyles, B. (1999). Reasons not to deploy RED. *Proceedings of the*

7th *International Workshop on Quality of Service (IWQoS'99),* 260-262.

Misra, V., Gong, W. B., & Towsley, D. (2000). Fluid-based analysis of a network of AQM routers supporting TCP flows with an application to RED. *ACM SIGCOMM Computer Communication Review,* 151-160.

Murthy, C. S., & Manoj, B. S. (2004). Transport layer and security protocols for ad hoc wireless networks. In *Ad Hoc Wireless Networks: Architectures and Protocol,* 451-504, Prentice Hall, New Jersey, USA.

Ohsaki, H., & Murata, M. (2004). On packet marking function of active queue management mechanism: should it be linear, concave, or convex? *Proceedings of SPIE's International Symposium on the Convergence of Information Technologies and Communications (ITCom 2004).*

Ott, T. J., Lakshman, T. V., & Wong, L. (1999). SRED: Stabilized RED. *Proceedings of the IEEE INFOCOM.*

Perkins, C., Royer, E. M., & Das, S. R. (2003). *Ad Hoc On-Demand Distance Vector (AODV) routing.* Internet-Draft, draft-ietf-manet-aodv-13.txt (Work in progress).

Pitsillides, A., Sekercioglu, Y. A., & Ramamurthy, G. (1997). Effective control of traffic flow in ATM networks using fuzzy logic based explicit rate marking (FERM). *IEEE Journal on Selected Areas in Communications, 15*(2), 209-225.

Plasser, E., Ziegler, T., & Reichl, P. (2002). On the non-linearity of the RED drop function. *Proceedings of the 15th International Conference on Computer Communication, 1,* 515-534.

Ren, F., Ren, Y., & Shan, X. (2002). Design of a fuzzy controller for active queue management. *Computer Communications, 25*(9), 874-883.

Rossides, L., Chrysostomou, C., Pitsillides, A., & Sekercioglu, Y. A. (2003). Fuzzy logic controlled

RED: Congestion control in TCP/IP differentiated services networks. *Soft Computing Journal,* *8*(2), 79-92.

Tseng, Y., Li, Y., & Chang, Y. (2003). On route lifetime in multihop mobile ad hoc networks. *IEEE Transaction on Mobile Computing, 2*(4), 366-376.

Wang, C., Li, B., Sohraby, K., & Peng, Y. (2003). AFRED: An Adaptive Fuzzy-based Control Algo-rithm for Active Queue Management. *Proceedings of 28th Annual IEEE International Conference on Local Computer Networks (LCN'03)* (pp. 12).

Yager, R. R., & Filev, D. P. (1994). *Essentials of fuzzy modeling and control*, 109-153, John Wiley & Sons, New Jersey, USA.

Yanfei, F., Fengyuan R., & Chuang, L. (2003). Design an active queue management algorithm based on fuzzy logic decision. *Proceedings of IEEE International Conference on Communication Technology (ICCT'03)*, 1, 286-289.

Chapter XVII
Risk Factors to Retrieve Anomaly Intrusion Information and Profile User Behavior

Yun Wang
Yale University, Yale-New Haven Health System & Qualidigm, USA

Lee Seidman
Qualidigm, USA

ABSTRACT

The use of network traffic audit data for retrieving anomaly intrusion information and profiling user behavior has been studied previously, but the risk factors associated with attacks remain unclear. This study aimed to identify a set of robust risk factors via the bootstrap resampling and logistic regression modeling methods based on the KDD-cup 1999 data. Of the 46 examined variables, 16 were identified as robust risk factors, and the classification showed similar performances in sensitivity, specificity, and correctly classified rate in comparison with the KDD-cup 1999 winning results that were based on a rule-based decision tree algorithm with all variables. The study emphasizes that the bootstrap simulation and logistic regression modeling techniques offer a novel approach to understanding and identifying risk factors for better information protection on network security.

INTRODUCTION

Statistically based anomaly intrusion detection systems analyze audit trail data to detect anomaly intrusion and profiling use behavior. Although the idea behind intrusion detection is simple (i.e., using normal patterns of legitimate user behavior

to identify and distinguish the behavior of an anomalous user) (Anderson, 1972, 1980; Denning, 1987; Helman & Liepins, 1993; Stallings, 2003), abnormal behavior detection is a difficult task to implement because of unpredictable attacks. The ideal intrusion detection system has four goals: (1) to detect a wide variety of intrusions;

(2) to detect intrusions in a timely fashion; (3) to present the analysis in a simple format; and (4) to be accurate (Bishop, 2003). Over the past two decades, statistical methods have been used for developing various intrusion detection systems, and achieving these goals has been attempted. Some previously studied methods include, for example, adaptive detection model (Teng, Chen, & Lu, 1990), principal component analysis (Shyu, Chen, Sarinnapakorn, & Chang, 2003), cluster and multivariate analysis (Taylor & Alves-Foss, 2001; Vaccaro & Liepins, 1989), Hidden Markov Model (Cho & Park, 2003; Gao, Ma, & Yang, 2002), data mining (Anderson, Frivold, & Valdes, 1995; Qu, Vetter, & Jou, 1997; Lee, Stolfo, & Mok, 1999), Bayesian analysis (Barbard, Wu, & Jajodia, 2001), and frequency and simple significance tests (Masum, Ye, Chen, & Noh, 2000; Qin & Hwang, 2004; Ye, Emran, Li, & Chen, 2001; Zhou & Lang, 2003). However, most previous studies have been focused mainly on the first two goals and have been conducted based on the use of all possible variables as independent variables to fit a model. Mukkamala et al. (2003) briefly addressed the data reduction issue, but the knowledge about the degree of significance of an individual variable associated with an attack still remains unclear, and accuracy of such association has not been addressed. A statistical model with a large number of independent variables may not guarantee a high ability of predicting power, and unnecessary variables could cause biases and could lead the model either to overestimate or to underestimate the predicted values. To address these gaps in knowledge, this study, using the bootstrap resample method (Efron & Tibshirani, 1994) and multiple stepwise logistic regression modeling technique (Hosmer & Lemeshow, 2000) sought to identify a small set of risk factors that are robust, statistically significant, and stable to use in detecting anomaly intrusion and profiling user behavior.

METHODS

Data Source

The study sample was drawn from the Third International Knowledge Discovery and Data Mining Tools Competition 1999 data (KDD-cup, 1999), which was created, based on the 1998 Defense Advanced Research Projects Agency (DARPA) Intrusion Detection Evaluation off-line database developed by the Lincoln Laboratory at Massachusetts Institute of Technology (Cunningham et al. 1999). The full KDD-cup data, which included seven weeks of TCP dump network traffic as training data that were processed into about five million connection records, two weeks of testing data, and 34 attack types, were generated on a network that simulated 1,000 Unix hosts and 100 users (Lippmann & Cunningham 2000). The test data do not have the same probability distribution as the training data and include additional specific attack types that were not in the training data. The data unit is a connection that consists of about 100 bytes of information and represents a sequence of TCP packets starting and ending at a fixed time window, between which data flow to and from a source IP address to a destination IP address under predefined protocols. Each connection record is identified as either normal or as a specific attack type. This study used 10% of the training data as a derivation dataset and the full test data as a validation dataset to identify and examine the risk factors.

Outcome and Independent Variables

The outcome of interest was a binary variable that labeled a connection as anomalous (yes/no), which could be any one of the included 38 attack types (24 in the derivation sample and an additional 14 new types in the validation sample). The independent variables included 41 initial variables or features (Stolfo, 2000) across four groups: (1) basic features of individual TCP/IP connections;

Table 1. Protocol and connection states

Name	Meaning
Protocol	
TCP	Transmission control protocol
UDP	User datagram protocol
ICMP	Internet control message protocol
Connection	
REJ	Connection attempt rejected
RST0	Connection established, originator aborted
RSTR	Connection established, responder aborted
S0	Connection attempt, no reply seen
S1	Connection established, not terminated
SF	Normal establishment and termination

(2) content features within a connection suggested by domain knowledge; (3) traffic features computed using a two-second time window; and (4) destination features. The type of protocol was categorized into three dummy variables: ICMP (yes/no), TCP (yes/no), and UDP (yes/no); normal or error status of the connection was divided into four dummy variables: REJ (yes/no), S0 (yes/no), SF (yes/no), and RSTO/RSTOS0/RSTR (yes/no) (Table 1); number of data bytes from source to destination and number of data bytes from destination to source were condensed by dividing the original values by 1,000 to match the scale for the other variables. The final number of potential independent variables, including the dummy variables, was 46.

Bootstrap Resample Method

A fundamental challenge in network anomaly intrusion detection area is to make probability-based inferences about a set of population characteristics (e.g., θ and σ that represent the true user behavior pattern based on the entire network traffic) based on a set of estimators (e.g., θ and σ that represent an observed user behavior pattern) using a sample acquired from the population. The bootstrap is a computer-based nonparametric simulation statistical method that aims for making better

statistical inferences and addresses the sample variability issue; it has been used widely in statistics and quantitative social science since 1979, when Bradley Efron published his first article on this method (Efron, 1979). Bootstrapping differs from the traditional parametric approach to inference in that it involves resampling the original data with replacement numerous times in order to generate an empirical estimate of the entire sampling distribution of an estimator rather than strong distributional assumptions and analytic formulas (Efron & Tibshirani, 1986; Mooney & Guval, 1993). This unique attribute allows researchers to make inferences in cases where such analytic solutions are unavailable and where such assumptions are untenable in anomaly detection. During bootstrapping, a new sample is generated by drawing n observations with replacement from the original data, and a new estimate is calculated. The resulting empirical distribution based on bootstrap analysis approximates the true user behavior pattern, which provides an approach to obtain an approximation of the estimate pattern in the absence of prior information about the true distribution of the estimate or the original data, a common situation of retrieving information in anomaly detection.

Multiple Logistic Regression Model

A logistic regression model, also known as logit model, is used for data in which the outcome variable is binary or dichotomous and is coded as 1 for the presence of an event and 0 for the absence of an event, and independent variables are binary, continuous, or categorical predictors. Its use has grown significantly during the past decade and has become the standard method for regression analysis of dichotomous data in many fields, including business, finance, criminology, engineering, and life science. Suppose that y_i, which has a 1 or 0 value, is the outcome variable for individual subject i, and p_i, is the probability that $y_i = 1$, for k independent variables and $i = 1,...,$

n individuals. The logistic regression model can be represented as:

$$\log\left[\frac{p_i}{1-p_i}\right] = \beta_0 + \beta_1 x_{i1} + \beta_2 x_{i2} + \cdots + \beta_k x_{ik} \quad (1)$$

$$p_i = \frac{\exp(\beta_0 + \beta_1 x_{i1} + \beta_2 x_{i2} + \cdots + \beta_k x_{ik})}{1 + \exp(\beta_0 + \beta_1 x_{i1} + \beta_2 x_{i2} + \cdots + \beta_k x_{ik})} \quad (2)$$

The expression on the left-hand side of the equation is usually referred to as the logit or log-odds, and has the desired property that no matter what the values of β_k and x_{ik}, p_i always ranges from 0 to 1. The parameter, β_k, is a logit coefficient that indicates the log-odds increase by β_k for every unit increase in the independent variable, x_{ik}. Exponentiating β_k yields an odds ratio (OR) that measures how much more likely (or unlikely) it is for the outcome to be present among those with $x_{ik} = 1$ than among those with $x_{ik} = 0$ for a binary independent variable or for every unit increase in which the independent variable is continuous. For example, assuming the outcome is an attack (yes = 1, no = 0), if x_{i1} denotes whether a connection is UDP, then OR = 1.5 estimates that an attack is 1.5 times as likely to occur among UDP connections than among non-UDP connections.

Statistical Analysis

The study was accomplished sequentially in three steps. The first step involved conducting a bivariate analysis for checking the frequency and association with the outcome for each of the 46 variables. Continuous variables with uneven distribution were normalized through the standardized z score transformation (observed value minus the mean value divided by the standard deviation of the values). The second step fitted 3,000 stepwise logistic regression models with 3,000 iterations of the bootstrapping simulation based on the derivation sample. Variables with a frequency > 0.1% that demonstrated a significant association with the outcome variable in the first step were eligible for loading into the forward stepwise logistic regression modeling process. A significance threshold of 0.01 for adding variables and an insignificance threshold of 0.05 for removing variables were used to select potential risk factors detecting potential attacks from the independent variable set. These thresholds ensure that a variable to be added into the model will be statistically significantly associated with the outcome at least 99% of the time, and a variable to be removed from the model will not be statistically significantly associated with the outcome at least 95% of the time.

The third step aimed to select final risk factors from the bootstrapping results. During each iteration of bootstrapping in the second step, a new sample was generated by drawing n observations with replacement from the original sample, and a stepwise logistic model was fitted, yielding a set of variables that were statistically significantly associated with the outcome. Thus, 3,000 iterations of the simulation yielded 3,000 sets of p-values, indicating the significance level for each variable's association with the outcome. A variable that was statistically significant at least 85% of the time (i.e., it ensured that a variable will have at least 0.85 probability of truly holding a significant association with the outcome for a given network traffic population) and had a Wald Chi-square absolute value of 10 or higher (i.e., it ensured that the significance level will be at least 0.001) was considered a robust risk factor for predicting attacks. The area under the receiver operating characteristic (ROC) curve was calculated for each fitted model per iteration to evaluate its discriminating power (Hosmer & Lemeshow, 2000). All of the statistical analyses were conducted using STATA version 8.0 (STATA Corporation, College Station, TX) and SAS version 8.12 (SAS Institute Inc. Cary, NC).

Classification

Risk factors identified by the bootstrap and stepwise logistic regression procedures were used to construct a final logistic model based on the derivation sample. The model yielding a set of parameters corresponding to each risk factor was used to calculate a probability of being an anomalous connection for each connection in both derivation and validation samples. By determining an appropriate threshold of being anomalous, this probability provided a standard to classify and profile user behavior into different groups (e.g., normal or anomalous). Sensitivity, specificity, ROC area, and correctly classified rate were used to measure the discrimination power and stability of the risk factors in classification and profile. Sensitivity measures the probability that a statistical test is positive for a true positive statistic, and specificity measures the probability that a statistical test is negative for a true negative statistic. In this study, a sensitivity value of 0.95 means that 95% of the detected events have been recognized correctly as normal connections, and a specificity value of 0.95 means that 95% of the abnormal activities have not been classified as normal. The relationship between values of sensitivity and specificity tends to be nonlinear and inversely proportional; increasing one value will systematically decrease the other. The ROC area, which measures the discriminating power of a model fitted by the predicted probability, ranges from 0.5 to 1.0. A model with no predictive power has a value of 0.5, and a perfect model has a value of 1.0. The correctly classified rate measures the proportion of connections that are normal and correctly identified as normal, and the proportion of connections that are anomalous and are correctly classified as anomalous. It is scaled as 1 when all the observed normal and abnormal connections are correctly classified, and 0 when there is 100% misclassification. The top KDD-cup 1999 winning entry (Elkan, 1999) that was conducted by using the C5 decision trees software was used as a benchmark to compare with classification results yielded by risk factors.

RESULTS

Characteristics of Data

The study sample included 805,050 network connections, within which the derivation sample had 494,021 (61.4%) connection records, and the validation sample had 311,029 (38.6%) records. Since each connection represented a two-second window, most records in both the derivation and the validation samples had exactly the same values across the 46 variables longitudinally. Most of these variables had very uneven distributions across the outcome, and 10 variables (19.6%), including connection from/to the same host/port, number of wrong fragments, number of urgent packets, number of hot indicators, number of failed login attempts, root shell is obtained, successfully root command attempted, number of shell prompts, number of outbound commands in an FTP session, and host login, were excluded from further stepwise modeling processes, because they had either zeros or very low frequencies or means. An additional five variables, including number of operations on access control files (ID = 16), rate of connections that have REJ errors (ID = 20), rate of the connection to the same service as the current connection that have SYN errors (ID = 24), rate of connections to the current host with RST errors (ID = 35), and rate of connections to the current host and specified service with RST errors (ID = 36), also were not eligible for stepwise regression analysis, because they had no statistically significant association with the outcome in the bivariate analysis (Table 2). The number of connections labeled *normal* was similar between the derivation and validation samples (19.7% vs. 19.5%). The abnormal con-

Table 2. Bivariate analysis based on the derivation sample

ID	Variables	Anomaly		Normal	
	Basic features of individual TCP connections				
1	Length (number of seconds) of the connection (mean, SD)	6.62	402.56	216.66	1359.21
	Type of protocol				
2	ICMP (yes/no [%, #])	71.16	282,314	1.32	1,288
3	TCP (yes/no [%, #])	28.55	113,252	78.96	76,813
4	UDP (yes/no [%, #])	0.30	1,177	19.71	19,177
5	Network service on the destination, HTTP (yes/no [%, #])	0.61	2,407	63.62	61,886
6	Number of data bytes from source to destination (per 1,000) (mean, SD)	3.48	1102.60	1.16	34.23
7	Number of data bytes from destination to source (per 1,000) (mean, SD)	0.25	31.80	3.38	37.58
	Normal or error status of the connection				
8	REJ (yes/no [%, #])	5.43	21,534	5.49	5,341
9	S0 (yes/no [%, #])	21.92	86,956	0.05	51
10	SF (yes/no [%, #])	72.27	286,731	94.28	91,709
11	RSTO or RSTOS0 or RSTR (yes/no [%, #])	0.35	1,395	0.10	98
	Content features within a connection suggested by domain knowledge				
12	Login successfully (yes/no [%,#])	0.83	3,298	71.9	69,939
13	Number of compromised conditions (mean, SD)	0.01	0.11	0.03	4.05
14	Number of root accesses (mean, SD)	0.00	0.11	0.06	4.53
15	Number of file creation operations (mean, SD)	0.00	0.04	0.00	0.20
16	Number of operations on access control files (mean, SD)	0.00	0.01	0.01	0.08
17	Guest login (yes/no, [%, #])	0.08	314	0.38	371
	Traffic features computed using a two-second time window				
18	Connections to the same host as the current connection (mean, SD)	411.76	156.27	8.16	17.71
19	Rate of connections that have SYN errors (mean, SD)	0.22	0.41	0	0.03
20	Rate of connections that have REJ errors (mean, SD)	0.06	0.23	0.06	0.23
21	Rate of connections to the same service (mean, SD)	0.74	0.42	0.99	0.09
22	Rate of connections to different services (mean, SD)	0.02	0.71	0.02	0.12
23	Connections to the same service as the current connection (mean, SD)	362.04	226.19	10.94	21.80
24	Rate of connections that have SYN errors (mean, SD)	0.22	0.41	0	0.03
25	Rate of connections that have REJ errors (mean, SD)	0.06	0.23	0.06	0.23
26	Rate of connections to different hosts (mean, SD)	0	0.05	0.13	0.28
	Destination				
27	Connections having the same destination host (mean, SD)	253.06	21.13	148.51	103.40
28	Connections having the same destination host and using the same service (mean, SD)	185.38	109.98	202.06	86.91
29	Rate of connections having the same destination host and using the same service (mean, SD)	0.73	0.43	0.84	0.31
30	Rate of different services on the current host (mean, SD)	0.02	0.08	0.06	0.18
31	Rate of connections to the current host having the same source port (mean, SD)	0.72	0.45	0.13	0.28
32	Rate of connections to the same service coming from different hosts (mean, SD)	0.00	0.04	0.02	0.05
33	Rate of connections to the current host with S0 errors (mean, SD)	0.22	0.41	0.00	0.03
34	Rate of connections to the current host and specified service with S0 errors (mean, SD)	0.22	0.41	0.00	0.02
35	Rate of connections to the current host with RST errors (mean, SD)	0.06	0.23	0.06	0.22
36	Rate of connections to the current host and specified service with RST errors	0.06	0.23	0.06	0.22

nections were categorized into four major attack types: *probe*—surveillance and other probing; *DoS*—denial of service; *U2R*—unauthorized access to local super user (root) privileges; and *R2L*—unauthorized access from a remote machine of connections. All these attack types had unbalanced distributions: 79.2% of the records were *DoS*; 19.7% represented *normal*; and the remaining 1.1% of the records was split among *Probe*, *R2L*, and *U2R*. The validation sample showed a remarkable difference in the distribution of the attacks with the initial derivation set after including the new attack types. Although the order of the most frequent attack types remained the same as the validation sample, there were remarkable frequency differences between the two samples throughout all attack types. The largest difference was *R2L*, increasing from 0.2% (n = 1,126) in the derivation sample to 5.2% (n = 16,189) in the validation sample; the next was *U2L*, from 0.01% (n = 52) to 0.07% (n = 228). The distributions in *normal* and *probe* were similar between the two samples (19.7% vs. 19.5% and 0.8% vs. 1.3%, respectively). *DoS* was reduced approximately 5.3 absolute percent points in the validation sample. The overall connections were distributed as 19.6% for *normal*, 1.0% for *probe*, 77.2% for *DoS*, 0.03% labeled *R2L*, and 2.2% labeled *U2R* (Table 3).

Risk Factors for Anomaly Intrusion

With non-parametric bootstrapping, 3,000 multiple logistic regression models have been fitted, based on random sampling with replacement from the original derivation data. These models yielded a mean ROC area value of 0.999 (95%CI, 0.99-1.00) and a mean Chi-square value of 516,490. Using the frequency rate of 85% as a threshold, 16 variables that were statistically significantly associated with the outcome and had a Wald Chi-square absolute value of 10 or higher were identified as robust risk factors. These variables were used to fit the final model to obtain the corresponding parameters for calculating the risk score for each connection (Figure 1). Among these factors, the frequency rate of being a robust risk factor range was from 85.2% (rate of connections to different services) to 100.0% (TCP, HTTP, RST, guest login, connections to the same host as the current connection, connections having the same destination host, connections having the same destination host and using the same service, rate of connections to the current host having the same source port, and rate of connections to the same service coming from different hosts). Overall, these risk factors demonstrated great associations with the outcome. Table 4 illustrates the coefficient, odds ratio, and a standardized estimate of each factor yield by the final model. A factor with a standardized estimate

Figure 1. Percentage of risk factors significantly associated with anomaly intrusion

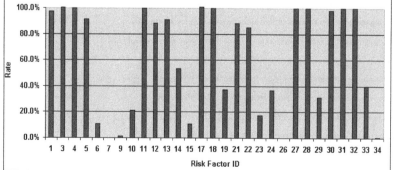

Table 3. Frequencies of major attacks by samples

Attack Types	Derivation (N=494,021)		Validation (N=311,029)		P value
	Total (#)	Rate (%)	Total (#)	Rate (%)	
Anomaly					
Surveillance and other probing (probe)	4,107	0.8	4,166	1.3	<0.001
Denial of service (DoS)	391,458	79.2	229,853	73.9	<0.001
Unauthorized access to local super user (root) privileges (U2R)	52	0.0	228	0.1	<0.001
Unauthorized access from a remote machine (R2L)	1,126	0.2	16,189	5.2	<0.001
Normal	97,278	19.7	60,593	19.5	0.021

less than 0 or an odds ratio less than 1 indicates that the factor had a negative association with the outcome, and a connection with this characteristic was unlikely to be an *anomaly*. Compared with Figure 1, which shows the likelihood of each risk factor being statistically significantly associated with the outcome, Table 4 shows the strength of each factor associated with the outcome. The areas under the ROC curve were 1.00 with an r-squared of 0.96 and a goodness-of-fit of 0.06 for the final model. Predictive ability ranged from 0.00 in the lowest deciles to 1.00 in the highest deciles, indicative that the model had good discrimination.

Classification

Based on Figure 1 and Table 4, an abnormal probability was calculated for each connection in both the derivation and the validation samples. The derivation sample-based probability had a mean of 0.35 with a standard deviation of 0.38 and a range of 0.00 to 1.00; the validation sample-based probability had a mean of 0.36 with a standard deviation of 0.44 and ranged from 0.00 to 1.00. The correlation coefficient of the probabilities between the two samples was 0.99. There were 70,600 (14.3%) connections that had a unique probability value in the derivation sample. Figure 2 illustrates the overall distributions of the risk factors-based probability of anomaly by the deri-

vation and the validation samples, emphasizing that by choosing an appropriate threshold, the risk factors are robust to distinguish the normal and anomaly groups. Figure 3 shows the association of different thresholds among sensitivity, specificity, and correctly classified rate based on the derivation sample. Note that these relationships were not linear—specificity was affected more than sensitivity and correctly classified rate by changes in classification threshold, and sensitivity tends to decrease as specificity increases, which is a common circumstance in traditional information retrieval. This figure clearly demonstrated the importance of a threshold in classification, and showed that the probability of 0.70 is the optimum value that provides an excellent sensitivity (98.9%), specificity (98.8%), and correctly classified (98.8%) values in the derivation sample. When applying this threshold to the validation sample, the sensitivity, specificity, and correctly classified value were 91.4%, 94.8%, and 92.1%, respectively. Compared with the KDD-cup 1999 top winning results, the risk factors-based classification showed similar ROC area (1.00 vs. 1.00), higher sensitivity (98.9% vs. 91.8%), similar specificity (98.8% vs. 99.5%) values, and higher correctly classified rate (98.8% vs. 93.3%) than the top winning results in the derivation sample, and similar sensitivity (91.4% vs. 91.8%), slightly low specificity (94.8% vs. 99.5%), ROC area (0.96 vs. 1.00), and comparable correctly

Table 4. Selected risk factors significantly associated with the outcome based on the derivation sample

ID	Risk Factors	Coefficient	Odds Ratio	95% Confidence Interval	P value	Standardized Estimate
	Intercept (β_0)	7.0326				
1	Length (number of seconds) of the connection	-0.1109	0.90	0.88 - 0.91	<0.001	-0.0611
2	ICMP (reference)		1.00			
3	TCP	-0.3732	0.69	0.60 -0.79	<0.001	-0.1001
4	UDP	-2.5541	0.08	0.07 -0.09	<0.001	-0.2799
5	HTTP	0.4891	1.63	1.47 -1.81	<0.001	0.0907
8	REJ (reference)		1.00			
11	RST	4.6891	108.61	81.16 -145.34	<0.001	0.1419
12	Login successfully	-0.3492	0.71	0.64 -0.78	<0.001	-0.0684
13	Number of compromised	0.0288	1.03	1.01 -1.05	<0.001	0.0159
17	Guest login	2.1580	8.65	7.26 -10.32	<0.001	0.0443
18	Connections to the same host as the current connection in the past two seconds	4.4714	87.48	73.69 -103.84	<0.001	2.4652
21	Rate of connections to the same service	-2.0776	0.13	0.12 -0.14	<0.001	-1.1455
22	Rate of connections to different services	-0.3198	0.73	0.71 -0.74	<0.001	-0.1763
27	Connections having the same destination host	0.7734	2.17	2.10 -2.23	<0.001	0.4264
28	Connections having the same destination host and using the same service	-1.2429	0.29	0.27 -0.30	<0.001	-0.6852
30	Rate of different services on the current host	-0.28880	0.75	0.73 -0.77	<0.001	-0.1588
31	Rate of connections to the current host having the same src port	1.2126	3.36	3.18 -3.56	<0.001	0.6686
32	Rate of connections to the same service coming from different hosts	0.3106	1.36	1.35 -1.38	<0.001	0.1712

Figure 2. Distributions of anomalous probability by the derivation and the validation samples

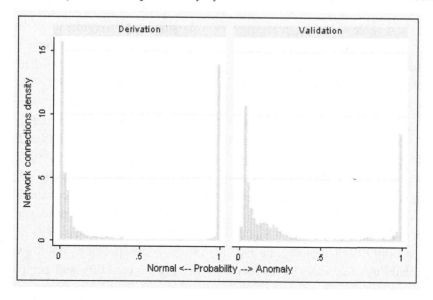

Figure 3. Impact of different thresholds on classification results

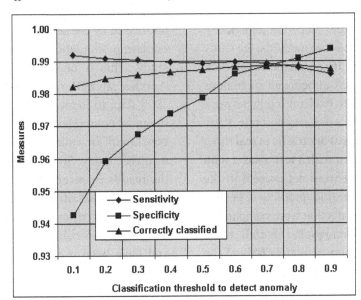

Table 5. Comparison with KDD-cup 1999 winning entry

Measure of classification	Predicted probability based on risk factors		KDD-cup 1999 winning entry
	Derivation sample	Validation sample	
ROC area	0.9974	0.9494	0.9960
Sensitivity (%)	98.90	91.44	91.81
Specificity (%)	98.84	94.77	99.45
Correctly classified rate (%)	98.80	92.10	93.30

classified rate (92.1% vs. 93.3%) with the winning results in the validation sample. Overall, this study demonstrated similar classification performances in comparison with the KDD-cup 1999 winning results but in a remarkably simple format, and it emphasized that the 16 risk factors are robust for better information retrieval on network security.

DISCUSSION

Anomaly intrusion detection is a communication process; an intrusion detection system can be considered a particular type of information retrieval system that acquires a set of symbols (information) from network traffic audit data and determines that one set of symbols has the same or a similar meaning as another. With the rapid advancement in computer and network technology and increased information and national security threats, the demand for better analysis of network traffic data and being able to improve interpretability of the structure of its symbols has intensified significantly. The primary contribution of the present study is that it applied the bootstrapping simulation and stepwise logistic regression modeling approaches to the intrusion detection area for meeting this demand. It demonstrated that the combination of using such modern statistical techniques could provide a novel solution for better information protection.

Furthermore, with the stepwise logistic regression model and bootstrap methods, the study identified and validated 16 risk factors for predicting and assessing the risk of being an anomalous intrusion for data stream exchanging in network traffic. Such risk factors are easy to collect and are available through network traffic in real time; they have been validated with a test dataset with novel attack types that were not present in the derivation sample, yielding predictive performance for anomaly events that were comparable to the original derivation results. Overall, these risk factors, reducing approximately 65% of the initial data dimension demonstrated, had similar performances in sensitivity, specificity, and correctly classified rate in comparison with the full dimension data and the KDD-cup 1999 winning results but in a remarkably simple format.

The benefit of using statistical methods is that they offer a wide availability of approaches, ranging from simple significance tests to complex analyses, including multidimensional scaling, multiple regression, cluster analysis, and factor analysis, to seek various solutions in retrieving anomaly intrusion information and profiling user behavior. However, the development of a sound statistical model and the identification of a set of robust risk factors to retrieve anomaly intrusion information present many challenges. There is no one gold-standard model that can be used to compare the performances; a stream of network traffic data with many positive risk factors might not represent a true attack, and a look-alike normal stream could present a novel attack due to uncertain factors and users changing their behavior. In general, increasing the sensitivity could reduce the false positive alarm rate, and increasing the specificity could reduce the false negative alarm rate. The objective of a good statistical model is to demonstrate high values in sensitivity, specificity, and correctly classified rate. To achieve this goal, the process of selecting risk factors must consider

the issues of sampling variability and stability of variables' statistical significance, which were addressed by the stepwise logistic modeling and bootstrap simulation techniques in the present study. This is one of strengths of this study. Another strength relies on the use of KDD-cup 1999 data to identify the risk factors, which is the most comprehensive and widely used public benchmark for testing intrusion detection systems available today. Since risk factors can influence the results in several ways, an ideal risk factor should be unaffected by scientific interpretation, widely accepted, and available on audit processes. Most of the 16 risk factors uphold these criteria and have been used widely in many intrusion detection studies.

Despite the strengths, the study has a number of limitations. First, the analyses were conducted based on cross-sectional but not longitudinal data, and, therefore, the estimated parameters may or may not perform well over time. Longitudinal statistical modeling techniques, which take into account changes in user behavior over time, should be considered as a future research direction. Second, despite the fact that KDD-cup intrusion detection evaluation data are the most widely used public benchmark for testing intrusion detection systems and the most comprehensive data available today, they have been criticized for lacking some important variables, such as timestamp and user-level information. The distribution of attack types (e.g., 79.2% of DoS vs. 19.7% of normal, and only 1.0% of data split among other attack types) also seems unrepresentative of real populations about which most researchers are aware. Thus, the performance of the risk factors and the corresponding parameters could be different in a new dataset that includes the missing variables and a fair distribution of attack types. Finally, this study did not take into account the between-system variance, since the KDD-cup data does not provide information at the individual network system level. The logistic regression model treated the between-system variance as zero. A disadvantage of this solution is that connections in one system tend to have similar outcomes and time-homogeneity but may not be representative of user behavior on other network systems (e.g., the data exchanging rate could be different between two network systems due to differences in network traffic or hardware configurations, and such differences could increase the variation of the connection time and impact on user behavior). A hierarchical random effects logistic regression modeling approach, which takes into account variation across different systems by allowing each system to have its own intercept, should be considered as a further direction when new benchmark data that include traffic from different networks become available.

This study could impact information retrieval at the network intrusion detection level in several aspects. The analysis approach to simplify the structure of information and to present the analysis in a simple format could be applied to different datasets and outcomes. The risk factors can be used as key elements to develop a neural network-based intrusion detection system; the risk factors and the corresponding parameters-based probability can be used as a principal solution to detect intrusion and profile users as a primary threshold to filter network traffic or as a key component assisting other intrusion detection techniques to develop a variety of hybrid-based detection systems. Since the probability risk score can be accomplished through common computer languages without interfacing with any typical software and statistical tool, it therefore can be widely adapted in a mobile computing environment and presents better intrusion detection information to network administrators for making more informed decisions in computer security.

ACKNOWLEDGMENT

The authors thank the anonymous reviewers and the editor-in-chief, for help with the manuscript, which has benefited greatly from their suggestions and comments. The authors also thank Dr. James Cannady at Nova Southeastern University for his comments, and Allyson Schulz, Director of R & D at Qualidigm, for her editorial commentary.

REFERENCES

Anderson, D., Frivold, T., & Valdes, A. (1995). *Next-generation intrusion detection expert system (NIDES): Summary report.* SRI International.

Anderson, P. J. (1972). *Computer security technology planning study volume II.* Bedford, MA: Air Force Systems Command.

Anderson, P. J. (1980). *Computer security threat monitoring and surveillance.* Fort Washington, PA: James P. Anderson Co.

Barbard, D., Wu, N., & Jajodia, S. (2001). Detecting novel network intrusions using Bayes estimators. In *Proceedings of the 1st SIAM International Conference on Data Mining* (pp. 24-29).

Bishop, M. (2003). *Computer security: Art and science.* Boston, MA: Addison-Wesley.

Cho, S. B., & Park, H. J. (2003). Efficient anomaly detection by modeling privilege flows using hidden Markov model. *Computer and Security, 22*(1), 45-55.

Cunningham, R. K., Lippmann, R. P., Fried, D. J., Garfinkle, S. L., Graf, I., Kendall, K. R., et al. (1999). Evaluating intrusion detection systems without attacking your friends: The 1998 DARPA intrusion detection evaluation. *SANS.*

Denning, D. (1987). An intrusion-detection model. *IEEE Transaction on Software Engineering, 13*(2), 222-232.

Efron, B. (1979). Bootstrap methods: Another look at the jackknife. *Annals of Statistics, 7,* 1-26.

Efron, B., & Tibshirani, E. R. (1986). Bootstrap methods for standard errors, confidence intervals, and other measures of statistical accuracy. *Statistical Science, 1*(1), 57-77.

Efron, B., & Tibshirani, E. R. (1994). *An introduction to the bootstrap.* London: Chapman & Hall.

Elkan, C. (2000). Results of the KDD'99 classifier learning contest. *ACM Transactions on Information and System Security, 3*(4), 262-294.

Gao, B., Ma, H., & Yang, Y. (2002). HMMS (hidden Markov models) based on anomaly intrusion detection method. In *Proceedings of the First International Conference on Machine Learning and Cybernetics* (pp. 381-385).

Helman, P., & Liepins, G. (1993). Statistical foundations of audit trail analysis for the detection of computer misuse. *IEEE Transactions on Software Engineering, 19*(9), 886-901.

Hosmer, D. W., & Lemeshow, S. (2000). *Applied logistic regression* (2nd ed.). New York: John Wiley & Sons.

KDD Cup. (1999). *Data available on the Web.* Retrieved February 19, 2005, from http://kdd.ics.uci.edu/databases/kddcup99/kddcup99.html

Lee, W., Stolfo, S., & Mok, K. (1999). A data mining framework for building intrusion detection models. In *Proceedings of the IEEE Symposium on Security and Privacy* (pp. 120-132).

Lippman, R., & Cunningham, S. (2000). Improving intrusion detection performance using keyword selection and neural networks. *Computer Networks, 34*(4), 594-603.

Masum, S., Ye, E. M., Chen, Q., & Noh, K. (2000). Chi-square statistical profiling for anomaly detection. In *Proceedings of the 2000 IEEE Workshop on Information Assurance and Security* (pp. 182-188).

Mooney, C. Z., & Duval, R. D. (1993). *Bootstrapping: A nonparametric approach to statistical inference.* Newbury Park, CA: Sage Publications.

Mukkamala, S., Tadiparthi, G. R., Tummala, N., & Janoski, G. (2003). Audit data reduction for intrusion detection. In *Proceedings of the IEEE 2003 International* Joint Conference on Neural Networks (pp. 456-460).

Qin, M., & Hwang, K. (2004). Frequent rules for intrusive anomaly detection with Internet datamining. In *Proceedings of the 13th USENIX Security Symposium* (pp. 456-462).

Qu, D., Vetter, B. M., & Jou, Y. F. (1997). Statistical anomaly detection for link-state routing protocols. In *Proceedings of the 1997 IEEE Symposium on Security and Privacy* (pp. 62-70).

Shyu, M., Chen, S., Sarinnapakorn, K., & Chang, L. (2003). A novel anomaly detection scheme based on principal component classifier. In *Proceedings of the IEEE Foundations and New Directions of Data Mining Workshop, in Conjunction with the 3rd IEEE International Conference on Data Mining (ICDM)* (pp. 172-179).

Stallings, W. (2003). *Network security essentials, applications and standards* (2nd ed.). NJ: Pearson Education.

Taylor, C., & Alves-Foss, J. (2001). "Low cost" network intrusion detection. In *Proceedings of the New Security Paradigms Workshop* (pp. 89-96).

Teng, H., Chen, K., & Lu, S. (1990). Adaptive real-time anomaly detection using inductively generated sequential patterns. In *Proceedings of the 1990 IEEE Symposium on Research in Security and Privacy* (pp. 278-284).

Vaccaro, H. S., & Liepins, G. E. (1989). Detection of anomalous computer session activity. In *Proceedings of the 1989 IEEE Symposium on Security and Privacy* (pp. 280-289).

Ye, N., Emran, S. M., Li, X., & Chen, Q. (2001). Statistical process control for computer intrusion detection. In *Proceedings of the DARPA Information Survivability Conference & Exposition (DISCEX II)* (pp. 397-343).

Zhang, Z., Li, J., Manikopoulos, C. N., Jorgenson, J., & Ucles, J. (2001). HIDE: A hierarchical network intrusion detection system using statistical preprocessing and neural network classification. In *Proceedings of the 2001 IEEE Workshop Information Assurance and Security* (pp. 85-90).

Zhou, M., & Lang, S. D. (2003). Mining frequency content of network traffic for intrusion detection. In *Proceedings of the IASTED International Conference on Communication, Network, and Information Security* (pp. 101-107).

This work was previously published in International Journal of Business Data Communications and Networking, Vol. 2, Issue 1, edited by J. Gutierrez, pp. 44-60, copyright 2006 by IGI Publishing, formerly known as Idea Group Publishing (an imprint of IGI Global).

Chapter XVIII
Network Setup for Secure Routing in Inter–Vehicle Communication Networks

Rania Wehbi
American University of Beirut, Lebanon

Ayman Kayssi
American University of Beirut, Lebanon

Ali Chehab
American University of Beirut, Lebanon

Zaher Dawy
American University of Beirut, Lebanon

ABSTRACT

In Inter-Vehicle Communication (IVC) networks, the high mobility and lack of infrastructure pose major challenges in designing secure routing protocols. In this work, we present a new secure routing protocol called SERVEN (SEcure Routing in VEhicular Networks) that can achieve near-instantaneous secure communication in IVC networks. In particular, we concentrate on the design of the network setup phase of the protocol and we present simulation results using Network Simulator version 2.28 (ns-2.28). Secure setup means the appropriate formation of a network whose nodes are aware of each other and of the right topology. This is especially important for location-based routing protocols in IVC networks.

INTRODUCTION

Inter-Vehicle Communication (IVC) networks will become an important building block for Intelligent Transportation System (ITS) applications (Tian, Han, Rothermel, & Cseh, 2003). IVC networks can serve as local wireless ad hoc networks for exchanging information between cars for cooperative driver assistance and other vehicle safety applications. Nevertheless, the design of effective inter-vehicular communication systems poses many technical challenges. First of all, IVC implies exchange of data between communication hosts whose location and velocity are changing continuously. Moreover, the communication patterns vary quickly as vehicles travel on different roads or in different areas. Therefore, routing of data in such a highly mobile wireless ad hoc network is liable to different attacks which motivate the research on new security mechanisms for IVC networks (Eishler, 2004). For example, the protection of route discovery is a critical prerequisite to ensure the robustness of the routing protocols. While security can be implemented at different levels, this paper focuses on the security mechanisms at the network level.

Secure routing protocols must be able to detect and isolate misbehaving nodes. A node may misbehave by agreeing to forward packets and then does not do so, because it is overloaded, selfish, malicious or broken. An overloaded node lacks the CPU cycles, buffer space or available network bandwidth to forward packets. A selfish node is unwilling to consume battery power, CPU cycles or available network bandwidth to forward packets not of direct interest to it. A malicious node launches a denial of service attack by dropping packets. A broken node might have a software fault that prevents it from forwarding packets. In addition to the routing challenges, IVC networks have to face many attacks on the security mechanisms, e.g., the key management mechanisms (Hubaux, Buttyan, & Capkun, 2001).

Before designing a secure routing protocol for an IVC network, the network setup should be properly executed. Proper or secure setup means the appropriate formation of a network whose nodes are aware of each other (correct node IDs) and of the right topology. After the secure formation of the network, the routing protocol should be able to maintain security and protect the network against possible attacks. The secure routing protocol SERVEN (SEcure Routing in VEhicular Networks), proposed in this paper,

handles both secure network setup and secure routing sustainability in an IVC network. SERVEN is thus divided into two phases: Phase 1 is concerned with the secure formation of an IVC network which is the topic of this paper, and phase 2, which is concerned with maintaining secure routing after successful secure network setup.

The rest of the paper is organized as follows: We start by outlining the related work. Then, the proposed protocol design for secure network setup is explained followed by simulation results and analysis. Finally, we draw our conclusions.

RELATED WORK

Several secure routing protocols for Mobile Ad-hoc Networks (MANETs) have been proposed in the literature (Hubaux, et al., 2001; Marti, Giuli, Lai, & Baker. 2000; Zhou & Haas, 1999; Zapata, 2001; Kong, Zerfos, Luo, Lu, & Zhang, 2001; Papadimitratos & Haas, 2002; Hu, Johnson, & Perrig, 2002a; Hu, Perrig, & Johnson, 2002b; Sanzgiri, Dahill, Levine, Shields, & Royer, 2002; Eichler, Schwingenschlögl, Dötzer, & Eberspächer, 2004) with protection capabilities against only specific attacks in MANETs. Most of this previous work focuses on providing secure routing based on cryptographic operations, such as symmetric and asymmetric cryptography. Some approaches focus on distributing the certificate authority based on the fact that no one single node in an ad hoc network can be trusted, due to low physical security and availability (Zhou & Haas, 1999; Kong, et al., 2001). Marti, et al. (2000) and Buchegger, et al. (2002) focus on mitigating routing misbehavior by rating and isolating the nodes according to their behavior. A different approach is to provide incentive to nodes so that they properly relay user data by introducing the concept of fictitious currency (Buttyan & Hubaux, 2000). Yi, et al. (2001) propose an approach to routing that incorporates security levels of nodes into traditional routing metrics. The protection of the route discovery process is regarded as an additional Quality-of-Service (QoS) issue.

Other previous work deals with routing approaches that are peculiar to IVC networks (Tian, et al., 2003; Sun, et al., 2000; Michael, 2001). However, these protocols do not consider security, which is the main concern in this paper. A recent paper addresses the issue of mobility in IVC networks (Chen & Cai, 2005), which was not the case in the other previous work. It proposes Local Peer Group (LPG) architecture to organize neighboring vehicles that have frequently changing neighbors and have no inherent relationships with one another. The paper presents also some open issues for ad hoc vehicle networking protocols.

PROTOCOL DESIGN

Before explaining SERVEN protocol design, certain aspects need to be defined. Each node (car) in the network has a unique ID. The network ID is determined by selecting the smallest ID of the nodes trying to initiate the network at the same time. Each node maintains four tables:

- Table of IDs (see Table 1) that stores the IDs of other nodes in the network along with relevant information.

Table 1 shows that *Car 1* is a node in Network *N1* that contains two nodes other than *Car 1*, *Car 2* and *Car 3*. *Car 2* and *Car 3* are in the same range of *Car 1* since they are only one hop away.

- APID table (see Table 2) that contains the IDs of the ACCEPT messages originated or received by the node. Each node maintains an AP Counter, which is set to 0 at start-up and is incremented by 1 each time the node accepts a new node. An APID is the ID of the ACCEPT message and is unique in the network. This ID is a combination of the node ID and the sequence number in the node's AP Counter. For example, the entries in Table 2 correspond to the IDs of two ACCEPT messages originated by *Car 1*.

- NAP table that includes information about unaccepted nodes. Table 3 displays the NAP table for node *Car 3*. This table reveals the fact that node *Car 4* tried to join the Network N1, but *Car 3* rejected it. The number of times *Car 4* was rejected by *Car 3* is only 1 since the "Count" field is set to 1. A node that is not accepted by two different nodes retains two entries in the NAP table, each corresponding to the node that rejects it. When a node is not accepted, the count relevant to the node that rejects it is incremented by one. When the summation of the counts for an unaccepted node reaches a threshold MAX_NAP_COUNT, the node is fired.

- GPS table (see Table 4) that contains entries given by the Global Positioning System (GPS). During the formation of the network, SERVEN takes advantage of the presence of a GPS receiver on every car participating in the network setup. This receiver provides the node with its position, velocity and time information.

Table 1. Table of IDs for node Car 1

Network ID = N1			
Node ID	Hop Count	Next Hop	Time Stamp
Car 1	0	-	Hh:mm:ss
Car 2	1	Car 2	Hh:mm:ss
Car 3	1	Car 3	Hh:mm:ss

Table 2. APID Table for node Car 1

APID
Car1,1
Car1,2

Table 3. NAP Table for node Car 3

Network ID = N1			
Unaccepted Node ID	**Sender ID**	**Count**	**Time Stamp**
Car 4	Car 3	1	hh:mm:ss

Secure Network Setup

The operation of SERVEN in the network formation phase will be clarified by explaining the ten different message types that SERVEN supports:

1. HELLO Message

This message is sent periodically (every *HELLO_INTERVAL* seconds) by the node that wants to initiate a network. Nodes that are accepted to join the network will be sending a HELLO message periodically as well. The HELLO message has a one-hop lifetime and is thus received by all cars that are in the range of the sender car. When a node receives a HELLO message, it first checks if the sending node is in the same network. If the sender belongs to another network, the node simply ignores the HELLO message. Each node maintains a timer *(Neighbor_Timer)* for every node in its range. This timer is rescheduled when the node receives a HELLO message from the corresponding node. Each time the node receives a HELLO message, it checks its table of IDs to make sure that it is aware of the presence of this node in its range. If this is the case, it just resets the relevant timer. If the node has just entered its range, it updates its table of IDs to set the hop count for this node to 1. If the timer expires

Table 4. GPS Table for node Car 1

Longitude	Latitude	Height	Velocity	Time
x_{11}	y_{11}	z_{11}	v_{11}	t_{11}
x_{12}	y_{12}	z_{12}	v_{12}	t_{12}
...	...	...	...	...
x_{1n}	y_{1n}	z_{1n}	v_{1n}	t_{1n}

before receiving a HELLO message from the relevant node, the node initiates a request process to find the new location of the node. The HELLO message contains the following fields: **ID of the source car** that originates the HELLO message, **Network ID** that the car belongs to or wants to initiate a network, **Position** of the car, **Velocity** of the car and **Time Stamp** (retrieved from the last entry in the GPS table). The flowchart in Figure 1 describes a node's reaction upon receiving a HELLO message.

2. REQUEST Message

When the timer *(Neighbor_Timer)* expires, the node realizes that the corresponding node is no longer in its range. It thus sends a REQUEST message asking for the new location of the node. This message contains a *Hop Count* field that determines the number of hops this message can progress. The *Hop Count* field is assigned a value equal to 5, based on the assumption that a node cannot traverse more than 5 hops in this short timespan while maintaining its availability in the network. When the node sends the request, it initiates a timer *(Find Timer)*. If it receives a REPLY message before this timer expires, the table of IDs is updated accordingly. Otherwise, it assumes that the node is no longer in the network and thus deletes it from the table of IDs. A node that receives the REQUEST message decrements the hop count by 1 and checks the ID of the node being requested. If this is not its ID, it sends the REQUEST further if the hop count is still greater than 0. If the ID requested is this node's ID, it sends a REPLY message to the node that originated the REQUEST. The reply contains a hop count field as well, but this time just to inform the receiver node of how many hops the sender is away from it. This value can be deduced by subtracting the final hop count value in the REQUEST message from 5. The REQUEST message contains the following fields: **ID of the Source node** that originated the REQUEST message, **Network**

Figure 1. Node processing of a HELLO message

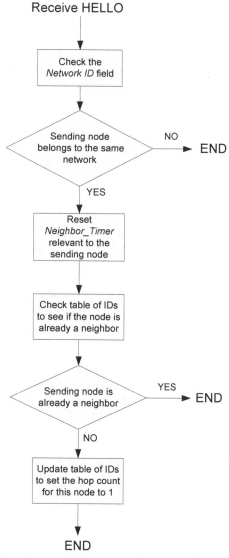

ID that the car belongs to, **ID of the Requested node** and **Hop Count**. The flowchart in Figure 2 describes a node's reaction upon receiving a REQUEST message.

3. REPLY Message

The node that receives a REQUEST message and notices that the requested node is itself sends a REPLY message to the node that sent the corresponding REQUEST message. It is assumed that

during REQUEST-REPLY, the network is stable. When a node other than the destination receives this message, it simply forwards it. When the destination node receives the REPLY, it updates its table of IDs accordingly. The fields contained in the REPLY message are the following: **ID of the Source** that originates the REPLY message, **Destination ID** (ID of the node that sent the REQUEST message), **Network ID** that the car belongs to and **Hop Count**. The flowchart in Figure 3 describes a node's reaction upon receiving a REPLY message.

4. JOIN Message

When a car receives a HELLO message, it replies with a JOIN message if it is willing to join the

Figure 2. Node processing of a REQUEST message

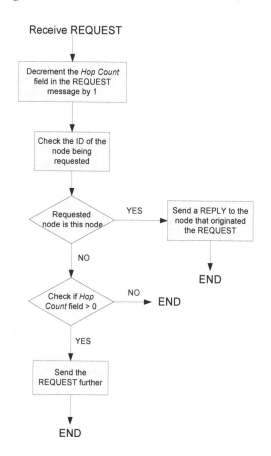

network. The ID of the car that sent the HELLO message is echoed back in the JOIN message as the destination ID. SERVEN takes into consideration the high mobility and assumes that a joining node should not traverse more than three meters from the time instant it asks to join the network until it is accepted or rejected by the nodes in the network. Taking a typical highway velocity range with maximum velocity set to 45 m/s, a node with maximum velocity needs approximately 0.067 s to traverse 3 m. Therefore, if a node receives various HELLO messages for the same network ID from different cars during the interval 0.067 s, then it should be challenged by all these HELLO sender nodes. Upon receiving the JOIN message, a node first checks its NAP table for entries corresponding to the node asking to join the network. If the NAP table contains relevant entries, the node checks the "Time Stamp" and "Count" fields. If the table contains more than one entry, the node checks each one separately. If it finds that there is a "Time Stamp" field such that (time stamp in JOIN message--time stamp in NAP table) < *UPDATE_INTERVAL*, it decides to reject the new node. This early rejection of the node may defeat a Denial-of-Service (DoS) attack that may be launched by a node trying to exhaust the network

Figure 3. Node processing of a REPLY message

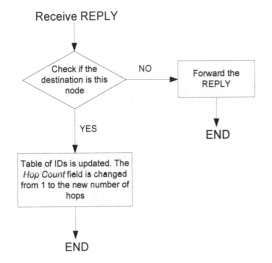

with CHALLENGE messages in response to the sent JOIN messages. The node also checks the "Count" field to determine if the new node has been fired. If this is the case, the new node will not be accepted. Otherwise, the node will process the JOIN message to check if this new node is launching an impersonation attack on any node in the network using the following procedure:

- The node checks the ID of the car sending the JOIN message. If it does not match its ID or any ID in its table of IDs, the node checks the *Destination ID* field.
  - If the *Destination ID* corresponds to the node itself, it knows that it is the node that should take the decision of accepting this node or not. It sets an *Alert_Timer* and broadcasts the received JOIN message to all nodes in the network. If the node does not receive any ALERT message before the *Alert_Timer* expires, it decides to challenge this node by checking the position information that is contained in the JOIN message.
  - If the Destination ID is not the same as the node's ID, the node performs no action.
- On the other hand, if the ID of the node sending the JOIN message matches the node's ID or any ID in its table of IDs (impersonation attack), the node checks the Destination ID field.
  - If the Destination ID corresponds to the node itself, it decides not to accept this node. It does not broadcast a NO-TACCEPT message since the true ID of the unaccepted node is not known. The new node is thus not accepted to join the network since no ACCEPT message is sent.
  - If the Destination ID is not the same as the node's ID, the node checks if it is a one-hop JOIN or a broadcasted

JOIN. If it is a one-hop JOIN, the node performs no action. Otherwise, it sends an ALERT to the node whose ID is contained in the Destination ID field; this is the node that should decide upon accepting the new node or not.

The flowchart in Figure 4 describes a node's reaction upon receiving a JOIN message.

The JOIN message contains the following fields: **ID of the source car** that originated the JOIN message, **Network ID** that the car belongs to or wants to initiate, **Destination ID** (ID of car that originally sent the HELLO message), **Position** of the car that corresponds to the last two entries in the GPS table, **Velocity** of the car that corresponds to the last two entries in the GPS table and **Time Stamp** retrieved from the last two entries of the GPS table.

5. CHALLENGE Message

As explained above, if the node that should decide upon accepting or rejecting a new node does not receive any ALERT message during the *ALERT_INTERVAL*, it decides to challenge the new node by checking the position information that are contained in the JOIN message. The CHALLENGE message is used by the accepting node to measure the time delay between itself and the node asking to join the network. The CHALLENGE message is not altered by the node requesting to join the network; the requesting node just resends it to the originator node. This message contains the time stamp set by the originator node. The two-way time delay is thus the difference between the time at which the CHALLENGE message arrives back at the originator node and the time when it was issued by the originator:

Figure 4. Node processing of a JOIN message

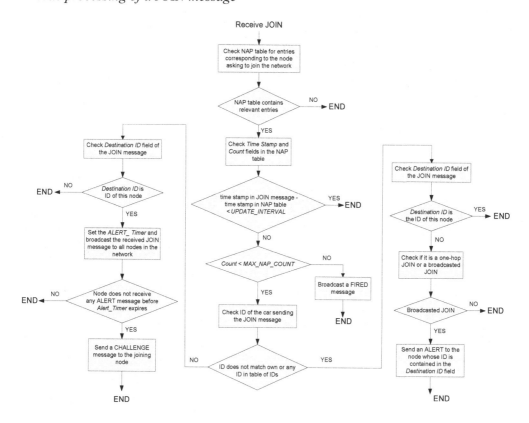

$$\Delta t_{measured} = t_{CHALLENGE\ returns} - t_{CHALLENGE\ sent}$$

$\Delta t_{measured}$ is obtained based on the assumption that the CHALLENGE message is not delayed due to traffic or retransmission that may occur because of collisions. The challenging node makes use of the time delay to calculate the two-way distance from the new node. This distance is obtained as follows:

$$\Delta t_{measured} = \frac{\Delta d_{measured}}{c} + \left(2 \times \frac{b_{Challenge}}{R_b} \right) + 2\varepsilon$$

$$\Delta d_{measured} = c \times \left(\Delta t_{measured} - \left(2 \times \frac{b_{Challenge}}{R_b} \right) - 2\varepsilon \right)$$

Where c is the speed of light, b is the number of bits of CHALLENGE packet, R_b is the bit rate and ε is the processing time. At this stage, the node has enough information about the new node to decide on accepting it or not. This information can be classified as:

- Accurate information from the CHALLENGE message ($\Delta t_{measured}$ and $\Delta d_{measured}$)
- Information obtained from the JOIN message. This represents the position, velocity and time given by the GPS system for the last two time instants (see message type 4). This information could be erroneous and need to be checked by the challenging node.

In order to illustrate the check process, consider a scenario of a new node (*Car 2*) asking to join an IVC network. *Car 1* is already in the network and happens to be in the range of *Car 2*. Therefore, *Car 1* has to decide whether to accept *Car 2* or not. From the CHALLENGE message that *Car 1* issues, it is able to determine the two-way time delay and relative distance ($\Delta t_{12measured}$ and $\Delta d_{12measured}$) as explained above. It gets information relevant to *Car 2* from the JOIN message it

received $[(x_{2(n-1)}, y_{2(n-1)}, z_{2(n-1)}, v_{2(n-1)}, t_{2(n-1)}), (x_{2n}, y_{2n}, z_{2n}, v_{2n}, t_{2n})]$. Several issues need to be resolved by *Car 1* in order to make the proper decision including the relative direction of the cars and the relation between their velocities. *Car 1* fetches its GPS table to obtain its position and velocity information at times $t_{1(m-1)}$ and t_{1m} equivalent to $t_{2(n-1)}$ and t_{2n}, respectively. We assume that the x-axis is used to determine the direction of motion. Therefore, we distinguish the following cases:

A. Cars Moving in the Same Direction

Car 1 checks for the direction as follows:

Assuming $t_{1(m-1)} = t_{2(n-1)}$ *and* $t_{1m} = t_{2n}$

If $x_{2n} - x_{2(n-1)} > 0$ & $x_{1m} - x_{1(m-1)} > 0$

or $x_{2n} - x_{2(n-1)} < 0$ & $x_{1m} - x_{1(m-1)} < 0$

$\Rightarrow$ *Car 1* and *Car 2* are moving in the same direction.

The condition that *Car 1* has to check depends on which velocity is greater and towards which car is the direction of motion. The equations in Figure 5 present all possible cases:

Car 1 then obtains the current position for *Car 2* as follows:

$$x_{2n\_current} = x_{2n} + (v_{2n} \times (t_{1n} - t_{2n}))$$

where $x_{2n\_current}$ is the position of the joining node at time retrieved from last entry of GPS table for this node, x_{2n} is the stored position of the joining node, v_{2n} is the stored velocity of the joining node, t_{1n} is the time in the last entry of the GPS table of this node and t_{2n} is the stored time.

Therefore, the current round-trip distance between the nodes can be calculated as shown in Figure 6.

Figure 5.

Motion towards Car 1 with $v_{1m} > v_{2n}$

$$\left[\begin{array}{l} \left(x_{2n} - x_{2(n-1)} > 0 \ \& \ x_{1m} - x_{1(m-1)} > 0 \ \& \ x_{1m} - x_{2n} > 0\right) \\ OR \\ \left(x_{2n} - x_{2(n-1)} < 0 \ \& \ x_{1m} - x_{1(m-1)} < 0 \ \& \ x_{1m} - x_{2n} < 0\right) \end{array}\right] \& \left[v_{1m} > v_{2n}\right] \qquad (1)$$

Motion towards Car 1 with $v_{1m} < v_{2n}$

$$\left[\begin{array}{l} \left(x_{2n} - x_{2(n-1)} > 0 \ \& \ x_{1m} - x_{1(m-1)} > 0 \ \& \ x_{1m} - x_{2n} > 0\right) \\ OR \\ \left(x_{2n} - x_{2(n-1)} < 0 \ \& \ x_{1m} - x_{1(m-1)} < 0 \ \& \ x_{1m} - x_{2n} < 0\right) \end{array}\right] \& \left[v_{1m} < v_{2n}\right] \qquad (2)$$

Motion towards Car 2 with $v_{2n} > v_{1m}$

$$\left[\begin{array}{l} \left(x_{2n} - x_{2(n-1)} > 0 \ \& \ x_{1m} - x_{1(m-1)} > 0 \ \& \ x_{2n} - x_{1m} > 0\right) \\ OR \\ \left(x_{2n} - x_{2(n-1)} < 0 \ \& \ x_{1m} - x_{1(m-1)} < 0 \ \& \ x_{2n} - x_{1m} < 0\right) \end{array}\right] \& \left[v_{2n} > v_{1m}\right] \qquad (3)$$

Motion towards Car 2 with $v_{2n} < v_{1m}$

$$\left[\begin{array}{l} \left(x_{2n} - x_{2(n-1)} > 0 \ \& \ x_{1m} - x_{1(m-1)} > 0 \ \& \ x_{2n} - x_{1m} > 0\right) \\ OR \\ \left(x_{2n} - x_{2(n-1)} < 0 \ \& \ x_{1m} - x_{1(m-1)} < 0 \ \& \ x_{2n} - x_{1m} < 0\right) \end{array}\right] \& \left[v_{2n} < v_{1m}\right] \qquad (4)$$

Where Δd_{GPS} is the round-trip distance obtained from the GPS table, x_{1n} and y_{1n} are the abscissa and ordinate in the last entry of the GPS table, y_{2n} is the stored ordinate of the joining node and $t_{current}$ is the current time. Now the condition that *Car 1* has to check is the following:

$$Is \quad \Delta d_{12measured} = \Delta d_{12GPS} - f(x,v) \\ \cdot \Delta v \cdot \Delta t_{12measured}$$

If $v_{1m} = v_{2n} = v$, then *Car 1* and *Car 2* have the same velocity and the above condition becomes: *Is* $\Delta d_{12measured} = \Delta d_{12GPS}$. If the conditions are satisfied, then *Car 1* decides to accept *Car 2*; otherwise it does not.

B. Cars Moving in Opposite Directions

Assuming $t_{1(m-1)} = t_{2(n-1)}$ *and* $t_{1m} = t_{2n}$

$$If \quad x_{2n} - x_{2(n-1)} > 0 \ \& \ x_{1m} - x_{1(m-1)} < 0$$
$$or \quad x_{2n} - x_{2(n-1)} < 0 \ \& \ x_{1m} - x_{1(m-1)} > 0$$

=> *Car 1* and *Car 2* are moving in opposite directions.

Therefore, *Car 1* has to check the following condition shown in Figure 7.

If $v_{1m} = v_{2n} = v$, then *Car 1* and *Car 2* have the same velocity and the condition shown in Figure 7.

$$Is \quad \Delta d_{12measured} = \Delta d_{12GPS} + \left(2 \cdot v \cdot \Delta t_{12measured}\right)$$

If the above conditions are satisfied, then *Car 1* decides to accept *Car 2*, otherwise it does not. The information fields contained in the CHALLENGE message are the following: **ID of the source car** that originated the CHALLENGE message, **Destination ID** (ID of the accepted

Figure 6.

$$\Delta d_{GPS} = 2 \times \left(\sqrt{\left(x_{1n} - x_{2n\_current} + \left(f(x,v) \times \Delta v \times \left(t_{current} - t_{1n} \right) \right) \right)^2 + \left(y_{1n} - y_{2n} \right)^2} \right)$$

$$\Delta v = \left| v_{1m} - v_{2n} \right|$$

$$f(x,v) = \begin{cases} +1 & \text{If} \quad equations\ (1)\ \&\ (3)\ are\ satisfied \\ -1 & \text{If} \quad equations\ (2)\ \&\ (4)\ are\ satisfied \end{cases}$$

Figure 7.

$$Is \quad \Delta d_{12measured} = \Delta d_{12GPS} + \left(2 \cdot v_{min} \cdot \Delta t_{12measured} \right) + \Delta v \cdot \Delta t_{12measured}$$

$$where \quad v_{min} = min\left[v_{1n}, v_{2n} \right] \quad \& \quad \Delta v = \left| v_{1n} - v_{2n} \right|$$

car), **Network ID** and **Time Stamp** (last entry in the GPS table). Note that the CHALLENGE message constitutes a core step in the execution of the secure setup phase of the protocol.

6. ACCEPT Message

When a node becomes certain of the position and time information sent by the joining node (see message type 5), it decides to accept the new node. The node thus increments its AP Counter by 1 and updates its table of IDs and APID table. It then checks for the new number of nodes in the network. If the number of nodes is still below the threshold (see message type 10 below), a one-hop ACCEPT message is sent that is received by all nodes in the same radio range. When the accepted node receives this ACCEPT message, a timer with *HELLO_INTERVAL* duration is set so that this node can start sending HELLO messages periodically. Any other node that is already part of the network and receives the ACCEPT message checks its NAP table. If there is an entry that corresponds to this node, it checks the "Time Stamp" field. If the table contains more than one entry, the node checks each one separately. If it finds that there is a "Time Stamp" field such that (time stamp in ACCEPT message - time stamp in NAP

table) < *UPDATE_INTERVAL*, it does not update its table of IDs. If this condition is not satisfied or no entries exist in the NAP table, the node updates its table of IDs and the APID table and checks for the new number of nodes in the network. If the number of nodes is still below the threshold, it resends the one-hop ACCEPT message after replacing the ID field with its ID and the table of IDs in the message with its updated one. The check that is done on the NAP table each time an ACCEPT message is received is intended to assure that a new node will not be accepted to join the network unless it is accepted by all network nodes from which it receives a HELLO during the interval 0.067 s. The following are the fields in the ACCEPT message: **ID of the car** currently sending the ACCEPT message, **Network ID**, **ACCEPT packet ID (APID)**, which is a combination of the ID of the node that originates the ACCEPT message and the AP Counter, **ID of the accepted node, Time Stamp** (last entry in the GPS table), **Table of IDs** and **Flag** set to 1.

7. NOTACCCEPT Message

When the challenge fails, the node decides not to accept the new node. It updates its NAP table. This table stores the *ID of the unaccepted node,* the *ID of the sender node* that does not accept this node, a *count* and a *time stamp* (see Table 3). A node that is not accepted by two different nodes retains two entries in this table, each corresponding to the node that rejects it. When a node is not accepted, the count relevant to the entry of the node that rejects it is incremented by 1. When the summation of the counts of all entries corresponding to an unaccepted node reaches a threshold *MAX_NAP_COUNT*, the node is fired. Otherwise, a NOTACCEPT message is broadcasted to all nodes in the network. When a node receives a NOTACCEPT message, it deletes the rejected node from its table of IDs and checks its NAP table. If it does not find an entry in the NAP table, it adds one, otherwise, it checks the ID of the sender field. If it finds an entry that corresponds to the NOTACCEPT message sender ID, it checks the count and determines the difference in time (current time-time stamp in this entry) for this entry. If it finds that this time difference is less than or equal to a predefined time delay *NAP_UP-DATE_INTERVAL*, it does not increment the count in this entry. Otherwise, it updates the entry and checks to decide whether to fire the node or not. Maintaining different entries for the same node in the NAP table is intended to defeat an attack that may be launched by a malicious node in an attempt to increase the count in a short duration of time and thus fire a certain node out of the network for the whole network lifetime. The fields contained in the NOTACCEPT message are the following: **ID of the source car** that originated the NOTACCEPT message, **Network ID, ID of the unaccepted node, Time Stamp** (last entry in the GPS table) and **Flag** set to 0.

8. FIRED Message

When the summation of the "Count" fields of all entries corresponding to an unaccepted node reaches the threshold MAX_NAP_COUNT, the node sends a FIRED message, which is broadcasted to all nodes in the network, notifying

them not to challenge and thus not to accept this node anymore. A node that receives the FIRED message sets the "Count" fields of all the entries relevant to the fired node in the NAP table to the threshold value MAX_NAP_COUNT. The fields contained in this message are the following: **ID of the source car** that originates the FIRED message, **Network ID** and **ID of the fired node**.

9. ALERT Message

As explained above, a node may receive a JOIN message from a new node trying to impersonate an already existing node in the network. In this case, the car sends an ALERT message, which is broadcasted to all nodes in the network notifying them that a certain node is being impersonated. The node that receives the ALERT is concerned with this message only if it is the node that should decide upon accepting or rejecting the new node. The fields contained in this message are the following: **ID of the source car** that originates the ALERT message and **ID of the node being impersonated**.

10. ENDPHASE Message

In order to launch the security mechanisms in the IVC network, SERVEN assumes that the number of nodes in the network reaches a predefined value *N*. *N* should be properly selected so that the applications supported by the established IVC network are able to function properly. These *N* nodes will collaborate in the second phase to maintain secure routing. Therefore, the routing protocol should be able to determine the end of the first phase. The ENDPHASE message supported by SERVEN undertakes this responsibility. As mentioned above, each time a node accepts a new node or receives an ACCEPT message for a node, it updates its table of IDs. Each time the ID table is updated, the node determines the number of nodes in the network as long as phase 1 is maintained. This number can be deduced from the number of entries in the table of IDs. When this value reaches the number *N*, the node broadcasts an ENDPHASE message to all nodes in the network. A node that receives this message will set the phase indicator to 1 and reject any further node asking to join the network for a duration t_2, during which the security mechanisms are launched in the network. The fields contained in this message are the following: **ID of the source car** sending the ENDPHASE message and **Time Stamp** (given by the GPS system).

SIMULATION RESULTS

We can clearly notice from the design presented in the Protocol Design Section that certain issues need to be specified for the protocol to work properly during its setup phase. This implies setting the timers and thresholds appropriately. The design explained in the previous section was implemented using Network Simulator 2.28 (*ns-2.28*). We take advantage of the fact that *ns-2.28* supports mobility to implement phase 1 of the protocol on top of the simulator. The timers that need to be specified are the following:

- The period of time (*HELLO_INTERVAL*) during which the HELLO message is sent.
- The time interval (*FIND_INTERVAL*) that is set to the *Find Timer* that is scheduled upon initiating a REQUEST message.
- The time interval (*UPDATE_INTERVAL*) that should be exceeded before challenging or accepting a node that was rejected this interval ago.
- The time interval (*ALERT_INTERVAL*) that is set to the *ALERT_Timer*, which is scheduled when a node broadcasts the JOIN received from a new node.
- The time interval (*NAP_UPDATE_INTERVAL*) that aims at defeating an attack launched by a malicious node in an attempt to increase the count in the NAP table in a

short duration of time and thus fire a certain node out of the network for the whole network lifetime.

Due to the space limitation, the exact procedures followed to deduce the values of these time intervals from the simulation results cannot be explained in detail. After performing extensive simulations on real IVC network scenarios, we obtained the following empirical values for the timers:

- HELLO_INTERVAL = 4 s
- FIND_INTERVAL = 0.02 s = 20 ms
- UPDATE_INTERVAL = 0.069 s = 69 ms
- ALERT_INTERVAL = 0.05 s = 50 ms
- NAP_UPDATE_INTERVAL = 0.005 s = 5 ms

In addition to these time intervals, the threshold (*MAX_NAP_COUNT*) that determines the number of times the node is allowed to be rejected before deciding that it should be fired is also set. In our implementation, we set this threshold to 20. This means that we allow a node to be un-accepted 20 times by one node or by different nodes before firing it from the network.

Time Analysis

Time analysis is performed to get the time needed by a normal joining node to be part of the network. Simulation results show that a new node needs around 0.02 s (20 ms) to be accepted and recognized by its one-hop neighbors, which obeys the requirement that the one-hop message transfer latency among vehicles should be less than 100 ms (Chen & Cai, 2005). For an IVC network with network diameter of 30 hops, we find out that the time needed to accept a joining node and make it recognized by all network nodes is around 0.35 s. It is worth mentioning that this time is obtained taking into account the processing time of a node in *ns-2.28*. Hence, if we consider

SERVEN's assumption that cars are equipped with powerful processors, then this time will decrease significantly. If we limit the network diameter to 30 hops, then the time of 0.35 s can be considered as the time needed for the network to converge as a new node is accepted.

Bandwidth Analysis

This subsection presents the analysis to determine the bandwidth consumed by SERVEN control messages during its operation in phase 1. We consider a scenario where five nodes happen to be in the same range and send their HELLO messages during a one second interval. The bandwidth consumed is the number of bits invoked in this one-hop during the 1 s interval, which is found to be equal to 1.84 kbps. We also considered the worst case scenario where 120 nodes happen to be in the same range and decide to join the network during the 1 s interval. Taking into account the HELLO messages sent by the five nodes that were already in the network and in the same range, the bandwidth consumed was found to be equal to 184.24 kbps. This implies that with a 2 Mbps bandwidth, 1.816 Mbps would be left for the application. We also considered the maximum number of nodes that could be in the same range in a four-lane scenario. This is found to be equal to 304 vehicles. The bit rate consumed by the HELLO messages sent by the 304 vehicles was found to be 111.872 kbps, which is also relatively small in comparison to a 2 Mbps bandwidth.

CONCLUSION

This paper addressed the issue of designing secure routing protocols for IVC networks. After presenting the need for security in such networks, we gave a detailed design of the protocol (SERVEN) during its setup phase. We explained the ten different message types that SERVEN supports to address the following three main security issues

during the setup phase: confidentiality of the car's location and time relevant information, prevention of external impersonation attacks and the limit of the network size. Each node is assumed to have a GPS receiver that provides it with the position, velocity and time information. We finally presented simulation results obtained from implementing SERVEN setup phase using *ns-2.28*. The results confirmed the proper operation of SERVEN for small and large IVC networks.

REFERENCES

Awerbuch, B., Holmer, D., Nita-Rotaru, C., & Rubens, H. (2002). An on-demand secure routing protocol resilient to byzantine failures, *ACM Workshop on Wireless Security (WiSe)*, Atlanta, GA (pp. 21-30).

Buchegger, S., & Boudec, J.Y.L. (2002). Nodes bearing grudges: Towards routing security, fairness, and robustness in mobile ad hoc networks. *Tenth Euromicro Workshop on Parallel, Distributed and Network-based Processing* (pp. 403-410).

Buttyan, L., & Hubaux, J.P. (2000). Enforcing service availability in mobile ad hoc WANs. *First Mobile Ad Hoc Networking and Computing (MOBIHOC)*. BA, MA (pp. 87-96).

Chen, W., & Cai, S. (2005). Ad hoc peer-to-peer network architecture for vehicle safety communications. *IEEE Communications Magazine*, 100-107.

Eichler, S. (2004). Security challenges in MANET-based telematics environments. Tenth *Open European Summer School and IFIP WG 6.3 Workshop* (pp. 196-203).

Eichler, S., Schwingenschlögl, C., Dötzer, F., & Eberspächer, J. (2004). Secure routing in a vehicular ad hoc network. *IEEE Vehicular Technology Conference: Wireless Technologies for Global Security,* Los Angeles, CA (pp. 3339-43).

Hu, Y.C., Johnson, D., & Perrig, A. (2002a). SEAD: Secure efficient distance vector routing for mobile wireless ad hoc networks. *Fourth IEEE Workshop on Mobile Computing Systems and Applications,* Callicoon, NY (pp. 3-13).

Hu, Y.C., Perrig, A., & Johnson, D. (2002b). Ariadne: A secure on-demand routing protocol for ad-hoc networks. *Eighth ACM International Conference on Mobile Computing and Networking (MOBICOM),* Atlanta, GA (pp. 21-38).

Hubaux, J.P., Buttyan, L., & Capkun, S. (2001). The quest for security in mobile ad hoc networks. *Third ACM Symposium on Mobile Ad Hoc Networking and Computing (MOBIHOC),* Long Beach, CA (pp. 146-155).

Kong, J., Zerfos, P., Luo, H., Lu, S., & Zhang, L. (2001). Providing robust and ubiquitous security support for mobile ad-hoc networks. *Ninth International Conference on Network Protocols (ICNP)* (pp. 251-260).

Marti S., Giuli, T., Lai, K., & Baker, M. (2000). Mitigating routing misbehavior in mobile ad hoc networks. *Sixth Annual International Conference on Mobile Computing and Networking (MOBI-COM),* Boston (pp. 255-265).

Michael, L. (2001). Adaptive layered data structure for inter-vehicle communication in ad-hoc communication networks. *Eighth World Congress on Intelligent Transportation Systems (ITS)* (pp. 1-11).

Papadimitratos, P., & Haas, Z. (2002). Secure routing for mobile ad hoc networks, *SCS Communication Networks and Distributed Systems Modeling and Simulation Conference* (pp. 27-31).

Sanzgiri, K., Dahill, B., Levine, B., Shields, C., & Royer, E. (2002). A secure routing protocol for ad hoc networks. Tenth *IEEE International Conference on Network Protocols (ICNP)* (pp. 78-87).

Sun, M.T., Feng, W.C., Lai, T.H., Yamada, K., & Okada, H. (2000). GPS-based message broadcast for adaptive inter-vehicle communications. *IEEE 52nd Fall Vehicular Technology Conference: Vol. 6* (pp. 2685-2692).

Tian, J., Han, L., Rothermel, K., & Cseh, C. (2003). Spatially aware packet routing for mobile ad hoc inter-vehicle radio networks. *IEEE 6th International Conference on Intelligent Transportation Systems (ITSC): Vol. 2* (pp. 1546-1551).

Yi, S., Naldurg, P., & Kravets, R. (2001). Security-aware ad hoc routing for wireless networks. *Second ACM Symposium on Mobile Ad Hoc Networking and Computing (MOBIHOC),* Long Beach, CA (pp. 299-302).

Zapata, M. (2001). Secure ad hoc on-demand distance vector (SAODV) routing. *IETF MA-NET Mailing List, Message-ID 3BC17B40. BBF52E09@nokia.com,* ftp://manet.itd.nrl.navy. mil/pub/manet/2001-10.mail, October 2001.

Zhou, L., & Haas, Z. (1999). Securing ad hoc networks, *IEEE Network Magazine,* Vol. 13, No. 6, pp. 24-30.

This work was previously published in International Journal of Business Data Communications and Networking, Vol. 2, Issue 4, edited by J. Gutierrez, pp. 1-17, copyright 2006 by IGI Publishing, formerly known as Idea Group Publishing (an imprint of IGI Global).

Chapter XIX
Metropolitan Broadband Networks:
Design and Implementation Aspects, and Business Models

Antonios Alexiou
Research Academic Computer Technology Institute and University of Patras, Greece

Christos Bouras
Research Academic Computer Technology Institute and University of Patras, Greece

John Papagiannopoulos
University of Aegean, Greece

Dimitrios Primpas
Research Academic Computer Technology Institute and University of Patras, Greece

ABSTRACT

This chapter presents the design principles that cover the implementation of broadband infrastructure in the region of Western Greece, by examining all the necessary parameters that arise while implementing such a critical developmental project. The broadband infrastructure that is deployed is either based on optical fiber (on big municipalities) or on wireless systems (OFDM based and WiFi cells). Furthermore, we present as two case studies all issues of the designing of the Metropolitan Area Network of Patras, the third largest city of Greece and the Wireless Access Network of Messatida. The major target of the broadband networks is to interconnect the buildings of the public sector in the city and also deploy infrastructure (fibers or wireless systems) that will create conditions of competition in providing both access and content services to the advantage of the end consumer. The usage of the broadband infrastructure by service providers will be based on the open availability of the infrastructure in a cost-effective way. Finally, we present the main characteristics of a proposed business plan that ensures financial viability of the broadband infrastructure and guarantees the administration, growth, and exploitation of infrastructure.

INTRODUCTION

This chapter presents the design principles that cover the implementation of broadband infrastructure in the region of Western Greece, by examining all the necessary parameters and studying all the issues that arise while implementing such a critical developmental project. In particular, we present the main principles that should be followed while developing such metropolitan area networks. Regarding the design guidelines, in this chapter we cover issues such as architecture of the broadband network, topology selection, requirements of the passive and active equipment, and requirements of the fiber and ducting infrastructure. Furthermore, we present as a case study critical issues regarding the design of the metropolitan area network of Patras, the third largest city of Greece. The main target of the MAN of Patras is to interconnect the buildings of the public sector in the city. The organizations that are going to be connected in the MAN are organizations of the sectors of public administration, education, health, culture, and so forth. The usage of the broadband infrastructure by service providers will be based on the open availability of the fiber optics infrastructure in a cost-effective way. Finally, we present the main characteristics of a proposed business plan that ensures financial viability of the broadband infrastructure and guarantees the administration, growth, and exploitation of the infrastructure.

Several related projects that implement neutral broadband infrastructure in cities are running across the world. For example, Ireland, Sweden, and New Zealand run such programs, where the local authorities design and fund the major part of the projects aiming to increase the broadband penetration with benefits to the end users (UTO-PIA, 2006; CityLink, 2006; Localret, 2006).

This chapter is structured as follows. We next describe broadband infrastructure in Europe and in Greece, then present the general guidelines for the design of municipal broadband networks. Following this, the methodology of work regarding the designing of the MANs is offered, and the overall architecture and topology of the MAN of Patras is briefly described. Additionally, the same section describes the architecture of smaller wireless networks that are implemented in smaller municipalities where the optical MANs are not profitable and presents a typical case study that is Messatida municipality. A presentation follows of the main characteristics of a business plan that ensures the financial viability of broadband infrastructure. Finally some concluding remarks and planned next steps are presented.

BROADBAND STATUS IN GREECE

The importance of broadband infrastructure worldwide is confirmed by the activities of certain advanced countries in order for the appropriate broadband infrastructure to be developed and adopted so as to contribute to economic growth and to tackle any possible cases of "technological exclusion" of citizens (Firth & Mellor, 2005).

The importance of broadband networks for the development of a country may also be confirmed by the intensiveness of the activities of many countries that set as their main strategic objective the implementation of such infrastructures. In addition, the development of such networks has also been adopted in the common European policy for the implementation of the Information Society. In eEurope 2005 as well as in i2010, broadband access is an important priority of the European Union (EC, 2002; Europa, 2004).

In the current situation, the proper infrastructure in Greece is owned only by the former public telecommunications provider (OTE), while the alternative providers seem only to have plans in expanding their network infrastructure within the big cities of Greece. The business plans of the alternative telecommunications companies and network carriers do not include the expansion of their network throughout Greece, since they are afraid that non-urban areas do not appear to have any business interest. Broadband access, as defined by the "Strategic Text on Broadband Access" of the relevant task force, requires the proper broadband infrastructure and the competition between the Internet service providers. Since broadband infrastructure is now being developed, the penetration of broadband usage has not been increased. Although these findings are pessimistic regarding the growth of broadband, the action line of the operational program "Information Society" appear to be a significant hope for the near future.

Unfortunately, the broadband penetration level has been very low in Greece. Greece has been the last country among the EU of 15, and remained last, in providing broadband access among the 25 countries of the EU (see Figure 1) (Europa, 2006). This is caused by the fact that there is no investment by the private sector, therefore there is no competition in the broadband market in the region.

The main issues that occur during this research for the current state of broadband in Western Greece could be divided in two main categories:

(a) the clients' side, as far as broadband demand is concerned; and (b) the providers' side, as far as broadband supply is concerned. Regarding the end users, the major issues are the following:

- High cost of broadband access regarding home usage
- Lack of broadband services that will take advantage of the infrastructure

The telecommunications companies have raised a number of issues that discourage them from investing in broadband infrastructure and services. Synoptically these issues are:

- Lack of the regulatory framework that adjusts and defines the market of broadband services, in order to ensure market and competition's functioning
- Difficulties in developing local loop unbundling (LLU)
- Lack of preparation in supporting the demand of broadband services by the former public telecommunications carrier (OTE)

Figure 1. Broadband penetration rates in EU25

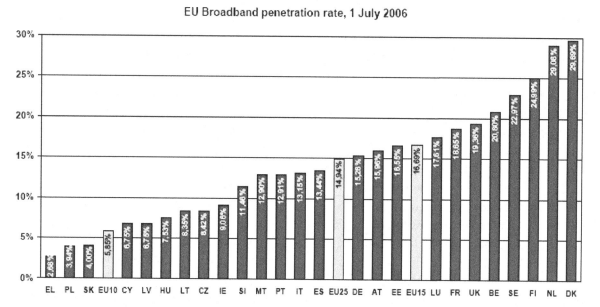

Since the start of 2005, the xDSL penetration has been rising. The current access network (copper cables) is being updated by installing xDSL technologies such as ADSL mainly and HDSL. According to OTE, 10,929 ADSL ports were installed in the region of Western Greece by the end of 2005 (and 270,000 throughout the country). In addition, wireless hotspots have been installed in public places, such as ports, entertainment parks, and so forth, through a project of the Information Society.

Another measure that is expected to boost ADSL use in the major cities of the country is the provision of ADSL Internet access at a diminished cost to university students. This measure was announced by the Greek government in June 2005, and it will begin at the start of the next academic year.

Taking into consideration the current state in the region of Western Greece where the telecommunications market still depends on the core fiber optics networks of the dominant provider (OTE) and all the above mentioned issues, it can be said that it is important for the Greek government authorities to update the telecommunication law of the country. This could secure the viability of the public and private telecommunication companies, and simultaneously the viability of the community-owned networks. To this end, the Greek government authorities, taking into consideration the issues mentioned in this section and the variability of the Greek telecommunications market, passed the new telecommunications law. This law aims to secure the telecommunications market and competition in Greece, and as a consequence, better services will be provided to the citizens. The new law provides the telecommunications firms with the conditions to enable the reduction of prices. The specific clauses clearly describe the functioning of the Regulatory Authority (EETT) in terms of independence and efficiency. The issues concerning the rights-of-way are also being defined (e.g., the rights-of-way of fiber optic through urban planning resources of different proprietors such as municipalities, individuals, institutions, and organizations), collocation issues, and the demarcation between public and private networks.

ISSUES ON DESIGNING BROADBAND INFRASTRUCTURE

This section presents the main principles that should be followed while designing such metropolitan area networks. In Western Greece (our case) the networks belong to cities, where in most of the cases the municipalities do not have the proper know-how of designing such networks. Therefore, a specialized technical consultant (the Research Academic Computer Technology Institute) has been selected in order to provide its know-how. In particular, the consultant works on conducting the studies of the networks' design and architecture, supervising the technical part of the construction of the networks and also designing the business plan that will be applied and will ensure the network's viability. The business plan proposes the scheme that will be responsible for the operation of the networks, according to the criteria and the guidelines of the EU (EC, 2002; Europa, 2004).

The expected result of these projects is the creation of broadband infrastructure in Greece, which in turn will create conditions of competition in Greece in advance of the end user. A common strategic design and implementation in a regional level is highly desirable. At the first stage, the main target of these networks, as metropolitan area networks, is to interconnect the buildings of the public sector of the cities in which they will be developed. The organizations that are going to be connected are those belonging on the education, health, and culture sectors, and so forth. During the second stage, this infrastructure will be available on network and content providers in a cost-effective way. The latter will create conditions of competition in broadband infrastructure and services that will benefit end users. The plan for deployment of the infrastructure encourages the public exploitation through the leasing of pairs of fiber optics. This fact provides revenue in a cost-effective way in order to cover all operating and maintenance costs.

The projects mainly consist of manholes, ducts, channels, fiber optics, points of interconnection, together with the installation of the passive and active equipment in order to provide the basic broadband access in the public sector buildings. In particular, a broadband infrastructure based on optic fibers will be installed across the cities, and several public collocation points will be created. The projects also fund some additional access infrastructure from public sector buildings to the collocation and aggregation points. This access infrastructure along with a small part of the cities' broadband infrastructure will be used to provide network connectivity to the public sector. The remaining broadband infrastructure (optic fibers and collocation points) will be available for the content and service providers to use, and it will provide broadband services to the citizens.

The major characteristics of the mentioned broadband infrastructure according to the European Commission (EC, 2003) should be the following:

1. **Open access:** The funded projects must be consistent with the new regulatory framework of electronic telecommunications and the rules of competition (public funding and antitrust). The appliance of these rules is a commitment in order to have clearly defined open access. In particular, the construction of the networks, as already mentioned, should be limited in the construction of infrastructure and equipment that will be open to any telecommunication carrier and service provider (ED, 2003; Magnago, 2004).

2. **Neutral operator:** The main principles in the deployment of the broadband infrastructure assign the network operator the obligation to retain the neutral character of the infrastructure. The network should be an open access installation to all the organizations that provide electronic networks and services with absolutely no discriminations against them (Economides, 1996).

3. **Infrastructure owner:** The municipality constructs the broadband infrastructure and obviously has specific benefits from these networks. Therefore, it is also responsible for planning the expansion of the current infrastructure in a controlled and rational way. Also its role is to solve all issues of the installed infrastructure and declare the rules of usage of the infrastructure by the providers.

METROPOLITAN AREA NETWORKS

This section is dedicated to describing the methodology that we followed in order to design the MAN of Patras. Furthermore, it presents the main characteristics of the MAN of Patras in terms of topology, architecture, and technology selection.

Designing Aspects

The overall architecture of the MAN is shown in Figure 2 (ITU, 2006). The topology is based on a three-level model: main network, distribution network, and access network. In turn, there are three types of nodes in the system: main nodes, distribution nodes, and access nodes.

The main network consists of a number of main nodes that are connected directly between each other. In the main network, there must be some direct redundancy between main nodes which are close together. This means that it must be possible from one main node to reach the main nodes next to it without passing through the active equipment of another node. The optical cables should be laid without a break between the main nodes,

Figure 2. General architecture

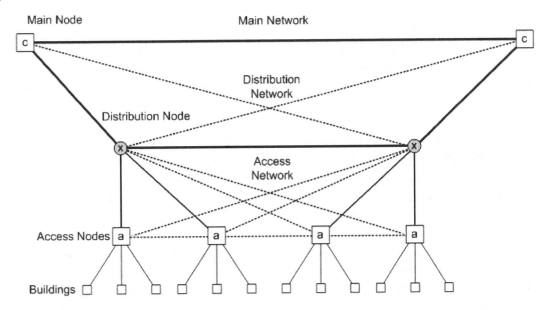

so as to achieve high operational dependability. The main network's optical cables that connect different main nodes are to be separately ducted. The number of fibers between the main nodes in the main network in a municipality ought to be not less than 72 per optical cable. This number results as follows: Each distribution node usually collects traffic from approximately eight access nodes, as designed in the technical studies for the development of the networks. Each access node gathers two pairs of fibers (one uplink and one backup), thus each optical cable should have at least 4 x 8 = 32 fibers, plus 32 for alternative routes in the distribution network. The available cables usually provide 48, 72, and 96 fibers, so 72 is the lower acceptable optical cable. If main nodes in different municipalities are long distances apart, with a smaller number of distribution nodes, the number of fibers may possibly be smaller if this is justified by great differences of fiber cost.

As far as the distribution network is concerned, it consists of the distribution nodes. A distribution node shall connect to a main node and shall be planned to have a redundant connection to another main node. The optical cables should be laid without a break from each main node to any distribution node. Alternatively, an optical cable loop is laid with two or three distribution nodes where the need for each distribution node is hived off. Over long distances this will be a cheaper but more vulnerable option. The number of fibers in the distribution network is affected by the following parameters:

• Number of access nodes connecting with each distribution node
• Number of operators needing connections in the distribution network
• Leasing of dark fiber to other actors

The number of fibers to each distribution node ought not to be less than 72 per optical cable, as already described.

The access network consists of the access nodes. A number of buildings are connected to an access node through a fiber cable with at least four fibers (two pairs of fibers, one uplink and one backup).

Regarding the fiber infrastructure, the additional optical cable will be installed, in order to handle situations of possible or anticipated penetration in the area, a large number of Internet operators active in the area, the positioning of active equipment, and the degree of redundancy in the networks. As a general rule, if existing ducting is to be used, a careful assessment must be made of the best way to use it. If the number of existing optical pipes is small, an optical cable with many fibers will have to be laid so as to make maximum use of the ducting.

For the part of the network that will provide connectivity to the public sector's buildings, the ethernet technology has been selected (Metro Ethernet Forum, 2006). Ethernet switches are used on access nodes and aggregate the traffic from the buildings. Each building has a 100 Mbps or 1 Gbps connectivity through Base-LX SFPs. The distribution nodes do not have any active equipment, only passive. The main nodes have gigabit ethernet switches with advanced features. Those switches connect the ethernet switches of access nodes as well as the buildings that have dedicated fiber connections. This choice has been done due to the fact that the public sector's buildings should use various service providers. In particular, the traffic from the connected schools in the MAN should be forwarded to the Greek School Network, the traffic from universities on Greek Research and Technology Network, and so forth. Therefore, the designing approach is to configure the equipment in such a way that will provide Transparent LAN services, connecting the building to their service provider transparently and "friendly" (Kompella & Rekhter, 2005). The latter means that the approach will eliminate the limitations that add to the network and service providers.

Methodology of Work

In order to handle the project work and secure the correctness and quality of the design, a specific methodology was followed. In particular the steps were the following:

- Several visits on municipalities took place, in order to finalize the location of the building, the points that the building will connect to the network, and the final mapping out of the ducts
- Design the network according to the three distinct levels (access, distribution, and main network)
- Design the requirements of the network's nodes and the equipment (passive and active)
- Write the first version of the analytical design study of the network
- Write the specific requirements of the network's components according to each municipality's needs
- Perform indicative cost accounting of the requirements and the overall design in order to ensure that it is compliant to the allocated budget
- Finally, optimize the network design and equipment requirements

The above mentioned methodology was used efficiently for eight different municipality networks in Western Greece. The case of MAN of Patras was the largest one and therefore the most complex.

The MAN of Patras

The city of Patras is the largest municipality in the region of Western Greece, the third largest city of Greece (its metropolitan area has a population of more than 200,000), an important commercial center, and a busy port—the second largest in Greece. Patras' MAN connects 210 public buildings in the city, among them three university institutes, six research centers, four hospitals, and 120 schools (primary and secondary).

Immediately benefiting from this network will be all the employees of institutions of education, research, health, and public administration in the region of Patras, while in effect all the citizens of a wider region of the city of Patras will profit. Additionally, all major Greek content and service providers can use (cost effectively) this infrastructure to provide broadband services to the citizens. Their interest is quite large as the local 'Patras' market is very attractive.

The MAN of Patras consists of five rings, while the total length of the ducts is 48 Km (see Figure 3). The used fiber cables (various types, 24/36/48/72 fibers) are approximately 230 Km. Among the rings, a star topology is used for the connections of the buildings to the access nodes. Additionally, 100% redundancy has been designed for the distribution and main network. More specifically the Patras MAN will consist of:

- Four (4) main nodes
- Eight (8) distribution nodes
- Twenty-two (22) access nodes
- Nine (9) wireless access nodes

Regarding the cost of the total investment, the Patras infrastructure cost approaches the value of 3 M€ which is absolutely comparable to the cost of the telecommunication services of the public sector of municipality of Patras. As shown in Table 1, this cost is approximately 2.2 M€ according to recent research for the municipality of Patras conducted by the Research Academic Computer Technology Institute. Consequently, the depreciation of the cost of the whole investment in the municipality of Patras will take no more than two years.

Wireless Municipal Networks

Additionally, the Information Society program funds similar smaller projects that are suitable for small municipalities (less than 10,000 citizens) that mainly are underpopulated. These projects have

Table 1. Telecommunications fees in the municipality of Patras (in K€)

	ORGANIZATION		SUM
Education–Research	Universities	2	880.41
	Technical Universities	1	73.37
	Research Institutes	6	117.39
	Elementary Schools	76	102.72
	High Schools	44	108.58
	Public occupational centers	2	5.57
Health	Hospitals	4	622.16
Government	Region	1	158.48
	Prefecture	1	70.43
	Municipalities	2	76.30
	Libraries	1	3.22
	Sum	**140**	**2218.6**

the same goals as the optical metropolitan area networks, but due to the local geography (difficult morphology), the underpopulation of these areas, and the small needs of the public sector, the deployment of optical infrastructure is unprofitable. Therefore, these special projects are carried out and are based on wireless technology.

The main design goal is the existence of backhaul connections based on multi-carrier OFDM that can succeed with large transmit rates over long distances and also support non-line-of-site (NLOS) connectivity. These systems are accompanied by WiFi products that are used in the densely populated areas in order to connect various sites of public sector (local authorities, schools, hospitals, etc.). Following this approach, small wireless networks can be implemented, investing a reasonable amount of money.

Those networks are designed in a three-level hierarchy (see Figure 4), where there are:

Figure 3. The general ducting schema in Patras MAN

Figure 4. The architecture of wireless broadband networks

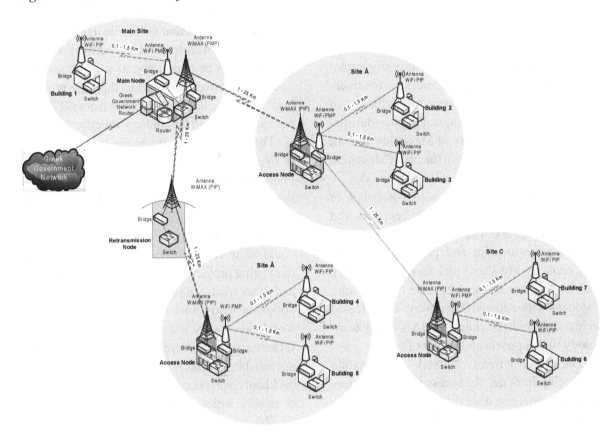

- Access nodes that provide connectivity through WiFi systems, or in special cases through multi-carrier OFDM (mainly WiMAX)
- Retransmission nodes that are used to connect main and access nodes when their immediate connection is not feasible
- Main nodes that aggregate the traffic from all connected sites and provide inter-municipal routing. Main nodes also support the interconnection with the global Internet through the appropriate providers in a federated way

Except for the basic connectivity between sites, those networks aim to provide inter-municipal VoIP calls for all public sector sites and connectivity with other federated networks that are higher in the hierarchy (for example, school networks,

national administrative networks). Additionally, the expansion of those networks is a continuous goal that can be succeeded either with wireless or optical connections. Finally, these networks will comprise the basis for the e-government and all the e-services of the new digital world that the European countries try to establish.

In the region of Western Greece, 19 small municipalities are going to implement such wireless metropolitan networks, aiming to limit their operational costs and increase the quality of the services provided to the citizens.

The Wireless Access Network of Messatida

This section presents a case of a municipal wireless access network—the case of Messatida. Messatida, in the western part of Peloponnesus and very close to Patras city. The population of the city is 11,873, and its area is 66.4 square kilometers.

The proposed municipal wireless access network covers the wider region of Messatida and constitutes a network that could be easily implemented since the covered distances are relatively small. This network will benefit institutions of education, research, health, and public administration in the municipality of Messatida, and all citizens of the wider region of the city of Messatida will have access to this broadband network.

The municipal wireless access network of Messatida consists of the backhaul network and the access network. The backhaul network consists of point-to-point and point-to-multipoint high capacity links (one and four respectively), with high-power transceivers able to cover long distances with a cost-effective way. The selected technology could be either WiMAX or any technology that supports multicarrier OFDM.

The whole wireless network of Messatida has one main node, six access nodes, and uses one retransmission node that is necessary due to the morphology. The total number of connected buildings is 22. As far as the access network is concerned, it consists of large-scale cell deployments implemented with point-to-multipoint WiMAX/multi-carrier OFDM technology, as well as WiFi hotspots where the cell radius is small enough. In particular, two access connections are implemented using WiMAX and six using WiFi systems.

Interconnection at a National Level

A major issue for the viability and exploitation of those networks is the interconnection between them in order to make a full connected broadband country. It is a key point for future years, but also a big challenge due to the morphology of Greece.

In a first stage, the interconnection of all the optical MANs and the wireless municipal networks from each "provider" of the public sector (school networks, Greek research and education networks,

the Greek government network) independently is an obvious solution. In this case, each provider will establish links that will route its traffic from the main node of each municipal network. But this solution must be temporary, as it is not scalable and cost effective due to the fact that each provider leases lines (or buys access lines from OTE) that are expensive and technology specific.

The outer goal should be the interconnection of those networks (not even for the needs of the public sector) through broadband infrastructure that will either be deployed or will be leased for a long time (at least 20 years). The solution for the deployment of interconnection infrastructure could be an easy solution, if we take advantage of existing projects for construction of highways and other roads. In this case, the deployment of optical infrastructure during the construction is worldwide a very cheap solution. Additionally, for solitary areas where the optical deployment is not feasible, alternative solutions such as wireless backhaul connections based on OFDM technology or satellite links can be studied.

This prospect will offer global connectivity through infrastructure compliant to specific technology standards and neutrality. Over this infrastructure, each provider will offer its services to its clients. The latter also applies for public sector needs.

Generally, it is a key point to study carefully this prospect of global national connectivity that will add value to these municipal broadband networks and will also expand their usage and viability.

BUSINESS MODEL

In order to secure the financial viability of the broadband infrastructure of Western Greece, it has to be supported by a business plan. Such business models have been proposed by several researchers and are used on other broadband municipal networks.

Figure 5. Basic business model's levels

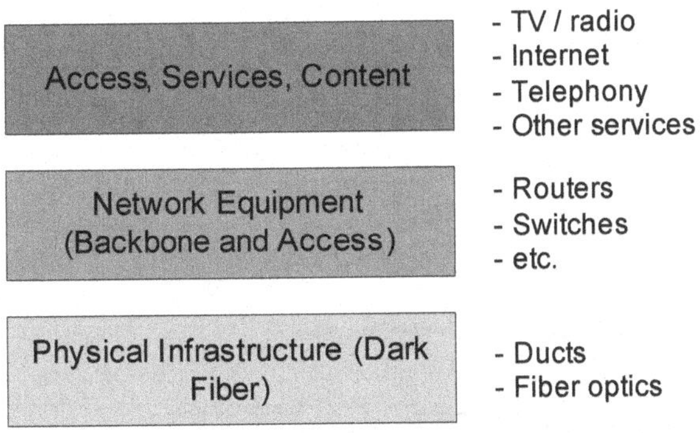

A business model defines the way a metropolitan public network should be exploited. It defines the role of the municipality or the public authorities, the handling of competition issues, the involvement of private companies, and so forth. Its intention is to provide the citizens with a viable metropolitan fiber optic network, including the proper resources for the maintenance and the expansion of the network (Monath, Kristian, Cadro, Katsianis, & Varoutas, 2003; Ecomomides, 1996). The main goal is the provision of better and less expensive services to the public (Henderson, Gentle, & Ball, 2005). Figure 5 presents the three basic levels of a business model:

- The first level refers to the physical infrastructure of the network (ducts, dark fiber, etc.) and to the organization that provides and exploits this broadband network infrastructure
- The second level refers to the active equipment of the network (e.g., routers, switches, etc.)
- The third level refers to who has access to the network, its services, and the provided content

By assigning each of the above mentioned levels to different organizations, consortiums, or companies, different business model cases can be proposed:

1. **Equal Access Model:** In this model the broadband infrastructure is built by the city or state and then it is leased or sold to an operating company or a consortium. The operating company adds the active equipment to the network and sells access to the operating broadband network to any service provider. The service providers pay the operating company a monthly fee per customer, while independent content providers are able to sell their content to the public or to business customers. This process is done through the operating company's portal, which is responsible for keeping billing records and having a direct billing relationship with the customer.

The role of the public authorities (municipality or government) in this model is to stimulate competition at the level of content and services. The government in this model has already invested in passive infrastructure, thus the cost for a service or content provider to enter the market is much lower. Through the operating company the government ensures an equal confrontation of all the service and content providers. In this model the roles and responsibilities of all the involved organizations must be clearly defined, because it may lead to complex structures and processes (Chlamtac, Gumaste, & Szabo, 2005).

The equal access model is followed by a number of international and EU countries. Examples of this model can be found in The Netherlands (Enschede) with the Dutch/German Internet Exchange (NDIX), in Canada (Alberta) with Axia, and in the United States (Grant County) with the Zipp Network. Variations of this model can also be found in the case of the city of Amsterdam, where the physical infrastructure already existed, and in Spain (region of Catalonia) and Italy (Infratel), where local government also set up the active infrastructure of the network.

Figure 6. The application of the proposed business model in network layers

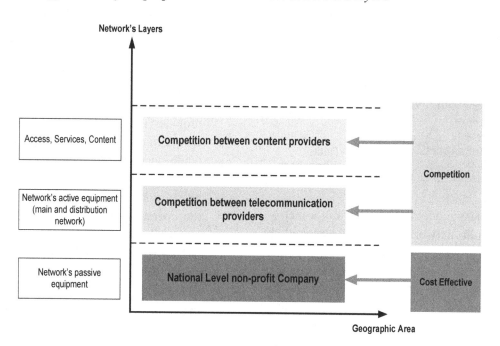

2. **Sole Private Provider Model:** This model is applicable for cases where no service and content providers preexist, and the broadband market has not created a critical mass of customers that would be able to generate sufficient revenue to a large number of involved companies. In this model the operating company is also the service provider. In this way, the development of broadband infrastructure can become more easily a viable project, but the customers experience a less wide range of services at a price that does not benefit the competition of companies. For this reason, the monopoly of the operating company should be maintained temporarily, in order to lead to an equal access model in a fixed period of time. This model requires a lower management complexity and is also more attractive to service providers as it becomes commercially viable much more quickly (Chlamtac et al., 2005). Examples of this model can be found in Sweden (Stokab–Stockholm) and The Netherlands with the Fiber Pilot program in Almere.

3. **Full Public Control Model:** In this model all the layers are managed by one or more public organizations, including the development of passive and active infrastructure and the provision of services. The private sector can also get involved in a variation of this model, by the creation of public-owned companies with private capital investment. This model is suitable in cases where the involvement of an operating company is not feasible and no service providers are activated. Most of the time, this is the case of rural or remote communities, with no prior broadband infrastructure (Chlamtac et al., 2005).

The main problem of this model, like the previous one, is that no competition is evolved between service and content providers. Moreover, the lack of technical expertise of the local government most of the time has as an effect of less innovation in the deployment of the network and its provided services. Finally, the cost of the total investment in building the network and providing the services is quite high for the local government.

Examples of this model can be found in Italy with Terrecablate in Siena and Acantho in the region of Emilia-Romagna, and in Austria with the Wienstrom in Vienna.

Proposed Business Model

The selection of the proper business model is essential for the viability and the success of the project. Regarding the metropolitan area networks, the use of the equal access business model based on a national level is the one that seems to fit most in the case of Greece. In this business model, the public sector is only the owner of the passive infrastructure (level one in the model presented in Figure 5) while in the upper two levels (Figure 5), competition is delivered between both telecommunications carriers that operate the networks and content and service providers.

The public sector's organization (which will operate on level one) will provide the fiber optics infrastructure, in a cost-effective way, to the telecommunication companies. The mission of this organization will be to establish competition conditions between the providers, and maintain and expand the network, where this will be necessary. In particular, it should have certain responsibilities, such as the information of the citizens, the recording of the needs during the use of the network infrastructures, in order to be able to maintain the networks and conduct the studies for their expansion. The requested revenue for the expansion of the network will come by the leasing of the existing infrastructure to telecommunication and service providers. Thus, the service and content providers will focus on their role by providing their competitive services in a cost-efficient way. The consumer will be able

to choose from among the competition a great variety of different services.

All in all, this model has some certain advantages regarding the design and the deployment of an overall broadband network in Greece. In this way, the service and content providers will provide their services at a low cost and in a continuously developing way. The service providers will also gain from this situation, as they will have access to national infrastructure through one organization and network operating schema. Additionally, there will be competition in the network level between telecommunication companies and competition in the access, services, and content level among the service and content providers (see Figures 5 and 6).

CONCLUSION

This chapter presented the basic design aspects for the broadband municipal infrastructure networks in the region of Western Greece. The proposed broadband networks will cover the needs of the eight major cities within the region of Western Greece and 61 other networks in other regions of Greece. These networks will interconnect the organizations of education, research, health, culture, and the sum of the buildings of public administration via high-speed connections, and will also establish public collocation points and exceeding fiber cables that can be used cost effectively by service and content providers. The projects are in the construction phase, and in the second half of 2008, the network will be up and running. Additionally, the case of the city of Patras, the largest case on the designed MANs, is described. Finally, the chapter discusses the proposed business models for the operation of those broadband networks and the one that we believe better suits the Greek case.

For future work, we already have plans to study and propose an appropriate business model to cover all technical and political aspects for the operation of those broadband infrastructure networks.

REFERENCES

Chlamtac, I., Gumaste, A., & Szabo, C. (2005). *Broadband services: Business models and technologies for community networks.* New York: Wiley Interscience.

CityLink. (2006). *New Zealand Wellington's case.* Retrieved June 14, 2006, from *http://www.citylink.co.nz*

EC (European Commission). (2002). *eEurope 2005: An information society for all.* Retrieved January 13, 2006, from http://ec.europa.eu/information_society/eeurope/2002/news_library/documents/eeurope2005/eeurope2005_en.pdf

EC. (2003). *Guidelines on criteria and modalities of implementation of structural funds in support of electronic communications.* Retrieved January 10, 2006, from http://ec.europa.eu/regional_policy/consultation/telecom_en.htm

Economides, N. (1996). The economics of networks. *International Journal of Industrial Organization, 14*(4), 673-699.

Europa. (2004). *Challenges for Europe's Information Society beyond 2005: Starting point for a new EU strategy.* Retrieved January 13, 2006, from http://europa.eu/rapid/pressReleasesAction.do?reference=IP/04/1383

Europa. (2006). *Broadband access in the EU: Situation at 1 July 2006.* Retrieved February 9, 2007, from http://forum.europa.eu.int/Public/irc/infso/cocom1/library?l=/public_documents_2006&vm=detailed&sb=Title

Firth, L., & Mellor, D. (2005). Broadband: Benefits and problems. *Telecommunications Policy, 29*(2-3), 223-236.

Henderson, A., Gentle, I., & Ball, E. (2005). WTO principles and telecommunications in developing nations: Challenges and consequences of accession. *Telecommunications Policy, 29*(2-3), 205-221.

ITU. (2006). *Construction, installation and protection of cables and other elements of outside plant.* Retrieved June 14, 2006, from http://www.itu.int/rec/T-REC-L/e

Kompella, K., & Rekhter, Y. (2005, December 28). *Virtual private LAN service.* Internet Draft (draft-ietf-l2vpn-vpls-bgp-06).

Localret. (2006). *The case of Barcelona.* Retrieved June 14, 2006, from http://www.localret.net/idiomes/english.htm

Magnago, A. (2004). Open access—business models and operational costs. *Proceedings of the Broadband Europe International Conference 2004,* Brugge, Belgium.

Metro Ethernet Forum. (2006). *Homepage.* Retrieved June 14, 2006, from http://www.metroethernetforum.org

Monath, T., Kristian, N., Cadro, P., Katsianis, D., & Varoutas, D. (2003). Economics of fixed broadband access network strategies. *Communications Magazine, 41*(9), 132-139.

UTOPIA (Utah Telecommunication Open Infrastructure Agency). (2006). Retrieved June 14, 2006, from http://www.utopianet.org/

KEY TERMS

Access Network: Part of the network architecture that consists of a number of access nodes.

Business Model: A plan that ensures the financial viability of the broadband infrastructure.

Distribution Network: Part of the network architecture that consists of a number of distribution nodes.

Main Network: Part of the network architecture that consists of a number of main nodes.

Optical Fiber Network: A type of network mainly based on fiber optics technology.

Wireless Access Network: Type of network mainly based on wireless technology.

This work was previously published in Handbook of Research on Global Diffusion of Broadband Data Transmission, edited by Y. Dwivedi, A. Papazafeiropoulou, and J. Choudrie, pp. 196-210, copyright 2008 by Information Science Reference, formerly known as Idea Group Reference (an imprint of IGI Global).

Compilation of References

A Guide to Network Topology. (2008). Retrieved January 26, 2008, from *http://learn-networking.com/network-design/a-guide-to-network-topology*.

Abutaleb, A., & Li, V. O. K. (1997). Paging Strategy Optimization in Personal Communication Systems. *Wireless Networks, 3*, 195-204. Amsterdam, The Netherlands: Baltzer.

Achem, N., Irmer, R., & Fettweis, G.P. (2000). Parallel interference cancellation with reduced complexity for multi-carrier spread spectrum FCDMA. *Proceedings of IEEE 6th International Symposium on Spread Spectrum Techniques and Applications*,353-357.

Adickes, D. M., Billo, E. R., Norman, A. B., Banerjee, S., Nnaji, O. B., & Rajgopal, J. (2002). Optimization of indoor wireless communication network layouts. *IIE Transactions, 34(9)*, 823-836.

Ahmed, I., Godbole, R., & Vishwanathan, S. (2004). An Open Standards Approach to Network-Centric Storage, Retrieved 12, July, 2005 from *www.netapp.com.*

Airjack. (n.d.). Retrieved March 29, 2006, from http://sourceforge.net/projects/airjack

Akyildiz, F., Mcnair, J., Ho J., Uzunalioglu, H., & Wang, W. (1998). Mobility Management in Current and Future Communications Networks. *IEEE Network Magazine,* July/August.

Akyildiz, I. F., Ho, J. S. M., & Lin, Y. B. (1996, August). Movement Based Location Update and Selective Paging for PCS Network. *IEEE/ACM Trans. Networking, 4*(4), 629-638.

Akyildiz, I. F., Mcnair, J., Ho, J. S. M., Uzunalioglu, H., & Wang, W. (1999). Mobility Management in Next Generation Wireless Systems. *Proc. IEEE, 87*(8), 1347-1385.

Alandjani, G., & Johnson, E. E. (2003). Fuzzy Routing in Ad Hoc Networks. *Proc. of IEEE Int'l Conf. on Per-*formance, Computing, and Communications, 525–530, Phoenix, AZ, April 9-11.

Alex, V. (1992). A good file system. In *Proceedings of USENIX File System Workshop* (pp. 1-12).

Alexandra, D-H., Holtzman, J., & Zvonar, Z. (1995). Multi-user detection for CDMA systems. *IEEE Personal Communications, 2*(2), 46-58.

Al-Frihat, J. (2005). Advanced queue management algorithms for computer networks. *Studies in Informatics and Control Journal, 14*(2) 111-116.

Allman, M., & Paxson, V. (1999, April). TCP congestion control. *Internet Engineering Task Force, RFC 2581.*

Almeida, J. M., Krueger, J., Pager, D. L., & Vernon, M. K. (2001). *Analysis of Educational Media Server Workloads.* Paper presented at ACM NOSSDAV. New York, USA.

Amram, M., & Kulatilaka, N. (1999). *Real options: Managing strategic investment in an uncertain world.* Boston: Harvard Business School Press.

Anderson, D., Frivold, T., & Valdes, A. (1995). *Next-generation intrusion detection expert system (NIDES): Summary report.* SRI International.

Anderson, P. J. (1972). *Computer security technology planning study volume II.* Bedford, MA: Air Force Systems Command.

Anderson, P. J. (1980). *Computer security threat monitoring and surveillance.* Fort Washington, PA: James P. Anderson Co.

Ang, S., & Straub, D. W. (1998). Production and Transaction economies and IS Outsourcing: A study of the US Banking Industry. *MIS Quarterly*, 535-552.

Anixter & Intel Corporation. (2003). *Gigabit Ethernet over Copper Cabling.* Retrieved June 17, from http://www.

personal.psu.edu/staff/r/y/ryb2/gige/Gigabit%20Ethern et%20over%20cabling.pdf

Antonelli, C. (1997). A regulatory regime for innovation in the communications industries. *Telecommunications Policy, 21*(1), 35-45.

Aoul, Y. H., Nafaa, A., Negru, D., & Mehaoua, A. (2004). FAFC: Fast Adaptive Fuzzy AQM Controller for TCP/IP Networks. *Proceedings of IEEE Global Telecommunications Conference, 3,* 1319-1323.

Applegate, L., & Montealegre, R. (1991). Eastman Kodak Organization: Managing Information System through Strategic Alliances. *Harvard Business School Case,* 9-192-030. Boston, Massachusetts.

Arias, J. R., Suárez, F. J, García, D. F., Pañeda, X. G., & García, V. G. (2002). *A Set of Metrics for Evaluation of Interactive News-on-Demand Systems.* Paper presented at ACM Multimedia Conference. Juan Les Pins, France

Arias, J. R., Suárez, F. J, García, D. F., Pañeda, X. G., & García, V. G. (2002). *Evaluation of Video Server Capacity with Regard to Quality of the Service in Interactive News-On-Demand Systems.* Paper presented at PROMS-IDMS2002. LNCS 2515. Coimbra, Portugal.

Artail, H., Safa, H., & Pierre, S. (2005). Database caching in MANETs based on separation of queries and responses. In *Proceedings of the IEEE International Conference on Wireless and Mobile Computing, Networking, and Communications* (pp. 237-244).

Asatani, K. (1998). Standardization on multimedia communications: Computer-telephony-integration-related issues. *IEEE Communications Magazine, 36*(7), 105-109.

Atilla, Eryilmaz, & Srikant R. (2006). Joint Congestion Control, Routing, and MAC for Stability and Fairness in Wireless Networks. *IEEE Journal on Selected Areas in Communications. 24*(8), 1514- 1524.

AudioVideoweb (2006). AudioVideoweb.com LLC, Retrieved 12th of November from http://www.audiovideoweb.com/

Awerbuch, B., Holmer, D., Nita-Rotaru, C., & Rubens, H. (2002). An on-demand secure routing protocol resilient to byzantine failures, *ACM Workshop on Wireless Security (WiSe),* Atlanta, GA (pp. 21-30).

Aweya, J., Ouellette M., & Montuno, D. Y. (2001). A control theoretic approach to active queue management. *Computer Networks, 36*(2-3), 203-35.

Bai, G., & Williamsom, C. (2004). *The effects of mobility on wireless media streaming performance.* Paper presented at Wireless Networks and Emerging Technologies (WNET), Banff, AB, Canada.

Bakes, C. M., Kim, C. M., & Ramos, C. T. (2003). An assessment of Gigabit Ethernet technology and its applications at the NASA Glenn Researcg Center: A case study. *Journal of Engineering and Technology Management, 20,* 245-272.

Balakrishnan, M., & Johnson, E. E. (2005). Fuzzy Diffusion for Distributed Sensor Networks. *Proc. of the IEEE Military Communications Conference,* 1–6, Oct. 17-20.

Baldwin, C., & Clark, K. (2000). *Design rules: The power of modularity.* MIT Press.

Bandara, J., Shen, X., & Nurmohamed, Z. (2000). A Fuzzy Resource Controller for Non-Real-Time Traffic in Wireless Networks. *Proc. of the IEEE Int'l Conf. on Communications, 1,* 75–79, June 18-22.

Bandara, J., Shen, X., & Nurmohamed, Z. (2002). Resource Allocator for Non Real-Time Traffic in Wireless Networks Using Fuzzy Logic. *Wireless Personal Communications,* Kluwer Academic Publishers, Netherlands, *21,* 329–344.

Banerjee, J. (2008). *Outsourcing Operator Networks—Strategic Options.* Executive Management Programme Dissertation, Management Development Institute, India.

Bansal, D., & Balakrishnan, H. (2000, May). TCP-friendly congestion control for real-time streaming applications. *Technical Report MIT-LCS-TR-806, MIT Laboratory for Computer Science.*

Bansal, D., & Balakrishnan, H. (2001, April). Binomial congestion control algorithms. *Proceedings of IEEE INFOCOM.*

Barbard, D., Wu, N., & Jajodia, S. (2001). Detecting novel network intrusions using Bayes estimators. In *Proceedings of the 1st SIAM International Conference on Data Mining* (pp. 24-29).

Bar-Noy, A., Kessler, I., & Sidi, M. (1995, July). Mobile users: To update or not to update?. *Wireless Networks, 1*(2), 175-185.

Barrett, D., & King, T. (2005). *Computer networking illuminated.* Jones and Bartlett Publishers, Inc.

Bazaraa, M. S., Sherali, H. D., & Shetty, C. M. (1993). *Nonlinear Programming: Theory and Algorithms* (2nd Ed.). New York: John Wiley & Sons.

Beigi, M., & Verma, V. (2001). Network prediction in a policy-based IP networks. In *Proceedings of the IEEE Globecom* (pp. 2522-2526). San Antonio, TX.

Beigi, M., Calo, S., & Verma, D. (2004). Policy transformation techniques in policy-based systems management. In *Proceedings of the Fifth IEEE International Workshop on Policies for Distributed Systems and Networks.* Yorktown, NY.

Bejerano, Y., Breitbart, Y., Garofalakis, M., & Rastogi, R. (2003). Physical Topology Discovery for Large Multi-Subnet Networks. *Bell Labs, Lucent Technologies, IEEE INFOCOM 2003.*

Bell, D., & Grimson, J. (1992). *Distributed database systems.* Addison-Wesley.

Bellavista, P., & Corradi, A. (2004). *A QoS management middleware based on mobility prediction for multimedia service continuity in the wireless internet.* Paper presented at IEEE Int. Symp. on Computers and Communications (ISCC) 2004, Alexandria, Egypt.

Bellavista, P., Corradi, A., & Giannelli, C. (2005). *Mobile proxies for proactive buffering in wireless internet multimedia streaming.* Paper presented at IEEE International Conference Distributed Computing Systems Workshops, Washington, DC.

Berry, M., & Linoff, G. (2000). Mastering Data Mining. Wiley & Sons.

Bersekas, D., & Gallager, R. (1992). *Data networks* (2nd ed.). Englewood Cliffs, NJ: Prentice Hall Publishers.

Bhattacharje, P. S., Saha, D., & Mukherjee, A. (2004, July). An Approach for Location Area Planning in a Personal Communication Services Network (PCSN). *IEEE Transactions on Wireless Communications, 3*(4), 1176-1187.

Bingham, J. (1990). Multi-carrier modulation for data transmission: An idea whose time has come. *IEEE Communication Magazine*, 5-14.

Bishop, M. (2003). *Computer security: Art and science.* Boston, MA: Addison-Wesley.

Black, F., & Scholes, M. (1973). The pricing of options and corporate liabilities. *Journal of Political Economy, 81*, 637-659.

Boleng, J., Navidi, W., & Camp, T. (2002). Metrics to Enable Adaptive Protocols for Mobile Ad Hoc Networks. *Proc. of the Int'l Conf. on Wireless Networks (ICWN '02)*, 293-298.

Bona, K. A. (1992). *AT&T to provide equipment to expand Philippine cellular system - AT and T Network Systems.* Retrieved Feb 20, 2008 from http://findarticles.com/p/articles/mi_m3457/is_n14_v10/ai_12445255.

Bonissone, P. P. (1992). A compiler for fuzzy logic controllers. *Proceedings of the International Fuzzy Engineering Symposium (IFES'91)*, 706-717, IOS Press.

Bos, L., & Leroy, S. (2001). Towards an all-IP-based UMTS system architecture. *IEEE Network*, 36-45.

Bourreau, M., & Dogan, P. (2001). Regulation & innovation in the telecommunications industry. *Telecommunications Policy, 25*(3), 167-184.

Braden, B. et al. (1998). Recommendations on queue management and congestion avoidance in the Internet. *Request for Comments (RFC) 2309.*

Brandauer, C., Iannaccone, G., Diot, C., Ziegler, T., Fdida, S., & May, M. (2001). Comparison of tail drop and active queue management performance for bulk-data and Web-like Internet traffic. *Proceedings of the 6th IEEE Symposium Computers and Communications,* Hammamet.

Brealey, R. A., & Myers, S. C. (2002). *Capital investment and valuation.* McGraw-Hill.

Brealey, R. A., Myers, S. C., & Allen, F. (2006). *Principles of corporate finance.* McGraw Hill.

Broch, J., Maltz, D. A., Johnson, D. B., Hu, Y. C., & Jetcheva, J. (1998). A performance comparison of multi-hop wireless ad hoc network routing protocols. In *Proceedings of ACM MobiCom* (pp. 85-97).

Brotherton, M. D, Huynh-Thu, Q., Hands, D. S., & Brunnström, K. (2006). Subjective Multimedia Quality Assessment. *IEICE Transactions on Fundamentals of Electronics, Communications and Computer Sciences,* Vol. E98-A, Number 11.

Bruneo, D., Villari, M., Zaia, A., & Puliafito, A. (2003). *VoD services for mobile wireless devices.* Paper presented at IEEE ISCC 2003, Kemer, Antalya, Turkey.

Buchegger, S., & Boudec, J.Y.L. (2002). Nodes bearing grudges: Towards routing security, fairness, and robustness in mobile ad hoc networks. *Tenth Euromicro*

Workshop on Parallel, Distributed and Network-based Processing (pp. 403-410).

Bucherer, M., Kaul, A., & Woerner, B. D. (1996). Analysis of DS-CDMA parallel interference cancellation with phase and timing errors. *IEEE Journal on Selected Areas in Communications, 4*(8), 1522-1535.

Busari, M., & Williamson, C. (2002). A Synthetic Workload Generation Tool for Simulation Evaluation of Web Proxy Caches. Computer Networks: *The International Journal of Computer and Telecommunications Networking, 38*(6), 779-794.

Buttyan, L., & Hubaux, J.P. (2000). Enforcing service availability in mobile ad hoc WANs. *First Mobile Ad Hoc Networking and Computing* (*MOBIHOC*). BA, MA (pp. 87-96).

CACI. (1999). COMNET III user's manual. *CACI Products Company.*

Cai, Y., & Hua, K. A. (2002). An adaptive query management technique for real-time monitoring of spatial regions in mobile database systems. In *Proceedings of 21st IEEE International Conference on Performance, Computing, and Communications* (pp. 259-266).

Calhoun, G. (1992). *Wireless Access and the Local Telephone Network*, Boston: Artech House.

Cao, G., Yin, L., & Das, C. R. (2004). Cooperative cache-based data access in ad hoc networks. *IEEE Computer Society, 37*(2), 32-39.

Carr, P. (1988). The valuation of sequential exchange opportunities. *Journal of Finance, 23*(5), 1235-1256.

Casale, G., Cremonesi, P., Serazzi, G., & Zanero, S. (2005). *Performance Issues in Video Streaming Environments.* Paper presented at IEEE QEST'05.

Casares-Giner, V., & Mataix-Oltra, J. (2002, May). Global Versus Distance-Based Local Mobility Tracking Strategies: A Unified Approach. *IEEE Trans. Veh. Technol., 51*, 472-485.

Casner, S., Frederick, R., Jacobsen, V., & Schulzrinne, H. (1996). *RTP: A transport protocol for real time applications.* ftp://ftp.isi.edu/in-notes/rfc1899.txt

Cayirci, E., & Akyildiz, I. F. (2003). Optimal Location Area Design to Minimize Registration Signalling Traffic in Wireless Systems. *IEEE Transactions on Mobile Computing, 2*(1), January-March.

Ceri, S., & Pelagatti, G. (1984). *Distributed databases: Principles and systems.* New York: McGraw-Hill.

Chan, B. Y., Si, A., & Leong, H. V. (1998). Cache management for mobile databases: Design and evaluation. In *Proceedings of the International Conference on Data Engineering (ICDE)* (pp. 54-53).

Chang, K., & Kim, D. (2001). Optimal prioritized channel allocation in cellular mobile systems. *European Journal of Operational Research, 28*, 345-356.

Chapin, S. J. (2001). *To InfiniBand ... And Beyond.* Retrieved May 27, 2003, from http://www.networkcomputing.com/1205/1205ws2.html

Chen, K., Xue, Y., & Nahstedt, K. (2003, May). On setting TCP's congestion window limit in mobile ad hoc networks. *Proceedings of the IEEE International Conference on Communication, Anchorage, Alaska.*

Chen, W., & Cai, S. (2005). Ad hoc peer-to-peer network architecture for vehicle safety communications. *IEEE Communications Magazine*, 100-107.

Cheng, J. Z., Yu, H.-C., & Sincoskie, W. D. (2005). Meeting the broadband access infrastructure demands: The promise of Gigabit Ethernet. *Technological Forecasting and Social Change, 72*(1), 1-10.

Cherkasova, L., & Gupta, M. (2004). Analysis of Enterprise Media Server Workload: Access Patterns, Locality, Content Evolution and Rates of Change. *IEEE/ACM Transactions on Networking*, 2004.

Cherkasova, L., Tang, W., & Singhal, S (2004). *An SLA-Oriented Capacity Planning Tool for Streaming Media Services.* Paper presented at DSN2004.

Chesire, M., Wolman, A., Voelker, G., & Lavy, H. (2001). *Measurement and Analysis of a Streaming-Media Workload.* Paper presented at USENIX Symposium on Internet Technologies and Systems.

Cheverst, K., Davies, N., Mitchell, K., & A., F. (2000). Experiences of developing and deploying a context-aware tourist guide. In *Proceedings of the 6th Annual International Conference on Mobile Computing and Networking* (pp. 20-31).

Chiang, T., & Huang, Y. (2004). Multicast Routing Representation in Ad Hoc Networks Using Fuzzy Petri Nets. *Proc. of the 18th Int'l Conf. on Advanced Information Networking and Applications, 2*, 420-423, March 29-31.

Chieng, D., Marshall, A., Ho, I., & Parr, G., (2001). Agent-Enhanced Dynamic Service Level Agreement in Future Network Environment. *Lecture Notes in Computer Science, 21*(16).

Chiussi, F. M., Khotimsky, D. A., & Krishnan, S. (2002, September). Mobility Management in Third-Generation All-IP Networks. *IEEE Communications Magazine, 40*(9), 124-135.

Chlamtac, I., Gumaste, A., & Szabo, C. (2005). *Broadband services: Business models and technologies for community networks.* New York: Wiley Interscience.

Cho, S. B., & Park, H. J. (2003). Efficient anomaly detection by modeling privilege flows using hidden Markov model. *Computer and Security, 22*(1), 45-55.

Chowdhry, P. (1997, September). Can Gigabit Ethernet and RSVP Beat ATM. *PCWeek Magazine.*

Christiansen, M., Jeffay, K., Ott, D., & Smith, F. D. (2001). Tuning RED for Web traffic. *IEEE/ACM Transaction on Networking, 9*(3), 249-264.

Chrysostomou, C., Pitsillides, A., Hadjipollas, G., Sekercioglu, Y. A., & Polycarpou, M. (2003). Fuzzy logic congestion control in TCP/IP best effort networks. *Proceedings of the Australian Telecommunications, Networks, and Applications Conference (ATNAC'03),* Melbourne, Australia.

Chrysostomou, C., Pitsillides, A., Rossides, L., Sekercioglu, Y. A., & Polycarpou, M. (2003). Congestion control in differentiated services networks using Fuzzy-RED. *IFAC Journal Control Engineering Practice, 11*(10), 1153-1170.

Chung, J., & Claypool, M., (2006). Empirical Evaluation of the Congestion Responsiveness of Real Player Video Streams. *Kluwer Multimedia Tools and Applications, 31*(2).

Cisco DOT11 MIB. (n.d.). Cisco DOT11 Association MIB. Retrieved March 29, 2006, from http://www.cisco.com

Cisco Systems. (2002). *Weighted random early detection on the Cisco 12000 Series Router.*

CityLink. (2006). *New Zealand Wellington's case.* Retrieved June 14, 2006, from *http://www.citylink.co.nz*

Comer, D. E. (1991). *Internetworking with TCP/IP* (Volume I). Englewood Cliffs, New Jersey: Prentice Hall

Cooper, G. R., & Nelleton, R. W, (1978). A spread spectrum technique for high capacity mobile commu-

nication. *IEEE Transaction on Vehicular Technology, 27,* 264-275.

Corman, H. T., Leiserson, E. C., Rivest, L. R., & Stein, C. (2001). *Introduction to Algorithms* (2nd Ed.). Boston: McGraw Hill.

Corporation, I. (2003). *Evolution of Gigabit Ethernet: From the Server to the Desktop.* Retrieved June 6, from http://www.intel.com/network/connectivity/resources/doc_library/white_papers/Gigabitevolution.pdf

Cosares, S., Deutsch, D., Saniee, I., & Wasem, O. (1995). Sonet toolkit: A decision support system for designing robust and cost-effective fiber-optic networks. *Interfaces, 25,* 20-40.

Costa, C., Cunha, I., Borges, A., Ramos, C., Rocha, M., Almeida, J., Ribeiro-Neto, B., (2005). Analyzing Client Interactivity in Streaming Media. *Paper presented at IEEE MMSP'05.*

Cox, J. C., Ross, S. A., & Rubinstein, M. (1979). Option pricing: A simplified approach. *Journal of Financial Economics,* 229-264.

Cranley, N., & Davis, M. (2005). *Performance evaluation of video streaming with background traffic over IEEE 802.11 WLAN networks.* First ACM Workshop on Wireless Multimedia Networking and Performance Modelling, Montreal, Quebec, Canada.

Cranley, N., & Davis, M. (2006). *Performance Evaluation of Video Streaming with Background Traffic over IEEE 802.11 WLAN Networks.* Paper presented at ACM WMuNEP'06, Montreal, Quebec, Canada.

Crow, B. P., Widjaja, I., Kim, L. G., & Sakai, P. T. (1997). *IEEE 802.11 Wireless Local Area Networks. IEEE Communication Magazine, 35*(9), 116–26.

Cunningham, R. K., Lippmann, R. P., Fried, D. J., Garfinkle, S. L., Graf, I., Kendall, K. R., et al. (1999). Evaluating intrusion detection systems without attacking your friends: The 1998 DARPA intrusion detection evaluation. *SANS.*

Curtin, M. (1997). Introduction to Network Security, Retrieved March 6, 2008 from *http://www.interhack.net/pubs/network-security/network-security.html.*

Dalal, A. C., &Perry, E., (2003). A New Architecture for Measuring and Assessing Streaming Media Quality. Paper presented at PAM 2003.

Das, S., Perkins, C., & Royer, E. (2000). Performance comparison of two on-demand routing protocols for ad hoc networks. In *Proceedings of IEEE INFOCOM* (pp. 3-12).

DaSilva, L. A., Midkiff, S. F., Park, J. S., Hadjichristofi, G. C., & Davis, N. J. (2004). Network Mobility and Protocol Interoperability in Ad Hoc Networks. *IEEE Communications Magazine.*

David, W. M., & Beibei, W. (2007). Efficient Statistical Parallel Interference Cancellation for DS-CDMA in Rayleigh Fading Channels. *IEEE Transaction on Wireless Communications, 6*(2), 566-574.

Davis, G., Ein-Dor, P., King, W., & Torkzadeh, R. (2006). IT Offshoring: History, Prospects and Challenges. *Journal of the Association for Information Systems, 7*(11), 770-795.

Deeter, L. D., & Smith, E. A. (1998). Economic design of reliable networks. *IIE Transactions, 30(12)*,1161-1174.

Demirkol, I., Ersoy, C., & Caglayan ,M. U., Delic, H. (2004, May). Location Area Planning and Cell-to-Switch Assignment in Cellular Networks. *IEEE Transactions on Wireless Communications, 3*(3), 880-890.

Denning, D. (1987). An intrusion-detection model. *IEEE Transaction on Software Engineering, 13*(2), 222-232.

Di Fatta, G., Hoffmann, F., Lo Re, G., Urso, A., (2003). A genetic algorithm for the design of a fuzzy controller for active queue management. *IEEE Transactions on Systems, Man, and Cybernetics--Part C, 33*(3), 313-324.

Divsalar, D., & Simon, M. (1996). A new approach to parallel interference cancellation for CDMA. *IEEE Proceedings of GLOBECOM, London, U.K, 1452-1457.*

Divsalar, D., Simon, M., & Raphaeli, D. (1998). Improved parallel interference cancellation for CDMA. *IEEE Transactions on Communication, 46*(2),258-268.

Dixit, A. K. & Pindyck, R. S. (1995). The options approach to capital investment. *Harvard Business Review.*

Dixit, A. K. (1989). Entry and exit decisions under uncertainty. *Journal of Political Economy, 97*(3), 620-638.

Dixit, A. K., & Pindyck, R. S. (1994). *Investment under uncertainty.* Princeton, NJ: Princeton University Press.

Doshi, B., Dravida, S., & Harshavardhana, P. (1995). Overview of INDT: A new tool for next generation network design. In *Proceedings of the IEEE Globecom.* Singapore.

Duong, H., Dadej, A., & Gordon, S. (2005). Proactive context transfer and forced handover in IEEE 802.11 wireless LAN based access networks. *ACM SIGMOBILE Mobile Computing and Communications Review, 9*, 32-44.

Dutta, A., & Kubat, P. (1999). Design of partially survivable network for cellular telecommunication systems. *European Journal of Operational Research, 118*(1), 52-64.

EC (European Commission). (2002). *eEurope 2005: An information society for all.* Retrieved January 13, 2006, from http://ec.europa.eu/information_society/eeurope/2002/news_library/documents/eeurope2005/eeurope2005_en.pdf

EC. (2003). *Guidelines on criteria and modalities of implementation of structural funds in support of electronic communications.* Retrieved January 10, 2006, from http://ec.europa.eu/regional_policy/consultation/telecom_en.htm

Economides, N. (1996). The economics of networks. *International Journal of Industrial Organization, 14*(4), 673-699.

Efron, B. (1979). Bootstrap methods: Another look at the jackknife. *Annals of Statistics, 7,* 1-26.

Efron, B., & Tibshirani, E. R. (1986). Bootstrap methods for standard errors, confidence intervals, and other measures of statistical accuracy. S*tatistical Science, 1*(1), 57-77.

Efron, B., & Tibshirani, E. R. (1994). *An introduction to the bootstrap.* London: Chapman & Hall.

Eichler, S. (2004). Security challenges in MANET-based telematics environments. Tenth *Open European Summer School and IFIP WG 6.3 Workshop* (pp. 196-203).

Eichler, S., Schwingenschlögl, C., Dötzer, F., & Eberspächer, J. (2004). Secure routing in a vehicular ad hoc network. *IEEE Vehicular Technology Conference: Wireless Technologies for Global Security,* Los Angeles, CA (pp. 3339-43).

Elbaum, R., & Sidi, M. (1996). Topological design of local area networks using genetic algorithms. *IEEE/ACM Transactions on Networking, 4*, 766-778.

Elkan, C. (2000). Results of the KDD'99 classifier learning contest. *ACM Transactions on Information and System Security, 3*(4), 262-294.

Elmargamid, A., Jing, J., Helal, A., & Lee, C. (2003). Scalable cache invalidation algorithms for mobile data access. *IEEE Transactions on Knowledge and Data Engineering, 15*(6), 1498-1511.

Europa. (2004). *Challenges for Europe's Information Society beyond 2005: Starting point for a new EU strategy.* Retrieved January 13, 2006, from http://europa.eu/rapid/pressReleasesAction.do?reference=IP/04/1383

Europa. (2006). *Broadband access in the EU: Situation at 1 July 2006.* Retrieved February 9, 2007, from http://forum.europa.eu.int/Public/irc/infso/cocom1/library?l=/public_documents_2006&vm=detailed&sb=Title

Fahmy, H., & Douligeris, C. (1995). END: An expert network designer. *IEEE Network*, 18-27.

Fall, K., & Floyd, S. (1996, July). Simulation-based comparisons of Tahoe, Reno, and SACK TCP. *Computer Communications Review.*

Fan, L., Cao, P., & Almeida, J. (1998). Summary cache: A scalable wide area web cache sharing protocol. In *Proceedings of ACM SIGCOMM*, ACM Press (pp. 254-265).

Fawer, U., & Aazhang, B. (1995). Multi-user receiver for code division multiple access communication over multipath channels. *IEEE Transactions on Communication, 43*(234), 1556-1565.

Federal Communications Commission. (2004). *Notice of proposed rulemaking in the matter of IP-enabled services.* WC Docket Number 04-36.

Feldmann, A., Caceres, R., Douglis, F., Glass, G., & Rabinovich, M. (1999). Performance of Web proxy caching in heterogeneous bandwidth environments. In *Proceedings of the 18th Conference of the IEEE Computer and Communications Society* (pp. 107-116).

Firth, L., & Mellor, D. (2005). Broadband: Benefits and problems. *Telecommunications Policy, 29*(2-3), 223-236.

Floyd S., & Fall, K. (1999, August). Promoting the use of end-to-end congestion control in the Internet. *IEEE/ACM Transactions on Networking, 7*(4), 458–472.

Floyd, S. (1995, October). TCP and explicit congestion notification. *ACM Computer Communication Review, 24*, 8-23.

Floyd, S., & Jacobson, V. (1993). Random early detection gateways for congestion avoidance. *IEEE/ACM Transaction Networking, 1*(4), 397-413.

Floyd, S., & Jacobson, V. (1993, August). Random early detection gateways for congestion avoidance. *IEEE/ACM Transactions on Networking, 1*(4).

Floyd, S., Gummadi, R., & Shenker, S. (2001). *Adaptive RED: An algorithm for increasing the robustness of RED's active queue management.* Retrieved January 18, 2008, from http://www.icir.org/floyd/red.html

Frogner, B., & Cannara, A. (1999). Monitoring and Prediction of Network Performance. In *the Proceedings of the International Workshop on Advance Issues of E-Commerce and Web-Based Information Systems* (pp. 122-129). Santa Clara, CA.

Ganslandt, M. (2001). *Strategic investment and market integration* (IUI Working Paper Series 560). The Research Institute of Industrial Economics.

Gao, B., Ma, H., & Yang, Y. (2002). HMMS (hidden Markov models) based on anomaly intrusion detection method. In *Proceedings of the First International Conference on Machine Learning and Cybernetics* (pp. 381-385).

García, M., Pañeda, X. G., García, D. F., García, D. F., García, V. G., & Arias, J. R, (2001). *A Tool for Performance Prediction of an HFC Operator Based on a Queuing Network Model Simulation.* Paper presented at SPECTS-2001. Orlando, USA.

García, R., Pañeda, X. G., García V., Melendi, D., & Vilas, M. (2007). Statistical characterization of a rela video on demand service: User behaviour and streaming-media workload analysis. *Simulation Modelling Practice and Theory.* Elsevier.

Gardiner, J., & West, B. (1995). *Personal Communication System and Technologies*, Boston: Artech House.

Gen, M., & Cheng, R. (2000). *Genetic Algorithm and Engineering Optimization*, New York: John Wiley & Sons.

Gerla, M., & Kleinrock, L. (1977). On the topological design of distributed computer networks. *IEEE Transactions on Communications, 25*, 48-60.

Gerla, M., & Tsai, J. T. C. (1995). Multicluster, mobile, multimedia radio network. *Wireless Networks, 1*(3), 255-265.

Gersht, A., & Weihmayer, R. (1990). Joint optimization of data network design and facility selection. *IEEE Journal on Selected Areas in Communications, 8*(9), 1667-1681.

Ghosh, J., Beal, M. J., Ngo, H. Q., & Qiao, C. (2006). *On profiling and predicting locations of campus-wide wireless network users.* Paper presented at ACM/SIG-MOBILE MobiHoc 2006, Florence, Italy.

Ghosh, S., Razouqi, Q., Schmacher, H. J., & Celmins, A. (1998). A Survey of Recent Advances in Fuzzy Logic in Telecomunications Networks and New Challenges. *IEEE Trans. on Fuzzy System*s, *6*(3), 443–447.

Gigabit Ethernet Alliance. (1998). *Gigabit Ethernet: Accelerating the standard for speed.* Retrieved June 6, 2003, from http://www.10gea.org/GEA-Acce1999_rev_wp.pdf

Ginnakis, G. B., Hua, Y., Stocia, P., & Tong, L. (2000). *Signal Processing Advances in Wireless and Mobile Communications VOL: 2 Trends in single- and Multi-user systems, Prentice Hall, New Jersey.*

Gomathy, C., & Shanmugavel, S. (2004). An Efficient Fuzzy Based Priority Scheduler for Mobile Ad hoc Networks and Performance Analysis for Various Mobility Models. *Proc. of the IEEE Wireless Communications and Networking Conference, 2,* 1087–1092, March 21-25.

Gomathy, C., & Shanmugavel, S. (2004). Effect of Packet Scheduling and Evaluation of Fuzzy Based Priority Scheduler on Ad hoc Network Unicast Communication. *Proc. of the IEEE Int'l Conf. on Signal Processing and Communications,* 506–510, Atlanta, USA, Dec. 11-14.

Gomathy, C., & Shanmugavel, S. (2005). Supporting QoS in MANET by a Fuzzy Priority Scheduler and Performance Analysis with Mixed Traffic. *Proc. of the 14th IEEE Int'l Conf. on Fuzzy Systems,* 31–37, Nevada, USA, May 22-25.

Gomathy, C., & Shanmugavel, S. (2005). Supporting QoS in MANET by a Fuzzy Priority Scheduler and Performance Analysis with Multicast Routing Protocols. *EURASIP Journal on Wireless Communications and Networking, 3,* 426–436.

Goodman, D. J. (1997). *Wireless Personal Communication Systems,* Boston: Addison Wesley.

Graham, J. R., & Harvey, C. R. (2002). How do CFOs make capital budgeting and capital structure decisions. *Journal of Applied Corporate Finance, 15*(1), 823

Grover, V., & Vaswani, P. (2000). Partnerships in the U.S. telecommunications industry. *Communications of the ACM, 43*(2), 80-89.

Grover, V., Cheon, M. J., & Teng, J.T.C.(1996). The effects of service quality and partnership on the outsourcing of information systems functions. *Journal of Management Information system, 12*(4), 89-116.

Guo, L., Tan, E., Chen, S., Xia, Z., Spatscheck, O., & Zhang, X. (2006). *Delving into Internet Streaming Media Delivery: A Quality and Resource Utilization Perspective.* Paper presented at IMC 2006.

Guoqing, L., & Hui, L. (2006). Resource Allocation for OFDMA Relay Networks With Fairness Constraints. *IEEE Journal on Selected Areas in Communications, 24*(11), 2061-2069.

Guoxioing, X., & Liangcai, G. (2005). Parallel interference cancellation with frequency diversity combining for multi-carrier DS-CDMA. *IEEE International Symposium on Microwave, Antenna, Propagation and EMC technologies for Wireless Communications.* (MAPE 2005), *1*(8-12), 297-300.

Gutting, R. H., Bohlen, M. H., Erwig, M., Jensen, C. S., Lorentzos, N. A., Schneider, M., & Vazierginiannis, M. (2000). A foundation for representing and querying moving objects. *ACM Transactions on Database Systems Journal, 25*(1), 1-42.

Habetha, J., & Walke, B. (2002). Fuzzy Rule-Based Mobility and Load Management for Self-Organizing Wireless Networks. *International Journal of Wireless Information Networks, 9*(2), 119-140.

Habib, S., & Parker, A. (2002). Computer-aided system integration tool for predicting enterprise network evolution. In *Proceedings of the Fifteen International Conference on Systems Engineering (ICSEng 2002),* Las Vegas, NV.

Habib, S., Parker, A., & Lee, D. (2002). Automated design of hierarchical intranets. *Computer Communications, 25*(11-12), 1066-1075.

Hadzic, I., & Szurkowski, E. S. (2005). High-Performance Synchronization for Circuit Emulation in an Ethernet MAN. *Journal Of Communication and Networks, 7*(1), pp.1-12.

Hara, T. (2002). Replica allocation in ad hoc networks with periodic data update. In *Proceedings of the 3rd International Conference on Mobile Data Management* (pp. 79-86).

Helix Server Project. (n.d.). Retrieved March 29, 2006, from https://helix-server.helixcommunity.org/

Helman, P., & Liepins, G. (1993). Statistical foundations of audit trail analysis for the detection of computer misuse. *IEEE Transactions on Software Engineering, 19*(9), 886-901.

Henderson, A., Gentle, I., & Ball, E. (2005). WTO principles and telecommunications in developing nations: Challenges and consequences of accession. *Telecommunications Policy, 29*(2-3), 205-221.

Herbert, J. (2003). *Issues in Resilient Network Design,* March 2003, International Network Services Inc.

Heusse, M., Rousseau, F., Berger-Sabbatel, G., & Duda, A. (2003). *Performance anomaly of 802.11b.* Paper presented at IEEE Infocom 2003, San Francisco.

Higgins, T. (2003). *Need-To-Know: Gigabit Ethernet - Part 1.* Retrieved June 6, from http://www6.tomshardware.com/network/20030304/Gigabit-04.html

Hiller, F., & Lieberman, G. (2005). *Introduction to Operations Research* (8th Ed.). New York: McGraw Hill.

Hills, A. (2001). Large-Scale Wireless LAN Design. *IEEE Communication Magazine, 39*(11), 98–104.

Hills, A. (2004). Radio Resource Management in Wireless LANs. *IEEE Radio Communications.* http://www.stat.sc.edu/~west/applets/binomialdemo.html

HNF, (1998). *High Performance Networking Forum,* Retrieved November, 17, 2007 from *www.hnf.org.*

Hochmuth, P. (2003). *Category 6 cabling not ready.* Retrieved May 27, from http://www.nwfusion.com/news/2002/128588_01-07-2002.html

Holland, G., & Vaidya, N. H. (1999, August). Analysis of TCP performance over mobile ad hoc networks. *Proceedings of the ACM MOBICOM, Seattle, WA, USA.*

Horstmann, I. J., & Markusen, J. R. (1987). Strategic investments and the development of multinationals. *International Economic Review, Department of Economics, University of Pennsylvania and Osaka University Institute of Social and Economic Research Association, 28*(1), 109-121.

Hosmer, D. W., & Lemeshow, S. (2000). *Applied logistic regression* (2nd ed.). New York: John Wiley & Sons.

Houdt, B. V., & Blondia, C. (2000). Performance Evaluation of the Identifier Splitting Algorithm with Polling in Wireless ATM Networks. *International Journal of Wireless Information Networks, 7*(2).

Hu, Y.C., Johnson, D., & Perrig, A. (2002). SEAD: Secure efficient distance vector routing for mobile wireless ad hoc networks. *Fourth IEEE Workshop on Mobile Computing Systems and Applications,* Callicoon, NY (pp. 3-13).

Hu, Y.C., Perrig, A., & Johnson, D. (2002). Ariadne: A secure on-demand routing protocol for ad-hoc networks. *Eighth ACM International Conference on Mobile Computing and Networking* (*MOBICOM*), Atlanta, GA (pp. 21-38).

Huang, C., Lai, W. K., Hsiao, S., & Liu, H. (2005). A Self-Adaptive Zone Routing Protocol for Bluetooth Scatternets. *Computer Communications,* Elsevier, *28*(1), 37-50.

Huang, C., Lai, W. K., Hsiao, S., Liuand, H., & Luo, R. (2004). A Bluetooth Routing Protocol Using Evolving Fuzzy Neural Networks. *International Journal of Wireless Information Networks,* Springer, Netherlands, *11*(3), 131-146.

Hubaux, J.P., Buttyan, L., & Capkun, S. (2001). The quest for security in mobile ad hoc networks. *Third ACM Symposium on Mobile Ad Hoc Networking and Computing* (*MOBIHOC*), Long Beach, CA (pp. 146-155).

Hughes-Jones, R., Clarke, P., & Dallison, S. (2005). Performance of 1 and 10 Gigabit Ethernet cards with server quality motherboards. *Future Generation Computer Systems, 21*(4), 469-488.

Hung, D. L. (1995). Dedicated digital fuzzy hardware. *IEEE Micro, 15*(4), 31-39.

Hurson, A. R., & Jiao, Y. (2005). Data broadcasting in mobile environment. In D. Katsaros, A. Nanopoulos, & Y. Manolopaulos (Eds.), *Wireless information highways.* London: IRM Press Publisher.

Hwang, I., Liu, C., & Wang, C. (2002). Link Stability-Based Clustering and Routing in Ad-Hoc Wireless Networks Using Fuzzy Set Theory. *International Journal of Wireless Information Networks, 9*(3), 201–212.

Iannaccone, G., May, M., & Diot, C. (2001). Aggregate traffic performance with active queue management and drop from tail. *ACM SIGCOMM Computer Communication Review,* July.

IDC. (2004). 2000 *Disk Storage System Forecast & Analysis (1999-2004),* Report (IDC #B23768).

IEEE 802.11 (1997). IEEE Standard. *Wireless LAN Medium Access Control (MAC) and Physical Layer (PHY) Specifications.*

IEEE 802.11a (1999). *IEEE standard. Wireless LAN Medium Access Control (MAC) and Physical Layer (PHY) Specifications: High Speed Layer in the 5 GHz Band.*

Intel Corporation. (2003). *Evolution of Gigabit Ethernet: From the Server to the Desktop.* Retrieved June 6, from http://www.intel.com/network/connectivity/resources/doc_library/white_papers/Gigabitevolution.pdf

Intel Corporation. (2003). *Gigabit Ethernet: Technology and Solutions.* Retrieved May 27, from http://www.intel.com/network/connectivity/resources/doc_library/white_papers/Gigabit_Ethernet/Gigabit_Ethernet.pdf

Intel. (2006). Accelerating High-Speed Networking with Intel® I/O Acceleration Technology, Retrieved January 10, 2008 from *http://www.idgconnect.com/networking/networkmanagement/accelerating_high_speed_networking_with_intel_i_o_acceleration_technology.*

ITU. (2006). *Construction, installation and protection of cables and other elements of outside plant.* Retrieved June 14, 2006, from http://www.itu.int/rec/T-REC-L/e

Ivanovici, M., & Beuran, R. (2006). *User Perceived Quality Assessment for Multimedia Applications.* Paper presented at OPTIM'06.

Jacobson, V. (1988, August). Congestion avoidance and control. *ACM Computer Communication Review, 18,* 314-329.

Janowski, D. D. (2003). Gigabit Ethernet: Making the Switch. *PC Magazine, 22,* 113-121.

Jayaputera, J., & Taniar, D. (2005). Data Retrieval for Location-Dependent Query in a Multi-cell Wireless Environment. *Mobile Information Systems: An International Journal,* IOS Press, *1*(2), 91-108.

Jayaputera, J., & Taniar, D. (2005). Query Processing Strategies for Location-Dependent Information Services. *International Journal of Business Data Communications and Networking, 1*(2), pp. 17-40

Jefery, G., Andrews, T., Meng, T. H. Y. (2004). Performance of multi-carrier CDMA with successive interference cancellation in a multipath fading channel. *IEEE Transactions on Communication Technology, 52*(5), 811-822.

Jin, S., & Bestavros, A., (2001). *GISMO, A Generator of Internet Streaming Objects and Workloads.* Paper presented at ACM SIGMETRICTS.

Jin, S., Guo, L., Matta, I., & Bestavros, A. (2001, July). A spectrum of TCP-friendly window-based congestion control algorithms. *Technical Report BU-CS-2001-015, Computer Science Department, Boston University.* Available at: http://www.cs.bu.edu/techreports/2001-015-spectrum-tcp-friendly.ps.Z.

Johnson, D., & Malta, D. (1996). Dynamic source routing in ad hoc wireless network. In *Mobile Computing,* edited by T. Imielinski & H. Korth, Kluwer Academic Publishers, Chapter 5, (pp. 153-181).

Johnson, H. (1987). Options on the maximum or the minimum of several assets. *Journal of Financial and Quantitative Analysis, 22*(3), 277-283.

Jung, II, D., You, Y. H., Lee, J. J., & Kim, K. (2002). Broadcasting and caching policies for location-dependent queries in urban areas. In *Proceedings of the of the 2nd International Workshop on Mobile Commerce* (pp. 54-59).

Kapp, S. (2002). 802.11: Leaving the wire behind. *IEEE Internet Computing, 6.*

Kassab, M., Belghith, A., Bonnin, J., & Sassi, S. (2005). *Fast preauthentication based on proactive key distribution for 802.11 infrastructure networks.* Paper presented at ACM WMuNeP 2005, Montreal, Quebec, Canada.

Katzela, I., & Schwarz, M. (1995). Schemes for Fault Identification in Communication Networks. *IEEE/ACM Transactions on Networking, 3*(6), 753–764.

Kauffman, R. J., & Li, X. (2005). Technology competition and optimal investment timing: A real options model. (forthcoming). *IEEE Transactions on Engineering Management, 52*(1), 15-29.

Kbar, G., & Mansoor, W. (2005). *Mobile Station Location based on Hybrid of Signal Strength and Time of Arrival.* International Conference on Mobile Business ICMB2205, Sydney. Australia July 11-13.

KDD Cup. (1999). *Data available on the Web.* Retrieved February 19, 2005, from http://kdd.ics.uci.edu/databases/kddcup99/kddcup99.html

Keynote (2006). Streaming Perspective StreamQ, Retrieved 12th of November from http://www.keynote.com/

Khanna, T., Palepu, K., & Vargas, I. (2003). Bharti Tele-Ventures. Case No: 9-704-426. Boston, MA: Harvard Business School.

Khoukhi, L., & Cherkaoui, S. (2005). FuzzyMARS: A Fuzzy Logic Approach with Service Differentiation for Wireless Ad hoc Networks. *Proc. of the IEEE Int'l Conf. on Wireless Networks, Communications, and Mobile Computing, 2,* 839–844, June 13-16.

Kirov, G. (2005). A simulation analysis of the TCP control algorithms. *Proceedings of the International Conference on Computer Systems and Technologies.*

Kokje, T., & Kakadia, V. (2007). Analysis of congestion control strategies for TCP variants using droptail and RED queuing disciplines. *Unpublished Technical Report, Department of Computer Science University of Southern California, Los Angeles.*

Kompella, K., & Rekhter, Y. (2005, December 28). *Virtual private LAN service.* Internet Draft (draft-ietf-l2vpn-vpls-bgp-06).

Kondo, S., & Milstein, B. (1994). Multi-carrier DS-CDMA systems in the presence of partial band interference. *IEEE Military Communication Conference, MILCOM-94, 2,* 588-592.

Kondo, S., & Milstein, L. B. (1996). Performance of Multicarrier DS-CDMA systems. *IEEE Transaction on Communication, 44*(2), 238-246.

Kong, J., Zerfos, P., Luo, H., Lu, S., & Zhang, L. (2001). Providing robust and ubiquitous security support for mobile ad-hoc networks. *Ninth International Conference on Network Protocols* (ICNP) (pp. 251-260).

Koucheryavy, Y., Moltachanov, D., & Harju, J. (2003). Performance evaluation of live video streaming in 802.11b WLAN environment under different load conditions. *Lecture Notes in Computer Science, 2889,* 30–41.

Koyama, A., Barolli, L., Capi, G., Apduhan, B. O., Arai, J. & Durresi, A. (2004). An efficient multi-purpose optimization method for qos routing using genetic algorithm. *Journal of Interconnection Networks, 5*(4), 409-428..

Krunz, M. (1998). Lecture Notes for ECE 564—fall 1998. *Broadband Networks and Multimedia Communications.* University of Arizona.

Kulatilaka, N., & Marks, S. (1988). The strategic value of flexibility: Reducing the ability to compromise. *American Economic Review, 78*(3), 574-580.

Kulatilaka, N., & Perotti, E. (1998). Strategic growth options. *Management Science, 44*(8), 1021-1031.

Kwan, M., Dogancay, K., & Jain, L. (2003). Fair Multipath Selection for Real-Time Video Transmission in Ad-Hoc Networks Using Artificial Intelligence. *Proc. of the Design and Application of Hybrid Intelligent System, 104,* 830-841, Melbourne, Australia, Dec. 14-17.

Kyriazakos, S., & Karetsos G.(2004). Practical resource management in wireless systems. *Book reviews IEEE Communications Magazine.*

Lacity, M. C., & Hirschheim, R. (1993). *Information Systems Outsourcing: Myths, Metaphors and Reality.* New York, NY: John Wiley & Sons.

Lacity, M. C., Willcocks, L. P. & Feeny, D. F. (1996). The value of selective IT outsourcing. *Sloan Management Review., 37,* 13-25.

Lai, K. C., & Shynk, J. J. (2000). Error-rate analysis of the adaptive successive interference canceller for DS-CDMA signals. *Proceedings of IEEE International Conference on Acoustics, Spread and Signal Processing (ICASSP)'2000.*

Latva-Aho, M., Juntti, M., & Heikkila, M. (1996). Parallel interference cancellation receiver for DS-CDMA systems in fading channels. *IEEE 8th International Symposium on Personal, Indoor and Mobile radio Communications, 2,* 559-564.

Lee, D. K., Xu, J., Zheng, B., & Lee, W. C. (2002). Data management in location-dependent information services. *IEEE Pervasive Computing, 2*(3), 65-72, July-Sept.

Lee, D. K., Zhu, M., & Hu, H. (2005). When location-based services meet databases. *Mobile Information Systems, 1*(2), 2005.

Lee, D., Choi, J., Choe, H., Noh, S. H., Min, S. L., & Cho, Y. (1997). Implementation and performance evaluation of the LRFU replacement policy. In *Proceedings of the 23rd Euromicro Conference* (pp. 106-111).

Lee, J. (2006). Outsourcing Alignment with Business Strategy and Firm Performance. *Communications of the Association of Information Systems, 17,* 1124-1146.

Lee, K. C. K., Leong, H. V., & Si, A. (2002). Semantic data access in an asymmetric mobile environment. In *Proceedings of the 3rd Mobile Data Management* (pp. 94-101).

Lee, W., Stolfo, S., & Mok, K. (1999). A data mining framework for building intrusion detection models. In *Proceedings of the IEEE Symposium on Security and Privacy* (pp. 120-132).

Leida, B. (1998). *A cost model of internet service providers: Implications for internet telephony and yield management.* MIT Master Thesis.

Li, J., Kameda, H., & Li, K. (2000, June). Optimal Dynamic Mobility Management for PCS Networks. *IEEE/ACM Trans. Networking, 8*(3), 319-327.

Li, M., Li, F., Claypool, M., & Kinicki, R. (2005). *Weather forecasting—predicting performance for streaming video over wireless LANs.* Paper presented at ACM NOSSDAV 2005, Stevenson, WA.

Li, Z., Zhang, Z., Addie R., & Clerot, F. (2003). Improving the adaptability of AQM algorithms to traffic load using fuzzy logic. *Proceedings of the Australian Telecommunications, Networks, and Applications Conference (ATNAC'03)*, Melbourne, Australia.

Liang, Q. & Ren Q. (2005). Energy and Mobility Aware Geographical Multipath Routing for Wireless Sensor Networks. *Proc. of the IEEE Wireless Communications and Networking, 3*, 1867–1871, March 13-17.

Liang, Q. (2003). A Design Methodology for Wireless Persona Area Networks with Power Efficiency. *Proc. of the IEEE Wireless Communications and Networking, 3*, 1475–1480, March 16-20.

Liang, Q. (2003). Designing Power Aware Self-Reconfiguring Topology for Mobile Wireless Personal Area Networks Using Fuzzy Logic. *IEEE Transactions on Systems, Man, and Cybernetics—Part C: Applications and Reviews, 33*(3), 390–394.

Liang, Q. (2003). Clusterhead Election for Mobile Ad Hoc Wireless Network. *Proc. of the 14th IEEE Proceedings on Personal, Indoor and Mobile Radio Communications, 2*, 1623–1628, Sept. 7-10.

Liang, Q. (2005). Fault-Tolerant and Energy Efficient Wireless Sensor Networks: A Cross-Layer Approach. *Proc. of the IEEE Military Communications Conference*, 1–7, Oct. 17-20.

Liao, Y., & Gao, L. (2006). *Practical schemes for smooth MAC layer handoff in 802.11 wireless networks.* Paper presented at IEEE WoWMoM 2006, Niagara Falls, Buffalo, NY.

Liberatore, V. (2002). Multicast scheduling for list requests". In *Proceedings of IEEE INFOCOM Conference* (pp. 1129-1137).

Lim, S. Y., Taniar, D., & Srinivasan, B. (2006). A taxonomy of database operations on mobile devices.

Handbook of Research on Mobile Multimedia, accepted for publication, 2006.

Lim, S., Lee, W. C., Cao, G., & Das, C. R. (2003). A novel caching scheme for internet based mobile ad hoc networks. In *Proceedings of the IEEE International Conference on Computer Communications and Networks (ICCCN)*, (pp. 38-43).

Lin, D., & Morris, R. (1997). Dynamics of random early detection. *Proceedings ACM SIGCOMM.*

Lin, F., & Milstein, L. B. (2000). Successive interference cancellation in multicarrier DS/CDMA. *IEEE Transactions on Communications, 48*(9),1530-1540.

Lin, W., Wong, A., & Dillon, T. (2005). A novel Fuzzy Logic Controller (FLC) for shortening the TCP channel roundtrip time by eliminating user buffer overflow adaptively. *Proceedings of the 28th Australasian Computer Science Conference (ACSC2005), 38*, 29-38, Newcastle, Australia.

Lippman, R., & Cunningham, S. (2000). Improving intrusion detection performance using keyword selection and neural networks. *Computer Networks, 34*(4), 594-603.

Liu, F., & Yang, C. (2004). Proxy Design for Improving the Efficiency of Stored MPEG-4 FGS Video Delivery over Wireless Networks. *Journal of Communication and Networks, 6*, 280-286.

Liu, H., Li, J., Zhang, Y., & Pan, Y. (2005). An Adaptive Genetic Fuzzy Multi-path Routing Protocol for Wireless Ad-Hoc Networks. *Proc. of the 1st ACIS Int'l Workshop on Self-Assembling Wireless Networks (SAWN 2005)*, 468–475, Maryland, USA, May 23-25.

Lo, E., Mamoulis, N., Cheung, D. W., Ho, W. S., & Kalnis, P. (2003). In *Processing ad-hoc joins on mobile devices.* Technical report, The University of Hong Kong (2003). Retrieved from http://www.csis.hku.hk/~dbgroup/techreport

Localret. (2006). *The case of Barcelona.* Retrieved June 14, 2006, from http://www.localret.net/idiomes/english.htm

Loguinov, D., & Radha, H. (2001). *Measurement Study of Low-bitrate Internet Video Streaming.* Paper presented at ACM SIGCOMM Internet Measurement Workshop. San Francisco, USA.

Loguinov, D., & Radha, H. (2002). Retransmission Schemes for Streaming Internet Multimedia: Evaluation

Model and Performance Analysis. *ACM SIGCOMM Computer Communication Review (CCR)*, *32*(2).

Loh, L., & Venkatraman, N. (1992). Diffusion of information technology outsourcing: influence sources and the Kodak effect. *Information Systems Research*, *3*, 334-58.

Loh, L., & Venkatraman, N. (1992). Determinants of IT outsourcing: A cross-sectional analysis. *Journal of Management Information Systems*, *9*, 7-24.

Lu, H., & Denko, M. K. (2004). Reliable data storage and dissemination in mobile ad hoc network. In *Proceedings of the International Workshop on Theoretical and Algorithmic Aspects of Wireless Ad Hoc, Sensor and Peer-to-Peer Networks* (pp. 81-86).

Lu, H., & Denko, M. K. (2005). Replica update strategies in mobile ad hoc networks. In *Proceedings of the 2nd IEEE/IFIP International Conference on Wireless and Optical Communications Networks* (WOCN 2005).

Luehrman, T. A. (1998). Strategy as a portfolio of real options. *Harvard Business Review*, 89-99.

Ma, H., Hu, Z., & Wang, G. (2004). A Reliable Routing Algorithm in Mobile Ad Hoc Networks Using Fuzzy Petri Net. *Proc. of the IEEE Global Telecommunications Conference Workshops*, 80–84, 29 Nov.-3 Dec..

Madhow, U., Honig, M. L., & Steiglitz, K. (1995). Optimization of Wireless Resources for Personal Communications Mobility Tracking. *IEEE/ACM Trans. Networking*, *3*(6), 698-707.

Madria, S. K., Bhargava, B., Pitoura, E., & Kumar, V. (2000). Data organisation for location-dependent queries in mobile computing. In *Proceedings of ADBIS-DASFAA* (pp. 142-156).

Magnago, A. (2004). Open access business models and operational costs. *Proceedings of the Broadband Europe International Conference 2004*, Brugge, Belgium.

Mahajan, V. & Peterson, R. (1985). *Models for Innovation Diffusion*, Sage Publications, Beverly Hills, CA.

Mahoney, J. T. (1992). Organizational economics within the conversation of strategic management. *Advances in Strategic Management*, *8*, 103-156.

Malinen, J. (n.d.). *HostAP driver*. Retrieved August 7, 2006, from http://hostap.epitest.fi/

Malladi, R., & Davis, K. C. (2002). Applying multiple query optimization in mobile databases. In *Proceedings*

of the 36th *Hawaii International Conference on System Sciences* (pp. 294-303).

Mamoulis, N., Kalnis, P., Bakiras, S., & Li, X. (2003). Optimization of spatial joins on mobile devices. In *Proceedings of the SSTD*.

Margrabe, W. (1978). The value of an option to exchange one asset for another. *Journal of Finance, 33*, 177-186.

Marlatt. (1998). IP telephony sees price wars. *Internet World*. http://www.interworld.com/ print/19998/04/06/ispworld/19980406-wars.html

Marti S., Giuli, T., Lai, K., & Baker, M. (2000). Mitigating routing misbehavior in mobile ad hoc networks. *Sixth Annual International Conference on Mobile Computing and Networking* (*MOBICOM*), Boston (pp. 255-265).

Martinez-Jerez, A., & Narayanan, V. G. (2006). Strategic Outsourcing at Bharti Airtel Limited. One Year Later. Case No: 9-107-003. Boston, MA: Harvard Business School.

Martinez-Jerez, A., & Narayanan, V.G. (2006). Strategic Outsourcing at Bharti Airtel Limited. Case No: 9-107-004. Boston, MA: Harvard Business School.

Marwaha, S., Srinivasan, D., Tham, C. K., & Vasilakos, A. (2004). Evolutionary Fuzzy Multi-Objective Routing for Wireless Mobile Ad Hoc Networks. *IEEE Congress on Evolutionary Computation (CEC2004)*, *2*, 1964–1971, USA, June 19-23.

Masum, S., Ye, E. M., Chen, Q., & Noh, K. (2000). Chi-square statistical profiling for anomaly detection. In *Proceedings of the 2000 IEEE Workshop on Information Assurance and Security* (pp. 182-188).

May, M., Bolot, J., Diot, C., & Lyles, B. (1999). Reasons not to deploy RED. *Proceedings of the 7th International Workshop on Quality of Service (IWQoS'99)*, 260-262.

McDonald, R., & Siegel, D. (1986). The value of waiting to invest. *Quarterly Journal of Economics*, *101*, 707-727.

McFarlan, F. W., & Nolan, R. L. (1995). How to manage an IT outsourcing alliance. *Sloan Management Review*, *36*, 9-22.

McKnight, L. W., & Bailey, J. P. (Eds.). (1997). *Internet economics*. Cambridge, MA: MIT Press.

McKnight, L. W., & Leida, B. (1998). Internet telephony: Costs, pricing, and policy. *Telecommunications Policy*, *22*(7), 555-569.

McNamara, K. (2001). *Gigabit Ethernet*. Retrieved June 17, 2003, from http://beradio.com/microsites/magazinearticle.asp?mode=print&magaszinearticleid=13

Meirosu, C., Golonka, P., Hirstius, A., Stancu, S., Dobinson, B., Radius, E., et al. (2005). Native 10 Gigabit Ethernet experiments over long distances. *Future Generation Computer Systems, 21*(4), 457-468.

Melendi, D. (2007). Configuración, despliegue y evaluación de servicios de audio y video en directo sobre redes heterogéneas *(Configuration, Deployment and Evaluation of Live Audio and Video Services over Heterogeneous Networks)*. PhD Thesis. University of Oviedo.

Mena, A., & Heidemann, J., (2000). *An Empirical Study of Real Audio Traffic*. Paper presented at IEEE Infocom, pp. 101-110. Tel-Aviv, Israel.

Menascé, D. A., & Almeida, V. A. F, (2000). *Scaling for E-Business: Technologies, Models, Performance and Capacity Planning*. Prentice Hall.

Merchant, A., & Sengupta, B. (1995, October). Assignment of Cells to Switches in PCS Networks. *IEEE/ACM Trans. Networking, 3*(5), 521-526.

Metro Ethernet Forum. (2006). *Homepage*. Retrieved June 14, 2006, from http://www.metroethernetforum.org

Mhatre, V., & Papagiannaki, K. (2006). *Using smart triggers for improved user performance in 802.11 wireless networks*. Paper presented at ACM Mobysis 2006, Uppsala. Sweden.

Michael, L. (2001). Adaptive layered data structure for inter-vehicle communication in ad-hoc communication networks. *Eighth World Congress on Intelligent Transportation Systems* (*ITS*) (pp. 1-11).

Michalewicz, Z. (1994) *Genetic algorithms + data structures = evolution programs*. Berlin, Germany: Springer-Verlag.

Mier, E. (1998). Voice-over-IP: Getting started. *Business Communications Review, 28*(5).

Mishra, A., Shin, M., & Arbaugh, W. (2003). An empirical analysis of the IEEE 802.11 MAC layer handoff process. *ACM SIGCOMM Computer Communication Review, 33*, 93–102.

Misra, V., Gong, W. B., & Towsley, D. (2000). Fluid-based analysis of a network of AQM routers supporting TCP flows with an application to RED. *ACM SIGCOMM Computer Communication Review*, 151-160.

Mitchell, B. (2008). Your Guide to Wireless/Networking, Retrieved January 28, 2008 from compnetworking.about.com/*od/hardwarenetworkgear/g/bldef_switch.htm*.

Mitra, D., Morrison, J., & Ramakrishnan, K. (1998). VPN Designer: A tool for design of multiservice virtual private networks. *Bell Labs Technical Journal, 3*(4), 15-31.

Mohsen, G., & Soleymani, M. R. (2002). Multi stage PIC with power and phase estimation. *Proceedings of IEEE Vehicular Technology Conference' 2002, 3,*1716-1726.

Monath, T., Kristian, N., Cadro, P., Katsianis, D., & Varoutas, D. (2003). Economics of fixed broadband access network strategies. *Communications Magazine, 41*(9), 132-139.

Mooney, C. Z., & Duval, R. D. (1993). *Bootstrapping: A nonparametric approach to statistical inference*. Newbury Park, CA: Sage Publications.

Moore, G. (1965). Cramming more components onto integrated circuits. *Electronics, 38*(8).

Moraru, B., Copaciu, F., Gabriel Lazar, G., & Dobrota V. (2007). Practical analysis of TCP implementations: Tahoe, Reno, NewReno. *Unpublished report, Technical University of Cluj-Napoca.*

Mukkamala, S., Tadiparthi, G. R., Tummala, N., & Janoski, G. (2003). Audit data reduction for intrusion detection. In *Proceedings of the IEEE 2003 International* Joint Conference on Neural Networks (pp. 456-460).

Murray, J. Y., & Kotabe, M. (1999). Sourcing strategies of US companies: a modified transaction—Cost analysis. *Strategic Management Journal, 20*, 791-809.

Murthy, C. S., & Manoj, B. S. (2004). Transport layer and security protocols for ad hoc wireless networks. In *Ad Hoc Wireless Networks: Architectures and Protocol*, 451-504, Prentice Hall, New Jersey, USA.

Murty, K. (1995). *Operations Research: Deterministic Optimization Models*. Upper Saddle River: Prentice Hall.

Myers, B. A., & Beigl M. (2003). Handheld computing. *IEEE Computer Magazine, 36*(9), 27-29.

Nagel, K., & Shreckenberg, M. (1992). A cellular automaton model for freeway traffic. *J. Phisique I, 2*(12), 2221-2229.

Natsheh E., Khatun S., & Jantan A. (2006). Adaptive Fuzzy Route Lifetime for Wireless Ad-hoc Networks. *The International Arab Journal of Information Technology (IAJIT)*, 3(4), 285-292.

Natsheh, E., Jantan, A. B., Khatun, S., & Subramaniam S. (2006). Fuzzy Reasoning Approach for Local Connectivity Management in Mobile Ad-hoc Networks. *International Journal of Business Data Communications and Networking (IJBDCN)*, 2(3), 1-18.

Natsheh, E., Jantan, A. B., Khatun, S., & Subramaniam S. (2007). Intelligent Reasoning Approach for Active Queue Management in Wireless Ad-hoc Networks. *International Journal of Business Data Communications and Networking (IJBDCN)*, 3(1), 16-33.

Natsheh, E., Jantan, A., Khatun, S., & Subramaniam S. (2005). A Fuzzy-Based Routes Lifetime Estimation for Ad-hoc Networks. *Proceeding of the 6th International Arab Conference on Information Technology (ACIT'2005)*, 413-419, Amman, Jordan, Dec. 6-8.

Netcraft Ltd. (2004). June 2004 Web Server Survey, Retrieved September 21, 2005 from *news.netcraft.com/archives/Web Server Survey.html*.

Network Level Resiliency for High Availability (HA) in Ethernet Networks, (2001). Retrieved January 11, 2008 from *www.znyx.com*.

Network Management Basics. (2006). Retrieved March 16, 2008 http://www.cisco.com/univercd/cc/td/doc/cisintwk/ito_doc/nmbasics.htm .

Network Simulator. (2005). Retrieved from http://www.isi.edu/nsnam/ns/

Nichols, J., Claypool, M., Kinicki, R., & Li, M. (2004). *Measurements of congestion responsiveness of Windows Media streaming media*. Paper presented at ACM NOSSDAV'04, Kinsale, County Cork, Ireland.

Nikaein, N., & Bonnet, C. (2002). ALM- Adaptive Location Management Incorporating Fuzzy Logic for Mobile Ad Hoc Networks. *Proc. of 1st Annual Mediterranean Ad Hoc Networking Workshop*, Sardegna, Italy, Sept. 4-6.

Nortel Networks. (2004). Designing a Resilient Network, Retrieved January, 10, 2008. From *http://www.nortel.com/products/01/passport/8600_rss/collateral/nn107680-031804.pdf*.

Nortel Networks. (2004). High-Availability Network for the Healthcare Industry, Retrieved February 19, 2008 from *www.nortelnetworks.com*.

Nowell D. L., & Kleinberg, J. (2003). The link prediction problem for social networks. In *Proceedings of the Twelfth Annual ACM International Conference on Information and Knowledge Management (CIKM'03)* (pp. 556-559). New Orleans, LA.

O'Hara, B., & Petrick, A. (1999). *The IEEE 802.11 Handbook: A Designer's Companion*. IEEE Press.

Odlyzko, A. (1998). The economics of the Internet: Utility, utilisation, pricing, and quality of service. *AT&T Labs – Research*.

Ohsaki, H., & Murata, M. (2004). On packet marking function of active queue management mechanism: should it be linear, concave, or convex? *Proceedings of SPIE's International Symposium on the Convergence of Information Technologies and Communications (ITCom 2004)*.

Ott, T. J., Lakshman, T. V., & Wong, L. (1999). SRED: Stabilized RED. *Proceedings of the IEEE INFOCOM*.

Ozakar, B., Morvan, F., & Hameurlain, A. (2005). Mobile join operators for restricted sources. *Mobile Information Systems*, 1(3).

Özsu, M. T., & Valduriez, P. (1999). Principles of distributed database systems (2nd ed.). Prentice Hall.

Pack, S., & Choi, Y. (2004). Fast handoff scheme based on mobility prediction in public wireless LAN systems. *IEEE Proceeding–Communications, 151*, 489–495.

Pañeda, X. G., García, R., Melendi, D., Vilas, M., García, V. (2007). Popularity analysis of a video-on-demand service with a great variety of subjects. Influence of the subject, video characteristics and new content publication policy. *International Journal of Advanced Media and Communication*. InderScience Inc.

Pañeda, X. G., Melendi, D., Vilas, M., García, R., García., V, & Rodríguez, I. (2007, September). FESORIA: An integrated system for analysis, management and smart presentation of audio/video streaming services. *Multimedia Tool and Applications*. DOI:

Pañeda, X., (2004). Análisis, modelado y configuración de servicios de video bajo demanda sobre redes de cable *(Analysis, modeling and configuration of video-on-demand services over cable networks)*. PhD Thesis. University of Oviedo.

Papadimitratos, P., & Haas, Z. (2002). Secure routing for mobile ad hoc networks, *SCS Communication Networks and Distributed Systems Modeling and Simulation Conference* (pp. 27-31).

Papadopoui, M., & Schulzrinne, H. (2001). Effects of power conservation, wireless coverage and cooperation on data dissemination among mobile devices. In *Proceedings of ACM MobiHoc* (pp. 117-127).

Pearlman, M. R., & Haas, Z. J. (1999). Determining the Optimal Configuration for the Zone Routing Protocol. *IEEE Journal of the Selected Areas in Communications, 17*(8), 1395–1414.

Pereira, F., (2005). *A Triple User Characterization Model for Video Adaptation and Quality of Service Experience.* Paper presented at IEEE MMSP'05.

Perkins, C. E., Belding-Royer, E. M., & Chakeres, I. (2003). Ad Hoc On Demand Distance Vector (AODV) routing. IETF Internet draft, draft-perkins-manet-aodvbis-00.txt, (Work in Progress).

Perkins, C., & Bhagwat, P. (1994). Highly Dynamic Destination-Sequenced Distance-Vector routing (DSDV) for mobile computers. In *Proceedings of ACM SIGCOMM* (pp. 234-244).

Perkins, C., Royer, E. M., & Das, S. R. (2003). *Ad Hoc On-Demand Distance Vector (AODV) routing.* Internet-Draft, draft-ietf-manet-aodv-13.txt (Work in progress).

Pierre S., & Legault, G. (1998). A genetic algorithm for design distributed computer network topologies, *IEEE Transactions on Systems, Man and Cybernetics, 28,* 249-258.

Pindyck, R. S. (1989). Irreversible investment, capacity choice, and the value of the firm. *American Economic Review, 2,* 969-985.

Pinnington, A., & Woolcock, P. (1995). How far is IS/IT outsourcing enabling new organizational structure and competences? *International Journal of Information Management, 15*(5), 353-365.

Pitsillides, A., Sekercioglu, Y. A., & Ramamurthy, G. (1997). Effective control of traffic flow in ATM networks using fuzzy logic based explicit rate marking (FERM). *IEEE Journal on Selected Areas in Communications, 15*(2), 209-225.

Plasser, E., Ziegler, T., & Reichl, P. (2002). On the non-linearity of the RED drop function. *Proceedings of the 15th International Conference on Computer Communication, 1,* 515-534.

Plessel, M. (1999). IEEE and Gigabit Ethernet Alliance Announce Formal Ratification of Gigabit Ethernet Over Copper Standard. *Gigabit Ethernet Alliance Press Release,* Published by the Institute of Electrical and Electronics Engineers, Inc.

Pospischil, R. (1998). Fast internet: An analysis about capacities, price structures and government intervention. *Telecommunications Policy, 22*(9), 745-755.

Prahalad, C. K., & Hamel, G. (1990). The Core Competence of the Corporation. *Harvard Business Review, 68*(3), 79-91.

Proakis, J. G. (1995). *Digital communications.* McGraw-Hill.

Pulin, P., & Holtzman, J. (1994). Analysis of a simple successive interference cancellation scheme in a DS/CDMA system. *IEEE Journal on selected areas in Communications, 12*(5),796-807.

Qin, M., & Hwang, K. (2004). Frequent rules for intrusive anomaly detection with Internet datamining. In *Proceedings of the 13th USENIX Security Symposium* (pp. 456-462).

Qu, D., Vetter, B. M., & Jou, Y. F. (1997). Statistical anomaly detection for link-state routing protocols. In *Proceedings of the 1997 IEEE Symposium on Security and Privacy* (pp. 62-70).

Quinn, J. B., & Hilmer, F. G. (1994). Strategic Outsourcing. *Sloan Management Review, Summer* 43-55.

Raju, G. & Hernandez, G. (2002). Routing in Ad Hoc Networks. *Proc. of the IEEE Int'l Conf. on Systems, Man and Cybernetics, 2,* 291-295, Oct. 6-9.

Raju, G. (2004). Intelligent Distributed Routing Under Constraints and Imprecise State Information. *Proc. of the IEEE Int'l Conf. on Systems, Man and Cybernetics, 4,* 3630-3634, Oct. 10-13.

Raju, G., Hernandez, G., & Zou Q. (2000). Quality of Service Routing in Ad Hoc Networks. *Proc. of the IEEE Wireless Communications and Networking Conference, 1,* 263-265, Sept. 23-28.

Ramani, I., & Savage, S. (2005). *SyncScan: Practical fast handoff for 802.11 infrastructure networks.* Paper presented at *IEEE Infocom* 2005, Miami, FL.

Ramesh, J., & Tsitsiklis, J. N. (2006). A Scalable Network Resource Allocation Mechanism With Bounded

Efficiency Loss. *IEEE Journal on Selected Areas in Commmunications, 24*(5), 992-999.

Rankin, T. (2004). *Cellular South Expands CDMA 1XRTT Network; Data Rollout Planned for Quarter Three.* Retrieved Feb 20, 2008 from http://findarticles.com/p/articles/mi_m0EIN/is_2004_June_1/ai_n6050795.

Rappaport, T. S. (1996). *Wireless Communications: Principles and Practice.* Upper Saddle River: Prentice Hall.

Rayward-Smith, V. J., Osman, I. H., Reeves, C. R., & Simth, G. D. (1996). *Modern Heuristic Search Methods.* New York: John Wiley & Sons.

Rea, S., & Pesch, D. (2004). Multi-metric Routing Decision for Ad Hoc Networks using Fuzzy Logic. *M-Zones White Paper June 04*, white paper 06/04, Ireland.

Rea, S., & Pesch, D. (2004). Multi-Metric Routing Decisions for Ad Hoc Networks using Fuzzy Logic. *Proc. of the 1st IEEE Int'l Symposium on Wireless Communication Systems,* 403–407, Mauritius, Sept. 20-22.

Rea, S., & Pesch, D. (2004). Fuzzy Logic based Multi-Metric Route Management for Ad-hoc Networks using Realistic Mobility Model. *Second International Workshop on Management of Ubiquitous Communications and Services (MUCS 2004),* Dublin, Ireland, Dec. 13-14.

Rea, S., & Pesch, D. (2005). Fuzzy Logic Routing with Load-Balancing using a Realistic Mobility Model. *Proc. of the IEEE 61st Vehicular Technology Conference,* 3, 2105–2109, 30 May-1 June.

RealNetworks (2002). Helix Universal Server Administration Guide.

Regnier, G. et al. (2004, September). TCP Onloading for Data Server. *IEEE Computer,* 46.

Ren, F., Ren, Y., & Shan, X. (2002). Design of a fuzzy controller for active queue management. *Computer Communications, 25*(9), 874-883.

Ren, Q., & Dunham, M. H. (2000). Using semantic caching to manage location-dependent data in mobile computing. In *Proceedings of the 6th International Conference on Mobile Computing and Networking* (pp. 210-221).

Rong, H., Zhigang H., & Hao, M. (2005). A Reliable Routing Algorithm Based on Fuzzy Applicability of F sets in MANET. *Proc. of the 11th Pacific Rim International Symposium on Dependable Computing (PRDC'05),* 245-249, Dec. 12-14.

Rossides, L., Chrysostomou, C., Pitsillides, A., & Sekercioglu, Y. A. (2003). Fuzzy logic controlled RED: Congestion control in TCP/IP differentiated services networks. *Soft Computing Journal, 8*(2), 79-92.

Rousskov, A., & Wessels, D. (1999). Cache digests. *Computer Networks and ISDN Systems, 30*(22-23), 2155-2168.

Rowitch, D. N., & Milstein, L. B. (1999). Convolutionally coded Multicarrier DS-CDMA systems in a multipath fading channel—Part II: Narrowband interference suppression. *IEEE Transaction on Communication, 47*(11), 1729-1736.

Rowitch. D. N., & Milstein, L. B. (1995). Convolutional coding for direct sequence multi-carrier CDMA. *IEEE Proceedings of Military Communication, San Diego, CA (pp.* 55-59).

RTSP Proxy Kit. (n.d.). Retrieved March 29, 2006, from http://sourceforge.net/projects/rtsp

Saarinen, T., & Vepsalainen, A. P. J. (1994). Procurement Strategies for Information Systems. *Journal of Management Information Systems, 11*(2), 187-208

Sailhan, F., & Issarny, V. (2003). Cooperative caching in ad hoc networks. In *Proceedings of the 4th International Conference on Mobile Data Management* (pp. 13-28).

Saksena, V. (1989). Topological analysis of packet networks. *IEEE Journal on Selected Areas in Communications, 7*, 1243-1252.

Saltenis, S., & Jensen, C. S. (2002). Indexing of moving objects for location-based services. *Proceedings of ICDE* (pp. 463-472).

Sanchez-Lacson, E. (2008). *Digitel earmarks $350M for expansion.* Retrieved Feb 20, 2008 from http://business.inquirer.net/money/breakingnews/view_article.php?article_id=113888

Sandro, B., Antonio, C., & Matteo, C. (2007). Radio Planning of Wireless Local Area Network. *Transactions on Networking, 15*(6), 1414-1427.

Sang, W. K., & Young-Jun, H. (2003). Log-Likelihood ratio based successive interference cancellation in CDMA systems. *IEEE vehicular Technology Conference'03,* 4, 2390-2392.

Sanzgiri, K., Dahill, B., Levine, B., Shields, C., & Royer, E. (2002). A secure routing protocol for ad hoc networks. Tenth *IEEE International Conference on Network Protocols (ICNP)* (pp. 78-87).

Saraydar, C. U., Kelly, O. E., & Rose, C. (2000, September). One-Dimensional Location Area Design. *IEEE/ACM Trans. Networking, 49*(5), 1626-1632.

Sarkar, N. I., Byrne, C., & Al-Qirim, N. (2006). Gigabit Ethernet implementation: the case of a large New Zealand organization. *International Journal of Business Data Communications and Networking, 2*(4), 59-77.

Scholtz, R. A. (1982). The origins of spread spectrum communication. *IEEE Transaction on Communication, 30*(5), 822-854.

Seada, K., & Helmy, A. (2002, March). Fairness evaluation experiments for multicast congestion control protocols. *Technical Report 02-757, University of Southern California, CS Department.*

Seada, K., Gupta, S., & Helmy, A. (2002, July). Systematic evaluation of multicast congestion control mechanisms. *Proceedings of the SPECTS.*

Sekercioglu, A., Pitsillides, A., & Vasilakos, A. (2001). Computational Intelligence in Management of ATM Networks: A Survey of Current State of Research. *Soft Computing Journal, 5*, 257-263.

Selsius Systems. (1998). A fundamental shift in telephony networks. Selsius Systems. http://www.selsius.com/literature/sales_literature/ip_pbx.pdf

Serenbetz, J. (1998). Assessing network infrastructure. *NetWorker, 2*, 40-46.

Seskar. I, Pedersen, K. J., Kolding. T. E., & Holtzman, J. (1998). Implementation aspects of successive interference cancellation. *ACM Wireless Networks.*

Seydim, A.Y., Dunham, M. H., & Kumar, V. (2001). Location-dependent query processing. In *Proceedings of the 2nd International Workshop on Data Engineering on Mobile and Wireless Access (MobiDE'01)* (pp. 47-53).

Sherali, H. D., Lee, Y., & Park, T. (2000). New modeling approaches for the design of local access transport area networks. *European Journal of Operational Research, 127(1)*, 94-108.

Shimon, M., & Bellcore. (1996). Multi-user detection for DS-CDMA communications. *IEEE Communications Magazine*, 124-136.

Shin, S., Forte, A. G., Singh, A., & Schulzrinne, H. (2004). *Reducing MAC layer handoff latency in IEEE 802.11 wireless LANs.* Paper presented at ACM MobiWAC 2004, Philadelphia.

Shinusuke, H., & Prasad, R. (1997). 'Overview of Multi-carrier CDMA. *IEEE Communications Magazine*, 126-133.

Shuster, M. S. (1998). Diffusion of network innovation: Implications for adoption of internet services. *MIT Internet Telephony Consortium Semiannual Meeting, Helsinki, Finland*, 20-22.

Shyu, M., Chen, S., Sarinnapakorn, K., & Chang, L. (2003). A novel anomaly detection scheme based on principal component classifier. In *Proceedings of the IEEE Foundations and New Directions of Data Mining Workshop, in Conjunction with the 3rd IEEE International Conference on Data Mining (ICDM)* (pp. 172-179).

Si, A., & Leong, H. V. (1999). Query optimization for broadcast database. *Data and Knowledge Engineering, 29*(3), 351-380.

Simon, V., Huszák, Á., Szabó, S., & Imre, S. (2003). Hierarchical Mobil IPv6 and Regional Registration Optimization, International Conference on Parallel and Distributed Computing. Euro-Par 2003, 26th-29th August, Klagenfurt, Austria, Published at Springer, Lectures Notes in Computer Sciences; 2790, ISBN 3-540-40788-X, pp. 1137-1140.

Simulator. (2000). ns-2 Network Simulator. Available at: http://www.isi.edu/nsnam/ns/.

Sing, S., & Dubey, R. (2004). *The World's Top Off-shoring Locations.* Business Standard, Retrieved 4 October 2004 from World Wide Web http://www.businessworld-india.com.

Sistla, A. P., Wolfson, O., Chamberlain, S., & Dao, S. (1997). Modeling and querying moving objects. In *Proceedings of the 13th International Conference on Data Engineering* (pp. 422-432).

Smit, H. T. J., & Trigeorgis, L. (1999). Growth options, competition and strategy: An answer to the market valuation puzzle. In L. Trigeorgis (Ed.), *Real options and business strategy: Applications to decision making.* Risk Books.

Song, M., Kang, S. W., & Park, K. (2005). On the design of energy-efficient location tracking mechanism in location-aware computing. *Mobile Information Systems, 1*(2), 109-127.

Spence, A. M. (1979). Investment strategy and growth in a new market. *Bell Journal of Economics, 10*(1), 119.

Sridhar, V. (2007). Growth of mobile services across regions of India. *Journal of Scientific & Industrial Research, 66,* 281-289.

Sridhar, V. (2008). *Changing Landscape of the IT Industry.* Retrieved 16 February 2008 from World Wide Web http://www.economictimes.com

Sridhar, V., & Bharadwaj, S. (2006). Growth of Outsourced IT Enabled Services in India: A System Dynamics Approach. In Kehal, H. S., and Singh, V. P. (Eds.) *Outsourcing & Offshoring in the 21st Century: A socio economic perspective.* Hershey, PA, U.S.A.: Idea Publishing, 282-301.

Sridhar, V., Malik, A. (2007). Turning Copper in to Gold: Bharti Airtel's Fixed Line Service in India. *Asia Case Research Centre, University of Hong Kong,* Case Reference No: 07/329C.

Stallings, W. (2003). *Network security essentials, applications and standards* (2nd ed.). NJ: Pearson Education.

Stallings, W. (2007). *Data and computer communications* (8th ed.). New Jersey: Prentice Hall.

Stevens, W. R. (1994, November). TCP/IP illustrated (Volume 1). Reading, MA: Addison-Wesley.

Stone, A. (2003). Has VoIP arrived? *IEEE Internet Computing,* 1011.

Stulz, R. (1982). Options on the minimum or the maximum of two risky assets. *Journal of Financial Economics, 10,* 161-185.

Suárez, F. Pañeda, X. G., & García, V. G. (2002). *Low Cost, Highly Available, High Performance Talks-on-Demand Sytems.* Paper presented at ACM International Multimedia Conference. Juan les Pins, France. 2002.

Sun, M.T., Feng, W.C., Lai, T.H., Yamada, K., & Okada, H. (2000). GPS-based message broadcast for adaptive inter-vehicle communications. *IEEE 52nd Fall Vehicular Technology Conference: Vol. 6* (pp. 2685-2692).

Sundaresan, K., Anantharaman, V., Hsieh, H-Y., & Sivakumar, R. (2003, January). ATP: A reliable transport protocol for ad hoc networks. *Proceedings of the ACM Mobihoc.*

Sweeney, T. (2000). *Gigabit Ethernet Over Copper: Time To Test That Cat-5 Cabling.* Retrieved June 17, 2003, from http://www.internetweek.com/indepth/indepth050800-1.htm

Tan, T. C. (2000). Gigabit Ethernet and structured cabling. *Electronics & Communication Engineering Journal, 12*(4), 156-166.

Tanenbaum, A. S. (1996). *Computer Networks,* 3rd ed. Prentice Hall, Inc.

Taylor, C., & Alves-Foss, J. (2001). "Low cost" network intrusion detection. In *Proceedings of the New Security Paradigms Workshop* (pp. 89-96).

TechFest. (2001). *TechFest Ethernet Technical Summary.* Retrieved May 27, 2003, from http://www.techfest.com/networking/lan/Ethernet1.htm

Telecom NZ Links. (2004). Retrieved June 3, 2004, from http://www.telecom.co.nz/content/

Teng, H., Chen, K., & Lu, S. (1990). Adaptive real-time anomaly detection using inductively generated sequential patterns. In *Proceedings of the 1990 IEEE Symposium on Research in Security and Privacy* (pp. 278-284).

Tero, O. (1997). Overview of multi-user detection / Interference cancellation for DS-CDMA. *IEEE International Conference on Personal Wireless Communications'97,* 115-119.

Thankakan, K., Thumthawatwom, T., & Santiprabhob, P. (2001). Intelligent Scheduling Management for QoS-Enabled Wireless Ad Hoc Network With Fuzzy Rule-Based System. *Proc. of the Joint 9th IFSA World Congress and 20th NAFIPS Int'l Conf., 5,* 2983-2988, Vancouver, Canada, July 25-28.

Thomos, H., & Schulz, W. (2002). Parallel interference cancellation applied to an asynchronous MC-CDMA systems. *Proceedings of IEEE Vehicular Technology Conference' 2002, 2,* 689-693.

Tian, J., Han, L., Rothermel, K., & Cseh, C. (2003). Spatially aware packet routing for mobile ad hoc inter-vehicle radio networks. *IEEE 6th International Conference on Intelligent Transportation Systems (ITSC): Vol. 2* (pp. 1546-1551).

Tirumula, A., Qin, F., Dugan, J., Ferguson, J., & Gibbs, K. (n.d.). *Iperf: Testing the limits of your network.* Retrieved March 29, 2006, from http://dast.nlanr.net/Projects/Iperf

Tolly, B. (2003). *Gig E to the desktop: Bargain or boondoggle?* Retrieved June 6, from http://www.nwfusion.com/columnists/2003/0217tolly.html

Tragantalerngsak, S., Holt, J., & Ronnqvist (2000). An exact method for the two-echelon, single-source, capacitated facility location problem. *European Journal of Operational Research, 123(3)*, 473-489.

Tran, D. A., Hua, K. A., & Jiang, N. (2001). A generalized design for broadcasting on multiple physical-channel air-cache. In *Proceedings of the ACM SIGAPP Symposium on Applied Computing (SAC'01)* (pp. 387-392).

Traupman, E., O'Connell, P., Minnis, J., Jadoul, M., & Huterer, M. (1999). The evolution of the existing carrier infrastructure. *IEEE Communications Magazine, 37(6)*, 134-139.

Triantafillou, P., Harpantidou, R., & Paterakis, M. (2001). High performance data broadcasting: A comprehensive systems "perspective." In *Proceedings of the 2nd International Conference on Mobile Data Management (MDM 2001)* (pp. 79-90).

Trigeorgis, L. (1996). *Real options: Managerial flexibility and strategy in resource allocation.* Cambridge, MA: MIT Press.

Tsai, J. T., & Hsiao, H. H. (2001). Performance of Movement-Based Location Update and One-Step Paging in Wireless Networks with Sparsely Underlaid Microcells. *Proceedings of IEEE GLOBECOM*, San Antonio, TX, Nov. pp. 642-647

Tsalgatidou, A., Veijalainen, J., Markkula, J., Katasonov, A., & Hadjiefthymiades, S. (2003). Mobile e-commerce and location-based services: Technology and requirements. In *Proceedings of the 9th Scandinavian Research Conference on Geographical Information Services* (pp. 1-14).

Tse, P. K. C., Lam, W. K., Ng, K. W., & Chan, C. (2005). An implementation of location-aware multimedia information download to mobile system. *Journal of Mobile Multimedia, 1(1)*, 33-46.

Tseng, Y., Li, Y., & Chang, Y. (2003). On route lifetime in multihop mobile ad hoc networks. *IEEE Transaction on Mobile Computing, 2(4)*, 366-376.

Uri, N. D. (2000). Measuring productivity change in telecommunications. *Telecommunications Policy, 24(5)*, 439-452.

Ush-Shamszaman, Z., & Abdur, R. M. (2005). A mobility management scheme in all-ip integrated network. *Proceedings of the 23rd IASTED International Multi-Conference Parallel and Distributed Computing And Networks.* 15-17.

UTOPIA (Utah Telecommunication Open Infrastructure Agency). (2006). Retrieved June 14, 2006, from http://www.utopianet.org/

Vaccaro, H. S., & Liepins, G. E. (1989). Detection of anomalous computer session activity. In *Proceedings of the 1989 IEEE Symposium on Security and Privacy* (pp. 280-289).

Van der Raadt, B., Gardin, T., & Yu, E. (2005). Exploring Web Services from a Business Value Perspective. Paper presented at IEEE RE'05.

Van, N. R., Awater, G., Morikura, M., Takanashi, H., MA Webster, M., & Halford, K. (1999). New High-Rate Wireless LAN Standards. *IEEE Communication Magazine, 37(12)*, 82–88.

Vanderlaan, P. (1999). *Installation Effects Upon Alien Crosstalk and Equal Level Far End Crosstalk.* Retrieved May 27, 2003, from http://bwcecom.belden.com/college/techpprs/ieacectp.htm

Varanasi, M. K., & Aazhang, B. (1990). Multistage detection in asynchronous Code Division Multiple Access communications. *IEEE Transactions on Communications, 38(4)*, 509-519.

Vekiarides, L., & Finkel, D. (1998). NETCAP: A tool for the capacity planning of ethernet LANs. In *Proceedings of the Sixth International Symposium on Modeling, Analysis and Simulation of Computer and Telecommunication Systems (MASCOTS 1998)* (pp. 198-203). Montreal, Canada.

Velayos, H., & Karlsson, G. (2004). *Techniques to reduce IEEE 802.11b handoff time.* Paper presented at IEEE ICC 2004, Paris.

Veloso, E., Almeida, V., Meira, W., Bestavros, A. & Jin, S. (2002, November). *A Hierarchical Characterization of a Live Streaming Media Workload.* Paper presented at ACM Internet Measurement Workshop (IMV)..

Venkatesh, C., Yadaiah, N., & Natarajan, A. M. (2005). Dynamic Source Routing Protocol Using Fuzzy Logic Concepts for Ad Hoc Networks. *Academic Open Internet Journal*, Bulgaria, *15*, 1–14.

Venken, V., Vleeschauwer, D., & Vriendt, J. (2001). Designing a DiffServ-capable IP-backbone for the UTRAN. In *Proceeding of the 2nd International Conference on 3G Wireless Beyond,* San Francisco.

Verdu, S. (1998). *Multi-user detection.* Cambridge Univ. Press.

Verma, D. (2002). Simplifying network administration using policy based management. *IEEE Network Magazine.*

Vicari, N., & Kohler, S., (2006). *Measuring Internet User Traffic Behaviour Dependent on Access Speed.* Paper presented at IP Traffic Measurement, Modelling and Management.

Vilas, M., Pañeda, X. G., Melendi, D., García, R., & García, V. (2006, May). *Influence of effective handoff latency on live streaming services.* Paper presented at CITA2006, Monterrey, Mexico.

Viterbi, A. (1995). *CDMA: Principles of spread spectrum communication.* Addison-Wesley.

Viterbi, A. J. (1971). Convolutional codes and their performance in communication systems. *IEEE Transaction on Communication, COM-19,* 751-772.

Vitharana, P., & Dharwadkar, R. (2007). Information Systems Outsourcing: Linking Transaction Cost and Institutional Theories. *Communications of the Association for Information Systems, 20,* 346-370.

Vivek, B., & Buehrer, M. R. (2001). Acquisition in CDMA systems using parallel interference cancellation. *IEEE 58th Vehicular Technology Conference' 2004, 2,*1078-1081.

Walsham, G. (1995). Interpretive case studies in IS research: Nature and method. *European journal of Information Systems, 4,* 74-81.

Walters, R. (1999). *Computer telephony integration.* Artech House, Inc.

Waluyo, A. B., Srinivasan, B., & Taniar, D. (2005). Research on location-dependent queries in mobile databases. *International Journal of Computer Systems Science & Engineering, 20*(3), 77-93, March.

Wang, C., Chen, S., Yang, X., & Gao, Y. (2005). Fuzzy Logic-Based Dynamic Routing Management Policies for Mobile Ad Hoc Networks. *Proc. of the IEEE Workshop on High Performance Switching and Routing,* 341–345, May 12-14.

Wang, C., Li, B., Sohraby, K., & Peng, Y. (2003). AFRED: An Adaptive Fuzzy-based Control Algorithm for Active Queue Management. *Proceedings of 28th Annual IEEE International Conference on Local Computer Networks (LCN'03)* (pp. 12).

Wang, J. (1999). A survey of Web caching schemes for the Internet. *ACM SIGCOMM, Computer Communication Review, 25*(9), 36-46.

Wang, L. & Olariu, S. (2004). A Two-Zone Hybrid Routing Protocol for Mobile Ad Hoc Networks. *IEEE Transactions on Parallel and Distributed Systems, 15*(2), 1105–1116.

Wang, Y. et al. (2005). A transparent cache based mechanism for mobile ad hoc networks. In *Proceedings of the 3rd International Conference on Inform Tech and Applications (ICITA'05)* (Vol. 2, pp. 305-310).

Wang, Z., & Crowcroft, J. (1991, January). A new congestion control scheme: Slow start and search (Tri-S). *ACM Computer Communication Review, 21,* 32-43.

Ward, M. (2002). Resilient Packet Ring, Retrieved March 1, 2008, from *http://searchnetworking.techtarget.com/sDefinition/0,,sid7_gci754865,00.html.*

Weiss, M. B. H., & Hwang, J. (1998). Internet telephony or circuit switched telephony: Which is cheaper? *The 26th Telecommunications Policy Research Conference,* Alexandria, VA.

Wessels, D., & Claffy, K. (1998). ICP and the squid Web cache. *IEEE JSAC, 16*(1998), 345-357.

Widmer, J., Denda, R., & Mauve, M. (2001, May). A survey on TCP-friendly congestion control. *IEEE Network.*

Wieland, K. (2006). The VoBB dilemma: What can incumbents do about voice over broadband? *Telecommunications Magazine.*

Willcocks, L. P., Fitzgerald, G., & Fenny, D. (1995). Outsourcing IT: The strategic implications. *Long Range Planning, 28*(5), 59-70.

William, L. C. (1993). *Mobile Communications Design Fundamentals,* (2nd Ed.). New York: John Wiley & Sons.

William, L. C. (2001). *Lee's Essentials of Wireless Communications.* New York: McGraw Hill.

Williamson, O. E. (1981). The Modern Corporation: Origin, Evolution, Attributes. *Journal of Economics Literature, 19,* 1537-1568.

Wolfson, O. (2002). Moving objects information management: The database challenge. In *Proceedings of the 5th Workshop on Next Generation Information Technology and Systems (NGITS)* (pp. 75-89).

Wong, V. W. S., & Leung, V. C. M. (2000, September). Location Management for Next-Generation Personal Communications Networks. *IEEE Network Magazine*, 18-24.

Wong, V., & Leung, V. (2001, October). An Adaptive Distance-Based Location Update Algorithm for Next Generation PCS Networks. *IEEE J. Select. Areas Commun., 19*, 1942-1952.

Wong, W. (1999). Telcos to push IP telephony in 1999. *CNET News*. http://www.news.com/News/Item/0,4,30542,00.html

Wong, Y. F., & Wong, W. C. (2002). A Fuzzy-Decision-Based Routing Protocol for Mobile Ad Hoc Networks. *Proc. of the 10th IEEE Int'l Conf. on Networks (Icon 2002)*, 317-322, Singapore, Aug. 27-30.

Wu, D., Hou, Y. T., Zhu, W., Zhang, Y., & Peha, J. (2001). Streaming video over the internet: Approaches and directions. *IEEE Transaction on Circuits and Systems for Video Technology, 11*, 282301.

Xia, X., & Liang, Q. (2005). Latency and Energy Efficiency Evaluation in Wireless Sensor Networks. *Proc. of the IEEE 62nd Vehicular Technology Conference, 3*, 1594–1598, Sept. 25-28.

Xiaodang, R., Shidong, Z., Yan, Y., & Zucheng, Z. (2003). A new successive interference cancellation for asynchronous CDMA. *IEEE GLOBECOM'03*, 1, 252-256.

Xie, H., Tabbane, S., & Goodman, D. (1993, May). Dynamic Location Area Management and Performance Analysis. *Proceedings of the 43rd IEEE Vehicular Technology Conference*, 533-539

Xie, Z., Short, R. T., & Rushforth, C. K. (1990). A family of suboptimum detectors for coherent Multi-user communications. *IEEE Journal on Selected Areas in Communication, 8*, 683-690.

Xu, J., Hu, Q., Lee, W. C., & Lee, D. L. (2004). Performance evaluation of an optimal cache replacement policy for wireless data dissemination. *IEEE Transaction on Knowledge and Data Engineering (TKDE), 16*(1), 125-139.

Xu, J., Tang, X., & Lee, D. L. (2003). Performance analysis of location-dependent cache invalidation schemes for mobile environments. *IEEE Transactions on Knowledge and Data Engineering (TKDE), 15*(2), 474-488.

Xu, J., Zheng, B., Lee, W. C., & Lee, D. L. (2003). Energy efficient index for querying location-dependent data in mobile broadcast environments. *Proceedings of the 19th IEEE International Conference on Data Engineering (ICDE '03)* (pp. 239-250).

Yager, R. R., & Filev, D. P. (1994). *Essentials of fuzzy modeling and control*, 109-153, John Wiley & Sons, New Jersey, USA.

Yanfei, F., Fengyuan R., & Chuang, L. (2003). Design an active queue management algorithm based on fuzzy logic decision. *Proceedings of IEEE International Conference on Communication Technology (ICCT'03)*, 1, 286-289.

Yang, D., Lee, T., Jan, K., Chang, J., & Sunghyun, C. (2006). Performance enhancement of multi-rate IEEE 802.11 WLANs with geographically-scattered stations. *IEEE Transactions on Mobile Computing, 5*, 907919.

Yang, G., Chen, L., Sun, T., Gerla, M., & Sanadidi, M. (2006). Smooth and efficient real-time video transport in presence of wireless networks. *ACM Transactions on Multimedia Computing, Communications, and Applications (TOMCCAP), 2*, 109–126.

Yang, R. Y., & Lam, S. S. (2000, November). General AIMD congestion control. *Proceedings of the ICNP*.

Yanping L., Yongbo Z., & Huakui, W. (2006). Partial parallel interference cancellation multi-user detection using recurrent neural network based on Hebb Learning Rule. *The Sixth world congress on Intelligent Control and Automation (2006) WCICA-2006*, 1, 2989-2992.

Ye, N., Emran, S. M., Li, X., & Chen, Q. (2001). Statistical process control for computer intrusion detection. In *Proceedings of the DARPA Information Survivability Conference & Exposition (DISCEX II)* (pp. 397-343).

Yemini, S., Kliger, S., Mozes, E., Yemini, Y., & Ohsie, D. (1996, May). High Speed and Robust Event Correlation. *IEEE Communications*.

Yeo, J., Youssef, M., Henderson, T., & Agrawala, A. (2005). *An accurate technique for measuring the wireless side of wireless networks*. Paper presented at WiTMeMo 2005, Seattle, WA.

Yi, S., Naldurg, P., & Kravets, R. (2001). Security-aware ad hoc routing for wireless networks. *Second ACM Symposium on Mobile Ad Hoc Networking and Computing (MOBIHOC)*, Long Beach, CA (pp. 299-302).

Yigal, B., Seung-Jae, H., & Li (Erran) Li (2007). Fairness and Load Balancing in Wireless LANs Using Association Control, IEEE. *IEEE/ACM Transactions on Networking, 15*(3), 560-573.

Yin, L., & Cao, G. (2006). Supporting cooperative caching in ad hoc networks. *IEEE Transactions on Mobile Computing, 5*(1), 77- 89.

Yin, R. (1994). *Case Study Research Design and Methods*: California: Sage Publications.

Yu, H., Zheng. D., Zhao, B. Y., Zheng, W., (2006). *Understanding User Behaviour in Large-Scale Video-on-demand Systems*. Paper presented at EuroSys2006.

Yusuf, M., & Haider, T. (2005). Energy-Aware Fuzzy Routing for Wireless Sensor Networks. *Proc. of the IEEE Int'l Conf. on Emerging Technologies*, 63–69, Islamabad, Pakistan, Sept. 17-18.

Zapata, M. (2001). Secure ad hoc on-demand distance vector (SAODV) routing. *IETF MANET Mailing List, Message-ID 3BC17B40.BBF52E09@nokia.com*, ftp://manet.itd.nrl.navy.mil/pub/manet/2001-10.mail, October 2001.

Zeadally, S., & Zhang, L. (2004). Enabling gigabit network access to end users. *Proceedings of the IEEE, 92*(2), 340-353.

Zenel, B. A. (1999). A general purpose proxy filtering mechanism for the mobile environment. *ACM Wireless Networks, 5*, 391409.

Zhang, X., Castellanos, J., & Campbell, A. (2002, March). Design and Performance of Mobile IP Paging, ACM Mobile Networks and Applications. *Special Issue on Modeling Analysis and Simulation of Wireless and Mobile Systems, 7*(2).

Zhang, X., Cheng, S., Feng, M., & Ding, W. (2004). Fuzzy Logic QoS Dynamic Source Routing for Mobile Ad Hoc Networks. *Proc. of the 4th IEEE Int'l Conf. on Computer and Information Technology (CIT'04)*, 652-657, Sept. 14-16.

Zhang, Z., Li, J., Manikopoulos, C. N., Jorgenson, J., & Ucles, J. (2001). HIDE: A hierarchical network intrusion detection system using statistical preprocessing and neural network classification. In *Proceedings of the 2001 IEEE Workshop Information Assurance and Security* (pp. 85-90).

Zhao, C., & Wang, G. (2004). Fuzzy-Control-Based Clustering Strategy in MANET. *Proc. of the Fifth World Congress on Intelligent Control and Automation, 2*, 1456–1460, June 15-19.

Zhao, C., & Wang, G. (2004). Routing Protocol Based on Fuzzy Regression for MANET. *Proc. of the 3rd Int'l Conf. on Machine Leaning and Cybernetics*, 1811–1815, Shanghai, China, Aug. 26-29.

Zheng, B., Xu, J., Lee, D. L. (2002). Cache invalidation and replacement strategies for location-dependent data in mobile environments. *IEEE Transactions on Computers, 51*(10), 1141-1153.

Zhenhua, X., Short, R. T., & Rushforth, C. K. (1990). A family of sub-optimal detectors for coherent multi-user communications. *IEEE Journal on Selected Areas in Communications*, SAC-8 (4), 683-690.

Zhigang, H., Rong, H., & Hao, M. (2005). A Route Reliability Algorithm for Mobile Ad Hoc Networks. *Proc. of the Int'l Conf. on Wireless Communications, Networking and Mobile Computing, 2*, 787–790, Sept. 23-26.

Zhou, L., & Haas, Z. (1999). Securing ad hoc networks, *IEEE Network Magazine*, Vol. 13, No. 6, pp. 24-30.

Zhou, M., & Lang, S. D. (2003). Mining frequency content of network traffic for intrusion detection. In *Proceedings of the IASTED International Conference on Communication, Network, and Information Security* (pp. 101-107).

ZNYX Networks, Inc. (2001). *Network Level Resiliency for High Availability (HA) in Ethernet Networks*. Retrieved January 30, 2008 from *www.znyx.com*

About the Contributors

Indranil Bose is associate professor of information systems at the School of Business, The University of Hong Kong. He holds a BTech from the Indian Institute of Technology, MS from the University of Iowa, MS and PhD from Purdue University. His research interests are in telecommunications, information security, data mining, and supply chain management. His publications have appeared in *Communications of the ACM*, *Communications of AIS*, *Computers and Operations Research*, *Decision Support Systems*, *Ergonomics*, *European Journal of Operational Research*, *Information & Management*, and *Operations Research Letters*. He is listed in the *International Who's Who of Professionals 2005-2006*, *Marquis Who's Who in the World 2006*, *Marquis Who's Who in Asia 2007*, *Marquis Who's Who in Science and Engineering 2007*, and *Marquis Who's Who of Emerging Leaders 2007*.

* * *

Abid Thyab Al-Ajeeli is a professor of computer science, University of Bahrain. His degrees include Bachelor of Computer Science, from the University of London, MSc in operational research from Southampton University, and PhD in software engineering from Keele University in 1990. He has worked at a number of places including oil industry, manufacturing industries, and at a number of universities all over the world. He is a member of a number of scientific societies. Professor Al Ajeeli has published a number of books and over 40 articles in reputed journals. His main areas of research are computerized manufacturing, networking, linguistics, and software engineering.

Yousif Al-Bastaki received a BSc degree from University of Bahrain, MSc degree from University of Leeds, UK and PhD degree from University of Nottingham, UK. Recently he has been appointed as an IT advisor of the deputy prime minister at the Kingdom of Bahrain and he previously worked as the Dean of College of IT at the University of Bahrain. Currently he is an associate professor at the University of Bahrain. His research interests are neural networks, genetic algorithms, and distance education.

Nabeel A. Y. Al-Qirim is the editor of three books in the area of e-business. He has published more than 70 research articles in refereed international outlets. He participated in panels and administered workshops. His research interests include IT and e-commerce strategy in businesses and in SMEs, e-government, health information systems and telemedicine, mobile commerce, outsourcing, supply chain management, and e-commerce in developing countries and in NGOs. He is on the editorial board of several journals. He chaired a conference (IIT'05), and several tracks and sessions at international conferences. Prior to joining Auckland University of Technology (Auckland, New Zealand) in 1999 and UAE University in 2004, he worked as an IT consultant since 1989 with multinational companies including IBM, Data General, Compaq, and Siemens Nixdorf.

Catherine Byrne is IT manager for an engineering consultancy company in New Zealand. She had been a teacher of mathematics and computer science before moving into the IT industry several years ago. Since then Catherine has specialised in IT infrastructure and systems management. Originally gaining a Bachelor of Computer Science in psychology and mathematics from Waikato University, she has in recent years completed a post graduate diploma in computer science from the Auckland University of Technology.

M. Chandrasekaran received his BE(Hons.) degree in electronics and communication engineering from University of Madras and his ME degree in computer science and engineering from Bharathiar University. He has submitted his PhD thesis in information and communication engineering at Anna University. He has more than 23 years of teaching experience. He has published papers in 7 national conferences and 6 international conferences conducted by IEEE. He has published papers in 6 international journals and one Asian journal. He is a member of ISTE and CSI. His research interests include neural networks, fuzzy logic, congestion control in TCP networks, and sensor networks. He has served as member of various committees representing AICTE and DOTE, Tamil Nadu for inspecting engineering colleges and polytechnics. He has served as a member of academic council. He has guided many BE, ME and MCA projects. Some of the projects have received awards from Tamil Nadu State Council for Science and Technology. He has worked as assistant professor in the Electronics and Communication Engineering department at Government College of Engineering, Salem. He is currently working as assistant director (planning) at the Directorate of Technical Education, Chennai, India.

Roberto García is telecommunications engineer from the Technical University of Madrid and PhD from the University of Oviedo. He is associated professor with the Department of Computer Science of the University of Oviedo and formerly associated professor with the Electronics Department in the University of Alcalá (Madrid). His current research interest is in the area of telecommunication systems and services, in performance analysis, modeling and simulation of telecommunication systems. He is also taking part in several research projects at national and European levels.

Victor García is telecommunications engineer from the Technical University of Madrid and PhD from the University of Oviedo. Nowadays, he is associated professor with the Department of Computer Science of the University of Oviedo. His current research interest is in the area of multimedia systems and services, in content distribution networks, digital TV services, mobile ad-hoc networks, wireless networks, performance analysis, modeling and simulation of telecommunication systems. He is also taking part in several research projects at national and European levels.

Sandor Imre received the MSc degree in telecommunication engineering from the Budapest University of Technology and Economics in 1993. In 1999 he received the PhD degree in electrical engineering. He is an associate professor at the Budapest University of Technology and Economics and the R&D director of the Mobile Innovation Center, Hungary. His research areas include IP mobility, routing, reliability, wireless LANs, software defined radio, and quantum computing.

Arumainayagam Ebenezer Jeyakumar was born in Dindigul, India in the year 1950. He received his master's degree from University of Madras, India in the year 1974 and PhD degree from Anna University, Chennai, India in the year 1992. His major field of studies focused on high voltage engineering. Later he developed good knowledge in the field of wireless communication and networking. He served as teaching faculty at various designations starting from lecturer to professor. Currently he is the principal of the Government College of Engineering, Salem, India. He has published more than 15 journal/conference papers in the area of electrical and electronics engineering. His current research interests include high voltage engineering, power systems, digital communication, signal processing, and wireless networking. He is a member of the Indian Society for Technical Education (ISTE) and a member of IEEE. He is also a syndicate member of Anna University, nominated by the Governor of Tamil Nadu, India for a period of three years.

Ghassan Kbar is associate professor of IT at the American University in Dubai (AUD). He has around eleven years of academic experience working at AUD and the University of New South Wales Sydney Australia, where he taught subjects related to computer networks including network operating system, routers, application servers, information security, and programming. He developed the master's security curriculum at AUD including course descriptions and syllabus. He has also more than seven years of industrial experience working as technical and project leaders at international telecommunication companies such Motorola and Sydney Open Telecommunication. He organized and chaired the ISSAF Security Workshop for 5 days presented by the Open Information Security Group (OISSG) at the American University in Dubai, 2007. He is a senior IEEE member, and has obtained CCNA and security CISCO academy instructor certificates. He has published more than 40 articles at international conferences and journals, and attended numerous seminars, forums, and workshops. His research interests include wireless networking, network security, high speed networks, and network protocols.

Wathiq Mansoor is associate professor of computer engineering at the American University in Dubai (AUD). He received his PhD degree (computer engineering) from University of Aston, UK. His research activities are in the areas of wireless networks, Web services, software agents, mobile databases, and neural networks. He has published a number of articles in international journals and conferences. He has more than twenty years of teaching experience in the fields of computer engineering, computer science, and information systems. He has organized many international workshops. He is an editor of several international journals.

David Melendi is computer science engineer and PhD from the University of Oviedo. Nowadays, he is associated professor with the Department of Computer Science of the University of Oviedo and member of the SYMM working group of the W3C. His current research interests are in the areas of multimedia systems and services, content distribution networks, digital TV services, mobile ad-hoc networks, performance analysis, and modeling and simulation of telecommunication systems. He is also taking part in several research projects at national and European levels.

John P. Mullen is an associate professor in the Department of Industrial Engineering and the assistant director of the Center for Stochastic Modeling at New Mexico State University, Las Cruces, New Mexico. He has extensive experience in academia, private industry, and the military. His research area is the application of operations research to problems in quality assurance and control, industrial safety, facilities design, industrial control, communications systems, information systems, and production systems.

Essam Natsheh obtained his PhD in communications and networks engineering from University Putra Malaysia in 2006. Currently, he is an assistant professor at the Computer Information Systems Department, College of Applied Studies and Community Services, King Faisal University (Saudi Arabia). Essam has more than ten years of teaching and research experience in Malaysia and Saudi Arabia. Also, he has more than 15 publications in refereed journals at international level. His research interest is in mobile ad-hoc networks, and the development of a new routing algorithm for this type of networking.

Joon-Yeoul Oh is an assistant professor in the Department of Accounting & Computer Information Systems at Texas A&M University-Kingsville. He has PhD degree in industrial engineering and his research interest is in the areas of data communications, information systems, operations research, focusing on algorithm development, simulation, and the telecommunication and manufacturing network systems optimization. In addition to his extensive consulting experience in private industry, he has served as an invited and contributed speaker at seminars and conferences such as Institute of Industrial Engineering, the Association of Operations Management, and Institute of Operations Research and Management Science.

Xabiel G Pañeda is computer science engineer and PhD from the University of Oviedo. Nowadays, he is associated professor with the Department of Computer Science of the University of Oviedo and member of the SYMM Working Group of the W3C. His current research interests are in the area of multimedia systems and services, content distribution networks, digital interactive TV services, and mobile ad-hoc networks. He is also taking part in several research projects at national and European levels.

Radhakrishnan Rathinavel is currently professor of electronics and communication engineering at Sri Ramakrishna Engineering College, in Tamil Nadu, India. He received the master's degree from P.S.G. College of Technology, Bharathiar University, Tamil Nadu, India in the year 1997 and currently pursuing PhD in Anna University, Chennai, India. His research interests include wireless communication, signal processing, and mobile communication. He is a member of Indian Society for Technical Education (ISTE), Institution of Electronics and Telecommunication Engineering (IETE), and Advanced Communication and Computing Society (ACCS).

Nurul Sarkar is a senior lecturer in the School of Computing and Mathematical Sciences at AUT University, Auckland, New Zealand. He has more than 13 years of teaching experience in universities at both undergraduate and postgraduate levels and has taught a range of subjects, including computer networking, data communications, computer hardware, and e-commerce. His first edited book entitled *Tools for Teaching Computer Networking and Hardware Concepts* has been published by IGI Global Publishing in 2006. Sarkar has published more than 70 research papers in international refereed journals, conferences, and book chapters, including the *IEEE Transactions on Education*, the *International Journal of Electrical Engineering Education*, the *International Journal of Information and Communication Technology Education*, the *International Journal of Business Data Communications and Networking*, *Measurement Science & Technology*, and *SIGCSE Bulletin*. Sarkar has received a best paper award for his paper (co-author: Roger McHaney) *Modeling and Simulation of IEEE 802.11 WLANs: A Case Study of a Network Simulator* at the IRMA'06 International Conference in Washington D.C. Sarkar's research interests are in multi-disciplinary areas, including wireless network architecture, performance modeling and evaluation of wireless networks, radio propagation measurements, network security, simulation and modeling, intelligent agents, and tools to enhance methods for teaching and learning computer networking and hardware concepts. Nurul is a member of IEEE Communications Society. He served as Chairman of the IEEE New Zealand Communications Society Chapter; Executive peer-reviewer of the SSCI indexed *Journal of Educational Technology & Society*; member of editorial review board of the *International Journal of Business Data Communications and Networking*, and the *International Journal of Information & Communication Technology Education*.

Kumarasamy Ramamoorthy Shankar Kumar is currently a professor at Sri Ramakrishna Engineering College, Tamil Nadu, India. He received the master's degree from Madras University, Chennai, India in the year 2000 and the PhD degree from the Indian Institute of Science, Bangalore, India in the year 2004. His research interests include future broadband wireless communication, multi-carrier communication systems, advanced signal processing for communication. He has published more than ten conference/journal papers in the field of CDMA systems. He is a member of Indian Society for Technical Education (ISTE), Institution of Electronics and Telecommunication Engineering (IETE). His research work has been supported by Swarnajayanti Fellowship, Department of Science and Technology (DST), Government of India.

Vilmos Simon received the MSc degree in telecommunication engineering from the Budapest University of Technology and Economics in 2003. He is currently pursuing the PhD degree in the Department of Telecommunications at the Budapest University of Technology and Economics. His research areas include location management in next generation mobile networks, IP mobility, modeling of multimedia traffic, and information spreading in biologically inspired networks.

Varadharajan Sridhar is professor in information management at the Management Development Institute, India. He received his PhD from the University of Iowa, USA. Sridhar's primary research interests are in the area of telecommunication management and policy and global software development. He has published his research work in *European Journal of Operational Research*, *Telecommunication Systems*, *International Journal of Business Data Communications and Networking*, *Applied Econometrics and International Development*, *Information Resource Management Journal*, *Journal of Global Information Management*, *Journal of Regional Analysis and Policy*, and *Journal of Information System Security*. He was the recipient of the Nokia Visiting Fellowship awarded by the Nokia Research Foundation. He is associate editor of *International Journal of Business Data Communications and Networking* and is on the editorial board of the *Journal of Global Information Management*.

R. S. D. Wahida Banu received her BE degree in electronics and communication engineering from University of Madras and her ME degree in applied electronics from University of Madras. She received her PhD in characterization & classification of partial discharges using GA based ANN from Anna University. She has more than 25 years of teaching experience. She has published more than 100 papers at various national/international conferences. She has published 20 papers in international journals. She is a member of ISTE, IE, SSI, and CSI. Her research interests include neural networks, fuzzy logic, computer networks, and genetic algorithms. She served as member of various committees representing AICTE, Anna University, and DOTE, Tamil Nadu for inspecting Engineering colleges and Polytechnics. She served as a member of the Academic Council. She guided many BE, ME, and MCA projects. She is the President of "Crimes against Employed Women", at Government College of Engineering, Salem,

Tamil Nadu, India. She has advised 3 PhD scholars and is currently supervising more than 20 PhD scholars. She is an approved supervisor recognized by universities such as Anna University, Madurai Kamaraj University, Mother Therasa University, Jawaharlal Nehru Technological University etc. She is currently working as Professor at the Electronics and Communication Engineering department of the Government College of Engineering, Salem, Tamil Nadu, India.

Manuel Vilas is telecommunications engineer from the University of Vigo and PhD from the University of Oviedo. Nowadays, he is an assistant professor with the Department of Computer Science, University of Oviedo. His current research interest is in the areas of multimedia systems and services, content distribution networks, digital TV services, wireless networks, performance analysis, and modeling and simulation of telecommunication systems. He is also taking part in several research projects at national and European levels.

Index

A

access point 169, 170
active queue management (AQM) algorithm 238,
    243, 244, 245, 246, 249, 250, 251, 252, 253,
    254, 255, 256
ad-hoc networks 231, 235, 236, 243, 244, 246, 249,
    251, 252
additive increase and multiplicative decrease (AIMD)
    algorithm 78, 79, 80, 81, 84, 94
availability 15, 49, 52, 58, 59, 65, 97, 126, 132, 176,
    204, 205, 206, 207, 208, 209, 212, 213, 215,
    234, 268, 273, 275, 284, 286, 287

B

binomial distribution 33, 204, 214

C

CacheData 218
CachePath 218
cellular network expansion 154, 155, 156, 158, 167
channel impulse response (CIR) 189
client strategy 128
computers, communication and compatibility (3Com)
    52, 53, 54, 55, 58, 59, 67
congestion control 78, 79, 80, 81, 82, 84, 88, 89, 90,
    91, 93, 94, 205, 237, 244, 246, 255
content provider 95, 96, 98, 99, 100, 101, 102, 109,
    297
convolutional code 195, 196, 197

D

direct sequence code division multiple access (DS-
    CDMA) 183, 184, 185, 186, 187, 188, 190,
    195, 188, 183, 187, 188, 195, 196, 200, 201,
    202, 203, 202
dumbbell topology 85

E

ethernet 27, 64, 66, 292
ethernet, gigabit (GigE) 66, 292

F

fault tolerance 208, 212, 213, 215
frame format 63, 64
frequency allocation 208
fuzzy reasoning algorithm (FRA) 231, 232, 233,
    234, 235, 238, 239

H

heuristics 141, 144, 154, 156, 158, 167, 236
heuristic search algorithm (HSA) 158, 159, 160,
    161, 164, 165, 166, 167
HybridCache 218

I

IEEE 802.3 (standard) 63, 65
initial feasible solution (IFS) 161
intelligent mobile devices 122
inter-vehicle communication (IVC) networks 272,
    273, 274, 279, 282, 283, 284
internet protocol telephony (IPT) 29, 30, 36, 37, 38,
    39

K

Knapsack Problem, The 154, 156
knowledge discovery and data mining tools competi-
    tion 1999 (KDD-cup 1999) data 258, 268
Kodak effect, The 5, 10

L

local exchange carrier (LEC) 28, 29, 34, 35, 36, 38,
    39, 40
local loop unbundling (LLU) 288